The Uppsala Edda

Snorri Sturluson

The Uppsala Edda

DG 11 4to

Edited with introduction and notes by
Heimir Pálsson

Translated by
Anthony Faulkes

VIKING SOCIETY FOR NORTHERN RESEARCH
UNIVERSITY COLLEGE LONDON
2012

© Heimir Pálsson 2012

ISBN 978-0-903521-85-7

Reprinted 2018

Printed by Short Run Press Limited, Exeter

Contents

Preface vii

Introduction xi
  1 Snorri Sturluson xi
    1.1 From Oddi to Reykjaholt xi
    1.2 The trip to Norway and return home (1218–20) xix
    1.3 Back to Norway (1237) xxiv
    1.4 The wrong horse backed xxv
    1.5 'Do not strike!' xxvi

  2 Manuscripts xxx
    2.1 DG 11 4to xxx
    2.2 Paper copies xxxiv
    2.3 Manuscript relations xlii

  3 How did the text of the *Edda* come into being? xliv
    3.1 Myths xliv
      3.1.1 Summary lv
    3.2 The language of poetry lvi
      3.2.1 Summary lxv

  4 One work or more than one? lxvii

  5 The DG 11 4to collection lxxiv
    5.1 Overview lxxiv
    5.2 *Skáldatal* lxxv
    5.3 *Ættartala Sturlunga* lxxvii
    5.4 *Lǫgsǫgumannatal* lxxviii
    5.5 *Skáldskaparmál* lxxx
    5.6 *Háttalykillinn*— second grammatical treatise lxxxi
    5.7 List of stanzas lxxxii
    5.8 *Háttatal* lxxxvi

  6 Headings and marginal notes xcii

  7 Empty space and additional material xcv

  8 Grammar and prosody c

  9 Summary cxvi

  10 Other editions of DG 11 4to cxx

  11 This edition cxxiv

Index of Manuscripts cxxvii
Bibliographical References cxxviii
Uppsala Edda 1
    Chapter Headings 2
    Prologue 6
    Gylfaginning 10
    Skáldatal 100
    Genealogy of the Sturlungs 118
    List of Lawspeakers 120
    Skáldskaparmál 124
    Second Grammatical Treatise 250
    Háttatal 260
Index of Names 308

Illustrations

Man with a sword 118
Female dancer (1) 118
Man with a stick 119
Female dancer (2) 119
Two dancers 120
Man riding a horse 121
Gangleri and the Three Kings 122
Circular diagram 252
Rectangular diagram 253

Preface

A quarter of a century has passed since the then textbook editor at Mál og Menning, Sigurður Svavarsson, asked me to undertake a school edition of Snorri's *Edda*. I was not particularly familiar with the Edda, but was grateful for the confidence shown in me and decided to produce a printed text closer to the manuscript than most. I borrowed a word-processor (as we called desktop computers then) from the printers at Oddi, had an intensive course in how to use it from the typesetter Hafsteinn, who expressed a sensible attitude to it by saying: 'Take it home with you and give me a ring when you get stuck.' It was actually thought such a novelty that a photographer from the Sunday newspaper was sent to my house to take a picture of it all.

It went better than might have been expected. I did indeed, like many others, make the great mistake of trusting blindly Finnur Jónsson's text of 1931, and in fact I had been given that by the publishers to start me off. Although I was able to take account of Anne Holtsmark and Jón Helgason 1953 too, my text would not have satisfied the demands of modern textual criticism. When a new edition was issued in 2003, I had the help of Bragi Halldórsson with the text, and besides there had been some progress in readers' editions of medieval texts with the publication of the Sagas of Icelanders by Svart á hvítu. In both my editions I was fixed in my view that the *Edda* ought to lie on the students' desks as a whole. *Skáldskaparmál* and *Háttatal* had to be included. It was not acceptable to print just *Gylfaginning* and stories from *Skáldskaparmál*. In the later edition the *þulur* were added too, though it is disputed where they belong.

It was only when I became lektor in Uppsala for the second time, in 2004, that I realised that there were many unsolved problems in the history of the *Edda*. This was after I had got to know the facsimile and transcription of the text of the Uppsala Edda, or DG 11 4to, published by Grape and Thorell.

During the years 1973–1976 Olof Thorell and I were colleagues in Old Norse studies at Uppsala University, and he was in fact my head. We never spoke together of Snorri's *Edda*, and yet it was precisely during these years that he was engaged on the final stages of his major work, making the word list and putting the finishing touches to his literal transcription of the text that had been published in facsimile by Anders Grape in 1962.

In 1929 the Swedish parliament had decided to give the Icelanders a gift in celebration of the millenium of the Alþingi in 1930 in the form of a facsimile of a major Icelandic manuscript in a Swedish Library. It can be deduced from Tönnes Kleberg's introductory remarks to the 1962 edition (pp. 1–2) that there had been some debate about the choice of manuscript for the gift, and it may be supposed that the Stockholm Homily Book had been a competing candidate along with the Uppsala Edda. It was the latter that triumphed, and the form in which it was produced turned out to be, as far as I am aware, a completely isolated experiment. The photographs were taken with equipment that had proved itself with, among other things, the publication of the Codex Argenteus in facsimile in 1927. But then this book was printed on vellum! A single copy was prepared which is now preserved in the National/University Library of Iceland.

It had been decided to provide copies of the photographs on paper for all the major libraries in Sweden, and at the same time as the vellum copy was made, 500 copies were printed on paper, and the majority of these were deposited in the University Library in Uppsala Carolina Rediviva 'för att användas som bytesmaterial, varigenom en spridning till viktigare forskningscentra garanterades' (to be used as exchanges by means of which dissemination to more important centres of research would be guaranteed), writes Kleberg in 1962. It has always been assumed that all these copies lay unbound and unpublished in the library from the time the vellum copy was made until they were used in Grape's edition of 1962.

But this is not so. It was due to chance that the present writer and his wife, Dr Eva Aniansson, who works in the Swedish Academy, discovered that there was in the Nobel library a bound copy on paper of the 1930 national gift with the same preface as the copy in the National Library of Iceland.

From the day-books of the bookbinder Gustav Hedberg, preserved in the Royal Library in Stockholm, it appears that in 1930, besides the copy that was printed on vellum and sent to Iceland, eighteen vellum bound copies of the Uppsala Edda printed on paper were made. At the time of writing the investigation is not finished, but what we know so far is that there is one copy in each of the following libraries: the Nobel library, the Royal Library in Stockholm, the University Library in Uppsala, the University Library in Lund, the National Parliament Library; two are preserved in the library of the Vetenskapsakademi in Stockholm, and besides these we know of one copy in private ownership in Iceland.[1] This makes altogether eight of the eighteen bound copies on paper that were made. They all have the same binding and the same preface as the one on vellum that was sent to Iceland.

The full edition that had been envisaged, according to Kleberg in the 1962 edition, was to include a transcription of the text, an exhaustive paleographical description and commentary, and the history of the manuscript. It was obviously going to be a long time before all this work could be completed, which was presumably why the 18 copies were bound

---

[1] It is in itself amusing that this copy was given to one of three Icelanders born in 1930 that were given the name Úlfljótur.

for immediate distribution in 1930, as a stopgap. In fact the work was not completed and published fully until 1977, when the second volume, with Thorell's research, appeared.

When I began my research on DG 11 4to in 2005, I sought help from my professor and colleague Henrik Williams, and eventually, with the help of Lasse Mårtensson and Daniel Sävborg, we got financial support from the Research Council during the years 2008 to 2011and were able to launch an investigation into the manuscript DG 11 4to (cf. Williams 2007). Maja Bäckvall and Jonathan Pettersson subsequently joined the project team. Part of the results of the team's research and of my discussions with my colleagues appears in this book.

I have spent most of my time over the last five years in study of the text of DG 11 4to. It has been most helpful to have Lasse Mårtensson, an expert in paleography, at my side, and his observations on the manuscript have been invaluable for the research that I have carried out on the text. Together we have tried to get as close to the scribe and redactor as possible (we are unsure whether these were the same man, and maybe it is not important to decide). We have certainly felt conscious that his legacy was entrusted to us, as Jón Helgason has expressed it, and both of us have felt that he had been unjustly judged by previous scholars.

The normalised spelling of this edition of the text of DG 11 4to follows to a certain extent the pattern in Íslensk fornrit. Yet *Norrøn ordbok* 2004 has been followed in the spelling of middle voice endings (*-st*, not *-sk*), to make it easier for foreign users.

Verses and poems are a particular problem in an edition such as this. I have chosen to reproduce what the manuscript has as closely as possible, without emendation. On the other hand I indicate in the notes the corrections that I consider reasonable or unavoidable, while trying to take account of what is on offer elsewhere. It is absolutely certain that a scribe at the beginning of the fourteenth century would not have understood all the verses that are quoted. But he would of course have had certain ideas about the text and must have realised that it was often just a question of giving an example of a kenning, however it fitted in.

Hereafter, the material is dealt with from all possible points of view. In the first section the authorship is discussed and a particular look is taken at what may conceivably explain the selection and treatment of the material in the *Edda*. In the second section the manuscript DG 11 4to is described and its special position among the manuscripts of the *Edda* is analysed. The theories of scholars about the relationships between the manuscripts are discussed. In the third section the chief aim is to show how the compilation of material for the *Edda* must have been carried out and how it must have taken a long time and conceivably been the work of more than one man. In the fourth section it is demonstrated that it leads to an impasse to think exclusively of the *Edda* as a single work. It consists of independent parts. In the fifth section it is shown that the redactor's attitude in DG 11 4to suggests most of all that his intention was to create two works, Liber primus and Liber secundus. In Sections 6 and 7 the additional material in DG 11 4to is dealt with, including marginal scribbles etc. In Section 8 the concepts the author makes use of are discussed, those that relate to both prosody and grammar. The conclusion reached is that Snorri Sturluson was not a great master of terminology. In Section 9 what has been shown in the preceding sections is drawn together. The present writer's conclusion is that it is perhaps possible to construct two stemmas of the manuscripts rather than one.

It is obvious that in a work like this the author builds on foundations laid by a host of earlier scholars, as will appear in fact from the bibliography. But there is one scholar still living to whom I owe a particular debt. Anthony Faulkes in his editions and researches has laid the foundation of most of what is written here. For the English edition of this book, he has besides been much more than my translator. A more accurate term would be guide. He has been generous with advice and positive criticism, and in fact taken an active part in the composition, especially in Section 8, where extensive footnotes are his work rather than mine, and the whole section has benefitted from his reliable knowledge of medieval European prosody and stylistics. For this my thanks, though I can never thank him fully.

Bergljót Soffía Kristjánsdóttir and Aðalsteinn Eyþórsson read my draft of the text both as regards normalisation and the interpretation of the verses. For this, I am greatly indebted to them, and the interpretations of the verses in *Skáldskaparmál* particularly have benefitted greatly from Bergljót's acuteness and understanding in the field of *dróttkvætt*.

Finally it is my pleasure to mention those colleagues of mine who have been tireless in responding to my queries and in discussing problems with me. I list only the chief of these in alphabetical order, since I owe them all my thanks in equal measure, and I have sought help from many others too, as will appear in what I have written below. The chief ones that must be mentioned are Böðvar Guðmundsson, Gunnar Karlsson, Helgi Skúli Kjartansson, Kristinn Jóhannesson, Veturliði Óskarsson and Vésteinn Ólason.

HEIMIR PÁLSSON

Introduction

1 Snorri Sturluson
1.1 From Oddi to Reykjaholt

So much has been written about Snorri Sturluson's life that it is pointless to add anything further. The most important biographical accounts are included in the bibliography. Yet here it is necessary to go over the main points, though we shall try to confine ourselves to what is most important for his *Edda*.

He was three (winters old) in 1181, but since the New Year at that period was reckoned to begin on 1st September, and we do not know whether he was born between then and 31st December or not, it is customary to say that by the modern reckoning Snorri was born in 1178/9. His nephew Sturla Þórðarson says he was five when his father died in 1183 (*Sturlunga saga* 1946: I 229) and he is supposed to have been 19 when his foster-father Jón Loptsson died on 1st November 1197 (*Sturlunga saga* 1946: I 237).

At the age of three he would have had no idea that he was a pawn in a game played by major powers, a sort of hostage. Jón Loptsson has reconciled his father Sturla Þórðarson (Hvamm-Sturla) with his arch-enemies in Reykholt, séra Páll Sǫlvason and especially the latter's wife Þorbjǫrg Bjarnardóttir. And to confirm the reconciliation, Jón offers to foster Sturla's youngest legitimate son. His name is Snorri, and thus he bears the name of the most renowned of his forefathers since the Settlement, Snorri goði Þorgrímsson.

It is always difficult to say what might have happened if things had been otherwise, and impossible to guess what would have happened if Snorri Sturluson had not been fostered by Jón Loptsson (according to *Íslenzkar æviskrár* born in 1124[1]). Jón has received the finest commendation of any secular leader in Iceland in the Middle Ages. *Sturlunga saga* (1946: I 51) says he was the greatest and most popular leader there had ever been in Iceland. If one reads *Sturlunga saga* and considers Jón's role as reconciler it is similarly clear that he was a fascinating, charismatic person, besides being gifted and peace-loving. A quarter of a man's nature is due to his nurture, according to the Icelandic proverb, and it is interesting to compare Snorri the man of peace with his kinsmen Sighvatr Sturluson and Sturla Sighvatsson as they are depicted in *Sturlunga saga*. Jón Loptsson's inclination to peacefulness has, one feels, set its mark on Snorri, toning down his family's violence somewhat.

But Jón was not just one of the Oddi people who had Sæmundr the Learned as his grandfather. His mother was King Magnús Bareleg of Norway's daughter Þóra. She and Loptr had married in Norway and Jón was born

---

[1] The year of his birth is doubtless based on Snorri's having said that Jón had been 11 years old in Konungahella in 1135, see below.

there and was with his parents in Konungahella when the town was laid in ruins in an invasion of Wends. Snorri describes the fighting (and is the only writer to do so), and writes (*Heimskringla* 1941–1951: I 288):

> Five winters after the death of King Sigurðr [Jórsalafari] great events took place in Konungahella. At that time the sheriffs there were Haraldr flettir's son Guthormr and Sæmundr húsfreyja. He was married to the priest Andréás Brúnsson's daughter Ingibjǫrg, their sons being Páll flípr and Gunni físs. Ásmundr was the name of Sæmundr's illegitimate son. Andréás Brúnsson was a very distinguished person. He officiated at Krosskirkja. His wife was called Solveig. Jóan Loptsson was then being fostered and brought up with them and was eleven years old. Jóan's father, the priest Loptr Sæmundarson, was also there then.

This is accompanied by a bloody account of the destruction of Konungahella and we who read it can hear the echo of what must have been the report of Loptr Sæmundsson and Jón Loptsson. They were in the town or at any rate very close to the scene of action. There is no doubt that the priest Andréás was highly commended in the account of the father and son if we consider his role in the disturbances. It is also worth noting that Jón Loptsson's daughter was named Solveig and his grandson Andréás—and that besides his son was named Sæmundr, who of course might have been named after either Sæmundr the Learned or Sæmundr húsfreyja in Konungahella.

The disputes between Jón Loptsson and Bishop Þorlákr are well known. The issues were at once personal, political and moral. Þorlákr was born in 1133, a little later, probably, than Jón. In *Þorláks saga* there is an account that has had a formative influence on people's conception of Oddi as a centre of learning. It says there (*Byskupa sögur* 1948: I 40–41):

> As his mother could see through her wisdom by God's providence what a glorious clergyman Þorlákr might become by his good conduct if his learning progressed, so the mother and her son entered the highest centre in Oddi under the tutelage of the priest Eyjólfr Sæmundarson, who had both great prestige and a high level of learning, goodness and intelligence in greater measure than most others, and we have heard the blessed Þorlákr bear this witness of him that he felt he had scarcely found such a glorious man as he was, and he demonstrated later that he did not want to let the good advice concerning his master go unheeded, which the blessed apostle Paul gave his disciples, saying thus to them in their hearing: 'Be imitators of me as I am of Christ', for it often happened when we praised his good conduct, that he said that was how his foster-father Eyjólfr Sæmundarson had behaved. It was fitting that he did this, though he honoured him greatly in his discourse, for it was due to him.

Eyjólfr Sæmundarson, who taught the budding bishop, was Snorri's foster-father Jón's uncle.

Apart from this rapturous depiction in *Þorláks saga*, we have only one testimony to the educational environment in Oddi: Snorri Sturluson's learning in native lore, law, history and poetry. Actually it is also worth noting what it says later in *Þorláks saga* (*Byskupa sögur* 1948: I 41–42; cf. Vésteinn Ólason 2008: 26) :

> He spent his time, when he was young, for long periods in study, and frequently in writing, in prayer in between, but learnt, when not occupied in anything else, what his mother was able to teach him, genealogy and history of individuals.

Þorlákr's mother passes on to him native lore of certain kinds. It may be that Snorri sought just as much to hear women chanting old poems, and Jón Loptsson will have taught him enough law to enable him to become Lawspeaker in 1215.

It is certainly an admissible procedure in writing the history of a school (and one much used in Iceland) to draw conclusions from the achievements of former pupils. But to characterise the whole school at Oddi on the basis of two pupils, St Þorlákr and Snorri, is pretty bold. It has, however been done, and at the same time it has been been assumed that the curriculum there would have been based on that of Church and monastery schools, the trivium and quadrivium. But about this there are simply no sources. *Þorláks saga* speaks of 'the highest centre' (*inn æðsta hǫfuðstað*) in Oddi, but does not actually mention any school, only the priest Eyjólfr.[1]

It makes no difference in this context that it is known that some members of the Oddi family studied in foreign schools. Obviously they must have guided the young people that were growing up at Oddi, but it is pointless to try to interpret that as education in the curriculum of monastic schools.

On through the mid twentieth century it was customary in Iceland for priests to hold some kind of private school to instruct promising young people, especially boys, in preparation for the entry examination to the Grammar Schools. The education at Oddi would clearly have been ideal for this purpose. St Þorlákr studied in both Paris and London. Páll, son of his sister and Jón Loptsson, went 'south to England and attended school there and acquired such great learning there that one could scarcely find any other example of a person acquiring as much learning or anything like it in the same period of time' (*Byskupa sögur* 1948: I 263).

Many have pointed out that *Heimskringla* lays great emphasis on the role of independent chieftains, so that they even rise up against the king that the saga is actually about. It can hardly be denied that the model for these chieftains was Snorri's foster-father, the man who answered the bishop himself in these terms when they were disputing the control of ecclesiastical foundations:

---

[1] It therefore seems to me that Sverrir Tómasson goes a step further than is justified by the sources when he says: 'When Snorri was growing up at Oddi the organisation of schools had probably been fully formalised both in the cathedral schools at Hólar and Skálholt and in educational centres such as Oddi, where known men of learning presided one after another' (1996a: 11).

> I can listen to the archbishop's command, but I am determined to disregard it completely, and I do not think he wants or knows any better than my forefathers Sæmundr the Learned and his sons. I am also not going to condemn the procedures of our bishops here in this country who honoured the custom of the country whereby laymen were masters of the churches that their forefathers had given to God, reserving for themselves and their issue control over them' (*Oddaverja þáttr*, in *Byskupa sögur* 1948: I 143).

—and used these words about it, when the bishop was going to excommunicate him for adultery with the bishop's sister:

> 'I know,' said Jón, 'that your condemnation is right and the offence justifies it. I will submit to your judgment to the extent of going into Þórsmǫrk or some such place where ordinary people will not be implicated by association with me, and I shall stay there with the woman you are complaining about for as long as I please, and your condemnation will not separate me from my difficult situation, nor will anyone do it by force, until God inspires me in my heart to to separate myself from it voluntarily. But consider your position to be such that I shall take care to see that you do not serve anyone else as you have served me' (*Oddaverja þáttr*, in *Byskupa sögur* 1948: I 158).

Obviously it would not occur to anyone to think these were actually Jón's words, but the *þáttr*'s account shows what picture people were constructing of this chieftain half a century or so after his death.[1] He was such as would probably have been the most important model for Snorri to follow as he grew up, and it was possibly even more important than his attendance at school.

On what Snorri studied at Oddi views have varied widely. Halldór Halldórsson (1975) assumed that Snorri would have learned at least the Latin system of classification of rhetorical features which would have been of great use in *Skáldskaparmál*. Anthony Faulkes (1993) casts great doubt on his knowledge of Latin. Vésteinn Ólason has expressed moderate and sensible ideas about what Snorri may conceivably have learnt in Oddi (2008: 26):

> Whatever plans Hvamms-Sturla may have had for Snorri, at any rate he became neither priest nor bishop. He learnt the ecclesiastical skills of reading and writing; doubtless he also learnt some Latin and other things that people learnt in the schools of the period. But the particular learning he displays in his writings relates to other things. It is a question of myths or mythological narratives, mythological poems in eddic metres, a huge mass of skaldic poems and doubtless a lot of oral tradition about both Icelandic and foreign matters. A part of all this Snorri got from books—we know this about the kings' saga material especially, and some poetry may well have been written down by others before Snorri got hold of it. But his comprehension of the material handed down by tradition and his immense knowlege must have deep roots.

---

[1] People have held very varying views about the reliability of *Oddaverja þáttr*. On its date I attach about equal importance to Guðni Jónsson's introduction to *Byskupa sögur* I (1948: xiii) and Ásdís Egilsdóttir's introduction to *Þorlákssaga* (1989: 28).

Introduction

Here the writer is treading very carefully, and the real question is: What did Snorri know, and what does that tell us about his upbringing?

Interest in the histories of Norwegian kings was of course great at Oddi. One can not only think of the king's daughter Þóra, Jón Loptsson's mother, we should also consider the poem *Noregs konunga tal*, which was composed during the early years of Snorri in honour of Jón. On the pattern of *Háleygjatal* and *Ynglingatal* the succession of kings from Hálfdan svarti to Magnús berfǿttr and his daughter is traced in 83 *kviðuháttr* stanzas, though not in the direct line (*Skj* A I 579–89; B I 575–590). There is no doubt that Snorri would have paid great attention to this poetry, though it is not necessary to give such a free rein to our imagination as to assume that he composed the poem at the age of 13–15.[1]

Jón Helgason provided a fine account of *Noregs konunga tal* in 1953 and in his discussion of the poem also gives an idea of what people were talking about over their ale cups in Snorri's early years at Oddi (1953: 115–116). He says this is a poem that

> ... lists his [Jón's] kinsmen, the kings of Norway, from Hálfdan svarti to Sverrir, 'who is now king' [thus the poem was composed after 1184]. The Norse rulers that are named in the poem are just 27, like the generations listed in the ancient poems [*Ynglingatal*, *Háleygjatal*]. Chronologically it forms a continuation of *Ynglingatal*, but in contrast to that poem and *Háleygjatal* it does not list a series of ancestors in the direct line. Like the ancient proptypes it tells mainly about the kings' deaths, and as a rule also states where they lie buried; for each king it gives the length of his reign, and it states explicitly that this information as far as Magnús góði is based on Sæmundr fróði. Undoubtedly this means a lost written work of his. Towards the end the poet passes over to speaking of the kings' daughter who 'in a lucky hour for the Icelanders' was married to the Icelandic chieftain, and praises both her son and the whole of his family. It is evident that the poet has studied the ancient genealogical poems; had they perhaps been written down at Oddi, and did Snorri, Jón Loptsson's foster-son, get to know them there?

In my transcription of the Uppsala Edda below there are 260 verse quotations, nearly all of them half-stanzas, though there are some couplets, but only exceptionally whole stanzas. Some stanza parts are used more than once, so the true figure is about 250. Of these, 50 stanza parts (generally half-stanzas, very seldom couplets) are preserved in other sources (chiefly Kings' Sagas). In other words, a fifth of these stanza parts would have been preserved if the *Edda* had not been compiled. The figures are even more striking if we look at the Codex Regius version. Here we shall make a rough comparison of the figures for these two versions.

---

[1] See among others Óskar Guðmundsson 2009: 47–49.

R includes nearly all the same stanza parts as U. There are a few additional ones, but not so many as to substantially alter the statistics. On the other hand, R contains several substantial quotations from longer poems: 20 stanzas (40 half-stanzas) of *Haustlǫng*, 19 stanzas (38 half-stanzas) of *Þórsdrápa*, four and a half stanzas (9 half-stanzas) of *Ragnarsdrápa*, the whole of *Grottasǫngr* (24 stanzas, 48 half-stanzas). In order to make a meaningful comparison with the Uppsala Edda version, it is of course necessary to count half-stanzas, not whole stanzas.

If we consider only these extra quotations, then the Codex Regius version has 135 half-stanzas more than the Uppsala Edda version, and so it is not far from the truth to say that there are about 400 half-stanzas in the Codex Regius version. Of these about the same number are preserved in other sources as of the half-stanzas in the Uppsala Edda version, that is 50. In other words about an eighth part of this poetry would have been preserved if the *Edda* had not been compiled.

It should be made clear that we have left out of account the *þulur*, which are only preserved in manuscripts of the *Edda*, especially R, A and B (cf. p. xxxiii below). With them a great deal of information would have been lost.

All this needs to be taken into account if an attempt is made to assess Snorri's part in the preservation of Old Norse culture. If the *Edda* had not been compiled it is likely that an immense number of sources, not only for Norse mythology but also for the Old Norse language, would have been lost.

There are cases in the *Edda* of poets being referred to who otherwise are completely unknown. For example, no poetry by Ásgrímr (assumed to be the Ásgrímr skáld of *Sturlunga saga* 1946: I 166 and 203 and the Ásgrímr Ketilsson said in *Skáldatal* in Kringla to have been a poet of King Sverrir) or Atli litli is known except the half-stanza that is attributed to each of them in Snorri's *Edda*, and there are other similar cases. On the other hand it is strange that 9 half-verses, attributed to Hallfreðr vandræðaskáld and assumed to be from his *Hákonardrápa* which is referred to only in *Hallfreðar saga*, are quoted in *Skáldskaparmál* but appear nowhere else. In DG 11 4to some of these half-verses are attributed to Hallvarðr, but this is probably only because in some earlier manuscript the name had been abbreviated. There are 6 quotations assumed to be from Kormakr Ǫgmundarson's *Sigurðardrápa* in DG 11 4to that are not in *Kormaks saga* or in any king's saga. They are easily distinguished, since Kormakr's verse form, *hjástælt* is rarely used.

It is now very difficult to get an idea of the corpus of poetry that Snorri had access to, though it must have been extensive. Clearly some poets were better preserved than others. Einarr skálaglamm, Einarr Skúlason and Þjóðólfr Arnórsson are much used, and actually the same may be said of Hofgarða-Refr, Bragi Boddason and Eyvindr skáldaspillir. Together these poets cover the period from about 850 on past the middle of the twelfth century. Einarr Skúlason doubtless wrote down his poems as he composed them, but it is highly unlikely that poets much before his time would have done so, especially Bragi Boddason and Einarr skálaglamm. There is evidence that Snorri used a written text of *Sexstefja* (see Lasse Mårtensson and Heimir Pálsson 2008), but many of the snippets that he used must have survived in oral tradition in his time like other pieces of well known poetry. It is certain that they would often have been attached to a story (like quatrains in twentieth-century Iceland), often the text would have become corrupted in people's memory and in transmission, but we are left with the idea of a huge corpus that must have been developing over a long period.

Snorri's interest in poetry developed early. In *Skáldatal* in Kringla he is reckoned among the poets who composed in honour of King Sverrir Sigurðarson, who died in 1202. If this poem was composed during the king's lifetime, Snorri cannot have been older than about twenty at the most when he wrote it. He sent a poem abroad to Earl Hákon galinn (died 1214) and received fine gifts as a reward, besides the earl according to Sturla commissioning a poem in praise of his wife, so he must have liked Snorri's poetry pretty well.[1] Nothing is preserved of these three poems, nor of any poems in praise of King Hákon or Earl Skúli except *Háttatal* and the *klofastef* ('split refrain') from a *drápa* about the latter. *Háttatal* is in fact the only complete praise poem preserved by this highly productive poet of princes, though there are six occasional verses in *dróttkvætt* plus one quatrain and a couplet (see *Skj* A II 77–79) that survive. That is all.

Sturla Þórðarson says of Snorri in *Íslendinga saga* that he *gerðist skáld gott* (lit. 'made himself a good poet') and this could of course be interpreted to mean that he had to work hard at it, though the phrase is probably simply an equivalent of 'became a good poet'. Sturla sees reason to mention this just at the point where he is saying how highly Snorri was regarded during his time at Reykjaholt before his journey abroad in 1218. He also emphasises that Snorri was 'skilled in everything he took up, and had the best instruction in everything that had to be done' (*Sturlunga saga* I 1946: I 269). It did require hard work and study to become good at court poetry. On this it suffices to call to mind Snorri's words to up-and-coming poets in his *Edda* about what they have to learn: 'But these things have to be told to young poets who desire to learn the language of poetry and to furnish themselves with a wide vocabulary using traditional terms or to understand what is expressed obscurely' (p. 90 below). It is necessary to learn the language of poetry, furnish oneself with a wide vocabulary and understand ancient poetry. It is by no means absurd to imagine that the compilation of *Skáldskaparmál*

---

[1] This is the poem *Andvaka*, which Snorri delivered to Kristín when he visited her and her second husband in Gautland in 1219 (*Sturlunga saga* 1946: I 271).

itself had been a part of Snorri's own study. It is on the other hand as clear as daylight when one looks at the *Edda* that its author had more faith in a good ear for poetry and extensive knowledge of language than in difficult theory. He was more of a student of poetry than one of literary theory.

Earl Hákon galinn had invited Snorri to visit him after his praise poem, but Sturla says: 'And Snorri had much of a mind to this. But the earl died about that time, and this caused his journey abroad to be delayed for a matter of a few winters. And yet he had decided on going, as soon as there was a suitable time for it' (*Sturlunga saga* 1946: I 269).

As will be mentioned later (Section 4), one might well imagine that at this period Snorri would have worked or had someone work at the gathering of material for both *Skáldskaparmál* and *Gylfaginning* and so compiled the first draft of his work.

The problem for the researcher is here as often elsewhere the lack of sources. We do not in fact know how the compilation of the *Edda* and later *Heimskringla* took place. In DG 11 4to it says that Snorri *hefir saman setta [Eddu]* 'has compiled the *Edda*' Sturla Þórðarson says of his namesake Sighvatsson: 'Now relations began to improve between Snorri and Sturla, and Sturla spent long periods then in Reykjaholt and took great trouble having books of history copied from the books that Snorri had compiled' (*Sturlunga saga* 1946: I 342). Snorri's words in his preface to *Heimkringlu* are also worth noting (*Hkr* I 3–4):

> In this book I have had written old stories about those rulers who have held power in the Northern lands and have spoken the Scandinavian language, as I have heard them told by learned men, and some of their genealogies according to what I have been taught, some of which is found in the records of paternal descent in which kings and other men of high rank have traced their ancestry, and some is written according to old poems or narrative songs which people used to use for their entertainment.

Though the *Edda* is not history in the same sense as *Heimskringla* is, it is composed of comparable short sections. Clearly Snorri had some written sources for both, but he bases his works also on poems and stories, in other words he had both written and oral sources.[1]

Oral sources are of course more difficult to describe than written ones. Yet it is tempting to point to examples in *Heimskringla* where an oral source is rather obvious. Bjarni Aðalbjarnarson points out in his introduction to *Hkr* III (pp. lx–lxi) that in *Magnúss saga blinda ok Haralds gilla* Snorri has added to the account he found in *Morkinskinna* and *Hryggjarstykki* everything that

---

[1] See Lasse Mårtensson and Heimir Pálsson 2008 on clear cases of written poems being quoted in the *Edda*.

is said in *Heimskringla* about the destruction of Konungahella (Chs 9–12). Then Bjarni continues (*Hkr* III lx):

> These events are briefly alluded to in *Ágrip*[1] but they are not referred to at all in *Morkinskinna* or *Fagrskinna*, and there is no likelihood that they were in any of the places where there are now lacunae in these texts. It is obvious where this account in *Heimskringla* is derived from. It is all described as if it were seen from the point of view of Jón Loptsson's foster-parents Andréás Brúnsson and his wife Solveig. Besides this couple and their relations only one person is named that was in Konungahella when it was destroyed, Haraldr flettir's son Guthormr. But all that is said of him is that he was sheriff there. It is likely that Jón Loptsson left Konungahella with his father before it was destroyed, and that Andréás met the pair later and told them what had happened. And it may well be that an account of the destruction of Konungahella was written which Snorri used. There is a clerical flavour to some parts of his account.

It is rather characteristic of scholars' aversion to the idea of oral sources that Bjarni should assume that there existed a written narrative to account for the 'clerical flavour' in this story. Even so, he has pointed out that Jón Loptsson must have got the story from the priest Andréás Brúnsson if he was not himself in the town when the Wends burned the church, though it seems to be just an assumption of Bjarni's that Jón and his father left the town.

As has been said above, Snorri refers to his informants in *Heimskringla*. Jón Loptsson was close to the scene of the events. We do not know whether Loptr Sæmundarson was still alive when Snorri came to Oddi, but Jón must certainly have passed on information from him about some events.

One does not need to have a particularly lively imagination to conceive how Jón and his father must have related the story when they got to Oddi. In memory it is mostly the horror of the events that stands out, and Snorri's conclusion is clear: 'The market town at Konungahella never recovered the same importance that it had before' (*Hkr* III 296). According to Swedish and Norwegian historians the development of Konungahella was greatest in the time of Hákon the Old, that is in the time of Snorri, but for the significance of the town in the twelfth century there are no reliable sources.[2]

1.2 The trip to Norway and return home (1218–1220)

In the four years that passed between the time when Snorri received the invitation from Earl Hákon galinn and when he actually went abroad, significant

---

[1] Here Bjarni seems to be referring to Ch. liii of *Ágrip* (*ÍF* XXIX: 48). It is not explicitly stated that this took place in Konungahella, but the same miracle story is the basis of it, about heathens who burn a church but flee before the cross, 'and then launched a boat and put the cross and the priest ashore'.
[2] See, for example, *Nationalencyklopedin*.

events took place. The people of Oddi had become involved in serious conflict with Norwegians. Jón Loptsson's grandson Páll Sæmundarson was killed in Norway and the people of Oddi took vengeance by putting great pressure on Norwegian merchants in the south of Iceland. This led to further killings in the Westman Islands, where Jón Loptsson's son Ormr was killed, and his son Jón, together with others. And here it is right to let Sturla Þórðarson tell the story (*Sturlunga saga* 1946: I 271–72):

> Snorri did not hear about Ormr being killed until he got to Norway—but then he went abroad from Hvítá. And there was hostile criticism of the people of Oddi's behaviour in the matter of the confiscations that had taken place at Eyrar. Those that demanded compensation for the killing of Ormr got a hostile response.
>
> When Snorri got to Norway, King Hákon and Earl Skúli had come to power. The earl received Snorri exceptionally kindly, and Snorri went to stay with the earl . . . Snorri stayed the winter with the earl.
>
> And the following summer he travelled east to Gautland to see the lawman Áskell and the Lady Kristín, who had previously been married to Hákon galinn. Snorri had composed a poem in praise of her called Andvaka, commissioned by Earl Hákon. And she received Snorri honourably and gave him many honourable gifts. She gave him the banner that had belonged to King Eiríkr Knútsson of the Swedes, who had had it when he brought about the fall of King Sǫrkvir at Gestilrein.
>
> Snorri returned to Earl Skúli in the autumn and stayed there a second winter, receiving very fine hospitality.

It is not known exactly where Áskell and Kristín lived. On the other hand it is quite certain that she was the grandchild of the Upplander St Eiríkr and it was probably from her that Snorri got his information about eastern Sweden, especially Uppsala and Uppland. She was born there and relatives of hers came from there, for instance her cousin Eiríkr Knútsson, whom Swedish sources do not actually state to have led the attack on Sǫrkvir at Gestilrein.[1] In fact *Sturlunga saga* is the only source for an important aspect of this event in Swedish history. To clarify the picture that we get from Swedish historiography, just one example will be given (Larsson 2005: 65–66):

> In the circumstances he was very well received in Västergötland, and before he travelled back to Norway in the autumn Lady Kristina gave him the banner that King Erik Knutsson of the Swedes had when he brought about the fall of King Sverker the Younger at Gestilrein nine years before—a truly royal gift that must have made the Icelandic nobleman swell with rapture.
>
> Where this renowned battle between the Sverker and the Erik dynasty took place would of course have been well known to both the lawman and his wife, and through them to Snorri too. Yet neither *Sturlunga saga*—the source that tells

---

[1] In fact there is no agreement about where Gestilrein was, and people have taken sides about it. The battle, on the other hand, was significant.

of his visit to Sweden—nor he himself has anything to say about the matter. Although he, as as a keen-sighted observer with an interest in high politics, would have been able to give us invaluable information about this event, he was not interested enough in it to describe it—it lay altogether too close in time for him and was already known to all.

The conflicts between Norwegians and the people of Oddi had caused great difficulties for Icelanders in Norway. Snorri obviously counted as one of the Oddi people, and of course he was foster-son of the head of the family, and one might well imagine that this was one of the reasons why he became a greater friend of Earl Skúli than of the young Hákon. The difference in their ages was substantial. Snorri and Skúli Bárðarson were both in the prime of life, the earl being perhaps ten years younger than Snorri (he is thought to have been born in 1288 or 1289), while Hákon was only fourteen when Snorri went abroad. But so harsh is fate that the young king was to be the instigator of both friends' deaths.

Sturlunga saga is our main source, in fact the only source for what happened in Norway in 1220. Sturla says this about it (*Sturlunga saga* 1946: I 277–78):

> Snorri Sturluson stayed two winters with Skúli, as was written above. King Hákon and Skúli gave him the honorary title of 'cupbearer' (*skutilsveinn*). Then in the spring, Snorri was planning to go to Iceland. But the Norwegians were great enemies of Icelanders and especially of people of Oddi, because of the confiscations that took place at Eyrar. So it came about that it was decided to make a raid on Iceland in the summer. Ships and the men to go in them were organised. But most people with more sense were not at all keen on this expedition and raised many difficulties about it . . .
>
> Snorri was very much against the expedition and declared the best course was to make friends with the best people in Iceland and maintained that he by his arguments would soon be able to bring it about that people would find it advantageous to turn to compliance with the rulers of Norway. He said that now there were apart from Sæmundr [Jónsson] no other greater men in Iceland than his brothers, and maintained that they would act pretty much in accordance with his recommendations when he got there.
>
> So after these representations the earl's mood softened and he put forward this advice, that the Icelanders should beg King Hákon to intercede for them so that the military expedition might not take place.
>
> The king was at this time young, and the lawman Dagfinnr, who was now his adviser, was a very great friend of Icelanders. And the result was that the king decided that the military expedition should not take place. And King Hákon and Earl Skúli made Snorri their thane; this was mostly engineered by the earl and Snorri. So Snorri was to try to persuade the Icelanders to be compliant with the rulers of Norway. Snorri was to send his son Jón abroad, and he was to stay as hostage with the earl, so that these conditions might be observed.

'They each trusted the other ill | Indeed there were few that trusted both' said Grímur Thomsen about Kálfr Árnason and Sveinn Álfífuson. Although Skúli and Hákon had made Snorri first 'cupbearer' and then thane, they trusted him no further than to insist that he send Jón murti as hostage 'so that these conditions might be observed'.

And there were others that mistrusted Snorri. When he reached land, battered by storm late in the autumn of 1220 on a ship given him by the earl with 'fifteen great gifts', the people of Oddi saw no reason to welcome him. 'They thought he must be put up by the Norwegians to oppose them, to prevent them from bringing a prosecution for the killing of Ormr. The most insistent on this was Bjǫrn Þorvaldsson, who was then living at Breiðabólstaðr and was considered an up-and-coming leader' (*Sturlunga saga* 1946: I 278). Bjǫrn was Gizurr Þorvaldsson's full brother and married to Hallveig, daughter of Ormr Breiðbǿlingr, son of Jón Loptsson's mistress. Hallveig would later become Snorri's wife and hold an equal share of his wealth. And the people of Oddi welcome Snorri with a lampoon.

Nothing is known about the authorship of this remarkable verse. Sturla says only that Þóroddr of Selvágr gave an unknown person a wether to compose it (*Sturlunga saga* 1946: I 278–79):

Oss lízk illr at kyssa	Unpleasant it seems to us to kiss
jarl, sás ræðr fyr hjarli,	the earl who rules the land,
vǫrr es til hvǫss á harra,	the lip is too sharp on the prince.
harðmúlaðr es Skúli.	Hard muzzled is Skúli.
Hefr fyr horska jǫfra	There has before wise rulers
hrægamms komit sævar	of the corpse-vulture of the sea come
—þjóð finnr lǫst á ljóðum—	—people find blemishes in the poetry—
leir aldrigi meira.	never more shit.

I have written about this lampoon in another place[1] and that will not be repeated here. Yet it may be pointed out that in the second half of the stanza we have the kenning *hrægamms sævar leir* (shit of the corpse-vulture of the sea), which appears to be a case of double tmesis and has to be read *hrægamms leir* (corpse-sea's vulture's shit); corpse-sea = blood, blood's vulture = eagle, eagle's shit (*arnarleir*) = doggerel (cf. *Skáldskaparmál*, Faulkes 1998: 5/1–7). *Arnarleir* is a rare expression and only known from one verse that is certainly earlier than the stanza in *Sturlunga saga*, and then in the form *leir ara ins gamla* (shit of the old eagle); this is in a lampoon by Þórarinn stuttfeldr (*Skj* A I 491: 2, 3; *Skaldic Poetry* II: 481). This verse of Þórarinn's was clearly the source of the anonymous verse about Snorri.

The word *arnarleir* itself, however, appears in DG 11 4to, where it tells of Óðinn's flight back to Ásgarðr with the mead of poetry in slightly different

[1] Heimir Pálsson 2010c.

terms from those of the Codex Regius version (p. 88 below; cf. Faulkes 1998: 5/1–7):

> Æsir settu út í garðinn ker sín. Óðinn spýtti miðinum í kerin. En sumum repti hann aptr, er honum varð nær farit ok hafa þat skáldfífl ok heitir arnarleir, en Suttunga mjǫðr þeir er yrkja kunna.
>
> The Æsir put their containers out in the courtyard. Óðinn spat the mead into the containers. But some of it he shat out backwards, since it was a close thing for him, and rhymesters have that and it is called eagle's shit, and [it is called] Suttungi's mead [what] those who are skilled at composing poetry [have].

In the other versions of the Edda the word does not appear, and the next example of its use that we have is by Arngrímr Brandsson, who says in *Guðmundardrápa*: 'eagle's shit have I to offer you' (*Skj* A II 349). Here we have reached nearly the middle of the fourteenth century, and it seems justifiable to assert that this was a rather rare word.

It has always been thought particularly humiliating to fall before one's own weapons. If the word *arnarleir* was Snorri's coinage, it is understandable that he should be upset when it was used of his own poetry—so he deletes the word from his *Edda*. *Skáldfíflahlutr* (poetaster's portion) is what applies.

It is clear that Snorri was angry about the lampoon. Sturla words it discreetly, indicating that he and Bjǫrn Þorvaldsson were on bad terms. 'He was annoyed at the mockery the people of the south had made of his poem' (*Sturlunga saga* 1946: I 284). Then Sturla says that some verses had been made in Stafaholt (where Snorri was living at this time), and all commentators have interpreted this to mean that it was Snorri that composed them. 'This is one of them,' says Sturla (*Sturlunga saga* 1946: I 284):

Björn frák brýndu járni	I heard that Bjǫrn with sharpened weapon
—bragð gótt vas þat—lagðan	—a good trick was that—was stabbed
—gerði Guðlaugr fyrðum	—Guðlaugr did men
geysihark—í barka.	great injury—in the windpipe.
Auðkýfingr lét ævi	The moneybags lost his life
óblíðr fyr Grásíðu:	unhappy before Grásíða:
hvöss var hon heldr at kyssa—	sharp was it to kiss—
harðmúlaðr vas Skúli.	hard muzzled was Skúli.

Guðlaugr Eyjólfsson had killed Bjǫrn Þorvaldsson with the spear Grásíða, thrusting it into his throat.

Though Snorri is often mentioned by Sturla in *Íslendinga saga* during the next few years, it is difficult to trace his career as an author from year to year. As is argued later, I find it extremely unlikely that he began compiling and writing the *Edda* only after his return to Iceland in 1220, much less after 1222, as Konráð Gíslason assumed and the sequence of composition according to Wessén seems to imply: *Háttatal* 〉 Commentary 〉 *Skáldskaparmál*, first version 〉 *Gylfaginning* 〉 Prologue 〉 *Skáldskaparmál*, second version. A different sequence is more likely.

On the other hand, around 1230 a lot of literary activity was going on in Reykjaholt. It was then that Sturla Sighvatsson 'took great trouble having books of history copied from the books that Snorri had compiled', as is mentioned above.

In the third decade of the century, however, it is very likely that Snorri reviewed drafts of the *Edda* that he had written previously. Now *Háttatal* is in existence or coming into existence, material has been added after his trip to Norway (maybe though mainly Icelandic material), his grasp of the material has improved, the narrative becomes sharper.

1.3 Back to Norway (1237)

The third and fourth decades of the thirteenth century were bloody ones in Iceland, with conflicts both between and within kin groups. Sturla Sighvatsson, he who took great trouble having books of history copied, goes abroad for absolution in 1233, calls at Norway on his way back, and his namesake Þórðarson tells us (*Sturlunga saga* 1946: I 364):

> Sturla met King Hákon in Túnsberg, and he was warmly welcomed, and stayed there for a long time during the second of the two winters that he was in Norway, and the king and Sturla were always talking together.

In his biography of Snorri, Sigurður Nordal shows how, according to his interpretation, events in Snorri's life were linked with the political turn of events (1973:17):

> With Sturla Sighvatsson's return to Iceland in the autumn of 1235 with a commission from King Hákon, a new chapter in the country's history opened. First Sturla set to work against Snorri.

Relations between the two kinsmen got worse and worse, but *Íslendinga saga* offers no explanation for Snorri's next trip to Norway (1237; *Sturlunga saga* 1946: I 408–9):

> Snorri Sturluson went abroad from Eyrar in the summer, and also Þórðr kakali, Þorleifr and Óláfr, and they came to the northern part of Norway and stayed the winter in Niðaróss.
>
> Snorri stayed with Duke Skúli's son Pétr, but the duke stayed in Oslo through the winter, both he and King Hákon. Things went reasonably well between father-in-law and son-in-law.

Sigurður Nordal interpreted this trip abroad like this (1973: 18): 'He must have realised that events were coming to a head in Iceland, and felt it better to be out of the way.' It might seem closer to the mark to pay attention to the

Introduction

fact that Sturla has now received the commission that Snorri reckoned was his from long before, and which he was now planning to ask for clarification about or for a renewal of. This might also explain why he kept himself further off from Hákon and closer to Skúli.

The author of *Hákonar saga*, who was also Sturla Þórðarson, knows that it is precisely in that year that Skúli got the title of duke. Now he is no longer just an earl, he is the first man in Norway to be a duke.

Just as during Snorri's earlier trip abroad, a significant event now took place in Iceland: the engagement at Ǫrlygsstaðir, the bloodiest civil conflict in the history of Iceland. Snorri's uncle Sighvatr fell, together with the latter's sons Sturla, Kolbeinn, Markús and Þórðr krókr, but another of his sons, Þórðr kakali learnt of the killings in Norway, like his uncle Snorri and Snorri's kinsmen Þorleifr Þórðarsson and Óláfr hvítaskáld. And again Sturla comments (*Sturlunga saga* 1946: I 439):

> When news of this reached Norway in the autumn, the deaths of the father and his sons were felt to be the most grievous loss, for they were very popular among merchants and others in the country. King Hákon was a great friend of Sturla's, for it was often said that he and Sturla had planned that the latter was to bring the country into subjection to King Hákon, and the king was to make him ruler of the country. King Hákon had warned Sturla particularly not to add to the number of killings in the country, but rather to force people abroad.

Snorri sends Þórðr kakali a well known verse after this (*Sturlunga saga* 1946: I 439–40):

Tveir lifið, Þórðr, en þeira
þá vas ǿðri hlutr brǿðra,
—rán vasa lýðum launat
laust—en sex á hausti.

Gera svín, en verðr venjask
vár ætt, ef svá mætti,
ýskelfandi, ulfar,
afarkaupum, samhlaupa.

And the editor, Magnús Finnbogason, paraphrases this: 'Now there still live [only] you two, Þórðr, but there were six of you last autumn, then the circumstances of you brothers were better—you achieved undiminished vengeance for the robbery. Warrior, the wolves cause the swine to group together if it can be done, but our family has to get used to harsh terms' (*Sturlunga saga* 1946: I 603). Even wild swine can defend themselves by uniting, but Sturlungar are unable to do that.

1.4 The wrong horse backed

It must have been obvious to Snorri that the king had taken a position in opposition to him. The conflicts between Hákon and Skúli are on the other hand getting worse, and it was gradually becoming clear that it would end in violence. One of them was going to win, and Snorri put his money on

Skúli, and again it is tempting to let Sturla Þórðarson tell the story (*Sturlunga saga* 1946: I 444):

> For the winter after the Ǫrlygsstaðir engagement, these three, Snorri Sturluson and his son Órœkja and [his cousin] Þorleifr Þórðarson stayed with Duke Skúli in Niðaróss, but Þórðr kakali was in Bjǫrgyn with King Hákon. But in the spring they got a ship belonging to Snorri's friend Guðleikr at Skartastaðir, and they prepared it for going to sea with the consent of the duke.
>
> But when they were ready and had made their way out below Hólmr, then men arrived from the king in the south, and with letters, which said this, that the king banned all Icelanders from leaving the country that summer. They showed Snorri the letters, and his answer was: 'I wish to leave.'
>
> And when they were ready, they were the guests of the duke before they took their leave. There were few men present at the duke and Snorri's talks. Arnfinnr Þjófsson and Óláfr hvítaskáld were with the duke, and Órœkja and Þorleifr with Snorri. And according to Arnfinnr, the duke gave Snorri the title of earl, and Styrmir inn fróði has noted: 'Anniversary of Snorri the secret earl's death'—but none of the Icelanders would confirm this.

The editors of *Sturlunga saga* 1946 correctly point out that Styrmir fróði was very likely in Snorri's confidence and would have considered himself free of all obligation to secrecy once Snorri was no more, but on the other hand the Icelanders that are mentioned, who were all relations of Snorri, would have had 'good reason to contradict this, since according to the law Snorri's wealth would have fallen to the royal treasury if he turned out to have really accepted an earldom from Duke Skúli, who just at this time was plotting a rebellion against the king' (*Sturlunga saga* 1946: I 571).

Sturla's account of the talks in Norway is an account of negotiations between two leaders. Each of them has with him two men, but it is in itself striking that one of the Duke's men is Snorri's nephew. Arnfinnr, on the other hand, is Norwegian and one of Skúli's friends. Here we see them working out plans for an empire in which Skúli would rule Norway, Snorri Iceland under Skúli's authority. This is of course high treason, and if Hákon got wind of the talks, the sequel is understandable.

1.5 'Do not strike!'

Snorri's last years in Iceland were sad ones. He enjoyed no luck with his children and now was a testing time. He has no one he can trust after the death of Hallveig Ormsdóttir in the summer of 1241, and Sturla gets involved in the story: 'Hallveig Ormsdóttir died in Reykjaholt, and Snorri felt that to be a great loss, as for him it was' (*Sturlunga saga* 1946: I 452). This is in fact very reminiscent of what Sturla says about Snorri when the latter learnt of the killing of Sighvatr at Ǫrlygsstaðir: 'He felt the death of his brother to be a very great loss, as it was, though they sometimes did not have the good fortune to see eye to eye together' (*Sturlunga saga* 1946: I 440).

Sigurður Nordal reckons one of the defects of Snorri's character to be 'tight-fistedness with money gained' (1973: 19). The traditional name for this was greed, *avaritia*, and it is one of the seven deadly sins. After Hallveig's death he shows for the last time that he is unfair in his dealings with his stepsons Klængr and Ormr Bjarnarson.[1] Division of the landed property does not proceed, and Snorri is very stubborn on this matter; if *Sturlunga saga* had been a novel one would have considered it a masterly stroke when the author chooses these words about it: 'So they divided the possessions and books, but with the landed property it did not work out' (*Sturlunga saga* 1946: I 452). The scholar has a short time to live when he is able to divide up his library. One would give a lot nowadays to get to know what books were shared out there.

But Snorri has to pay for his unreasonableness about the sharing of the inheritance. Hallveig's sons were nephews of Gizurr Þorvaldsson, and he said it was 'not right that they had not got a fair sharing out with Snorri, saying that he would give them his backing to get it too' (*Sturlunga saga* 1946: I 452).

When Sturla Þórðarson traces the events of the year 1240, he expresses himself thus (*Sturlunga saga* 1946: I 447):

> That summer Eyvindr brattr and Árni óreiða came out with letters from King Hákon, and little notice was taken of them. They also told of the hostilities there had been in Norway during the winter, and the fall of Duke Skúli.

The clouds are gathering. Skúli has fallen, Hallveig dies, a warning arrives from Álftanes on Mýrar. They are sitting in a small parlour in Sauðafell, Snorri, Sturla Þórðarson and Órœkja Snorrason, while Tumi Sighvatsson the Younger is pouring out drinks (*Sturlunga saga* 1946: I 453):

> Beer had been brought in there from the ship. Snorri told about his dealings with Hallveig's sons. He also had there a letter that Oddr Sveinbjarnarson had sent him from Álftanes. It contained secret writing (*stafkarlaletr*), and they could not read it, but it seemed to them to have some kind of warning in it. Snorri said he did not trust the people of the south of Iceland, 'and yet I shall go to the south first and see to my estate,' he said, 'and then go to the west and then stay for the most part at Hólar, but some of the time at Saurbœr.'
>
> A great deal was discussed there, and they all rode together in to Hjarðarholt. And from there Snorri rode south and they west.

It is probable that the *stafkarlaletr* that they could not understand except partially was some kind of code. The editors of the 1946 edition explain it as 'secret runes'. The word is a hapax legomenon (cf. *ONP*) and can scarcely be said to be transparent. The writer of the letter was educated as a deacon

---

[1] See *Sturlunga saga* 1946: I 452, and cf. Sigurður Nordal 1973: 19.

and we have to assume that he was literate. It is therefore unsafe to assume that the letter was simply illegible.

Now one might think of it as a game and suggest there was wordplay involved. Readers of *Auðunar þáttr vestfirzka* will remember his pilgimage to Rome and how he took up a beggar's way of life (*stafkarls stígr*). Pilgrims walked with a pilgrim's staff (*stafkarls stafr*). Is it conceivable that the kinsmen over their beer-cups were joking about *stafkarlaletr* (= *stafkarls stafir*? — *stafr* can mean both staff and stave or *letr*) simply because they could not understand Latin? *Letr* means not only script (letters) but also what is written, as can be seen from Fritzner's dictionary, where these passages are quoted under *letr* 2):[1]

> má þessor orð vel eptir þí, sem letrit ljóðar, af Zabulons ætt skilja *Stj.* 232^{24}; sá maðr, sem þessa luti fær svá vel — skilit eptir því, sem letrit heyrist ljóða, at — Stj. 29^{19}; svá finnst í fögru letri skrifat í latínu, at — *Æf.* 48^1; ef hann náir því letri, sem þar um er gert, skal hann skera þat í sundr ok brenna í eldi *Klm.* 548^{16}; ljóst er vorðit af letrum þeim, er lærðir menn leifðu eptir sik— at *Thom.* 295^3; sem ljósliga stendr í þess háttar letrum *Stj.* 4^{10}.

If Deacon Oddr wrote in Latin it was so that any dishonest rogues that got hold of the letter would not understand it. But he forgot to consider that Snorri had only a limited amount of Latin and Sturla probably had next to none too.[2]

Snorri said he did not trust the people of the south of Iceland, yet he took incredibly few precautions in Reykjaholt, and not much intelligence reached him about what was going on (*Sturlunga saga* 1946: I 453):

> When Gizurr came down from Kjölr, he summoned men to come to him. The brothers Klængr and Ormr were there, the bishop's son Loftr and Árni óreiða too. He then brought out the letters that Eyvindr and Árni had brought from Norway. They said that Gizurr was to make Snorri go to Norway, whether he pleased or not, or otherwise he was to kill him because he had left Norway under the king's ban. Hákon declared Snorri a traitor to himself. Gizurr said he was no way going to act against the king's letter, but said he knew that Snorri would not go abroad without being forced. Gizurr now wanted to go and seize Snorri.

[1] On Snorri's interest in wordplay see *Skáldskaparmál* (Faulkes 1998) ch. 72.

[2] On the two kinsmen's knowledge of Latin the least said the better, as has been suggested before. Nothing that is said of their studies throws any light on the problem. Zealous attempts to find Latin models for the *Edda* have yielded no results (see for example Dronke and Dronke 1977 and Faulkes 1993). No Latin words appear in the writings of Snorri (the apparent Latin accusative ending in *Trójam*, p. 8 below, is hardly an exception; the other MSS have *Troan*, which is likely to be a misunderstanding of *Trojana*, cf. Faulkes 1978–79, 101 n. 36) or in those of Sturla either to indicate the extent of the acquaintance with Latin either of them had. It is an old habit to reckon all literate men in the Middle Ages able to read and write Latin, but if that were so, why is the First Grammatical Treatise written in Icelandic without any mixture of Latin terms?

The sequence of events on the 23rd of September 1241 is straightforward but peculiar. Gizurr Þorvaldsson (formerly Snorri's son-in-law), the bishop's son Loptr (son of Páll son of Jón Loptsson) and Snorri's stepson Kløngr Bjarnarson gather supporters. Sturla takes seventy men, presumably by the shortest route, Okvegur, and seems to arrive at a more or less undefended Reykjaholt. There is no mention of anyone else being there but Snorri and the priest Arnbjǫrn, who seems to have been pretty easily taken in when Gizurr gets him to show him where Snorri is hiding, saying that 'they would not be able to be reconciled if they did not meet' (*Sturlunga saga* 1946: I 454). Gizurr does not bloody his hands, but sends five fighting men into the cellar to kill Snorri. They must have been the source of the report later that Snorri said nothing else but 'Eigi skal hǫggva!' ('Do not strike!)' twice.

Much has been written about these last words. Some consider that they bear witness to Snorri's faint-heartedness (see the excellent surveys in Stefán Karlsson 1989 and Lýður Björnsson 1978), others consider them a sign of the fearlessness that counts it right to remind people of the Ten Commandments. It is worth noting Lýður Björnsson's point (1978: 162) about the similarity between these words of Snorri's and those of Duke Skúli in *Hákonar saga* (1977: 134): 'Do not strike me in the face, for it is not the custom to treat noblemen so.' It was the same author that wrote *Hákonar saga* and *Íslendinga saga* and he was well aware of the friendship between Skúli and Snorri.

The next day it seems clear that the large number of men gathered for this attack was because there is expectation of terrible vengeance for Snorri. Sturla Þórðarson tells about this vengeance, which mostly misfired, in *Íslendinga saga*, and in fact he himself took part in the attempted vengeance and claims on his property with his cousin Órœkja (see *Sturlunga saga* 1946: I 454–72).

The most famous Icelandic writer and in fact the foremost medieval author of Scandinavia is no more. His life is in many ways a riddle, about his works we know less than we would choose. There is no shortage of romantic pictures of him. Here is one of them (Ivar Eskeland 1992: 17):

> [One] cannot tell, a good eight hundred years later, whether we would have got immortal works from Snorri Sturluson's head and hand if his father had not accepted Jon Loptsson of Oddi's offer. Perhaps our ancient history of Norway would then have been no different from the one that we know. Maybe we would then not have had the sparkling picture gallery of our ancient rulers that this Snorri came to give us; depictions of people that will live in the minds of all Scandinavians as long as Scandinavians are to be found. Neither might his compatriots have had the monumental work about Snorri Sturluson's great ancestor, savage and poet Egill Skallagrímsson.

Perhaps it was just the spirit from the peaceable chieftain at Oddi that was echoed in Snorri's dying words.

2 Manuscripts
2.1 DG 11 4to

The vellum manuscript that bears the catalogue number DG 11 4to and is preserved in the University Library Carolina Rediviva in Uppsala, is always reckoned to have been written in the first quarter of the fourteenth century. It is not known where, but the contents suggest the area of the Sturlungs' supremacy in the west of Iceland. Nothing is known about the history of the manuscript until it turns up in Denmark in the possession of Vice-Principal Brynjólfur Sveinsson, later bishop at Skálholt in Iceland, having presumably been brought from Iceland by him. In the winter of 1636–37 Jón lærði Guðmundsson, then in Copenhagen, made a copy of it at Brynjólfur's request.[1] Some copies had, however, been made of the vellum before it left Iceland. Jón Sigurðsson had examined one of them, which was then in the Árni Magnússon collection in Copenhagen and now has the catalogue number AM 157 8vo in the Árni Magnússon Institute for Icelandic Studies in Reykjavík.[2] Jón Sigurðsson seems not to have realised that this copy had been made before the vellum began to get seriously damaged, and thus offers readings that make it possible to fill gaps in the text in a more reliable way now than has been done previously. AM 157 8vo will be discussed in a separate section below.

When DG 11 4to is dated to the early fourteenth century, this is based on the handwriting as well as orthography and word forms. The script is Gothic and the letter forms point to about 1300. The scribe was clearly acquainted with the svarabhakti vowel -*u*-, but reveals this only by his inverse spellings such as *dóttr, móðr* instead of *dóttur, móður*. The long *i*-umlauted vowels ǿ and æ have fallen together, not to mention the short *ö*-sounds, ǫ and ø.[3] Everything points to the first part of fourteenth century, and rather close to its beginning. This places it among the earliest manuscripts of *Snorra Edda*, together with GkS 2367 4to and AM 748 I b 4to.

DG 11 4to contains altogether 56 leaves. It was paginated (wrongly) in recent times so that f. 1 is unnumbered, and f. 2r numbered p. 1. Here reference will be made primarily to the (actual) folio numbers rather than to the marked page numbers unless there is a particular reason to use the latter.

The division into gatherings is rather unusual. The first has ten leaves, then there are five of eight leaves and one of six. Both the first and the last

---

[1] See Einar G. Pétursson 1998: 121. Jón's copy is preserved in the Bodleian Library, Oxford, as Marshall 114.

[2] See *Edda Snorra Sturlusonar* 1848–87: III 248–49.

[3] In Lasse Mårtensson's forthcoming book an exhaustive account of the palaeographical evidence for the date of the manuscript will be given.

gatherings are thus anomalous. Guðvarður Már Gunnlaugsson has considered the case of the first (2009: 343–44):

> I have no good explanation to hand of why the first gathering has ten leaves, but it has occurred to me that originally the scribe had intended to bind this Edda of his ... up with some other book already written. But when he had got started on the first gathering, he reconsidered and decided that he was dealing with a separate book. But if this was so, he needed a flyleaf, since he had already begun to write on the leaf which would otherwise have to be f. 1r. How was he to find a solution? OK, he gets a new sheet and folds it round the quarto gathering that he has begun to write on, and then, when he has filled eight leaves, he continues writing on the second half of the new sheet and fills that and thus ends up with a ten folio gathering in which the first leaf is completely blank and the text begins on f. 2r ... The outermost folios of this gathering are perhaps slightly smaller than the others as a result.

As often happens in these studies, we have in other words to accept a little ingenuity, and we can go further down that road. As is mentioned later, the scribe seems to have intended that the first three gatherings should constitute an independent entity, a book (in the sense in which this word was used in the Middle Ages, as a major division of a lengthy work). So perhaps he soon realised that the work would not quite fit onto three gatherings, so he made use of the expedient of wrapping a new sheet round the first gathering, and thus got everything to work out.[1]

The last gathering has only six leaves, and there is nothing to suggest that it was ever intended to be greater. The text ends in line 10 of f. 56r and it does not appear that the scribe had any more than the fifty-six stanzas that he has written. There could be various explanations for this, and they are discussed below. Anyway it seems clear that the scribe considered his job to be finished.

It may be considered thanks to the sheet wrapped round the first gathering that the text in DG 11 4to appears to be uncurtailed. It begins on a page that has always been protected and ends on a recto page, which of course would have been protected too. Thus DG 11 4to has become the only uncurtailed manuscript surviving of *Snorra Edda*, that is to say it lacks nothing either at the beginning or the end. Three of its leaves are, however badly damaged. There are large holes in ff. 32, 33 and 34 so that there are lacunae in the text. These are the three last leaves of the fourth gathering. The holes in ff. 32 and 33 are in corresponding places, but the last leaf in this gathering, f. 34, is worst affected, 'with extensive lacunae and and a great deal of the parchment lost' (Grape et al. 1977: ix).

[1] Presumably this would have happened before he had begun writing f. 5r of the original gathering (p. 11 of the existing manuscript), as otherwise he would probably have inserted the new sheet in the middle of his first gathering. If he had done that, the break between the third and fourth gatherings would of course have been less manageable, as there would have been another leaf to fill with his first book.

Mould is usually blamed for this damage, but casual inspections by Guðvarður Már Gunnlaugsson and his colleagues at the Árni Magnússon Institute point rather to some kind of corrosive liquid eating it away.[1] At any rate it seems clear that these three leaves were all damaged together. The damage will be discussed in greater detail in Section 2.2.

When Brynjólfur Sveinsson had to go to Iceland, whether he wanted to or not, to take up the office of bishop in 1639, he gave the manuscript to his friend St. J. Stephanius, principal at Sorø Akademi. Later, in 1662, the bishop sent his king, Frederik III, both what became the Codex Regius of the eddic poems and what became the Codex Regius of *Snorra Edda* (GkS 2365 4to and GkS 2367 4to). Another scholar, Arngrímur Jónsson the Learned, gave Ole Worm the book that has since borne the name of its owner and is known as Wormianus or Wormsbók (Ormsbók) and has the catalogue number AM 242 fol. and is a most splendid manuscript in many ways. Codex Wormianus is later than the Uppsala manuscript, probably not earlier than 1350.[2]

When Stephanius died in 1650, he left behind a family in dire financial straits. His widow, Thale Eisenberg, put his library up for sale and an offer came from Gustav II Adolf's daughter Queen Kristina of Sweden. She was crowned in the year of Stephanius's death, and planned to set up a royal library in Uppsala. The wealthy Magnus Gabriel De la Gardie was an intermediary and underwrote the purchase of books. It took some time, and it was not until 1652 that the manuscript of *Snorra Edda* reached Sweden and was ultimtely deposited in the University Library in Uppsala.[3]

The history and use of DG 11 4to is so exhaustively treated in Grape 1962 that there is no need to go over it again here. It is relevant, however, to draw attention to the fact that scholars in Uppsala in the eighteenth century and even in the early nineteenth century assumed that DG 11 4to was conceivably the original manuscript of the work, but this was very firmly denied by Rasmus Kristian Rask in his introduction to the edition of 1818 (pp. 8–9):

> Some scholars have regarded the Uppsala Edda as the author's own original; but on the contrary, it seems to me obvious that it is the latest of the three, and a kind of epitome of the others.[4]

[1] In an email to me of 8th October 2010, Guðvarður spoke of his and conservation specialist Hersteinn Brynjólfsson's impressions, though to be sure the latter had only seen reproductions of the manuscript.

[2] This manuscript came into the possession of Árni Magnússon in 1706. See Finnur Jónsson 1931: viii.

[3] It was probably from Johan Ihre, professor in Uppsala in the eighteenth century, that Jón Sigurðsson got the mistaken idea into his head that Jón Rúgmann had brought DG 11 4to to Uppsala (*Íslenzkt fornbréfasafn* I: 499).

[4] In Rask's time the Utrecht manuscript was unknown and thus he speaks of just three (complete) versions.

Rask's proof is threefold. The headings in DG 11 4to cannot be original, for otherwise they would appear in the Codex Regius and Codex Wormianus as well; the scribe has misunderstood some things, so his text cannot be the original; and shortening has sometimes led to the text of DG 11 4to meaning nothing or else being just wrong. It may be said that everyone is now in agreement with Rask on this point. DG 11 4to is not the original, not even a copy of the original. On the other hand there is still disagreement about shortenings and lengthenings.

A copy of one medieval manuscript was made on paper just before the end of the sixteenth century (1595) and the copy is preserved in Utrecht in Holland (Codex Trajectinus or Trektarbók, Utrecht University Library no 1374[1]). The manuscript it was copied from is now lost, but it was closely related to the Codex Regius.

Parts of the *Prose Edda* are preserved in AM 757 a 4to, AM 748 I b 4to and AM 748 II 4to (all three now in Reykjavík). They all have some leaves missing, but the first two contain independent redactions of parts of the *Edda*, and the text of the third, as far as it goes, is similar to that of GkS 2367 4to.[2] In the late Middle Ages a copy of Codex Wormianus was made, of which parts survive in AM 756 4to.

This is a considerably varied collection of manuscripts, which is no less remarkable for the fact that one can say that apart from the Utrecht manuscript and AM 748 II 4to, each manuscript offers a separate version or redaction of the work. Thus GkS 2367 4to has *þulur* that are not in Codex Wormianus or the Uppsala manuscript and two poems, *Jómsvíkingadrápa* and *Málsháttakvæði*, that are not in any other manuscript of the *Edda*; AM 242 fol. has four so-called grammatical treatises, an extended version of the prologue, parts of a variant version of the second part of *Skáldskapamál* and part of *Rígsþula*; DG 11 4to one of the grammatical treatises and a version of *Skáldatal* and other additional material; AM 757 a 4to and 748 I b 4to texts of parts of *Skáldskaparmál* that vary considerably from the other manuscripts and *þulur* that are not in either GkS 2367 4to or Codex Trajectinus.[3] AM 757 a 4to also has parts of the third grammatical treatise and some religious (Christian poems), AM 748 1 b 4to also has parts of the third grammatical treatise and part of a fifth and *Íslendingadrápa*. AM 748 II 4to contains passages from *Gylfaginning* and *Skáldskaparmál* with a text that is most similar to that in the Codex Regius, and the same Sturlung

---

[1] An inaccurate diplomatic edition was published by von Eeden in 1913, and Anthony Faulkes prepared a facsimile edition in 1985.

[2] See Guðrún Nordal 2001: 45. The texts of these manuscripts can be seen in *Edda Snorra Sturlusonar* 1848–87: II 397–494 (AM 748 I b 4to), 501–572 (AM 757 a 4to) and 573–627 (AM 748 II 4to).

[3] These *þulur* are printed along with those of the Codex Regius in *Skj* A I 649–690.

genealogy as is found in the Uppsala manuscript. The only manuscript that is free from 'interpolations' seems therefore to be the Codex Trajectinus. Hereafter the discussion will centre mainly on the Codex Regius version (R) and the Uppsala Edda version (U), and an attempt will be made to distinguish between versions and manuscripts by referring to the former as R and U and the latter by their catalogue numbers.

In itself it is quite natural that there should be so many different versions if one bears in mind that *Snorra Edda* is a textbook. It belongs to that genre of writing that is always being revised, always work in progress. Thus it is far from the case that the rewriting of the Edda ends with the Middle Ages. This is demonstrated by, for example, the works of Jón lærði and Magnús Ólafsson of Laufás.[1] In this book it is first and foremost the version of *Snorra Edda* that is preserved in DG 11 4to and was conceivably made in its present form about the middle of the thirteenth century or earlier that will be discussed.

2.2 Paper copies

As was pointed out above, there are three leaves of DG 11 4to that are seriously damaged. That means that it is very important to find copies that had been made before the damage occurred. The paper copies that have been most used in editions up to now were all made after the vellum left Iceland, which must have been during the time Brynjólfur Sveinsson was in Roskilde (1632 onwards). While Jón lærði Guðmundsson was in Copenhagen in 1636–37 he made a copy for Brynjólfur (now Marshall 114 in the Bodleian Library in Oxford), and in fact it is by far the most likely thing that Brynjólfur had taken the vellum with him from Iceland in 1631, when he went to Denmark to continue his studies and take up his post in Roskilde. Most other known copies are in Sweden, and it has generally been copies made by Jón Rúgmann, Harald Wijsing, Erik Sotberg and Jón Sigurðsson that have been used to fill the gaps in the text of the vellum (see Grape et al. 1977: xix). When the 1977 edition was completed, Jón lærði's copy was still not known, but on the other hand the importance of the manuscript to the discussion of which considerable space will be devoted here, AM 157 8vo, has been overlooked for a long time.

AM 157 8vo is now preserved in the Árni Magnússon Institute in Iceland. In Kålund's catalogue the manuscript was numbered 2368 and its description and dating is straightforward: 'Paper 16 × 10·2 cm. 24 leaves. 17th century.

---

[1] These will not be discussed further here, nor any other adaptations from the post-Medieval period, though there would be good reason to do so. For Jón Lærði's *Eddurit* see Einar G. Pétursson 1998 and for the so-called *Laufás Edda* see Anthony Faulkes 1977–79: I.

Binding covered with parchment with writing on the inside.' His description of the contents is clear and precise:

1) Ff. 1–21v 'An*n*ar eddu partur er kalladur Skällda edur kiennyngar'. Corresponds (with some omissions) to pp. 302–82 in the Arnamagnæan edition of Codex Upsaliensis; ends in Refhvörf.

2) Ff. 21v–22r 'Nockur staf ro': *Seven alphabets in code, arranged in tabular form.*

3) Ff. 22v–23v Skáldatal. *Arranged in columns.*

4) Ff. 23v–24 Lögsögumannatal á Íslandi.

This is in its way a quite satisfactory description of the contents, but could well have been more detailed. Altogether we are speaking of 25 numbered openings, 50 pages of text.

F. 1r to f. 16v, l. 8: *Skáldskaparmál*. Corresponds to DG 11 4to, Grape et al. 1977: 51–87. Apparently without abbreviations, but with a fair number of scribal errors and a few emendations. To begin with the headings are included, though they are not always identical to those in DG 11 4to, and when they are omitted there is always a space left for them. Heading on f. 1r: An*n*ar eddu partur er kalla*ð*ur Skällda e*ð*ur kien*n*yngar.

F. 16v, l. 9 to f. 17v, l. 12: Part of the second grammatical treatise, from the circular diagram of the alphabet. Corresponds to DG 11 4to, Grape et al. 1977: 89–91.

F. 17v, l. 13 to f. 21v, l. 10: 'Hätta tal biriast'. The list of verses in *Háttatal* as in DG 11 4to, Grape et al. 1977: 93 continues as far as f. 18r, l. 4. Then, after the heading 'drott kuæda hattr', the text corresponding to DG 11 4to, Grape et al. 1977: 94 — 101 'til rietts maals at færa'. These are the first 17 stanzas of *Háttatal* with commentary.

F. 21v, l. 11: 'Hier eptir skrifast Nockur staf ro með ø*ð*ru fleira til gagns þe*i*m Brúka vilja.' This comprises eight alphabets tabulated in an oblong grid. Undir the grid on the right hand-side is written: 'Á þessari opnu stendr f*yrst* almen*n*ingur, þar næst tven*n* málrún*n*a*r* staf ro og 3 torken*n*ing 4 ramvillyng*ur* 5 villu letr 6 ſprÿnglet*ur* siounda sliturs stafir.' There is nothing corresponding to this in DG 11 4to.

F. 22v to f. 23v, in the left column: *Skáldatal* corresponding to DG 11 4to, Grape et al. 1977: 43–47.

F. 23v to f. 24v, l. 4, in the right column: *Lögsögumannatal* corresponding to DG 11 4to, Grape et al. 1977: 48–49.

On a piece of paper with the manuscript Árni Magnússon has written: 'Convenire puto cum Edda Upſalenſi', i.e. 'I believe this agrees with the Uppsala Edda'.

All this is fine and good. Árni was certainly correct in implying that here we are concerned with a copy of DG 11 4to, and Jón Sigurðsson confirmed this with the following statement (*Edda Snorra Sturlusonar* 1848–87: III 249):

Hic codex ex insula Flatey occidentalis Islandiæ in possessionem Arnæ pervenisse videtur, sed ex codice Upsaliensi profectus est, nam non solum multa habet Upsaliensi peculiaria, sed præsertim sub calcem addit resensum poëtarum, huic codici in plurimis consentientem, sed magnopere depravatum, addita insuper serie legiferorum ejusdem codicis. Non igitur dubitamus hunc librum ex ipso codice Upsaliensi, dum in Islandia erat, vel ex ejus apographo descriptum esse; neque enim pauca nobis indicia relicta sunt, quæ luculenter demonstrent, plura apographa hujus codicis ante tempora Arnæ Magnæi in tractu Borgarfjordensi et Dalensi exstitisse, iis præsertim locis, ubi posteri familiæ Sturlungorum habitasse præsumi possunt.

This manuscript seems to have come into Árni's possession from the island of Flatey in the west of Iceland, but is derived from Codex Upsaliensis, for not only does it have much that is peculiar to Codex Upsaliensis, but in particular it adds near the end *Skáldatal* agreeing with that manuscript in many details, though extremely corrupt, with the addition as well of the list of lawspeakers in the same manuscript. We therefore have no doubt that this book was transcribed from Codex Upsaliensis itself while it was in Iceland, or else from a copy of it; for we have surviving no few indications that demonstrate splendidly that many copies of that manuscript existed before the time of Árni Magnússon in the region of Borgarfjörður and Dalir, particularly in those places where the descendants of the family of the Sturlungs may be presumed to have lived.

It is not known where Jón got the information from that the manuscript came from Flatey, unless he is there just thinking of the 'many copies of that manuscript' that he claimed to know had existed round Borgarfjörður. Nothing is known of these copies. Particular variations in the spelling in AM 157 8vo in fact indicate that the scribe was not from Borgarfjörður or Dalir. This point will be returned to later.

Since Jón Sigurðsson was clearly aware that DG 11 4to was the main source of AM 157 8vo, it is odd that he should not have looked into whether the seventeenth-century scribe had other manuscripts available to him and used them to supplement DG 11 4to, and also whether his copy could perhaps provide fuller information about the text where DG 11 4to was damaged. For Jón Sigurðsson must have been fully aware of the damaged pages, since he had himself made a copy of the manuscript while on his visit to Uppsala.

The first question is soon answered. There are no signs that the scribe of AM 157 8vo consulted other manuscripts than DG 11 4to or better copies of it. This is obvious from the errors that are reproduced, and also from the way he omits where he cannot improve. Three examples will suffice.

On f. 27r, l. 23 of DG 11 4to a space was left to write the fragment of a verse by Þjóðólfr hvinverski, but in AM 157 the space is closed up:

DG 11 4to (f. 27r, l. 21; p. 126 below)   AM 157 8vo (f. 1r, line 5 from below)
Svá kvað Úlfr Uggason: Ríðum at vilgi   So kvað Úlfr Uggason: Ríðum at vigli
víðu, víðfrægr, en menn líða, Hroptatýr,   víðum víðfrægr en menn líða, Hroptatýr
um hapta hróðrmál, sonar báli. Svá kvað   að hapta hróðr mál, sonar báli. So kvað
Þjóðólfr hvinverski: Hallfreðr vandræðaskáld: Sannyrðum
                                              spenr sverða snarr þiggjandi viggjar bar-
Svá kvað Hallfrøðr: Sannyrðum spenr   haddaða byrjar biðkván und sig Þriðja.
sverða snarr þiggjandi viggjan barhod-
daða byrjar biðkván und sik Þriðja.

If the scribe had had either the Codex Regius version or the Codex Wormianus version before him, he could have filled the gap with the quatrain of Þjóðólfr and emended *ríðum* to *ríðr* in Úlfr's verse. *Vigli* for *vilgi* is on the other hand a not unparalleled kind of transposition of letters with this scribe. But *viggjar* is his emendation for the meaningless *viggjan*.

In the same way it is interesting to look at examples where a seventeenth-century scribe had fewer options (the letters in round brackets are represented by indeterminate abbreviation signs in DG 11 4to):

DG 11 4to (f. 41r, l. 24; p. 228 below).   AM 157 8vo (f. 12v, line 9 from below)
Tveir eru fuglar þeir er eigi þarf annan veg Tveir eru fuglar þeir er eÿ þarf annan
að kenna en kalla blóð eða hræ ⟨drykk⟩   veg að kenna en kalla blóð eður hræ
þeira. Þat er hrafn eða ǫrn. Alla aðra fugla þeirra og er það hrafn og örn. Alla aðra
karlkenda má kenna við blóð. Sem Þjóðólfr   fugla karlkennda má kenna við blóð,
kvað: Blóðorra lætr barri bragningr ara   sem Þjóðólfur kvað: Blóðorra lætr barri
fagna; Gauts berr sík á sveita svans verð   bragningr ara fagna Gauts berr sÿk og
konungr Hǫrða; Geirsoddum lætr grøðir   sveita svans verð konungr Hörða.
g(runn) h(vert) st(ika) ⟨sunnar⟩ h(irð)
þ(at) ⟨er⟩ h(ann) s(kal) v(arða) hrægamms
ara s(ævar).
Krákr, Huginn, Muninn, borginmóði,   Krákur, Huginn, Muninn og Borgin-
árflognir, ártali, holdboði.   móði, árflognir, ártali. holdboði.

The opening sentence is truly strange and probably corrupt in DG 11 4to, but no attempt is made to emend it in AM 157 8vo. The abbreviations in Þjóðólfr Arnórsson's verse would have been incomprehensible unless one had seen the complete lines just before or knew the verse by heart. So it would have been quite natural to omit the quatrain if the scribe did not have a text of either the Codex Regius version or the Codex Wormianus in front of him.

An example can also be pointed out where an obvious error in DG 11 4to is reproduced in AM 157 8vo:

DG 11 4to (f. 33r, l. 23; p. 170 below)   AM 157 8vo (f. 6v, l. 10)
Kona er kend til gulls, kǫlluð selja gulls.   Kona er kennd til gulls kölluð selja gulls
Sem kvað Hallar-Steinn: Svalteigar mun   sem kvað Hallar Steinn: Sval teigar mun

selju salts Viðblindi galtar rǫfkastandi   selju sjallt Viðblindi galtar rauf[1] kastandi
rastar reyrþvengs muna lengi. Hér eru   rastar reyrþvengs muna lengi. Hér eru
hvalir kallaðir Viðblindi galtar. Viðblindi   hvalir kallaðir Viðblindi galtar. Viðblindi
var jǫtunn og dró hvali upp í hafi sem   var jötunn og dró hvali í hafi upp sem fiska.
fiska. Teigr hvala er sær, rǫf sævar er gull.   Teigur fiska er sær. Rauf sævar er gull; kona
Kona er selja gulls, þess er hún gefr. Selja   er og selja gulls þess er hon gefur. Sel⟨j⟩a
heitir tré. Kona er ok kend við allskyns tré   heitir trje. Kona er kennd við allskyns trje
kvenkend. Hon er lág kǫlluð þess er hon   kvenkennd, hon er lág kölluð þess er hon
lógar. Lág heitir tré þat er fellt er í skógi.   lagar. Lág heitir trje það sem fellt er úr skógi.
Svá kvað Gunnlaugr ormstunga: Sem kvað Gunnlaugur ormstunga:

The context makes it clear that whereas both manuscripts have 'Viðblindi galtar', it ought to be 'Viðblinda galtar' as in the Codex Regius. Thus we get the kenning *svalteigr Viðblinda galtar*, as in fact is made clear in the prose comments.

This list might be extended, but it is unnecessary to discuss the matter further. AM 157 8vo is a copy, or a copy of a close copy, of DG 11 4to.

This having been established, the next step is obviously to examine the parts of this manuscript that are copied from the damaged pages in DG 11 4to, ff. 32r–34v, which are the last three leaves of the fourth gathering in that manuscript. The complete text of these pages will appear later in this edition, but here we shall just look at the holes in DG 11 4to where lines are worst affected. The parts of the text that have disappeared from DG 11 are enclosed in square brackets. The text where the manuscripts do not quite agree is underlined.

DG 11 4to (f. 32r, l. 15; p. 166 below).   AM 157 8vo (f. 6r, l. 5).

Eyss land[r]eki [l]jósu lastvar Kraka barri   Eys landrek⟨i⟩ ljósu lastvar kraka bari
á hlémildra holdi hoskir [ká]lfur m[ér   á hlæmildra holdi hoskur kálfur mér
sjálfum. Svá kvað Sk[úl]i Þorsteinsson: sjálfum. So kvað Skúli Þorsteinsson:
Þá er ræfrvita Reifn[i]s rauð eg f[yrir Sǫl   Þá er ræfurvita reipnis rauðir (rauð
til auðar] herfylgnis bar ek Hǫlga haugþak   mér?) fyrir sól til auðar. Í Bjarkamálum
saman b[augum. Í Bjarkam]álum eru tǫlð   er töld öll gulls heiti. So segir þar:
mǫrg gulls heiti. Svá segir þar: G[ramr hinn   Gramr hinn g⟨j⟩öflasti[2] gladdi hirð sína
gǫfga]sti gladdi hirð sína Fenju forverki,   Fenju forverki, Fofnis miðgarði, Glasis
Fáfnis miðgarð[i, Gla]sis glóbarri, Grana   glóbarði, Grana fagra byrði, Draupnis
fagrbyrði, Draupnis dýrsveita.   dýrsveita.

Unfortunately some (quite readable) text is omitted in AM 157 8vo, and not all difficulties can be resolved. For example, it cannot be seen from AM 157 8vo whether it should be *baugum* or *bauga* in Skúli Þorsteinsson's verse,

---

[1] In DG 11 4to *rǫf* is written *ravf*. The scribe of AM 157 8vo usually uses ǫ for this sound, but appears not to have recognised the word and wrote *rauf* instead.

[2] See Grape et al. 1977: 142.

Introduction

since the scribe of AM 157 8vo omits the second couplet. On the other hand, Jón Rúgmann's reading *gjǫflasti* in *Bjarkamál* is supported by AM 157 8vo.

DG 11 4to (f. 32v l. 15; p. 170 below)　　　　AM 157 8vo (f. 6v, l. 3.)

Maðr er kallaðr brjótr gulls, sem kvað Ót[t]arr: Góðmenni[s] þar[f] ek gunnar gullbrjótanda at nj[ó]ta, hé[r er almenn]is inni inndrótt með gram svinnum. Svá kvað [Einarr skálaglamm: G]ullsendir l[æ]tr grundar <u>glaðar þengill her[drengi, hans mæti]</u> kná ek hljóta hljó⟨t⟩, Yggs mjaðar njóta. En [gullvǫrpuðr se]m Þorleikr kvað: Hirð viðr grams með gerðum gullvǫrpuðr [sér ho]lla. Svá kvað Þorvaldr blǫnduskáld: Gullstríðir verpr glóðum, gefr auð konungr rauðan, óþjóðar bregðr eyðir, armleggs, Grana farmi.

Maður er kallaður brjótur gulls sem kvað Óttar: Góðmennnis þarf ek gunnar gullbrjótandi að njóta, hann hefur almennis inni inndrótt með gram svinnum. Sem kvað Einar skálaglamm: Gull sendis lætur g⟨r⟩undar <u>glaður þeingill so leingi hans ek</u> kná ek hljóta hlio Yggs mjaðar njóta. Gullvørpuður sem Þorleikur kvað: Hirð viður grams með gerðum gullverpendr sér holla. Sem kvað Þorvaldur blönduskáld: Gullstirður verpur blöðum gefr (?) konungur ⟨rauðan⟩[1] óþjóðar bregðr eyðir armleggs Grana farmi.

The way this gap is filled by editors is largely supported by AM 157 8vo, but the words *glaður þeingill so leingi hans ek* in AM 157 8vo suggest that the scribe saw something quite different from what Jón Rúgmann saw, and is supported by both the Codex Regius and Codex Wormianus.

DG 11 4to (f. 33r, l. 15; p. 174 below)　　　　AM 157 8vo (f. 6v, l. 5 from below)

En stirðmálugr sta[rð]i storðar leggs fyrir borð[i fróns á] fólka reyna fránleitr ok blés eitri. Viðr [ok] meiðr sem [kvað Korm]akr: Meiðr er mǫrgum ǿðri morðreins í dyn flein[a; hjǫrr fær hildi]bǫrrum hjarl Sigurði jarli. Lundr sem kvað Hallfreðr [vendræða]sk[áld]. Alþol[lum] stendr Ullar austr að miklu trausti rǫkilundr hi[nn] ríki [ra]ndfárs brynjaðr harri.

En stirðmálugur starði storðar legg fyrir borði fróns á flóka reynir fránleitr og blés eitri. Viður og meiður sem Kormákr kvað: Meiður er mörgum æðri morðreins í dyn fleina . . . ~~bövom~~ börvom hall Sigurði jalli. Lundur sem Hallfreður vandræðaskáld kvað: Alþollum stendr Ullar austur með miklu trausti ræki lundur hinn ríki randfárs brynjaðr hari.

It is odd that here the scribe of AM 157 8vo should leave out the words *hjǫrr fær hildi* which would have been in the middle of where the hole is in DG 11 4to, while on f. 33v he clearly makes a guess about what should be there.

DG 11 4to (f. 33 v, l. 15; p. 178 below)　　　　AM 157 8vo (f. 7r, l. 19)

Vápn ok herklæði skal kenna til o[r]ustu ok til Óðins ok valm[e]ygja ok [h]er[konunga], kenna hjálm hǫtt þ[eira] e[ða] fald, en brynju serk eða skyr[tu, en skj]ǫld tjald. [E]n s[kja]ldb[or]g er kǫlluð hǫll eða ræfr, veg[r eða gólf. S]kildir eru kallaðir, ok

Vopn ok herklæði skal kenna til orustu og til Óðins og valmeyja og herkonunga og kalla hjálminn hött þeirra eður fald, brynju serk eður skyrtu en skjöld tjald en skjaldborg er kölluð höll, ræfur eður veggur, <u>gólf eður brík.</u> Skildir eru kenndir

---

[1] This word is added in the margin (by the same hand?) with an indicative sign.

kendir við herski[p], sól eða tung[l eða við herskip, sól eður tungl, loga eður blik lauf] eða [b]lik eða garðr skipsins. Skjǫldr eður garður skipsins. Skjöldur er kallaður er kallaðr skip Ull[a]r eða fó[ltr Hr]ungnis, skip Ullar eður fóta Hrugnis er hann stóð er hann stóð á skildinum. á skildinum.

The letters that lay on the verso side of this leaf opposite *hjǫrr fær hildi* on the recto side are *r eða gólf. S* in DG 11 4to. It looks as though the scribe of AM 157 could read or thought he could read what was there, and interpreted it as *gólf eður brík*. *Brík* is found as the baseword in kennings for shield and in the sense of 'board' would fit in with *ræfur*, *veggur* and *gólf*. It may be noted that he is apparently the only one to read *loga* where the editors print *lauf*, which is the reading in Jón Rúgmann's copy as well as the Codex Regius and Codex Wormianus. His reading *(skip) fóta Hrungnis* fits better with skaldic usage than *fótr Hrungnis*. The shield was what Hrungnir put under the soles of his feet.

The last leaf in the fourth gathering of DG 11 4to is, as one would expect, the worst affected of the three. On the upper part of the leaf there is damage that the editors have, what is more, given up trying to emend. Thus Grape et al. 1977 print the quatrain by Hallfreðr (p. 65) with the difficulties unresolved: 'und ſvrſ ſv ... ivlſ [r]v̄ŋvm'. The scribe of AM 157 has no apparent problem reading it, for he writes: 'Unnfúrſ imal runnum'. Certainly it has to be admitted that the words are difficult to interpret, but he must have thought he could read something.

Before he gets to the largest hole, the scribe of AM 157 gets in a mess. He jumps over four lines in his exemplar, so we find nothing out about the legibility of the manuscript here. On the other hand there is in little doubt that he read what followed without difficulty.

DG 11 4to (f. 34r, l. 14; p. 180 below)   AM 157 8vo (f. 7v, l. 4)

Hlýrtungl sem [hér segir]: Dagr var fríðr sá er fǫgrum fleygjendr alimleygjar á hran[feril h]ringa hlýrtu[ngli m]ér þrungðu. Garðr skips, sem hér segir: [S]vo [for geg]n í gǫgn[u]m   Garður skips sem hér segir: So fór í gegn [garð stei]nfarinn barða, sá var, gunnstǿrir   gögnum grandsteirn farinn branda sá vör geira gu[nnar]hǿ[f]r, se[m næfrar]. Askr Ullar   gunnstærir geira gunnar hæfir sem næfra. sem Þjóðólfr kvað. Ganga él um yng[va]   Askr Ullar, sem Þórólfur kvað: Ganga él [Ullar skips með full]u, þar er samnaglar   um yngva Ullar skips með fullu þar er siglur slíðrdúkaðar ríða. Ilja [blað] Hrungnis,   samnaglar siglu slíðurdúkaðar ríða. Ilja se[m] kvað Bragi.   blað Hrungni⟨s⟩ sem Bragi kvað.

In fact there is a lot that is odd about this page and its legibility. Jón Rúgmann was able to read the words *Ullar skips með fullu* (see Grape et al. 1977: 154), and Sotberg's copy in Cod. Ups. R 684 (S) includes them too, but Jón Sigurðsson on the other hand could read nothing there. Thorell points out

Introduction

that this may be taken to mean that this place was relatively undamaged in Jón Rúgmann's time, but he adds (Grape et al. 1977: 154):

> To a certain extent this is contradicted . . . by the fact that Jón Rúgmann in the corresponding place on the next page has left an open space for three words (*en vondur viðris*) that were not filled in until later, the third word wrongly. How S, on the other hand, has, as far as one can judge at the first attempt, been able to produce a relatively correct reading remains to be explained.

So we have to turn the page.

DG 11 4to (f. 34v, l. 10; p. 184 below)	AM 157 8vo (f. 7v, l. 11 from below)
Spjót er kallaðr ormr, sem Refur kvað: Kná [my]rkdreki markaðr mi[nn] þar er ýtar finna øfr á aldar lóf[um eikinn b]orðs á leika. Ǫrvar eru kallaðar hagl boga eða strengjar eða h[lífa] eða orrostu, sem Einarr kvað: Brak-Rǫgna skóg bogna barg óþ[ly] rmir var[g]a hagl úr Hlakkar seglum hjǫrs rakliga fjǫrvi. Orrosta er kǫlluð Hjað[nin] ga veður eða él, en vopn Hjaðninga eldr eða vendir. Orrosta er [veðr Ó]ðins, sem fyrr er ritat. Svá kvað Ví[ga-Glú]mr: Rudd[a ek se]m [ja]rðar <u>orð lék á því forðum</u> með veðr[stǫfum V]iðris vand[ar] mér til handa. Viðris veður er orrosta [en vǫndur vígs sver]ðið, en menn stafir sverðsins. Hér er b[æði <u>vápn</u>] ok or[rusta k]e[nt] ok haft til kenningar mannsins, ok er [þat] rekit kallat er svá er ort. Skjǫldr [er] land vápnanna en vápn eru hagl eða regn þess [lands] ef nýge[r]vinga[r er] ort.	Spjót er kallað ormur sem Refur kvað: Kná myrkdreki markaður minn þar ýtar finna æfur á aldar lofum eikiborðs á leiki. Örvar eru kenndar hagl boga eður strengja eður hlífa eður orustu sem Einar kvað: Brak rögna <u>skók</u> bogna ok bjarg óþyrmir varga hagl úr Hlakkar seglum hjörs raklega fjörvi. Orusta er kölluð Hjaðninga veður eður él, en vopn Hjaðninga eldur eður v⟨e⟩ndir. Orusta er og kölluð veður Óðins sem fyr var ritað sem kvað Víga-Glúmur: Rudda eg sem jarðar á veðurstöfum Viðris vandils mér til handa Viðris[1] veður er orusta en vígs vöndur er sverðið en menn stafir sverðsins. Hér er bæði <u>veður</u> og orusta kent og haft til kenningar mannsins og er það rekið kallað er so er ort. Skjöldur er land voknanna[2] en vopn eru hagl eður regn þess land⟨s⟩ ef nýgervingar er ort.

Apart from the fact that the scribe omits a whole line of Víga-Glúmr's verse that is fully legible in DG 11 4to (*orð lék á því forðum*), the text in AM 157 8vo may be said to be complete and accurate (except for *vandils*, which may have been in DG 11 4to, see p. 186 note 3 below) and the only explanation can be that the exemplar was undamaged when the copy was made.

It seems therefore, after what has been said, that the obvious thing to do is to use AM 157 8vo when gaps have to be filled in *Skáldskaparmál* in DG 11 4to. On the other hand, some things suggest that the damage had at any rate started to take place on ff. 33 and 34 before that copy was made.

---

[1] It would be more normal to expand the abbreviation to *viðar*.
[2] According to Maurer 1888: 284–88, this spelling indicates that the scribe grew up in the Eastern fjords or the south-east of Iceland rather than in Borgarfjörður or Dalir.

2.3 Manuscript relations

Here is not the place to describe the other manuscripts of *Snorra Edda* in detail. On the other hand it is necessary to point out that what is here referred to as the Codex Regius version is largely the foundation of the texts in four manuscripts. The Utrecht manuscript was copied from a now lost sister-manuscript to GkS 2367 4to, the Codex Regius. Codex Wormianus, AM 242 fol., is largely derived from a manuscript with basically the same text as GkS 2367 4to, but has readings and reworkings of some parts that indicate an independent redactor who occasionally introduces readings that appear to be closely related to the Uppsala Edda version.[1] Since Codex Wormianus is definitely much later than DG 11 4to, one obviously cannot rule out the possibility that the scribe of Codex Wormianus had access to a text that was at any rate more closely related to the Uppsala Edda version. AM 748 II 4to contains two fragments of *Skáldskaparmál* with a text very similar to that of the Codex Regius. The Codex Regius version and the Uppsala Edda version may be regarded as the two main versions of the *Edda* and will hereafter be referred to as R and U respectively.

The fragmentary manuscripts AM 757 a 4to and AM 748 I b 4to contain a quite different and independent version of parts of *Skáldskaparmál* that seem generally to be closest to R, though there are readings in them that indicate a relationship to U. AM 756 4to, as was said above, contains parts of *Gylfaginning* and *Skáldskaparmál* derived from Codex Wormianus.

The greatest difference between R and U is in length. Some mythological narratives in the Uppsala Edda version are much briefer than in the Codex Regius version, the material is ordered differently and the lengthy quotations from *Þórsdrápa*, *Haustlǫng*, *Ragnarsdrápa* and *Grottasǫngr* are not in U, but on the other hand DG 11 4to contains material that is not to be found in precisely the same form in other manuscripts: *Skáldatal*,[2] a genealogy of the Sturlungs,[3] a list of lawspeakers, the second grammatical treatise[4] and a list of stanzas of *Háttatal*.

For a good century the relationship of these manuscripts has been a matter of dispute among scholars. It has generally been accepted as certain that all versions are ultimately derived from the same archetypal manuscript, and then there seemed to be only two possibilities: either the Uppsala Edda version is a shortening of the Codex Regius version or the latter is an expansion of the former.

---

[1] Cf. Faulkes (1998: xl): 'in chapter 65 there are rather a lot of agreements between W and U'.

[2] A version of *Skáldatal* was also in the *Heimskringla* manuscript Kringla and is preserved in copies of it.

[3] The Sturlung genealogy in AM 748 II 4to is almost identical.

[4] Also in Codex Wormianus.

Introduction

The problem in this debate has always been that it is possible to use the same examples to support either theory, and as is pointed out in Section 3.1 below, Zetterholm, after a detailed investigation (1949), reached the conclusion that in the narrative of Þórr's journey to Útgarða-Loki the text of the Uppsala Edda version was a shortening and the text of the Codex Regius version was an expansion of the original story.

In my essay *Tertium vero datur* (DIVA, http://uu.diva-portal.org/smash/record.jsf?pid=diva2:322558) I tried to sort out these theories and reached the conclusion that in fact there was a third possibility that was by far the most likely. Snorri himself made two versions of his Edda, and so the two main versions that survive are derived from different originals. This is an ancient idea, expressed most clearly in the doctoral dissertation of the German scholar Friedrich W. Müller in 1941 (*Untersuchungen zur Uppsala-Edda*). The author fell in the First World War and did not live to follow up his ideas, and in most of what has been written since on this topic they are dismissed as an interesting hypothesis incapable of proof and in fact rather improbable. There is, however, a particular reason in this context to mention Zetterholm's research (1949) again, and it will be discussed further later. His is the most scholarly criticism of Müller's method I have seen.

Walter Baetke's variation of Müller's theory in his essay *Die Götterlehre der Snorra-Edda*, which first appeared in 1950 and was reprinted in *Kleine Schriften* in 1973, is interesting. Baetke accepts the arguments of Müller and earlier Mogk (1925) that the Uppsala Edda version must retain much from the original version, but then adds (1973: 234):

> I am not so convinced about Müller's thesis, at least insofar as it pertains to the Prologue, that both versions, X [= R] and U, derive from Snorri himself; I am more inclined to see in some of the additions of X the hand of a later redactor.

In other words the revision was not necessarily made entirely by the original author, rather by someone else.

3 How did the text of the *Edda* come into being?

About the answer to this question there is little or nothing known. All an investigator can do is keep asking himself what is most likely, how must it have been, what can be deduced from the manuscripts and texts. When Finnur Jónsson rejected the theory that the U text was a copy of some kind of rough draft that the archetype of the other manuscripts had been based on, he grasped at among other things the argument that it 'conflicts ... with everything that is otherwise known about book production in Iceland' (1931: xxxi). But the fact is that we know almost nothing about how a work like *Snorra Edda* would come into being. It is easy to imagine that *Njáls saga* was based on oral tradition, because there is something there to catch hold of. *Egils saga* follows the pattern of a biography, *Gunnlaugs saga* is a love story with triangular relationships. *Hrafnkels saga* is a novella about a power struggle. These works have some coherence. The *Edda* has no storyline except that based on *Vǫluspá* in *Gylfaginning*. Though it states that it is a book to teach young poets (ch. 34 in the U version), it has no precedent as an *ars poetica* that it bears any similarity to. So we can only use guesswork about the origin of the work.

The first main part of the *Edda*, *Gylfaginning*, is a collection of mythological stories and pieces of information about Norse mythology that cannot have existed in systematic form in a Christian society before the time of the *Edda*. The author's sources in this part must have been oral tales in prose or poetry that existed here and there, the same stories in various places but not identical in any two.

The second major part, *Skáldskaparmál*, is a systematic presentation of poetical language with examples from earlier poets that would not all have been preserved in any one place either. We have no reason to think that there were not collections of material, lists of names, *þulur* and so forth, in existence before Snorri's time. On the other hand, we have good reason to assume that he created his own personal system, arranging the sources in a new way.

Both these things are quite different from anything we have reason to assume about the creation of other narrative works of the Middle Ages in Iceland.

3.1 Myths

I based my arguments in *Tertium vero datur* on a detailed comparison of narrative passages in GkS 2367 4to and DG 11 4to. Word counts seemed to show that theories of shortening and lengthening were pretty far-fetched, since the comparison of the proportional differences in length indicated that three explanations would be required. This can be illustrated in three tables. The numbers in the first column show the order in which these passages appear in the text. In the first table was have the passages in which DG 11 4to has practically the same number of words as GkS 2367 4to, or at least 85%:

No	This edition	Faulkes	Contents	Words in DG 11 4to	Words in GkS 2367 4to	U as % of R
2	Pp. 22–46	2005 15/5	Bifrǫst – Forseti (prose and verse)	3255	3559	91·5
3	Pp. 46–50	2005 26/35	Loki and family	1153	1158	99·5
4	Pp. 50–54	2005 29/17	Gyðjur introduced	463	520	89·0
15	Pp. 90–94	1998 20/18	Þórr and Hrungnir	1063	1109	95·8
16	Pp. 94–96	1998 24/17	Þórr and Geirrøðr	612	593	103·0
17	Pp. 236–238	1998 41/29	Sif's hair and other dwarves' work	709	723	98·0
18	Pp. 238–240	1998 45/3	Andvari's gold	491	553	88·8
19	Pp. 240–242	1998 58/4	Hrólfr kraki	641	754	85·0

Obviously the texts in this table are of such similar length that they could as far as that goes be copied from the same exemplar. Yet the matter is not so simple. Passages 15–19 are all from the original collection in *Skáldskaparmál*, but only nos 2–4 are from *Gylfaginning*. In passage 2, the description of the scene and the circumstances, there also appear some strange abbreviations in DG 11 4to, which Maja Bäckvall (2007) and Lasse Mårtensson and Heimir Pálsson (2008) have shown cannot be derived from the same exemplar as was used for GkS 2367 4to. They are in this quotation from *Vǫluspá*:

    Þá gengu v.   Þá gengu regin ǫll
    A. s   á rǫkstóla,
    g. h. g.   ginnheilug goð
    ok um þat g'   ok um þat gættust
    h' skyldi dverga   hverr skyldi dverga
    drótt um spekja   dróttir skepja
    ór brimi blóðgu   ór Brimis blóði
    ok Bláins leggium.   ok ór Bláins leggjum

The text on the right shows the whole stanza as we know it from the Codex Regius of the eddic poems (GkS 2365 4to), but obviously there is no way of understanding the abbreviations in DG 11 4to unless the first four lines (which are the first refrain in the poem) have appeared earlier, as they have in GkS 2365 4to. Then it is natural to abbreviate the refrain the second time it comes, as is done in GkS 2365 4to, f. 1, l. 19, but it is not abbreviated in any manuscript of *Snorra Edda* except DG 11 4to, where it has not appeared before. The same thing happens in other places with verse quotations in DG 11 4to.[1] How did such abbreviations get into this manuscript? They cannot derive from GkS 2365 4to, for there the refrain is abbreviated in a different way, and *Hauksbók*, of course, does not come into question here if only because of its age, and anyway the refrain is not abbreviated there either. The only possible explanations are that a scribe had omitted an earlier occurrence of the verse in his exemplar, or that he knew the lines from some other source, and since he was making the manuscript for his own personal use, he abbreviated the lines as an *aide-mémoire* and relied on his memory ro recall the full text. This might have been done by Snorri himself.

In the next table there are narratives where the text of DG 11 4to has about 60–75% of the number of words in GkS 2367 4to, and here it is only stories from *Gylfaginning* that are concerned:

No	This edition	Faulkes	Contents	Words in DG 11 4to	Words in GkS 2367 4to	U as % of R
0	Pp. 6–10	2005 3/1	Prologue	1007	1725	58·4
1	Pp. 12–20	2005 8/26	Creation story	1693	2562	66·1
6	Pp. 56–60	2005 32/3	People and everyday life in Valho̧ll	473	627	75·0
7	Pp. 60–62	2005 34/27	The builder of the fortification; origin of Sleipnir	392	586	66·8
8	Pp. 64–72	2005 37/3	Þórr and Útgarða-Loki	2207	3468	63·5
11	P. 78	2005 48/15	Loki's punishment	334	522	64·0
12	Pp. 78–84	2005 49/18	Fimbulvetr, ragnarøkkr (prose)	729	1230	59·3

Now the picture gets more complicated.

The Prologue will be discussed later. But however one looks at this text it is difficult to see a common original for all versions. A particular problem is that the Prologue conflicts with *Gylfaginning* when we get to the origin of Óðin.[2]

---

[1] See Lasse Mårtensson and Heimir Pálsson 2008.
[2] See Heinrich Beck 2004 and 2009.

Certainly it is possible to imagine that someone has retold stories and shortened a great deal, but it is certainly not the same person as edited the stories on p. xlv above. Boer (1924) suggested different editors, and of course this is a possible explanation, but as far as I know has no parallel within the same work. We find various editors at work in for example Hauksbók, but each keeps within his own area. Here one would have to assume editors each intruding on another's work. So it is tempting to look for another explanation.

The most detailed examination of one of these pieces of narrative was carried out by D. O. Zetterholm in his *Studier i en Snorre-text. Tors färd till Utgård* (1949). Zetterholm described shortenings in Sagas of Icelanders and Kings' Sagas, and also in Hauksbók, but his careful study of the texts of GkS 2367 4to and DG 11 4to led to an unexpected conclusion in the middle of his essay about lengthening and shortening: 'My answer must be: lengthening in R and shortening in U' (p. 54). This gives a splendid picture of the problem that arises. The arguments can be turned back and forth according to how the wind blows. If one assumes shortening in U, it is at the same time tempting to assume lengthening in R.

A third picture arises when the texts in the next table are examined. Here the number of words in DG 11 4to are less than 50% of that in GkS 2367 4to. The first five narratives are in the *Gylfaginning* part of DG 11 4to, but nos 13 and 14 are in *Skáldskaparmál* in the Codex Regius version. The Grotti story is in *Skáldskaparmál* in both versions:

No	This edition	Faulkes	Contents	Words in DG 11 4to	Words in GkS 2367 4to	U as % of R
5	P. 54	2005 30/38	Freyr and Gerðr (prose and verse)	147	454	32·4
9	Pp. 72–74	2005 44/3	Þórr and the Miðgarðsormr	292	655	44·5
10	Pp. 74–76	2005 45/16	Death of Baldr	610	1242	49·0
13	Pp. 86–88	1998 1	Iðunn and Þjassi	452	996	45·7
14	P. 88	1998 4/8	Mead of poetry	392	924	42·4
20	P. 244	1998 51/29	Grotti	81	337	24·0

Here it should be noted that in most cases we are dealing with key myths about the gods. It was bound to be reckoned a basic element in a textbook about poetry to give information about the mead of poetry.[1] Freyr's love story was

[1] See my article about the Gunnlǫð story (2010b).

awe-inspiring. And we also know from other sources that Þórr's encounter with the Miðgarðsormr was one of the most popular of all the stories about the gods.[1] And the death of Baldr and the theft of Iðunn's apples were no small affairs. The story of Grotti is a strange one and *Grottasǫngr* an unusual poem. In view of this it is difficult to see any good reason for shortening in these cases, and it is natural to demand an explanation if people want to believe in that theory.

Now it is of course pointless to discuss medieval texts of the Edda without trying to understand the sources and possible origins of the work. It has already been pointed out that Snorri's main sources for his myths must have been oral. Of course, mythological poems are often invoked as sources in *Gylfaginning*, but if the text is examined, there are actually very few poems named there that we know from the collection of eddic poems that we have. In DG 11 4to only *Vǫluspá* and *Grímnismál* are mentioned by name. A poem called *Heimdallargaldr* is also mentioned, but it is otherwise unknown. Verses are quoted that we know as part of *Vafþrúðnismál*, but the poem's name does not appear in DG 11 4to and in GkS 2367 4to it is only said once that 'so says the giant Vafþrúðnir' (Finnur Jónsson 1931: 13). In DG 11 4to single verses are quoted from *Fáfnismál*, *Lokasenna*,[2] *Hyndluljóð*[3] and *Hávamál*[4] (pp. 30, 35–36, 16 and 12).

It is as clear as daylight that the structure of *Gylfaginning* is based on that of *Vǫluspá*. The order of topics is the same, and the quotations from the poem are numerous, though there are more in the Codex Regius version than in the Uppsala Edda. On the other hand, scholars have sometimes been remarkably bold in using Snorri and his *Edda* to explain the *Vǫluspá* of the Codex Regius poems. For example, there is no way that the words of *Vǫluspá* 24, 'brotinn var borðveggr | borgar Ása' can be taken as referring to events leading up to the story of the building of the gods' fortification, as is commonly done, except by invoking *Snorra Edda*, since the next element in the *Vǫluspá* narrative simply tells that Freyja (not the sun and moon as in *Snorra Edda*) had been given to the giants, and there is no mention there of the building of the fortification or Sleipnir. While it is clear that Snorri had a different version of *Vǫluspá* from the one we know from GkS 2365 4to,

[1] See for example Preben Meulengracht Sørensen 2002.

[2] In fact stanzas 21, 29 and possibly 47 of the poem we know by this name.

[3] In GkS 2367 this quotation is attributed to 'the short *Vǫluspá*' (Finnur Jónsson 1931: 12–13), which is taken to be stt. 29–44 of the poem otherwise known as *Hyndluljóð*.

[4] This quotation is rather doubtful. *Hávamál* is not named, and this would be the only quotation from an eddic poem put into the mouth of Gylfi (and it is also rather inaccurate, though less so in GkS 2367 4to). On this see Heimir Pálsson 1994.

Introduction

or else used an oral source that we do not know, we probably ought to tread very warily in using his *Edda* to interpret *Vǫluspá*.

Many have been ready to reckon the skaldic poems *Ragnarsdrápa*, *Þórsdrápa*, *Húsdrápa* and *Haustlǫng* among Snorri's sources. From Bragi Boddason's *Ragnarsdrápa* he is supposed to have taken various stories, probably especially those about Hjaðningavíg, Sǫrli and Hamðir and Gefjun's ploughing—for Þórr and the Miðgarðsormr he had so many sources that were in agreement that not much could have been added from Bragi. On Hjaðningavíg there is this to be said, that in DG 11 4to as in other versions of the *Edda*, there is a fairly full account of Hildr, Heðinn and Hǫgni. If it is compared with the quotation from *Ragnarsdrápa* in GkS 2367 4to (DG 11 4to does not include it), there are no verbal correspondences, though the story is undoubtedly the same.

Sǫrli and Hamðir are only mentioned in kennings in the Uppsala Edda. In the Codex Regius the passage about them is in the section devoted to the story of the Niflungs. About this Finnur Jónsson says (1931: lvi): 'This whole story is without doubt based on the old *Sigurðarsaga* (*Fáfnisbana*), which is given this name by Snorri in his commentary to *Háttatal* (p. 231).' Since this is an important matter, it is tempting to compare the texts of *Háttatal* 35 and its commentary (but only including half-stanzas):

DG 11 4to (p. 294 below)	GkS 2367 4to (Faulkes 2007: 18)	AM 242 fol.
	Þessi háttr er hin forna skjálfhenda:	
Reist at Vágsbrú vestan, varrsíma bar fjarri, heitfastr hávar rastir hjálm-Týr svǫlu stýri . . .	Reist at Vágsbrú vestan (varrsíma bar fjarri) heitfastr hávar rastir hjálm-Týr svǫlu stýri . . .	Reist at Vágsbrú vestan varrsíma bar fjarri heitfastr hávar rastir hjálm-Týr svǫlu stýri . . .
Hér er skjálfhent eða aðalhending í þriðja vísuorði í hvárum helmingi, en at ǫðru sem dróttkvætt. Þenna hátt fann fyrst Þorvaldr veili. Þá lá hann í útskeri nokkuru, kominn af skipsbroti ok hafði fátt klæða, en veðr kalt. Þá orti hann kvæði er kǫlluð er Kviðan skjálfhenda eða Drápan steflausa.	Hér er skjálfhent með aðalhending í þriðja vísuorði í hvárum tveggja helmingi, en ⟨at⟩ ǫðru sem dróttkvætt. Þenna hátt fann fyrst Veili. Þá lá hann í útskeri nokkvoru, kominn af skipsbroti, ok hǫfðu þeir illt til klæða ok veðr kalt. Þá orti hann kvæði er kallat er kviðan skjálfhenda eða drápan steflausa, ok kveðit eptir Sigurðar sǫgu.	Hér er skjálfhenda með aðalhendingum hið þriðja vísuorð í ⟨h⟩várum helmingi, en at ǫðru sem dróttkvætt.

Introduction

The last five words in GkS 2367 4to here are absent in Codex Trajectinus, so *Sigurðar saga* is only named in the one manuscript, and the scribe or editor of Codex Wormianus seems moreover rather confused about *skjálfhenda*, putting the account of Veili/Véli after the otherwise nameless stanza (which is not in *skjálfhenda*) that appears as st. 38 in DG 11 4to, at the end of the poem and without commentary too in GkS 2367 4to, not at all in Codex Trajectinus (which, however, lacks the end of the poem), but after st. 54 in Codex Wormianus (the last sentence describes the form of this stanza, not of *skjálfhenda*):[1]

> Farar snarar fylkir byrjar,
> freka breka lemr á snekkjum
> vaka taka vísa rekkar
> viðar skriðar at þat biðja . . .

> Þenna hátt fann sá maðr er Véli hét þá er hann kom ór skipsbroti, þá er hann var í skeri einu. Þá orti hann kvæði er hann kallaði kviðuna skjálfhendu eða drápuna steflausu. Hér eru þrjár hendingar í vísuorði ok skothent í fyrsta ok þriðja vísuorði en þriðja hending ok fylgir samstafa hverri hendingu.

All this confusion leaves us unclear whether the author of the *Edda* knew this famous work *Sigurðar saga* at all. The title is not recorded elsewhere, but it is taken to be an early version of *Vǫlsunga saga*. In any case, if the author of the *Edda* had known *Hamðismál* he would be more likely to have based the little he says about Hamðir and Sǫrli on that poem.

Gefjun and her encounter with Gylfi is not mentioned in DG 11 4to. This story may have been little known in Iceland before Snorri paid his visit to lawman Áskell and his wife Kristín in 1219.

Eilífr Guðrúnarson's *Þórsdrápa* is a long and unusual poem, and it is only preserved in *Snorra Edda* (Codex Regius, Codex Trajectinus and Codex Wormianus), which have nineteen stanzas in a row (Faulkes 1998: 25–30), though there are two quatrains that are preserved in DG 11 4to as well as in the other three which could belong to the poem and were included as part of it by Finnur Jónsson in *Skjaldedigtning* (A I: 151 and 152), bringing the number to 21.

Although *Þórsdrápa* is an obscure poem, there is no doubt that it is about Þórr's journey to Geirrøðargarðar, and all uncertainty is removed at the end of the narrative in DG 11 4to (and the other manuscripts), where it says: 'Eilífr Guðrúnarson has composed an account based on this story in *Þórsdrápa*.' Here it is tempting to quote what Finnur Jónsson says in his edition of *Snorra Edda* (1931: lv):

> Ch. 27 [in his edition] contains Þórr's journey to Geirrøðr and the killing of the latter, the same material as Eilífr Goðrúnarson treated in his remarkable and difficult poem Þórsdrápa, which is included in RWT, but lacking in U. There can scarcely

---
[1] In fact the deleted words should probably stand, since the description applies to lines 1 and 3, but not to lines 2 and 4.

be any doubt that the poem is a (later) interpolation; but Snorri did know the poem, for he quoted a couple of half-verses from it elsewhere. There is really nothing in Snorri's account that definitely seems to go back to the poem. A verse in *ljóðaháttr* (about the river Vimur) is quoted; this and the whole account is obviously based on an ancient oral tradition. There is actually a contradiction between Snorri and the poem, since Snorri explicitly says that Þórr had neither his hammer nor his girdle of might, whereas in the poem he strikes the giant with his 'bloody hammer' (v. 90).[1]

In fact Finnur also points out that the account of Þórr's breaking the backs of the giant's daughters could be based on st. 14 of *Þórsdrápa*, but then that is all there is, he says. On the other hand he fails to mention that DG 11 4to attributes a second *ljóðaháttr* stanza to Þórr, thus making him a more productive poet than he is in the other manuscripts.

Another quatrain that has been used as an example is as follows (st. 39 in DG 11 4to, st. 44 in GkS 2367; Faulkes 1998: 15; p. 140 below):

> Reiðr stóð Rǫsku bróðir
> vá gagn faðir Magna.
> Skelfra [DG 11: Skalf eigi . . .] Þórs né Þjálfa
> þróttar steinn við ótta.

It is easy to regularise the pattern of alliteration by reading *Vreiðr* and *Vrǫsku*. Though Icelandic poets in Eilífr's time usually ignore vr- at the beginning of words, they would definitely have known enough examples of its being required to be able to capitalise on the variation. What is much more surprising is that in the long quotation from *Þórsdrápa* in the Codex Regius version the first couplet does not appear. The second couplet, which may perhaps be a *stef*, does (though it does not occur elsewhere in the poem as it is recorded), but with the verb in the past tense (*skalfa*) in all manuscripts (Faulkes 1998: 28/7–8). Whatever the explanation of this may be, it suggests that the quatrain quoted above is derived from a different source from that used for the long quotation.

Jón Sigurðsson put forward the conjecture that the scribe of DG 11 4to had intended the last part of f. 22v and ff. 23r–26v to contain Eilífr's *Þórsdrápa*.[2] It would then have had to be a long *drápa*, for the nineteen stanzas in the Codex Regius would have filled only one leaf in DG 11 4to. It seems much more sensible to accept Finnur Jónsson's idea that the quotation was interpolated into the Codex Regius version, and anyway it is clear that *Skáldatal*, the genealogy and list of lawspeakers were included in the Uppsala Edda version according to a preconceived plan.

[1] In a lively interpretation of *Þórsdrápa* in *Speculum Norroenum* 1981, Margaret Clunies Ross makes a great deal out of this and conjectures that it referred to an initiation rite in which Þórr gained possession of his hammer.

[2] *Íslenzkt fornbréfasafn* I: 499; cf. Grape 1962: 11.

About *Húsdrápa* Finnur Jónsson was in no doubt. From it Snorri had got information about Þórr's encounter with the Miðgarðsormr: 'It is not difficult to point to the sources used here. They are Úlfr's *Húsdrápa*, poems by Eysteinn Valdason and possibly others, together with *Hymiskviða*' (1931: liii). Finnur also refers to Mogk's account (1880). Now it is obvious that this was a well known story throughout the Germanic linguistic area and would have been often retold. Moreover it appears that two differing versions were current, so that there is no way that we can nail down the particular sources used by Snorri in this instance.[1]

Of course this does not mean that we can put forward the idea that Snorri did not know *Húsdrápa*, that powerful poem that Úlfr Uggason is supposed to have composed when transported with delight at the images depicted on the walls of the hall at Hjarðarholt, as it says in *Laxdæla saga*. But it is one thing to be acquainted with a poem, or even to know it, and quite another to use it as a source. This can be illustrated by a simple example.

Both Finnur Jónsson (1931: liii) and Mogk reckoned it obvious that Baldr's death and funeral was described according to the account in *Húsdrápa*. This of course cannot be disproved, but even so, the difference between the two accounts is rather striking. Úlfr Uggason said this according to *Skáldskaparmál* in DG 11 4to:

Ríðr á borg til borgar
boðfróðr sonr Óðins,
Fr[eyr], ok fólkum stýrir,
fyrstr enum gulli bysta.

Something has gone wrong in the genealogy here. As is well known, Freyr was not Óðinn's son. The Codex Regius version has *sonar*, and then presumably the lines mean 'Freyr rides on a boar to the pyre of Óðinn's son'. But in *Gylfaginning* it says in both the Codex Regius version and the Uppsala Edda version: 'Freyr sat í kerru ok var þar beittr fyrir goltrinn Gullinbusti eða Sligrutanni [GkS 2367 4to: Slíðrugtanni]. Heimdallr reið Gulltopp.' It therefore seems unsafe to assume that the account of the funeral in *Gylfaginning* is based on the wording of Úlfr Uggason. There is a difference between coming riding on a boar and harnessing it to a chariot.[2] It is however clear that the narrator in the Uppsala Edda version knew *Húsdrápa*, and it is enough to point to his wording of how Loki and Heimdallr fought over

---

[1] In DG 11 4to it is clearly stated that Þórr decapitated the giant, while in the Codex Regius version alternative endings to the story are referred to.

[2] Yet we must be a little cautious here, because in DG 11 4to it says this about Freyja: 'En er hon ríðr þá ekr hon á köttum sínum ok sitr í reið (p. 42 below). In GkS 2367 4to it says: 'En er hon ferr, þá ekr hon köttum tveim ok sitr í reið' (Faulkes 2005: 2 5).

Brísingamen: 'Úlfr Uggason kvað í Húsdrápu langa stund eptir þessi frásǫgn ok er þess þar getit at þeir vóru í sela líki' (p. 146 below).

In DG 11 4to, Þjóðólfr hvinverski's *Haustlǫng* is mentioned once, and then with recognisable wording: 'Eftir þessi sǫgu hefir ort Þjóðólfr enn hvinverski í Haustlǫng.' The story referred to is the encounter of Þórr and the giant Hrungnir, which in the Uppsala Edda version has been moved and placed at the end of *Gylfaginning*. In the Codex Regius version there is a quotation comprising seven stanzas of the poem.

But in addition, in the Codex Regius version there is an even longer quotation from *Haustlǫng* after the answer to the question 'Hvernig skal kenna Iðunni?' In Faulkes's edition the answer is as follows (1998: 30):[1]

> Kalla hana konu Braga ok gætandi eplanna, en eplin ellilyf Ásanna; hon er ránfengr Þjaza jǫtuns, svá sem fyrr er sagt at hann tók hana braut frá Ásum. Eptir þeiri sǫgu orti Þjóðólfr hinn hvinverski í Haustlǫng.

Thirteen stanzas follow, and actually there is much that is odd in this material. The story has been told at the beginning of *Skáldskaparmál* in the Codex Regius version, and the reference to *Haustlǫng* would have fitted in better there. In DG 11 4to the story is told at the end of *Gylfaginning*. There it is briefer and more compact than in the Codex Regius version, and it will be helpful to compare the two versions. The passage is characteristic of many of the stories that are shorter in DG 11 4to. Italics indicate wording that has the greatest similarity in the two versions, underlining emphasises the greatest differences.

DG 11 4to (p. 86 below)

Bragi segir Ægi frá mǫrgum tíðindum:

Óðinn, Loki ok Hǿnir <u>fóru um fjall</u>, <u>fundu øxnaflokk</u>, <u>taka eitt nautit</u> ok *snúa til seyðis*, <u>rjúfa tysvar seyðinn</u> ok var eigi soðit. *Þá sá þeir ǫrn yfir sér ok lézk hann valda at eigi var soðit.*

Gefit mér fylli ok mun soðit. Þeir játa því. Hann lætr sígast á seyðinn, <u>tók annat uxalærit ok bóguna báða</u>.

GkS 2367 4to (Faulkes 1998: 1–2)

Hann hóf þar frásǫgn at 'þrír Æsir fóro heiman, Óðinn ok Loki ok Hœnir, ok <u>fóru um fjǫll ok eyðimerkr</u> ok var ilt til matar. <u>En er þeir koma ofan í dal nakkvarn</u>, <u>sjá þeir øxna flokk ok taka einn uxann</u> ok *snúa til seyðis*. En er þeir hyggja at soðit mun vera, <u>raufa þeir seyðinn ok var ekki soðit. Ok í annat sinn er þeirr raufa seyðinn</u>, þá er stund var liðin, ok var ekki soðit. Mæla þeir þá sín á milli hverju þetta muni gegna. *Þá heyra þeir mál í eikina upp yfir sik ok sá er þar sat kvazk ráða því er eigi soðnaði á seyðinum.* Þeir litu til ok sat þar ǫrn eigi lítill. Þá mælti ǫrninn:

' *"Vilið þér gefa mér fylli mína af oxanum, þá mun soðna á seyðinum."*

'*Þeir játa því. Þá lætr hann sígask ór trénu ok sezk á seyðinn* ok <u>leggr upp þegar it fyrsta lær oxans tvau</u>

---

[1] Three quatrains from the poem appear in the section on kennings in *Skáldskaparmál* in DG 11 4to.

Loki þreif upp stǫng ok laust á bak erninum. En hann brá sér upp við hǫggit ok flýgr. Stǫngin var fǫst við bak erninum, en hendr Loka voru fastar við annan stangar enda. Ǫrninn flýgr svá at <u>fœtr Loka námu niðri við jǫrðu ok grjóti.</u> En hendr hugði hann slitna mundu ór axlarliðum ok biðr friðar. Ǫrninn lézt hann eigi mundu lausan láta nema Iðunn kœmi þar með epli sín. Loki vill þetta ok ferr brott með eiði. Hann teygir hana eptir eplunum ok biðr hana hafa sín epli, ok hon fór. <u>Þar kom Þjazi jǫtunn í arnarham ok flaug með hana í Þrúðheim.</u> Æsir gerðust ófrir mjǫk ok spurðu hvar Iðunn væri. En er þeir *vissu var Loka heitit bana nema hann fǿri eptir henni meðr valsham Freyju. Hann kom til Þjaza jǫtuns er hann var róinn á sœ. Loki brá henni í hnotar líki ok flaug með hana.* Þjazi tók arnar ham ok flaug eptir þeim. *En er œsir sá hvar valrinn fló þá tóku þeir byrði af lokar spánum ok slógu eldi í.* Ǫrninn fekk eigi stǫðvat sik at fluginum ok *laust eldi í fiðrit,* ok drápu þeir jǫtuninn fyrir innan Ásgrindr.

<u>ok báða bógana.</u> Þá varð Loki reiðr ok greip upp mikla stǫng ok rekr á kroppinn erninum. Ǫrninn bregzk við hǫggit ok flýgr upp. Þá var fǫst stǫngin við kropp arnarins ok hendr Loka við annan enda. Ǫrninn flýgr hátt svá at <u>fœtr taka niðr við grjótit ok urðir ok viðu,</u> [en] *hendr hans hyggr hann at slitna muni ór ǫxlum. Hann kallar ok biðr allþarfliga ǫrninn friðar, en hann segir at Loki skal aldri lauss verða nema hann veiti honum svardaga at koma Iðunni út of Ásgarð með epli sín,* en Loki vil þat. Verðr hann þá lauss ok ferr til lagsmanna sinna ok er eigi at sinni sǫgð fleiri tíðindi um þeira ferð áðr þeir koma heim. En at ákveðinni stundu teygir Loki Iðunni út um Ásgarð í skóg nokkvorn ok segir at hann hefir fundit epli þau er henni munu gripir í þykkja, ok bað at hon skal hafa með sér sín epli ok bera saman ok hin. <u>Þá kemr þar Þjazi jǫtunn í arnarham ok tekr Iðunni ok flýgr braut með ok í Þrymheim til bús síns.</u>

'En Æsir urðu illa við hvarf Iðunnar ok gerðusk þeir <u>brátt hárir ok gamlir.</u> Þá áttu þeir Æsir þing ok [spyrr hver annan] hvat síðarst vissi til Iðunnar, en þat var sét síðarst at hon gekk ór Ásgarði með Loka. *Þá var Loki tekinn ok fœrðr á þingit ok var honum heitit bana eða píslum.* En er hann varð hræddr, þá kvazk hann mundu sœk⟨j⟩a eptir Iðunni í Jǫtunheima ef Freyja vill ljá honum valshams er hon á. Ok er hann fær valshaminn flýgr hann norðr í Jǫtunheima ok *kemr einn dag til Þjaza jǫtuns. Var hann róinn á sœ*, en Iðunn var ein heima. *Brá Loki henni í hnotar líki ok hafði í klóm sér ok flýgr sem mest.* [E]n er Þjazi kom heim ok saknar Iðunnar, tekr hann arnarhaminn ok flýgr eptir Loka ok <u>dró arnsúg í flugnum. En er Æsirnir sá er valrinn flaug</u> með hnotina ok hvar ǫrninn flaug, þá gengu þeir út undir Ásgarð ok báru þannig byrðar af lokarspánum, ok þá er valrinn flaug inn of borgina, lét hann fallask niðr við borgarvegginn. Þá slógu Æsirnir eldi í lokarspánu en ǫrninn mátti eigi stǫðva er hann misti valsins. *Laust þá eldinum í fiðri arnarins* ok tók þá af fluginn. Þá váru Æsirnir nær ok drápu Þjaza jǫtun fyrir innan Ásgrindr ok er þat víg allfrægt.

There is much here that may be found curious. It is, for example, worth observing that the Uppsala Edda version has the eagle put away one of the ox's hams and both shoulders (note that the gods are three in number), but in both the Codex Regius version and *Haustlǫng* he puts away both hams and both shoulders (Þjóðólfur refers to them as 'fjóra þjórhluti' (four quarters). The Codex Regius version and *Haustlǫng* similarly agree that the Æsir became *hárir ok gamlir* (hoary and old), whereas the Uppsala Edda version has only one adjective, *ófrir*, which means 'furious(ly angry)'. Of course one can point out that *hárir ok gamlir* might well have been a fixed phrase and does not have to be a literal quotation. The Codex Regius version and Þjóðólfr both use the otherwise unknown noun *arnsúgr* when describing Þjazi's flight in eagle shape (cf. Faulkes 2005: 20/36–38) while DG 11 4to just says that he flies after Loki and Iðunn.

Iðunn is actually dealt with very strangely in the *Edda*. In *Gylfaginning* (both versions) she is introduced as wife of Bragi, though it is added that she 'varðveitir í eski sínu epli þau er guðin skulu á bíta, þá er þau eldask'. Gangleri observes that this is a great responsibility and the gods have much at stake on 'gæzlu Iðunnar ok trúnaði'. And now comes a unique reply (p. 44 below):

> Þá mælti Hár ok hló við: Nær lagði þat óføru einu sinni. Kunna mun ek þar af at segja. En nú skalt þú heyra fleiri nǫfn guðanna.

This is early in *Gylfaginning*, and it is as if Iðunn is now forgotten, though one would have thought that the story of the theft of the apples would have been given some prominence in the history of the gods. But it is held back in the Codex Regius version until *Skáldskaparmál*, while in the Uppsala Edda version it has been transferred along with other stories from *Skáldskaparmál* to *Gylfaginning*. That there should be no reference to Þjóðólfr when the story of the theft of the apples is narrated is, to tell the truth, not good evidence that his poem was a major source.

This survey of Snorri's sources for his mythology seems to me to indicate decidedly that for this part of his work he relied heavily on oral tradition. Eddic poems in particular were preserved in this way, though indications can be found of there having been written versions in the cases of *Vǫluspá* and *Sexstefja*.[1] But there are four skaldic poems that he used very little, at least early on. In Section 3.2 below his references to his sources in *Skáldskaparmál* will be considered.

3.1.1 Summary

From what has been said above it seems clear that it is not always the same source that underlies the myths as they are told in the Codex Regius version and the Uppsala Edda version. There are simply too many differences between the two versions of important events like the death of Baldr or

[1] See Lasse Mårtensson and Heimir Pálsson 2008.

the theft of Iðunn's apples for it to be possible for the two versions to have come about by the shortening of one or the lengthening of the other. A much more natural explanation is that the two versions were based on different oral narratives that varied in quality and were told by different storytellers. This is made much clearer if one compares this situation with stories that are told in almost identical words in both versions and are undoubtedly derived from the same original (for instance Þórr's journey to Geirrøðargarðar).

Sometimes it can be assumed that more than one source has been used for a story even in a single version of the Edda. This is clear as day in parts of the story of Creation (see Heimir Pálsson 1999) or Óðinn's genealogy in the Prologue and *Gylfaginning* (see Heinrich Beck 2009). It may be pointed out that *Háttatal* 13 seems to accept the account of creation in *Vǫluspá* as valid (either the original creation or the recreation of the earth after *ragnarøkkr*). The *forn minni* (traditional statements) in this verse are *Stóð sær á fjǫllum* and *Skaut jǫrð úr geima*.

Just a few of the eddic poems have definitely provided the main material and structure for the narrative in *Gylfaginning*. There are few cases where it is possible to assert that the version that we know best, that found in the Codex Regius (GkS 2365 4to), was the basis, and it is sometimes clear that the Codex Regius version and the Uppsala Edda version have not followed the same version of a poem.

Oral prose stories have much more often provided the basis for episodes than verse narratives in *dróttkvætt*. Þórr's journey to Geirrøðargarðar is thus not told in accordance with *Þórsdrápa*, though the author of the *Edda* clearly knew that poem.

Þórr's journey to Útgarða-Loki is told in neither any eddic nor any skaldic poem. Yet it is clear from *Lokasenna* and *Hymiskviða* that it was a well known story. Thus there are valid grounds that tend to support the idea that in the twelfth and thirteenth centuries all sorts of stories about the gods were told for entertainment, probably just like other folk tales. This was the richest source of mythological stories for the author of the *Edda*.

3.2 The language of poetry

In the Uppsala Edda four mythological narratives, those about the origin of the mead of poetry, the battle between Þórr and Hrungnir, the kidnapping of Iðunn and Þórr's visit to Geirrøðargarðar, have been moved from *Skáldskaparmál* and made into the closing chapters of *Gylfaginning*. In doing this, the redactor seems to have been trying to separate the mythological narratives from the account of poetical language, and takes this further than the author had originally done. The original intention had probably been to tell first in *Skáldskaparmál* about the origin of poetry and then to list the kennings for

Óðinn and the other gods. But the story of Iðunn and Þjazi is a false start. Both in the Uppsala Edda version and the Codex Regius version it breaks in rather like a thief in the night as the first of all Bragi's stories (DG 11 4to f. 19r; p. 86 below; Faulkes 1998: 1). The narrative in DG 11 4to ends with one of the well known kennings for gold: 'En er synir Auðvalda tóku arf, tók hverr munnfylli af gulli. Er nú gullit kallat munntal jǫtna, en í skáldskap mál þeirra' (p. 88 below). In the Codex Regius version it is expressed more clearly: 'En þat hǫfum vér orðtak nú með oss at kalla gullit munntal þessa jǫtna, en vér felum í rúnum eða í skáldskap svá at vér kǫllum þat mál eða orðtak, tal þessa jǫtna' (Faulkes 1998: 3).

It may be said to be a rule in *Skáldskaparmál* that first there is the question 'hvernig skal kenna' and this is answered by 'svá at kalla'. But there is an important and remarkable departure from this rule in the Codex Regius version. It is never asked how Óðinn should be referred to in kennings (cf. Faulkes 1998: 5). The texts are presented in parallel below. In the Uppsala Edda version the question is indeed expressed indirectly, but the answer follows the regular pattern.

The two versions correspond closely in the kennings for Óðinn in *Skáldskaparmál*, though subject to this reservation, that the intention is to treat of the kennings for poetry, in DG 11 4to with the introductory words 'Enn skal láta heyra dǿmin hvernig skáldin hafa sér látit líka at yrkja eptir þessum heitum ok kenningum' (p. 124 below), and in the Codex Regius 'Enn skal láta heyra dœmin hvernig hǫfuðskáldin hafa látit sér sóma at yrkja eptir þessum heitum ok kenningum' (Faulkes 1998: 6). Then there follow full and fairly similar lists of examples of kennings for Óðinn.

On the other hand it is remarkable that both versions leave the reader pretty well in limbo with the words *eftir þessum heitum ok kenningum*, since they do not relate to anything and come in oddly as the two versions have come down to us. In the Uppsala Edda version, supplementary material has come in (Þórr's encounter with Hrungnir, Þórr's journey to Geirrøðargarðar, *Skáldatal, Ættartala Sturlunga, Lǫgsǫgumannatal*), in the Codex Regius version an interpolation from *Trójumanna saga* (see Finnur Jónsson 1931: 86–88 and Faulkes 1998: xxiii). The texts can be compared as follows:

DG 11 4to (pp. 90 and 124 below)	GkS 2367 4to (Faulkes 1998: 5/9–33, 6/30–33)
Þá mælti Ægir: Hvé mǫrg eru kyn skáldskaparins?	Þá mælir Ægir: 'Hversu á marga lund breytið þér orðtǫkum skáldskapar, eða hversu mǫrg eru kyn skáldskaparins?'
Bragi segir: Tvenn: mál ok háttr.	
Ægir spyrr: Hvat heitir mál skáldskaparins?	Þá mælir Bragi: 'Tvenn eru kyn þau er greina skáldskap allan.'
Bragi segir: Tvent, kent ok ókent.	Ægir spyrr: 'Hver tvenn?'

Ægir segir: Hvat er kent?
Bragi segir: At taka heiti af verkum manns eða annarra hluta eða af því er hann þolir ǫðrum eða af ætt nokkurri.
Ægir segir: Hver dǿmi eru til þess?
Bragi segir: At kalla Óðin fǫður Þórs, Baldrs eða Bezlu eða annarra barna sinna. eða ver Friggjar, Jarðar, Gunnlaðar, Rindar eða eiganda Valhallar eða stýranda guðanna, Ásgarðs eða Hliðskjálfar, Sleipnis eða geirsins, óskmeyja, einherja, sigrs, valfalls; gervandi himins ok jarðar, sólar. Kalla hann aldinn Gaut, hapta guð, hanga guð, farma guð, Sigtýr.
En þat er at segja ungum skáldum er girnast at nema skáldskapar mál ok heyja sér orðfjǫlða með fornum heitum eða skilja þat er hulit er ort, þá skili hann þessa bók til skemtanar. En ekki er at gleyma eða ósanna þessar frásagnir eða taka ór skáldskapnum fornar kenningar er hǫfuðskáldin hafa sér líka látið. En eigi skulu kristnir menn trúa né á sannast at svá hafi verit.
[. . .]
Enn skal láta heyra dǿmin hvernig skáldin hafa sér látit líka at yrkja eptir þessum heitum ok kenningum. Svá sem segir Arnórr jarlaskáld at Óðinn heiti Alfǫðr.

Bragi segir: 'Mál ok hættir.'
'Hvert máltak er haft til skáldskapar?'
'Þrenn er grein skáldskaparmáls.'
'Hver?'
'Svá: at nefna hvern hlut sem heitir; ǫnnur grein er sú er heitir fornǫfn; in þriðja málsgrein er kǫlluð er kenning, ok ⟨er⟩ sú grein svá sett at vér kǫllum Óðin eða Þór eða Tý eða einhvern af Ásum, eða álfum, at hverr þeira er ek nefni til, þá tek ek með heiti af eign annars Ássins eða get ek hans verka nokkvorra. Þá eignask hann nafnit en eigi hinn er nefndr var, svá sem vér kǫllum Sigtý eða Hangatý eða Farmatý, þat er þá Óðins heiti, ok kǫllum vér þat kent heiti. Svá ok at kalla Reiðartý.'
En þetta er nú at segja ungum skáldum þeim er girnask at nema mál skáldskapar ok heyja sér orðfjǫlða með fornum heitum eða girnask þeir at kunna skilja þat er hulit er kveðit: þá skili hann þessa bók til fróðleiks ok skemtunar. En ekki er at gleyma eða ósanna svá þessar sǫgur at taka ór skáldskapinum for[nar ke]nningar þær er hǫfuðskáld hafa sér líka látit. En eigi skulu kristnir menn trúa á heiðin goð eða ok eigi á sannyndi þessar sagnar annan veg en svá sem hér finnsk í upphafi bókar er sagt er frá atburðum þeim er mannfólkit viltisk frá réttri trú, ok þá næst frá Tyrkjum, hvernig Asiamenn þeir er Æsir eru kallaðir fǫlsuðu frásagnir þær frá þeim tíðindum er gerðust í Troju til þess at landfólkit skyldi trúa þá guð vera.
[Here comes the interpolation from *Trójumanna saga*]
Enn skal láta heyra dǿmin hvernig hǫfuðskáldin hafa látit sér sóma at yrkja eptir þessum heitum ok kenningum, svá sem segir Arnórr jarlaskáld at hann heiti Alfǫðr.

In content, these passages are very comparable, though the Codex Regius version seems clearly to have a more mature textbook style, and it is extremely difficult to imagine the Uppsala Edda version as having derived from it.

In *Skáldskaparmál* in the Uppsala Edda version, there are, as was stated above, 260 numbered verse quotations in my transcription. Some are the same text repeated, so that it would be more accurate to speak of 250. They are nearly always half-stanzas (four lines). It is rather unlikely that people learnt verses in this form. They were more often composed as eight-line

Introduction

stanzas than as quatrains, and probably very often had a story attached. It is of course conceivable that Snorri knew all these examples and all the additional examples in *Heimskringla* too, though with those he would have had great help in earlier Kings' Sagas. Yet it is very remarkable that of 600 or so verses in *Heimskringla* only twenty-four are found in *Skáldskaparmál* in the form in which it appears in DG 11 4to. From this I can draw only one rational conclusion. There were two different collections of verses (corpuses) that were used. Of course these two collections could have resided in the same man's head, but after a hundred years of literacy in Iceland this becomes rather less plausible than earlier. People have in fact long realised that Snorri had a different version of *Vǫluspá* from the ones we see in the Codex Regius or Hauksbók.[1] It probably became ever commoner for poems to be composed so to speak direct onto parchment. In an article of 2008, I pointed out that the redactor of the Uppsala Edda version clearly had a written text of Þjóðólfr Arnórsson's *Sexstefja* before him.[2]

The compilation of verse examples must have taken quite a long time, and we really don't know whether it was the work of more than one man. At Oddi there seem to have been a large number of people during Snorri's formative years, and it is very likely that he had help with this work. The results, on the other hand, were variable. By far the majority of the verse examples in *Skáldskaparmál* are in the first part, where kennings are discussed. The concept itself is not explained there, but if one looks at the material, it is clear that sometimes it is a question of metaphors (*ægis jódraugar* = seamen; *gullmens pǫll* = woman), sometimes simply of human relationships or attributes (Þórr is called Óðinn's son, Bragi Iðunn's husband).[3] On the other hand, it is quite clear that the collection of examples has gaps. If the number of verse examples for each kenning concept is calculated, we get the following picture (figures in brackets are the number of verse examples):

Óðinn (22), poetry (14), Þórr (15), Baldr (0), Njǫrðr (0), Freyr (3), Heimdallr (0), Týr (0), Bragi (0), Viðarr (0), Váli (0), Hǫðr (0), Ullr (0), Hǿnir (0), Loki (0), Frigg (0), Freyja (0), Iðunn (0); sky (11), earth (5), sea (10), sun (2), wind (1), fire (0), winter (2), summer (1); man (0), gold (17), man in terms of gold (4), woman in terms of gold (8), man in terms of trees and weapons (9); battle (7), weapons and armour (22), ship (11); Christ (10), kings (5), ranks of men (15).

[1] Sophus Bugge noted this and gave detailed variants in *Norrœn fornkvæði* 1867.
[2] See Lasse Mårtensson and Heimir Pálsson 2008.
[3] Bergsveinn Birgisson has recently written very intelligently about kennings in his doctoral dissertation (2008), especially in the third and fourth chapters (Kjenningteori and Estetikk). See also his article in *Skírnir* (Spring 2009). There is a very clear treatment of Snorri's concepts in Faulkes's introduction to *Skáldskaparmál* (1998), especially the section The analysis of poetic diction (pp. xxv–xxxvii).

It is quite clear that two of the gods, Óðinn and Þórr, provided the best harvest. Most of the other divine figures are without examples. It becomes a bit more lively when when we get to the kennings for gold, weapons and armour, ships, men and women. Obviously this is explained by the characteristic topics of the poems. So much was composed about battles and seafaring, men and women, that it must have been easy to find material for these sections in the collection of examples.

With *heiti* there are generally few examples. Poetry and the gods get five examples each, but otherwise only the sons of Hálfdan stand out. There were eighteen of them, and Snorri gives twenty-one examples of the use of their names to mean 'king'. But he has something remarkable to say about *heiti* for sky (p. 206 below):

> Þessi nǫfn himins[1] eru rituð en eigi hǫfum vér funnit í kvæðum ǫll þessi. En þessi heiti þikki mér óskylt at hafa nema kveðit[2] sé til.

In Icelandic, when something is said to be written ('ritat'), it means that there is a written source. Unfortunately the author here does not say where these names for 'sky'were written, but what follows shows that it was a very comprehensive list:

> Hann heitir himinn, hlýrnir, heiðþyrnir, leiptr, hrjóðr, víðbláinn.
>
> Hverninn skal kenna himininn? Kalla hann Ymis haus, ok erfiði ok byrði dverga, hjálm Austra, Vestra, Norðra, Suðra; land sólar ok tungls ok himintungla, vápna eða veðra, hjálm eða hús lopts ok jarðar.

The question about how the sky is to be referred to in kennings has been raised before. The reply was basically the same, but not quite identical (p. 150 below):

> Svá at kalla hann Ymis haus, ok þar af jǫtuns haus, ok erfiði eða byrði dverganna eða hjálm Vestra ok Austra, Suðra, Norðra; land sólar ok tungls ok himintungla, vápna ok veðra; hjálmr eða hús lopts ok jarðar ok sólar.

Here it seems that it can be fairly safely asserted that both extracts have the same source (or sources), since in both places there is the same obvious error of *vápna* for (probably) *vatna*. 'Land of weapons' is a well known kenning for 'shield', but very strange as a kenning for the sky. But it appears in these two places in DG 11 4to, ff. 30r and 37v. In the second of these the leaf is damaged, and all that can be read is *va₀₀na*. Jón Rúgmann assumed the same form to be intended in both places, but Jón Sigurðsson suggested

---

[1] It is an obvious scribal error when we find *heims* in the text here, and also in the heading. From what follows it is obvious that it ought to be *himins*.

[2] e is sometimes written for æ in medieval manuscripts, and it may be that *kvæðit* was intended. This would correspond more closely to the reading of GkS 2367 4to, which has 'nema áðr finni hann í verka hǫfuðskálda þvílík heiti' (Faulkes 1998: 85).

reading *vatna* on the second occurrence, and indeed weather and waters go better together than weather and weapons. AM 157 8vo seems, however, to resolve all doubt. The reading was *vápna*. It can of course be pointed out, as an excuse for the scribe, that *veðr* is a very common element in kennings for 'battle'. The manuscripts of the Codex Regius version (GkS 2367 4to, AM 242 fol. and Codex Trajectinus) have *vagna* instead of *vápna*, which may be regarded as authentic, whether it related to the constellation Charles's wain or Þórr's and Freyja's chariots (see verse 59 in *Skáldskapamál*, where Ormr Barreyjarskáld calls the sky *vagnbraut*). On the other hand there is an odd coincidence if one looks at the text of AM 757 a 4to (*Edda Snorra Sturlusonar* 1848–87: II 526), since there we find *vagna* as in the Codex Regius version, but under the heading *Kenningar heimsins*, the same error as DG 11 4to on f. 37r, *Um nǫfn heimsins*. It is highly unlikely that two scribes would make the same error with an interval of a century between them. Here as elsewhere, the redactor of the AM 758 I b 4to /AM 757 a 4to version seems to follow partly the Uppsala Edda version and partly the Codex Regius version.[1]

In the second quotation above there is an interesting grammatical anomaly. The kennings listed are all objects of the verb *kalla* (or complements of the phrase *kalla hann*), but at *hjálmr eða hús* we suddenly have the nominative case instead of the normal accusative (*land* is ambiguous as regards its case). This is not an isolated example. It occurs many times in the lists in *Skáldskaparmál*, for instance in the list of kennings for 'poetry' (p. 132 below):

> Svá sem hér: at kalla Kvasis dreyra eða dverga skip, mjǫð jǫtna, mjǫð Suttunga, mjǫð Óðins ok ása, fǫðurgjǫld jǫtna; lǫgr Óðrøris ok Sónar ok Boðnar, ok lǫgr Hnitbjarga, fengr ok fundr ok farmr ok gjǫf Óðins.

The first six kennings have the expected accusative, but from *lǫgr Óðreris* onwards, the basewords are nominative. It is of course possible to explain the anomaly as the incompetence of scribes, as many commentators have been ready to do. Finnur Jónsson liked the word *vilkårlig* (capricious) when characterising all the stupidities that he thought the scribe of DG 11 4to was guilty of. But here the explanation may be much more straightforward. If the scribe (note that it need not have been the scribe of DG 11 4to) had a list of kennings before him, where the possibilities were tabulated, then the list may have looked something like this, with all the basewords in the nominative:

> Kvasis dreyri, dverga skip, mjǫðr jǫtna, mjǫðr Suttunga, mjǫðr Óðins ok ása, fǫðurgjǫld jǫtna, lǫgr Óðrøris ok Sónar ok Boðnar, ok lǫgr Hnitbjarga, fengr ok fundr ok farmr ok gjǫf Óðins.

---

[1] See Finnur Jónsson 1931: xxxviii; Faulkes 1998: xliv–l.

When he needed to adapt the list to fit its new context, after the introductory 'At kalla . . .' he may have read the first line of his exemplar as a whole, and written it down, and then the second line, forgetting now to change the case of all the basewords. This has happened in various places in *Skáldskaparmál* and not only in the Uppsala Edda version,[1] and is a very natural error for a scribe or redactor to make. But then we would have to assume the use of written lists as sources.

Lists of names that appear in a fixed order may indicate the same sort of thing. For instance the gods are listed three times in DG 11 4to in almost identical order, as can be seen here (the differences in order are italicised):

Introduction in *Gylfaginning*	Ægir's feast	Kennings in *Skáldskaparmál*
Þórr	Þórr	Þórr
Baldr		Baldr
Njǫrðr	Njǫrðr	Njǫrðr
Freyr	Freyr	Freyr
Týr	*Týr*	*Heimdallr*
Bragi	*Heimdallr*	*Týr*
Heimdallr	*Bragi*	*Bragi*
Hǫðr	Viðarr	Viðarr
Viðarr	Váli	Váli
Áli / Váli		Hǫðr
Ullr	Ullr	Ullr
	Hœnir	Hœnir
Forseti	Forseti	
Loki	Loki	Loki

Hǫðr and Baldr are absent from Ægir's feast,[2] but otherwise the order is very similar. There is some swapping of positions halfway down the lists, but in general the arrangement is the same in each case. The same is true of the Codex Regius version, which also has the same swapping of positions.

Although considerably less is said about goddesses than gods in the *Edda*, it is interesting to look at how they are introduced in the two versions. In DG 11 4to they are introduced as follows (pp. 50–52):

---

[1] The mixture of cases occurs in R and T too, rather more often than in U. See Faulkes 1998, note to 14/25–30. It is suggested there that this may have arisen when additions were made to the lists.

[2] Of course one might imagine that this is because the feast takes place after the death of Baldr (cf. Faulkes 1998, note to 1/9–11), though we cannot expect rational chronology in mythological stories from the pre-literary period. W.Ong has some interesting comments on this in *Orality and Literacy* (1982).

Frigg er ǫzt ... Ǫnnur er Saga ... Eir ... Gefjun ... Fylla ... Freyja ... Sjǫfn ... Lofn ... Vár ('Vavr') ... Vǫr ('Vavr') ... Syn ... Hlín ... Snotra ... Gná.

But in the Codex Regius version it says (Faulkes 2005: 29–30):

Frigg er œzt ... Ǫnnur er Sága ... Þriðja er Eir ... Fjórða er Gefjun ... Fimta er Fulla ... Freyja ... Sjaunda Sjǫfn ... Átta Lofn ... Níunda Vár ... Tíunda Vǫr ... Ellipta Syn ... Tólfta Hlín ... Þrettánda Snotra ... Fjórtánda Gná.

Some conclusions may perhaps be drawn from the numbering in the Codex Regius. It is definitely more likely that such numbering was added than that it was deleted. Apart from the fact that somewhere in the history of the Uppsala Edda version, the goddesses Vǫr and Vór have been combined into one, or at any rate not distinguished, the list is the same. Since length in vowels was rarely indicated by medieval scribes, the names of Vǫr and Vór would often have been spelt the same.

It is interesting to see how the kennings for Loki are listed in the Uppsala Edda version compared with the Codex Regius version. Neither gives any examples from poetry and so it is tempting to assume that both are based on prose compilations of some kind, not necessarily the same one in each case. The words that are in the wrong case are italicised.

DG 11 4to, f. 29v 15–23 (p. 148 below)
Hversu skal kenna Loka?

Kalla hann son Fárbauta ok ~~Heljar~~ Laufeyjar ok Nálar, bróður Býleifst ok Helblinda; *faðir* Vánargands, þat er Fenrisúlfur, ok Jǫrmungands, þat er Miðgarðs ormr, ok Heljar ok Nara ok Ála; ok frænda ok fǫðurbróður, vársinna ok sessa Óðins ok ása ok kistuskrúð Geirraðar; *þjófr* jǫtna haf⟨r⟩s ok Brísingamens ok Iðunnar epla; Sleipnis frænda, ver Sigunar, gaða (= goða?) dólg, hárskaða Sifjar, bǫlva smið; *hinn slǿgi áss, rǿgjandi* ok *vélandi* guðanna, *ráðbani* Baldurs, *hinn búni* (= *bundni*?) *áss, þrætudólgr* Heimdallar ok Skaða.

GkS 2367 4to (Faulkes 1998:19–20)
Hvernig skal kenna Loka?

Svá at kalla son Fárbauta ok Laufeyjar, Nálar, bróður Býleists ok Helblinda, fǫður Vánargands (þat er Fenrisúlfr) ok Jǫrmungands (þat er Miðgarðsormr) ok Heljar ok Nara, ok Ála frænda ok fǫðurbróður, sinna ok sessa Óðins ok Ása, heimsœki ok kistuskrúð Geirrøðar, *þjófr* jǫtna, hafrs ok Brísingamens ok Iðunnar epla. Sleipnis frænda, *verr* Sigynjar, goða *dólgr, hárskaði* Sifjar, bǫlva *smiðr, hinn slægi Áss,* rœgjanda ok *vélandi* goðanna, *ráðbani* Baldrs, hinn bundni, *þrætudólgr* Heimdala⟨r⟩ ok Skaða.

The Uppsala Edda version calls Loki Óðinn's *vársinni* (though the length of the first vowel is not indicated in DG 11 4to). This word is unknown from elsewhere and has actually not got into the dictionaries, except the *ONP* word list, where it is given in the form *varsinni*. Finnur Jónsson (1931) records the readings (the word in the accusative case) of U and T as *varsin(n)a* and that of AM 757 a 4to as *ver sinna*. Two editors of the *Edda* in normalised spelling, Magnús Finnbogason and Árni Björnsson, read *vársinna*, glossed by the latter 'foster-brother'. Taking account of *Lokasenna* and the role of the goddess Vár, one might suppose that *vársinni* had some sexual connotation, and we may recall that in the prose with *Helgakviða Hjǫrvarðssonar* it says: 'Helgi ok Sváva veittust várar ok unnust furðumikit' (Bugge 1867: 176). The scribes of GkS 2367 4to and AM 242 fol. presumably did not know the word, but were well acquainted with *sinni* 'companion', and thought that would do.

The *þulur* in GkS 2367 4to and other manuscripts are of course good evidence that word lists of various kinds existed. There are few *þulur* in DG 11 4to, though there are enough of them to show that they were a natural and independent collection of sources. The *þula* of terms for groups of men, for instance, is interesting (p. 216 below, cf. Faulkes 1998: 106–107):

> Maðr heitir einn hverr,
> ái ef tveir eru, (R: tá ef tveir ró)
> þorp ef þrír eru,
> fjórir eru fǫruneyti,
> flokkr fimm menn,
> sveit ef sex eru,
> sjau fylla sǫgn,
> átta fylla ámælisskor, (R: átta bera ámælisskor)
> nautar eru níu,
> tugr eru tíu, (R: dúnn ef tíu eru)
> ærir eru ellefu,
> toglǫð tólf,
> þyss er þrettán,
> ferð er fjórtán,
> fundr er þar er fimmtán finnast,
> seta eru sextán,
> sók⟨n⟩ eru sautján,
> ørnir þikkja óvinir þeim er átján møta,
> neyti eru nítján, (R: neyti hefir sá er nítján menn ⟨hefir⟩)
> drótt er tuttugu,
> þjóð eru þrír tigir,
> fólk er fjórir tigir,
> fylki eru fimm tigir,
> samnaður sex tigir,
> svarfaðr sjau tigir, (R: sørvar eru sjau tigir)
> aldir átta tigir,
> herr er hundrað.

This list is nearly the same in the two versions, and it is noteworthy that a term for ninety men is lacking in both.[1]

---

[1] See Faulkes 1998: 106–7.

In *Den norsk-islandske skjaldedigtning* (*Skj* A I 652), Finnur Jónsson prints two stanzas from DG 11 4to under the heading 'Þulur'.[1] They are, however, quite different from most of the other *þulur*, in that they are composed in *dróttkvætt* and were obviously added to fill in an empty space on f. 45r (see below, p. 246), but they are fine examples of collections of words:

> Blíð er mær við móður,
> mála drekkr á ekkju,
> kvíðir kerling eiðu,
> kveðr dóttir vel beðju,
> opt finnr ambátt hǫptu,
> æ er frilla grǫm sværu,
> kiljar kvæn við elju,
> [k]ann nipt við snǫr skipta.

> Brottu er svarri ok sværa,
> sveimar rýgr ok feima,
> brúðr er í fǫr með fljóði,
> fat ek drós ok man kjósa,
> þekki ek sprund ok sprakka,
> spari ek við hæl at mæla,
> firrumst ek snót ok svarra,
> svífr mér langt frá vífi.

One can almost see a schoolboy or his master trying to collect all the terms for 'woman' into some memorable form. These two stanzas are followed by a third that is a conventional *mansǫngsvísa* ('love poem') where the poet complains of his lady's failure to reciprocate his love. These three verses are clearly an independent addition or space-filler on f. 45r, after the end of *Skáldskaparmál*, unequivocally in the same hand as the main text, although they are obviously not part of the section of the *Edda* that has just been written any more than they are of what follows, for on the next page begins the second grammatical treatise. In AM 748 I b 4to the two stanzas of terms for women together with three *dróttkvætt* stanzas containing names of islands, two of which are attributed to Einarr Skúlason in Faulkes 1977–79: I 267, come near the end of a large collection of *þulur*. The two containing terms for women, moreover, have the same heading as was used on the previous page, 'Kvenna heiti ókend' (*Edda Snorra Sturlusonar* 1848–87: II 489–490).

3.2.1 Summary

The material we have in *Skáldskaparmál* is remarkably varied. Some of it must come from independent verses (*lausavísur*) preserved orally. In the Middle Ages

---

[1] There is actually also a sub-heading 'Forskellige—ikke sammenhængende—vers' ('Various—unconnected—stanzas'). Note that the two stanzas are also in AM 748 I b 4to.

as later in Iceland, men and women would have had various scraps of verse they were able to quote for their entertainment when there was not much else available.

It is likely that long before the time of Snorri, people had made for their convenience lists of different kinds to help them in composing poetry. These would have been *þulur* of various terms that could be continually extended and added to. Some of these would doubtless have been written down early, some may have remained oral mnemonics. These were the equivalent of modern rhyming dictionaries for poets, and it would be absurd not to assume that medieval poets would have tried to lighten their labours with such aids.

The poet Þórarinn Eldjárn sent me by email (24th September 2010, quoted here with the writer's permission) some entertaining thoughts on this topic. In it he wrote among other things:

> A very long time ago I made myself a resource that I call a rhymefinder. In it are the Icelandic consonants in alphabetical order, and to each of them are added all the possible consonants that can stand as a group at the beginnings of words, for example b, bj, bl, blj, br, brj and so on. To find rhyming words, set the word that it has to rhyme with after each consonant. Let us say we have the word *ól*. Then under b you have the possibility of *ból, bjól, blól, bljól, ból, brjól*. Most of these words do not actually exist, but the possibilities are at any rate exhaustively listed.
>
> In *Kyrr kjör* I put it as if Guðmundur Bergþórsson had worked this out for himself, and not I. And maybe he just did it too. Who can tell? But obviously you are right that people of all periods must have tried to help themselves out like this. Snorri too.

It is not known whether the author of the *Edda* had access to any writings of this kind in Iceland, but it has to be assumed that he worked from various materials according to his own wit and understanding. We know nothing of any assistants he may have had, but they may have been numerous. Still, it is clear that one mind was behind all the working out, though as will be discussed later, the work was a long time developing.

4 One work or more than one?

After Konráð Gíslason (1869) had dated *Háttatal* to 1222–1223 ('neither sooner or later', says Wessén) and Elias Wessén had written his famous introduction to the facsimile of the Codex Regius (1940), there has been fairly good agreement among scholars that the *Edda* was to be regarded as an integral work that was compiled between 1222 and 1225. Wessén began his discussion with a rhetorical question (1940: 14):

> Why does Snorri's poetics embody precisely the works that it actually does? How is it that he begins with a mythology, and passes on to stylistics and metrics? Can Snorri be imagined to have had this plan clearly before him already from the beginning?

Then Wessén discusses *Háttatal*, *Skáldskaparmál*, *Gylfaginning* and the Prologue (in this order) and then reaches his conclusion (p. 30):

> While writing the commentary on *Háttatal* it became clear to [Snorri] that there was much more that a skald should know. He then conceived the idea of writing *Skáldskaparmál*, and later *Gylfaginning*. Indeed, it seems improbable that he should have proceeded in any other order during the composition. That he should have b e g u n by writing a mythology when it was his intention to write a manual for skalds would be quite incomprehensible. On the other hand, it is only natural that later on, when the work was completed, the most entertaining part, *Gylfaginning*, should be placed at the beginning.

Wessén does indeed assume that *Skáldskaparmál* has been 'revised and enlarged on several occasions' and is in its present form later than *Gylfaginning*. A decade later, Anne Holtsmark wrote the introduction to her and Jón Helgason's edition in the series Nordisk filologi, which is probably the edition that has been most used in Scandinavian universities, and her imaginative paraphrase of Wessén's theory has been very influential (1950: xii–xiii):

> Snorri came back from a visit to the Norwegian king Hákon Hákonarson and Jarl Skúli in 1220. He composed a poem about them both, the content of which is unremarkable, but its form all the more exceptional; it is 102 stanzas in 100 different verse forms. The poem is called *Háttatal* and was finished in 1222–23. For this poem he wrote a metrical commentary . . . one can express oneself in three ways, he says, call something by its name, use a 'heiti' or a 'kenning'. He compiled examples of how skalds used heiti and kennings and arranged them systematically. But many of the kennings could not be understood unless he told the stories that they were derived from, including both tales of gods and heroes . . . While he was engaged on that, he must have got the idea of writing *Gylfaginning*. It was the whole of heathen mythology he now decided to write . . . When the Prologue and *Gylfaginning* were finished, Snorri went back to *Skáldskaparmál*. He creates a frame story for that too, in *Gylfaginning* he was inspired by *Vafþrúðnismál*, here it is *Lokasenna* that provides the frame.

This has become the standard view and is repeated in work after work. There is a good example in Marlene Ciklamini (1978: 43): 'Snorri first conceived and executed a part of the work that today is read only by specialists, a long poem of metrical commentary named *Háttatal, "Enumeration of Poetical Meters"*. In modern editions and in the manuscripts this part is the third and last section of the work, a position which indicates that the composition lacks intrinsic interest.' Later on, Ciklamini does indeed state, in opposition to Holtsmark, that it is *Skáldskaparmál* that is under the influence of *Vafþrúðnismál*.

When Sigurður Nordal wrote his *Litteraturhistoria* (Nordisk kultur VIII B) he was more circumspect than the scholars that have been quoted here (1953: 219):

> Edda (*Snorra Edda*) is the only one of Snorri's works that is attributed to him in a surviving manuscript of the book itself. Its last section is *Háttatal*, finished in the winter of 1222–23. That his *Edda* was completed around this time, but on the basis of earlier preparatory work, can be regarded as more or less certain.

This is judicious caution, and in fact Wessén had assumed that the compilation of material for *Skáldskaparmál* had taken a very long time, but after 1223.

On the other hand the fact is that there is much that is unclear and some that is uncertain in this dating. Firstly, it is improbable that the commentary to *Háttatal* was made before *Skáldskaparmál* and absurd to think that it would have accompanied the poem when it was sent abroad. That would have been pure bad manners to the two rulers. In fact there is no basis for the assumption that *Háttatal* was composed in one go, and the latter part of the poem could well have been composed later than 1223.

Secondly, comparison of the commentary in GkS 2367 4to with that in DG 11 4to reveals that it is considerably fuller in the former than in the latter, not least in regard to the names of verse-forms. The commentary seems in other words to expand with time, and moreover this is much more likely than that information should be deleted, and is thus clear evidence of the work having been subject to continual development and reworking.

Thirdly, it is very suspicious that the author should not use a single example from *Háttatal* to illustrate poetical language in *Skáldskaparmál*.

Fourthly, there is so little reference in *Gylfaginning* to *Skáldskaparmál* or vice versa, that there is no way to see with certainty which was compiled first. The following passage in the Codex Regius version is often quoted in this connection (Faulkes 1998: 5):

> En eigi skulu kristnir menn trúa á heiðin goð ok eigi á sannyndi þessar sagnar annan veg en svá sem hér finnsk í upphafi bókar er sagt er frá atburðum þeim er mannfólkit viltisk frá réttri trú, ok þá næst frá Tyrkjum, hvernig Asiamenn þeir er Æsir eru kallaðir fǫlsuðu frásagnir þær frá þeim tíðindum er gerðusk í Troju til þess at landfólkit skyldi trúa þá guð vera.

But actually it is far from clear that the reference here is to anything other than the Prologue, and the Uppsala Edda version simply says 'E[n] eigi skulu kristnir menn trúa né á sannast at svo hafi verit' (p. 90 below):[1] Here there is no mention of the beginning of the book. On the other hand, both versions of *Skáldskaparmál* agree that Heimdallr can be referred to as *sonr níu mæðra* or *vǫrðr goða* 'as was said/written before' (p. 146 below; Faulkes 1998: 19). These words clearly refer to *Gylfaginning*, where Heimdallr actually is called *vǫrðr guða* and *níu systra sonr* (p. 44 below; Faulkes 2005: 25–26). If this reference is taken seriously, it indicates unequivocally that *Gylfaginning* is earlier than *Skáldskaparmál*, or that *Skáldskaparmál* was revised after *Gylfaginning* was written.

Fifthly, it should be mentioned that the poet of *Háttatal* is clearly very well up in poetic theory. This indicates that he has at any rate studied poetry and thought carefully about it over a long period. No one doubts that he must have paid careful attention when *Noregs konunga tal* was being composed in praise and honour of his foster-father in Oddi, though the idea seems to me rather unlikely that Snorri composed this poem at the age of 15.[2]

Sixthly one might ask whether it is likely that the procedure of a writer of a textbook would have been to begin by compiling the answers and then search for the evidence that fitted them. *Háttatal* is more likely to be the conclusion than the starting out point.

Bjarni Aðalbjarnarson pointed out in the introduction to his edition of *Heimskringla* (1941–51: I xxiv) that in the years preceding his trip to Norway in 1218 Snorri would have had plenty of time to compose his *Edda*, apart from *Háttatal*. In my article 'Fyrstu leirskáldin' (2010c) I demonstrated the likelihood that the version of the story of the mead of poetry that appears in DG 11 4to had been known from Snorri's work before 1220. I pointed out there that the use of the term *arnarleir* of the 'poetaster's portion' is unknown from other medieval manuscripts of the *Edda*, but that it was actually used in a satirical verse about Snorri when he returned from his first trip to Norway (cf. p. xxii above). Then I drew attention to the fact that the unusual expression *taka hein úr pússi sínum* ('to take a whetstone from one's pouch') occurs in both the Uppsala Edda and Sturla Þórðarson's *Íslendingasaga (Sturlinga saga* 1946: I 284), where it is put into the mouth of Snorri's brother Sighvatr. Other versions of the story have the whetstone on Óðinn's belt. Naturally, individual words can never be regarded as proof, but they can add weight to the evidence.

The main question, of course, is whether the *Edda* is so obviously a unity that the author must have conceived it as a whole before he began the work. This

---

[1] Cf. also AM 757 a 4to, *Edda Snorra Sturlusonar* 1848–87: II 533.
[2] Cf. Óskar Guðmundsson 2009: 47–58.

seems to me not to be the case. The three main parts of the work, *Gylfaginning*, *Skáldskaparmál* and *Háttatal*, are all so separate that they could each stand on their own. This is confirmed by the existence of two manuscripts, AM 748 I b 4to (from the first quarter of the fourteenth century) and AM 757 a 4to (from about 1400) that contain versions of *Skáldskaparmál* without either *Gylfaginning* or *Háttatal*. People have obviously thought that it was possible to get the full benefit of reading *Skáldskaparmál* without the other sections. The same attitude can be seen in AM 157 8vo, a paper manuscript from the beginning of the seventeenth century with a relatively accurate transcript of *Skáldskaparmál* in DG 11 4to.[1] The opening words of this manuscript show that *Skáldskaparmál* had already by about 1600 come to have a separate name, 'Skálda', a hypocoristic term for *Skáldskaparmál*, to which it obviously refers in the heading 'Annar Eddu partur er kallaður Skálda eður kenningar'. It was probably about the same time that the author of *Qualiscunque descriptio Islandiae* writes about two works, one called *Skálda*, the other *Edda*.[2] This name *Skálda* sticks with *Skáldskaparmál* for a long time; one only has to look at Rask's edition of 1818, where the name is printed on the title page of *Skáldskaparmál*.

A great deal has been written about the Prologue, and in fact it is only preserved complete in DG 11 4to and AM 242 fol. (though this version has long interpolations), but Anthony Faulkes has reconstructed a very convincing picture of the original beginning in GkS 2367 4to, using four seventeenth-century manuscripts derived from it before its first leaf was lost.[3] The Prologue in DG 11 4to is considerably shorter than in the other versions, but could certainly be derived from the same root. It is in the Prologue that euhemerism is introduced. The Æsir were mortals that were worshipped as gods after their deaths. This idea is attributed to the Greek philosopher Euhemeros, who lived about three hundred years BC. His *Sacred History* has only survived in extracts quoted by later writers, but his ideas were frequently reproduced in patristic writings and became widespread in Europe in the Middle Ages. They reached Iceland early, for they can be traced in Ari's genealogy of the Ynglings.[4] Saxo Grammaticus, an older contemporary of Snorri, also made use of the theory, and it doubtless added weight to the idea that our heathen forefathers should be regarded as intellectual beings who were not themselves given to worshipping evil spirits (the concept of 'the noble heathen').

---

[1] Sverrir Tómasson's observation is worth noting: 'Textual evidence that *Skáldskaparmál* was originally an independent work need not affect the judgment that the Prologue, *Gylfaginning* and *Skáldskaparmál* were regarded as three independent units in a single coherent work' (1996a: 4, footnote 3).

[2] See Sverrir Tómasson 1996a: 55.

[3] See Faulkes 1979. The reconstructed text is printed in Faulkes 2005 (first edn Oxford: Clarendon Press 1982).

[4] See *Íslendingabók* 1968: 27–28.

But Snorri used euhemerism not only in his *Edda*, but also in *Ynglinga saga* in his *Heimskringla*, and there it is used very differently. The narrative in *Ynglinga saga* is much more lively and varied; moreover the narrator there was probably more practised and experienced and his purpose different. Among other things, he has got hold of the entertaining little episode of Gefjun and Gylfi the Swede. This story may well have titillated his ears during his visit to lawman Áskell and Kristín in Gautland in 1219. It does not show very great geographical knowledge to think of Lake Mälar in Sweden as having come into being when Sjælland was ploughed up and carried off. The correspondence the story suggests is between the nesses in Sjælland and the bays in Lake Vänern, not those in Lake Mälar. The story was probably interpolated into the Codex Regius version of the *Edda*, for DG 11 4to contains no mention of Gefjun's dealings with Gylfi, and obviously Bjarni Aðalbjarnarson is thinking of the Codex Regius of the *Edda* when he writes in a footnote in his edition of *Heimskringla* (1941–51: I 14–15): 'Snorri neglected to introduce Gefjun and Gylfi to his readers since he had already spoken of them in *Gylfaginning*.'

It has long been disputed whether the Prologue is the work of the same person as wrote *Gylfaginning*. Here no attempt will be made to give an account of this controversy, but reference may be made to Heinrich Beck's articles of 2004, 2008 and 2009. In the last of these, Beck points out that it is difficult to imagine that the same person, at the same stage of his intellectual development, compiled both of these texts:

The Prologue in DG 11 4to (p. 8 below)	*Gylfaginning* in DG 11 4to (pp. 16–17 below)
Konungr hét Menon. Hann átti dóttur Prjámuss konungs Trójam. Sonr þeira hét Trór er vér kǫllum Þór. Þá var hann tólf vetra er hann hafði fullt afl sitt. Þá lypti hann af jǫrðu tíu bjarnstǫkum senn. Hann sigraði marga berserki senn ok dýr eða dreka. Í norðrhálfu heimsins fann hann spákonu eina er Sibil hét, en vér kǫllum Sif. Engi vissi ætt hennar. Sonr þeira hét Lórriði, hans sonr Vingiþórr, hans sonr Vingenir, hans sonr Móða, hans sonr Magi, hans sonr Sefsmeg, hans sonr Beðvig, hans sonr Atra, er vér kǫllum Annan, hans sonr Ítrman, hans sonr Eremóð, hans sonr Skjaldun, er vér kǫllum Skjǫld, hans sonr Bjáf, er vér kǫllum Bǫr, hans sonr Jat, hans sonr Guðólfr, hans sonr Finnr, hans sonr Frjálafr, er vér kǫllum Friðleif, hans sonr Vodden, er vér kǫllum Óðin.	Næst var þat er hrím draup at þar varð af kýrin Auðumla. Fjórar mjólkár runnu ór spenum hennar ok fǿddi hon Ymi. En kýrin fǿddist er hon sleikti hrímsteina er saltir voru. Ok enn fyrsta dag er hon sleikti kom ór manns hár, annan dag hǫfuð, enn þriðja allr maðr er Buri hét, fǫðr[1] Bors, er átti Beyzlu, dóttur Bǫlþorns jǫtuns. Þau áttu þrjá sonu, Óðin, Víli, Vé, ok þat ætlum vér, segir Hár, at sá Óðinn ok hans brǿðr munu vera stýrandi heims ok jarðar, ok þar er sá eptir her⟨r⟩ann[2] er vér vitum nú mestan vera.

[1] This form of the word could be either nominative or accusative.
[2] This word is discussed at length in Grape et al. 1977: 115.

Beck in fact leaves it open whether Snorri could have written the two accounts at different periods of his life. Besides, one must remember that the first story, the one in the Prologue, is intended to explain the migration of the Æsir, the other is the story they themselves have made up to deceive Gylfi about the gods they profess to worship, and they are undoubtedly based on different kinds of sources, the former on pseudo-historical genealogies, the latter (presumably) on mythological folktales. Vésteinn Ólason has pointed out (2001) that the second story is put into the mouths of Æsir who in any case are telling fictions, and so can invent what picture they like of the origin of Óðinn. This is an acute observation. To be sure Hár, Jafnhár and Þriði will have made up the story that suits them.

There is no denying that we may easily imagine that the interpretation of Euhemerism that we find in the Prologue could well be older than the *Edda*. We know, as has been said before, that the concept was known in Iceland, and it may well be that Snorri used the work of other writers when he was compiling ('setti saman') the work that we see in the manuscripts. About this we can say nothing with certainty, but if it were true it would explain why his use of Euhemerism is so different in his accounts of the origin of Óðinn in the Prologue from those in *Gylfaginning* and *Ynglinga saga*.

Finnur Jónsson has brought forward good arguments to show that the story of Gefjun and Gylfi did not belong to the *Edda* from the beginning (1931: xix):

> It is incomprehensible what the contents of this chapter have to do with *Gylfaginning* or the *Edda* as a whole. It falls completely outside the work's narrative frame, takes no account of anything inside it and has no consequences in what follows. A proper skaldic verse is quoted, which happens nowhere else in *Gylfaginning*, apart from the little quatrain in the next chapter which stands much closer to Eddic verse.

Besides this, Finnur points out that Gylfi is introduced into the story twice in Codex Wormianus, though here he assumes that the redactor of the Uppsala Edda version had corrected its text as regards the introduction of Gylfi, but regarded it as very significant that the chapter about Gefjun and Gylfi was completely lacking in the Uppsala Edda version.

In accordance with the above, I consider it most natural to regard each of the main sections of the *Edda* as a separate work. In the Uppsala Edda version this is emphasised by the putting together of a compilation that includes other unconnected items. This is actually a feature of AM 748 I b 4to and 757 a 4to too. In both a major part of *Skáldskaparmál* is copied out and placed as if it were a continuation of Snorri's nephew Óláfr hvítaskáld's treatise on rhetoric (the so-called third grammatical treatise). This is stated in AM 748 I b 4to in the following way (*Edda Snorra Sturlusonar* 1848–87: II 427–28):

Introduction

Hér er lykt þeim hlut bókar er Óláfr Þórðarson hefir samansett ok upphefr skáldskaparmál ok kenningar[1] eptir því sem fyrri fundit var í kvæðum hǫfuðskálda ok Snorri hefir síðan samanfœra látit.

(Here is concluded the part of the book that Óláfr Þórðarson has compiled, and begins Skáldskaparmál and kennings according to what was earlier found in poems of major poets and Snorri has since had put together.)

But this is not the end of the story, for between Óláfr's treatise and *Skáldskaparmál* comes a short list of kennings that is far from identical with what Snorri compiled.[2]

In AM 748 I b 4to and 757 a 4to (as also in DG 11 4to and Codex Wormianus), *Skáldskaparmál* is regarded as belonging with grammatical (or rhetorical) treatises. This is by no means arbitrary as regards the third and fourth treatises, for both use poetry to exemplify their categories. We may quote the words of Björn Magnússon Ólsen (1884: vi):

> It is not difficult to understand why the Icelandic grammarians got their illustrations from skaldic poetry. Icelandic examples of acknowledged authenticity were required, and such were to be found in skaldic poems. The Bible could not come into consideration, since there was no authorised Icelandic translation. It was naturally not without influence on this choice of Icelandic examples either, that in the classical or medieval authors that were available, there were found examples taken from Latin poets. Added to this, there was the fact that skaldic verse more readily stuck in the reader's or student's mind than examples taken from Icelandic prose, as well as that they could be assumed to be already known to most or at any rate to many readers.

The authors of these treatises would therefore probably have been able to agree with what Einar Sigurðsson of Eydalir wrote:

> Kvæðin hafa þann kost með sér
> þau kennast betur og lærast ger.
>
> (Poems have this virtue in them
> they are more easily taught and more readily learnt.)

---

[1] It is interesting to compare this with the heading to *Skáldskaparmál* in AM 157 8vo: 'Annar eddu partur er kalladur Skällda edur kiennyngar'.

[2] There is an excellent comparison of the contents of *Skáldskaparmál* in DG 11 4to, AM 748 I b 4to and AM 757 a 4to in Faulkes 1998: xlix–l.

5 The DG 11 4to compilation

5.1 Overview

The arrangement of material in DG 11 4to is, as has appeared in the above, considerably different from that in the other principal manuscripts of the *Edda*. A list of the contents is given below, but it needs to be made clear that the manuscript seems to me really to divide into two parts, Liber primus and Liber secundus.

Prologue (pp. 6–10 below).
Gylfaginning, scene 1 (pp. 10–86 below).
Gylfaginning, scene 2 (pp. 86–96 below).
Skáldatal (pp. 100–116 below).
Ættartala Sturlunga (p. 118 below).
Lǫgsǫgumanntal (p. 120 below).
Skáldskaparmál (principally *kenningar* and *heiti*; ends with three *dróttkvætt þulur* (pp. 124–246 below). Lasse Mårtensson (2010) suggests that this section should be divided into three parts, and in regard to the palæography this would be reasonable).
Háttalykillinn (Second grammatical treatise: phonology; pp. 250–256 below).
List of stanzas in *Háttatal* stt. 1–36 (p. 260 below).
Háttatal stt. 1–56 (text with rhetorical and metrical commentary; pp. 262–306 below).

Where it departs from convention here (see for example Krömmelbein 1992 and Guðrún Nordal 2001) is that I regard what has sometimes been called *Bragarœður* as a part of *Gylfaginning* (rather than of *Skáldskaparmál*), with just a change of scene.[1] This is justified by the fact that no major break is indicated at the point where Gylfi emerges from the scene of his deception in Valhǫll and the Æsir sit down at the feast with Ægir (or Hlér) and begin to listen to Bragi's stories. Then of course I regard the list of stanzas in *Háttatal* as an independent work, and Lasse Mårtensson (2010) has demonstrated that it is derived from a different source from the text of *Háttatal* that follows. Below it is also pointed out that there are more names of verse forms (or rhetorical features) in the list of stanzas than in the corresponding part of the text of the poem that follows, and they are closer to the Codex Regius version of the text. The break between Liber primus and Liber secundus is after *Lǫgsǫgumanntal* and is actually emphasised by the placing of the fine picture of Hár, Jafnhár and Þriði and supported by Guðvarður Már

---

[1] Rask, in his edition (1818), continued the chapter numbering from *Gylfaginning* through *Bragarœður* (the last being ch. 58). Thus the Þjazi story and the origin of the mead of poetry are made to tag on to the end of *Gylfaginning*, while the stories of Hrungnir and Geirrøðr keep their places in *Skáldskaparmál*. *Edda Snorra Sturlusonar* 1848–87: I follows this arrangement, though both editions are based on the text of GkS 2367 4to, not DG 11 4to.

Gunnlaugsson's demonstration (2009) that ff. 26v and 27r have not always been consecutive.[1]

What happened in DG 11 4to in Liber primus and makes the manuscript really different from other manuscripts that contain both *Gylfaginning* and *Skáldskaparmál* (it is hardly possible to compare it with manuscripts that contain only the latter) is that most of the stories about the gods have been moved from *Skáldskaparmál* so that very little of them remains in Liber secundus, and that afterwards three independent lists (two of them are rather short) which are all linked in content and character with the Sturlungs have been added. These are *Skáldatal*, *Ættartala Sturlunga* and *Lǫgsǫgumanntal*. This indeed fits very well with what has been said earlier about the *Edda* as a textbook being 'subject to continual development and reworking'. It was a work in progress.

5.2 Skáldatal

Skáldatal ('List of poets), which lists court poets under the names of the rulers in whose honour they composed, is indissolubly linked with Snorri's works. It was included in the Kringla manuscript of *Heimskringla*, probably at the end. Surviving copies show that it was there virtually the same as what we have in DG 11 4to. Yet some important changes were made in it in the course of time, and it is necessary to discuss them briefly, and also the role of *Skáldatal* in the *Edda*. Guðrún Nordal has discussed both these matters with great perception and shrewdness.

On the role of *Skáldatal* I largely agree with what she says (2001: 126):

> As a result of the new arrangement of *Skáldskaparmál* in U, no skaldic verse has so far been cited in the vellum to illustrate the wealth of the poetic diction, and therefore *Skáldatal* serves to lay the groundwork for the poets' testimony.[2] The citations and references to the poets in the latter part of *Skáldskaparmál* are therefore to be placed in the context of the chronology of the kings of Scandinavia, and with a particular reference to *Heimskringla*.[3]

---

[1] I do not know whether it has been pointed out before that the the two pages are so different in surface texture and cleanness that the best explanation is that f. 26v was once the last page of a book. Guðvarður Már drew attention to this when we examined the manuscript together in Uppsala, and has since confirmed this in conversation with me.

[2] A part of the 'new arrangement' spoken of here must be the supposed removal of the long quotations from the skaldic poems *Þórsdrápa*, *Haustlǫng* and *Húsdrápa* from the Uppsala Edda version of *Skáldskaparmál*. But if the contrary view, that they were interpolated into the Codex Regius version, is adopted, part of the argument would fall to the ground: the absence of the long quotations would be irrelevant, and only the transference of the Þórr narratives to Gylfaginning would affect the relevance of the list.

[3] When one remembers how few of the same quotations from skaldic verse appear in both the *Edda* and *Heimskringla*, it looks as though it may have been the list of kings rather than the list of poets that was important.

There seems to me to be no doubt that it is correct that *Skáldatal* is included as a kind of reference work. It actually is easy to work out from the list of kings in *Skáldatal* when each poet was composing, that is the good half of the poets quoted that are mentioned in *Skáldatal*.[1] Thus *Skáldatal* has clear relevance at just this point. Eilífr Guðrúnarson, however, the last poet to be mentioned in Scene 2, is not included in *Skáldatal*.

Guðrún's observation that many Icelandic poets composed in praise of high ranking men that were not kings or earls is no less important. Actually, Þorleifr hinn spaki is the only one in this class that is named in Kringla, perhaps because he was the first of many chieftains of this kind in *Heimskringla*. Guðrún comments (2001: 126):

> These men do not belong to the royalty and therefore are excluded from (or omitted in) the catalogue in *Kringla*. The writer of [*Skáldatal* in U], however, has no such qualms, and lists eighteen additional chieftains starting with Arinbjǫrn hersir, Egill's friend, and concluding with the thirteenth-century chieftain and adviser to the king, Gautr of Mel.

Of course it casts rather a shadow over this that Snorri composed an insulting verse about Gautr of Melr at the instigation of Duke Skúli (*Skj* A I 78, v. 4). On the other hand, Gautr was a good supporter of Sturla Þórðarson, as is related in *Sturlu þáttr* in *Sturlunga saga*.

It is actually odd that Kringla makes Snorri a poet of King Sverrir, but DG 11 4to doesn't. There could be various explanations for this, but the simplest is just to assume a mistake in DG 11 4to, for there one of Sverrir's poets is Snorri Bútsson, about whom nothing is known, though he could be a member of the Sturlung family. Perhaps the scribe's eye skipped from one Snorri to the other (haplography).

Guðrún Nordal considered it safe to date *Skáldatal* in the Uppsala Edda version late (2001: 122):

> The list is longer in [*Skáldatal* in U], not only because [*Skáldatal* in Kringla] finished counting by about 1260 and [*Skáldatal* in U] by about 1300, but also owing to the addition of English kings and Norwegian chieftains to the list.

This is presumably based on the fact that the latest poet named is Jón murti Egilsson, who is reckoned to have died about 1320 or later (*Edda Snorra Sturlusonar* 1848–87: III 686). He must then have been very old by the standard of the time, for he was named after Jón murti Snorrason, who was killed in Norway in 1231, and so could hardly have been born much later than that. Nothing is known of his poetry, but according to *Skáldatal*, he composed about Eiríkr Magnússon, who ruled from 1281 to 1299. There is nothing in *Skáldatal* to suggest that the king was dead, so the source of the statement that Jón murti was his poet could have been from the 1280s. Of course there is nothing that makes it impossible for *Skáldatal* in the Uppsala

---

[1] In DG 11 4to I calculate that 35 poets of the 62 that are quoted are listed in *Skáldatal*.

Edda version to have been brought up to date when DG 11 4to was being written, though the bulk of it had been compiled much earlier.

The dating of these supplementary items will become important when later on an attempt is made to give an account of the conceivable evolution of the Uppsala Edda version.

On f. 24r–v there are notable gaps in *Skáldatal*. Five earls are mentioned, Ormr Eilífsson, Hákon Ívarsson, Sigurðr Hávarsson, Eiríkr Sigurðarson and Philippus Birgisson, but have no poets attached to them. In this there is no difference between *Skáldatal* in Kringla and *Skáldatal* in the Uppsala Edda. But in the Uppsala Edda version Hákon Eiríksson has just one poet, Bersi Torfuson, who in the Kringla version is only reckoned to be a poet of Sveinn Hákonarson (see *Edda Snorra Sturlusonar* 1848–87: III 257). If this is correct, it makes Earl Hákon a sixth earl that has no poets. I have not come across any attempt to account for the inclusion of the names of these rulers in *Skáldatal* at all, and there seems really to be only one reasonable explanation: originally this was not a list of poets but a list of rulers. In other words, it was one of the resources that Snorri or some other writer of King's Sagas used for reference. But before Kringla was written the list had been changed and rulers' poets were inserted. When it came to earls without poets, their names were not deleted, but were allowed to keep their place although there were no poets to put under them.

5.3 *Ættartala Sturlunga*

The genealogy of the Sturlung family ends with Snorri and his siblings, including his sister Helga, mother of Egill and Gyða, and this Egill is actually the father of Jón murti and son of Sǫlmundr austmaðr. Guðvarður Már Gunnlaugsson has recently (2010) argued that the genealogy must have been compiled at the request of Sǫlmundr or Helga, and that Egill and Gyða were probably still living with their parents. This would then probably have been considerably earlier than 1230. It is easy to find further general reasons for thinking that the genealogy might be connected with Sǫlmundr. He was probably Norwegian and had emigrated to Iceland, and everyone who goes to live in a foreign country knows that it is a problem getting used to all the identities and relationships that one is confronted with then. Sǫlmundr would thus probably have found the Sturlung genealogy very helpful, particularly the latter part of it.

There is a similar genealogy, but reaching further on in time, in AM 748 II 4to (printed in *Edda Snorra Sturlusonar* 1848–87: III lxxiii–lxxiv). It extends as far as Pétr Jónsson, who will have been descended from people of Vatnsfjǫrðr and was a descendant of Snorri, and probably alive about 1400, when this manuscript was written (cf. Finnur Jónsson 1931: xiii). The variations from the genealogy in DG 11 4to are so insignificant that they can both be taken to be derived from the same roots, with this version updated to 1400.

It is interesting really to compare this genealogy, which covers at least 69 generations, with the one that was found adequate in *Sturlunga saga*. That one is more realistic, and it goes back only as far as Snorri goði, from whom Snorri Sturluson and his sister Helga were the seventh generation. *Sturlunga saga* looks back only as far as the Settlement of Iceland, but in the *Edda* manuscripts the line is taken back through Haraldr blátǫnn to Óðinn and from him back to Adam. The line from Óðinn down to the Skjǫldung kings is from *Skjǫldunga saga* (one of Snorri's sources in *Ynglinga saga* and his *Edda*). From Óðinn back to Ses(c)ef is derived from Anglo-Saxon genealogies (constructed in Christian times in England), from Ses(c)ef to Þórr uses various Icelandic mythological names, all linked with Þórr in some way, and Þórr is made a grandson of King Priam of Troy, using some names from *Trójumanna saga*. All of this is almost identical with the genealogy from Munon/Mennon down to Oðinn in the Prologue to the *Edda*, and may have been constructed by Snorri himself. From Priam back to Celius father of Saturn appears in the version of the Prologue in Codex Wormianus and is ultimately based on Classical sources, and may have reached Iceland via a writer such as Honorius of Autun. Cretus and Ciprus have a suspicious resemblance to the names of two islands in the Mediterranean, and these links to the biblical names, which supply the rest of the line back to Adam, are also found in fourteenth-century Welsh genealogies. The genealogy in the Uppsala Edda and AM 748 II 4to was probably the earliest to include the whole line from medieval Icelanders back to Adam, whether or not Snorri was concerned in its construction. The prehistoric series of names is clearly a learned fiction which would hardly have been taken seriously in the thirteenth century.[1]

5.4 *Lǫgsǫgumannatal*

The list of Lawspeakers ends with Snorri Sturluson where he took up that office for the second time, and Guðvarður Már (2010: 34–36) correctly points out that it is not stated how long he served, though that is done for his first period of office, as it is for all others who held it. This indicates unequivocally that the list was compiled while Snorri was still serving his second stint, 1222–1231.

For by far the greater part, *Lǫgsǫgumannatal* agrees with the information that can be gleaned from Ari's *Íslendingabók* and the Annals. Jón Sigurðsson compared these sources and his results appeared posthumously in 1886 (marked JS in the table below). As will be seen from the upper parts of the columns below, the disagreements can be explained as the result of the misreading of Roman numerals. There has been confusion of u (v) and ii on more than one occasion, and this has been the cause of a twelve-year discrepancy by the time Ari's list ends. After that *Lǫgsǫgumannatal* agrees with the Annals except that

---

[1] On the versions of the Old Icelandic *langfeðgatal* see Faulkes 1978/79: 91–106.

Introduction

the same kind of misreading gives Styrmir Kárason only two years of office instead of five. Apart from that it all works out.

Lawspeakers in DG 11 4to	Number of years	Year given	Lawspeakers according to Ari	Number of years	Years according to JS	Roman numerals in U	Roman numerals in JS
Hrafn Høingsson	20		Hrafn Høngsson	20	930–949		
Þórarinn Ragabróðir	20		Þórarinn Ragabróðir	20	950–969		
Þorkell máni	12		Þorkell máni	15	970–984	xij	xu
Þorgeirr frá Ljósavatni	14	1000[1]	Þorgeirr að Ljósavatni	17	985–1001	xiu	xuij
Grímr frá Mosfelli	2		Grímr að Mosfelli	2	1002–1003		
Skapti Þóroddson	24	1030[2]	Skapti Þóroddsson	27	1004–1030	xxiu	xxuij
Steinn Þorgeirsson	3		Steinn Þorgestsson	3	1031–1033		
Þorkell Tjǫrvason	20		Þorkell Tjǫrvason	20	1034–1053		
Gellir Bǫlverksson	9		Gellir Bǫlverksson	9	1054–1062		
Gunnarr inn spaki	3		Gunnarr hinn spaki	3	1063–1065		
Kolbeinn Flosason	3	1066[3]	Kolbeinn Flosason	6	1066–1071	iij	uj
Gellir Bǫlverksson (second time)	3		Gellir Bǫlverksson	3	1072–1074		
Gunnarr inn spaki (second time)	1		Gunnarr hinn spaki	1	1075		
Sighvatr	8		Sighvatr Surtsson	8	1076–1083		
Markús Skeggjason	24	1083[4]	Markúss Skeggjason	24	1084–1107		
Gunnarr Úlfheðinsson[5]	9		Úlfheðinn Gunnarsson	9	1108–1116		
Bergþórr Hrafnsson	6		Bergþórr Hrafnsson	6	1117–1122		
Gunnarr Þorgeirsson	12		Guðmundr Þorgeirsson	12	1123–1134		
Hrafn Úlfheðinsson	4				1135–1138		
Finnr Hallsson	7				1139–1145		
Gunnarr Úlfheðinsson	10				1146–1155		
Snorri Húnbogason	15				1156–1170		
Styrkárr Oddason	10				1171–1180		
Gizurr Hallsson	22				1181–1200		
Hallr Gizurarson	4				1201–1209		
Styrmir Kárason	2				1210–1214	ij	u
Snorri Sturluson	4				1215–1218		
Teitr Þorvaldsson	2				1219–1221		
Snorri Sturluson (second time)					1222–1231		

[1] 'Á hans dǫgum kom Kristni til Íslands.'
[2] 'Hann andaðist á inu sama ári ok Óláfr konungr inn helgi fell.'
[3] 'Þat sumar sem hann tók lǫgsǫgu fell Haraldr konungr á Englandi.'
[4] 'tók lǫgsǫgn þat sumar er Gizurr biskup hafði verið einn vetr hér á landi.'
[5] Here the generations have gone astray. It ought to be Úlfheðinn Gunnarsson.

It is the same with both the genealogy and the list of lawspeakers, that it is difficult to see what business they have in a textbook on poetry. The most likely explanation is that someone in the Sturlung family was having material collected into a single volume that lay in booklets or on loose leaves and was connected with the family, or was relics of Snorri.

5.5 *Skáldskaparmál*

Liber secundus in DG 11 4to begins with *Skáldskaparmál* and in this part there is not an enormous difference between the two main versions of the Edda. Yet there are cases of divergence that make it safe to assert that the same exemplar could not have been the source of both the Uppsala Edda version and the Codex Regius version of *Skáldskaparmál*. I have elsewhere (Lasse Mårtensson and Heimir Pálsson 2008) spoken of the abbreviations in a stanza (or *stef*?) from *Sexstefja*. Sometimes the texts of verse quotations are so different that there seems no way one can assume simple misreadings or copying errors. On the other hand, it is clear as daylight that scribes around 1300 experienced great difficulties in understanding *dróttkvætt* verses. It is sufficient to point out all the emendations that modern editors have felt it necessary to make. Finnur Jónsson selected readings from different manuscripts, but often reckoned he needed to propose alterations. Anthony Faulkes tries to keep to the Codex Regius text, but frequently finds it necessary to advise acceptance of the emendations of Kock or Finnur. If one tries to keep to the unemended text of DG 11 4to, it is certainly often possible, but the meaning becomes considerably different from what has been read in GkS 2367 4to. To illustrate this would take more space than is available here, and the reader is referred to the interpretations accompanying the normalised texts below. Just one example will, however, be given here.

DG 11 4to, v. 184 (p. 198 below)	GkS 2367 4to, v. 286 (Faulkes 1998: 81)
Þeygi var sem þessum	Þági var sem þessum
þengill, á jó sprengir	þengils á jó strengjar
mjǫk fyrir, mála kveðjur	mjǫð fyrir málma kveðju
mær⟨r⟩ heiðingjum bæri.	mær heiðþegum bæri.

In this quatrain there are no more and no fewer than seven words that are different either in meaning or form in the two versions. The verse is by Sighvatr of Apavatn, and is no 42 in *Óláfs saga helga* in *Heimskringla* (*Hkr* II 63). Bjarni Aðalbjarnarson, whose text is based largely on Kringla, which is identical here to the text of GkS 2367 4to except for having *heiðþægum* in the fourth line, interprets the verse as follows: 'This was not like when a maiden serves these king's followers mead on a ship before battle'. Faulkes writes (1998: 204):

The picture painted is unusual (mead being served on board ship by a woman before the battle); but if *fyrir* means 'instead of' we have the conventional contrasting of battle with peaceful activities. It also depends on how the adverbial phrases are ordered; possibly 'It was not then on the ship like when a maid served mead . . . instead of (or in return for?) battle.'
Here no doubt shall be cast on the fact that the text of GkS 2367 4to is closer to the original than the text of DG 11 4to, but on the other hand it is quite possible that the scribe or redactor of the Uppsala Edda version interpreted the verse differently from modern scholars (maybe it was difficult to read in his text of *Heimskringla*), for it is possible to read the text in prose word order as 'Þeygi var sem mærr þengill bæri þessum heiðingjum mála kveðjur; mjǫk sprengir fyrir á jó.' And a conceivable interpretation might be: 'It was not like a renowned prince bringing these paid troops (empty) promises of pay; the horse was on the point of collapsing (under the weight of what he was bringing them)'. Then word-play would have to be assumed, 'heiðingi' ('heathen') = 'heiðþegi' ('pay-receiver'), but that is no more far-fetched than is often found in skaldic verse. The horse with its load of money would also be a nice echo of Grani's burden = gold.

In general, the order of material in the Codex Regius version of *Skáldskaparmál* is the same as in the Uppsala Edda version. Yet various thing have become confused because the stories that were moved into *Gylfaginning* in the Uppsala Edda version are apparently kept in their original places in the Codex Regius version, and the long verse quotations there make a considerable difference. The main aim in every case is to deal with kennings first, and after than *heiti*. This works out better in the Codex Regius version than in the Uppsala Edda version, and various things indicate that the Uppsala Edda version was put together from various sources.

5.6 *Háttalykillinn* — second grammatical treatise

Skáldskaparmál deals with vocabulary, poetical language. Before his task was over, it is clear that the redactor of the Uppsala Edda version felt it necessary to deal with phonology. For this he chose an essay that later became the second one in Codex Wormianus and is usually referred to as the second grammatical treatise. Understandably, this is not the title it has in DG 11 4to, which has no more than this one treatise (Codex Wormianus does not give it any title at all). It is likely that the scribe of DG 11 4to made up his title himself, calling it 'Háttalykill', obviously basing it on the repeated use of the word *lykill* = key in the treatise itself (p. 250 below):

> Muðrinn ok tungan er leikvǫllr orðanna. Á þeim velli eru reistir stafir þeir er mál allt gera ok hendir málit ýmsa, svá til at jafna sem hǫrpu strengir eða eru læstir lyklar í simphónie.

This is emphasised later in the text when the oblong diagram is being explained (p. 256 below):

> Stafa setning sjá sem hér er rituð er svá sett til máls sem lyklar til hljóðs ⟨í⟩ músika ok regur fylgja hljóðstǫfum svá sem þeir lyklum. Málstafir eru ritaðir með hverri regu bæði fyrir ok eptir, ok gera þeir mál af hendingum þeiri[1] sem þeir gera við hljóðstafina fyrir eða eptir. Kǫllum vér þat lykla sem þeir eru í fastir, ok eru þeir hér svá settir hér sem í spacioni sem lyklar í simphoníe ok skal þeim kippa eða hrinda ok drepa svá regustrengina ok tekr þá þat hljóð sem þú vilt haft hafa . . . Hér standa um þvert blað ellifu hljóðstafir, en um endilangt blað tuttugu málstafir. Eru þeir svá settirs sem lyklar í simphoníe, en hljóðstafir sem strengir. Málstafir eru tólf þeir sem bæði hafa hljóð hvárt sem kipt er eða hrundit lyklinum. En átta þeir er síðarr eru ritaðir hafa hálft hljóð við hina. Sumir taka hljóð er þú kippir at þér, sumir er þú hrindir frá þér.

Some kind of hurdy-gurdy was known in the Middle Ages (at least from the eleventh century), and it is clearly this kind of instrument that is meant by the word *simphonía* here. They are probably right who reckon that the grammatical treatises were intended to help people understand how rhyme worked.[2] It was probably helpful to use among other things the analogy of musical harmony.

But it is another question whether this Háttalykill would be a help to anyone in understanding the kind of rhyme that Snorri calls *hending*. Yet it contains an important discussion of length of sounds, which as is well known, was all-important in *dróttkvætt* and in fact very significant in other kinds of verse.

The second grammatical treatise is short (though it is longer in Codex Wormianus, the latter part of which version is replaced by diagrams in DG 11 4to), filling scarcely five pages in the manuscript, of which the diagrams take up the equivalent of more than one complete side. About its age it is difficult to be certain, but Lasse Mårtensson's observations suggest that the letter forms are early rather than late, and there are indications that it may have followed the recommendations of the first grammatical treatise in the use of small capitals to represent long consonants. It has not been possible to find any model at all for this treatise, but the imagery used points unequivocally to foreign textbooks which may have been used in Iceland for the classification of Icelandic speech sounds, and the learned tone is unmistakable.

5.7 List of stanzas

The treatise ends with line 19 of the fifth page (f. 47v), and to begin with nothing else was written on this page, but completely different material was begun on the next leaf. There is no heading, but there is a coloured initial: 'Fyrst er dróttkvæðr háttr'. Thus begins the strange list of stanzas, giving the first lines only of thirty-five stanzas of *Háttatal*.

---

[1] Error for *þeim*?
[2] On this see Sverrir Tómasson 1996a: 5–6.

Finnur Jónsson saw no problem explaining the list (1931: xxx):
> The scribe just wants to make an abstract. He starts with the beginning of the stanza and the name of the verse form. When he had done about a third of the poem, he reconsiders (because he now has more time?), and writes down the whole poem with commentary,[1] but now only gets as far as st. 56. And with that the scribe is at last definitely finished.

Now, when palaeographical study has shown that the list of stanzas was not made from the same exemplar as was used for the poem itself in DG 11 4to,[2] it is clear that Finnur's theory is mistaken. It was not the scribe of DG11 4to who compiled the list. I cannot either accept without reservations Anthony Faulkes's way of putting it (2007: xxii):

> Since many of the names of verse-forms are omitted from the other manuscripts, this is a most welcome addition to the text, whether or not the names derive from Snorri. It is, however, difficult to see any possible purpose in this arrangement of the text other than as an *aide-mémoire* to someone who knew the text of the poem by heart, but wanted to be reminded of the order of the verses and of the names of the verse-forms. It may have been used either in conjunction with performance, or, perhaps more likely, in conjunction with an oral discussion or lecture on the various metres represented. The reason for stopping with st. 36 is not apparent. Other material in the Uppsala manuscript (*Skáldatal*, the Sturlung genealogy, the list of lawspeakers) suggests that the manuscript is derived from a compilation made from Snorri's working papers.

It is a debatable issue whether the list of names of verse forms includes names that 'are omitted from the other manuscripts' (it would have been better to have written 'are absent from or illegible in the other manuscripts'),[3] but the rest is absolutely correct. Such a list is an aid to memory for teachers or reciters. Guðrún Nordal has pointed out to me that Holm Perg. 8vo nr 4 in the Royal Library in Stockholm contains a similar list of stanzas for *Heimsósómi*.[4] If this list is compared with Jón Þorkelsson's *Kvæðasafn eftir nafngreinda menn frá miðöldum og síðari öldum* (1922–27: 238–44), one can see that a half or the whole of the first line of each stanza is written in the arrangement of the poem in AM 713 4to, and the list is on ff. 11v to 12r, or on a single opening. This can hardly be anything other than a memory sheet for a performer of the poem or

---

[1] Finnur says in a footnote: 'There is no ground for supposing that here [i.e. in the text of *Háttatal*] a different manuscript has been used from when he wrote down the first lines.'

[2] See Lasse Mårtensson 2010.

[3] From the table below and Lasse Mårtensson's survey it can be seen that the list most often has the same names for verse forms as GkS 2367 4to. It seems to me that when one version has information that is not in other manuscripts, it has been added there, not deleted from the others, so I cannot agree with the use of the term *omitted*. On the other hand it is easy to agree with the suggestion that Faulkes has made to me in an email: 'I think the names in the list in U have been compiled from the commentary in a manuscript that had a text rather different from that of RTW (or U).'

[4] Jón Samsonarson mentions this in his typewritten observations on Icelandic manuscripts in Sweden (typescript in Stofnun Árna Magnússonar í íslenskum fræðum).

for a teacher who wanted to use this splendid poem when teaching morals, but did not want to make mistakes in the rhymes. The names of the verse-forms of *Háttatal* (some of which can better be described as the names of the rhetorical features in the verses) in the list, those in *Háttatal* itself in DG 11 4to and those in GkS 2367 4to (which in many cases are found in the commentary rather than in headings to the stanzas) appear as can be seen in the table below. It seems clear to me that the list is based on a much fuller source than *Háttatal* in DG 11 4to itself. It is extremely unlikely in textbook material that information should be omitted, much more likely that it should be amplified as the work is used.

DG 11 4to, first lines of text	DG 11 4to headings and commentary[1]	List of stanzas in DG 11 4to	GkS 2367 4to names
1. Lætr sá er Hákon heitir	*Dróttkvæðr háttr	Dróttkvæðr háttr	Dróttkvæðr háttr
2. Fellr um fúra stilli	*Kendr háttr	Kendr háttr	Kendr háttr
3. Úlfs bága verr ægis	*Rekit	Rekit[2]	
4. Stinn sár þróast stórum	*Sannkent	Sannkent	
5. Oðharða spyr ek eyða	*Tvíriðit	Tvíriðit	Tvíriðit
6. Sviðr lætr sóknar naðra	*Nýgjǫrvin[ga]r	Nýgervingar	Nýgjǫrvingar
7. Hjálms fylli spekr hilmir	*Oddhent	Oddhent	Odd-hendingar
8. Klofinn spyr ek hjalm fyrir hilmis	*Ǫnnur oddhending		
9. Vex iðn. Vellir roðna	*Sextánmælt	Sextánmælt	Sextánmæltr
10. Jǫrð verr siklingr sverðum	Át[t]mæltr háttr	Áttmælt	Áttmælt
11. Ýskelfir kann úlfum	Inn þriðji	Fjórðungalok	Hinn þriði
12. Hákon veldr ok hǫlðum	Enn fjórði/fimmti	Stælt	Stælt
13. Manndýrðar fær mærðar		Hjástælt	Hjástælt
14. Hákon ræðr með heiðan	Inn sjáundi	Langlokum	Inn sjaundi
15. Þeim er, grundar grímu		Afleiðingum	Inn átti
16. Setr um vísa vitran	Drǫgur	Drǫgur	Drǫgur
17. Síks glóðar ver søkir	*Refhvǫrf	Refhvǫrf	Refhvǫrf
18. Blóð fremr hlǫkk at háðist	A[nna]t refhvarf[3]	Ǫnnur refhvǫrf	Ǫnnur refhvǫrf
19. Segl skekr of hlyn, Huglar	Mestu refhvǫrf	Þriðju refhvǫrf	In mestu refhvǫrf
20. Hélir hlýr fyrir stáli			In minni refhvǫrf
21. Lung frá [ek] lýða þengils		Ǫnnur en minni	Ǫnnur in minni

[1] * means that the name appears both as a heading and in the commentary.

[2] Anthony Faulkes has pointed out to me that *tvíkent, rekit, sannkenning* and *tvíriðit*, and many other names too, in both versions, are more stylistic features than names of verse forms. Many stanzas that Snorri makes into different verse forms are in our eyes just stylistic variations. Moreover, although st. 3 illustrates *tvíkent*, and there are individual examples of *rekit* in stt. 2/1–2 (*stillir fúra fleinbraks*) and 3/4 (*brún rúna Míms vinar*), there are no stanzas illustrating *rekit* or *tvíriðit*, even though both GkS 2367 and Codex Trajectinus add *Þetta er tvíriðit kallat* before st. 5 (which illustrates *stuðning*); so making *rekit* and and *tvíriðit* into headings to stanzas is a mistake.

[3] In the commentary (f. 101/11) it appears that this is *in mestu refhvǫrf*, though this name appears again with st. 19. In the commentary in GkS 2367 4to, stt. 17, 18 and 19 are all said to be *in mestu refhvǫrf*.

Introduction   lxxxv

22. Himinglæva strýkr hávar		En þriðja	In minstu refhvǫrf
23. Firrist hǫnd með harra		Refhvarfabróðir	Refhvarfabróðir
24. Hreintjǫrnum gleðr horna		Dunhent[1]	
25. Ræst gaf ǫðlingr jástar		Tilsagt	Tilsagt
26. Fúss brýtr fylkir eisu		Orðskviðuháttr	Orðskviðuháttr
27. Ískalda skar ek ǫldu		Álagsháttr	Álagsháttr
28. Vandbaugs veiti sendir[2]		Tvískelft	Tvískelft
29. Tvær man eg hilmi hýrum		Detthent	Detthendr háttr
30. Þoll bið eg hilmis hylli		Draugsháttr	Draugsháttr
31. Stáls dynblakka støkkvi		Bragarháttr	Bragarbót
32. Él þreifst skarpt um Skúla		Liðhendum	Riðhendur
33. Lífs var rán at raunum		Veggjat	Veggjat
34. Flaust bjó fólka treystir		Flagðalag	Flagðaháttr
35. Reist at Vágsbrú vestan[3]		[st. 35 is omitted]	Inn forna skjálfhenda
36. Hristist hvatt þá er reistist		Príhent	Príhent
37. Vann, kann virðum banna			Hinn dýri háttr
38. Farar snarar fylkir byrjar			
39. Ok hjaldrreifan hófu			Tiltekit
40. Hverr fremr hildi barra			Greppaminni
41. Velr ítrhugaðr ýtum[4]			Liðhendur
42. Alrauðum drífr auði			Rétthent
43. Samþykkjar fremr søkkum	Minni alhenda		In minni alhenda
44. Frama skotnar gramr, gotnum			Alhent
45. Lætr undir brot brotna	Stamhent		Stamhendr háttr
46. Virðandi gefr virðum			Samhent
47. Seimþverrir gefr seima			Iðurmælt
48. Auðkendar verr auði			Klifat
49. Hjaldrremmir tekr Hildi			Stúfr
50. Yggs drósar rýfr eisa[5]			Meiri stúfr
51. Herstefnir lætr hrafn[6]			Hinn mesti stúfr
52. Sær skjǫldungs niðr skúrum			Skothendr
53. Stjóri venst at stóra[7]			Liðhendur
54. Skýtr at Skǫglar veðri			
55. Hverr sér jǫfri ǿgri			Torf-Einars háttr
56. Hverr ali blóði bysta			Egils háttr

[1] In the commentary to st. 47 in both versions 'afhending sem í dunhendum hætti' is mentioned, so it is clear that the concept was known.

[2] Here the word *skjalfhenda* appears in the commentary, but can hardly be a name.

[3] In the commentary it is stated that this was the form used by Þorvaldr veili in his *Kviðan skjálfhenda*.

[4] In the commentary it is said what *liðhendur* are, but the word is not the name of a verse form there.

[5] In the commentary it is clear that this contains catalectic ('stýfðr') lines.

[6] Both versions here speak of a *háttafǫll* (metrical fault).

[7] In the commentary in DG 11 4to *liðhendur* are spoken of.

The list of stanzas, as has been said, seems to come from a different source, or at least a different manuscript, from the text of *Háttatal* in DG 11 4to. The explanation of why the first lines of only thirty-five stanzas were included in the list, could of course be that originally these were written on a verso page and the continuation was later lost, but it is also conceivable that no more were written because, for example, the user (the teacher or the student) did not think that he needed to know any more. About that we obviously cannot know anything further. And the next section of the manuscript presents us with no fewer problems.

5.8 *Háttatal*

On DG 11 4to f. 48v begins a poem which is given this heading in red: 'Háttatal er Snorri Sturluson orti um Hákon konung ok Skúla hertuga'. This is more or less identical with the main heading on f. 2r except that there it has *hefir ort* instead of *orti*. As will be discussed further in the section on headings in DG 11 4to (Section 6 below), it is important to note that in both places Skúli is called *hertogi*, a title he did not receive until 1237,[1] which presumably gives a *terminus post quem* for the headings. It is clear from *Skáldatal* that this title was thought to be of some significance, for there Snorri is listed first as one of Earl Skúli's poets, and then as one of Duke Skúli's poets (DG 11 4to, f. 24v). Historians believe that as *Hákonar saga* claims, Skúli was the first person to hold this title in Norway (see Hamre 1961). In GkS 2367 4to it says: 'Hertogi heitir jarl ok er konungr svá kallaðr ok fyrir því er hann leiðir her til orrostu' (Faulkes 1998: 100). This sentence is not in DG 11 4to, and nor is the example from Þjóðólfr Arnórsson that follows it in GkS 2367 4to (and Codex Trajectinus, AM 757 a 4to and AM 748 II 4to according to Finnur Jónsson 1931: 180). The word itself is older than Skúli's time in the sense 'war-leader, army leader, general', and it is in this older sense that it is used in *Háttatal* 40/5 and 66/2 (though here too of Skúli), as well as, of course, in Þjóðólfr and many other skaldic poets. The new sense (which was derived from Middle Low German) is found in prose from the first half of the thirteenth century, but in verse for the first time in Sturla Þórðarson's *Hákonarkviða* 26/8 (again of Skúli). It therefore seems certain that while the headings to *Háttatal* and to the *Edda* as a whole in DG 11 4to must be later than 1237, *Háttatal* itself, and *Skáldskaparmál* (at any rate in the Codex Regius version), which only have the older meaning of *hertogi*, are definitely earlier, when the word as a title was still unknown.

Háttatal in DG 11 4to is oddly curtailed, having only 56 stanzas. It seems it can be taken as certain that it was the same in the scribe's exemplar,

---

[1] See *Hákonar saga* ch. 90; cf. also Faulkes 2007: x.

because the writing stops in the middle of a recto page and the scribe had chosen a gathering of six leaves as the final one in the book. In other words, he had never intended to write any more of the poem. There can be various reasons for this. The most likely is that the rest of the poem was missing in the scribe's exemplar, which may have had leaves lost at the end. This is a common problem in Icelandic manuscripts, and it is often blamed on their being kept in poor conditions. A second possible explanation is of course that the redactor of the Uppsala Edda version found it sensible to stop at this point. Most of the variants of the *dróttkvætt* form have been exemplified, and as Guðrún Nordal has pointed out (2001: 124), the last verse form in this manuscript is *Egils háttr* and it would be quite fitting to close the poem with a reference to the poet's noble ancestor. The snag is that the name of the verse form does not appear in this manuscript and has to be sought in the Codex Regius version, and besides, it is st. 66, not 56, that can be taken as the last example of *dróttkvætt* in *Háttatal*. A third possibility is that a copy had been made of *Háttatal* when its composition had only reached this point. Snorri might easily have paused in his task for a shorter or longer period of time. In the discussion of its dating above it was pointed out that we have no reliable evidence that *Háttatal* was the first part of the *Edda* to be written, and in fact there is very little that helps to date it other than the usual (modern) assumption that it is polite to express one's thanks for hospitality before too long has passed from the time of the visit. This has long been accepted, but of course it is not impossible that Snorri had only finished the poem after his decision to make his second trip to Norway in 1237. This idea is no doubt precluded by the closing stanza, which speaks of the king and the *earl*, as well as the use of the word *hertogi* in stt. 40 and 60 discussed above. Yet one must bear in mind that after the first third of the poem, much more is said about Skúli than about Hákon. The analysis of the relative space devoted to each ruler in Faulkes 2007: vii is certainly correct:

> The first section [of *Háttatal*], stt. 1–30, is about Hákon, the second, stt. 31–67, is about Skúli, exept for st. 67, which is about both rulers; in the third, stt. 68–95 are also mainly about Skúli, stt. 96–102 again seem to relate to both rulers.

This itself also means that the space devoted to each ruler in the part of the poem that is in DG 11 4to is about equal. It is in the third section that it all becomes unbalanced.

In the account in *Sturlunga saga* and *Hákonar saga* of Snorri's trips to Norway, it becomes clear that the friendship that develops between Snorri and Skúli is much stronger and closer than that between Snorri and Hákon. This comes out very entertainingly when Snorri and his cousins Þorleifr Þórðarson and Óláfr Þórðarson hvítaskáld travel to Norway in 1237 as it is told by Sturla in *Sturlunga saga* 1946: I 408–409):

> Snorri Sturluson went abroad from Eyrar in the summer, and Þórðr kakali, Þorleifr and Óláfr, and they came to land in the northern part of Norway and stayed the winter in Niðarós.
>
> Snorri stayed with Duke Skúli's son Pétr, but the duke stayed in Oslo for the winter, both he and King Hákon too. Relations between father- and son-in-law were good. Órækja was now staying with the Duke.

It makes no difference though Skúli stays with Hákon that winter. Snorri finds himself better off with the former's son Pétr.

They are more of an age, Snorri and Skúli than Snorri and Hákon; when Snorri first came to Norway in 1218, he was scarcely forty, and Skúli about thirty, while Hákon was only fourteen. This is one of the explanations that has often been given of why the role of Hákon in *Háttatal* is so meagre. There is a limit to what can be said in praise of the warlike achievements of a teenage boy. It may also have been a factor that Skúli came much closer to Snorri's concept of the ideal ruler in *Heimskringla* than Hákon.

All the manuscripts that contain *Háttatal* (DG 11 4to, GkS 2367 4to, Codex Wormianus and Codex Trajectinus) have an accompanying commentary, varying in the amount of detail and yet all clearly closely related. Faulkes (2007: viii) lists at least ten places where the commentary in the Codex Regius version has discrepancies from the text of the poem. Seven of them are also in DG 11 4to, so we shall consider those.

Faulkes's first example is from the comment on st. 15. In DG 11 4to the text reads (p. 278 below):

> Hér er enn fyrri vísuhelmingr leiddr af inni fyrri vísu ok fylgir þat vísuorð er afleiðingum er kallat, er síðast var í enni fyrri vísu. Þessum vísuhelmingi er svá breytt ok er sá vísuhelmingur eigi ella réttr at máli.
>
> (Here the first half-stanza is dependent on the preceding stanza, and the line that is known as *afleiðingar* (antecedent), which was last in the preceding stanza, links with it. This half-stanza is thus changed and the half-stanza is otherwise not correct in expression (it is incomplete).)

The Codex Regius version has to a large extent the same comment, at any rate in the first sentence, though there it reads 'þat málsorð er afleiðing er kǫlluð' ('the word that is known as *afleiðing*'), and it is clearly more accurate to speak of 'word' rather than 'line' here, for it is the word *konungdómi* (st. 14/8) that is referred to, not the whole of the line. St. 14 has the feature that is described in DG 11 4to like this: 'Hér hefr upp mál í inu fyrsta vísuorði, en lýkr í inu síðarsta, ok eru þau sér um mál' ('Here a sentence begins in the first line and is completed in the last, and they make up a separate statement'). This refers to the sentence 'Hákon ræðr með heiðan . . . orðrómi konungdómi' which is split over st. 14/1 and 8 and continues in st. 15/1 with 'þeim er . . . átti áðr hans faðir ráða'. The commentator is pointing out that the relative pronoun *þeim er* goes with the antecedent (*afleiðing*) *konungdómi* at the end of the preceding stanza. The compilers of dictionaries have understood the meaning of the sentence, but Cleasby-Vigfússon translates *afleiðing* in this sentence as simply *continuation*, and *Norrøn ordbok* (2004) gives this as the third meaning of *afleiðing* and adds: 'det relative pronomenet når det er første ord i ei strofe og viser til et ord i den føregåande' ('the relative pronoun when it is the first word in a stanza and relates to a word in the preceding stanza'). The problem is that the commentator says it is *konungdómi* that is referred to as *afleiðing* ('þat (vísu)orð ... er síðarst var í enni fyrri vísu'), not the relative pronoun that is first in the next stanza. *Afleiðing* therefore cannot here be translated 'continuation', as the etymology ('leading from') and other occurrences of the word would suggest, but must mean 'antecedent' ('that which has consequences'?). The dative *afleiðingum* in DG 11 4to can perhaps be regarded as instrumental, but this would not be normal usage. The dictionary definitions are obviously based on this one occurrence and cannot be regarded as having a scholarly basis. The meaning of the sentence is not in doubt, but the word chosen for the phenomenon seems inappropriate to the context, and this is doubtless what Faulkes means by 'the commentary not fitting the verse' (2007: x), though this may be somewhat of an exaggeration. On the other hand this is probably a good example of the commentator struggling to describe a phenomenon for which the language of his time did not have the necessary resources.

Faulkes's second example relates to the comment on *refhvǫrf* before st. 17. In DG 11 4to the text reads thus (p. 280 below):

Þessi [háttr] er inn tíundi, er vér kǫllum refhvǫrf. Í þeim hætti skal velja [sama]n þau orðtǫk er ólíkust eru at greina ok hafa þó einnar tíðar f[al]l bæði orð, ef vel skal vera. Nú er til þessa háttar vant at finna ǫll orð gagnstaðlig, ok eru hér því sum orð dregin til hǿginda. En sýnt er þat í þessi vísu at orðin munu finnast, ef vandliga er at leitat, ok mun þat sýnast at flest frumsmíð stendr til bóta. Sem hér er kveðit:

  Síks glóðar verr søkir
  slétt skarð ha[f]i jarðar,
  hlífgranda rekr hendir
  heit kǫld loga ǫldu.
  Fljót⟨t⟩ válkat skilr fylkir
  friðlæ rǫðuls sævar,
  ránsið ræsir stǫðvar,
  reiðr, glaðr, frǫmum meiðum.

About this Faulkes says (2007: viii) that 'none of the possible meanings of *tíðar fall* seems to fit the pair of words exemplifying *refhvǫrf* in stt. 17–22'. This is quite right if we only take account of the meanings we know for Old Norse *tíð* and *fall*.[1] If we examine the examples it becomes fairly clear what

---

[1] Both Sverrir Tómasson (1993: 212) and Faulkes (2007: 53) point out that the Prologue to the first grammatical treatise in Codex Wormianus has the similar phrase 'fall eða tíma', which is translated 'quantitas sive tempus' in *Edda Snorra Sturlusonar* 1848–87: II 4–5.

the writer is getting at: *hafa einnar tíðar fall* means simply 'belong to the same word class'. Although there are at least half a dozen examples of the words of opposed meaning not belonging to the same word class (i.e. they are not both either nouns or adjectives or verbs) in the six stanzas in question, the rule is largely followed. In st. 17, for example, there is one exception (*slétt* : *skarð*). In st. 18, there are two (*skelfr* : *harðr*, *svalr* : *brandr*), and so on. It is true that it is difficult to see how *tíðar fall* can come to mean 'word class', but in spite of all the interest shown in grammar and rhetoric in medieval Iceland, it is clear that technical terms were very arbitrarily chosen in Icelandic, and there was no widely accepted terminology in these fields, as also appears if we look at Snorri's words relating to prosody.

Tíð is also involved in Faulkes's third example. This is concerned with the comment on st. 23, which begins with the words: 'Hér er í ǫðru vísuorði ok inu fjórða þau er gagnstaðlig orð eru hvárt ǫðru sem refhvǫrf, en standa eigi saman, ok er ein samstafa milli þeira, ok lúkast eigi bæði ⟨í⟩ eina tíð' (p. 286 below). In the stanza that the comment relates to the contrasted words appear thus: *vetr at sumri, hvíld at gǫngu, hǫll it rétta* and *tóm en fulla*. The distinguishing feature of these pairs of words is obvious: the first in each pair is monosyllabic, the second is disyllabic. Between each pair is an unstressed particle that fits well into the metre according to Craigie's Law about the third syllable from the end of the line being unstressed.[1] *Eigi bæði í ein tíð* must refer to the contrasted words not agreeing in having the same number of syllables, i.e. not being of the same length (*einn* = same).

Faulkes's examples 4–6 all relate to comments that seem to be in the wrong place, and would fit better with different stanzas from the ones they purport to belong with, and it is possible to accept his view in each case.

The seventh and last example (st. 32/9–10) that is found in DG 11 4to probably means that the commentator overinterprets what is in his text. It is the internal rhymes that are being discussed, and it says: 'Hér skiptir háttum í ǫðru ok fjórða vísuorði. Standa hendingar nær enda ok lúkast báðar í einn hljóðstaf ok er betr at samhljóðandi sé eptir aðra.' ('Here the verse forms are varied in the second and fourth line. The rhyme syllables come near the end, and they both have the same vowel in the ending, and it is better that one of them is followed by a consonant.') Line 2 obeys this rule with the rhymes *snarvinda* : *lindar*, but in line 4 *dynbrunnum* : *runnin* the vowels in the ending are different and both words end in a consonant. Since in the commentary, 'second and fourth line' always means 'in each half-verse', the rule ought to apply in lines 6 and 8 too, but line six has *ilstafna* : *hrafni*, with different vowels in the ending and no consonants following, line 8 has

[1] Craigie 1900: 381.

þrábarni : *arnar* with different vowels in the ending, though here again one word does have a consonant at the end. Of course it might occur to someone to read *dynbrunni* : *runnin* in line 4, but nothing can save lines 6 and 8. It is as if the commentator only looked closely at the first example. Anyway, he does only say that it is better to have both words ending with a consonant, not obligatory.

There are reliable sources for Snorri Sturluson having composed *Háttatal* in honour of King Hákon Hákonarson of Norway and Earl, later Duke Skúli. This is stated in red in two places (ff. 2r and 48v in DG 11 4to), and besides that also in the third grammatical treatise by Snorri's nephew Óláfr Þórðarson and in *Hákonar saga* (by his other nephew Sturla Þórðarson), and in the additions to *Skáldskaparmál* in Codex Wormianus and in the heading in Codex Trajectinus.[1] On the other hand, there is no medieval manuscript that states that he compiled the commentary to *Háttatal* (the statement in DG 11 4to that the *Edda* was composed by Snorri 'in the manner in which it is arranged here' cannot be taken to apply literally to every part of the compilation in that manuscript), and it could well be the work of others, though it may be based on draft notes deriving from Snorri.

---

[1] See Faulkes 2007: vii.

6 Headings and marginal notes

DG 11 4to is the only medieval manuscript of the complete *Edda* that sports preserved headings. GkS 2367 4to did have quite a number of coloured headings and large initials, but they have now become difficult to read. In all there are 117 headings in DG 11 4to written by the same hand as the main text, but in red ink, which is always considered a sign that they were added later, and that an empty space had been left for them.[1] The headings are of very different lengths, which probably means that they were copied from the scribe's exemplar, so that he would know how much space they were going to need. In fact there is really no need to argue this point, as will soon become apparent.

When Gylfir has turned his back on his adventure in Valhǫll, there is a brief heading: 'Frá heimboði ása með Ægi' (f. 19r). It need not make much difference whether the feast that is going to be the frame of what follows was held by Ægir or the Æsir, but soon after this heading comes another: 'Hér segir frá því at æsir sátu at heimboði at Ægis ok hann spurði Braga hvaðan af kom skáldskaprinn. Frá því er Kvasir var skapaðr. Hér hefr mjǫk setning skáldskapar' (f. 19v), and again on the next page: 'Hér segir hversu skilja skal skáldskap' (f. 20r). This conflicts directly with what comes seven leaves later: 'Hér hefr skáldskapar mál ok heiti margra hluta' (f. 27r). The most likely explanation of this conflict is that the redactor/scribe has transferred these chapters from their original place without adjusting the headings for the new arrangement, but carried them over with the narratives as they were, and this results in the duplication of the opening of *Skáldskaparmál*.

There can be little doubt about why this transfer of material took place. It was the redactor's intention to collect all the mythological stories together in Liber primus. Finnur Jónsson realised this, and from his wording it can be detected that he did not see this as particularly sensible (1931: xxvii):

> There is only one explanation for the phenomenon that is found here. The scribe has wished to collect all the myths, place them together. Therefore he takes these two myths about Þórr and the two giants out of their original context and gives them as an immediate supplement to his mythology. One can only think that his intention was not to be going to copy any more at all. If that was the case, he nevertheless changed his mind, and later continued his copying.

Intentionally or not, Finnur in fact overlooked the myths of Iðunn and Þjassi, and of the mead of poetry, which were also transferred, nor did he try to find any rational explanation for the transference of the myths.

In the margin in AM 748 I b 4to a reader has written on f. 25r: 'Gud g*ie*fe mier at læra þ*ess*a bok m*e*d odru godu enn hon er vond Gud fad*er* mijkvne

---

[1] Thorell (Grape et al. 1977: xv) counts 116 headings. He seems to have missed one.

[= miskunne].'[1] ('God grant me to study this book with other good things but it is evil God the father have mercy.') It can scarcely be doubted that *vondr* here means 'dangerous' or 'corrupting'. It is thus natural to think that a pious teacher wanted to have the heathen myths gathered together in Liber primus, since in Liber secundus there was contained in quite compact form all the material that the student/pupil needed to learn. Liber primus could thus be a handbook for the teacher, though of course it would be useful for the student to refer to *Skáldatal*.

Now we must of course bear in mind that we know little about teaching methods in medieval schools, not to speak of upbringing. It may have been the intention of this teacher to read aloud from the book, just as it is said of Gísli Finnsson in *Jóns saga helga* (*Byskupa sögur* 1948: II 36):

> When master Gísli preached God's Word before the people on feast days, then he did not speak many things without a book in front of him or trust much to his memory, rather he explicated the writings of the holy fathers from the book that lay on the lectern before him. This sensible and prudent man did this largely for the sake of humility, so that whereas he was young in age, those who were listening would be more impressed when they saw that he derived his teachings from holy and significant writings, and not just from the efforts of his mind and his wisdom.

Book learning is an instrument of power, and the teacher perhaps wanted to keep part of his teaching material to himself.

It has long been clear that the headings in DG 11 4to cannot derive from any imagined archetype, the actual original *Edda*. If they did, one would expect to see evidence of them in other manuscripts (see the summary of Rask's views, p. xxxiii above). But really there is no need of such arguments. It is sufficient, as has been indicated before (p. lxxxvi above), to look at two of the headings (pp. 6 and 262 below):

> Bók þessi heitir Edda. Hana hefir saman setta Snorri Sturluson eptir þeim hætti sem hér er skipat. Er fyrst frá ásum ok Ymi, þar næst skáldskapar mál ok heiti margra hluta. Síðast Háttatal er Snorri hefir ort um Hákon konung ok Skúla hertuga.

and

> Háttatal er Snorri Sturluson orti um Hákon konung ok Skúla hertuga.

Earl Skúli was not duke (*hertugi*) until 1237, and before that this wording is out of the question. It seems most sensible to lump all the headings in DG 11 4to together and say that they cannot have come into the picture before about 1240–50. *Skáldatal* considers Snorri a poet of Earl Skúli as well as of Duke Skúli, so it is unsafe to assume amendment or updating of the headings. They were clearly inserted in a version of the *Edda* that was much more like the Codex Regius version than the Uppsala Edda version, as is pointed out by Sverrir Tómasson (1992: 534):

[1] See Elias Wessén's comment (1945: 14).

This arrangement of the material [in the main heading of DG 11 4to] does not correspond with the manuscript itself, for there the text of *Skáldskaparmál* is interrupted, first by *Skáldatal* and then *Lǫgsǫgumannatal* down to Snorri Sturluson, and after *Skáldskaparmál* comes the second grammatical treatise, then comes *Háttatal*, which actually is not linked closely with the other material in the *Edda* in Codex Wormianus, for there the poem stands after the grammatical treatises. In the Codex Regius the arrangement of the material is closest to what it says in Codex Upsaliensis.[1]

This is absolutely correct, and the obvious conclusion is that the headings were not put into the Uppsala Edda version as we know it from DG 11 4to, but rather into an earlier version which in its arrangement of material stood closer to the Codex Regius version.

By far the majority of the headings follow a fixed pattern: *Hér segir frá Múspellsheimi ok frá Surti* (p. 14 below), *Frá því er synir Burs drápu Ymi* (p. 18 below), or *Frá Fenrisúlfi ok ásum* (p. 48 below). And when it comes to the kennings, use is made of a formula: *Kennd jǫrðin* (p. 152 below), *Kendr maðrinn* (p. 160 below), and in the *heiti* section: *Um nǫfn guðanna* (p. 204 below). The headings to the major parts, *Gylfaginning* and *Skáldskaparmál* have a different form: *Hér hefr Gylfa ginning frá því er Gylfi sótti heim Alfǫðr í Ásgarð með fjǫlkyngi ok frá villu ása ok frá spurningu Gylfa* (p. 10 below) and *Hér hefr skáldskapar mál ok heiti margra hluta* (p. 124 below). The verb *hefja* is a sign that something more than a short passage is in the offing, and probably that is why the longest story is the one that gets to benefit from it: *Hér hefr sǫgu Þórs ok Útgarða-Loka* (p. 64 below). The main heading to *Háttatal* has no introductory verb phrase: *Háttatal, er Snorri Sturluson orti um Hákon konung ok Skúla hertuga* (p. 262 below). There are only 14 headings within *Háttatal* and nearly all are names of verse forms without verbs. The exceptions are *Hér segir af sextán málum* (p. 274 below), *Hér segir um refhvǫrf* (p. 280 below) and *Hér segir hversu skipta skal hættinum* (p. 286 below).

When one looks at the whole, the headings are obviously intended to facilitate an overview of the contents, they are planned from the point of view of the work as a textbook and clearly made with the needs of the teacher as a guide.

It is worth noting that in AM 157 8vo, copied from DG 11 4to, the headings are treated rather freely. The first is simply: 'Hversu skal kenna skáldskap', and corresponds to 'Hér hefr skáldskapar mál ok heiti margra hluta' in DG 11 4to (p. 124 below). The exemplar seems nevertheless to be followed in outline, as was said before.

---

[1] Sverrir does not mention the Sturlung genealogy nor the list of stanzas in *Háttatal*, which are also clearly separate from the parts that are mentioned in the heading.

But the headings are not the only thing that brings out the textbook character of the work. Especially in one gathering, the first in *Skáldskaparmál* and the fourth in the book, by far the majority of the verse examples are marked in the margin with a *v*. The same is done in a few places in the *Gylfaginning* part, but there the *v*'s appear with much greater regularity and are spread more evenly between chapters. On the last page of the fourth gathering (f. 34r) it is as if the scribe loses heart, and on the first page of the fifth gathering the *v* is only to be seen twice and after that it never appears again.

In AM 157 8vo these marks in the margin are reproduced fairly accurately on the first four openings of this manuscript, which corresponds to DG 11 4to f. 27r to f. 28v, line 20. After that they become rather scattered, but on the other hand they do not come to an end as they do in DG 11 4to at the end of its fourth gathering, but carry on with varying regularity right to the end of *Skáldskaparmál*. In *Háttatal* there is only one mark in the margin in AM 157 8vo (f. 19r).

Similar marking of the verses can be seen in other manuscripts, such as manuscripts containing sagas, like Möðruvallabók, and there they are probably intended as a help to those reading aloud, but in DG 11 4to it seems most natural to regard them as reminders of the contents, and if so they are again a mark of the textbook nature of the work. Olaf Thorell was convinced that it was the scribe himself that entered the marks (Grape et al. 1977: xv), and then they would probably have been in his exemplar (or exemplars), for he seems to have added little off his own bat.

7 Empty space and additional material

In the place where the scribe of DG 11 4to worked there was no shortage of parchment. There are many examples of his ending a chapter in the middle of a page, and leaving the rest of the page empty when it could easily have been used. Sometimes it has been filled with something else, probably at a later time, but not much later. Some of this additional material will be mentioned here.

On f. 22v the scribe has finished a section with the words *Eptir þessi sǫgu hefir ort Eilífr Guðrúnarson í Þórsdrápu* in line 20, leaving almost a third of a page empty, and on the opposite page, where *Skáldatal* begins, there was also a bit of empty space. In the sixteenth or seventeenth century someone has made use of these spaces and written in them verses from *rímur*, but here the parchment is so dirty that it has been difficult to decipher them (see Grape 1962: 15).

Skáldatal ends on f. 25r in column 2. Part of column 2 and the whole of Column 3 is empty, and an artist has then used the space to depict two dancers, a woman and a man (with a knife), and another person with a stick, perhaps conducting the performance (see pp. 118–19.below).

The list of lawspeakers ends on f. 26r, line 12. The rest of the page was left empty, as was the next page, and both were later used for drawings, another dancing woman on f. 26r, and on 26v the well known drawing of Gangleri and the three kings (see pp. 119 and 122 below).

On f. 37v the enumeration of *heiti* and kennings breaks off with the moon and sun, the final kenning for the latter being 'eldr himins ok lopts'. That is in line 16 of the left hand page, and the rest of the page was left blank and later filled with the amusing drawing of a knight on his horse with the caption 'Hér ríðr maðr, Jón mágr!' ('Here rides a man, kinsman-in-law Jón!'; see p. 121 below). F. 38r then begins with an unusually elaborate initial capital, and clearly the scribe regarded this as a real chapter break, and now begins the account of King Hálfdan and his eighteen sons.

On f. 45r *Skáldskaparmál* ends with the words 'Hafa hér eptir skáldin kveðit, sem fyrr er ritat' ('The poets have used this (or 'these things') in poems, as is written above'). This is in line 16, and there is nearly half a page left. The space is filled, probably by the same scribe, with the *dróttkvætt* verses containing terms for women that were mentioned earlier (p. lxv), and are also in AM 748 I b 4to. Next there is this beautiful love complaint:

Stendr þat er stórum grandar	This troll-wife's storm (passionate emotion)
sterkviðri mér Herkju,	that greatly disturbs thought resides in my
í hneggverǫld hyggju;	heart-world (breast);
hefi ek stríð borit víða.	I have borne strife (anxiety) far and wide.
Þar kemr enn ef un⟨n⟩a	It may reach the point yet if
ítr vildi Bil skáldi	the beautiful goddess (lady) would love the poet
at blíðr grør Gríðar	that the giantess's merry wind (joyful thoughts)
glaumvindr í sal þindar.	will grow happily in my diaphragm's hall (breast).

In prose word order this can perhaps be: *Þat Herkju sterkviðri er stórum grandar hyggju stendr mér í hneggverǫld; ek hefi borit stríð víða. Þar kemr enn, ef ítr Bil vildi unna skáldi, at Gríðar glaumvindr grør blíðr í sal þindar.* The strange kennings for thought or feeling are variations of the unexplained kenning for thought in *Skáldskaparmál* (Faulkes 1998: 108/28–30; p. 220, ch. 84 in the present edition). The audience might well be amused at the giantess's merry wind in the poet's diaphragm's hall and wonder whether this hall was above or below the diaphragm. The poet is saying that he has suffered love-longing for a long time, but that he could be happy if the lady would return his passion.

The second grammatical treatise ends on f. 47v in line 19 and the list of stanzas in *Háttatal* begins on the next page and ends in line 22. On both pages of the opening there was a considerable mount of space left, and this has been used. It looks as though it was the scribe of DG 11 4to wrote the beginnings of coded texts on both pages. This is the simplest and commonest method of encoding: instead of the vowels, the next consonant in the alphabet is written, thus b for a or á, f for e or é, k for i or í and so on. Thus under the list of stanzas he wrote *Hfr fr rktbðr hblfr fkprðktxgr hbttb* and this can be read 'Hér er ritaðr hálfr fjórði tugr hátta', and on the opposite page stands (when decoded): *Gunnarr á mik, vel má þú sjá mik, ekki mátt þú taka mik, ekki mun þat saka þik*. Finnur Jónsson suggested emending *ekki* to *ella* (*Småstykker* 1884–91: 188), and Einar Ól. Sveinsson then put this emended ownership formula arranged as a quatrain on the half-title page of *Fagrar heyrði eg raddirnar* (1942 and 1974). This undoubtedly improved the sense. The readings that Yelena Sesselja Helgadóttir chose (2007: 204), *upp* for *ekki* and *mátt* for *má*, have no support in the manuscript; ϝccϝ means *ecce* and *mb* means *má*.

Finnur Jónsson printed the ownership formula in *Småstykker* 1884–91: 188–89 (this part published in 1886) and said there:

> This sentence or one very like it appears very frequently in later manuscripts. Here it has a twofold significance, since it 1) shows the phrase's relatively great age, 2) shows that the manuscript's first owner (and scribe?) was a certain Gunnarr, but who this person was, it is hardly possible to say with any certainty.

The same year, Finnur's 'Præfatio' appeared in the third volume of *Edda Snorra Sturlusonar* 1848–87, and there he said with less hesitation (p. lxiv): 'sine dubio hoc est nomen possessoris, ejusdemque scriptoris' (without doubt this is the name of the owner, the same person as the scribe). Although he here speaks of the identification as an undeniable fact, Finnur still refers in a footnote to his words in *Småstykker*.

Grape (1962) seems to have been of the same opinion, regarding Gunnarr as both scribe and owner of the manuscript. His argument for this, however, had rather more to it, as he considered it obvious that the scribe had in fact been copying from an earlier manuscript in the encoded passages. His grounds for this were that in the code used for the Gunnarr passage, the scribe used *c* and *f* instead of *k* and ϝ, which was his usual practice elsewhere. What Grape failed to note was that the scribe of DG 11 4to knew both *c* and *k*, *f* and ϝ and in this encoding *k* was used to mean *i*, while ϝ stood for *e* (cf. ϝccϝ = *ekke*, i.e. *ekki*) and it was necessary to make do with *f* for *f*.[1] The next scribe (see below) has got confused about this and writes for example *stffnk*, which clearly ought to read *stϝfnk* = *stefni*.

Actually, any hypothesis about the identity of Gunnarr is invalidated by the fact that the ownership formula and the blessing of the scribe that follows it (see below) both belong in a colophon at the end of a manuscript, and in DG 11 4to this is not where they are. They must therefore have been copied from (and apply to) some other manuscript. They are irrelevant here.

That the sentence about Gunnarr is in the main scribe's hand is confirmed not only by the formation of the letters, but also by the fact that it is followed

---

[1] Lasse Mårtensson drew my attention to Grape's false reasoning.

by the words *Dextera scriptoris benedicta sit omnibus horis* ('Blessed be the right hand of the scribe at all times'). This is still encoded. But then another scribe takes over, and has perhaps just learnt the code, though now the content is quite different. On the left hand page stands:

> Sýkvandi djǫfull, sigraz aldri á allzherjar þingi. Rekinn muntu ór guðs dómi, skolli, ok rekinn verða með hundum helvízkum. Ek stefni þér af blóðgri bráð ok af þessi einkunn ór þessi landeign at guðs lofi.

> Illness-causing devil, may you never be victorious at the general assembly. You will be driven from God's court, you fox, and be chased by hellish dogs. I call you off this bloody food and off (animals) with this mark (of ownership), to leave this property by God's will.

And on the right hand page:

> Allt it illa skal þér áfast vera, óhreinn andi, í heljar myrkrum sem ⟨h⟩reistr á fiski; í hungri helvítis, í heitum eldi geri ek þik sekjan, ó⟨h⟩reinn andi, ok allar þær meinvættir er þessum fjárskǫðum valda. Nú stefni ek yðr at orðfullu ok lǫgfullu at guðs lofi.

> Everything evil shall attach itself to you, unclean spirit, in the darkness of hell like scales on a fish; in the hunger of hell, in hot fire I declare you guilty, unclean spirit, and all the noxious creatures that cause this loss of animals. Now I challenge you with correct wording and correct legal proceeding by God's will.

Both texts appear to be curses, the first conceivably against the fox, who is being driven off the property, the second, a very necessary one for a farming community, against the kind of devil that attacks domestic animals.

Loss of *h* before *r* in *reistr* = *hreistr* and *óreinn* = *óhreinn* could be interpreted as Norwegian influence and could give a slight indication of the origin, but is probably too little to carry much weight.[1]

As was said above, st. 56 of *Háttatal* ends in the middle of f. 56r, and in the space left the same artist has been at work as on f. 25r and elsewhere (see p. 120 below).

On the empty front page of the manuscript (f. 1r) three verses have been written in the fifteenth or sixteenth century. The first seems to be an independent stanza, the second and third belong together. The text is very difficult to read, but Finnur Jónsson (1884–91: 192–93), Thorell (in Grape et al.1977: xvii), and Yelena Sesselja Helgadóttir (2007: 97–100 and 201) have wrestled with it. According to Yelena's reading, the verses go as follows (I follow her normalisation). Both she and Finnur assume that the first is supposed to be spoken by a ghost (a man buried alive, Finnur says) while the other two are by a living poet. In the interpretation of the first verse, I have permitted myself to depart considerably from the previous explicators.

---

[1] On Norwegianisms see Stefán Karlsson 2000: 173–187; 2004: 48.

Introduction

Dauðr vark hemlis hlíðar	I was dead (maimed) in my hawk-perch (arm) and yet I
haukstalls viku alla,	was alive, for the whole stage of Hemlir's (sea-king's)
segit þat blindu bandi[1]	hillside (sea), i.e. the whole length of the voyage; tell that
bifþorns ok þó lifði.	to the blind god[1] (Hǫðr) of the quivering thorn (spear),
Nú emk jarla kóngr orðinn	i.e. to the warrior; now I, wounded, have become king of
undigr svana grundar,	the earls of the swans' ground (sea), i.e. of the sea heroes;
kvikr þreyk naðrs inn nøkkvi	alive, I, the naked one, descendant of the unburied one
niðr ógrafins þriðja.	(living man), long for Þriði's (Óðinn's) serpent (spear).

Yelena Sesselja calls the other two verses battle verses, and she interprets them thus (2007: 201):

Koma mun okkur fyrir ekki	It will do us no good,
Eyvindur þó a[ð] vér skyndim	Eyvindur, though we hasten
undan ýta fundi	the storm of shield-men (battle)
él rand í dag manna.[2]	away from the meeting of men (engagement) today.
Bíðum hér þ[eirrar] hríðar,	Let us wait here for this battle,
hlaðs, verðum nú stansa,	we must now halt,
brosa mun lind í landi	the land-wise linden (tree) of the head-band (lady)
láðsvinn,[3] ef við vinnum.	will smile if we win.
Nú tekur F[reyr] að færa	Now the Freyr of battle-cloud (shield, whose god is the
fólk skýs að bæ mínum	warrior), the keeper of Glammi's (a seaking's) horses
gætir glamma s[ót]a	(ships), i.e. the viking, begins to bring his war-anchor
gunnakkeri sunnan.[4]	(sword) from the south to my dwelling.
Gera munu þeir [. . .] þekja	They will thatch the wolf's . . .
þrýmlinns boðar minni	battle snake's . . .
randa [. . .] og rjúfa	of shields . . . and tear down
ræfur dreyrfáum næfri.	the roofs with bloodstained thatching.

This reading accords well with Finnur Jónsson's interpretation in *Småstykker* (1884–91: 192–93), cf. Grape et al. 1977: xvii, note 1.

It is obvious that these verses tell us nothing about the origin of the manuscript or of the *Edda* either. They are merely a sign that empty spaces called for something to be written or drawn.

Spaces of half or whole pages of course show not only that there was plenty of parchment, they are also a sign of carefully thought out chapter divisions in the work.

[1] Though *bǫnd* (pl.) is common meaning 'gods' in Old Icelandic verse, the sg. *band* is not found elsewhere with this sense, but it seems to be so here. The 'blind god' can of course only be Hǫðr.

[2] Reading *él randmanna* as a kenning for battle. Finnur Jónsson emends to *ǫlranns nanna*, a kenning for woman.

[3] Finnur Jónsson emends to *látsvinn* 'sensibly behaved'.

[4] The kennings in the first four lines follow Finnur Jónsson's interpretation of the kennings. The last four lines are difficult to make much sense of. Finnur suggests the kenning *randa drífa* 'battle' is involved.

8 Grammar and prosody

There is no doubt that in the Middle Ages people in Iceland looked upon the *Edda* as part of the Ars grammatica, the school subject that included what we now call grammar as well as rhetoric. Donatus's work, which was used in most schools in Europe throughout the Middle Ages, included sections on both. Thus four independent 'grammatical' treatises were inserted between *Skáldskaparmál* and *Háttatal* in Codex Wormianus, and *Háttalykillinn* or the second grammatical treatise in DG 11 4to. *Skáldskaparmál* also circulated on its own, as was mentioned before, in AM 748 I b 4to and AM 757 a 4to, both of which also contain parts of the third grammatical treatise. On the other hand, *Gylfaginning*, which is now considered the most entertaining and most significant part of the *Edda*, seems not to have been considered essential material for the student. Though *Skáldskaparmál* was rich in examples of kennings involving heathen gods, and could have raised worries in young people, as can be seen from the marginal note in in AM 748 I b 4to mentioned above (pp. xcii–xciii), yet the Æsir seem to have become largely fit for home entertainment by the fourteenth century and even earlier. Snorri called his booth at the Alþingi Valhǫll and also Grýla (a frightening monster), whether for fun or to make people respect it. In verses in *Sturlunga saga* Óðinn and Freyr appear in jokes, and when the priest at Reykjaholt's wife Þorbjǫrg stabbed the knife into Hvamm-Sturla's face, wanting to make him look like Óðinn 'whom you want to resemble most' (*Sturlunga saga* 1946, I 109), presumably it should not be taken as a sign that even women of her status believed in Óðinn in the twelfth century. Dream verses before great events in *Sturlunga saga*, however, indicate that the picture of Ragnarǫk in *Vǫluspá* was alive, at any rate in folk-belief.

In the Codex Wormianus there is an interesting prologue to the grammatical treatises, and Sverrir Tómasson has called it the redactor's manifesto (1996a: 16). Part of this prologue is based on the statement of purpose in the *Edda* where young poets are addressed and urged on to achievement, and at the same time it is stated that Christian people should not believe in superstitions. DG 11 4to expressed it thus (p. 90 below; cf. p. lxviii above): 'En ekki er at gleyma eða ósanna þessar frásagnir eða taka ór skáldskapnum fornar kenningar er hǫfuðskáldin hafa sér líka látit. En eigi skulu kristnir menn trúa né á sannast at svo hafi verit', but the prologue to the treatises in Codex Wormianus uses these words (Ólsen 1884: 152):

> Skal þó eigi at heldr láta þat únýtt vera, sem fornskáldin hafa fundit, er efni ok grundvǫllr er alls skáldskapar. En eigi skulu menn þessum frásǫgnum trúa framar en skynsamligt er, eftir því sem segir í fyrsta hlut bókarinnar.

> What ancient poets have invented, which is the material and foundation of all poetry, must not, however, be taken to be of no account. But people must not believe these stories any more than is reasonable, in accordance with what is stated in the first part of this book.

Introduction

Later on it says (Ólsen 1884: 153):

> En nú skal lýsa hversu skáld ok frǿðimenn, ok einkanlega klerkarn⟨ir⟩ vilja lofast láta, hversu kveða skal, ok ónýta eigi at heldr þat er fornir menn hafa framit, utan þat sem klerklegar bǿkr banna, því at þat er náttúruligt at menn sé nú smásmuglari sem frǿðibǿkurnar dreifast nú víðara.[1]
>
> So now it shall be shown how poets and scholars, and especially the clergy, are willing to permit themselves to compose and still not disregard what ancient poets have achieved, except in the case of what clerical books forbid, for it is natural for people to be more particular the more widely the learned books are disseminated.

This prologue was probably written one or two generations later than DG 11 4to. We do not notice from the remarks of poets that the *Edda* then was considered particularly dangerous, but perhaps some conclusions can be drawn from Abbot Arngrímr Brandsson's *Guðmundardrápa* and Eysteinn Ásgrímsson's *Lilja*. Arngrímr is reckoned to have composed his poem in 1345 and says this (*Skj* B II 372, *Skj* A II 348):

Rædda ek lítt við reglur Eddu	In accordance with the rules of the *Edda*
ráðin mín, ok kvað ek sem bráðast	I have not uttered my teaching much, and I have
vísur þær, er vil ek ei hrósa,	spoken my verses very hastily, I will not praise it,
verkinn erat sjá mjúkr í kverkum;	the work is not so smooth in the throat;
stirða hefir ek ár til orða,	I have a stiff oar (or rudder, i.e. tongue) for words,
ekki má af slíku þekkjaz,	one cannot please in such a way,
arnar leir hefig yðr at færa,	eagle's shit have I to offer you,
emka ek fróðr hjá skáldum góðum.	I am not learned compared with good poets

Apart from the fact that the abbot implies that the rules of the *Edda* ought to be observed, note that he uses the term *arnarleir* about what all versions of the *Edda* except the Uppsala Edda version call *skáldfíflahlutr*.[2] But the most important thing in this cliché-filled apology for his poetry is that he refers to the rules of the *Edda* as if that is an obvious thing to do, and everyone will know what he is talking about. And the same attitude appears when Brother Eysteinn expresses his apology in *Lilja* (*Skaldic Poetry* VII 2: 672; cf. *Skj* B II 415 and A II 394):

Veri kátar nú virða sveitir;	Be joyful now, companies of men;
vættig þess, í kvæðis hætti	I trust now that you will forgive
várkynni, þóat verka þenna	that I compose this work in poetic form
vandag miðr, en þætti standa;	with less care than might have seemed right;
varðar mest til allra orða,	what is most important is that for all the words
undirstaðan sé réttlig fundin,	the foundation should be correctly found.
eigi glǫgg þóat eddu regla	even though the rule of the *Edda*, not clear,
undan hljóti at víkja stundum.	must sometimes be departed from.

The editor and explicator in *Skaldic Poetry*, Martin Chase, says about the words 'eigi glǫgg': 'The sense seems to be not that the rules themselves are not clear, but that the observance of them darkens the clarity of the text.'

---

[1] Cf. p. xxiii above and Sverrrir Tómasson 1996a: 16–18.
[2] On the word *leirburður* see Sverrir Tómasson 1996b: 67.

And on 'eddu regla' he says: 'The reference to *SnE* (rather than to traditional poetic rules in general) attests to the influence this work still held at the time *Lil* was composed' (*Skaldic Poetry* VII 2: 673).

To tell the truth, it is hard to say whether the poet of *Lilja* is speaking of *Snorra Edda* in particular. Both he and Arngrímr Brandsson may simply mean the rules of poetic art in general.[1] He complains in st. 98 about the bad practice of filling poems with obscure and obsolete words, and very little space is devoted to poetic language in *Lilja*, where hardly any kennings are used. That is indeed the direct policy of the poet (*Skaldic Poetry* VII 2: 673):

Sá, er óðinn skal vandan velja,	He who chooses to make a poem carefully
velr svá mǫrg í kvæði at selja	chooses to put in his poem so many
hulin fornyrðin, at trautt má telja,	obscure old words, they can hardly be counted,
tel eg þenna svá skilning dvelja.	I reckon that this interferes with understanding.

Arngrímr's language in *Guðmundardrápa* has quite another flavour. He calls his tongue his 'oar' or 'rudder for words', the King of Heaven is 'Prince of the heavens', Mary the 'shrine of the Prince of the sun', and so on.

On these topics otherwise see Sverrir Tómasson's, article (1996a) 'Nýsköpun eða endurtekning? Íslensk skáldmennt og Snorra Edda fram til 1609', in the collection *Guðamjöður og arnarleir*. In the same volume there is Bergljót Soffía Kristjánsdóttir's '"Gunnlöð ekki gaf mér neitt af geymsludrykknum forðum ..." Um Steinunni Finnsdóttur, Hyndlurímur og Snækóngsrímur'. Steinunn was a poetess of the seventeenth century. Bergljót points out a remarkable innovation in Steinunn's love poetry and says (1996: 212):

> Her choice of material and poetic language are evidence that she combines in her work knowledge of Old Icelandic poetic theory and of poems in which the poetic language lived on and flowered; of *rímur* which seem to have been mostly composed by men, and folk tale poems that would rather more likely have been composed by women. With regard to *Snorra Edda*, the most important thing is that this woman, Steinunn Finnsdóttir, sheds new light on the work and shows that its author followed the conventional line that expected poetry to be an exclusively male activity. And at the same time as she aims her artillery directly at the main work of Icelandic poetic theory, she chooses material and orders her language in such a way that they focus on woman and those of her adventures that are not to be found in the world of gods and heroes of that work.

What Bergljót is here saying applies equally well to all versions of *Snorra Edda*. The role of women is minor. It is only in two myths that goddesses play a small part, the Iðunn story and the story of Sif's hair, but in both cases they are victims. True, the role of Frigg, the defending and sorrowing mother in the myth of the death of Baldr, is of course considerable. The giant maidens Gerðr and Skaði are important in the love stories they are involved in. In *Skáldatal* three women are named, Ragnarr loðbrók's wife Áslaug, the poetess Vilborg

---

[1] Cf. Faulkes 1977: 34.

who composed about Óláfr kyrri, and Steinvǫr Sighvatsdóttir who composed about Gautr of Melr. No poetry composed by these women is preserved. Of course one might say that the poetic language of the *Edda* reflects the reality of the Middle Ages: in poetical conventions that were mostly shaped in the royal court and in warfare, women played little obvious part.

Anthony Faulkes has written a clear account of Snorri's conceptual categories in relation to poetic language in his introduction to *Skáldskaparmál* (1998), especially in the section 'The analysis of poetic diction' (pp. xxv–xxxvii). The same author has also dealt very fully with Snorri's possible models in classical tradition in 'The Sources of Skáldskaparmál: Snorri's intellectual background' (1993). In the latter, Faulkes points out that where one might have expected echoes from classical leaning, there is nothing to be seen (p. 65):

> His account of *nýgjǫrvingar* makes it clear that with this term he is thinking of someting like extended metaphor or allegory, but Snorri in general shows little interest in metaphor and figures of speech—strange if he had read any of the standard classical or medieval treatises on rhetoric. He sees poetical language largely in terms of substitutions of one name for another, rather than in terms of transference of meaning.

It is worth noting that the passage in *Snorra Edda* that Faulkes considers most reminiscent of classical poetic theory has its closest parallel in Aristotle, who was probably quite unknown in Iceland in Snorri's time, and it is so different in DG 11 4to that all similarity with Aristotle disappears:

DG 11 4to (p. 90 below)	GkS 2367 4to (Faulkes 1998: 5)
Þá mælti Ægir: Hvé mǫrg eru kyn skáldskaparins?	Þá mælir Ægir: 'Hversu á marga lund breytið þér orðtǫkum skáldskapar, eða hversu mǫrg eru kyn skáldskaparins?'
Bragi segir: Tvenn: Mál ok háttr.	Þá mælir Bragi: 'Tvenn eru kyn þau er greina skáldskap allan.'
Ægir spyrr: Hvat heitir mál skáldskaparins?	Ægir spyrr: 'Hver tvenn?'
Bragi segir: Tvent, kent ok ókent.	Bragi segir: 'Mál ok hættir.'
Ægir segir: Hvat er kent?	'Hvert máltak er haft til skáldskapar?'
Bragi segir: At taka heiti af verkum manns eða annarra hluta eða af því er hann þolir ǫðrum eða af ætt nokkurri.	'Þrenn er (R: eru) grein skáldskaparmáls.'
Ægir segir: Hver dǿmi eru til þess?	'Hver?'
Bragi segir: At kalla Óðin fǫður Þórs, Baldrs eða Bezlu eða annarra barna sinna, eða ver Friggjar, Jarðar, Gunnlaðar, Rindar eða eiganda Valhallar eða stýranda guðanna, Ásgarðs eða Hliðskjálfar, Sleipnis eða geirsins, óskmeyja, einherja, sigrs, valfalls; gervandi himins ok jarðar, sólar. Kalla hann aldinn Gaut, hapta guð, hanga guð, farma guð, Sigtýr.	'Svá: at nefna hvern hlut sem heitir; ǫnnur grein er sú er heitir fornǫfn; in þriðja málsgrein er kǫlluð er kenning, ok ⟨er⟩ sú grein svá sett at vér kǫllum Óðin eða Þór eða Tý eða einhvern af Ásum eða álfum, at hverr þeira er ek nefni til, þá tek ek með heiti af eign annars Ássins eða get ek hans verka nokkvorra. Þá eignask hann nafnit en eigi hinn er nefndr var, svá sem vér kǫllum Sigtý eða Hangatý eða Farmatý, þat er þá Óðins heiti, ok kǫllum vér þat kent heiti. Svá ok at kalla Reiðartý.'

The passage in Aristotle's *Poetics* (XXI. 11–13) that deals with this figure of speech is as follows (he is speaking of metaphor used 'in the way of analogy'):

> When, of four terms, the second bears the same relation to the first as the fourth to the third; in which case the fourth may be substituted for the second and the second for the fourth. And sometimes the proper term is also introduced besides its relative term. Thus a cup bears the same relation to Bacchus as a shield to Mars. A shield therefore may be called the cup of Mars and a cup the shield of Bacchus. Again, evening being to day what old age is to life, the evening may be called the old age of the day and old age the evening of life.

There is a clear similarity between this and the text in GkS 2367 4to, but it disappears when we look at the text of DG 11 4to.

Faulkes draws attention to the fact that actually Snorri only discusses his categories at the beginning and end of *Skáldskaparmál*, and uses very few terms to distinguish them. In speaking of kennings and *heiti* he uses only seven terms, *kenning*, *heiti*, *kent heiti*, *ókent heiti*, *við(r)kenning*, *sannkenning* and *fornafn*. And since *kent heiti* is synonymous with *kenning* and *ókent heiti* with *heiti*, there are actually only five, though some have interpreted *sannkenning* and *fornafn* as synonymous too.

Háttatal gives more definitions, and all the relevant texts can be compared in what follows:

Concept	Definition in DG 11 4to P. 90 below, cf. p. ciii	Definition í GkS 2367 4to Faulkes 1998: 5
kenning, kent heiti (*Skáldskaparmál*)	Ægir segir: Hvat er kent? Bragi segir: At taka heiti af verkum manns eða annarra hluta eða af því er hann þolir ǫðrum eða af ætt nokkurri. Ægir segir: Hver dǿmi eru til þess? Bragi segir: At kalla Óðin fǫður Þórs, Baldrs eða Bezlu eða annarra barna sinna, eða ver Friggjar, Jarðar, Gunnlaðar, Rindar, eða eiganda Valhallar eða stýranda guðanna, Ásgarðs eða Hliðskjálfar, Sleipnis eða geirsins, óskmeyja, einherja, sigrs, valfalls; gervandi himins ok jarðar, sólar. Kalla hann aldinn Gaut, hapta guð, hanga guð, farma guð, Sigtýr.	... kenning, ok ⟨er⟩ sú grein svá sett at vér kǫllum Óðin eða Þór eða Tý eða einnhvern af Ásum eða álfum, at hverr þeira er ek nefni til, þá tek ek með heiti af eign annars Ássins eða get ek hans verka nokkvorra. Þá eignask hann nafnit en eigi hinn er nefndr var, svá sem vér kǫllum Sigtý eða Hangatý eða Farmatý, þat er þá Óðins heiti, ok kǫllum vér þat kent heiti. Svá ok at kalla Reiðartý.

Introduction

	P. 266 below	Faulkes 2007: 5
kenning (*Háttatal*)	Kenningar eru með þrennu móti greindar. Fyrst heita kenningar, annat tvíkent, þriðja rekit. Þat er kenning at kalla fleinbrak orrostuna. Þat er tvíkent að kalla fleinbraks fúr sverðit, en þá er rekit, ef lengra er.	Kenningar eru með þrennum háttum greindar: fyrst heita kenningar (R: renn-), annat tvíkent, þriðja rekit. Þat er kenning at kalla fleinbrak orrostu, en þat er tvíkent at kalla fleinbraks ⟨fúr⟩ sverðit, en þá er rekit ef lengra er.
	Pp. 216–218 below	Faulkes 1998: 107
viðkenning	Þat eru viðkenningar at nefna annan hlut réttu nafni ok kalla þann er hann nefnir til þess er hann er eigandi, eða svá at kalla hann réttu nafni þess er hann nefndi, fǫður hans eða afa. Ái heitir, sonr, arfuni, arfi; bróð[ir] heitir blóði, lifri, niðr, nefi, komr [sic], kundr, kynstafr, niðjungr, ættstuðill, æt⟨t⟩bornir, afspringr . . . Þessi kǫllum vér viðrkenningar, ok þó at maðr sé kendr við bǿi sína eða skip, eða þat er nafn á, eða eign sína, þá er eignarnafn á.	Þat eru viðkenningar at nefna annan hlut réttu nafni ok kalla þann er hann vill nefna eiganda eða svá at kalla hann þess er hann nefndi fǫður eða afa; ái er hinn þriði. Heitir ok sonr ok arfuni, barn, jóð ok mǫgr, erfingi. Heitir ok bróðir blóði, barmi, hlýri, lifri. Heitir ok niðr nefi, áttungr, konr, kundr . . . Þessi heiti kǫllum vér viðkenningar ok svá þótt maðr sé kendr við bœ sinn eða skip sitt þat er nafn á eða eign sína þá er einkarnafn er gefit.
	P. 218 below	Faulkes 1998: 107
sannkenning (*Skáldskaparmál*)	Þetta kǫllum vér sannkenningar at kalla mann spekimann, ætlanarmann, orðspakan, ráðsnjallan, auðmildingur, úslǿkinn, gæimann, glæsimann. Þetta eru forn nǫfn.	Þetta kǫllum vér sannkenningar at kalla mann spekimann, *ætlunarmann, orðspeking, ráðsnilling, auðmilding, óslœkinn, gæimann, glæsimann. Þetta eru fornǫfn.
	P. 268 below	Faulkes 2007: 6
sannkenning (*Háttatal*)	Þat er sannkenning að styðja svá orðið meðr réttu efni at kalla stinn sár, því at hǫfug eru stór sár, en rétt er mælt at þróist. Ǫnnur sannkenning er sú at sárin þróast stórum. Nú er eitt vísuorð ok tvær sannkenningar.	Þat er sannkenning at styðja svá orðit með sǫnnu efni, svá at kalla stinn sárin, því at hǫfug eru sár stór; en rétt er mælt at þróask. Ǫnnur sannkenning er sú at sárin þróask stórum. Nú er eitt vísuorð ok tvær sannkenningar. Í ǫðru vísuorði er kǫlluð sterk egg en framir seggir. Í inu þriðja er svá, at hvast skerr, hlífin er traust; ok í fjórða orði at kalla konunginn

		mikinn, en líf hans framligt, þar næst at kalla hreint sverð ok harðliga roðit, en einnhverr liðsmanna ok væri rétt mál þótt maðr væri nefndr. Gǫfugr er konungrinn kallaðr, rǫndi⟨n⟩ var kostig ok furaðisk undarliga
	Nú fer svá með sama hætti unz ǫll er uppi vísan, ok eru hér sextán sannkenningar sýndar í átta vísuorðum. En þó fegra⟨r⟩ þat mjǫk í kveðandi að eigi sé jammjǫk eptir þeim farit.	skjótt; konungrinn unði glaðr frœknu hjarta. Nú eru hér sýndar sextán sann[kenningar í átta] vísuorðum, en þó fegra þær mjǫk í kveðandi at eigi sé svá vandliga eptir þeim farit.
	Sannkenningar hafa þrenna grein, heitir ein stuðning, ǫnnur sannkenning, þriðja tvíriðið.	Sannkenningar hafa þrenna grein: heitir ein sannkenning, ǫnnur stuðning, þriðja tvíriðit.
	P. 216 below	Faulkes 1998: 107/12
fornafn (*Skáldskaparmál*)[1]	Enn eru þær kenningar er menn láta ganga fyrir nǫfn manna. Þat kǫllum vér fornǫfn manna.	Enn eru þau heiti er menn láta ganga fyrir nǫfn manna. Þat kǫllum vér viðkenningar eða sannkenningar eða fornǫfn.
	P. 264 below	Faulkes 2007: 4
fornafn (*Háttatal*)	Þá má ok hlýða at hljóðstafr standi fyrir optar í fornǫfnum ...	Þá má ok hlýða at hljóðstafr standi fyrir optar í fjórðungi í fornǫfnum ...

[1] 'Fornafn' appears in *Skáldskaparmál* under *sannkenning* above ('These [sannkenningar] are called *fornǫfn*'), and some have assumed that this means that they are synonyms, but a few lines above that, the definition here is given ('Also there are the kennings/*heiti* that men let stand for people's names'). Faulkes (1998: xxix) has suggested that *fornafn* is a loan translation of the Latin term *pronominatio* 'the substitution of an epithet or appellative for a person's proper name'. This would include *viðkenningar* and *sannkenningar* and any other kennings or *heiti* when they stand for person's names; this type of kenning and *heiti* is extremely common. The corresponding Greek term *antonomasia* is defined thus in the third grammatical treatise in AM 748 I b 4to and Codex Wormianus (*Edda Snorra Sturlusonar* 1848–87: II 166, 422): 'Antonomasia setr sameiginligt nafn fyrir eiginligu nafni ('Antonomasia puts a common noun for a proper name'). In *Háttatal* 'fornafn' means 'pronoun' (Latin *pronomen*), as it does in Modern Icelandic and sometimes in the third grammatical treatise in Codex Wormianus (*Edda Snorra Sturlusonar* 1848–87: II 90). This of course is a related concept, for pronouns are also used to replace proper names. Thus *fornafn*, as a translation of *pronominatio* or *pronomen* (to both of which it is etymologically an exact equivalent), would cover all the examples in *Skáldskaparmál*, as well as those in *Háttatal* and the third grammatical treatise (which uses *fornafn* in both senses). Both *pronomen* and *pronominatio* were basic terms of Latin grammar and rhetoric, and the merest acquaintance with the trivium would explain Snorri's knowledge of it.

	P. 268 below	Faulkes 2007: 6
stuðning	Hér fylgir stuðning hverri sannkenning, sem eggin er kǫlluð óðhǫrð en fullhvatir menn. Þat er sannkenning: hǫrð egg en hvatir menn. Þat er stuðning er annat sannanarorð fylgir sannkenningu.	Hér fylgir stuðning hverri sannkenning, svá sem kǫlluð er eggin óðhǫrð, en fullhvatir menninir. Þat er sannkenning: hǫrð egg, en hvatir menn. Þat er stuðning er annat sǫnnunarorð fylgir sannkenning.
	P. 218 below	Faulkes 1998:107–108.
ókent heiti	Þessi eru kvenna nǫfn úkend: víf, brúðr. Fljóð heita þær konur er mjök fara með dramb eða skart. Snótir heita þær er orðnøfrar eru. Drósir heita þær konur er kyrrlátar eru. Svarri ok svarkr þær er mikillátar eru. Ristill heitir sú kona er skǫruglynd er. Rýgr heitir sú er ríkust er. Feima heitir sú er ófrǫm er sem ungar meyjar ok þær konur er údjarfar eru. Sæta heitir sú kona er bóndi hennar er af landi farinn. Hæll heitir sú kona er bóndi hennar er veginn utanlands. Ekkja heitir sú kona er bóndi hennar er andaðr, þær konur eljur er einn mann eigu. Kona er kǫlluð beðja eða mála ok rúna bónda síns, ok er þat viðkenning.	Þessi eru kvenna heiti ókend í skáldskap: Víf ok brúðr ok fljóð heita þær konur er manni eru gefnar. Sprund ok svanni heita þær konur er mjǫk fara með dramb ok skart. Snótir heita þær er orðnæfrar eru. Drósir heita þær er kyrrlátar eru. Svarri ok svarkr, þær eru mikillátar. Ristill er kǫlluð sú kona er skǫruglynd er. Rýgr heitir sú kona er ríkust er. Feima er sú kǫlluð er ófrǫm er svá sem ungar meyjar, eða þær konur er ódjarfar eru. Sæta heitir sú kona er búandi hennar er af landi farinn, hæll er sú kona kǫlluð er búandi hennar er veginn. Ekkja heitir sú er búandi hennar varð sóttdauðr. Mær heitir fyrst hver, en kerli⟨n⟩gar er gamlar eru. Eru enn þau kvinna heiti er til lastmælis eru ok má þau finna í kvæðum þótt þat sé eigi ritat. Þær konur heita eljur er einn mann eigu. Snǫr heitir sonar kván. Sværa heitir vers móðir. ⟨Heitir ok móðir,⟩ amma, þriðja edda. Eiða heitir móðir. Heitir ok dóttir ok barn, jóð. Heitir ok systir dís, jóðdís. Kona er ok kǫlluð beðja, mála, rún⟨a⟩ búanda síns ok er þat viðrkenning.

cviii   Introduction

		Faulkes 1998: 41
nýgerving (Skáld-skaparmál)		... hin yngri skáld hafa ort eptir dœmum hinna gǫmlu skálda, svá sem stóð í þeira kvæðum, en sett síðan út í hálfur þær er þeim þóttu líkar við þat er fyrr var ort. svá sem vatnit er sænum en áin vatninu en lœkr ánni. Því er þat kallat nýgervingar alt er út er sett heiti lengra en fyrr finnsk, ok þykkir þat vel alt er með líkindum ferr ok eðli.
	P. 270 below	Faulkes 2007: 7
nýgerving, nykrat (Háttatal)	Þat eru nýgervingar at kalla sverðit ⟨orm⟩ ok kenna rétt, en kalla slíðrar gǫtur hans, en fetlana ok umgerð hams hans. Þat heldr til náttúra hans ormsins, at hann skríðr ór hamsi ok til vatns. Því er svá at hann ferr at leita blóðs bekkjar ok skríðr hugar stígu, þat eru brjóst manna. Þá eru nýgervingar vel kveðnar at þat mál er upp er tekit halldist um alla vísuna. En ef sverðit er ormr kallat, en síðan fiskr eðr vǫndr eður annan veg breytt, þat kalla menn nykrat ok þikkir þat spilla.	Þat eru nýgjǫrvingar at kalla sverðit orm ok kenna rétt, en slíðrirnar gǫtur hans, en fetlana ok umgjǫrð hams hans. Þat heldr til ormsins náttúru, at hann skríðr ór hamsi svá at hann skríðr mjǫk til vatns. Hér er svá sett nýgjǫrving at hann ferr leita blóðs bekkjar, at þar er hann skríðr hugar stígu, þat eru brjóst manna. Þá þykkja nýgjǫrvingar vel kveðnar ef þat mál er upp er tekit haldi of alla vísulengð. *En *ef sverð *er (R: Svá sem seerð sé) ormr kallaðr, ⟨en síðan⟩ fiskr eða vǫndr eða annan veg breytt, þat kalla menn nykrað, ok þykkir þat spilla.
leyfi	Pp. 270–274	Faulkes 2007: 7–8
	Twelve examples of licence.	*Twelve examples of licence.*

On the whole the two versions are very close. The Codex Regius version, however is noticeably fuller, especially in the number of examples (for instance under *ókent heiti*). It is significant that there are comments under *sannkenning* on all eight lines of the stanza in GkS 2367 4to, but in DG 11 4to only on the first line, which is made to do duty for the other seven. It is very tempting to conclude that the version with fuller explanations represents a later version of the textbook.

Anthony Faulkes points out (1998: xxvii–xxviii) that the term *nýgerving* is used slightly differently in *Skáldskaparmál* and *Háttatal*,[1] but in both,

---

[1] On this see also Bergsveinn Birgisson 2008: 94–95.

the basic meaning sems to be the making of new meanings for words, i.e. metaphors. In *Háttatal* the example is of extended metaphor or allegory, while in *Skáldskaparmál* ch. 33 (in the Codex Regius version) the example is of varying the determinant with near synonyms (sea – lake – river – stream) or with synonyms of homonyms (Ægir – ægir – sea; = *ofljóst*), in chs 50 and 69–70, it is of the use of metaphorical base-words (some of these examples become extended metaphors too). In DG 11 4to the difference is less noticeable, since the definition in ch. 33 in the Codex Regius is absent, and only the examples in chs 50, 69 and 70 (Faulkes 1998: 74 and 108) are included. The story told in *Skáldskaparmál* in the Codex Regius version that leads up to the definition there is also not in the Uppsala Edda version. The four examples that are found there of the use of the figure are very close to the way that the term is used in *Háttatal* (pp. 218–220 below):

> Eyru heita hlustir. Þau má svá kenna at kalla land eða jarðar heitum nokkurum eða munn eða sjón, augu heyrnarinnar ef nýgervingar eru.
>
> Munn skal svo kenna at kalla land eða hús tungu eða tanna eða góma, varra, ok ef nýgervingar eru, þá kalla menn munn skip, en varrar borð eða tungu rǿðit eða stýrit.
>
> **Hér segir enn frá nýgervingum**
>
> Hugr heiti sefi, ást, elskugi, vilji [*written* villi], munr. Huginn má svá kenna at kalla vind trollkvenna ok rétt at nefna hverja er vill, ok svá at nefna jǫtna eða kenna þá til konu hans eða móður hans eða dóttur.
>
> Hǫnd má kalla jǫrð vopna eða hlífa, við axla ok erma, lófa, hreifa, jǫrð gullhringa ok vals ok hauks ok allra heita hans, ok í nýgervingum fót axla ok baugnauð.

All four of these examples are of referring to parts of the body by other things with analogical functions, while in *Háttatal*, similar analogies are made between the characteristics of a sword and a snake. The clearest example is perhaps that of the mouth, which can be referred to as a ship in which the lips are its gunwales and the tongue its oar or rudder (cf. Arngrímr's verse on p. ci above).

There are various indications that Snorri did not have a great number of categories to choose from, and there were few conventions about how to use them. It is for example interesting to look at the examples given of *sannkenning* in DG 11 4to (p. cv above): 'Þetta kǫllum vér sannkenningar at kalla mann spekimann, ætlanarmann, orðspakan, ráðsnjallan, auðmildingr, úslǿkinn, gæimann,[1] glæsimann. Þetta eru forn nǫfn.' ('We call these appropriate descriptions to say a person is a man of wisdom, a thinker . . . These are *fornǫfn*').

---

[1] Thus GkS 2367 4to. DG 11 4to has *geimann*. In this as in other manuscripts, e is occasionally written for æ. Cf. note 2 on p. lx above.

This seems fairly clear: they are true descriptions, not metaphorical ones. Óláfur Þórðarson hvítaskáld, who undoubtedly knew his uncle's work, seems to be saying something quite different in his grammatical treatise here (Ólsen 1884: 102–103; cf. *Edda Snorra Sturlusonar* 1848–87: II 158–160):

Metaphora er framføring orða eða hluta í aðra merking. Hon verðr á .iiij. leiðir:[1] Af andligum hlut til andligs hlutar sem hér:	Metaphor is transference of words or things to a different meaning. It happens in four ways: from a living thing to a living thing, as here:
En skinnbjarta skortir, skapið kannaz mér svanna, dýr er hon hætt at hváru, hálmein Njǫrun steina.[2]	But the skin-bright goddess of jewels (lady) — her nature is known to me, in any case she is a dangerous beast, — lacks the damager of straw (fire).
Hér er dýr kǫlluð konan. Er þar framføring eiginligs hlutar, konunnar, í annarliga merking, sem dýrit er. Úeiginlig líking er þat millum dýrs ok konu, þvíat dýrit er skynlaust kvikendi en maðrinn skynsamligt. Fyrir fegurðar sakir þótti skáldinu betr fara málit ok úberari verða lǫstrinn, at kalla margláta konu heldr dýr en greina sér hvern hlut, þann er hon gerði úmannliga. Með þeim hætti eru þær kenningar er vér kǫllum sannkenningar í skáldskap, at kalla manninn Ása heitum ok kenna svá til vápna eða skipa eða nokkurn Ása annars nafni ok kenna þá við eign sína nokkura, sem Eyvindr kvað:	Here the woman is called a beast. This is transference of a particular thing, the woman, to a different meaning, which the animal is. This is an improper comparison between animal and woman, for the animal is an irrational creature, but a human is rational. For beauty's sake, poets thought the language better and the vice more apparent to call a loose woman an animal rather than to specify each thing in which she behaved unlike a human. This how the kennings are constructed that we call *sannkenningar* in poetry, calling a man by the names of Æsir and then referring to him in terms of weapons or ships or calling one of the Æsir by the name of another and then referrring to him by some property of his, as Eyvindr said:
Farma týs fjǫrvi næmði Jarðráðendr á Ǫglói.[3]	... of the Týr of cargoes land rulers deprived of life at Ǫgló.
Hér er farma Týr Óðinn kallaðr. Svá eru ok jǫtnar ok dvergar kallaðir menn eða konungar bjarga eða steina sem Skrautoddr kvað:	Here Óðinn is called Týr of cargoes. Similarly giants and dwarves are called men or kings of rocks of stones, as Skrautoddr said:

[1] Donatus (whom Óláfr is actually translating here) says: 'Metaphor is transference of things and words. This is done in four ways, from animate to animate, from inanimate to inanimate, from animate to inanimate, from inanimate to animate.' Cf. Ólsen 1884: 102.

[2] Parts of this verse are difficult to understand. See *Lexicon Poeticum* under the word *halmein*.

[3] Only the second half of the stanza is quoted. The object of the verb was in the first half (Sigurðr), as was the base word of the kenning *svanr Farmatýs*.

Bǫls munat bǫr at dylja Berg-Þórs nǫsum órum.	One must not conceal the misfortune ... mountain-Þórr's (giant's) ... [1]
Þessi figúra er optast svá sett í norrǿnum skáldskap, at þeir hlutir, er framfǿrast, eru kenndir við nǫkkur tilfelli sín, en þó finnst hvártveggja, sem þar er hverr konungr er kallaðr Yngvi eða Þengill ok annat þvílíkt fyrir tignar sakir fornkonunga. En í latínu er metaphora svá optast sett, at framfǿrðir hlutir eru úkenndir, en þó finnst hvártveggja, sem Ovidius segir:	This figure in Norse poetry is usually constructed so that the things that are transferred are referred to by some 'accident' of theirs, and yet both types are found, as when some king is called Yngvi or Þengill or something else similar, because of the reputation of ancient kings. But in Latin metaphor is usually constructed so that the transferred things are without a determinant, though both types are found, as Ovid says:
Tiphys et Automedon dicar amoris ego.	I may be called called the Tiphys and Automedon of love.
Hann kallar kerrugæti eða stýrimann ástar.	He calls himself the charioteer or helmsman of love.

This is very different from the way that *sannkenningar* is explained in *Skáldskaparmál*, and it seems that Óláfr considered himself fully entitled to use the concept of *sannkenning* in quite a different way from what Snorri did.[2] Perhaps they had been discussing the matter.[3]

Faulkes says correctly that *við(r)kenning* is the least problematical of Snorri's terms. It is clear that he uses it to mean referring to people in terms of their possessions or relationships, and it is also clear, he says, 'that nearly all kennings for people which are designed to specify an individual person are in this category' (1998: xxvi). The verb phrase *kenna við e–t* certainly lies behind *viðkenningu*, but Snorri also use *kenna til e–s* in the same sense.

[1] The remaining words were linked with words in the unquoted part of the stanza.

[2] Sverrir Tómasson writes about Óláfr (1992: 530): 'It does happen ... that he uses fully Icelandic terms such as *sannkenning* as if he seems to have understood it in a different way from his uncle Snorri and linked it more closely with Latin rhetoric'.

[3] On the other hand, this sentence on *sannkenningar* (Ólsen 1884: 103) comes in Óláfr Þórðarson's account of metaphor (*framfǿring*), which is only extant in the version of the third grammatical treatise in AM 242 fol.; AM 748 I b 4to and AM 757 a 4to do not contain it. In *Edda Snorra Sturlusonar* 1848–87: II 160 it is suggested that *sannkenningar* here is an error for *mannkenningar*. There are three other occurrences of *sannkenning* in this treatise (Ólsen 1884: 100, 107–8), and in all three it is the equivalent of *epitheton* ('an adjective or phrase expressing a characteristic quality or attribute of the person or thing mentioned'), and there is no conflict with the use of *sannkenning* in the *Edda*. *Háttatal* 5/3–6 is quoted in Ólsen 1884: 107 in illustration of *epitheton*. The word *mannkenning* does not seem to be recorded elsewhere, but the examples given in the treatise are very similar to the description of the kenning in Faulkes 1998: 5/18–24, quoted above, p. ciii; indeed Farmatýr is mentioned in both accounts; cf. also 40/5–16. In view of this, perhaps the views of Snorri and his nephew were not so very dissimilar after all. It would in any case be strange for Óláfr to use the term *sannkenning* in a discussion of metaphor.

After pointing out that Snorri has no passages on kennings or *heiti* for giants in *Skáldskaparmál* although there are lots of such kennings in the poems he quotes, Faulkes says (1998: xxx):

> It is important to remember that Snorri's *Edda* is not a treatise on earlier Norse poetry; it is a book of instruction for young poets of his day illustrated from the work of earlier poets. It was no part of the requirement of young poets in the thirteenth century to be able to compose about giants (or indeed to write satire): their function was to learn to praise kings. It is this that determines the content of the Prose Edda, which not surprisingly does not well represent or cover the whole range of skaldic verse, and generally concentrates on the kinds of kennings that would be most useful for praising kings.
>
> This is also probably the reason why Snorri shows so little interest in metaphor and figures of speech. He sees poetical language largely in terms of substitutions of one name for another, rather than in terms of tranference of meaning. The latter he describes as *nýgervingar* and exemplifies in a number of places in both *Skáldskaparmál* and *Háttatal*, but always with the implication that it is somewhat exceptional.

Terms for aspects of alliteration, rhyme and rhythm do not appear until the commentary to *Háttatal*. The comments on st. 1 lay the foundation (p. 264 below):

> Ǫnnur stafasetning er sú er fylgir setning hljóðs þess er hátt gerir ok kveðandi. Skal sú grein í dróttkvæðum hætti vera at fjórðungr vísu skal þar saman fara at allri stafa setning ok hljóða. Skal í fyrra vísuorði svá greina þá setning:
>
> > Jǫrð kann frelsa fyrðum
>
> Hér er svá: jǫrð, fyrð. Þá er ein samstafa í hvárri ok fylgir sinn hljóðstafr hvárri ok svá hǫfuðstafr, en einn stafr hljóðs er í hváru orðinu ok inn sami málstafr eptir hljóðstaf. Þessa setning hljóðfalls kǫllum vér skothending. En í ǫðru vísuorði er svá:
>
> > Friðrofs konungr ofsa
>
> Svá er hér rofs ok ofs. Þat er einn hljóðstafr ok svá þeir er eptir fara í báðum orðunum. En upphafsstafrinn greinir orðin. Þetta heita aðalhendingar. Svá skal hendingar setja í dróttkvæðum hætti at in síðari hending í hverri vísu⟨orði⟩, sú er heitir viðrhending, hon skal standa í þeiri samstǫfu er ein er síðarr. En sú er frumhending heitir stendr stundum í upphafi orðs ok kǫllum vér þá oddhending, en stundum í miðju orði ok kǫllum vér þá hluthending. Þessi er dróttkvæðr háttr. Með þessum hætti er flest ort þat er vandat er. Þessi er upphaf allra hátta svá sem málrúnar eru fyrir ǫðrum rúnum.

Gradually the list of terms emerges quite clearly, and many have remained standard in Icelandic prosodic discourse since the days of Snorri. In DG 11 4to these terms for features of prosody, phonology and grammar are used:

Prosody

hending	rhyme, assonance (both end-rhyme and internal rhyme)
aðalhending	chief rhyme, full rhyme
skothending	half-rhyme, assonance

frumhending	anterior rhyme, the first of two in a *dróttkvætt* line
oddhending	front rhyme, one that comes at the beginning of a line
hluthending	mid-rhyme, one that is not at the beginning of a line
viðrhending	accessory rhyme, the second of two internal rhymes in a line
samhending	'coincidental rhyme', one falling on the same syllable as the alliteration, producing identical syllables
afhending	use of the same rhyme-syllable in even lines as at the end of the preceding odd lines
háttleysa	lack of form, a stanza with no hendings
vísuorð	line of verse (sometimes abbreviated *orð*)
stafr	alliterating sound, stave
stafasetning	alliteration, internal rhyme
hǫfuðstafr	chief alliterating stave
stuðill	alliterating stave in the odd lines of a *dróttkvætt* verse
leyfi	permission, licence; cf. *skáldaleyfi* 'poetic licence' in Modern Icelandic

Phonology

samstafa	syllable
skjót samstafa	unstressed or short syllable
sein samstafa	long syllable?[1]
hǫrð samstafa	strong or accented syllable
lin samstafa	weak, unaccented syllable
hljóðstafr	vowel
samhljóðandi	consonant

Grammar

fornǫfn	pronouns
málfylling	particle

In this list it is worth noting that *fornǫfn* has a different meaning in *Háttatal* from what it has in *Skáldskaparmál*. There DG 11 4to actually has the reading *forn nǫfn*, but this obviously has to be emended to *fornǫfn*. If *fornafn* in *Skáldskaparmál* means *pronominatio* (see note 1 on p. cvi above), i.e. an expression that replaces a proper noun, then *sannkenning* might well be regarded as a type of *fornafn*.

To be able to speak of the features that constitute the *dróttkvætt* form there is no need for more terminology than this. This does not mean that Snorri or some other author of the commentary had been able to work out all the rules

[1] One would expect *seinn* to mean 'long' in the description of st. 7, but the passage is actually about how the use of contraction can reduce the number of syllables in a line from six to five. *Seinn* perhaps means here that the remaining syllables are spoken so slowly that they take as long to speak as a normal line of six syllables. *Seinn* is used of long vowels in the second grammatical treatise.

of this verse form. He is, for instance, unable to give a satisfactory account of resolution. On the other hand, one can say that as material for teaching purposes the commentary is remarkably clear and discerning.

But although there is so much that is similar in the two versions of *Háttatal*, which are obviously closely related, it is clear that the scribe of DG 11 4to did not understand everything that he wrote, and possibly he had a much worse exemplar than the scribe of GkS 2367 4to. There are considerably more errors in the commentary in DG 11 4to, and here it will be a good thing to look at the differences where it is clear that GkS 2367 4to is considerably more correct. Variations in wording are ignored here, and note is taken only of the places where the wording of the comments in DG 11 4to conflicts with the verses. The number of the examples corresponds to the numbering of the verses, so that they will easily be found in the text.

Verse 8:
U: Sétta [leyfi] at hafa í dróttkvæðum hætti samhendingar eða *hluthendingar*.
R: Sétta leyfi er þat at hafa í dróttkvæðum hætti samhendingar eða *liðhendingar*.

Verse 12:
U: En annat ok it þriðja vísuorð *er sér um mál kallat*.
R: En annat ok it þriðja vísuorð *er sér um mál, ok er þat stál kallat*.

Verse 18:
U: Þessi eru *ǫnnur vísuorð*, ok eru hér hálfu færi vísuorð þau er refhvǫrfum eru sett, ok eru þau tvenn í ǫðru vísuorði ok eru þau kǫlluð en mestu.
R: Þessi eru *ǫnnur refhvǫrf* ok eru hér hálfu færi vísuorð þau er refhvǫrfum eru ort, ok eru þau tvenn í ǫðru vísuorði, ok eru fyrir því kǫlluð in mestu.

Verse 27:
U: Hér hefr upp annat ok it fjórða vísuorð með fullu orði ok einni samstǫfu, ok *leiðir orð af inum fyrra vísuhelmingi ok orðinu*. En þær fimm samstǫfur er þá eru um mál er eftir eru.
R: Hér hefr upp annat ok hit fjórða vísuorð með fullu orði ok einni samstǫfu, ok *leiðir þat orð af hinu fyrra vísuorði*, en þær fimm samstǫfur er þá eru eptir eru sér um mál.

Verse 31:
U: Hér skiptir háttum *í ǫðru ok þriðja vísuorði*.
R: Þetta heitir bragarbót. Hér skiptir háttum *í fyrsta ok þriðja vísuorði*.

Verse 39:
U: *Hér skiptir háttum í fjórða vísuorði*.
R: *Hér skiptir háttum it fimta vísuorð*.

Verse 46:
U: Hér eru þær hendingar er í *ǫðru ok fjórða vísuorði svá settur sem skothendur í dróttkvæðum hætti*.

R: *Hér eru þær hendingar er vér kǫllum samhendur, því at þessar eru allar með einum stǫfum ok eru í ǫðru[1] ok þriðja vísuorði svá settar sem skotendur í dróttkvæðum hætti.*

Verse 48:
U: Hér halda samhendingar *um alla vísulengð*
R: Hér halda samhendingar *of allan vísuhelming*

Verse 49:
U: Hér er *í fyrsta orði stýft ok tekin af sú samstafa er dróttkvæðum hætti skal leggja með hending.*
R: Hér er *it fjórða vísuorð stýft ok tekin af samstafa er í dróttkvæðum hætti skal setja með hending.*

Of course there are only nine examples, and five of them relate to numerals. It may be that misreading of Roman numerals can explain some of these, and this is common in other manuscripts, but it should be noted that none of the manuscripts that we have use Roman numerals in these places. It would then have to be the manuscript from which DG 11 4to was copied that had inherited them from the archetype. Actually this could well be the explanation.

The remaining discrepancies are (the first word in each pair is the reading of DG 11 4to): *hluthendingar* : *liðhendingar*, *ǫnnur vísuorð* : *ǫnnur reflhvǫrf*, *fyrri vísuhelmingr* : *fyrra vísuorð*; in addition there are two cases where words have dropped out (verses 12 and 46). All these are characteristic scribal errors, common today as they have always been.

I think it has been demonstrated that the technical terminology in the different versions of the *Edda* is by no means an established one, and it is often unclear; it is as though the redactors have been feeling their way forward. But it was continually in process of development and extension. It was adequate for its task and impressive in its range and independence of Latin sources.

---

[1] It is worth noting that here DG 11 4to, GkS 2367 4to and Codex Trajectinus all share the same error. The word ought to be *fyrsta*, and so it is in Codex Wormianus. See Faulkes 2007: 44. In his edition it is emended.

9 Summary

In conclusion, what has been said about the history of the *Edda* in this introduction will be summarised, and for clarity's sake set out in numbered paragraphs.

1. Material in the *Edda* must have been being collected together over quite a long period of time, and there is no reason not to assume that this collecting began during Snorri's years at Oddi.
2. There is little indication that the *Edda* was planned as a whole at the outset. The main sections, *Gylfaginning* and *Skáldskaparmál*, are in content and style independent, and of course the same applies to *Háttatal*.
3. There is no way of proving that the sections of the *Edda* were written in reverse order. Wessén's idea about how it was compiled, which has been supported by others after him, is a theory only, interesting but unprovable and rather improbable.
4. Some of what appears in DG 11 4to cannot be derived from the same archetype as the Codex Regius version is dervied from. This applies particularly to the very different texts of verses in *Skáldskaparmál* and extremely different tellings of stories in *Gylfaginning* and *Skáldskaparmál*. Those who favour the idea of the text having been shortened in the Uppsala Edda need to explain how these differences have come about.
5. Some of the abbreviations (suspensions) must derive from the original *Edda*, since it is hard to imagine how they could have come about from a text that was written out in full (a scribe does not write 'g. h. st'.' for 'grunn hvert stika sunnar', if the latter stands in his exemplar). If the abbreviations were in the original, the version that has the full text must be derived from a different source unless it was made by someone who new the verses by heart. It is rather improbable that abbreviations of this kind could survive many recopyings.
6. DG 11 4to is derived from a version of the *Edda* independent of the Codex Regius version, the *Uppsala Edda version, not from the 'original' *Edda*. Nevertheless various things in it could have their roots in first drafts of teaching materials about poetic theory made by Snorri.
7. Snorri had probably begun to compose both *Gylfaginning* and *Skáldskaparmál* before he went to Norway in 1218.
8. DG 11 4to is a compilation, but also a carefully thought out manuscript textbook. This is apparent both from redactorial decisions such as the transfer of mythological stories from *Skáldskaparmál* across to the second scene of *Gylfaginning*, the headings and the supplementary material.
9. It is very unlikely that the headings in DG 11 4to are from before 1237 (when Skúli was made duke). Since they are fairly certainly earlier than DG 11 4to itself, it is most natural to assume that the Uppsala Edda

Introduction

version was made about 1240–50. This would then be the required intermediate link between the first draft and DG 11 4to. In *Skáldatal* Snorri is said to be poet of Earl Skúli and of Duke Skúli.

10. There is no way to prove that DG 11 4to does not present us with a shortened version of the *Edda*, but it is definitely not a shortened version of the *Edda* that we know from the Codex Regius version in GkS 2367 4to, AM 242 fol. and Codex Trajectinus.

On this basis it is tempting to set out a suggestion for a kind of genealogy of DG 11 4to, but it must be emphasised that no attempt will be made to draw a stemma of the relationships between these four manuscripts, any attempt do which is doomed to failure. Nor will any suggestions be made about the relationship of AM 748 I b 4to and AM 757 a 4to with DG 11 4to. But it is clear that there are in places links between these two manuscripts and the Uppsala Edda version.

It is assumed here that Snorri had compiled some drafts of the *Edda* before 1218, and that they included *Gylfaginning* and *Skáldskaparmál* in a similar form to that we find in the Uppsala Edda version later. Afterwards Snorri (or someone else) reviewed these drafts, probably having better sources for some of the material, maybe some new narratives and more verse, and collected them together. This is the version that becomes the archetype of the Codex Regius version, but it is impossible to see it as the source of the Uppsala Edda.

A conceivable history of the Uppsala Edda version can be shown in tabular form thus:

Stages	Content	Comments
S1 (before 1218)	Gylfaginning Skáldskaparmál	Both parts similar to what appears later in the Codex Regius version
U1 (about 1240–50, at any rate after 1237)	Prologue Gylfaginning Skáldskaparmál Háttatal with commentary	Headings added. Order of material unchanged from S1. *Háttatal* has been composed and partially provided with commentary, and now some or all of this has been inserted into the poem.
DG 11 4to	Liber primus: Formáli Gylfaginning scene 1 Gylfaginning scene 2 Skáldatal Sturlung genealogy List of lawspeakers Liber secundus: Skáldskaparmál Háttalykill (2nd grammatical treatise) List of stanzas Háttatal as in U1	Here the mythological narratives are transferred from *Skáldskaparmál* into what I have called scene 2 of *Gylfaginning* (to get rid of the problematical title Bragaræður). The compilation is complete (having been commissioned) and the material divided into Liber primus and Liber secundus.

S1 comprises Snorri's first drafts of *Gylfaginning* and *Skáldskaparmál*. U1 is the earliest version of the Uppsala Edda, perhaps the exemplar from which DG 11 4to was copied for the four sections named here.

The table makes clear the compilatory nature of DG 11 4to, and the textbook development that takes place is brought out.

In all versions of the *Edda* the textbook character of the work is apparent. The Codex Regius and Codex Trajectinus add *þulur*, Codex Wormianus the grammatical treatises, and in DG 11 4to material of various kinds is added from different quarters, and the order of the material is changed. And about the same time as DG 11 4to was being written, the version of *Skáldskaparmál* that we have in AM 748 I b 4to was compiled. Already, Óláfr hvítaskáld has written his grammtical/rhetorical treatise, based largely on foreign sources, but with some ideas derived from his uncle Snorri. All this happened, it appears, within a century of Snorri's first drafts, and the conclusion may well be drawn that by then the Edda had become a well known and popular textbook, and that the material in it was considered useful. Research into its reception (see Sverrir Tómasson 1996a) has shown that copying and rewriting continued through the following centuries, and although *rímur* poetry did not introduce many new metaphorical kennings, it played its part in the preservation of the eddic language and style.

An obvious question, of course, is why the Uppsala Edda version (U1) was made when it was known that there was a 'better' version available. There is no rational answer to this, other than 'the teacher'. A person who had used the draft version for teaching and doubtless added to it as necessary off his own bat, maybe knew better texts of the mythological narratives and was pretty well content with the list of kennings in *Skáldskaparmál*, would not have needed the revised version. It is well known that established textbooks are renewed slowly; moreover it is sometimes maintained nowadays that it takes anything up to half a century for new knowledge to be introduced into the classroom.

On the other hand, whoever it was that put U1 together nevertheless had *Háttatal* available. This almost certainly already had its heading (f. 2r): 'Síðast Háttatal er Snorri hefir ort um Hák[on] konung ok Skúla hertug[a]'.

It seems clear that some commentary had been added to *Háttatal* in the *Edda* in U1, but it is a very improbable, if not absurd, idea to imagine that it accompanied the poem from the start. On the other hand, it is extremely difficult to work out whether it was by the poet himself or by someone working for him. Above (p. xci), an attempt was made to steer a middle path by assuming that Snorri had drafted some comments. The concepts used do not suggest that much was sought in foreign writers on rhetoric; they seem to be rather primitive ad hoc ideas.

DG 11 4to is a compilation, and thus offers us an independent version of the *Edda*. An accurate, though not all that acute, scribe, has received a commission which would seem to have looked like this. The book was to be in two parts.

1. Mythological stories are to be collected together into the first part.
2. *Skáldatal*, the Sturlung genealogy and the list of lawspeakers are to be copied. That concludes the first part, Liber primus.
3. *Skáldskaparmál* is to follow, with *Háttalykillinn* (second grammatical treatise).
4. An old list of stanzas in *Háttatal* is to be copied.
5. *Háttatal* itself in its present form comprises the final part of the work. That concludes Liber secundus.

This commission has been followed in every detail without the text of the material the scribe had to hand being revised at all. Thus the headings have become misleading and in some cases absolutely wrong, once passages have been moved. This is most noticeable in scene 2 of *Gylfaginning*, to which narratives had been moved from the *Skáldskaparmál* section.

There is no way of knowing why *Háttatal* only has 56 stanzas in DG 11 4to, but it looks as though there was no more in the scribe's exemplar.

Although we cannot tell who the person that commissioned the manuscript was, or where he lived, it is suggestive that it first turns up in the hands of Brynjólfur Sveinsson, who had been educated in Skálaholt, where there had probably been a school since the Middle Ages. Árni Þorláksson was bishop in Skálaholt 1269–1298, and he was succeeded by Árni Helgason (died 1320).

Lasse Mårtensson's research on the handwriting and scribal characteristics of DG 11 4to have shown that the scribe was a very careful scribe who never once corrected what he did not understand. The same is apparent when what he wrote in the most difficult part of his task, the verse quotations in *Skáldskaparmál* and *Háttatal*, are examined objectively. In the present edition an attempt has been made as far as possible to interpret these quotations without emendation, though frequently more straightforward alternatives are pointed out. The scribe of DG 11 4to undoubtedly believed he understood most of what he wrote, but he also paid his predecessors the compliment of not altering what he did not understand.

10 Other editions of DG 11 4to

The first serious attempt to edit *Snorra Edda* from the Uppsala manuscript was the theologian Johan Göransson's edition of *Gylfaginning* in 1746.[1] Göransson was a staunch disciple of Rudbeck and a supporter of his doctrine about the cradle of civilisation having been Sweden. His ideas about the *Edda* come out clearly from his title:

DE
YFVERBORNA ATLINGARS,
ELLER,
SVIOGÖTARS ok NORDMÄNNERS,
EDDA,
Det är Stammodren för deras, uti Hedendomen, både andliga ok verldsliga vishet; nu första gången på Svensko översatt, med Latinsk uttolkning försed; jämte et företal om EDDANS ålder ok innehåld, m.m. samt om de äldsta ok rätta, Skythar, Getar, Götar, Kämpar, Atlingar, Yfverborna, Karlar, ok alla dessas stamfader, Gomer: Utgifven efter en urgamal, ok ganska fullkomlig Upsala Academie tilhörig, på Götisko, handskrifven Permebok.

Rudbeck had Swedicised the Greek racial name Ὑπερβόρεοι (Hyperboreans), Appollo-worshippers who lived in luxurious well-being beyond Boreas, the north wind, calling them 'de Yferborna' and transferring them to Sweden.

Göransson's Latin and Swedish translations, however, did little to arouse people's interest in the Uppsala Edda at that time. Perhaps its origin, as Göransson presented it, was rather off-putting. Briefly, he seems to have imagined that the *Edda* had been written in Uppsala in the time of Moses (1746: xxxii). His comparison of the Uppsala text with Resen's edition (based on Laufás Edda[2]) led him to a confident conclusion (1746: xxxiv–xxxv; cf. Grape 1962: 43 note):[3]

Den handskrefna Boken, som man nu följt, är skrefven vid Sturlossons tid. Vid första påseendet ser man, at hon är ganska gamul; ok Götiskan uti detta ok Resenii Manuskripter äro ganska olika. Ty Resenii Böker äro uti språket mycket lika Jsländskan; men uti denna vår Handskrefna Bok är språket enehanda, med det här i Riket på gamla Runstenar förvarade språket . . . Hon *bör heta, icke Jsländares utan Sviogötars, ok Nordmänners Edda*. Emedan des språk kommer mera öfverens med Götiskan, än Jsländskan; ok hon är sammansatt vid Upsala, men icke på Jsland; så ser man, att hon helt orätt kallas Edda Jslandorum. At Sviogötar kallas Nordmänner, så väl som de Norske, är en klar sak af Historien.

[1] On this edition and its editor see Grape 1962: 41–51.
[2] See Faulkes 1977–1979.
[3] It is rather uncertain exactly when Göransson's edition appeared. It is undated, but Grape points out that in a lecture on 25th june 1746 Göransson speaks of his Edda as having been published in that year. Rask, who dated it 1745, presumably assumed that it was that year because that was when Göransson had DG 11 4to on loan.

But that was not the end of his romancing. In his introduction Göransson says (1746: xxxi–xxxii):

> Semunder ok Snorre hafva icke diktat Eddan, utan afskrifvit henne efter gamla Runoböker. Detta vil man vidlöftigare bevisa när man kommer till Sibillas spådom. Men nu i korthet märka, at uti Olof Skötkungs tid, då Christendomen kom in i Svearike, hafver Påfven skrifvit til bemälte Konung, och föregifvit at Runorna ok de gamle Runobökerna, hindrade Christendomen emedan de syntes fulla med trulldom: Kung Olof holt Riksdag, ok då, denne sak blef foredragen, stannade man uti det slut, at Runorna skulle bortläggas; alla Runoböker upbrännas; hvilket skedde. Då en stor hop gamla handlingar blevo upbrände, dem undantagne, som någre hedningar med sig utförde på Island.[1]

In essence this absurd story derives from some of Rudbeck's more extreme theories and was spread about to explain why there had survived no Swedish texts from heathen times. Göransson's edition thus had nationalistic and political significance. It was part of a program of rehabilitation of Sweden's past.

Rasmus Rask dismissed Resen and Göransson very summarily in his edition, referring first to Schlötzer's comment that Resen's Edda 'was a fine example of how one should not edit a text', and then continuing (1818: 13):

> Svo aum sem þessi útgáfa er, svo er þó *Jóhans Göranssonar* Edduútgáfa (Uppsölum 1745 í 4:rablf.) hálfu verri; Hèr er fyrst hrínglandi vitlaus formáli á svensku, sem t.d. sannar »að Edda sè samansett og skrifuð þegar Móyses gamli var á dögum« (bls. 32.). Af textanum finnst hèr einúngis Gylfaginníng, tekin úr *U*. Enn af því útgefarinn gat ecki lesið böndin í skinnbókinni, er varla sú lína, sem ekki sè einhvör málleysa á, t.d. á fyrstu línu: Bok þessi heiter Edda *henna* hever *sam*setta o.s.frv. Hvorki get eg heldr hrósað hans lát[ínsku] nè svensku útleggíngu, af því hann hefir svo optliga misskilið textann.

It appears that Göransson had planned to make a diplomatic edition of DG 11 4to (cf. Grape 1962: 42), but nothing came of it, and as Rask said, his edition only included *Gylfaginning*.

---

[1] Magnus Alkarp (2009: 60–67) traces this story and points out that one of the earliest versions of the book-burning episode must be the one that is linked to Pope Sylvester II and Óláfr Tryggvason (it is not mentioned in *Heimskringla*), and the Swedish historian Erik Johannes Schroderus (1609–37) names four Scandinavian poets whose books are supposed to have been destroyed. These books were those of 'Iorunderi, Gissuri et Schulemontani . . . Atheri magni'. These have been identified as Jórunn skáldmær, one of the few poetesses that are named in *Skáldskaparmál*, Gizurr svarti, a poet of King Óláfr the Swede according to *Skáldatal* in Kringla (*Edda Snorra Sturlusonar* 1848–87: II 252), or Gizurr gullbrárskáld, who was with Óláfr Tryggvason according to *Skáldatal* in DG 11 4to (f. 23v), Einarr Skúlason, who was of course quite a lot later, and Óttarr svarti, who was a poet of King Óláfr the Swede according to both versions of *Skáldatal* and of King Óláfr the Saint in the Kringla version. There are, however, problems with these identifications, and more research is needed.

In places Göransson could not read the manuscript, and occasionally he adopted readings from Resen in preference to it, though this seems to have been chiefly when he felt that something had dropped out in DG 11 4to, such as the myths of Winter and Summer.

Rather interesting are the examples shown here, where the texts of Resen, DG 11 4to and Göransson are set side by side:

Resen VI. Dæmeſaga	P. 20 below	Göransson 1746: 20
Wrmes Ymes Høffde	Or ymiſ holldi	Or Ymis holldi
Er Jørð skopud/	Var iorþ vm ſkopvð.	Var jorþ um skopud.
Enn vr Sveita Siôr/	En or ſveite ſior.	En or sveita sior
Biørg vr Beinum	b. or. b.	Biorg or beinum.
Bedur vr Haare	b or. h.	Badmr or hari
Enn vr Hauſe Himen.	En or h.h.	En or hause himin
Resen XIII. Dæmeſ.	P. 24 below	Göransson 1746: 26–27.
Thå geingu Reigen øl la Rogstôla/	Þa gengv v. A. ſ.	Þa gingu V. A. S.
Ginnheilog God/	g. h. g.	G. H. G.
og vm thad gettus/	ok vm þat g.'	Ok um þat g.
huer ſkillde Duerga	h.' ſkylldi dverga	h. skylldi Dverga
drott off skepia.	drott vm spekia	Drott um ſpekia

Here Göransson fills out the incomprehensible abbreviations of DG 11 4to in lines 4 and 5 of the first verse, replacing *beðr* by *baðmr* in line 5, probably from Resen's footnote k, but leaves the abbreviations V. A. S. G. H. G., perhaps because the text of this verse is hidden in a long footnote in Resen's edition. Resen's footnotes contain readings from Codex Wormianus, the Codex Regius of *Snorra Edda*, and from the Poetic Edda. Sometimes he uses sigla, but in the two above cases there are none, and the readings do not agree with any one of these manuscripts.

Rask held a rather negative view of the Uppsala version, considering DG 11 4to the latest and worst of all the redactions. His edition indeed pointed the way to an eclectic text where the editor would adopt readings from any of the manuscripts as he thought fit, though chiefly following the Codex Regius, and when the Uppsala version was very different from the others, generally no account was taken of it.

The next edition of DG 11 4to, and the first that can be regarded as in any way complete, appeared in *Edda Snorra Sturlusonar* 1848–87: II–III. In the second volume (pp. 250–296) was printed the main body of the text, Prologue, *Gylfaginning*, *Skáldskaparmál*, the second grammatical treatise and *Háttatal*, and in the third volume (pp. 259–269) *Skáldatal* was added. Details were also given of all the poets listed in *Skáldatal*, both in the version in DG 11 4to and the one in Kringla. The original spelling was preserved, but no indication was given of abbreviations. There remained excluded for the time being the genealogy of the Sturlungs and the list of lawspeakers, but Jón Sigurðsson printed the first in *Íslenzkt fornbréfasafn* 1857–1972, I and the second in Safn til sögu Íslands II 1 (1886).

The texts in these editions were always conscientiously prepared; there are no translations, but the commentary on *Skáldatal* has not been done better elsewhere.

In Göransson's edition the eighteenth century had acquired an edition of the Uppsala Edda, though it was severely flawed. In the Arnamagnæan edition the nineteenth century got a much better one, and in Grape (et al.) 1962 and 1977 the study of the manuscript was carried out in a proper scholarly manner with detailed commentary. Olof Thorell's list of word forms is excellent, though it lacks notes. The twentieth century had got its Uppsala Edda.

With still greater technical accuracy than ever before, a further step forward will be taken with Lasse Mårtenson's forthcoming MENOTA edition. The Icelandic reader's edition currently in preparation with interpretations of the verses will make the text more accessible to Icelandic readers, and it is hoped that in the mean while the present edition with English translation and introduction and notes in English will be of benefit to Anglophone students and scholars unaccustomed to diplomatic editions.

11 This edition

The spelling of DG 11 4to has been normalised in the conventional way, in the main as in *Norrøn ordbok*. The intention has been to give an impression of the stage of linguistic development in the time of Snorri Sturluson rather than of that of the scribe of the manuscript. Thus the distinction has been kept between ǫ and ø and between æ and œ (the latter here printed ǿ).

Scribes in the Middle Ages did not have a fixed standard of spelling to adhere to: they would generally follow the rules they were taught in the scriptorium where they were trained. These rules would vary from place to place and at different times. Scribes would also sometimes be influenced by the spelling of the manuscript they were copying. Consequently, two different scribes could often use very similar spellings, and the same scribe could on different occasions use different spellings of the same word. Generally we can see what word is meant by the various spellings, though there are often doubtful cases, and these are discussed in the notes on the text. Here an example can be given from *Skáldskaparmál*. In verse 84, there is a word written *vnaþ* in the manuscript. The scribe does not often indicate length of vowels, so *v* can be used for the vowels *u* and *ú* as well as for the consonant, and *a* for *a* and *á*; and he frequently writes þ where the modern rule requires ð. The reader therefore has a choice whether to take the word as *unað* 'delight' or *únáð (ónáð)* 'trouble'—and indeed it makes a difference.

It may also be mentioned that some consonants have more than one function. For instance, the scribe uses *z* in the following ways:

α) As the equivalent of *st*, especially finally in the middle voice or reflexive forms of verbs (e.g. *fannz = fannst*).

β) As the equivalent of the genitive *-s* after a dental consonant (e.g. *landz, mannz*) and of *s* before a dental consonant (*harþſveipaþaztan*).

γ) As the equivalent of the sound of *ts* or *ðs* (e.g. *bezt* from *betst*, *lézt* from *létst*, *hundraz* for *hundraðs*). *Múzpell* (elsewhere written *Múspell*), probably derived from Old Saxon *mutspelli* 'end of the world', is probably the same phenomenon.

δ) As the equivalent of tst (e.g. *hellz* for *heltst*).

ε) Exceptionally, to represent the sound usually written ð (in ꜰagr ſkjolldvzvſtvm = *fagrskjǫlduðustum*, biartveɢivzvſtv = *bjartveggjuðustu*); this only occurs in these two words, and maybe the rare superlative past participles confused the scribe, though *z* is not used in the other two examples of such forms in *Háttatal* st. 34.

In such cases, the editor frequently has to use his judgment. Little is known, for instance, about how the middle voice endings were pronounced at the beginning and end of the thirteenth century. When texts are normalised with Old Icelandic spelling, for instance in *Íslenzk fornrit,* it is often printed *-sk* in texts believed to be early, but *Norrøn ordbok* has opted for *-st,* and this practice has been followed here.

Many variations in spelling can be regarded as spellings to be normalised rather than errors requiring emendation. For instance scribes do not always distinguish d, ð and þ, or o, ǫ and ø, or œ, æ and e or é, and some do not distinguish v, y and ý, or e, é and ei; p and f can interchange, probably mainly as a result of misinterpreting insular f (ꝼ) as p. *Meyja* can be spelt *meygja*. Long or double consonants are often written for short or single ones and vice versa. A series of minims in Gothic script can be misread, thus confusing *in* and *ni*, *im* and *un* etc. There are examples of all these variations in this text.

Normalising spelling does not necessarily involve normalising word forms. Here alternative forms such as *hvernig, hvernveg, hvern veg, hvernenn* are retained.

A scribe's spelling can give some indication of the stage of linguistic development at the time he was working. The scribe of DG 11 4to was acquainted with the epenthetic vowel *u* in words like *hestur* for earlier *hestr*. But this does not mean that he would write *hestur*. His rule was clearly not to indicate the epenthetic vowel, and this has led him sometimes to be 'hypercorrect', so that he often wrote *systr, móðr, bróðr, fǫðr* instead of *systur, móður, bróður, fǫður* in inflections where the *u* is not epenthetic but represents the original vowel of the ending. He even finds himself writing *stjǫrnr* for the plural instead of *stjǫrnur*. On these so-called inverted spellings see the word list (Ordförrådet) in Grape et al. 1977. There every occurrence of every word form is conscientiously listed. Here the spelling is corrected to the grammatically correct forms.

In nearly all editions of *Snorra Edda*, readings are adopted from various manuscripts. This is not usually done here except in the notes. The text is emended as little as possible, and when it is, it is always noted. This has a great effect on the explanations of the verses, but here I have assumed that the scribe generally considered that he understood what he wrote. The intention is not to reconstruct the original text of Snorri Sturluson, much less that of the poets that he quoted, but rather to examine exhaustively the text that the anonymous scribe set down on parchment around the year 1300. All the interpretations of the verses are compiled with this aim in mind, and so are very often quite different from what one finds in other editions. To facilitate comparisons all the verse quotations in *Skáldskaparmál* are numbered twice, with the number in brackets corresponding to that in the editions of Finnur Jónsson (1931) and Anthony Faulkes (1998). They are both based primarily on GkS 2367 4to (the Codex Regius) and so correspond to each other. In *Gylfaginning* the quotations from Eddic poems are referred to the stanza numbers in Hans Kuhn's 1962 edition (who follows the numbering in Bugge 1867).

In compiling the interpretations I have naturally relied heavily on earlier editions as far as possible, but I alone am responsible for any deviations. *Lexicon Poeticum* has of course been the greatest help, but I have also benefitted from the explanations in Anthony Faulkes's careful edition of the *Edda*, and have often sought ideas in Hermann Pálsson 1954.

The text is based on Grape (et al.) 1962 and 1977, but the chapter divisions are as in *Edda Snorra Sturlusonar* 1848–87: II. The folio numbers and pagination of the manuscript are shown in the margins. Pointed brackets are used round letters that seem to have been accidentally omitted by the scribe, square brackets round letters that are no longer legible or were apparently deliberately omitted. In textual notes, words in inverted commas are printed with the spelling of the manuscript, those in italics are in normalised spelling. Round brackets are used to expand abbreviations (where necessary).

Index of Manuscripts

AM 132 fol. (Möðruvallabók; Stofnun Árna Magnússonar, Reykjavík): xcv

AM 242 fol. (Codex Wormianus, W; Det Arnamagnæanske Institut, Copenhagen); printed in Finnur Jónsson 1924; facsimile in *Codex Wormianus*, ed. Sigurður Nordal 1931 (CCIMA II): xxxii, xxxiii, xlii, lxiv, lxx, lxxiii, lxxxviii, cxvii, cxviii

AM 713 4to (Stofnun Árna Magnússonar, Reykjavík): lxxxiii

AM 748 I b 4to (A; Stofnun Árna Magnússonar, Reykjavík); printed in *Edda Snorra Sturlusonar* 1848–87: II 397–494; facsimile in *Fragments of the Elder and the Younger Edda*, ed. E. Wessén 1945 (CCIMA XVII): xvi, xxx, xxxiii, xlii, lxx, lxxii, lxxiii, xcii, c, cxvii, cxviii

AM 748 II 4to (C; Stofnun Árna Magnússonar, Reykjavík); printed in *Edda Snorra Sturlusonar* 1848–87: II 573–627 (there referred to as AM 1 e β fol.); facsimile in *Fragments of the Elder and the Younger Edda,* ed. E Wessén 1945 (CCIMA XVII): xxxiii, xlii, lxxvii, lxxviii, lxxxvi, xcii

AM 756 4to (Stofnun Árna Magnússonar, Reykjavík); a part printed in *Edda Snorra Sturlusonar* 1848–87: II 495–500: xxxiii, xlii

AM 757 a 4to (B; Stofnun Árna Magnússonar, Reykjavík); printed in *Edda Snorra Sturlusonar* 1848–87: II 501–72: xvi, xxxiii, xlii, lxx, lxxii, lxxiii, lxxxvi, c, cxvii

AM 157 8vo (Stofnun Árna Magnússonar, Reykjavík): xxx, xxxiv, xxxvi, xxxvii, xxxviii, xxxix, xl, xli, lxx, xciv, xcv

DG 11 4to (Codex Upsaliensis, U; University Library, Uppsala); printed in *Edda Snorra Sturlusonar* 1848–87: II 250–396; Grape et al. 1977; facsimile in Grape 1962: xvi, xxx, xxxi, xxxii, xxxiii, xxxiv, xxxvi, xxxvii, xxxviii, xl, xli, xlii, xliv, lxx, lxxiii, lxxiv, lxxxviii, xcii, xcv, c, cxvi, cxviii

GkS 2365 4to (Codex Regius of the eddic poems; Stofnun Árna Magnússonar, Reykjavík); printed in Kuhn 1962; facsimile in *Codex Regius of the Elder Edda*, ed. A. Heusler 1937 (CCIMA I): xxxii, xlv, xlvi, xlviii, lvi

GkS 2367 4to (Codex Regius of the Prose Edda, R; Stofnun Árna Magnússonar, Reykjavík); printed in Finnur Jónsson 1931; Anthony Faulkes 1998, 2005 and 2007; facsimile in *Codex Regius of the Younger Edda*, ed. E. Wessén 1940 (CCIMA XIV): xv, xvi, xxx, xxxii, xxxiii, xlii, xliv, xlv, xlvi, xlvii, lxviii, lxx, lxxxviii, xcii, cxvii, cxviii

Perg. 8vo nr 4 (Royal Library, Stockholm): lxxxiii

Marshall 114 (Bodleian Library, Oxford): xxx note 1, xxxiv

MS No. 1374 (Codex Trajectinus, T; University Library, Utrecht); printed in W. van Eeden (ed.), *De Codex Trajectinus van de Snorra Edda*, Leiden 1913; Árni Björnsson (ed.), *Snorra Edda*, Reykjavík 1975; facsimile in *Codex Trajectinus*, ed. Anthony Faulkes, Copenhagen 1985 (Early Icelandic Manuscripts in Facsimile XV): xxxii note 4, xxxiii, xxxiv, xlii, lxxxviii, cxvii, cxviii

R 684 (S; Uppsala University Library): xl

Bibliographical References

Ágrip af Nóregskonunga sǫgum. Fagrskinna—Nóregs konunga tal. 1984. Ed. Bjarni Einarsson. Reykjavík. Íslenzk fornrit XXIX.

Alkarp, Magnus. 2009. *Det Gamla Uppsala. Berättelser & metamorfoser kring en alldeles särskild plats*. Uppsala: Institutionen för arkeologi och antik historia. Occasional papers in archaeology 49.

Árni Björnsson (ed.). 1975. *Snorra Edda*. Reykjavík: Iðunn.

Ásdís Egilsdóttir (ed.). 1989. *Þorláks saga helga. Elsta gerð Þorláks sögu helga ásamt jarteinabók og efni úr yngri gerðum sögunnar*. Reykjavík: Þorlákssjóður.

Ásgeir Blöndal Magnússon. 1989. *Íslensk orðsifjabók*. Reykjavík: Orðabók Háskólans.

Baetke, Walter. 1973. 'Die Götterlehre der Snorra-Edda'. *Kleine Schriften. Geschichte, Recht und Religion in germanischem Schrifttum*, 206–46. Weimar: Hermann Böhlaus Nachfolger.

Beck, Heinrich. 2004. 'Zur Diskussion über den Prolog der Snorra-Edda'. In Karin Hoff et. al. (eds). *Poetik und Gedächtnis. Festschrift für Heiko Uecker zum 65. Geburtstag*, 145–54. Frankfurt am Main: Peter Lang.

Beck, Heinrich. 2008. 'Die Uppsala-Edda und Snorri Sturlusons Konstruktion einer skandinavischen Vorzeit'. *Scripta Islandica* 58: 5–32.

Beck, Heinrich. 2009. '*Gylfaginning*: Anmerkungen zu Versionen und Interpretationen'. *Analecta Septentrionalia*. Berlin: Walter de Gruyter.

Bergljót Soffía Kristjánsdóttir. 1996. '"Gunnlöð ekki gaf mér neitt af geymsludrykknum forðum . . ." Um Steinunni Finnsdóttur, Hyndlurímur og Snækóngsrímur'. In Sverrir Tómasson (ed.). *Guðamjöður og arnarleir. Safn ritgerða um eddulist*, 165–219. Reykjavík: Háskólaútgáfan.

Bergsveinn Birgisson. 2008. *Inn i skaldens sinn. Kognitive, estetiske og historiske skatter i den norrøne skaldediktningen*. Bergen: Universitetet i Bergen.

Bergsveinn Birgisson. 2009. 'Konuskegg og loðnir bollar'. *Skírnir* 183: 106–57.

Björn K. Þórólfsson. 1925. *Um íslenskar orðmyndir á 14. og 15. öld og breytingar þeirra úr fornmálinu*. Reykjavík: Fjelagsprentsmiðjan.

Boer, R. C. 1924. 'Studier over Snorra Edda'. *Aarbøger for nordisk Oldkyndighed og Historie*, 145–272.

Bugge, Sophus (ed.). 1867. *Norræn fornkvæði. Sæmundar Edda hins fróða*. Christiania: Malling.

Byskupa sögur I–III. 1948. Ed. Guðni Jónsson. Reykjavík: Íslendingasagnaútgáfan.

Bäckvall, Maja. 2007. *Völuspá i Uppsala-Eddan. En nyfilologisk undersökning*. MA thesis in Swedish/Norwegian language at Uppsala University. http://urn.kb.se/resolve?urn=urn:nbn:se:uu:diva-8258.

CCIMA: Corpus codicum Islandicorum medii aevi I–XX. 1930–56. Copenhagen: Munksgaard.

Ciklamini, Marlene. 1978. *Snorri Sturluson*. Boston: Twayne Publishers.

Cleasby, Richard and Guðbrandur Vigfússon. 1957. *An Icelandic–English Dictionary*. 2nd. edition. With a Supplement by W. A. Craigie. Oxford: Clarendon Press.

Clunies Ross. Margaret. 1981. 'An interpretation of the myth of Þórr's encounter with Geirrøðr and his daughters'. Ursula Dronke et al. (ed.). *Speculum Norroenum. Norse Studies in Memory of Gabriel Turville-Petre*, 370–91. Odense: Odense University Press.

Craigie, William A. 1900. 'On some Points in Skaldic Metre'. *Arkiv för nordisk filologi*. Ny följd 12: 341–84.

Dronke, Ursula and Peter. 1977. 'The Prologue of the Prose *Edda*: Explorations of a Latin Background'. In Einar G. Pétursson and Jónas Kristjánsson (eds) *Sjötíu ritgerðir helgaðar Jakobi Benediktssyni 20. júlí 1977*, 153–76. Reykjavík: Stofnun Árna Magnússonar.

Edda Snorra Sturlusonar I–III. 1848–87. Ed. Jón Sigurðsson et al. Hafniæ: Sumptibus Legati Arnamagnæanæ.

Egils saga Skalla-Grímssonar. 1933. Ed. Sigurður Nordal. Reykjavík. Íslenzk fornrit II.

Einar G. Pétursson. 1998. *Eddurit Jóns Guðmundssonar lærða. Þættir úr fræðasögu 17. aldar.* Reykjavík: Stofnun Árna Magnússonar.

Einar Ólafur Sveinsson (ed.). 1942, 1974. *Fagrar heyrði eg raddirnar*. Reykjavík: Mál og Menning.

Eskeland, Ivar. 1992. *Snorri Sturluson: Ein biografi*. Oslo: Grøndahl og Dreyer.

Faulkes, Anthony (ed.). 1977. 'Edda'. *Gripla* II: 32–39.

Faulkes, Anthony (ed.). 1977–79. *Two Versions of Snorra Edda from the 17th Century*. I. *Edda Magnúsar Ólafssonar (Laufás Edda)*. II. *Edda Islandorum. Vǫluspá. Hávamál. P. H. Resen's Edition of 1665*. Reykjavík: Stofnun Árna Magnússonar.

Faulkes, Anthony. 1978–79. 'Descent from the gods'. *Mediaeval Scandinavia* 11: 92–125.

Faulkes, Anthony. 1979. 'The Prologue to Snorra Edda. An Attempt at Reconstruction'. *Gripla* III: 204–13.

Faulkes, Anthony. 1993. 'The Sources of Skáldskaparmál: Snorri's Intellectual Background'. In Alois Wolf (ed.). *Snorri Sturluson. Kolloquium anläßlich der 750. Widerkehr seines Todestages.* Tübingen: Gunter Narr.

Faulkes, Anthony (ed.). 1998. Snorri Sturluson. *Edda: Skáldskaparmál*. London: Viking Society for Northern Research.

Faulkes, Anthony (ed.). 2005. Snorri Sturluson. *Edda: Prologue and Gylfaginning*. London: Viking Society for Northern Research.

Faulkes, Anthony (ed.). 2007. Snorri Sturluson. *Edda*: *Háttatal*. London: Viking Society for Northern Research.
Finnur Jónsson (ed.). 1884–91. *Småstykker* 1–16. København: Samfund til udgivelse af gammel nordisk litteratur.
Finnur Jónsson. 1920–24. *Den oldnorske og oldislandske Litteraturs Historie* I–III. København: G. E. C. Gad.
Finnur Jónsson (ed.). 1931. *Edda Snorra Sturlusonar*. København: Gyldendal.
Fritzner, Johan. 1886–96. *Ordbog over det gamle norske Sprog* I–III. Kristiania: Den Norske Forlagsforening.
Gísli Sigurðsson (ed.). 1998. *Eddukvæði*. Reykjavík: Mál og menning.
Grape, Anders (ed). 1962. *Snorre Sturlasons Edda. Uppsala-handskriften DG 11*. Stockholm: Almqvist och Wiksell.
Grape et al. (eds). 1977. *Snorre Sturlassons Edda. Uppsala-handskriften DG 11*. Transkriberad text och Paleografisk kommentar av Anders Grape, Gottfried Kallstenius och Olof Thorell. Inledning och Ordförråd av Olof Thorell. Uppsala: Almquist och Wiksell.
Guðvarður Már Gunnlaugsson. 2009. 'Hvernig leit Uppsalabók út í öndverðu?' In Agneta Ney et al (eds). *Á austrvega. Saga and East Scandinavia*. Preprint papers of the 14th International Saga Conference, 343–45. Gävle: Gävle University Press.
Guðvarður Már Gunnlaugsson. 2010. 'Helga Sturludóttir og Sölmundur austmann'. In Gísli Sigurðsson et al. (eds). *Guðrúnarstikki kveðinn Guðrúnu Nordal fimmtugri 27 september 2010*, 34–37. Reykjavík: Menningar- og minningarsjóður Mette Magnussen
Göransson, Johan. [1746]. *De Yfverborna Atlingars, eller, Sviogötars ok Nordmänners, Edda*. Upsala.
Hákonar saga Hákonarsonar. 1977. Ed. Marina Mundt. Oslo: Norsk historisk kjeldeskrift-institutt. Norrøne tekster 2.
Halldór Halldórsson. 1975. *Old Icelandic* heiti *in modern Icelandic*. Reykjavík: Institute of Nordic Linguistics.
Hamre, Lars. 1961. 'Hertig. Noreg'. *Kulturhistorisk lexikon för nordisk medeltid* VI: 516–17.
Heimir Pálsson. 1994. 'Þekkti Snorri Hávamál?' In Gísli Sigurðsson, Guðrún Kvaran and Sigurgeir Steingrímsson (eds). *Sagnaþing helgað Jónasi Kristjánssyni sjötugum 10. apríl 1994*, 365–75. Reykjavík: Hið íslenska bókmenntafélag.
Heimir Pálsson. 1999. 'Að sætta heimildir. Lítið eitt um starfsaðferðir Snorra Sturlusonar'. In Haraldur Bessason and Baldur Hafstað (eds). *Heiðin minni. Greinar um fornar bókmenntir*, 159–79. Reykjavík: Heimskringla.
Heimir Pálsson (ed.). 2003. *Snorra-Edda*. Reykjavík: Mál og menning.

Heimir Pálsson. 2004. 'Dalfiskar með salti – ellert ormar med en nypa salt.' In Unn Hellsten et al. *Språkets vård och värden, en festskrift till Cahharina Grünbaum* 302–09. Stockholm: Norstedt Ordbok.

Heimir Pálsson. 2010a. 'Tertium vero datur'. http://uu.diva-portal.org/smash/record.jsf?pid=diva2:322558.

Heimir Pálsson. 2010b. 'Alltaf sama sagan?' *Tímarit Máls og menningar* 71/4: 65–78.

Heimir Pálsson. 2010c. 'Fyrstu leirskáldin'. *Són* 8: 25–37.

Heimir Pálsson. 2010d. 'Vísur og dísir Víga-Glúms'. *Gripla* 21: 169–95.

Hermann Pálsson. 1954. 'Vísnaskýringar við Snorra-Eddu'. In Guðni Jónsson. *Eddulyklar*. Akureyri: Íslendingasagnaútgáfan.

Hkr: Snorri Sturluson 1941–51. *Heimskringla* I–III. Ed. Bjarni Aðalbjarnarson. Reykjavík: Hið íslenzka fornritafélag. Íslenzk fornrit XXVI–XXVIII.

Holtsmark, Anne. 1949. 'Myten om *Idun og Tjatse* i Tjodolvs *Haustlǫng*'. *Arkiv för Nordisk Filologi* 64: 1–73.

Holtsmark, Anne. 1960. 'Grammatisk litteratur på modersmålet'. *Kulturhistoriskt lexikon för nordisk medeltid* V: 414–19.

Holtsmark, Anne. 1964. *Studier i Snorres mytologi*. Oslo: Universitetsforlaget.

Holtsmark, Anne and Jón Helgason (eds). 1950. Snorri Sturluson. *Edda: Gylfaginning og prosafortellingene av Skaldskaparmál*. København: Munksgaard. Nordisk Filologi A. Tekster. I.

Hreinn Benediktsson. 1963. 'Phonemic Neutralization and Inaccurate Rhymes'. *Acta philologica Scandinavica* XXXVI: i–ii, 1–18.

Ihre, Johan. 1772. *Bref till herr Cancelli-rådet Sven Lagerbring, rörande then Isländska Edda, och egentligen then handskrift theraf, som på Kongl. Bibliotheket i Uppsala förvaras*. Upsala: Joh. Edman.

Íslendingabók. Landnámabók. 1968. Ed. Jakob Benediktsson. Reykjavík. Íslenzk fornrit I.

Íslenzkar æviskrár I–V. 1948–52. Ed. Páll Eggert Ólason. Reykjavík: Hið íslenzka bókmenntafélag

Íslenzkt fornbréfasafn I–XVI. 1857–1972. Kaupmannahöfn: Hið íslenzka bókmenntafélag.

Jón Helgason. 1953. 'Norges og Islands digtning'. In *Nordisk kultur* VIII B. *Litteraturhistorie. Norge og Island*, 3–179. København.

Jón Helgason (ed.). 1962. *Eddadigte* I. *Vǫluspá. Hávamál*. København: Munksgaard. Nordisk filologi 4.

Jón Samsonarson. Icelandic manuscripts in Sweden.

Jón Sigurðsson. 1886. *Lögsögumannatal og lögmanna á Íslandi*. Kaupmannahöfn. Safn til sögu Íslands II.1.

Jón Þorkelsson (ed.). 1922–27. *Kvæðasafn eftir nafngreinda menn frá miðöld*. Reykjavík: Hið íslenzka bókmenntafélag.

Jónas Kristjánsson. 1992. 'Heiðin trú í fornkvæðum'. In Úlfar Bragason (ed.) *Snorrastefna* 25.–27. júlí 1990, 99–112. Reykjavík: Stofnun Sigurðar Nordals.

Kock, Ernst A. 1946–49. *Notationes Norrœnæ*. Lund: Gleerup.

Konráð Gíslason. 1869. 'De ældste Runeindskrifters sproglige Stilling'. *Aarbøger for nordisk Oldkyndighed og Historie*, 35–148.

Krömmelbein, Thomas. 1992. 'Creative Compilers. Observations on the Manuscript Tradition of Snorri's *Edda*'. In Úlfar Bragason (ed.). *Snorrastefna* 25.–27. júlí 1990, 113–29. Reykjavík: Stofnun Sigurðar Nordals.

Kuhn, Hans (ed.). 1962. *Edda* I. Heidelberg: Carl Winter.

Larsson, Mats G. 2005. *Minnet av vikingatiden. De isländska kungasagorna och deras värld*. Stockholm: Atlantis.

Lexicon Poeticum: Sveinbjörn Egilsson. 1931. *Lexicon Poeticum Antiquæ Linguæ Septentrionalis*. Rev. Finnur Jónsson. København.

Lind, E. H. 1905–31. *Norsk-isländska dopnamn och fingerade namn från medeltiden*. Uppsala: Lundequistska bokhandeln.

Lýður Björnsson. 1978. 'Eigi skal höggva'. *Skírnir* 152: 162–65.

Lönnroth, Lars. 1978. *Den dubbla scenen. Muntlig diktning från Eddan till ABBA*. Stockholm: Prisma.

Magnús Finnbogason (ed.). [1952]. *Edda Snorra Sturlusonar*. Reykjavík: Bókaverslun Sigurðar Kristjánssonar.

Maurer, Konrad. 1888. 'Vokn und Vopn'. *Arkiv för nordisk Filologi*, 284–88.

Meissner, Rudolf. 1921. *Die Kenningar der Skalden*. Bonn und Leipzig: Kurt Schroeder. Rheinische Beiträge I.

Meulengracht-Sørensen, Preben. 2002. 'Þórr's Fishing Expedition'. In Paul Acker and Carolyne Larrington (eds). *The Poetic Edda: Essays on Old Norse Mythology*, 119–37. London: Routledge.

Mogk, Eugene A. 1879. 'Untersuchungen über die Gylfaginning'. *Beiträge zur Geschichte der deutschen Sprache und Literatur*, 477–537.

Mogk, Eugene A. 1880. 'Untersuchungen über die Gylfaginning. Zweiter teil'. *Beiträge zur Geschichte der deutschen Sprache und Literatur*, 203–334.

Mogk, Eugene A. 1925. 'Zur bewertung des Cod. Upsaliensis der Snorra-Edda'. *Beiträge zur Geschichte der deutschen Sprache und Literatur*, 402–14.

Müller, Friedrich W. 1941. *Untersuchungen zur Uppsala-Edda*. Dresden: Dittert.

Mårtensson, Lasse. 2010. 'Översikten över Háttatal i DG 11 4to – dess funktion och ursprung'. *Gripla* 21: 105–45.

Mårtensson, Lasse and Heimir Pálsson. 2008. 'Anmärkningsvärda suspensioner i DG 11 4to (Codex Upsaliensis av Snorra Edda) – spåren av en skriven förlaga'. *Scripta Islandica* 59: 135–55.

Nationalencyklopedin. 1989–96: Stockholm: Bra böcker.

Naumann, H.-P. 1999. 'Grotta söngr'. *Reallexikon der Germanischen Altertumskunde* 13: 98–100.

Nordal, Guðrún. 2001. *Tools of literacy. The role of skaldic verse in Icelandic textual culture of the twelfth and thirteenth centuries*. Toronto: University of Toronto Press.
Nordal, Sigurður (ed.). 1933. *Egils saga Skalla-Grímssonar*. Reykjavík. Íslenzk fornrit II.
Nordal, Sigurður. 1953. 'Sagalitteraturen'. In *Nordisk kultur* VIII B. *Litteraturhistorie. Norge og Island*, 180–273. København.
Nordal, Sigurður. 1973. *Snorri Sturluson*. Reykjavík: Helgafell.
Noreen, Adolf. 1923. *Altisländische und Altnorwegische Grammatik*. Halle: Max Niemeyer.
Norrøn ordbok. 2004. Compiled by Leiv Heggstad, Finn Hødnebo and Erik Simensen. [4th edition of *Gamalnorsk ordbok*] Ed. Leiv Heggstad and Alf Torp. Oslo: Det norske samlaget.
Ólafur Briem (ed.). 1968. *Eddukvæði*. Reykjavík: Skálholt.
Ólafur Halldórsson. 1990. 'Snjófríðar drápa'. In *Grettisfærsla* 217–32. Reykjavík: Stofnun Árna Magnússonar á Íslandi.
Ólsen, Björn Magnússon (ed.). 1884. *Den tredje og fjærde grammatiske afhandling i Snorres Edda tillige med de grammatiske afhandlingers prolog*. København: Samfundet til udgivelse af gammel nordisk litteratur.
Ong, Walter. 1982. *Orality and literacy: the technologizing of the word*. London: Methuen.
ONP: Ordbog over det norrøne prosasprog. http://dataonp.hum.ku.dk/index.html.
Óskar Guðmundsson. 2009. *Snorri. Ævisaga Snorra Sturlusonar 1179–1241*. Reykjavík: JPV útgáfa.
Paasche, Fredrik. 1922. *Snorre Sturlason og Sturlungene*. Kristiania: H. Aschehaug.
Raschellà, Fabrizio D. (ed.). 1982. *The So-called Second Grammatical Treatise. An Orthographic Pattern of Late Thirteenth-Century Icelandic*. Firenze: F Le Monnier. Filologia Germanica. Testi e Studi 2.
Rask, Rasmus Kristian (ed.). 1818. *Snorra-Edda ásamt Skáldu og þarmeð fylgjandi ritgjörðum*. Stockhólm.
Skáldatal, sive recensus poëtarum Septentrionalium. Ed. Jón Sigurðsson. In *Edda Snorra Sturlusonar* 1848–87: III 205–498.
Skaldic Poetry of the Scandinavian Middle Ages. II: *Poetry from the Kings' Sagas 2. From c. 1035 to c. 1300*. 2009. Ed K. E. Gade; VII: *Poetry on Christian subjects*. 2007. Ed. Margaret Clunies Ross. Turnhout: Brepols.
Skj: Finnur Jónsson (ed.). 1912–15. *Den norsk-islandske Skjaldedegtning* A I–II, B I–II. København: Gyldendal.
Stefán Karlsson. 1989. 'Eigi skal höggva'. In *Véfréttir sagðar Vésteini Ólasyni fimmtugum*, 81–82. Reykjavík.

Stefán Karlsson. 2000. 'Om norvagismer i islandske håndskrifter'. In Guðvarður Már Gunnlaugsson (ed.). *Stafkrókar*. Reykjavík: Stofnun Árna Magnússonar.

Stefán Karlsson. 2004. *The Icelandic Language*. London: Viking Society for Northern Research.

Sturlunga saga I–II. 1946. Ed. Jón Jóhannesson, Magnús Finnbogason and Kristján Eldjárn. Reykjavík: Sturlunguútgáfan.

Sverrir Tómasson. 1992. 'Snorra Edda'. In Vésteinn Ólason (ed.). *Íslensk bókmenntasaga* I: 534–42.

Sverrir Tómasson. 1993. 'Formáli málfræðiritgerðanna'. *Íslenskt mál* 15: 221–40. Reprinted in *Tækileg vitni* 2011: 199–217. Reykjavík: Stofnun Árna Magnússonar.

Sverrir Tómasson. 1996a. 'Nýsköpun eða endurtekning? Íslensk skáldmennt og Snorra Edda fram til 1609'. In Sverrir Tómasson (ed.). *Guðamjöður og arnarleir. Safn ritgerða um eddulist*. Reykjavík: Háskólaútgáfan: 1–64.

Sverrir Tómasson. 1996b. '"Suptungs mjöðurinn sjaldan verður sætur fundinn". Laufás Edda og áhrif hennar'. In Sverrir Tómasson (ed.). *Guðamjöður og arnarleir. Safn ritgerða um eddulist*. Reykjavík: Háskólaútgáfan: 65–89.

Sävborg, Daniel. 2009. 'Redaktionen av *Skáldskaparmál* i Codex Upsaliensis'. In Agneta Ney et al. (eds). *Á austrvega. Saga and East Scandinavia*. Preprint papers of the 14th International Saga Conference, 837–44. Gävle: Gävle University Press.

Vésteinn Ólason (ed.). 1992. *Íslensk bókmenntasaga* I. Reykjavík: Mál og menning.

Vésteinn Ólason. 2001. 'List og tvísæi í Eddu'. *Gripla* XII: 41–65.

Vésteinn Ólason. 2008. 'Snorri Sturluson: tiden, mannen og verket'. In John Ole Askedal and Klaus Johan Myrvoll (eds). *Høvdingen: om Snorre Sturlasons liv og virke*, 21–40. Oslo: Vidarforlaget.

Viðar Pálsson. 2008. 'Pagan Mythology in Christian Society'. *Gripla* XIX: 123–58.

Wessén, Elias (ed.). 1940. *Codex Regius of the Younger Edda*. Copenhagen: Munksgaard. CCIMA XIV.

Wessén, Elias (ed.). 1945. *Fragments of the Elder and the Younger Edda*. Copenhagen: Munksgaard. CCIMA XVII.

Williams, Henrik. 2007. 'Projektet Originalversionen av Snorre Sturlassons Edda? Studier i Codex Upsaliensis. Ett forskningsprogram'. *Scripta Islandica* 58: 85–99.

Yelena Sesselja Helgadóttir (ed.). 2007. *Lausavísur frá svartadauða til siðaskipta*. Reykjavík: Háskólaútgáfan.

Zetterholm, D. O. 1949. *Studier i en Snorre-text. Tors färd til Utgård*: *Codices Upsaliensis DG 11 4to och Regius Hafn. 2367 4to*. Stockholm: Geber. Nordiska texter och undersökningar 17.

Snorra Edda
The Uppsala Manuscript
DG 11 4to

Chapter Headings:

1. Bók þessi heitir Edda. Hana hefir saman setta Snorri Sturluson eptir þeim hætti sem hér er skipat. Er fyrst frá ásum ok Ymi, þar næst skáldskapar mál ok heiti margra hluta. Síðast Háttatal er Snorri hefir ort um Hákon konung ok Skúla hertuga......6
2. Hversu greind er verǫldin í þrjá staði......8
3. Frá því er Óðinn kom á norðrlǫnd......8
4. Frá því er Óðinn kom í Svíþjóð ok gaf sonum sínum ríki......10
5. Hér hefr Gylfa ginning frá því er Gylfi sótti heim Alfǫðr í Ásgarð með fjǫlkyngi ok frá villu ása ok frá spurningu Gylfa......10
6. Frá spurningu Ganglera......12
7. Hér segir frá Múspellsheimi ok frá Surti......14
8. Hér segir er guðin skǫpuðu Ymi jǫtun......14
9. Frá því er skǫpuð var kýrin Auðumla......16
10. Frá því er synir Burs drápu Ymi......18
11. Burs synir skǫpuðu Ask ok Emlu......20
12. Frá Nóra jǫtni ok Nótt dóttur hans......20
13. Hér segir frá Bifrǫst......22
14. Hér segir frá helgistað guðanna......26
15. Frá aski Ygdrasils......30
16. Hér segir frá Álfheimum......32
17. Hér segir frá nǫfnum Óðins ok ríki......34
18. Hér segir frá Þór ok ríki hans ok Bilskirni......38
19. Frá bǫrnum Njarðar......42
20. Hversu biðja skal ásinn ok frá Braga ok Heimdall......42
21. Hér segir frá æsi Loka......46
22. Frá Fenrisúlfi ok ásum......48
23. Frá ásynjum......50
24. Freyr fekk Gerðar......54
25. Frá vist ok drykk með ásum......56
26. Frá því er er Loki gat Sleipni við Svaðilfera......60
27. Hér þegir Þriði......64
28. Hér hefr sǫgu Þórs ok Útgarða-Loka......64
29. Hér segir frá því er Þórr fór at draga Miðgarðsorminn......72
30. Frá lífláti Baldrs ok fǫr Hermóðs til Heljar......74
31. Frá fimbulvetri ok Ragnarøkkrum......78
32. Frá heimboði ása með Ægi......86
33. Hér segir frá því at æsir sátu at heimboði at Ægis ok hann spurði Braga hvaðan af kom skáldskaprinn. Frá því er Kvasir var skapaðr. Hér hefr mjǫk setning skáldskapar......88
34. Hér segir hversu skilja skal skáldskap......90
35. Saga Þórs ok Hrungnis......90
36. Frá Geirrøð jǫtni ok Þór......94

[Skáldatal]......100

[Ættartala Sturlunga] ... 118
[Lǫgsǫgumannatal] ... 120
37 Hér hefr skáldskapar mál ok heiti margra hluta ... 124
38 Frá því eptir hverjum heitum skáldin hafa kveðit ... 124
39 Hér segir hversu skáldin hafa kent skáldskapinn ... 132
40 Frá kenningu Þórs ... 138
41 Frá kenningu Baldrs ... 144
42 Frá kenningu Njarðar ... 144
43 Frá kenningu Freys ... 144
44 Frá kenningu Heimdalls ... 146
45 Frá kenningu Týs ok Braga ... 146
46 Frá kenningu Viðars ok Vála ... 146
47 Kendr Hǫðr ok Ullr ... 146
48 Frá kenningu Hǿnis ok Loka ... 148
49 Kend Frigg ok Freyia ... 148
50 Frá kenningu Iðunnar ... 148
51 Hversu kenna skal himininn ... 150
52 Kend jǫrðin ... 152
53 Frá kenningu sjóvarins ... 154
54 Frá kenningu sólar ... 158
55 Kendr vindrinn ... 158
56 Kendr eldr ... 160
57 Vetrinn ... 160
58 Kent sumar ... 160
59 Kendr maðrinn ... 160
60 Kent gullit ... 162
61 Kendr maðrinn ... 170
62 Kend konan til gulls ... 170
63 Kend orrostan ... 176
64 Kend vápnin ... 178
65 Frá kenningu skips ... 186
66 Hversu kenna skal Krist ... 190
67 Hér segir frá konungum ... 194
68 Hér segir hverir fremstir eru ... 196
69 Hér segir hversu kend er setning skáldskapar ... 202
70 Um nǫfn guðanna ... 204
71 Um nǫfn heimsins ... 206
72 Um nǫfn stundanna ... 206
73 Hér segir um nǫfn sólar ok tungls ... 206
74 [No title] ... 208
75 Capitulum ... 210
76 [Greppar] ... 214
77 Hér segir fornǫfn ... 214
78 Hǿverskra manna nǫfn ... 216
79 Hér segir frá viðrkenningum ... 216

80	Frá sannkenningu	218
81	Frá kvenna nǫfnum úkendum	218
82	Hversu kenna skal hǫfuðit	218
83	Kendr muðr	218
84	Hér segir enn frá nýgervingum	220
85	Hér segir hversu heitir hǫndin	220
86	Hversu kendir eru fǿtrnir	220
87	Kent málit	220
88	Kendr vargrinn	222
89	Kendr bjǫrn	224
90	Frá hirti ok hesta nǫfnum ágætum	224
91	Frá hestum	226
92	Frá orma heitum	228
93	[Hræfuglar (Carrion Birds)]	228
94	Frá kenningu arnarins	230
95	Kendr eldr	232
96	Hér segir frá bardaga Heðins ok Hǫgna	234
97	Hér segir um kenning gulls	234
98	Frá vélum dvergsins við Loka	236
99	Frá kenningu gulls	238
100	Loki drap Otr son Hreiðmars	238
101	Frá því er Hrólfr seri gullinu	240
102	Capitulum	242
103	Hér segir hví gull er kallat Fróða mjǫl	244
104	Hér segir hví gull er kallat haugþak Hǫlga	244
105	Hér segir af setningu háttalykilsins	250
106	[The circular diagram]	254
107	[The rectangular diagram]	256

[List of verses] 260
Háttatal, er Snorri Sturluson orti um Hákon konung ok Skúla hertuga 262
Dróttkvæðr háttr i 262
Kendr háttr ij 264
Rekit iij 266
Sannkent iiij 266
Tvíriðit v 268
Nýgjǫrvingar vj 268
Oddhent vij 270
Ǫnnur oddhending 272
Hér segir af sextán málum 274
Áttmæltr háttr 274
Hér segir um refhvǫrf 280
Annat refhvarf 282
Hér segir hversu skipta skal hættinum 286
Hættir fornskálda 304

Part I

Gylfaginning

1 **Bók þessi heitir Edda. Hana hefir saman setta Snorri Sturluson eptir þeim hætti sem hér er skipat.** Er fyrst frá ásum ok Ymi, þar næst skáldskapar mál ok heiti margra hluta. **Síðast Háttatal er Snorri hefir ort um Hákon konung ok Skúla hertuga.**

Almáttigr Guð skapaði himin ok jǫrð ok alla hluti er þeim fylgja, ok síðast menn, er ættirnar eru frá komnar, Adam ok Evu, ok dreifðust ættirnar um heiminn síðan.

En er frá liðu stundir újafnaðist fólkit. Sumir vóru góðir, sumir lifðu eptir girndum sínum. Fyrir þat var drekt heiminum nema þeim er meðr Nóa vóru í ǫrkinni. Eptir þat bygðist enn verǫldin af þeim. En allr fjǫlðinn afrǿktist þá Guð. En hverr mundi þá segja frá Guðs stórmerkjum er þeir týndu Guðs nafni? En þat var víðast um verǫldina er fólkit villtist. En þó veitti Guð mǫnnum jarðligar giptir, fé ok sælu ok speki at skilja jarðliga hluti ok greinir þær er sjá mátti lopts ok jarðar. Þat undruðust þeir er jǫrðin ok dýr hǫfðu saman náttúru í sumum hlutum, svá ólíkt sem þat var.

Þat er eitt er jǫrðin er grǿn í hám fjalltindum ok sprettr þar upp vatn ok þurfti þar eigi lengra at grafa en í djúpum dal. Svá er ok dýr eða fuglar, at jamlangt[1] er til blóðs í hǫfði sem í fótum.

Ǫnnur[2] náttúra er sú jarðarinnar at á hverju ári vex á henni gras ok blóm ok á sama ári fellr þat. Svá ok dýr eða fuglar at því vex hár eða fjaðrar ok fellr á hverju ári.

Þat er en þriðja náttúra jarðarinnar at hon er opnuð þá grǿr gras á þeiri moldu er efst er á jǫrðunni. Þeir þýddu bjǫrg ok steina móti tǫnnum ok beinum.

Svá skilðu þeir af þessu at jǫrðin væri kvik ok hefði líf með nokkurum hætti, er hon fǿddi ǫll kvikvendi ok eignaðist allt þat er dó. Þangat til hennar tǫlðu þeir ættir sínar.

Sá þeir þat at ójafn var gangr himintungla, sum gengu lengra en sum. Þat grunaði þá at nokkurr mundi þeim stýra, ok mundi sá vera ríkr ok ætluðu hann mundu verit hafa fyrri en himintunglin. Ætluðu hann ráða mundu skini sólar ok dǫgg jarðar ok vindum ok stormi. En eigi vissu þeir hverr hann var. En því trúðu þeir at hann ræðr ǫllum hlutum ok til þess at þeir mætti muna, þá gáfu þeir ǫllum hlutum nafn með sér, ok síðan hefir | átrúnaðr breyzt á marga vega, sem menn skiptust eða tungur greindust.

En allt skilðu þeir jarðliga því at eigi hǫfðu þeir andliga gipt ok trúðu at allt væri af nokkuru efni skapat eða smíðat.

---

[1] The element *jafn-* is written 'jam-' nine times and 'jafn-' fifteen times.
[2] The manuscript has 'ǫnnr'. Cf. Introduction p. cxxv.

1 This book is called Edda. Snorri Sturluson has compiled it in the manner in which it is arranged here. First it is about Æsir and Ymir, next Skáldskaparmál ('poetic diction') and (poetical) names of many things. Finally Háttatal ('enumeration of verse forms') which Snorri has composed about King Hákon and Duke Skúli.

Almighty God created heaven and earth and all things in them, and lastly humans from whom generations are descended, Adam and Eve, and these generations spread over the world afterwards.

But as time passed, the people became diverse. Some were good, some lived according to their lusts. Because of this the world was drowned except for those that were with Noah in the ark. After that the world was settled again by them. But the vast majority then neglected God. But who was there then to tell of God's great wonders when they had forgotten God's name? So it was in most parts of the world that the people went astray. And yet God granted them earthly blessings, wealth and prosperity and wisdom to understand worldly things and the details of everything that could be seen in the sky and on earth. They were amazed that the earth and animals had common characteristics in some things, being so different.

This is one, that the earth is green on high mountain peaks and water springs up there and there was no need to dig further there than in a deep valley. So it is too with animals and birds, that it is just as far to blood in the head as in the feet.

It is a second property of the earth that each year vegetation and flowers grow on it and it falls in the same year. So it is too with animals and birds, that hair or feathers grow on them and fall each year.

It is the third property of the earth that [when] it is opened, then grass grows on the soil that is uppermost on the earth. They interpreted rocks and stones as the equivalent of teeth and bones.

They understood from this that the earth was alive and had life after a certain fashion, since it fed (gave birth to?) all creatures and took possession of everything that died. To it they traced their ancestry.

They saw that the courses of the heavenly bodies were various, some travelled further than some. They suspected that someone must control them, and he must be powerful, and they thought he must have existed before the heavenly bodies. They thought he must rule the shining of the sun and the dew of the earth and the winds and storm. But they did not know who he was. But this they believed, that he rules all things, and so that they might remember, then they gave each thing a name among themselves, and religion has since changed in many ways as men dispersed and languages branched.

But they understood everything in an earthly way because they did not have spiritual grace and believed that everything was created or made from some material.

2 Hversu greind er verǫldin í þrjá staði

Verǫldin verðr greind í þrjár hálfur. Einn hlutr var frá suðri til vestrs ok um Miðjarðarsjá. Sá heitir Affríka. Enn syðri hlutr er heitr svá at þar brennr af sólu. Annarr hlutr frá vestri til norðrs ok inn til hafs heitir Evrópa eða Enea. En nerðri[1] hlutr er þar kaldr ok vex eigi gras ok eigi má byggja. Frá norðri um austrhálfuna til suðrs heitir Asía. Í þeim hluta veraldarinnar er ǫll fegrð ok eignir, gull ok gimsteinar. Þar er mið verǫldin, ok svá sem þar er betra en í ǫðrum stǫðum, svá er þar ok mannfólkit meirr tignat en í ǫðrum stǫðum at spekt ok afli, fegrð ok ǫllum kostum. Þar var sett Rómaborg er vér kǫllum Tróju. Í Tróju vóru tólf konungdómar ok einn yfir ǫllum ǫðrum, þar vóru tólf hǫfuðtungur.

Konungr hét Menon. Hann átti dóttur Príamus konungs Trójam. Sonr þeira hét Trór er vér kǫllum Þór. Þá var hann tólf vetra er hann hafði fullt afl sitt. Þá lypti hann af jǫrðu tíu bjarnstǫkum senn. Hann sigraði marga berserki senn ok dýr eða dreka. Í norðrhálfu heimsins fann hann spákonu eina er Sibil hét, en vér kǫllum Sif. Engi vissi ætt hennar. Sonr þeira hét Lórriði, hans sonr Vingiþórr, hans sonr Vingenir, hans sonr Móða, hans sonr Magi, hans sonr Sefsmeg, hans sonr Beðvig, hans sonr Atra, er vér kǫllum Annan, hans sonr Ítrman, hans sonr Eremóð, hans sonr Skjaldun, er vér kǫllum Skjǫld, hans sonr Bíaf, er vér kǫllum Bǫr, hans sonr Jat, hans sonr Guðólfr, hans sonr Finnr, hans sonr Frjálafr, er vér kǫllum Friðleif, hans sonr Vodden, er vér kǫllum Óðin.

3 Frá því er Óðinn kom á norðrlǫnd

Þessi Óðinn hafði mikinn spádóm. Kona hans hét Frigida, er vér kǫllum Frigg. Hann fýstist norðr í heim með mikinn her ok stórmiklu fé, ok hvar sem þeir fóru þótti mikils um þá vert ok líkari goðum en mǫnnum. Þeir kómu í Saxland, ok eignaðist Óðinn þar víða landit ok þar setti hann til landsgæzlu þrjá syni sína. Vegdreg réð fyrir[2] Austr-Saxlandi. Annarr sonr hans hét Beldeg, er vér kǫllum Baldr. Hann átti Vestrfál, þat ríki er svá heitir. Þriði sonr hans hét Sigi, hans sonr Rerir faðir Vǫlsungs er | Vǫlsungar eru frá komnir.[3] Þeir réðu fyrir Frakklandi. Frá ǫllum þeim eru stórar ættir komnar.

Þá fór Óðinn í Reiðgotaland ok eignaðist þat ok setti þar son sinn Skjǫld, fǫður Friðleifs er Skjǫldungar eru frá komnir. Þat heitir nú Jótland er þeir kǫlluðu Reiðgotaland.

[1] Written thus, i.e. *nyrðri*.
[2] Written 'firir' on this one occasion, elsewhere, 'fyrir'.
[3] Vǫlsungr is not mentioned here in other manuscripts of *Snorra Edda*, and his father's name is not mentioned elsewhere in *Snorra Edda* in any manuscript. His descent from Rerir, Sig(g)i and Óðinn is described in *Vǫlsunga saga*.

2 How the world is divided into three areas

The world is divided into three regions. One part was from south to west and over the Mediterranean sea. This is called Africa. The southern part is hot so that there it is burned by the sun. The second part from west to north and in to the sea is called Europe or Enea. The northern part there is cold, and vegetation does not grow and habitation is impossible. From the north over the eastern region to the south is called Asia. In that part of the world is all beauty and wealth, gold and jewels. The middle of the world is there, and just as it is better there than in other places, so too mankind there is more blessed than in other places with wisdom and strength, beauty and all good qualities. There the City of Rome was situated, which we call Troy. In Troy there were twelve kingdoms and one over all the others; there were twelve chief languages there.

There was a king called Menon. He was married to King Priam's daughter Trója. Their son was called Trór, whom we call Þórr. He was twelve when he had his full strength. Then he lifted from the ground ten bearskins at once. He defeated many berserks at once, and wild animals and dragons. In the northern part of the world he came across a prophetess called Sibyl, but we call her Sif. No one knew her ancestry. Their son was called Lórriði, his son Vingiþórr, his son Vingener, his son Móða, his son Magi, his son Sefsmeg, his son Beðvig, his son Atra, whom we call Annarr, his son Ítrmann, his son Eremóð, his son Skjaldun, whom we call Skjǫldr, his son Bjáf, whom we call Bǫrr, his son Jat, his son Guðólfr, his son Finnr, his son Frjálafr, whom we call Friðleifr, his son Wodden, whom we call Óðinn.

3 About how Óðinn came to northern lands

This Óðinn had great prophetic powers. His wife was called Frigida, whom we call Frigg. He became eager [to go] to the north of the world with a great army and a huge amount of property, and wherever they went they were thought a great deal of and more like gods than men. They came to Saxony, and Óðinn gained possession of extensive territory there and put in charge of the land there three of his sons. Vegdreg ruled over East Saxony. His second son was called Beldeg, whom we call Baldr. He had Westphalia, the kingdom that is known by this name. His third son was called Sigi, his son Rerir, father of Vǫlsungr whom the Vǫlsungs are descended from. They ruled over the land of the Franks. From all these, great dynasties are descended.

Then Óðinn went to Reiðgotaland and gained possession of it and established there his son Skjǫldr, father of Friðleifr whom the Skjǫldungs are descended from. It is now called Jutland that they called Reiðgotaland.

4 Frá því er Óðinn kom í Svíþjóð ok gaf sonum sínum ríki

Þaðan fór Óðinn í Svíþjóð. Þar var sá konungr er Gylfi hét, ok er hann frétti til Asíamanna er æsir vóru kallaðir, fór hann í móti þeim ok bauð þeim í sitt ríki. En sá tími fylgði ferð þeira, hvar sem þeir dvǫlðust í lǫndum, þá var þar ár ok friðr, ok trúðu menn at þeir væri þess ráðandi, því at ríkis menn sá þá ólíka flestum mǫnnum ǫðrum at fegrð ok viti. Þar þótti Óðni fagrir vellir ok landskostir góðir, ok kaus sér þar borgarstað sem nú heita Sigtún. Skipaði þar hǫfðingja í þá líking sem í Tróju. Vóru settir tólf hǫfðingjar at dœma landslǫg.

Síðan fór Óðinn norðr þar til er sjór tók við honum, sá er hann ætlaði at lægi um ǫll lǫnd, ok setti þar son sinn til ríkis, er Semingr hét,[1] en nú heitir Noregr, ok telja Noregs konungar ok svá jarlar þangat ættir sínar. Með Óðni fór Yngvi er konungr var í Svíþjóðu eptir hann ok Ynglingar eru frá komnir.

Þeir æsirnir tóku sér kvánfǫng þar innan lands ok urðu þær ættir fjǫlmennar um Saxland ok um norðrhálfuna. Þeirra tunga ein gekk um þessi lǫnd, ok þat skilja menn at þeir hafa norðr hingat haft tunguna í Noreg ok Danmǫrk, Svíþjóð ok Saxland.

5 Hér hefr Gylfa ginning frá því er Gylfi sótti heim Alfǫðr í Ásgarð með fjǫlkyngi ok frá villu ása ok frá spurningu Gylfa

Gylfir[2] var maðr vitr ok hugsaði þat er allir lýðir lofuðu þá ok allir hlutir gengu at vilja þeira, hvárt þat mundi af eðli þeira vera eða mundi guðmǫgnin valda því. Hann fór til Ásgarðs ok brá á sik gamals manns líki. En æsirnir vóru því vísari at þeir sá ferð hans ok gjǫrðu í móti sjónhverfingar. Þá sá hann háva hǫll. Þak hennar vóru þǫkt gylltum skjǫldum sem spánþak. Svá segir Þjóðólfr:[3]

1 (1)   Á baki létu blíkja,
          barðir vóru grjóti,
          Svǫlnis salnæfrar:
          seggir hyggjandi.

Gylfir sá mann í hallardyrum er lék at handsǫxum, ok vóru sjau senn á lopti. Sá spurði hann fyrri at nafni. Hann nefndist Gangleri ok kominn | af rifilsstigum ok spyrr hverr hǫllina átti. Hann segir at sá var konungr þeira ok mun ek fylgja þér at sjá hann.

[1] *er Semingr hét* obviously ought to come after *son sinn*.

[2] Gangleri's real name appears only twice in the actual text of *Gylfaginning* and both times in the form 'Gylfir', not 'Gylfi'. On the other hand, the form 'Gylfi' appears in the heading above and in the preceding chapter, where it refers to a king.

[3] In Fagrskinna and Flateyjarbók these four lines are attributed, as here, to Þjóðólfr (inn hvinverski), but in *Heimskringla* (*Ynglingasaga*) they are attributed to Þorbjǫrn hornklofi; they are thought to be from his poem known as *Haraldskvæði* or *Hrafnsmál*. They seem to describe ironically Haraldr harðráði's opponents at Hafrsfjǫrðr using their shields to protect their backs as they fled.

4 About how Óðinn came to Sweden and gave his sons rule

From there Óðinn went to Sweden. There was there a king that was called Gylfi, and when he heard about the men of Asia who were called Æsir, he went to meet them and invited them into his kingdom. And such success attended their travels, in whatever country they stopped, then there was prosperity and peace there, and people believed that they were responsible for it, because people that had power saw they were unlike most other men in beauty and wisdom. Óðinn found the fields there beautiful and the conditions in the country good, and selected as a site for his city there the place that is now called Sigtún. He organised rulers there on the same pattern as in Troy. Twelve rulers were set up to administer the laws of the land.

Then Óðinn went north to where he was faced by the sea, the one that he thought encircled all lands, and set a son there over the realm that was called Semingr, but is now called Norway, and kings of Norway and also earls trace their ancestry back to him. With Óðinn went Yngvi, who was king in Sweden after him and whom the Ynglings are descended from.

The Æsir found themselves marriages within the country there, and these families became numerous over Saxony and over the northern region. Their language alone became current over all these countries, and people understand that they have brought the language here to the north, to Norway and Denmark, Sweden and Saxony.

5 Here begins the befooling of Gylfi, about how Gylfi paid a visit to All-father in Ásgarðr with magic and about the Æsir's heresy and about Gylfi's questioning.

Gylfir was an intelligent man and pondered about how all peoples praised them and all things went according to their will, whether this would be because of their nature or whether the divine powers would be responsible. He travelled to Ásgarðr and assumed the form of an old man. But the Æsir were the wiser in that they saw his movements and prepared deceptive appearances for him. Then he saw a high hall. Its roof was covered with gilded shields like tiles. So says Þjóðólfr:

1   On their backs they let shine—
     they were bombarded with stones—
     Svǫlnir's (Óðinn's) hall-shingles (shields):
     sensible men!

Gylfir saw a man in the doorway of the hall who was juggling with knives, and there were seven in the air at a time. This man spoke first and asked him his name. He said his name was Gangleri (Walk-Weary) and that he had travelled trackless ways and asks whose hall it was. He says that it was their king—'and I shall take you to see him.'

Þar sá hann margar hallir ok mǫrg gólf ok margt fólk. Sumir drukku en sumir léku. Þá mælti Gangleri, er honum þótti þar margt ótrúligt:

2 (2) Skatnar allir
áðr ne[1] gangim fram
um skygnast skuli,
því at óvíst er at vita
hvar óvinir
sitja á fletjum fyrir.[2]

Hann sá þrjú hásæti ok hvert upp af ǫðru ok sátu þar maðr í hverju. Þá spurði hann hvert nafn hǫfðingja þeira væri. Sá sagði, er hann leiddi inn: Sá er í neðsta sæti sitr er konungr ok heitir Hár, ok þar næst Jafnhár. En sá er efstr er heitir Þriði.

Hann spyrr Ganglera hvat fleira væri eyrinda, en heimill er matr ok drykkr.

Gangleri segir at fyrst vill hann spyrja ef nokkurr er fróðr maðr inni.

Hár segir at hann komi eigi heill út ef[3] hann er fróðari.

3 (3) Ok stattu fram
meðan þú fregn.
Sitja skal sá er segir.

6 Frá spurningu Ganglera

Gangleri hóf svá sitt mál: Hverr er ǿztr eða elztr með goðum?

Hár segir: Sá heitir Alfǫðr at váru máli. En í Ásgarði hefir hann tólf nǫfn: Alfǫðr, Herjann, Nikaðr, Nikuðr, Fjǫlnir, Óski, Ómi, Riflindi, Sviðurr, Sviðrir, Viðrir, Sálkr.

Þá svarar Gangleri: Hvar er sá guð eða hvat má hann eða hvat hefir hann unnit til frama?

Hár svarar: Lifir hann um aldr ok stjórnar ǫllu ríki sínu, stórum hlutum ok smám.

Þá svarar Jafnhár: Hann smíðaði himin ok jǫrð ok lopt.

Þá mælti Þriði: Hitt er meira er hann smíðaði himin ok jǫrð at hann smíðaði mann ok gaf honum ǫnd at lifa. Þó skal líkamr fúna ok skulu þá allir búa með honum réttsiðaðir þar sem heitir Gimlé. En vándir menn fara til Heljar ok þaðan í Niflheim niðr í níunda heim.

[1] *ne* is redundant, unless it is emphasising the implied negative in *áðr*, or is an error for *en*.

[2] This is the only verse in *Gylfaginning* put into the mouth of anyone other than one of the Æsir (or the narrator). Though it is clearly related to *Hávamál* 1, it must be from a different version from that in GkS 2365 4to and other manuscripts of *Snorra Edda*, which read *Gáttir allar | áðr gangi fram* in the first two lines.

[3] Other manuscripts have *nema* 'unless'.

He saw there many halls and many apartments and many people. Some were drinking and some were playing games. Then said Gangleri, when he found that many things there were incredible:

2   All men
    before we enter
    should look round carefully,
    for one cannot know for certain
    where enemies
    may be sitting waiting inside.

He saw three thrones, one above the other, and a man sat there in each. Then he asked what the name of their ruler was. The one who had led him in said:

'The one that sits in the lowest seat is a king and is called Hár (High), and next to him Jafnhár (Just-as-high). But the one that is at the top is called Þriði (Third).

He asks Gangleri what further business he had—'but you are welcome to food and drink'. Gangleri says that first he wants to find out if there is any learned person in there.

High says that he will not get out unscathed if he is more learned.

3   'And stand out in front
    while you ask.
    He that tells shall sit.'

6 About Gangleri's questioning

Gangleri began his questioning thus: 'Who is the highest or most ancient among the gods?'

'High says: He is called All-father in our language. But in Ásgarðr he has twelve names: All-father, Herjann, Nikaðr, Nikuðr, Fjǫlnir, Óski, Ómi, Riflindi, Sviðurr, Sviðrir, Viðrir, Sálkr.'

Then replies Gangleri: 'Where is this god, and what power has he and what has he achieved to gain distinction?'

High replies: 'He lives for ever and rules all his kingdom, great things and small.'

Then replies Just-as-high: 'He made heaven and earth and sky.'

Then spoke Third: 'This is a geater achievement, when he made heaven and earth, that he made man and gave him a soul to live. Yet body shall decay and then all righteous shall dwell with him in the place called Gimlé. But wicked men go to Hel and from there on to Niflheimr down in the ninth world.'

Þá segir Gangleri: Hvat hafðist hann áðr at en himinn ok jǫrð vóru skǫpuð?
Þá svarar Hár: Þá var hann með hrímþussum.[1]
Gangleri segir: Hvat var upphaf eða hversu hófst hann?
Hár segir: Svá segir í Vǫluspá:[2]

4 (4)   Ár var alda
          þar er ekki var,
          vara sandr né sjór
          né svalar undir.
          Jǫrð fannst eigi
          né upphiminn,
          gap var ginnunga
          en gras hvergi.

Þá svarar Jafnhár: Þat var mǫrgum vetrum fyrri en jǫrð var skǫpuð er Niflheimr var gerr. Ok í honum miðjum liggr bruðr sá er Hergelmir heitir, ok þaðan falla þær ár er svá heita: Kvǫl, Gundró, Fjǫrni, Fimbulþul, Slíðr ok Hríðr, Sylgr ok Ylgr, Víðleiptr. Gjǫll er næst Helgrindum.

7 Hér segir frá Múspellsheimi ok frá Surti

Þá segir Þriði: | Fyst var þó Múspellsheimr, sá er svá heitir. Hann er ljóss ok heitr ok ófǿrt er þar útlendum mǫnnum. Surtr ræðr þar fyrir ok sitr á heimsenda. Hann hefir loganda sverð í hendi, ok í enda veraldar mun hann koma ok sigra ǫll goðin ok brenna heiminn með eldi. Svá segir í Vǫluspá:[3]

5 (5)   Svartr ferr sunnan
          með sviga lævi,
          skínn af sverði
          sól valtíva,
          grjótbjǫrg gnata
          en guðar hrata
          traða halir helvega
          en himinn klofnar.

Gangleri segir: Hversu skipaðist áðr en ættirnar yrði ok aukaðist mannfólkit?

8 Hér segir er guðin skǫpuðu Ymi jǫtun

Þá segir Hár: Ár þær er heita Élivágar eru svá langt komnar frá uppsprettunum at eitrkvikan sú er þar fylgði harðnaði sem sindr í afli. Þat varð íss ok nam

---

[1] Always written thus in DG 11 4to, never *-þurs*.
[2] Cf. *Vǫluspá* 3.
[3] Cf. *Vǫluspá* 52.

Then says Gangleri: 'What was he doing before heaven and earth were created?'

Then replies High: 'Then he was with frost giants.'

Gangleri says: 'What was the beginning and how did he start?'

High says: 'So it says in *Vǫluspá*:

4   It was at the beginning of time,
      where nothing was;
      sand was not, nor sea,
      nor cool waves.
      Earth did not exist,
      nor heaven on high;
      the mighty gap was,
      but nowhere growth.'

Then replies Just-as-high: 'It was many winters before the earth was created when Niflheimr was made, and in its midst lies the spring that is called Hvergelmir, and from it flow the rivers that are called: Kvǫl, Gundró, Fjǫrni, Fimbulþul, Slíðr and Hríðr, Sylgr and Ylgr, Víðleiptr. Gjǫll is next to the gates of Hel.'

7 Here it tells of Múspellsheimr and of Surtr

Then says Third. 'But first there was Múspellsheimr, that which is so called. It is bright and hot and impassable for those that are not native there. Surtr is ruler there and sits at the frontier of the world. He has a flaming sword in his hand, and at the end of the world he will come and defeat all the gods and burn the world with fire. So it says in *Vǫluspá*:

5   Svartr travels from the south
      with the stick-destroyer (fire);
      shines from his sword
      the sun of the gods of the slain;
      rock cliffs crash
      and gods tumble down,
      heroes tread the paths of Hel
      and heaven splits.

Gangleri says: 'What were things like before generations came to be and the human race was multiplied?'

8 Here it tells how the gods created the giant Ymir

Then says High: 'The rivers that are called Élivágar are come so far from the sources that the poisonous flow that accompanied them has gone hard like clinker in a furnace. It turned into ice and came to a halt and stopped flowing.

hann staðar ok rann eigi. Þá héldi yfir þannug ok þat er af stóð eitrinu fraus ok jók hvert hrímit yfir annat, allt í Ginnungagap.

Þá mælti Jafnhár: Ginnungagap, þat er vissi til norðrættar, fylltist með þunga ok hǫfugleik, með ⟨h⟩rími ok ís ok inn frá úr ok gustr. En syðri hlutr Ginnungagaps léttist móti síum ok gneistum er flugu ór Múspellsheimi.

Þá segir Þriði: Svá sem kalt stóð ór Niflheimi ok grimmt, svá var allt þat er vissi námunda Múspellsheimi heitt ok ljóst, en Ginnungagap var létt sem lopt vindlaust. Ok þá er blærinn hitans mǿtti hríminu, svá at bráðnaði ok draup af, ok með krapti þeim er stýrði, varð manns líkindi á. Sá hét Ymir, en hrímþussar kalla hann Aurgelmi, ok þaðan eru þeira ættir, sem hér segir:[1]

6 (6) Eru vǫlvur allar
       frá Viktólfi,
       vættir allar
       frá Vilmeiði
       jǫtnar allir
       frá Ymi komnir.

Ok enn segir svá at[2]

7 (7) Ór Élivágum
       stukku eitrdropar
       ok vǫxtr vinds
       ok varð jǫtunn ór.
       Þær einar ættir
       koma saman.

Þá mælti Gangleri: Hvernig uxu ættir þaðan eða trúi þér hann guð vera?

Þá svarar Jafnhár: Eigi trúum vér hann guð. Illr var hann ok hans ættmenn, þat eru hrímþussar. Ok er hann svaf fekk hann sveita, ok undir vinstri hendi hans óx maðr ok kona, ok annarr fótr hans gat son við ǫðrum, ok þaðan kómu ættir.

Þá mælti Gangleri: Hvar bygði Ymir eða við hvat lifði hann?

9 Frá því er skǫpuð var kýrin Auðumla

Hár svarar: Næst var þat er hrím draup at þar varð af kýrin Auðumla. Fjórar mjólkár runnu ór spenum hennar ok fǿddi hon Ymi. En kýrin fǿddist er hon sleikti hrímsteina er saltir vóru. Ok enn fyrsta dag er hon sleikti kom ór manns hár, annan dag hǫfuð, enn þriðja allr maðr er Buri hét, fǫðr[3] Bors,

---

[1] Cf. *Hyndluljóð* 33 (*Vǫluspá in skamma* 5).

[2] Cf. *Vafþrúðnismál* 31.

[3] *fǫðr* is occasionally found as a nominative form, as a simplex as well as in compounds like *Alfǫðr*.

Then it frosted over in that direction and what was rising from the poison froze and this rime increased layer upon layer right over Ginnungagap.'

Then spoke Just-as-high: 'Ginnungagap, the part that faces in a northerly direction, was filled with weight and heaviness, with rime and ice, and inwards from it vapour and blowing. But the southerly part of Ginnungagap cleared up in the face of the molten particles and sparks that came flying out of the world of Múspell.'

Then says Third: 'Just as out of Niflheimr there arose coldness and grimness, so everything that was facing close to the world of Múspell was hot and bright, but Ginnungagap was weightless as a windless sky. And when the blowing of the warmth met the rime, so that it thawed and dripped from it, then by means of the power that controlled it there came to be a figure of a man in it. He was called Ymir, but the frost giants call him Aurgelmir, and from him are descended their generations, as it says here:

6   All sibyls are
       from Viktólfr,
       all supernatural beings
       from Vilmeiðr,
       all giants
       [are] come from Ymir.

And further it says this, that

7   From Élivágar
       shot poison drops
       and the growth of wind,
       and a giant came into being from them.
       Only these generations
       converge.'

Then spoke Gangleri: 'How did generations grow from these, or do you believe him to be a god?'

Then Just-as-high replies: 'We do not believe him to be a god. He was evil, and his descendants, they are frost giants. And as he slept he sweated, and under his left arm grew a male and a female, and one of his legs begot a son with the other, and descendants came fom them.'

Then spoke Gangleri: 'Where did Ymir live and what did he live on?'

9 About how the cow Auðumla was created

High replies: 'The next thing was, when the rime dripped, that from it came into being the cow Auðumla. Four rivers of milk flowed from its udder, and it fed Ymir. But the cow fed as it licked the rime-stones, which were salty. And the first day as it licked, there came out a man's hair, the second day a head, and the third a complete man, who was called Buri, father of Borr,

er átti Beyzlu, dóttur Bǫlþorns jǫtuns. Þau áttu þrjá sonu, Óðin, Vili, Vé, ok þat ætlum vér, segir Hár, at sá Óðinn ok hans brǿðr munu vera stýrandi heims ok jarðar, ok þar er sá eptir her⟨r⟩ann[1] er vér vitum nú mestan vera.

10 Frá því er synir Burs drápu Ymi

Synir Burs drápu Ymi ok hljóp ór honum þat blóð at þeir drektu með því allri ætt hrímþussa, nema einn komst undan með sínu hyski. Þann kalla jǫtnar Bergelmi. Hann fór á lúðr sinn ok helzt þar, ok þaðan eru komnar hrímþussa ættir.

8 (8)   Ørófi vetra[2]
        áðr jǫrð væri um skǫpuð
        þá var Bergelmir borinn.
        Þat ek fyrst um man
        at fróða jǫtunn[3]
        á var lúðr um lagiðr.

Þá mælti Gangleri: Hvat hǫfðust þá Burs synir at, er þú trúir guð vera?

Hár segir: Eigi er þat lítit. Þeir fluttu Ymi í mitt Ginnungagap ok gerðu af honum jǫrð, af blóði hans sæ ok vǫtn, bjǫrg af beinum, grjót af tǫnnum ok af þeim beinum er borin[4] vóru, ok af blóðinu, er ór sárunum rann, þá gerðu þeir sjá þann er þeir festu jǫrðina í. Síðan tóku þeir hausinn ok gerðu ór himininn ok settu yfir jǫrðina með fjórum skautum, ok undir hvert horn settu þeir dverg, Austr⟨a⟩, Vestra, Norðra, Suðra. Þá tóku þeir síur ór Múspellsheimi ok settu í mitt Ginnungagap ofan ok neðan á himininn at lýsa jǫrðina. Þeir gáfu staði ǫllum eldingum. Þaðan af vóru dǿgr greind ok ára tal. Svá segir:[5]

9 (9)   Sól þat ne vissi
        hvar hon sali átti,
        máni þat ne vissi
        hvat hann megins átti,
        stjǫrnur þat ne vissu
        hvar þær staði áttu.

Þá mælti Gangleri: Mikil merki eru þetta ok mikil smíð.

Hár svarar: Kringlótt er jǫrð ok liggr um enn djúpi sær, ok með þeim strǫndum gáfu þeir bygð jǫtnum. En fyrir innan á jǫrðina gerðu þeir borg fyrir ófriði jǫtna umhverfis jǫrðina ok hǫfðu þar til brár Ymis ok kǫlluðu borgina Miðgarð. Þeir kǫstuðu heilanum í loptit ok gerðu af skýin. Svá sem hér segir.

[1] There is a long discussion of this word in Grape et al. 1977: 115.
[2] Cf. *Vafþrúðnismál* 35.
[3] This line is ungrammatical. It should either be *at fróði jǫtunn* 'that the wise giant' or *at fróða jǫtun* 'after the wise giant'.
[4] GkS 2367 4to has *brotin* 'broken' here.
[5] Cf. *Vǫluspá* 5/5–10.

who was married to Beyzla, daughter of the giant Bǫlþorn. They had three sons, Óðinn, Vili, Vé, and it is our opinion,' says High, 'that this Óðinn and his brothers must be rulers of the world and the earth, and he remains the lord there, whom we now know to be greatest.'

10 About how Burr's sons killed Ymir

'Burr's sons killed Ymir and there flowed out of him so much blood that with it they drowned all the race of frost giants, except that one escaped with his household. Giants call him Bergelmir. He went onto his ark, and from him are descended the races of frost giants.

8   Countless winters
before the earth was created
then was Bergelmir born.
That is the first I remember,
that the wise giant
was laid on a box.'

Then spoke Gangleri: 'What did Burr's sons do then, if you believe them to be gods?'

High says: 'That is no small thing. They transported Ymir to the middle of Ginnungagap and out of him made the earth, of his blood the sea and lakes, rocks of his bones, stones of his teeth and of the bones that were carried, and of the blood that flowed from his wounds they then made the sea that they fastened the earth in. Then they took his skull and out of it made the sky and set it above the earth with four points, and under each corner they set a dwarf, Austri, Vestri, Norðri, Suðri. They took molten particles out of Múspellsheimr and set them in the midst of Ginnungagap above and below in the sky to illuminate the earth. They assigned positions to all the lights. By means of them days were distinguished and the count of years. So it says:

9   The sun did not know
where its dwelling was,
the moon did not know
what power it had,
the stars did not know
where their places were.'

Then spoke Gangleri: 'These are very remarkable things and great creations.'

High replies: 'The earth is circular, and round it lies the deep sea, and along the shores they gave dwellings to giants. But on the earth on the inner side they built a fortification round the world against the hostilities of giants, and for it they used Ymir's eyelashes, and they called the fortification Miðgarðr. They threw his brains into the sky and of them made the clouds. As it says here:

10 (10) Ór Ymis holdi[1]
 var jǫrð um skǫpuð,
 en ór sveita sjór
 b. ór b.
 b. ór h.
 en ór h. h.

11 (11) En ór hans brám
 gerðu blíð regin
 Miðgarð manna sonum,
 ok ór hans heila
 vóru þau in harðmóðgu
 ský ǫll um skǫpuð.

11 Burs synir skǫpuðu Ask ok Emlu

Þá er þeir gengu með sjóvar strǫndu, Burs synir, fundu þeir tré tvau ok skǫpuðu af mann; gaf inn fyrsti ǫnd, annarr líf, þriði heyrn ok sýn ok hét maðr Askr en konan Emla. Óx þaðan af mannkindin er bygð var gefin undir Miðgarði.

Síðan gerðu þeir í miðjum heimi Ásgarð. Þar bygði Óðinn ok ættir þeira er várar ættir eru frá komnir.[2]

Enn segir Hár: Þar er einn staðr er Hliðskjálf heitir, ok er Alfǫðr sezt þar í hásæti sér hann um heim allan ok hvers manns athæfi. Kona hans er Frigg Fjǫrgynsdóttir, ok af þeiri ætt er ása ætt er bygði Ásgarð inn forna, ok er þat goðkunnig ætt. Því heitir hann Alfǫðr at hann er faðir allra guðanna. Jǫrðin var dóttir hans ok var þeira sonr Ása-Þórr.

12 Frá Nóra jǫtni ok Nótt dóttur hans

Nóri jǫtunn bygði fyrst Jǫtunheima. Dóttir hans var Nótt. Hon var svǫrt. Hon giptist Naglfara. Sonr þeira hét Auðr. Síðan var hon gipt Ónar ok var Jǫrð þeira dóttir. Hana átti Dǫglingr ok var Dagr sonr þeira. Hann var fagr sem faðir hans. Þá tók Alfǫðr Nótt ok Dag ok setti á himin ok gaf þeim tvá hesta ok kerrur ok ríða þau umhverfis jǫrðina.[3] Nótt ríðr Hrímfaxa. Hann dǫggvir jǫrðina með méldropum sínum. Dagr á Skinfaxa ok lýsir lopt ok jǫrð af faxi hans.

Mundilferi átti tvau bǫrn. Máni hét sonr hans en Sól dóttir ok átti hana Glórnir. Goðin reiddust því ofdrambi er þau hétu svá, ok settu þau upp á himin ok draga þau kerru sólar þeirar er goðin hǫfðu skapat af þeiri síu er

---

[1] Cf. *Grímnismál* 40–41. On the abbreviations cf. Introduction pp. xlv–xlvi.

[2] Here one would have expected the feminine form *komnar*.

[3] There does not seem to be the same distinction between *aka* 'drive' and *ríða* 'ride' here as there is in Modern Icelandic. Cf. ch. 19 below: *En er hon ríðr þá ekr hon á kǫttum sínum ok sitr í reið*. See Introduction p. lii.

10   From Ymir's flesh
     was earth created,
     and from blood, sea.
     rocks of bones,
     trees of hair,
     and from his skull, the sky,
11   and from his eyelashes
     the joyous gods made
     Miðgarðr for sons of men,
     and from his brains
     were those cruel
     clouds all created.'

11 Burr's sons created Askr and Emla

'As they were walking along the sea shore, Burr's sons, they found two logs and created a man from them; the first gave breath, the second life, the third hearing and sight, and the man was called Askr and the woman Emla. There grew from them the mankind to whom the dwelling place was given under Miðgarðr.

'Afterwards they built in the middle of the world Ásgarðr. There dwelt Óðinn and their descendants from whom our family lines are come.'

High says further: 'There is one place there that is called Hliðskjálf, and when All-father sits down in the high seat there he sees over the whole world and what everyone is doing. His wife is Frigg, daughter of Fjǫrgynn, and from that ancestry is the race of Æsir who dwelt in the old Ásgarðr, and that race is of divine origin. And the reason why he is called All-father is that he is father of all the gods. The earth was his daughter and their son was Þórr of the Æsir.'

12 Of the giant Nóri and his daughter Nótt

'The giant Nóri first of all lived in the world of giants. His daughter was Nótt (Night). She was black. She was married to Naglfari. Their son was called Auðr. Afterwards she was married to to Ónarr, and Jǫrð (Earth) was their daughter. Dǫglingr married her and Dagr (Day) was their son. He was fair like his father. Then All-father took Nótt and Dagr and put them in the sky and gave them two horses and chariots and they ride around the earth. Night rides Hrímfaxi. He bedews the earth with the drips from his bit. Dagr has Skinfaxi and light is shed over sky and earth from his mane.

'Mundilferi had two children. His son was called Máni (Moon) and his daughter Sól (Sun), and Glórnir married her. The gods got angry with this arrogance of giving them these names, and put them up in the sky, and they draw the chariot of the sun that the gods had created of the molten particle

flaug ór Múspellsheimi. Máni tók bǫrn tvau af jǫrðu, Bil ok Hjúka, er þau fóru frá brunni þeim er Byggvir heitir. Sárinn hét Sǿgr en Simul stǫngin. Viðfiðr hét faðir barnanna. Þau bǫrn fylgja Mána sem sjá má af jǫrðunni.

Þá mælti Gangleri: Skjótt ferr sólin sem hon sé hrædd.

Þá svarar Hár: Nær gengr sá er hana leiðir. Úlfar tveir gera þat, Skoll ok Hatti Hróðrvitnisson.

Þá mælti Gangleri: Hver er ætt úlfanna?

Hár segir: Gýgr ein býr fyrir austan Miðgarð í skógi þeim er Járnviðr heitir, ok svá heita þær trǫllkonur er þar byggja. Gamla trǫllkona er móðir margra jǫtna ok allir í vargs líkjum. Þaðan kom Mánagarmr. Hann fylltist með fjǫrvi feigra manna ok gleypir tunglit en stǫkkvir blóði himininn. Þá týnir sól skini sínu, svá sem hér segir:[1]

12 (12)   Austr býr in arma
í Járnviði.
ok fǿðir þar
Fenris kindir.
Verðr af þeim ǫllum
íma nokkur
tungls tregari
í trǫlls hami.

13 (13)   Fyllist fjǫrvi
feigra manna
rýðr ragna | sjǫt
rauðum dreyra.
Svǫrt verða sólskin
um sumur eptir
verðr ǫll va. ly.
V. einn ok h.

13 Hér segir frá Bifrǫst

Þá spyrr Gangleri: Hver er leið til himins af jǫrðu?

Hár segir hlæjandi: Eigi er nú fróðliga spurt. Er eigi þat sagt er goðin gerðu brú af jǫrðu til himins er heitir Bifrǫst? Hana muntu sét hafa. Kann vera at þú kallir hana regnboga. Hon er með þrim litum ok mjǫk sterk ok ger með mikilli list meiri en aðrar smíðir. En svá sterk sem hon er, þá mun hon brotna, þá er Múspells megir fara at ríða hana, ok svima hestar þeira yfir stórar ár. Svá koma þeir fram ferðinni.

Þá segir Gangleri: Eigi þóttu mér goðin gera hana af trúnaði er hon skal brotna, ok megi þau þó gera sem þau vilja.

[1] Cf. *Vǫluspá* 40–41. On the abbreviations see Introduction pp. xlv–xlvi.

that flew out of Múspellsheimr. Máni took two children from the earth, Bil and Hjúki, as they were going from the spring called Byggvir. The tub was called Sǿgr and the carrying-pole Simul. The children's father was called Viðfiðr. These children accompany Máni, as can be seen from earth.'

Then spoke Gangleri: 'The sun moves fast as if it is afraid.'

Then High replies: 'He goes close who is leading her. Two wolves are doing that, Skoll and Hatti Hróðrvitnisson.'

Then spoke Gangleri: 'What is the wolves' ancestry?'

High says: 'A certain giantess lives to the east of Miðgarðr in the forest that is called Járnviðr, and that is what the trollwives that live there are called. The old trollwife is mother of many giants and all of them in the form of wolves. From them was descended Mánagarmr. He filled himself with the lifeblood of dying men and will swallow the moon and spatter the heavens with blood. Then the sun will lose its shine, as it says here:

12   In the east lives the wretched one,
in Járnviðr
and breeds there
Fenrir's kind.
From them all comes
a certain she-wolf,
causer of grief to the sun (or moon)
in troll's guise.

13   It gorges the lifeblood
of dying men,
reddens gods' halls
with red gore.
Dark will sunshine become
for summers after,
all weathers hostile.
Do you alone know, and what?'

13 Here it tells about Bifrǫst

Then Gangleri asks: 'What way is there to heaven from earth?'

High says, laughing: 'That is not an intelligent question. Is it not told how the gods built a bridge from earth to heaven that is called Bifrǫst? You must have seen it. It may be that you call it a rainbow. It has three colours and is very strong and built with great art, more so than other constructions. But strong as it is, yet it will break when Múspells lads go to ride it, and their horses will swim across great rivers. That is how they will carry out their journey.'

Then says Gangleri : 'It seems to me the gods did not build it in good faith if it is going to break, and yet they can do as they please.'

Þá segir Hár: Eigi eru goðin ámælis verð at þessi smíð. Góð brú er Bifrǫst. En engi hlutr er sá í þessum heimi er sér megi treystast þá er Múspells megir herja. Gangleri segir: Hvat hafðist Alfǫðr þá at er gerr var Ásgarðr?

Hár segir: Í upphafi setti hann stjórnarmenn í sæti ok beiddi þá at dǿma ørlǫg manna ok ráða. Dómrinn var þar sem heitir Iðavǫllr í miðri borginni. Þat er it fyrsta þeira verk at gera hof þat er sæti þeira tólf standa í, nema þat sæti er Alfǫðr átti. Þat hús er bezt gert á jǫrðu ok mest. Allt er þat útan ok innan sem gull eit⟨t⟩ sé. Í þeim sal kalla menn Glaðheim. Annan sal gerðu þeir er hǫrgr var í er gyðjur áttu ok var hann allgott hús ok fagrt. Hann kalla menn Vindglóð. Þar næst smíðuðu þeir hús er þeir lǫgðu afl í, ok þar til smíðuðu þeir hamar ok tǫng ok steðja ok þaðan af ǫll tól ǫnnur. Ok því næst smíðuðu þeir málm, stein ok tré ok svá gnógliga þann málm er gull heitir at ǫll borðgǫgn ok reiðigǫgn hǫfðu þeir af gulli. Ok er sú ǫld kǫlluð gullaldr, áðr en spillist af tilkvámu kvennanna. Þær kómu ór Jǫtunheimum.

Þar næst settust guð upp í sæti sín ok réttu dóma sína ok mintust hvaðan dvergarnir hǫfðu kviknat í moldu niðri í jǫrðunni, svá sem maðkar í holdi. Dvergarnir hǫfðu skapast fyrst ok tekit kviknan í holdi Ymis ok vóru þá maðkar. Ok af atkvæði guðanna urðu þeir vitandi mannvits ok hǫfðu manns líki ok búa þó í jǫrðu ok í steinum. Móðsognir var ǿttztr[1] þeira ok annarr Durinn. Svá segir í Vǫluspá:[2]

14 (14)   Þá gengu v.[3]
A. s.
g. h. g.
ok um þat g'
h' skyldi dverga
drótt um spekja[4]
ór brimi blóðgu
ok Bláins leggjum.[5]

15 (15)   Þeir mannlíkun
mǫrg um gerðu
dvergar í jǫrðu
sem þeim Dyrinn[6] kendi.

Ok segir þeim nǫfn þeira:

---

[1] Presumably = ǿðstr or ǿztr. Cf. Vǫluspá 10: Þar var Mótsognir | mæztr um orðinn.
[2] On the list of dwarfs, cf. Vǫluspá 9–16.
[3] regin ǫll 'all the powers' the Codex Regius version and Vǫluspá.
[4] skepja 'create' the Codex Regius version and Vǫluspá.
[5] On the abbreviations see Introduction pp. xlv–xlvi.
[6] It seems that this is the same person as Durinn, and moreover that it is he that is listing the names of dwarfs (Grape et al. 1977: 194). Insular u and y are quite often confused in manuscripts.

Then says High: 'The gods are not deserving of blame for this work. Bifrǫst is a good bridge. But there is nothing in this world that will be secure when Múspell's lads attack.'

Gangleri says: 'What did All-father do then, when Ásgarðr was built?'

High says: 'In the beginning he put rulers on thrones and bade them decide the destinies of men and be in charge. The judicial court was in the place called Iðavǫllr in the centre of the city. It was their first act to build the temple that their twelve thrones stand in, except for the throne that belonged to All-father. This building is the best that has been built on earth and the largest. Outside and inside it seems like nothing but gold. This place is called Glaðheimr. They built another hall in which was the sanctuary that belonged to goddesses, and it was a very fine building and beautiful. It is called Vindglóð. The next thing they did was raise a building that they put forges in, and for them they made hammer and tongs and anvil, and with these all other tools. After that they worked metal, stone and wood, using so copiously the metal that is known as gold that they had all their furniture and utensils of gold. And this age is known as the Golden Age until it was spoiled by the advent of the women. They came out of the world of giants.

'Next gods took their places on their thrones and instituted their courts and discussed where the dwarfs had been generated from in the soil down in the earth like maggots in flesh. The dwarfs had taken shape first and acquired life in the flesh of Ymir, and were then maggots. But by decision of the gods they became conscious with intelligence and had human shape and yet they live in the earth and in rocks. Móðsognir was the most eminent of them, and the second was Durinn. So it says in *Vǫluspá*:

14 Then went [the powers]
    to their judgment seats,
    most holy gods,
    and deliberated on this,
    who was to soothe
    the troop of dwarfs
    from bloody surf
    and Bláinn's bones.

15 They made
    many human images,
    dwarfs in the earth
    as Durinn taught them.

'And he tells them their names:

16 (16) Nýi, Niði,
         Norðri, Suðri,
         Austri, Vestri,
         Alþjófr, Dvalinn,
         Nani, Niningr, Dani,
         Bivur, Bǫrr,
         Bambǫrr, Nori,
         Orr, Annarr,
         Onni, Mjǫðvitnir.[1]
17 (16) Viggr ok Gandálfr,
         Vindálfr, Þorinn,
         Fili, Kili,
         Fundinn, Váli,
         Þjór,[2] Þorinn,
         Vitr ok Litr,
         Nýráðr,
         Rekkr, Ráðsviðr.

Þessir eru dvergar ok búa í steinum, en enir fyrri í moldu.

18 (17) Dramir, Dolgþvari,
         Hár, Hugstari,
         Hleiðólfr, Glóni,
         Dori,[3] Óri,
         Dúfr, Andvari,
         Heptifili.

Hár segir: En þessir kómu frá Svarnishaugi til Aurvanga á Jǫruvǫllu, ok þaðan er kominn Lofarr. En þessi eru nǫfn þeira:

19 (18) Skirfir, Virfir,
         Skafiðr, Ái,
         Álfr, Yngvi,
         Eikinskjalli,
         Falr, Frosti,
         Fiðr, Ginarr.

14 Hér segir frá helgistað guðanna

Þá spyrr Gangleri: Hvat er hǫfuðstaðr eða helgistaðr guðanna?
  Hár svarar: Þat er at aski Ygdrasils. Þá skulu goðin eiga dóma sína hvern dag.

[1] The names here could be normalised *Náni, Níningr, Dáni, Bívur, Nóri, Ǫrr, Ǫnni*.
[2] *Váli, Þjór* written *Valiþior*.
[3] Or *Dóri*.

16 Nýi, Niði,
　　Norðri, Suðri,
　　Austri, Vestri,
　　Alþjófr, Dvalinn,
　　Nani, Niningr, Dani,
　　Bivur, Bǫrr,
　　Bambǫrr, Nor,
　　Orr, Annarr,
　　Onni, Mjǫðvitnir.

17 Viggr and Gandálfr,
　　Vindálfr, Þorinn,
　　Fili, Kili,
　　Fundinn, Váli,
　　Þjór, Þorinn,
　　Vitr and Litr,
　　Nýráðr,
　　Rekkr, Ráðsviðr.

'These are dwarfs and live in rocks, whereas the previous ones [live] in soil.

18 Dramir, Dolgþvari,
　　Hár, Hugstari,
　　Hleiðólfr, Glóni,
　　Dori, Óri,
　　Dúfr, Andvari,
　　Heptifili.'

High says: 'But these came from Svarnishaugr to Aurvangar on Jǫruvellir, and from them is descended Lofarr. And these are their names:

19 Skirfir, Virfir,
　　Skafiðr, Ái,
　　Álfr, Yngvi,
　　Eikinskjalli,
　　Falr, Frosti,
　　Fiðr, Ginarr.'

14 Here it tells of the gods' holy place

Then Gangleri asks: 'What is the chief centre or holy place of the gods?'

　　High answers: 'It is at the ash Yggdrasill. There the gods must hold their courts each day.'

Þá mælti Gangleri: Hvat er at segja frá þeim stað?

Jafnhár segir: Askrinn er allra trjá mestr ok beztr. Limar hans dreifast um heim allan ok standa yfir himni. Þrjár røtr trésins halda því upp ok standa afar breitt. Ein er með ásum, ǫnnur með hrímþussum, þar sem forðum var Ginnungagap. Þriðja stendr yfir Nif⟨l⟩heim[1] ok undir þeiri rót er Hvergelmir. En Níðhǫgr gnagar neðan rótina. En undir þeiri rót er til hrímþussa horfir er Mímisbrunnr, er spekt ok mannvit er í folgit, ok heitir sá Mímir er á brunninn. Hann er fullr af vísendum fyrir því at hann drekkr ór brunninum ór Gjallarhorni. Þá kom Alfǫðr ok beiddist eins drykkjar af brunninum. En hann lagði auga sitt í veð. Svá segir í Vǫluspá:

20 (19) Allt veit ek Óðinn
hvar þú auga falt
í þeim enum mæra
Mímisbrunni.
Drekkr mjǫð Mímir
morgin hverjan
af veði Valsfǫðr.
Viti þér enn eða hvat?

Þriðja rót asksins stendr á himnum ok undir þeiri rót er Urðarbrunnr. Þar eiga goðin dómstað. Hvern dag ríða æsir þar upp um Bifrǫst. Hon heitir ok Ásabrú. Þessi eru nǫfn hestanna ása: Sleipnir er beztr, hann á Óðinn. Hann hefir átta føtr. Annarr Glaðr, þriði Gyllir, fjórði Skeiðbrimir, fimti Slintoppr, sétti Sinir, sjaundi Gils, átti Falófnir, níundi[2] Gullltoppr, tíundi Léttfeti. Baldrs hestr var brendr með honum. En Þór⟨r⟩ gengr at dómi ok veðr þar at[3] er svá heita:[4]

21 (20) Kǫrmt ok Ǫrmt
ok Kerlaugar tvær,
þær skal Þórr vaða
hvern dag
er hann døma ferr
at aski[5] Ygdrasils,
því at Ásbrú
brennr ǫll loga,
en heilǫg vǫtn flóa.

Þá mælti Gangleri: Brennr eldr yfir Bifrǫst?

Hár segir: Þar er þú sér í regnboganum rautt er eldr brennandi upp á himin. Þá mundi ganga bergrisar Bifrǫst ef ǫllum væri ferð[6] at er fara vildi.

---

[1] Here written 'Nifheim' but elsewhere always 'Nifl-'.
[2] The manuscript has '.x.', but this must be an error for '.ix.'
[3] Probably an error for þær ár (ár þær GkS 2367 4to).
[4] Cf. *Grímnismál* 29.
[5] Written 'askæ'; æ for unstressed e/i is found on eight other occasions in DG 11 4to.
[6] Other manuscripts have *fǿrt* here, which gives better sense: 'if it was crossable'.

Then spoke Gangleri: 'What is there to tell about that place?'

Just-as-high says: 'The ash is of all trees the biggest and best. Its branches spread out over all the world and extend across the sky. Three of the tree's roots support it and extend very very far. One is among the Æsir, the second among the frost giants, where Ginnungagap once was. The third extends over Niflheimr, and under that root is Hvergelmir. And Níðhǫggr gnaws the root from below. And under that root that reaches towards the frost giants is Mímir's spring, that has wisdom and intelligence contained in it, and the one that is master of the spring is called Mímir. He is full of learning because he drinks of the spring from Gjallarhorn. Then All-father came and asked for a single drink from the spring. And he placed his eye as a pledge. So it says in *Vǫluspá*:

20   I know it all, Óðinn,
    where you deposited your eye
    in that renowned
    well of Mímir.
    Mímir drinks mead
    every morning,
    from Valsfǫðr's pledge.
    Know you yet, or what?

'The third root of the ash extends to the heavens, and under that root is Urðr's spring. There the gods hold their court. Every day the Æsir ride there up over Bifrǫst. It is also called the Æsir's bridge. These are the names of the Æsir's horses: the best is Sleipnir, it is Óðinn's. It has eight legs. Second Glaðr, third Gyllir, fourth Skeiðbrimir, fifth Slintoppr, sixth Sinir, seventh Gils, eighth Falófnir, ninth Gulltoppr, tenth Léttfeti. Baldr's horse was burned with him. But Þórr walks to the court and wades the rivers whose names are:

21 (20)   Kǫrmt and Ǫrmt
    and two Kerlaugs,
    these must Þórr wade
    every day
    when he goes to judge
    at the ash Ygdrasill,
    because Áss-bridge
    burns all with flame
    and holy waters flood.'

Then spoke Gangleri: 'Does fire burn over Bifrǫst?'

High says: 'Where you see red in the rainbow, it is fire flaming up to heaven. Mountain giants would then walk Bifrǫst if there were travel there for all that wanted to go.

Margir staðir eru á himni fagrir ok er þar allt guðlig vernd fyrir. Þar stendr staðr einn undir askinum við brunninn ok ór þeim sal koma þrjár meyjar er svá heita: Uðr, Verðandi, Skuld. Þær meyjar skapa mǫnnum aldr. Þat kǫllu vér nornir. En⟨n⟩ eru fleiri nornir þær er koma til hvers barns er fǿtt er, at skapa aldr. Þær eru goðkyndar,[1] en aðrar álfa ættar, en enar þriðju dverga ættar, svá sem hér segir:[2]

22 (21)   Sundrbornar
hygg ek nornir vera
eigut þær ætt saman.
Sumar eru áskyndar,
sumar álfkyndar,
sumar eru dǿtr Dvalins.

Þá mælti Gangleri: Ef nornir ráða ørlǫgum manna, þá skipta þær geysi misjafnt. Sumir hafa gott líf ok ríkuligt, en sumir hafa lítit lén ok lof, sumir langt líf, sumir skamt.

Hár segir: Góðar meyjar ok vel ættaðar skapa góðan aldr. En þeir menn er fyrir óskǫpum verða, þá valda því illar nornir.

15 Frá aski Ygdrasils

Þá mælti Gangleri: Hvat er at segja fleira frá askinum?

Hár segir: Margt er þar af at segja. Ǫrn einn sitr á limum asksins ok er hann margs vitandi, en millum augna honum sitr haukr sá er heitir Veðrlaufnir. Íkorni sá er heitir Ratakostr rennr upp ok niðr eptir askinum ok berr ǫfundarorð millum arnarins ok Níðhǫgs. En fjórir hirtir renna í limum asksins ok bíta bast. Þeir heita svá: Daninn, Dvalinn, Dyneyrr, Dyraþrór. En svá margir ormar eru í Hvergelmi með Níðhǫgi at engi tunga má telja. Svá sem hér segir:[3]

23 (22)   Askr Ygdrasils
drýgir erfiði
meira en menn um viti:
Hjǫrtr bítr neðan[4]
en á hliðu fúnar,
skerðir Níðhǫgr neðan.

Ok enn segir hér svá:[5]

[1] Written *goþkynþar*, in the verse *-kyndar*.
[2] Cf. *Fáfnismál* 13
[3] Cf. *Grímnismál* 35.
[4] The other manuscripts have *ofan*.
[5] Cf. *Grímnismál* 34.

'There are many beautiful places in heaven, and everywhere there has divine protection round it. One place stands there under the ash by the spring, and out of this hall come three maidens that are called U⟨r⟩ðr, Verðandi, Skuld. These maidens shape men's lives. We call them norns. There are also other norns that visit every child that is born, to shape their lives. These are of divine origin, while others are of the race of elves, and a third group are of the race of dwarfs, as it says here:

22   Of diverse parentage
     I consider norns to be,
     they do not have a common ancestry.
     Some are descended from Æsir,
     some descended from elves,
     some are daughters of Dvalinn.'

Then spoke Gangleri: 'If norns determine the destinies of men, then they allot terribly unfairly. Some have a good life and a prosperous one, while some have little success and glory, some long life, some short.'

High says: 'Good maidens, ones of noble parentage, shape a good life. But the people that become the victims of misfortune, then it is evil norns that are responsible.'

15 Of the ash Yggdrasill

Then spoke Gangleri: 'What else is to be said of the ash?'

High says: 'A great deal is to be said of it. An eagle sits on the ash's branches, and it has knowledge of many things, and between its eyes sits a hawk that is called Veðrlaufnir. A squirrel that is called Ratakostr runs up and down through the ash and carries malicious messages between the eagle and Níðhǫggr. And four stags run in the branches of the ash and feed on the bark. They are called Daninn, Dvalinn, Dyneyrr, Dyraþrór. And so many snakes are in Hvergelmir with Níðhǫggr that no tongue can enumerate them. As it says here:

23   The ash Yggdrasill
     suffers hardships
     more than people realise:
     a stag bites from below,
     and at the sides it rots,
     Níðhǫggr eats away at it from below.

'And it says further here:

24 (23) Ormar fleiri
liggja undir aski Ygdrasils
en þat um hyggi hverr ósvinnra apa.
Góni ok Móni
þeir eru Grafvitnis liðar.
Grábakr ok Grafvǫlduðr.
Ófnir ok Sváfnir
hygg ek | at æ muni
meiðs kostum má.[1]

Þat er enn sagt at nornir þær er byggva við Urðarbrunn taka hvern dag vatn ór brunninum ok aurinn með, þann er liggr um brunninn ok ausa upp yfir askinn til þess at eigi skulu limar hans fúna eða tréna. En þat vatn er svá heilagt at allir er þar koma eru svá hvítir sem hinna sú er skjall heitir er liggr innan um eggskurmsl. Svá sem hér segir:[2]

25 (24) Ask veit ek standa
heitir Ygdrasill
hár borinn heilagr
hvíta auri.
Þaðan koma dǫggvar
þær í dali falla.
Stendr yfir grein
Urðarbrunni.

Sú dǫgg er þaðan af kemr kalla menn hunangsfall ok þaðan af fǿðast býflugur. Fuglar tveir fǿðast í Urðarbrunni er svanir heita, ok af þeim fuglum hefir þat fuglakyn komit er svá heitir síðan.

16 Hér segir frá Álfheimum

Þá mælir Gangleri: Mikil tíðindi kantu segja af honum. Hvat er þar fleira hǫfuðstaða en at Urðarbrunni?

Hár segir: Margir staðir eru þar gǫfugligir. Sá er þar staðr er kallaðr er Álfheimar. Þar byggvir fólk þat er ljósálfar heita. En dǫkkálfar búa niðri undir jǫrðu ok eru þeir ólíkir sýnum ok enn ólíkari reyndum. Ljósálfar eru hvítari en sól sýnum, en dǫkkálfar svartari en bik.

Þar er ok sá staðr er Breiðablik heitir ok engi er þar fegri staðr.

Þar er ok sá staðr er Glitnir heitir ok eru veggir hans ok steðr allar af rauðu gulli ok þak hans er af gulli.

[1] Codex Regius of the *Poetic Edda* has *meiðs kvistu* (acc.) *má* (eat away). Other manuscripts of *Snorra Edda* have *kvistum* ('twigs'), only DG 11 4to has *kostum* ('condition, state').
[2] Cf. *Vǫluspá* 19.

24 More snakes
    lie beneath the ash Yggdrasill
    than any one of the stupid apes thinks.
    Góni and Móni,
    they are Grafvitnir's followers,
    Grábakr and Grafvǫlduðr,
    Ófnir and Sváfnir
    I think will for ever
    damage the tree's being.

'It is also said that the norns that dwell by Urðr's spring take water from the spring each day and with it the mud that lies round the well and pour it up over the ash so that its branches may not decay or rot. And this water is so holy that all those that come there are as white as the membrane that is called the skin that lies round the inside of an eggshell. As it says here:

25 I know that an ash stands,
    it is called Yggdrasill,
    tall, holy, poured over
    by white mud.
    From it come the dews
    that fall in the valleys.
    A branch stands above
    Urðr's spring.

'The dew that falls from it, people call it honeydew, and from it bees feed. Two birds feed in Urðr's spring that are called swans, and from these birds has come the species of bird that has since been called that.'

16 Here it tells of the world of elves

Then speaks Gangleri: 'You are able to give a great deal of information about it. What other chief centres are there besides the one at Urðr's spring?'

High says: 'Many splendid places are there. There is a place there that is called the world of elves. The folk live there that are called light-elves. But dark-elves live down under the earth, and they are unlike in appearance and even more unlike in nature. Light-elves are whiter than the sun to look at, but dark-elves blacker than pitch.

'There is also the place there that is called Breiðablik, and there is no fairer place there.

'There is also the place there that is called Glitnir, and its walls and columns are all of red gold, and its roof is of gold.

Þar er sá staðr er Himinbjǫrg heita. Sá stendr á himins enda við brúar sporð, þar er Bifrǫst kemr til himins.

Þar er enn mikill staðr er Valaskjálf heitir. Þann gerðu ok þǫktu skíru silfri.[1] Þar er ok Hliðskjálf í þeim sal, þat hásæti er svá heitir. Þá er Alfǫðr sitr í því hásæti sér hann um heim allan.

Á sunnanverðum heims enda er sá staðr er allra er fegrstr ok bjartari en sólin, er Gimlé heitir. Hann skal standa þá er himinn ok jǫrð fyrirfarast, ok byggva þann stað réttlátir menn um aldir alda. Svá segir í Vǫluspá:[2]

26 (25) Sal veit ek standa
 sólu fegra
 gulli þaktan
 á Gimlé.
 Þar skulu dyggvar
 dróttir byggja
 ok um aldrdaga
 ynðis njóta.

Þá mælti Gangleri: Hverr gætir þess staðar þá er svartalogi brennir himin ok jǫrð?

Hár segir: Svá er sagt at annarr himinn sé suðr ok upp frá þessum ok heitir sá heimr Víðbláinn, en hinn þriði sé upp frá þeim ok heitir sá Ǫndlangr, ok á þeim himni hyggju vér þenna stað vera. En ljósálfar einir hyggju vér at nú byggi | þá staði.

17 Hér segir frá nǫfnum Óðins ok ríki

Þá mælti Gangleri: Hverir eru æsir þeir er mǫnnum er skylt at trúa á?

Hár svarar: Tólf eru æsir goðkunnigir.

Þá mælti Jafnhár: Eigi eru ásynjur óhelgari, ok eigi megu þær minna.

Þá mælti Þriði: Óðinn er ǿztr ok elztr ásanna. Hann ræðr ǫllum hlutum ok svá sem ǫnnur goðin eru máttug, þá þjóna honum ǫll svá sem bǫrn fǫður. En Frigg kona hans veit ok ørlǫg manna, þótt hon segi engar spár, sem sagt er at Óðinn sjálfr mælti við þann ás er Loki er nefndr:[3]

27 (27) Ærr ertu nú orðinn
 ok ørviti,
 hví floptir þú Loptr?

[1] The subject of this sentence is missing, but is presumably to be understood as *guðin* 'the gods', as in the other manuscripts.

[2] Cf. *Vǫluspá* 64.

[3] Cf. *Lokasenna* 21, 29, and perhaps 47. The stanza is easier to understand in the other manuscripts (cf. Faulkes 2005: 21), which are almost the same as in GkS 2365 4to. *Floptir* is not a recognisable word.

'There is the place there that is called Himinbjǫrg. It stands at the edge of heaven by the bridge's end, where Bifrǫst reaches heaven.

'There is also a large place there that is called Valaskjálf. They built this and roofed it with pure silver. Hliðskjálf is also there in that hall, the throne of that name. When All-father sits on that throne he can see over all the world.

'At the southernmost end of heaven is the place that is fairest of all and brighter than the sun, which is called Gimlé. It shall stand when heaven and earth are destroyed, and righteous people shall live in that place for ever and ever. So it says in *Vǫluspá*:

26   I know a hall standing
fairer than the sun,
roofed with gold
at Gimlé.
There shall virtuous
men dwell
and for all ages
enjoy delights.'

Then spoke Gangleri: 'Who will protect this place when the dark fire burns heaven and earth?'

High says: 'They say there is another heaven south of and above this one of ours, and that one is called Víðbláinn, and that a third one is above that one and it is called Ǫndlangr, and it is in that heaven that we believe this place to be. But we believe it is only light-elves that inhabit these places for the time being.

17 Here it tells of Óðinn's names and rule

Then spoke Gangleri: 'Which are the Æsir that men ought to believe in?'

High replies: 'There are twelve Æsir whose nature is divine.'

Then spoke Just-as-high: 'No less holy are the Ásynjur, nor is their power less.'

Then spoke Third: 'Óðinn is highest and most ancient of the Æsir. He rules all things, and mighty though the other gods are, yet they all submit to him like children to their father. But his wife Frigg also knows men's destinies though she does not prophesy, as it is said that Óðinn himself said to the Áss who is named Loki:

27   Mad have you now become,
and out of your wits,
why do you . . . , Loptr?

Ørlǫg manna
Frigg hygg ek at þau viti
því at henni sjálfgi segir.

Óðinn heitir Alfaðir því at hann er faðir allra goðanna. Hann heitir ok Valfǫðr, því at hans óskasynir eru allir þeir er í val falla. Þeim skipar hann Valhǫll ok Vingólf ok heita þeir þá einherjar. Hann heitir ok Hangaguð ok Happaguð ok Farmaguð. Ok enn nefnist hann á fleira vega; þá er hann var kominn til Geirraðar konungs segir hann svá:[1]

28 (28)   Hétumst Grímr
ok Gangleri,
Herjann, Hjálmberi,
Þekkr, Þriði,
Þuðruðr,
Helblindi, Hár.

29   Saðr, Svipall,
Sanngetall,
Herteitr, Hnikarr,
Bileygr, Báleygr,
Bǫlverkr, Fjǫlnir,
Grímnir, Glapsviðr, Fjǫlsviðr.

30   Síðhǫttr, Síðskeggr,
Sigfǫðr, Atríðr,
Hnikuðr, Alfǫðr, Farmatýr,
Óski, Ómi,
Jafnhár, Biblindi,
Geldnir, Hárbarðr,
Sviðurr, Sviðrir,
Jálkr, Kjalarr, Viðurr,
Þrór, Gautr,
Jálkr, Veratýr.

Þá mælti Gangleri: Geysi mǫrg nǫfn hafi þér gefit honum, ok þat veit trú mín at þat mun vera mikill fróðleikr sá er kann skyn ok dǿmi hverir atburðir orðit hafa til hvers þessa nafns.

Hár segir: Mikil skynsemi er at rifja þat vandliga upp, en þó er þat skjótast at segja at flest heiti hafa verit gefin af þeim a⟨t⟩burðum at svá margar eru greinir tungna í verǫldinni, þá þikkjast allir þjóðir þurfa at breyta nafni hans

[1] Cf. *Grímnismál* 46–50.

Destinies of men,
I think that Frigg knows them
because she herself does not tell her.

'Óðinn is called All-father, for he is father of all the gods. He is also called Valfǫðr (father of the slain), since all those that fall in battle are his adoptive sons. He assigns them places in Valhǫll and Vingólf, and they are then known as Einherjar. He is also called Hangaguð and Happaguð and Farmaguð. And he calls himself by still other names; when he was come to King Geirrøðr he says this:

28 I called myself Grímr
and Gangleri,
Herjann, Hjálmberi,
Þekkr, Þriði,
Þuðruðr,
Helblindi, Hár.

29 Saðr, Svipall,
Sanngetall,
Herteitr, Hnikarr,
Bileygr, Báleygr,
Bǫlverkr, Fjǫlnir,
Grímnir, Glapsviðr, Fjǫlsviðr.

30 Síðhǫttr, Síðskeggr,
Sigfǫðr, Atríðr,
Hnikuðr, Alfǫðr, Farmatýr,
Óski, Ómi,
Jafnhár, Biblindi,
Geldnir, Hárbarðr,
Sviðurr, Sviðrir,
Jálkr, Kjalarr, Viðurr,
Þrór, Gautr,
Jálkr, Veratýr.'

Then spoke Gangleri: 'A terrible lot of names you have given him, and by my faith, one would need a great deal of learning to be able to give details and explanations of what events have given rise to each of these names.'

High says: 'It is very instructive to go closely into all this, but to put it most briefly, most names have been given him as a result of the fact that with all the branches of languages in the world all nations find it necessary

til sinnar tungu til bǿnaferlis sjálfum sér.[1] En sumir atburðir til þessa heita hafa gerzt í ferðum hans ok er þat fǿrt í frásagnir, ok muntu eigi mega fróðr maðr heita ef þú skalt eigi kunna at segja frá þessum stórtíðindum.

Gangleri segir: Hver eru nǫfn annarra goðanna eða ásanna, eða hvat hafa þeir gert til frama?

18 Hér segir frá Þór ok ríki hans ok Bilskirni

f. 8r, p. 13 Hár segir: | Þórr er þeira framarst, sá er kallaðr er Ása-Þórr eða Ǫku-Þórr. Hann er sterkastr ása ok allra guðanna ok manna. Hann á þar ríki er Þr⟨úð⟩vangr heitir. En hǫll hans heitir Bilskirnir. Í þeim sal eru fimm hundruð gólfa ok fjórir tigir. Þat er hús mest svá at menn viti. Svá segir í Grímnismálum:[2]

31 (29) Fimm hundruð gólfa
 ok fjóratugu
 svá hygg ek Bilskirni með bogum.
 Ranna þeira
 er ek ræfr vita
 míns veit ek mest magar.

Þórr á hafra tvá ok reið eina. Svá heita hafrarnir: Tangnjóstr ok Tangrisnir. Þórr ekr í reiðinni þá er hann ferr í Jǫtunheima, en hafrarnir draga reiðina. Því heitir hann Ǫku-Þórr.

Hann á ok þrjá kostgripi. Einn er hamarrinn Mjǫlnir er hrímþussar ok bergrisar kenna er á lopt kemr. Ok er þat eigi undarligt því at þar með hefir hann lamðan margan haus á feðrum þeira ok frændum.

Annan grip á hann beztan, megingjarðir, ok er hann spennir þeim um sik vex honum ásmegin hálfu.

Þriðja grip á hann þann er mikill gripr er í. Þat er járngreipr. Þeira má hann eigi missa við hamarskaptit. En engi er svá frægr at telja kunni hans stórmerki. En segja kann ek þér mǫrg tíðindi, at dveljast mun dagr áðr en sagt er allt þat er ek veit.

Þá mælti Gangleri: Spyrja vil ek at fleirum sonum hans.

Hár svarar: Annarr sonr hans er Baldr inn góði ok er frá honum gott at segja. Hann er beztr ok hann lofa allir. Hann er svá fagr álitum ok svá bjartr at lýsir

---

[1] *Bǿnaferli* seems to be hapax legomenon, and does not appear in any dictionary except *ONP*, which gives it as a variant reading. Gunnar Karlsson has pointed out to me that there are many similar compounds in Old Norse, e.g. *atferli*, *búferli*, *orðferli*. These suggest that the meaning is 'religious activity, act of prayer'. Helgi Skúli Kjartansson has pointed out to me that the Stockholm Homily book says that one gets one's prayer fulfilled 'at ſa feʀ rétt bǿninı ſvaſem dominuſ dici<i>t</i> ſiálfr.' This wording is unique, and so it is not far-fetched to imagine that *bǿnaferli* was such a rare word in the thirteenth century that the scribe of the original of the Codex Regius version of *Snorra Edda* avoided using it, and replaced it with *til ákalls og bǿna*.

[2] Cf. *Grímnismál* 24.

to adapt his name to their language for praying for themselves. But some events giving rise to these names have taken place in his travels and have been made the subject of stories, and you cannot claim to be a learned person if you are unable to tell of these important happenings.'

Gangleri says: 'What are the names of the other gods and Æsir, and what glorious works have they done?'

18 Here it tells of Þórr and his rule and Bilskirnir

High says: 'Þórr is the most outstanding of them. He is called Þórr of the Æsir or Qku-Þórr (Driving-Þórr). He is the strongest of the Æsir and of all the gods and men. His realm is a place called Þrúðvangr. But his hall is called Bilskirnir. In that hall there are five hundred and forty apartments. It is the largest hall as far as men know. So it says in *Grímnismál*:

31   Five hundred apartments
        and forty,
        I think are in Bilskirnir in all.
        Of the buildings
        whose roofs I know,
        I know my son's is the greatest.

'Þórr has two goats and a chariot. The goats are called thus: Tangnjóstr and Tangrisnir. Þórr drives in his chariot when he goes to the world of giants, and the goats draw the chariot. This is why he is called Qku-Þórr.

'He also has three special possessions. One is the hammer Mjǫllnir, well known to frost giants and mountain giants when it is raised aloft. And that is not to be wondered at, for with it he has smashed many a skull for their fathers and kinsmen.

'Another possession he has that is very valuable, a girdle of might, and when he buckles it on, his Áss-strength is doubled.

'He has a third possession that is a most important possession. This is a pair of iron gauntlets. He must not be without these when he holds the hammer-shaft. But no one is so famous that he can recount all his exploits. But I can tell you many stories so that it will be a long day before all that I know is told.'

Then spoke Gangleri: 'I would like to hear about more of his sons.'

High replies: 'His second son is Baldr the Good, and there is good to be told of him. He is the best and all praise him. He is so fair in appearance

af honum, ok eitt gras er svá hvítt at jafnat er við brá Baldrs. Þat er allra grasa hvítast ok þar eptir máttu marka fegrð hans, bæði á hár ok á s̶i̶l̶k̶i̶ líkam. Hann er hvítastr ása ok fegrst talaðr ok líknsamastr. En sú náttúra fylgir honum at eigi má haldast dómr hans. Hann byggvir þann stað er Breiðablik heitir ok fyrr er nefndr. Hann er á himni. Í þeim stað má eigi óhreint vera, svá sem hér segir:[1]

32 (30) Breiðablik heitir
þar er Baldr hefir
sér um gerva sali
á því landi
er ek liggja veit
fæsta fæingstafi.[2]

Enn þriði áss er sá er Njǫrðr heitir. Hann býr þar sem heitir Nóatún. Hann ræðr þar fyrir gǫngu vinds ok stillir sjó ok vind ok eld. Á hann skal heita til sæfara ok veiða. Hann er svá auðigr eða fésæll at hann má gefa þeim land ok lausafé er hann vill. Á hann skal til þess heita.

Eigi er Njǫrðr ása ættar. Hann var upp føddr í Vanaheimi. En vanir gísluðu hann guðum ok tóku í móti þann er Hønir hét. | Þat varð at sætt með guðum ok vǫnum.

Njǫrðr átti þá konu er Skaði heitir, dóttir Þjaza jǫtuns. Hon vildi hafa bústað þann er faðir hennar hefir át⟨t⟩. Þat er á fjǫllum nokkurum, þar er heitir Þrúðheimr. En Njǫrðr vill vera nær sæ. Þau sættast á þat at þau skulu vera níu nætr í Þrúðheimi en þrjár í Nóatúnum. En er Njǫrðr kom aptr til Nóatúna af fjallinu, þá kvað hann þetta:

33 (31) Leið erumst fjǫll
varkata ek lengi hjá,
nætr einar níu.
Úlfa þytr
mér þótti illr vera
hjá sǫngvi svana.

Þá kvað Skaði:

34 (32) Sofa ek máki[3]
sævar beðjum á
fugls jarmi fyrir;
sá mik vekr
er af víði kemr
morgin hvern: már.

[1] Cf. *Grímnismál* 12.
[2] Doubtless an error (perhaps a mishearing) for *feiknstafi* (so other manuscripts).
[3] *máki* clearly should be a negative form, i.e. *máka*; *-i* is not normally negative. GkS 2367 4to has *máttak*, which is not a negative form either (emended to *máttigak* in Faulkes 2005). Codex Wormianus has *ne mátta*, Codex Trajectinus *ek mátka*.

and so bright that light shines from him, and there is a plant so white that it is compared to Baldr's eyelash. It is the whitest of all plants, and from this you can tell his beauty both in hair and body. He is the whitest of the Æsir and the most beautifully spoken and most merciful. But it is one of his characteristics that no decision of his can be carried out. He lives in a place that is called Breiðablik and has been mentioned before. It is in heaven. No unclean thing is permitted to be in that place, as it says here:

32   It is called Breiðablik
      where Baldr has
      built himself halls,
      in that land
      where I know to be
      fewest evil intents.

'The third Áss is the one that is called Njǫrðr. He lives in a place called Nóatún. He rules there over the motion of the wind and moderates sea and wind and fire. It is to him one must pray for voyages and fishing. He is so rich and wealthy that he can grant land and possessions to whomever he wishes. One must pray to him for this.

'Njǫrðr is not of the race of Æsir. He was brought up in the world of the Vanir. But the Vanir gave him as hostage to the gods and took in exchange the one called Hǿnir. This came to be the settlement between the gods and Vanir.

'Njǫrðr had a wife that is called Skaði, daughter of the giant Þjazi. She wanted to have the home that her father has had. This is in certain mountains, in a place called Þrúðheimr. But Njǫrðr wants to be near the sea. They agreed on this, that they shall be nine nights in Þrúðheimr and three in Nóatún. But when Njǫrðr came back to Nóatún from the mountain, then he said this:

33   I hate mountains,
      I was not long near them
      just nine nights.
      Wolves' howling
      I thought ugly
      compared with the swans' song.

'Then said Skaði:

34   I cannot sleep
      on the sea's beds
      for the birds' screaming;
      he wakes me
      who comes from out at sea
      every morning: that gull.

Þá fór Skaði upp á fjall ok bygði á Þrúðheimi ok ferr hon mjǫk með boga ok skíðum ok skýtr dýr. Hon heitir ǫndurguð eða ǫndurdís. Svá segir:[1]

35 (33) Þrúðheimr heitir
þar nú Þjazi býr
sá enn mátki jǫtunn.
En nú Skaði bygg⟨i⟩r,
skír brúðr guma,
fornar toptir fǫður.

19 Frá bǫrnum Njarðar

Njǫrðr í Nóatúnum gat síðan tvau bǫrn. Hét annat Freyr er einn er ágætastr með guðum. Hann ræðr fyrir regni ok skini sólar ok þar með jarðar ávexti. Á hann er gott at heita til árs ok friðar. Hann ræðr friði ok fésælu manna.

Annat barn hans er Freyja. Hon er ágætust af ásynjum. Hon á þann bǿ á himnum er Fól⟨k⟩vang⟨r⟩ heitir, ok hvar sem hon ríðr til vígs á hon hálfan val allan en hálfan Óðinn. Svá segir:[2]

36 (34) Fólkvangr heitir
en þar Freyja ræðr
kosta beztum sal.
Hálfan val
hon kýss hvern dag,
en hálfan Óðinn á.

Sessvarnir heitir ok salr hennar.[3] En er hon ríðr þá ekr hon á kǫttum sínum ok sitr í reið.[4] Hon er nákvæmust mǫnnum til áheita ok af hennar nafni er þat tignar nafn er ríkiskonur eru kallaðar frúr. Henni líkaði vel mansǫngr. Á hana er gott at heita til ásta.

Þá mælti Gangleri: Miklir þikki mér þessir fyrir sér æsirnir. Ok eigi er undr at mikill kraptr fylgi yðr er þér skuluð kunna skyn guðanna ok vita hvern biðja skal hvers hlutar eða hverrar bǿnar, eða eru fleiri guðin?

20 Hversu biðja skal ásinn ok frá Braga ok Heimdall

Hár svarar: Þá er enn áss er Týr heitir. Hann er djarfastr ok breythugaðr[5] ok hann ræðr mjǫk sigri í orrostum. Á hann er gott at heita hreysti mǫnnum. Þat

---

[1] Cf. *Grímnismál* 11. Other manuscripts read *er Þjazi bjó* 'where Þjazi lived' in line 2, which makes better sense. In both GkS 2365 and the other manuscripts of *Snorra Edda*, Þjazi is called *(h)inn ámátki jǫtunn*, and that probably means something similar to *enn mátki jǫtunn*, perhaps 'very powerful', 'very terrible' or 'filled with supernatural power' (see Gísli Sigurðsson 1998: 73).

[2] Cf. *Grímnismál* 14.

[3] The hall is called *Sessrúmnir* in other manuscripts and here on p. 148 below.

[4] Cf. note 3 on p. 20 above.

[5] GkS 2367 has *bezt hvgaðr* 'most courageous'.

'Then Skaði went up onto the mountain and lived in Þrúðheimr, and generally travels with a bow and skis and shoots game. She is called ski-deity or ski-goddess. So it says:

35   It is called Þrúðheimr,
there Þjazi now lives,
that mighty giant.
But now Skaði inhabits,
bright bride of men,
her father's old abode.'

19 Of Njǫrðr's children

'Njǫrðr of Nóatún had afterwards two children. One was called Freyr, who is particularly glorious among the gods. He is ruler of rain and sunshine and thus of the produce of the earth. It is good to pray to him for prosperity and peace. He rules peace and wealth of men.

'His other child is Freyja. She is the most glorious of the Ásynjur. She has a dwelling in the heavens that is called Fólkvangr, and wherever she rides to battle she gets half of all the slain, and Óðinn gets the other half. So it says:

36   There is a place called Fólkvangr,
and there Freyja is in charge
of the hall that is finest in its accommodation.
Half the slain
she chooses each day,
and half Óðinn has.

'Her hall is also called Sessvarnir. And when she rides, then she drives with her cats and sits in a chariot. She is the most approachable one for people for invoking, and from her name is derived the honorific title whereby noblewomen are called 'frúr' (ladies). She was very fond of love songs. It is good to pray to her concerning love affairs.'

Then spoke Gangleri: 'Most important these Æsir seem to me to be. And it is no wonder that great power is with you when you claim to be acquainted with details about the gods and know which one must be prayed to for each thing and for each request, but are there more of the gods?'

20 How one should pray to the Áss and of Bragi and Heimdallr

High replies: 'Then there is also an Áss that is called Týr. He is the bravest and changeable in his mind and he has a lot of control over victory in battles. It is good for men of action to pray to him. There is a saying

er orðtak at sá er týhraustr er umfram er aðra. Ok þat er eitt mark um hraustleik hans ok djarfleik, | þá er æsir lokkuðu Fenrisúlf til þess at leggja á hann fjǫturinn Gleifni,[1] þá trúði hann þeim eigi at þeir mundi leysa hann fyrr en þeir lǫgðu honum at veði hǫnd Týs í munn hans. En er æsirnir vildu eigi leysa hann, þá beit hann af hǫndina þar sem nú heitir úlfliðr ok er hann einhendr. Hann er svá vitr at þat er ok mælt at sá sé týrspakr. En ekki er hann kallaðr sættir manna.

Bragi er einn ássinn. Hann er ágætr at speki ok mest at málsnilld ok orðfimi. Hann kann mest af skáldskap, ok af honum er bragr kallaðr skáldskaprinn. Ok af hans nafni er sá kallaðr bragarmaðr, karla eða kvenna, er orðsnilld hefir framarr en aðrir.

Kona Braga heitir Iðunn. Hon varðveitir í eski sínu epli þau er guðin skulu á bíta, þá er þau eldast. Ok verða þá allir ungir, ok svá mun verða til Ragnarøkkrs.

Þá segir Gangleri: Allmikit þikki mér guðin eiga undir gæzlu Iðunnar eða trúnaði.

Þá mælti Hár ok hló við: Nær lagði þat ófǿru einu sinni. Kunna mun ek þar af at segja. En þú skalt nú heyra fleiri nǫfn guðanna.

Heimdallr heitir einn. Hann er kallaðr inn hvíti áss. Hann er mikill ok heilagr. Hann báru at syni níu meyjar ok allar systr. Hann heitir ok Hjálmskíði ok Gullintanni. Tenn hans vóru af gulli. Hestr hans heitir Gulltoppr. Hann býr þar sem heitir Himinbjǫrg við Bifrǫst. Hann er vǫrðr guða ok sitr þar við heims enda at gæta brúar fyrir bergrisum. Hann þarf minna svefn en fugl. Hann sér jamt um nótt sem um dag hundrað rasta frá sér. Hann heyrir ok þat er gras vex á jǫrðunni ok ull á sauðum ok allt þat er lætr. Hann hefir lúðr þann er heitir Gjallarhorn ok heyrir blástr hans í heima alla. Svá segir:[2]

37 (35) Himinbjǫrg heitir,
    en þar Heimdallr býr,
    kveða valda véum,
    vǫrðum guða.
    Drekkr í væru ranni
    glaðr en⟨n⟩ góða mjǫð.

Ok enn segir í sjálfum Heimdallargaldri:

38 (36) Níu em ek meyja mǫgr
    níu em ek systra sonr.

Hǫðr heitir enn einn ássinn. Hann er blindr. Ørit er hann sterkr. En vilja mundi goðin ok menninir at þenna ásinn þyrfti eigi at nefna, því at hans handa verk munu lengi hǫfð at minnum.

[1] The fetter's name is usually *Gleipnir*, as in ch. 22. Insular f (ꝼ) and p are easily confused.
[2] Cf. *Grímnismál* 13. Lines 2–5 in GkS 2365 4to and other manuscripts of *Snorra Edda* read *en þar Heimdall kveða valda véum. Þar vǫrðr goða drekkr* ... ('and there they say Heimdallr rules the holy places. There the gods' watchman drinks ...'), so having the usual break after line 3.

that a man is *týr*-valiant who surpasses others. And it is one proof of his valour and bravery, when the Æsir were luring Fenriswolf so as to get the fetter Gleifnir on him, then he did not trust them that they would let him go until they placed Týr's hand in his mouth as a pledge. And when the Æsir refused to let him go, then he bit off his hand at the place that is now called the wolf joint, and he is one-handed. He is so intelligent that it is also said that so-and-so is *týr*-wise. But he is not considered a promoter of settlements between people.

'Bragi is one Áss. He is renowned for wisdom and especially for eloquence and command of language. He is especially knowledgeable about poetry, and because of him the poetry is called *bragr*. And from his name a person is said to be a *bragr* ('chief') of men, both male and female, who has eloquence beyond others.

'Bragi's wife is called Iðunn. She keeps in her casket the apples that the gods have to feed on when they age. And then they all become young, and so it will go on until the twilight of the gods.'

Then says Gangleri: 'It seems to me that the gods are staking a great deal on Iðunn's care and trustworthiness.'

Then spoke High, laughing: 'It nearly led to disaster on one occasion. I shall be able tell you about that. But you must now hear more names of the gods.

'There is one called Heimdallr. He is known as the white Áss. He is great and holy. Nine maidens bore him as their son, all of them sisters. He is also called Hjálmskíði and Gullintanni. His teeth were of gold. His horse is called Gulltoppr. He lives in a place called Himinbjǫrg by Bifrǫst. He is the gods' watchman and sits there at the end of the world to guard the bridge against mountain giants. He needs less sleep than a bird. He can see, just as well by night as by day, a distance of a hundrd leagues. He can also hear grass growing on the earth and wool on sheep and everything that makes a sound. He has a trumpet called Gjallarhorn and its blast can be heard in all worlds. So it says:

37 There is a place called Himinbjǫrg,
    and there Heimdallr dwells,
    they say he controls the guardianship
    for the holy places of the gods.
    He drinks in the pleasant hall,
    merry, the good mead.

'And moreover he says in Heimdallargaldr itself:

38 Offspring of nine maidens am I,
    of nine sisters am I the son.

'There is another Áss that is called Hǫðr. He is blind. Only too strong is he. And the gods and men would prefer that this Áss did not need to be named, for his handiwork will long be kept in mind.

Viðarr heitir inn þǫgli áss. Hann hefir skó þykkan. Næst því er hann sterkr sem Þórr. Af honum hafa goðin mikit traust í allar þrautir.

Áli eða Váli heitir einn, sonr Óðins ok Rindar. Hann er djarfr í orrostum ok mjǫk hagskeytr.

Ullr heitir einn, son Sifjar, stjúpsonr | Þórs. Hann er bogmaðr svá góðr ok skíðførr svá vel at engi má við hann keppa. Hann er fagr áliti ok hann hefir hermanns atgervi. Á hann er gott at heita í einvígjum.

Forseti heitir sonr Baldrs ok Nǫnnu Nefsdóttur.[1] Hann á þann sal á himni er Glitnir heitir. En allir er til hans koma með sakavendræði þá fara allir sáttir á brott. Sá er dómstaðr beztr með goðum ok mǫnnum:[2]

39 (37)   Glitnir heitir salr,
          hans[3] er g(ulli) s(tuddr)
          ok silfri s(ama).
          En þar Forseti
          byggvir f(lestan) d(ag)
          ok svefr allar sakar.

21 Hér segir frá æsi Loka

Sá er einn talðr með ásum er sumir kalla rógbera ásanna eða frumkveða flærðar ok vamm allra guða ok manna. Sá er nefndr Loki eða Loptr, son Fárbauta jǫtuns. Móðir hans heitir Laufey eða Nál. Brøðr hans heita Býleiptr ok Helblindi. Loki er fríðr ok fagr sýnum, illr í skaplyndi, mjǫk fjǫlbreytinn at háttum. Hann hefir þá speki mjǫk um fram aðra menn er slǿgð heitir ok vélar til allra hluta. Hann kom ásum jafnan í fullt vendræði ok opt leysti hann þeira vendræði með vélum. Kona hans hét Sigyn, sonr hans hét Nari eða Narfi.

Enn átti Loki fleiri bǫrn. Angrboða heitir gýgr í Jǫtunheimum. Við henni gat Loki þrjú bǫrn. Eitt er Fenrisúlfr, annat er Jǫrmungandr, þat er Miðgarðsormrinn, þriðja er Hel.

En er þessi þrjú systkin, bǫrn Loka, fǿddust upp í Jǫtunheimum ok guðin rǫktu til spádóma at af þessum bǫrnum mundi þeim mikit úhapp standa, ok þótti ǫllum ills af ván, fyrst af móðerninu en verra af fǫðurnum, þá sendi Alfaðir guðin eptir bǫrnunum ok lét fǿra sér. Ok er þau kómu til hans þá kastaði hann orminum í inn djúpa sæ er liggr um lǫnd ǫll, ok óx sá ormr svá at hann liggr um lǫnd ǫll í miðju hafi ok bítr í sporð sér.

Hel kastaði hann í Niflheim ok gaf henni vald yfir níu heimum, at hon skyldi skipta vistum með þeim er til hennar koma. En þat eru sóttdauðir

---

[1] Other manuscripts call her *Nepsdóttir*. Another example of insular f instead of p.
[2] Cf. *Grímnismál* 15.
[3] Must be an error for *hann*.

'Viðarr is the name of the silent Áss. He has a thick shoe. He is almost equal in strength to Þórr. He is a source of great support to the gods in all dangers.

'Áli or Váli is the name of one, son of Óðinn and Rindr. He is bold in battles and a very good shot.

'Ullr is the name of one, son of Sif, stepson of Þórr. He is such a fine archer and so good at skiing that no one can compete with him. He is beautiful in appearance and he has a warrior's accomplishments. He is a good one to pray to in single combats.

'Forseti is the name of the son of Baldr and Nanna Nefsdóttir. He has a hall in heaven that is called Glitnir. And all who come to him with difficult legal disputes, then they all leave with their differences settled. It is the best place for judgment among gods and men

39 There is a hall called Glitnir,
  it is held up by golden pillars
  and by silver ones likewise.
  And there Forseti
  dwells most days
  and settles all disputes.'

21 Here it says about the Áss Loki

'There is one reckoned among the Æsir that some call the calumniator of the Æsir or the originator of falsehoods and the disgrace of all gods and men. His name is Loki or Loptr, son of the giant Fárbauti. His mother is called Laufey or Nál. His brothers are called Býleiptr and Helblindi. Loki is pleasing and handsome in appearance, evil in nature, very capricious in behaviour. He possesses to a greater degree than others the kind of learning that is called cunning, and tricks for every purpose. He was always getting the Æsir into a complete fix and he often got them out of their fix by tricks. His wife was called Sigyn, his son was called Nari or Narfi.

'Loki had other offspring too. There was a giantess called Angrboða in the world of giants. With her Loki had three children. One is Fenriswolf, the second is Jǫrmungandr, that is the Miðgarðr serpent, the third is Hel.

'And when these three siblings, Loki's children, were being brought up in the world of giants, and the gods traced prophecies to the effect that from these children great disaster would arise for them, and they all felt evil was to be expected from them, to begin with because of their mother's nature and worse because of their father's, then All-father sent the gods to fetch the children and had them brought to him. And when they came to him, then he threw the serpent into the deep sea that lies around all lands, and this serpent grew so that it lies around all lands in the midst of the ocean and bites on its own tail.

'Hel he threw into Niflheimr and gave her authority over nine worlds so that she had to administer board and lodging to those that come to her. These are

menn ok ellidauðir. Hon á þar mikla bólstaði ok eru garðar hennar forkunnliga hávir en grindr stórar. Eljúðnir heitir salr hennar, Hungr diskr, Sultr knífr, Ganglati þræll, Ganglǫt ambátt, Fallanda forað grind, Þolmóðnir þreskǫldr er inn gengr, Kǫr sæing, Blíkjandbǫl ársalr hennar eða tjald. Hon er blá hálf, en hálf með hǫrundar lit. Því er hon auðkend ok heldr gnúpleit ok grimlig.

22 Frá Fenrisúlfi ok ásum

f. 10r, p. 17 Úlfinn føddu æsirnir heima ok hafði Týr einn til djǫrfung at gefa honum mat. En guðin sá hvé mikit hann óx hvern dag ok allar spár sǫgðu at hann mundi vera lagðr til skaða þeim. Þá fengu æsirnir þat ráð at þeir gerðu fjǫtur allsterkan, er þeir kǫlluðu Lǿðing ok báru hann til úlfsins ok báðu hann reyna afl sitt viðr fjǫturinn. En úlfi þótti sér þat ekki ofrefli ok lét þá fara með sem þeir vildu. En it fyrsta sinn er hann spyrndi við, brotnaði fjǫturrinn, ok leystist hann svá ór Lǿðingi.

Því næst gerðu æsirnir annan fjǫtur, hálfu sterkara, er þeir kǫlluðu Dróma ok báðu úlfinn reyna enn þenna fjǫtur ok tǫlðu hann verða mundu ágætan af afli, ef slík stórsmíði mætti eigi halda honum. En úlfrinn hugsaði at þessi fjǫturr var sterkr mjǫk ok þat með at honum hafði vaxit afl síðan er hann braut Lǿðing. Kom þat í hug at hann mundi verða at leggja sik í hættu ef hann skal frægr verða, ok lætr leggja á sik fjǫturinn. Ok er æsirnir tǫlðust búnir, þá hristi úlfrinn sik ok laust fjǫtrinum á jǫrðina ok knúðist at fast, spyrnir at fast ok braut fjǫturinn svá at fjarri kom niðr hlutirnir. Svá drap hann sik ór Dróma. Þat er síðan orðtak at leysi ór Lǿðingi eða drepi ór Dróma, þá er einn hverr hlutr er ákafliga sóttr.

Eptir þat óttuðust æsirnar at þeir mundi eigi fá bundit hann. Þá sendi Alfǫðr þann mann er Skírnir hét í Svartálfaheim til dverga nokkurra ok lét gera fjǫtur þann er Gleipnir heitir. Hann var gjǫrr af sex hlutum, af dyn kattarins ok af skeggi konunnar, af rótum bjargsins ok sinum bjarnarins, af anda fisksins ok af hráka fuglsins. En þó at þú vitir eigi áðr þessi tíðindi, þá máttu nú finna hér skjótt sǫnn dǿmi at eigi er logit, at þér munuð séð hafa at konan hefir eigi skegg, ok engi dynr verðr af hlaupi kattarins, ok eigi eru rǿtr undir bjargi. Ok þat veit trúa mín at jamsatt er þat allt er ek hefi sagt þér, þótt þeir sé sumir hlutir er þú mátt eigi reyna.

Þá mælti Gangleri: Þetta má ek at vísu sjá er nú segir þú frá ok þú hefir nú til dǿma tekit. En hvernig varð fjǫturrinn smíðaðr?

Hár segir: Þat kann ek þér vel segja. Fjǫturr var sléttr ok blautr sem
f. 10v, p. 18 silkirǿma, en svá traustr ok sterkr sem nú máttu heyra. Þá er fjǫturrinn | var fǿrðr ásum þá þǫkkuðu þeir vel sendimanninum sitt eyrindi. Þá fóru æsirnir út í vatn þat er Ámsvarnir heitir, í hólm þann er Lyngvi er kallaðr, ok kǫlluðu

those that die of sickness or old age. She has great mansions there and her walls are exceptionally high and the gates huge. Her hall is called Eljúðnir, Hunger her dish, Famine her knife, Ganglati her slave, Ganglǫt her serving maid, Stumbling block her gate, Þolmóðnir the threshold where you enter, Sickbed her bed, Gleaming-bale her bed-curtains or hangings. She is half black and half flesh coloured. Thus she is easily recognisable, and rather downcast and fierce-looking.'

22 Of Fenriswolf and the Æsir

'The Æsir brought up the wolf at home, and it was only Týr that had the boldness to give it food. But the gods saw how much it grew each day, and all the prophecies said that it was destined to cause them harm. Then the Æsir adopted this plan, that they made a very strong fetter, which they called Løðingr, and brought it to the wolf and suggested he should try his strength on the fetter. And the wolf decided that it was not beyond his strength and let them do as they wished with it. And the first time he kicked at it, the fetter broke, and thus he freed himself from Løðingr.

'Next the Æsir made a second fetter, twice as strong, which they called Drómi, and and asked the wolf to try this fetter too, and declared that he would become famous for his strength if such mighty pieces of engineering could not hold him. And the wolf thought to himself that this fetter was very strong, and also that his strength had grown since he broke Løðingr. It occurred to him that he would have to take some risks if he is to become famous, and allows the fetter to be put on him. And when the Æsir declared they were ready, then the wolf shook himself and knocked the fetter on the ground and strained hard, kicked at it hard and broke the fetter so that the fragments landed far away. Thus he struck himsef out of Drómi. It has since been a saying to loose from Lǿðingr or dash oneself out of Drómi when something is achieved with great effort.

'After this the Æsir began to fear that they would not manage to get him bound. Then All-father sent someone called Skírnir to the world of black elves to some dwarfs and had a fetter made called Gleipnir. It was made of six things, of the sound of the cat and of the woman's beard, of the roots of the mountain and the sinews of the bear, of the fish's breath and of the bird's spittle. And even if you do not already know this information, yet you can now find immediate proof that you have not been deceived in this, in that you must have seen that the woman has no beard, and no noise comes from the cat's running, and there are no roots under a mountain. And I declare by my faith that everything I have told you is just as true even if there are some things that you cannot test.'

Then spoke Gangleri: 'This I can indeed see that you are now telling me of and you have now given as examples. But what was the fetter made like?'

High says: 'I can easily tell you that. The fetter was smooth and soft like a silken ribbon, but as firm and strong as you shall now hear. When the fetter was brought to the Æsir, then they thanked the messenger heartily for carrying out their errand. Then the Æsir went out onto a lake that is called Ámsvartnir to an island that is called Lyngvi, and summoned the wolf with them, showed

með sér úlfinn, sýndu honum silkibandit ok báðu hann slíta, kóðu[1] vera mundu nokkuru traustara en líkindi þóttu á vera fyrir digrleiks sakir, ok seldi hverr ǫðrum ok treysti með handaflinu ok slitnaði eigi. En þó kvóðu þeir úlfinn mundu slíta.

Þá svarar úlfrinn: Svá lízt mér á þenna dregil sem enga frægð mega ek af hljóta þó at ek slíta í sundr svá mjótt band. En ef þat er gert með list eða vél þótt band sýnist lítit, þá kemr eigi band á mína fǫtr. Þá svǫruðu æsir at hann mundi skjótt í sundr slíta svá mjótt silkiband, er hann hafði skjótt í sundr brotit sterka járnfjǫtra. En ef þú fær eigi skjótt í sundr brotit, þá muntu ekki hrætt fá guðin. Skulu vér þá leysa þik.

Úlfrinn svarar: Ef þér bindið mik svá at ek fæ eigi leyst mik, skil ek at ek mun seint taka af yðr lausn. Em ek úfúss at láta þat band á mína leggi. En heldr en þér frýið mér hugar, þá rétti einn hverr yðarr hǫnd sína í munn mér at veði at þetta sé falslaust gert. En hverr ásanna sá til annars ok þóttu nú vera tvau vendræði ok vildi engi sína hǫnd fram selja, fyrri en Týr lét fram ena hǫgri hǫnd sína ok leggr í munn úlfinum.

Þá tóku þeir festina ór fjǫtrinum, er Gelgja heitir, ok drápu henni í gegnum hellu mikla, sú heitir Gjǫll, ok festum[2] helluna langt í jǫrð niðr. Þá tóku þeir enn mikinn stein, er Þviti heitir, ok skutu honum enn lengra niðr ok hǫfðu hann fyrir festarhæl. Þá er æsirnir sá at úlfrinn var bundinn með fullu ok er hann spyrndi við þá harðnaði bandit, ok því harðara er hann brauzt um, því skarpara var bandit, þá hlógu allir nema Týr; hann lét hǫnd sína.

Úlfrinn gapti ákafliga ok vildi bíta þá ok fekst um mjǫk. Þeir skutu í munn honum sverði nokkuru. Nema hjǫltin við neðra kjǫptinn en inn efra gómínn blóðrefillinn. Þat er gómsparri hans. Hann grenjar illiliga ok slefa renn ór munni hans. Þat er á sú er Vam heitir. Þar liggr hann til Ragnarøkkrs.

f. 11r, p. 19   Þá mælti Gangleri: Furðu illa barna eign gat Loki, en ǫll | þessi systkin eru mikil fyrir sér. En fyrir hví drápu æsirnir eigi úlfinn er þeim er ills af honum ván?

Hár segir: Svá mikils virðu guðin vé sín ok griðastaði at eigi vildu þau saurga þá með blóði úlfsins, þótt svá segði spárnar fyrir at hann mundi verða at bana Óðni.

23 Frá ásynjum

Gangleri mælti: Hverjar eru ásynjur?

Hár segir: Frigg er øzt; hon á þann sal er Fensalir heita, ok er hann allvegligr.

---

[1] Third person plural past of *kveða* occurs three times, and is written 'qvaþo', 'qvoþv' and 'koþv'. See Noreen 1923 § 498 and § 77.11.

[2] The *-m* is written as a nasal stroke and is probably redundant. The verb should be third person plural, rather than first.

him the silky band and bade him tear it, declaring it to be rather firmer than seemed likely, judging from its thickness, and passed it from one to the other and tried it by pulling at it with their hands, and it did not break. And yet, they said, the wolf would break it.

'Then the wolf replies: "It looks to me with this ribbon as though I will gain no fame from it though I tear apart such a slender band. But if it is made with art or trickery, then even if a band does look thin, a band is not going on my legs."

'Then the Æsir replied that he would soon tear apart such a slender silken band, when he had soon broken apart strong iron fetters.

'"But if you cannot soon manage to break it apart, then you will not be able to frighten the gods. We shall then set you free."

'The wolf replies: "If you bind me so that I am unable to release myself, then I realise that I would have to wait a long time for you to release me. I am reluctant to let this band onto my legs. But rather than that you should question my courage, let one of you put out his hand into my mouth as a pledge that this is done in good faith."

'But all the Æsir looked at each other and found themselves in a dilemma, and none wished to offer their hand until Týr put forward his right hand and put it into the wolf's mouth.

'Then they took the cord coming from the fetter, which was called Gelgja, and thrust it through a great stone slab, this is called Gjǫll, and fastened the slab far down in the earth. Then they again took a great rock that is called Þviti, and flung it still further down and used it as an anchoring peg. When the Æsir saw that the wolf was thoroughly bound, and when he kicked against it, then the band grew harder, and the harder he struggled, the tougher became the band, then all laughed except Týr; he lost his hand.

'The wolf stretched its jaws tremendously and tried to bite them and reacted violently. They thrust into its mouth a certain sword. Its hilt pushes against its lower jaw and its point against its upper gums. This is its gum-prop. It howls horribly and saliva runs from its mouth. This is the river that is called Vam (blemish, disgrace). There it lies until the twilight of the gods.'

Then spoke Gangleri: 'It was an amazingly nasty family that Loki begot, and all these siblings are important. But why did not the Æsir kill the wolf since they can expect evil from it?'

High says: 'So greatly did the gods respect their holy places and places of sanctuary that they did not want to defile them with the wolf's blood, even if the prophecies foretold that it will be the death of Óðinn.

23 Of the Ásynjur

Gangleri spoke: 'Who are the Ásynjur?'

High says: 'The highest is Frigg; she has a dwelling that is called Fensalir, and it is very splendid.

Ǫnnur er Saga;[1] hon býr á Søkkvabekk.

Eir; hon er læknir með ásum.

Gefjun heitir ein. Henni þjóna þær er meyjar andast.

Fylla; hon er mær ok ferr laust hár hennar ok gullband um hǫfuð ok berr eski Friggjar ok gætir skóklæða hennar ok veit leynd ráð með henni.

Freyja er tignust með Frigg. Hon giptist þeim manni er Óðr hét. Dóttir þeira er Hnoss. Hon giptist þeim manni er Óir hét. Hon var svá fǫgr at af hennar nafni eru þeir hlutir hnossir kallaðir er gersimar eru. Óðr fór á brott langar leiðir, en Freyja grætr eptir. Tár hennar eru rautt gull. Freyja á mǫrg nǫfn en sú sǫk er til þess, at hon gaf sér mǫrg nǫfn er hon kom með ymsum þjóðum at leita Óðrs. Hon heitir Marþǫll ok Hæn, Gefn, Sýr. Freyja átti ok Brísingamen. Hon er ok kǫlluð Vanadís.

Sjǫfn; hon gerir mjǫk til at snúa hugum manna til ásta, kvenna ok karla, ok af hennar nafni er elskuginn kallaðr sjǫfni.

Lofn; hon er gott[2] til áheita ok mild, ok hon fær leyfi til samgangs manna með Alfǫðr eða Frigg þó at áðr sé bannat. Af hennar nafni er lof kallaðr.

Vár;[3] hon hlýðir á eiða manna ok einkamál er menn veita sín í millum, karlar ok konur. Því heita þau mál várar.

Vǫr er vitr ok spurul svá at ekki má hana leyna. Þat er orðtak at kona verði vǫr.

Syn; hon gætir dyra í hǫllinni ok lýkr fyrir þeim er eigi skulu inn ganga. Hon er sett til varnar á þingum fyrir þau mál er maðr vill ósanna. Því er þat orðtak at syn er fyrir sett, þá er maðr neitir.

Hlín; hon er sett til gæzlu þeim mǫnnum er Frigg vill forða við háska nokkurum. Þaðan af er þat orðtak at sá hleinir er forðast.

Snotra er vitr ok látprúð. Af hennar heiti er kǫlluð snotr kona eða karlmaðr.

Gná; hana sendir Frigg í ymsa staði at eyrindum sínum. Hon á hest þann

f. 11v, p. 20 er rennr lopt ok lǫg ok heitir | Hófvarpnir. Þat var eitt sinn er hon reið at vanr nokkurr sá hana ok ferð hennar, er hon reið í loptinu. Hann mælti:

40 (38)   Hvat þar flýgr
eða hvat þar ferr
eða hvat at lopti líðr?

Hon svarar:

41 (39)   Eigi ek flýg
þó ek ferk
þó ek at lopti líð

[1] This name is usually taken to be Sága.

[2] The feminine form *góð* would be more normal here, though the neuter can be taken to be adverbial.

[3] Both this name and Vǫr in the next paragraph are written 'Vavr'. Since length of vowels was rarely indicated in medieval manuscripts, the names Vǫr (later Vár) and Vǫr would often have been spelt the same.

'Second is Saga; she dwells at Søkkvabekkr.
'Eir; she is physician among the Æsir.
'One is called Gefjun. She is served by those that die virgins.
'Fylla; she is a virgin and her hair flows free and there is a gold band round her head, and she carries Frigg's casket and looks after her footwear and shares hidden counsels with her.
'Freyja is highest in rank along with Frigg. She was married to someone called Óðr. Hnoss is their daughter. She was married to someone called Óir. She was so beautiful that from her name those things that are treasures are called *hnossir*. Óðr went off on long travels, and Freyja stayed behind weeping. Her tears are red gold. Freyja has many names, and the reason for this is that she adopted many names when she came among various peoples in search of Óðr. She is called Marþǫll and Hæn, Gefn, Sýr. Freyja owned the necklace of the Brísingar. She is also known as Lady of the Vanir.
'Sjǫfn; she does a great deal to turn people's thoughts to love, men and women, and it is from her name that affection is called *sjǫfni*.
'Lofn; she is good to pray to and kind, and she gets leave for people's union from All-father or Frigg even if before it was forbidden. It is from her name that it is called *lof* (permission).
'Vár; she listens to people's oaths and private agreements that people make between each other, men and women. Thus these contracts are called *várar*.
'Vǫr is wise and enquiring, so that nothing can be concealed from her. There is a saying that a woman becomes *vǫr* (aware).
'Syn; she guards the doors in the hall and shuts them against those who are not to enter. She is appointed as a defence at assemblies against the cases that it is desired to refute. Thus there is a saying that *syn* (denial) is made when one says no.
'Hlín; she is given the function of protecting people whom Frigg wishes to save from some danger. From this comes the saying that one who escapes *hleinir* (finds refuge?).
'Snotra is wise and courteous. From her name a woman or a man is said to be *snotr* (sensible).
'Gná; Frigg sends her to various places on errands for her. She has a horse that runs through sky and sea and is called Hófvarpnir. It was on one occasion when she was riding that a certain Vanr saw her and her travelling, when she was riding in the sky. He said:

40 What is it flying there
   and what is it travelling there
   and what is it passing through the sky?

'She replies:

41 I am not flying
   though I travel
   though I pass through the sky

á Hófvarpni
þeim er hátt strýkr
gakk um garð vóru.¹

Af Gnár nafni er þat mælt at þat gnæfar er hátt ferr.

Sól ok Bil eru með ásum,² ok eru þær aðrar er þjóna í Valhǫllu, bera drykk ok gæta borðbúnaðar ok ǫlgagna. Svá heita þær í Grímnismálum:³

42 (40) Hrist ok Mist
vil ek at mér horn beri.
Skegǫld ok Skǫgul
Hildr ok Þrúðr
Hlǫkk ok Herfjǫtra
Gjǫll ok Geirahǫð
ok Randgríðr ok Ráðgríðr
ok Reginleif,
þær bera einherjum ǫl.

Þessar heita valkyrjur. Þær sendir Óðinn til orrostu. Þær kjósa feiga menn ok ráða sigri. Guðr ok Rósta ok norn en yngsta, er Skuld heitir, ríða jafnan at kjósa val ok ráða vígum.

Jǫrð, móðir Þórs, ok Rindr, móðir Vála, eru talðar með ásynjum.

24 Freyr fekk Gerðar

Gymir hét maðr en kona hans Ǫrboða; hann var bergrisa ættar. Dóttir þeira var Gerðr, allra kvenna vænst.

Þat var einn dag at Freyr gekk í Hliðskjálf ok sá um heim allan. Ok er hann leit í norðrætt þá sá hann á einum bø mikit hús, ok þar gekk kona út ok lýsti af hári hennar bæði lopt ok lǫg. Ok svá hefndi honum þat mikillæti er hann settist í þat at⁴ helga sæti at hann gekk brott fullr af harmi, ok ekki svaf hann er hann kom heim ok þeir Skírnir hittust. Þá fór Skírnir at hitta Gerði ok kom saman ástum þeira.

Hann fekk Skírni í hendr sverð sitt. En hann hafði þá ekki sverð er þeir Beli hittust. En drepa mátti hann Bela með hnefa sínum. En verra er honum þat þá er hann missir sverðsins er Múspells megir herja ok hann berst við þá.

---

¹ In lines 4–6, the Codex Regius version has: *á Hófhvarfni* | *þeim er Hamskerpir* | *gat við Garðrofu*. The text of DG 11 4to must be wrong, but can hardly be scribal error based on the same archetype as the Codex Regius version. It can make some sense if *vóru* is read *vórn*.

² Here some text is missing, though there is no gap in the manuscript. The Codex Regius version has: *Sól og Bil eru talðar með ásynjum en sagt er fyrr (frá) eðli þeirra. Enn eru þær aðrar* . . . ('Sól and Bil are reckoned among the Ásynjur, but their natures have been spoken of above. There are still others . . .').

³ Cf. *Grímnismál* 36.

⁴ Doubtless an error for *it* (definite article neuter).

on Hófvarpnir
who dashes off.
Go through our fence!

'From Gnár's name something is said to *gnæfa* (tower) when it goes high up.

'Sól and Bil are with the Æsir, and there are these others that serve in Valhǫll, serve drink and look after the tableware and drinking vessels. This is what they are called in *Grímnismál*:

42 Hrist and Mist
    I want to bring me drinking horns.
    Skegǫld and Skǫgul
    Hildr and Þrúðr
    Hlǫkk and Herfjǫtra
    Gjǫll and Geirahǫð
    and Randgríðr and Ráðgríðr
    and Reginleif
    they serve the Einherjar with ale.

'These are called valkyries. Óðinn sends them to battle. They choose men to be doomed and determine the victory. Guðr and Rósta and the youngest norn, who is called Skuld, always ride to choose the slain and determine the slayings.

'Þórr's mother Jǫrð and Váli's mother Rindr are reckoned among the Ásynjur.'

24 Freyr united with Gerðr

'There was a man called Gymir and his wife Ǫrboða; he was of the race of mountain giants. Their daughter was Gerðr, of all women the finest.

'It happened one day that Freyr went into Hliðskjálf and saw over all the world. And when he looked in a northerly direction, then he saw a large house in a certain homestead, and a woman went out there and from her hair light shone over both sky and sea. And his punishment for his presumption in having sat in that holy seat was that he went away full of grief, and he did not sleep when he got home and he and Skírnir met. Then Skírnir went to see Gerðr and united their loves.

'He handed over to Skírnir his sword. So he did not have a sword when he and Beli met. But he was able to kill Beli with his fist. But it will be worse for him when he is without his sword when Múspell's lads wage war and he fights with them.'

25 Frá vist ok drykk með ásum

Þá segir Gangleri: Hvat hefir Óðinn at fá svá mǫrgu fólki sem þar er, ef allir vápndauðir menn koma til hans?

Hár segir: Þar er mikit fjǫlmenni, ok mun þó eigi ofmikit þikkja þá er úlfrinn kemr. En aldri er svá mikit fjǫlmenni at eigi má endast flesk þat er Sæhrímnir heitir. | Hann er soðinn hvern dag ok heill at aptni. En fáir munu þetta kunna at segja þér. Andrímnir heitir steikarinn, en Eldrímnir ketillinn. Sem hér segir:[1]

43 (42)   Andrímnir lætr
          í Eldrímni
          Særímni soðinn,
          fleska bezt
          en þat fáir vitu
          við hvat einherjar alast.

Þá mælti Gangleri: Hvárt hefir Óðinn þat sama borðhald sem einherjar?

Hár segir: Þá vist er stendr á hans borði gefr hann tveim úlfum er hann á ok svá heita: Geri ok Freki. En enga vist þarf hann. Vín er honum bæði matr ok drykkr. Sem hér segir:[2]

44 (43)   Gera ok Freka
          seðr gunntanigr[3]
          hróðigr herjafeðr.[4]
          En við vín eitt
          vápngaffiðr[5]
          Óðinn æ lifir.

Hrafnar sitja tveir á ǫxlum hans ok segja honum ǫll tíðindi í eyru hans þau er þeir sjá eða heyra. Þeir heita svá: Huginn ok Muninn. Þá sendir Óðinn í dagan at fljúga um heima alla ok koma aptr um dagverð. Því heitir hann hrafna guð. Sem hér segir:[6]

45 (44)   Huginn ok Muninn
          fljúga hvern dag
          jǫrmungrund yfir.
          ⟨Ó⟩unz ek Hugin
          at hann aptr kemr,
          þó sjámz ek meir um Muninn.

[1] Cf. *Grímnismál* 18.
[2] Cf. *Grímnismál* 19.
[3] So DG 11 4to; *gunntamigr* GkS 2367 4to, *gunntamiðr* GkS 2365 4to, Codex Wormianus and Codex Trajectinus; only the last makes any sense ('accustomed to battle').
[4] *-feðr* is normally dat. sg. or nom. acc. pl.
[5] *-gafigr* GkS 2367 4to and Codex Trajectinus, *-gǫfugr* GkS 2365 4to and Codex Wormianus.
[6] Cf. *Grímnismál* 20. GkS 2365 4to, GkS 2367 4to, Codex Wormianus have *ne* in l. 5.

25 Of food and drink with the Æsir

Then says Gangleri: 'What has Óðinn to offer so many people as are there, if all men that die from weapons come to him?'

High says: 'There is a great number there, and yet they will not seem too many when the wolf comes. But there will never be such a large number that the pork that is called Sæhrímnir will not be sufficient. It is cooked every day and whole again by evening. But there must be few that are able to tell you this. The cook is called Andhrímnir and the pot Eldhrímnir. As it says here:

43   Andhrímnir
      in Eldhrímnir
      has Sæhrímnir cooked,
      best of meats,
      but there are few that know
      on what the Einherjar feed.'

Then spoke Gangleri: 'Does Óðinn have the same fare as the Einherjar?'

'High says: 'The food that stands on his table he gives to two wolves that he has and that are called Geri and Freki. But he needs no food. Wine is for him both meat and drink. As it says here:

44   Geri and Freki
      the battle-accustomed
      triumphant father of hosts feeds.
      But on wine alone
      splendidly weaponed
      Óðinn ever lives.

'Two ravens sit on his shoulders and speak into his ears all the news they see or hear. Their names are Huginn and Muninn. Óðinn sends them out at dawn to fly over all the worlds and they return for dinner. Thus he is called raven-god. As it says here:

45   Huginn ok Muninn
      fly each day
      over the mighty earth.
      I fear for Huginn
      lest he come back,
      yet I am afraid more about Muninn.'

Þá segir Gangleri: Hvat hafa einherjar at drykk er þeim endist jamgnógliga sem vistin, eða er þar vatn drukkit?

Hár segir: Undarliga spyrðu, at Alfǫðr mundi bjóða til sín konungum eða jǫrlum ok mundi hann gefa þeim vatn at drekka. Margr kemr sá til Valhallar er dýrt mundi þikkjast kaupa vatnsdrykkinn ef eigi væri betra fagnaðar þangat at vitja, sá er áðr þolir sár ok sviða til banans. Geit sú er Heiðrún heitir stendr uppi á Valhǫll ok bítr barr af limum trés þess er Léraðs heitir. En ór spenum hennar rennr mjólk er hon fyllir með skaptkerit. Þær[1] eru svá miklar at allir einherjar verða fulldrukknir af.

Þá segir Gangleri: Haglig geit er þat. Góðr viðr mun þat vera er hon bítr af.

Þá segir Hár: Meira er vert um hjǫrtinn Takþyrni, er stendr á Valhǫll ok bítr af limum þessa trés. En af hornum hans verðr svá mikill drogi[2] at niðr kemr í Hvergelmi ok þaðan falla þær ár er svá heita: Síð, Víð, Søkin, Ækin, Svoll,[3] Gundró, Fjǫrni, Fimbulþul, Gipul, Gjǫful, Gǫmul, Geirumul. Þessar falla um ásabygðir. Þessar eru enn nefndar: Fýri, Vinþǫll, Holl, Gráð, Gundró, Nǫt, Reytt, Nǫnn, Hrǫnn, Vina,[4] Veglun, Þjóðnunja.

Þá segir Gangleri: Mikit hús mun Valhǫll vera | ok þrǫngt fyrir dyrum.

Þá segir Hár:[5]

46 (45) Fimm hundruð dyra
ok fjóra tugu
svá hygg ek á Valhǫllu vera.
Átta hundruð einherja
ganga ór einum dyrum
þá er þeir ganga við vitni at vega.

Þá segir Gangleri: Mikit fjǫlmenni er í Valhǫllu eða hvat ⟨er⟩ skemtun einherja þá er þeir drekka eigi?

Hár segir: Þá er þeir hafa klæzt ganga þeir í garðinn út ok berjast ok fellir hverr annan. Þat er leikr þeira, ok at dagverði ríða þeir til Valhallar ok drykkju sem hér segir:[6]

47 (46) Allir einherjar
Óðins túnum í
hǫggvast hvern dag.
Val þeir kjósa
ok ríða vígi frá,
sitja meirr um sáttir saman.

---

[1] Presumably *ár* (rivers) are imagined to run from Heiðrún's udder. Cf. ch. 9 above.
[2] Presumably an error for *dropi*, which is what the Codex Regius version has.
[3] Perhaps read *Svǫl*.
[4] Or *Vína*.
[5] Cf. *Grímnismál* 23.
[6] Cf. *Vafþrúðnismál* 41.

Then says Gangleri: 'What do the Einherjar have as drink that lasts them as plentifully as the food, or is water drunk there?'

High says: 'That is a strange question you are asking, whether All-father would invite kings and earls to his house and would give them water to drink. Many a one comes to Valhǫll who would think he had paid a high price for his drink of water if there were no better cheer to be got there who had previously endured wounds and burning pain leading to his death. There is a goat that is called Heiðrún stands up on top of Valhǫll and feeds on the foliage from the branches of the tree that is called Léraðr. And from its udder flows milk with which it fills the vat. They (the rivers) are so large that all the Einherjar can drink their fill from it.'

Then says Gangleri: 'That is a handy goat. It must be a good tree that it feeds on.'

Then says High: 'There is more significance in the stag Takþyrnir that stands on Valhǫll and feeds on the branches of that tree. And from its horns there comes such a great dripping that it comes down into Hvergelmir, and from there flow the rivers that are called Síð, Víð, Søkin, Ækin, Svoll, Gundró, Fjǫrni, Fimbulþul, Gipul, Gjǫful, Gǫmul, Geirumul. These flow through where the Æsir live. These are the names of others: Fýri, Vinþǫll, Holl, Gráð, Gundró, Nǫtt, Reytt, Nǫnn, Hrǫnn, Vina, Veglun, Þjóðnunja.'

Then says Gangleri: 'Valhǫll must be a large building and crowded at the doorways.'

Then says High:

46 'Five hundred doors
    and forty,
    that is what I think are in Valhǫll.
    Eight hundred Einherjar
    will go out of one doorway
    when they go to fight the wolf.'

Then says Gangleri: 'There is a large number in Valhǫll, so what entertainment do the Einherjar have when they are not drinking?'

High says: 'When they have got dressed they go out into the courtyard and fight, and they fell each other. That is their sport, and at dinner they ride to Valhǫll and the drinking, as it says here:

47 All Einherjar
    in Óðinn's courts
    fight each day.
    They select their victims
    and from battle ride,
    sit the more at peace together.'

Gangleri segir: Hvaðan kemr ~~eldr~~ vindr? Hann er sterkr, hann hrørir stór hǫf ok leysir eld. Engi má hann sjá, því er hann undarliga skapaðr.

Hár segir: Á norðanverðum heims enda sitr jǫtunninn Hræsvelgr í arnarham. Ok er hann beinir flug stendr vindr undan vængjum hans. Sem hér segir:[1]

48 (26) Hræsvelgr heitir jǫtunn,
  hann sitr á himins enda,
  jǫtunn í arnarham.
  Af hans vængjum
  kveða vind standa
  alla menn yfir.

Ok enn segir:[2]

49 (47) Askr Ygdrasils
  er øztr viða
  en Skíðblaðnir skipa,
  Óðinn ása
  en jóa Sleipnir,
  Bifrǫst brúa
  en Bragi skálda,
  Hábrók hauka
  en hunda Garmr.

Gangleri segir: Hvaðan kom hestrinn Sleipnir?

26 Frá því er er Loki gat Sleipni við Svaðilfera

Hár segir: Smiðr nokkurr kom til ása ok bauð at gera þeim borg á þrim misserum þá er úrugg væri fyrir bergrisum. En hann mælti til kaups at eiga Freyju, ok hafa vill hann Sól ok Mána. Þá rǫddu æsirnir at ef nokkurr hlutr væri vangerr at borginni sumardag inn fyrsta, þá skyldi hann af kaupinu, ok engi maðr skyldi honum lið veita. Hann beiddist at hafa lið af hesti sínum Svaðilfera, ok olli því tillagi Loki.

Hann gerði borgina ok dró til grjót um nætr á hestinum. Undr þótti ásunum hvé stór bjǫrg hann fǿrði til. Hálfu meira gerði hestrinn en smiðrinn. En at kaupinu vóru sterk vitni, því at jǫtunninn þóttist griðalauss með ásum, ef jǫtunninn væri þar er Þórr kǿmi heim. En hann var farinn í Austrveg at berja trǫll. Borgin var sterk ok há svá at eigi mátti á þat leita.

En er þrír dagar vóru eptir smíðarinnar, þá settust guðin í sæti sín ok spurði hverr annan hverr því réði at | gipta Freyju í Jǫtunheima, eða spilla loptinu ef himinninn døk⟨k⟩tist ef sól eða tungl væri í brott tekin ok gefit jǫtnum.

[1] Cf. *Vafþrúðnismál* 37.
[2] Cf. *Grímnismál* 44.

Gangleri says: 'Where does the wind come from? It is strong, it stirs great seas and makes fire go free. But no one can see it, so it is marvellously made.'

High says: 'At the northernmost end of the world sits the giant Hræsvelgr in the shape of an eagle. And when he starts to fly, wind arises from under his wings. As it says here:

48   There is a giant called Hræsvelgr,
he sits at heaven's end,
a giant in eagle's shape.
From his wings
they say wind arises
over all men.

'And further it says:

49   The ash Ygdrasill
is foremost of trees,
and Skíðblaðnir of ships,
Óðinn of Æsir,
and of horses Sleipnir
Bifrǫst of bridges,
and Bragi of poets,
Hábrók of hawks
and of dogs Garmr.'

Gangleri says: 'Where did the horse Sleipnir come from?'

26 Of how Loki begot Sleipnir with Svaðilferi

High says: 'A certain builder came to the Æsir and offered to build them a fortification in three seasons that would be safe against mountain giants. But he stipulated as payment the possession of Freyja, and he wishes to have Sól (the sun) and Máni (the moon). Then the Æsir spoke about it, that if anything was unfinished in the fortification on the first day of summer, then he should forfeit his payment, and no man was to give him help. He asked to have help from his stallion Svaðilferi, and Loki was behind their agreement to this.

'He built the fortification and hauled up stone at night with his stallion. It seemed amazing to the Æsir what great rocks he brought up. The stallion did twice as much as the builder. But at their agreement were mighty witnesses, for the giant felt without a guarantee of safety among the Æsir if the giant should be there when Þórr came home. But he was gone to eastern parts to thrash trolls. The fortification was strong and high so that it could not be stormed.

'But when three days remained for the building, then the gods took their places on their thrones and asked each other who had been responsible for giving Freyja in marriage to the world of giants and spoiling the sky if the heaven were to go dark if sun and moon were taken away and given to giants.

En þat kom nú ásamt með þeim at Loki þótti ráðit hafa. Létu hann verðan ills dauðdaga ef eigi hitti hann ráð til at smiðrinn væri af kaupinu ok veittu nú Loka atgǫngu. En er hann varð hræddr, svarði hann eið at hann mundi svá til haga at smiðrinn væri af kaupinu, hvat sem hann kostaði til.

En er smiðrinn ók eptir grjótinu með hestinum Svaðilfera, þá hljóp ór skógi merr nokkur ein samt ok hrein ok hvein við. En hestrinn kendi hvárt hrossit var ok ørðist ok sleit í sundr reipin ok hljóp til merarinnar, en hon til skógar undan ok smiðrinn eptir ok vill taka hestinn. En hrossin hlaupa alla nóttina ok dvelst smíðin þá nótt, ok eptir um daginn varð ekki svá smíðat sem fyrri. En er hann sér at eigi má smíðat verða, fǿrðist hann í jǫtunmóð. En er æsirnir sá þat, var eigi þyrmt eiðunum ok nefndu Þór, ok þegar kom hann ok fǿrði á lopt hamarinn ok guldu þá smíðarkaupit, ok laust hann í Hel ok sendu í Niflheim.

En Loki hafði þá fǫr til Svaðilfera at hann bar fyl. Þat var grátt at lit ok hafði átta fǿtr. Sá hestr var beztr með guðum ok mǫnnum. Svá segir í Vǫluspá:[1]

50 (48) þ. g' c. a.
A. r. s.
gin h. gvþ,
ok v. þat g.
hverr hefði lopt
lævi blandit
eða ætt jǫtuns
óskmey gefna.

51 (49) Á gengust eiðar
orð ok sǿri,
mál ǫll meginlik
er á meðal fóru.
Þórr einn þar vá
þrunginn móði;
hann sjaldan sitr
er hann slíkt of fregn.

Þá spyrr Gangleri: Hvat er sagt frá Skíðblaðni, er hann bezt skipa?

Hár segir: Hann er beztr ok hagligastr, en Naglfari er mestr. Þat eiga Múspells megir. Dvergar nokkurir gerðu Skíðblaðni ok gáfu Freyju.[2] Hann er svá mikill at allir mega skipa hann meðr herbúnaði ok hefir byr þegar segl er dregit upp, hvert er fara vill. En ef eigi skal honum á sæ fara, þá er hann gerr af svá mǫrgum hlutum at hann má vefja saman ok hafa í pungi sínum.

[1] Cf. Vǫluspá 25–26. On the abbreviations see Introduction pp. xlv–xlvi.
[2] In the other manuscripts (and in Skáldskaparmál in DG 11 4to too) and in Grímnismál 43 it is Freyr who has Skíðblaðnir, though it is Óðinn's ship in Hkr I 18.

But there was agreement among them that Loki seemed to have advised it. They declared him worthy of an evil kind of death if he did not find a scheme whereby the builder would forfeit his payment, and offered to attack Loki. And when he got afraid, he swore an oath that he would manage things so that the builder would forfeit his payment, whatever it cost him to do it.

'So when the builder drove out for stone with the stallion Svaðilferi, then there ran out of a wood a certain mare all on its own and neighed and whinnied at him. And when the stallion recognised what kind of horse it was, it went frantic and tore apart the tackle and ran to the mare, and she away to the wood and the builder after her and tries to catch the stallion. But the horses ran around all night, and the building was held up for that night, and the next day not as much building was done as previously. And when he realises that building cannot be done, he got into a giant rage. So when the Æsir saw this, the oaths were disregarded and they invoked the name of Þórr, and immediately he came and raised his hammer aloft, and then they paid the builder's wages and struck him into Hel, and sent him to Niflheimr.

'But Loki had such dealings with Svaðilferi that he gave birth to a foal. It was grey in colour and had eight legs. This horse was the best among gods and men. So it says in *Vǫluspá*:

| 50 | Then went all [the powers] to their judgment seats, most holy gods, and deliberated on this, who the sky had with darkness tainted and to the giant's family given the beloved maiden. |
| 51 | Oaths were gone back on, pledged words and promises, all the solemn vows that passed between them. Þórr alone fought there, bursting with wrath; he seldom sits idle when he learns such things.' |

Then asks Gangleri: 'What is told about Skíðblaðnir, is it the best of ships?'

High says: 'It is the best and handiest, but Naglfari is the biggest. It belongs to Múspell's lads. It was some dwarfs made Skíðblaðnir and gave it to Freyja. It is so big that they can all go aboard it with war gear and it gets a fair wind as soon as its sail is hoisted, wherever it is desired to go. But if it is not wanted to take it to sea, then it is made of so many parts that it can be folded up and kept in one's pocket.

Þá segir Gangleri: Gott skip er Skíðblaðnir, en fjǫlkyngi mun við vera
hǫfð áðr svá væri gert.

27 Hér þegir Þriði[1]

Gangleri segir enn: Hvárt hefir Þórr hvergi þar komit at honum væri ofrefli
fyrir fjǫlkyngi | sǫkum?

Hár segir: Fáir munu frá því segja kunna. En margt hefir honum harðfǿrt
þótt. En þótt nokkurr hlutr hafi svá rammr orðit at hann fengi eigi sigrat, þá
er eigi skylt at segja frá, því at mǫrg eru dǿmi til þess ok því eru allir skyldir
at trúa at hann er mátkastr.

Þá mælti Gangleri: Svá lízt mér at þess hlutar muna ek spurt hafa er engi
er til ór at leysa.

Þá svarar Jafnhár: Heyrt hǫfum vér sagt frá því er oss þikkir ótrúligt. En
nær sitr sá er veit, ok muntu því trúa at hann mun eigi ljúga nú it fyrsta sinn,
er alldrigi ló fyrri.

Þá svarar Gangleri: Hér hlýði ek svǫrum þessa máls.

28 Hér hefr sǫgu Þórs ok Útgarða-Loka

Hár segir: Þat er þá upphaf at Ǫku-Þórr fór með hafra sína ok meðr honum
Loki ok koma at kveldi til eins bónda. Tók Þórr hafrana ok skar, ok vóru
þeir flegnir ok bornir til ketils. Ok er soðit var, settist Þórr til matar ok bauð
bónda til nótturðar ok bǫrnum hans. Son hans hét Þjálfi en Rǫska dóttir.
Þá lagði Þórr hafrstǫkurnar útar frá eldi ok mælti at bǫrnin skyldu kasta
beinunum á stǫkurnar. Þjálfi, son bónda, laust lærlegg hafrsins með knífi
sínum ok spretti til mergjar.

Þórr var þar um nóttina ok í óttu stóð hann upp ok klæddist, tók Mjǫlni ok
brá upp ok vígði hafrstǫkurnar. Stóðu hafrarnir upp ok var annarr haltr eptra
fǿti. Þórr fann þat, lét bónda eða hjú hans eigi mundu hafa skynsamliga með
farit beinunum, lét brotinn legg hafrsins. Bóndinn varð hræddr er Þórr lét
síga brúnina fyrir augun. En þat er hann sá til augnanna hugðist hann falla
mundu fyrir sjónunum einum saman. Hann herði hendrnar at hamarskaptinu
svá at hvítnuðu knúarnir. Bóndi ok hjú hans báðu sér friðar ok buðu bǿtr
þær er hans[2] vildi.

Ok er hann sá hræzlu þeira mikla, gekk af honum móðrinn ok tók af bónda
bǫrn hans, Þjálfa ok Rǫsku, ok þjónuðu þau honum síðan.

Hann lét þá eptir hafra sína ok fór í Jǫtunheima ok allt til hafsins ok svam
yfir þat it djúpa haf, ok er hann kom til lands þá gekk hann upp ok með honum
Þjálfi ok Rǫskva ok Loki. Ok er þau vóru litla hríð farin varð mǫrk stór fyrir

---

[1] This heading is rather odd. In the Codex Regius version, the narrator in the next
chapter is Þriði. Cf. Faulkes 2005: 37/2.

[2] Error for *hann*.

Then says Gangleri: 'Skíðblaðnir is a good ship, but magic must be made use of before something like that is made.'

27 Here Third is silent

Gangleri goes on to say: 'Has Þórr never found himself somewhere where it was beyond his power because of magic?'

High says: 'Few will be able to tell about that. But many things he has found difficult to deal with. But even if something has been so powerful that he has not managed to defeat it, still there is no need to speak of it, for there is much evidence to show, and everyone is bound to believe, that he is mightiest.'

Then spoke Gangleri: 'It looks to me as though I must have asked something that there is no one available to answer.'

Then replies Just-as-high: 'We have heard tell about what seems to us incredible. But not far off is sitting one who knows, and you can be confident that he will not lie now for the first time who never lied before.'

Then replies Gangleri: 'Here I shall listen to the replies to this question.'

28 Here begins the story of Þórr and Útgarðaloki

High says: 'This is then how it started, that Qku-Þórr set off with his goats and with him Loki, and they arrived in the evening at a peasant's. Þórr took his goats and slaughtered them, and they were skinned and put in the pot. And when it was cooked, Þórr sat down to his food and invited the peasant to an evening meal and his children. His son was called Þjálfi and his daughter Rǫska. Then Þórr placed the goatskins on the other side of the fire and said that the children were to throw the bones onto the skins. The peasant's son Þjálfi struck the goat's ham-bone with his knife and split it open for the marrow.

'Þórr stayed there the night, and just before dawn he got up and dressed, took Mjǫllnir and raised it and blessed the goatskins. The goats got up and one was lame in its hind leg. Þórr noticed this, said the peasant or one of his people must have not treated the bones with proper care, said the goat's leg was broken. The peasant was afraid when Þórr made his brows sink down over his eyes. But what he saw of his eyes, he thought he would collapse at just the very sight. He clenched his hands on the shaft of the hammer so that the knuckles went white. The peasant and his household begged for mercy and offered whatever atonement he wanted. And when he saw their great terror, his wrath left him and he accepted from the peasant his children Þjálfi and Rǫskva, and they were his servants afterwards.

'He then left his goats behind and went to the world of giants and all the way to the sea and swam across that great deep sea, and when he reached land, then he went ashore and with him Þjálfi and Rǫskva and Loki. And when they were gone a little way, they were faced by a huge forest. They walked through the

þeim. Gengu daginn til myr|krs. Þjálfi var manna skjótastr. Hann bar kýl Óðins Þórs.[1] En til vista var eigi gott. Þá er myrkt var, leituðu þeir sér náttstaðar ok fundu skála nokkurn í mǫrkinni, mikinn. Vóru dyrr á enda ok jambreiðar skálanum. Þar vóru þeir um nóttina. En um miðnætti varð landskjálpti mikill ok gekk jǫrðin undir þeim skykkjum ok skalf húsit. Þá stóð Þórr upp ok hét á félaga sína ok leituðust fyrir ok fundu afhús til hǿgri handar á miðjum skálanum ok fóru þangat. Settist Þórr í dyrnar, en þau vóru innar frá honum ok hrædd mjǫk. En Þórr helt hamarskaptinu ok hugði at verja sik. Þá heyrðu þeir ym mikinn ok gný.

Ok er komit var at dǫgun, kom Þórr út ok sá mann hvíla í skóginum skamt frá sér ok var eigi lítill ok hraut sterkliga, ok þóttist Þórr skilja hvat látum verit mun hafa um nóttina. Hann spennir sik megingjǫrðum ok óx honum ásmegin. Ok í því bili vaknar sá maðr. Stóð upp skjótt. Þá varð Þór bilt at slá meðr hamrinum ok spurði hann at nafni, en hann nefndist Skrýmir. En eigi þarf ek at spyrja at þú ert Ása-Þórr, eða hefir þú dregit á brott hanzka minn? Seilist þá Skrýmir til ok tók hanzkann. Sér Þórr at þat hafði verit um nóttina skálinn, en afhúsit var þumlungrinn hanzkans. Skrýmir spurði ef Þórr vildi at þeir fǿri allir saman, en Þórr játti því. Þá tók Skrýmir ok leysti nestbaggann ok bjóst at eta, en Þórr í ǫðrum stað ok hans menn. Þá bauð Skrýmir at þeir legði í einn stað baggana ok legði á bak sér, ok svá gerðu þeir. Ok nú leggr Skrýmir á bak sér ok stígr heldr stórum. Ok at kveldi leitaði hann náttstaðar undir eik einni.

Þá mælti Skrýmir til Þórs at hann vill leggjast niðr undir eikina at sofa, en þeir taki nestbaggann ok búi til matar sér. Því næst sofnar Skrýmir ok hraust[2] fast. En Þórr tók nestbaggann ok vill leysa. Ok ótrúligt er þat at segja at engan knút fekk hann leyst. Ok er hann sér þat, grípr hann hamarinn ok lýstr í hǫfuð Skrými. Hann vaknar ok spyrr hvárt laufsblað felli í hǫfuð honum eða hvárt þeir sé mettir. Þórr lét at þeir mundi | sofa undir annarri eik.

At miðri nótt heyrir Þórr at Skrýmir hrýtr. Þá tekr Þórr hamarinn ok lýstr í hǫfuð honum í miðjan hvirfilinn ok søkk hamarrinn. Þá vaknar Þórr Skrýmir ok spyrr: Hvárt fell axkorn í hǫfuð mér, eða hvárt vakir þú Þórr? Hann lézt vera vaknaðr.

Nú ætlar Þórr at slá hann þriðja sinni, reiðir upp hamarinn af ǫllu afli ok lýstr á þunnvangan⟨n⟩ er upp vissi. Søkkr hamarrinn at skaptinu. En Skrýmir sezt upp ok strýkr um vangann ok ennit ok mælti:

Hvárt munu fuglar vera nokkurir í trénu yfir mér. Mér þótti sem fjǫðr nokkur felli af trénu í hǫfuð mér. Ok spurði: Hvárt vakir þú Þórr? Mál mun vera upp at standa ok klæðast. Þér eigið nú ekki langt til borgar er

---

[1] Both names are written clearly, and no attempt was made to indicate a correction.
[2] Error for *hraut*.

day until it was dark. Þjálfi was the fastest of runners. He carried Óðinn's Þórr's knapsack. But there was little in the way of lodgings to be found. When it was dark they looked for somewhere to spend the night and found a certain hall in the forest, a large one. There was an entrance at one end and it was the full width of the building. There they stayed the night. But about midnight there was a great earthquake and the ground under them moved in shudders and the building shook. Then Þórr got up and called to his companions and they searched around and found a side-chamber on the right hand side halfway down the building and went to it. Þórr positioned himself in the doorway and they were further in behind him and very fearful. But Þórr clasped the shaft of his hammer and planned to defend himself. Then they heard a great rumbling and groaning.

'And when dawn came, Þórr came out and saw a man lying in the forest a short way off, and he was no midget and was snoring mightily, and Þórr realised what the noise must have been in the night. He buckles on his girdle of might and his Áss-strength grew. And at that moment this man awoke. He got up quickly. Then Þórr hesitated to strike with his hammer and asked him his name, and he said his name was Skrýmir.

' "But I do not need to be told that you are Þórr of the Æsir., but have you been making off with my glove?"

'Then Skrýmir reaches over and picked up his glove. Þórr realises that it had been his hall during the night, and the side-chamber was the thumb of the glove. Skrýmir asked if Þórr would like them all to travel together, and Þórr agreed. Then Skrýmir went and undid his knapsack and began to eat, and so did Þórr and his people in another place. Then Skrýmir suggested that they should put the bundles together in one and put them on his back, and they did so. So now Skrýmir put them on his back and took rather long strides. And in the evening he found a place to spend the night under an oak.

'Then spoke Skrýmir to Þórr that he wants to lie down under the oak to sleep, but they should take the knapsack and get on with their food. Next Skrýmir falls asleep and snored hard. Bur Þórr took the knapsack and tries to undo it. And it is beyond belief to have to say that not a single knot could he get undone. And when he realises this, he grasps the hammer and strikes on Skrýmir's head. He wakes up and asks whether a leaf of foliage had fallen on his head, and whether they had eaten. Þórr said that they would sleep under another oak.

'At midnight Þórr hears that Skrýmir is snoring. Then Þórr takes his hammer and strikes on his head in the centre of the crown and the hammer sank in. Then Skrýmir wakes up and asks:

' "Did an ear of wheat fall on my head, and are you awake, Þórr?"

'He said he had woken up. Now Þórr plans to strike him a third time, swings the hammer up with all his might and strikes on the temple that was facing upwards. The hammer sinks in up to the shaft. But Skrýmir sits up and strokes his cheek and forehead and said:

' "Can there be some birds in the tree above me? It seemed to me as though some feather fell from the tree onto my head."

'And he asked: "Are you awake, Þórr? It must be time to get up and dress. You do not now have far to go to the castle that is called Útgarðr, but I have

Útgarðr[1] heitir, en ek hefi heyrt kvis yðart at yðr þikkir ek heldr mikill maðr. En sjá megu þér þar stœrri menn. Ræð ek yðr heilt: Látið ekki mikit yfir yðr. Illa mun þat þolat slíkum kǫgursveinum,[2] eða hverfið aptr ok er yðr sá betri. Ella stefni þér í austrætt ef þér vilið til borgarinnar. En ek á norðr leið. Tekr nestbaggann, leggr á bak sér ok snýr á skóginn, ok er eigi getit at æsirnir biði hann heilan fara.

Þeir ganga til Miðgarðs[3] ok sjá borg standa á vǫllum nokkurum ok settu hnakka á bak sér áðr þeir fengi yfir sét. Grind var fyrir borgarhliði. Þórr fekk eigi upp komit ok smugu millum svalanna.[4] Þeir sá hǫll mikla, gengu inn ok sá þar œrit stóra menn. Þeir kvǫddu Útgarða-Loka er þeir kómu fyrir hásæti. Hann leit til þeira seint ok glotti við tǫnn ok mælti:

Seint er um langan veg at spyrja sǫnn tíðindi, er sveinstauli einn er orðinn at Ǫku-Þór. En meiri muntu en mér lízt, eða við hverjum íþróttum eru þér búnir félagar? Engi mun sá með oss vera er eigi kunni nokkurar[5] íþróttir.

Loki segir: Engi mun sá hér innan hirðar er skjótara muni eta en ek.

Þá svarar Útgarða-Loki: Íþrótt er þetta ef þú efnir, ok reyna skal þetta. Hann kallar á bekkinn á þann mann er Logi er nefndr ok biðr hann freista sín móti Loka. Þá var tekit trog eitt mikit ok sett á hallargólfit, fullt | af slátri, ok settist Loki at ǫðrum enda en Logi at ǫðrum megin, ok át hvártveggi sem tíðast ok mœttust í miðju troginu. Hafði Loki etit slátr allt af beinum, en Logi hafði etit slátr allt ok beinin ok svá trogit, ok vann Logi leikinn.

Þá spurði Útgarða-Loki hvat sá enn ungi maðr kynni leika. Þjálfi segir at hann mun freista at renna skeið við einn hvern hirðmann hans. Hann svarar: Þat er góð íþrótt, ok lét hann vel búinn at skjótleik ef hann skal þessa íþrótt vinna, ok freista skal. Gengr hann út á gott s⟨k⟩eið, kallar til sín sveinstaula nokkurn er Hugi hét, ok bað hann renna við hann fyrsta skeið, ok er Hugi því framarr at hann snýst aptr í móti honum at skeiðs enda.

Þá mælti Útgarða-Loki: Þurfa muntu at leggja þik meirr fram. En þó hafa hér komit ekki ófljótari menn.

Þá taka þeir annat skeið ok er Hugi kemr til skeiðs enda snerist hann aptr, ok er þá langt kólfskot til Þjálfa. Þá mælti Útgarða-Loki: Vel þikki mér Þjálfi renna. En eigi trúi ek honum nú at hann vinni leikinn. En nú mun reyna er

[1] First written 'miþgarþr' but corrected to 'vtgarþr' (see Grape et al. 1977: 126).
[2] The word kǫgursveinn appears only here (in both versions) and in ch. 29 in DG 11 4to only (where the Codex Regius version has *lítill ok ungmenni eitt* ('small and just a youth'), and in *Hárbarðsljóð* 13, where Þórr uses the word of Hárbarðr. But kǫgurbarn is found in *fornaldarsögur* and in *Maríu saga*. Ásgeir Bl. Magnússson suggests it means 'a child held in the folds of a skirt, child in arms'.
[3] Error for *Útgarðs*. No attempt was made to correct it.
[4] *Svalanna* means 'of the balcony'. It must be an error for *spalanna* 'rails or bars of a gate' (confusion of insular w (p) and þ?).
[5] Written 'nockvrvrar'.

heard your whispers that you find me rather a big man. But there you will be able to see bigger men. I will give you good advice. Don't act big. That will not be put up with easily from such babies, or else turn back, and that will be better for you. Otherwise make for the east if you want to go to the castle. But my way lies to the north."

'He takes the knapsack, puts it on his back and turns into the forest, and it is not reported that the Æsir bade him farewell.

'They walk on to Miðgarðr and see a castle standing on some open ground and had to bend their heads back to touch their spines before they managed to see over it. There was a gate across the castle entrance. Þórr could not manage to get up over it and they squeezed between the bars. They saw a great hall, went in and saw there men that were big enough. They greeted Útgarða-Loki when they came before the throne. He was slow to turn to them and bared his teeth in a smile and said:

' "Accurate news travels slowly over long distances, since a little boy has turned into Ǫku-Þór. But you must be bigger that it appears to me, so what are the feats that your party are able to perform? There can be no one staying with us who does not know some feats."

'Loki says: "There will be no one here in the court that will eat more quickly than I."

'Then Útgarða-Loki replies: "That is a feat if you can perform it, and it shall be put to the test."

'He calls to the bench to the man that is called Logi (flame) and bids him try his prowess against Loki. Then a long trencher was fetched and put on the hall floor, full of meat, and Loki sat down at one end and Logi on the other side, and each ate as quickly as he could and they met in the middle of the trencher. Loki had eaten all the meat off the bones, but Logi had eaten all the meat and the bones and also the trencher, and Logi won the contest.

'Then Útgarða-Loki asked what that young man there could perform. Þjálfi says that he will attempt to run a race with one of the men of his court. He replies:

' "That is a good feat," and declares him well endowed with speed if he is to perform this feat, and "it shall be put to the test."

'He goes out onto a fine running track, calls to him a certain little boy that was called Hugi (thought), and bade him run the first race with him, and Hugi is so far ahead that he turns back to meet him at the end of the course. Then Útgarða-Loki said:

' "You will have to make a greater effort. And yet men have come here that are no less fast."

'Then they start a second race, and when Hugi comes to the end of the course he turns back, and Þjálfi is now a good arrow shot behind. Then spoke Útgarða-Loki:

' "I think Þjálfi runs well. But I do not now have any confidence in him that he will win the contest. But now we shall see when they run the third race."

þeir renna it þriðja skeiðit. Ok nú er Hugi er kominn til skeiðs enda er Þjálfi eigi kominn á mitt skeið. Nú er þetta reynt.

Þá mælti Útgarða-Loki: Hvat íþrótt kantu Þórr? Muntu vera fyrir þeim, svá mikit sem menn hafa gert um þín stórvirki. Hann svaraði at helzt vill hann þreyta drykkju við nokkurn mann hans. Útgarða-Loki segir at þat má vel vera. Gengr í hǫllina ok biðr taka vítishorn er hirðmenn eru vanir af at drekka. Hann sýnir Þór ok segir at þat þikkir vel drukkit at drekka af í einu. En sumir drekka í tveimr en engi svá vesall at eigi drekki af í þrimr.

Þór sýnist hornit eigi mikit ok þó mjǫk langt. Hann var þyrstr mjǫk. Setr á munn sér ok svalg stórum ok ætlar at hann skal eigi lúta optarr í hornit. Ok er hann þraut eyrindi ok sér í hornit at nú er litlu minna í en áðr. Þá segir Útgarða-Loki: Vel er drukkit en eigi til mikit. Munda ek eigi trúa ef mér væri sagt frá Ása-Þór at hann drykki eigi meira. Þú munt drekka ǫðru sinni.

Þórr svaraði engu, setr hornit á munn sér ok ætlar af at drekka, þreytir á drykkjuna sem honum vanst til eyrindi. Ok enn sér hann at stikillinn hornsins vill eigi upp, ok sér í ok ætlar nú minna hafa þorrit en it fyrra sinn. Er nú gott beranda borð á horninu.

Þá svarar Útgarða-Loki: Hvat er nú Þórr? Muntu nú eigi, Þórr, spara þér til eins drykkjar meira en þér mun hǫgst vera? Svá lízt mér ef þú skalt drekka inn þriðja drykkinn, sem þessi mun mestr ætlaðr vera. En ekki máttu hér heita svá mikill maðr sem æsir kalla þik ef þú gerir eigi meira af þér um aðra hluti. Þá varð Þórr reiðr mjǫk, setr hornit á munn sér ok þreytir mest. Ok er hann leit í hornit, þá hafði lengst á gengit. En er hann sér þat, gefr hann upp ok vill eigi drekka lengr.

Þá mælti Útgarða-Loki: Auðsætt er þat at máttr þinn er ekki mikill. Viltu leika fleira?

Þórr segir: Freista mun ek enn um fleiri leika. En undarligt mundi mér þikkja, ef ek væri heima með ásum, ef slíkir drykkir væri þar litlir kallaðir. En hvat leik vili þér bjóða?

Þá svarar Útgarða-Loki: Þat er ungra sveina at hefja upp af jǫrðu katt[1] minn. En eigi munda ek slíkt kunna at mæla við Ása-Þór ef ek hefða eigi séð at hann er minni maðr en mér er sagt.

Þá hljóp fram kattr grár á hallargólfit mikill heldr. Þórr tók hendinni undir kviðinn niðr ok lypti upp. En kattrinn beygði kenginn ok svá sem hann rétti upp hǫndina lypti kattrinn einum fǿtinum.

Þá mælti Útgarða-Loki: Svá fór sem mik varði. Kattrinn er heldr mikill, en þú ert lágr ok lítill.

Þórr segir: Svá lítill sem ek em, þá gangi til einn hverr yðarr at fást viðr mik, nú er ek em reiðr.

---

[1] In this part of the story the forms *katt* and *kattr* are used in DG 11 4to, but at the end of the narrative Útgarða-Loki uses the *u*-mutated form 'kottenn', i.e. *kǫttinn*. This is the normal Old Norse form; *katt(r)* may be formed by analogy with genitive *kattar*.

'And now when the end of the course is reached, Þjálfi had not got to the middle of the course. Now this one is decided.

'Then spoke Útgarða-Loki: "What feat do you know, Þórr? You must be superior to them, when people have made so much of your mighty deeds."

He replied that he would most willingly compete at drinking with one of his men. Útgarða-Loki says that that would be fine. He goes into the hall and orders the forfeit-horn to be fetched that the men of his court were accustomed to drink from. He shows it to Þórr and says that it is considered to be well drunk to drink it off in one.

' "But some drink it in two, but no one [is] so poor that he does not drink it off in three."

'The horn looks not large, and yet very long, to Þórr. He was very thirsty. He puts it to his mouth and took great gulps, and intends not to address the horn again. And when he ran out of breath, he sees in the horn that now there is not much less in it than before. Then says Útgarða-Loki:

' "That was a good drink, and not excessive. I would not have believed it if I had been told about Þórr of the Æsir that he would not drink more. You will take another drink."

'Þórr made no reply, puts the horn to his mouth and intends to drink it off, struggles with the drink as long as his breath held out. And still he finds that the point of the horn will not go up, and looks into it and thinks it has now gone down less than the time before. The level is now far enough down for the horn to be carried easily without spilling.

'Then Útgarða-Loki answers: 'What is it now, Þórr? Will you not, Þórr, be saving for yourself for one drink more than will be most convenient for you? It seems to me if you are going to drink a third draught as if this one will be intended to be the biggest. But you cannot here be reckoned such a great man as the Æsir say you are if you do not put up more of a showing in other things. Then Þórr got very angry, puts the horn to his mouth and struggles his mightiest. And when he looked in the horn, then it had gone down furthest. So when he sees that, he gives up and will not drink any more.

'Then spoke Útgarða-Loki: "It is obvious that your strength is not great. Will you try more contests?"

'Þórr says: "I may as well have a try at still more contests. But it would seem strange to me, if I were at home with the Æsir, if such drinks were reckoned small there. But what game do you want to offer?"

'Then Útgarða-Loki replies: "It is for young lads to lift up my cat off the ground. But I would not know how to mention such a thing to Þórr of the Æsir if I had not seen that he is a lesser man that I have been told."

'Then a grey cat ran out onto the hall floor, rather a big one. Þórr put his hand down under its belly and lifted it up. But the cat arched its back and as he stretched up his hand the cat raised one paw.

'Then spoke Útgarða-Loki: "It went just as I expected. The cat is rather large, but you are short and small."

'Þórr says: "Small as I am, just let one of you come up and wrestle with me, now that I am angry."

Útgarða-Loki segir ok litast um. Eigi sé ek hér þann mann at eigi mun lítilræði í þikkja at glíma við þik. Kalli higat kerlingu fóstru mína, ok fást þú við hana. Fellt hefir hon stǿrri sveina ok þá er mér lítast hvergi ósterkligri en þú. Ekki er þar af annat sagt en því harðara er Þórr knýst at því fastara stóð hon. Þá tók kerling at leita til bragða. Þórr varð lauss á fótum ok váru sviptingar harðar, ok fell Þórr á kné ǫðrum fǿti, ok þá bað Útgarða-Loki þau hætta ok lét hann eigi fleirum þurfa at bjóða fang. Ok vóru þeir þar um nóttina.

En um morgininn bjuggust æsirnir á brott ok leiddi hann þá á gǫtu | ok spurði hvernveg Þór þǿtti fǫr sín orðin. Þórr segir at þeir mundi kalla hann lítinn mann.

Þá segir Útgarða-Loki. Nú skal segja þér it sanna, er þú ert kominn út af borginni. Eigi hefðir þú komit í hana ef ek hefða vitat þik svá mikils háttar sem þú ert.

En sjónhverfingar vóru gervar, fyrst á skóginum, ok kom ek fyrst til fundar við yðr. Ok er þú vildir leysa nestbaggann var hann bundinn meðr gresjárni.[1] En þú fant eigi hvar upp var at lúka. Þá laust þú mik með hamri þínum þrysvar sinnum, ok var it fyrsta minst ok þó svá mikit at mér mundi unnit hafa at fullu ef á hefði komit. En þar er þú sátt hjá hǫll minni setberg ok þar í ofan þrjá dali ferskeytta ok einn djúpastan, þat vóru hamarspor þín. Setberginu brá ek fyrir hǫggin.

En Loki þreytti leik við eld um átit. En Þjálfi tók hlaup við huginn ok mátti hann eigi ok engi annarr þat viðr hann þreyta.

Þat var þó mest undr er þú drakt af horninu er annarr endir var í ægi. Því eru orðnar fjǫrurnar.

En þar lyptir þú upp Miðgarðsorminum er þú tókt kǫttinn. En þá hræddust allir er þat sá er þú lyptir einum fǿtinum á kettinum.

En þú fekst þar við Elli er þú hugðist við kerlinguna eiga. Henni hefir engi á kné komit.

En þér komit mik eigi optarr heim at sǿkja.

Þá bregðr Þórr upp hamrinum, ok nú sér hann hvergi Útgarða-Loka ok eigi heldr borgina.

29 Hér segir frá því er Þórr fór at draga Miðgarðsorminn

Eptir þenna atburð snýrr Þórr heimleiðis. Ætlar nú at hitta Miðgarðsorminn ok kom til jǫtuns nokkurs er Eymir er nefndr.

En um morgininn bjóst jǫtunn at fara til fiskjar. Þórr vill fara með honum. En jǫtunn lét ekki gagn mundu at kǫgrsveini þeim. Mun þik kala ef ek sit lengi ok útarla á miðum sem ek em vanr.

[1] *Gresjárn* 'magic wire'. Cf. Old Irish *grés* 'handicraft'.

'Útgarða-Loki says, looking around: "I do not see here anyone that will not think it demeaning to wrestle with you. Call here the old woman, my nurse, and you fight with her. She has brought down bigger boys, and ones that have seemed to me in no way less strong-looking than you."

'Nothing other is told about it than that the harder Þórr strained at it, the firmer she stood. Then the old woman started to try tricks. Þórr began to lose his footing, and there were hard wrenchings, and Þórr fell onto the knee of one leg, and then Útgarða-Loki told them to stop and said there was no need for him to challenge more people to a wrestling match. And they stayed there the night.

'And in the morning, the Æsir got ready to leave and he took them out onto the road and asked how Þórr thought he thought his expedition had turned out. Þórr says that they would call him a person of little account.

'Then says Útgarða-Loki: "You shall be told the truth, now that you are come out of the castle. You would not have come into it if I had known you to be of such great significance as you are.

' "But you have been deceived by appearances, to begin with in the forest, and it was I that came to meet you first of all. And when you tried to undo the knapsack, it was tied with trick wire. And you could not find where it had to be unfastened. Then you struck me three blows with your hammer, and the first was the smallest, and yet so hard that it would have done for me completely if it had landed on me. But where you saw near my hall a table mountain and down in it three square valleys and one of them deepest of all, these were the marks of your hammer. I moved the table mountain in front of your blows.

' "But Loki competed at a sport with fire about the eating. And Þjálfi ran a race with the thought and he could not, nor anyone else, compete at that with it.

' "Yet that was the greatest marvel when you drank from the horn whose other end was in the ocean. From that the tides have originated.

' "But there you were lifting up the Miðgarðr serpent when you seized the cat. And then everyone that saw it was terrified when you raised one of the cat's paws.

' "But you were fighting Elli (old age) when you thought you were having to do with the old woman. No one has brought her to her knees.

' "But you will not come to visit me again."

'Then Þórr swung up his hammer, and now he can see Útgarða-Loki nowhere nor the castle either.'

29 Here it tells about how Þórr went to fish for the Miðgarðr serpent

'After this episode Þórr turned to go home. He plans now to find the Miðgarðr serpent and arrived at a giant's that is called Eymir.

'And in the morning the giant got ready to go fishing. Þórr wants to go with him. But the giant said that this baby would be no use.

' "You will get cold if I stay a long time and far out on the fishing banks, as I am used to doing."

Þórr reiddist honum mjǫk ok kvað þat eigi víst ok spurði hvat þeir skyldi hafa at beitum. Eymir bað hann fá sér beitur. Þórr tok uxann er heitir Himinrjóðr, er Eymir átti, ok sleit af hǫfuðit ok settist í austrrúm, ok þótti Eymi hann heldr róa mikit ok lét þá komna á þær vastir sem hann var vanr ok bað þá eigi róa lengra. Þórr lézt vildu enn miklu lengra róa. Eymir kvað þat hætt við Miðgarðsorminn. Þórr vill róa. | Eymir varð ókátr.

Þórr greiddi vaðinn ok lét koma á uxahǫfuðit á ǫngulinn ok fór til grunns. Miðgarðsormrinn beit á ǫnglinum ok kom í góminn. En ormrinn brá við fast svá at báðir hnefar Þórs skullu við borðinu. Þá fǿrðist Þórr í ásmegin, spyrndi við fast svá at hann hljóp báðum fótum í gegnum skipborðit ok spyrndi við grunni. Dró þá at sér orminn ok upp viðr borðinu. En engi hefir sá séð enar ógrligstu sýnir er eigi hefir þat er Þórr hvesti augun á orminn. En hann starði neðan á móti ok blés eitrinu.

Jǫtunninn varð litverpr er hann sá orminn, ok særinn fell inn nokkut. En er Þórr greip hamarinn, fálmaði jǫtunninn til agnsaxins ok hjó við borðinu vað Þórs. En ormr søkk í sæinn. En Þórr kastaði hamrinum ok laust við eyra jǫtninum svá at hann steyptist at borðinu ok laust af honum hǫfuðit við háunum. En Þórr óð til lands.

Þá mælti Gangleri: Mikit afrek var þetta.

30 Frá lífláti Baldrs ok fǫr Hermóðs til Heljar

Hár svaraði: Meira var hitt vert, er Baldr enn góða dreymði hættligt ok sagði ásum. Frigg beiddi honum griða at eigi grandaði honum eldr né járn né vǫtn, málmr né steinar né viðir, sóttir né dýr, fuglar né eitrormar.

Ok er þetta var gert, var þat skemtan Baldrs at hann stóð upp á þingum. Skyldu sumir skjóta at honum en sumir hǫggva, sumir grýta. Hann sakaði ekki.

En er Loki sá þat, líkaði honum illa, gekk til Fensala til Friggjar til Fensala[1] ok brá sér í konu líki. Spyrr Frigg, ef hann vissi hvat menn hǫfðust at á þinginu. Hann sagði at allir skutu at Baldri en hann sakar ekki. Þá mælti Frigg: Eigi munu vápn né viðir bana Baldri. Eiða hefi ek af ǫllum tekit.

Þá mælti konan: Hafa allir hlutir eiða unnit at eira Baldri?

Frigg svaraði: Viðarteinungr einn vex fyrir vestan Valhǫll er heitir mistilteinn. Sá þótti mér ungr at krefja eiðsins.

Þá hverfr konan. En Loki gengr til ok tekr mistilteininn ok slítr upp með rótum. Gengr til þingsins. En Hǫðr stóð utarliga í mannhringinum, er hann var blindr. Þá mælti Loki við hann: Hví skýtr þú eigi at Baldri? Hann svarar: Því at ek sé ekki, ok þat annat at ek em vápnlauss.

Loki mælti: Gerðu í líking annarra manna ok veit honum atsókn. Ek mun vísa þér til hans. Skjót þú at honum vendi þessum.

[1] So DG 11 4to.

'Þórr got very angry with him and said that was not certain and asked what they were to use as bait. Eymir told him to get himself baits. Þórr took an ox that is called Himinrjóðr that belonged to Eymir, and tore off its head and seated himself in the well of the boat and Eymir thought he was rowing rather hard and said they were come to the fishing ground that he was accustomed to and said they were not to row further. Þórr said he wanted to row much further yet. Eymir said that was dangerous with the Miðgarðr serpent. Þórr wants to row. Eymir became unhappy.

'Þórr got out his line and fastened the ox-head onto the hook and it went to the bottom.

'The Miðgarðr serpent bit on the hook and it went into its gum. And the serpent jerked away so hard that both Þórr's knuckles banged down on the gunwale. Then Þórr summoned up his Áss-strength, pushed down so hard that he forced both feet through the ship's side and braced them against the sea-bed. He then hauled the serpent towards him and up to the gunwale. And no one has seen the horriblest sights who has not [seen] how Þórr fixed his eyes on the serpent. And it stared up at him and spat poison.

'The giant changed colour when he saw the serpent, and the sea flowed in somewhat. But when Þórr grasped his hammer, the giant fumbled for his bait-knife and cut Þórr's line at the gunwale. And the serpent sank into the sea. But Þórr threw his hammer and struck at the giant's ear so that he was hurled against the gunwale and struck off his head by the rowlocks. But Þórr waded ashore.'

Then spoke Gangleri. 'That was a great achievement.'

30 Of Baldr's death and Hermóðr's journey to Hel

High replied: 'That was of greater significance when Baldr the Good dreamed danger-boding things and told the Æsir. Frigg requested immunity for him so that there should not harm him fire nor iron nor liquids, metal nor stones nor wood, sicknesses nor animals, birds nor poisonous snakes.

'And when this was done, it was an entertainment for Baldr that he stood up at assemblies. Some were to shoot at him and some strike him, some stone him. He was not harmed.

'But when Loki saw this, he was not pleased, he went to Fensalir to Frigg to Fensalir and changed his appearance to that of a woman. Frigg asks if he knew what people were doing at the assembly. He said that everyone was shooting at Baldr but he is not harmed. Then spoke Frigg:

' "Neither weapons nor wood will kill Baldr. I have taken oaths from them all."

'Then spoke the woman: "Have all things sworn oaths not to harm Baldr?"

'Frigg replied: "There is one shoot of a tree growing to the west of Valhǫll that is called mistletoe. It seemed young to me to demand the oath from."

'Then the woman disappears. But Loki goes up and and takes the mistletoe and tears it up by the roots. He goes to the assembly. And Hǫðr was standing at the edge of the circle of people, as he was blind. Then Loki spoke to him:

' "Why do you not shoot at Baldr?"

'He replies: "Because I cannot see, and secondly because I have no weapon."

'Loki spoke: "Follow other people's example and make an attack on him. I will direct you to him. Shoot this stick at him."

Hǫðr tók mistilteininn ok skaut í gegnum Baldr, ok var þat mest óhappaskot með guðum ok mǫnnum.

Nú sá hverr til annars ok allir með grimmum hug til þess gert hafði. En engi mátti þar hefna í griðastaðnum.

Allir báru illa harminn, en Óðinn verst. Var þar grátr fyrir mál. Þá spurði Frigg hverr sá væri með ásum er eignast vildi ástir hennar ok ríða á Helvega at ná Baldri meðr útlausn. Hermóðr, son Óðins, fór ok reið Sleipni.

Baldr var lagðr í skipit Hringhorna, ok ætluðu guðin fram at setja með bálgerð, ok tókst þat eigi fyrri en Hyrrokin kom til. Hon reið vargi, ok vargar vóru at taumum. Ok nú fengu eigi berserkir haldit taumunum. Hon dró framm skipit ok at fyrsta viðbragði hraut skipit ór hlunnunum. Þá vildi Þórr ljósta hana. En guðin banna þat.

Lík Baldrs var borit á bálit. Nanna Nefsdóttir sprakk er hon frá. Þórr vígði bálit með Mjǫlni, ok hann spyrndi dvergnum Lit á bálit.

Þeir[1] vóru þá ǫll guðin. Freyr sat í kerru ok var þar beittr fyrir gǫltrinn Gullinbusti eða Sligrutanni. Heimdallr reið Gulltopp. En Freyja[2] ók kǫttum sínum. Þar vóru ok hrímþussar. Óðinn lagði á bálit Draupni ok hest Baldrs með ǫllum reiða.

Hermóðr reið níu nætr til Gjallarár ok á gulli hlaðna brú. Móðguðr gætti brúarinnar, ok hon mælti: Fyrra dag reið Baldr hér með fimm hundruð manna. En eigi glymr miðr undir þér einum.

Þá reið hann at Helgrindum ok sá þar bróður sinn. Hann bar framm boð sín. En sú ein var ván um brottkvámu hans ef allir hlutir gráta hann með ásum, kykvir ok dauðir. En ella haldist með Helju.

Baldr fekk honum hringinn Draupni. En Nanna sendi Frigg fald, en Fullu fingrgull. Þá fór Hermóðr aptr í Ásgarð ok segir tíðindi.

Þá báðu guðin alla hluti gráta Baldr ór Helju, menn ok kykvindi, jǫrð ok steina. Tré ok allr málmr grétu Baldr, sem þú munt séð hafa at þessir hlutir gráta allir í frosti ok hita. Þat er sagt at guðin finna gýgi í helli nokkurum er Þǫkt nefndist, biðja hana gráta sem allt annat Baldr ór Helju. Hon svarar:

52 (50)   Þǫkt[3] mun gráta
        þurrum tárum
        Baldrs helfarar
        kyks eða dauðs.[4]
        Haldi Hel því er hefir.

Þar var Loki raunar.

---

[1] Doubtless an error for *þar*.

[2] Written 'freyio'.

[3] The Codex Regius version has the rather more meaningful name *Þǫkk* ('thanks').

[4] The Codex Regius version has here the expected fifth line of this *ljóðaháttr* stanza: *nautka ek karls sonar* 'No good got I from the old one's (Óðinn's) son'.

'Hǫðr took the mistletoe and shot it through Baldr, and that was the unluckiest shot among gods and men.

'They all looked at each other and all with grim thought towards the one [that] had done this. But no one could take vengeance there in the place of sanctuary.

'They all bore their grief badly, but Óðinn worst. There was weeping in place of speech. Then Frigg asked who there was among the Æsir that wished to earn her love and ride the roads to Hel to get Baldr back by ransom. Óðinn's son Hermóðr went and rode Sleipnir.

'Baldr was laid in the ship Hringhorni, and the gods were intending to launch it with a funeral pyre, and this could not be done until Hyrrokin came up. She was riding a wolf and wolves were holding the reins. And now berserks could not manage the reins, She dragged the ship forward and at the first pull the ship flew from the slipway. Then Þórr wanted to strike her. But the gods forbade that.

'Baldr's body was carried onto the pyre. Nanna Nefr's daughter collapsed when she heard. Þórr consecrated the pyre with Mjǫllnir, and he kicked the dwarf Litr onto the fire.

'Now all the gods were there. Freyr sat in a chariot and the boar Gullinbusti or Sligrutanni was harnessed in front of it. Heimdallr rode Gulltoppr. But Freyja drove her cats. Frost giants were there too. Óðinn laid Draupnir on the pyre and Baldr's horse with all its harness.

'Hermóðr rode nine nights to the river Gjǫll and onto a bridge covered with gold. Móðguðr was guarding the bridge, and she said:

' "The other day Baldr rode here with five hundred men. But it does not clatter less under just you."

'Then he rode to the gates of Hel and saw his brother there. He put forward his request. But the only hope of him getting away was if all things weep for him with the Æsir, alive and dead. But otherwise he is kept with Hel.

'Baldr gave him the ring Draupnir. And Nanna sent Frigg a headdress and Fulla a finger ring. Then Hermóðr went back to Ásgarðr and tells what has happened.

'Then the gods bade all things weep Baldr out of Hel, men and animals, earth and stones. Trees and all metal wept for Baldr, as you must have seen that these things all weep in frost and heat. It is said that the gods find a giantess in a certain cave who called herself Þǫkt, ask her to weep Baldr out of Hel like everything else. She replies:

52   Þǫkt will weep
       dry tears
       for Baldr's funeral
       alive or dead.
       Let Hel keep what she has.

'It was Loki really.

Þá er guðin vissu þat, vóru þau reið Loka, ok fal hann sik á fjall⟨i⟩ nokkuru ok vóru fjórar dyrr á húsi hans, at hann sæi í allar ættir. En um daga var hann í Fránangsforsi í laxs líki. Honum kom í hug at æsirnir mundi setja vél fyrir hann. Tók síðan língarnit ok reið moskva, sem net er gert. Þá sá hann æsi þangat fara. Óðinn hafði sét hann ór Hliðskjálf. Loki hljóp í ána, en kastaði netinu á eldinn.

Kvasir gekk inn fyrstr er vitrastr var. Þá skilði hann at þetta mundi vél til fiska, ok gerðu eptir folskanum er netit brann. Fara í forsinn ok helt Þórr oðrum netshálsi, en allir æsir oðrum. En Loki lagðist millum steina tveggja ok drógu þeir netit yfir hann framm. Fara oðru sinni ok binda svá þungt við at eigi mátti undir fara. Þá fór Loki fyrir netinu ok er skamt var til sjóvar hleypr hann yfir upp þinulinn ok rennir upp í forsinn.

Nú sjá æsirnir hvar hann fór, skipta nú liðinu í tvá staði. Þórr veðr eptir miðri áinni ok fara svá út til sjóvar. Ok er Loki sér lífs háska á sæinn at fara, þá hleypr hann yfir netit. En Þórr greip hann hondum. En hann rendi í hondum honum ok nam hondin staðar í sporðinn. Ok er fyrir þá sok laxinn aptrmjór.

Loki var nú tekinn griðalauss ok fœrðr í helli nokkurn. Ok tóku hellur þrjár ok settu á enda, lustu á rauf á hverri. Þá vóru teknir synir Loka, Váli ok Nari, ok brugðu Vála í vargs líki ok reif hann í sundr Nara. Þá tóku æsir þarma hans ok bundu Loka með yfir þrjá eggsteina. Stóð einn undir herðum, annarr undir lendum, þriði undir knésbótum, ok urðu bondin at járni. Skaði festi eitrorm yfir andlit honum. En Sigyn helt munlaug undir eitrdropana, ok slær út eitrinu, ok þá drýpr í andlit honum er full er munlaugin, ok kippist hann þá svá hart við at jorð skelfr. Þar liggr hann til Ragnarøkkrs.

31 Frá fimbulvetri ok Ragnarøkkrum

Hvat segir þú frá fimbulvetri? segir Gangleri.

Hár segir: Drífr þá snjór ór ollum áttum. Þá eru frost mikil ok vindar. Ekki nýtr sólar. Þeir vetr fara þrír saman, en ekki sumar í milli. En áðr ganga aðrir þrír vetr þeir er um alla verold eru. Orrostur | dreifast niðr fyrir ágirni ok engi þyrmir feðr né syni í manndrápum eða sifjum. Svá segir:[1]

53 (51)   Brœðr munu berjast
ok at bonum verða,
munu systrungar
sifjum spilla.
Hart er í heimi
hórdómr mikill,
skeggold, skálmold,
skildir klofna,

[1] Cf. *Voluspá* 45.

'When the gods knew this, they were angry with Loki, and he hid himself on a certain mountain, and there were four doors in his house, so that he could see in all directions. But in the daytime he was in Fránangr's waterfall in the form of a salmon. It occurred to him that the Æsir would set a trap for him. Then he took the linen thread and worked it into a mesh, as a net is made. Then he saw Æsir coming there. Óðinn had seen him from Hliðskjálf. Loki leapt into the river, but threw the net onto the fire.

'Kvasir went in first, who was most intelligent. Then he realised that this must be a device to catch fish, and he made one on the pattern of the ashes where the net was burning. They go to the waterfall and Þórr held one corner of the net and all the Æsir the other. But Loki lay down between two stones and they dragged the net forward over him. They go a second time and tie such weights to it that nothing could go under it. Then Loki went in front of the net and when it was a short way to the sea he leapt up over the top of the net and slipped up into the waterfall.

'Now the Æsir see where he went. They now divide their party into two groups. Þórr wades along the middle of the river and so out to the sea. And when Loki sees mortal danger in going into the sea, then he leaps over the net. But Þórr grabbed him in his hands. But he slid in his hands and his hand got a grip on the tail. And this is why the salmon tapers towards the tail.

'Loki was now captured without quarter and taken to a certain cave. And they took three stone slabs and set them on edge, knocking a hole in each one. Then Loki's sons were fetched, Váli and Nari, and they turned Váli into the form of a wolf and he tore Nari to pieces. Then the Æsir took his guts and bound Loki with them over [the] three sharp-edged stones. One stood under his shoulders, the second under his loins, the third under the hollows of his knees, and the bonds turned to iron. Skaði fixed a poisonous snake over his face. But Sigyn held a basin under the poison drops and pours away the poison, and then it drips into his face when the basin is full, and he jerks away so hard that the earth shakes. There he will lie until the twilight of the gods.'

31 Of the mighty winter and twilights of the gods

'What have you to say about the mighty winter?' says Gangleri.

High says: 'Snow will drift from all directions. Then there will be great frosts and winds. The sun will do no good. There will be three of these winters and no summer between. But before that there will come three other winters that will be over all the world. Battles will spread down because of greed and no one will show mercy to father or son in killings or relationships. So it says:

53   Brothers will fight each other
           and become each other's killers,
           cousins will
           break the bonds of kinship.
           It will be hard in the world,
           much depravity,
           age of axes, age of swords,
           shields will be cloven,

vindǫld, vargǫld,
unds verǫld steypist.
Mun enn[1] maðr
ǫðrum þyrma.

Úlfrinn gleypir sólina ok er mein sýnt mǫnnum. Þá gleypir annarr úlfrinn tunglit. Stjǫrnur hverfa. Jǫrðin skelfr. Bjǫrg ok viðir losna ór jǫrðunni ok hrynja. Fjǫtrar ok bǫnd brotna. Þá verðr Fenrisúlfrinn lauss. Þá geysist hafit á landit því at Miðgarðsormrinn snýst í Jǫtunheima. Þá losnar skipit Naglfari er gert er ór nǫglum dauðra manna. Því skal maðr eigi deyja með óskornum nǫglum, at sá eykr mikil efni til skipsins Naglfara er guðin vildu at seint yrði gert ok svá menninir. En í þessum sævargangi flýtr Naglfari. Hrymr stýrir honum. Fenrisúlfr ferr með gapanda munninn, ok er inn neðri keptr[2] með jǫrðu en inn efri með himni. Gapa mundi han⟨n⟩ meira ef rúmit væri til.

Miðgarðsormrinn blæss eitri ok aðra hlið uppi yfir honum þá klofnar himinninn. Ok í þessum gný ríða Múspells megir. Surtr ríðr fyrst. Fyrir honum ok eptir er eldr brennandi. Sverð hans er svá bjart sem sól. En þá er þeir ríða brotnar Bifrǫst. Múspells megir ríða á vǫllinn Vígriðinn, Fenrisúlfr ok Miðgarðsormrinn. Þar er ok Loki ok Hrymr með honum. Loka fylgja ok hellurnar.[3] Múspells megir hafa einir sér fylking ok er sú bjǫrt. Vǫllrinn Vígriðinn er hundrað rasta víðr á hvernig.

Heimdallr blæss í Gjallarhorn ok vekr upp ǫll guðin til þingsins. Óðinn ríðr til Mímisbrunns ok tekr af Mími ráð fyrir sér. Þá skelfr askr Ygdrasils ok engi hlutr er þá óttalauss á himni ok á jǫrðu. Æsir herklæðast til þingsins ok allir einherjar koma á vǫllinn. Óðinn ríðr með gullhjálminn fyrstr ok hefir geirinn Gungni í hendi ok stefnir á móti Fenrisúlfinum. Þórr berst við Miðgarðsorminn, Freyr móti Surti ok fellr hann er hann hefir eigi sverðit góða.

Hundrinn Garmr er þá lauss frá Gnipalundi ok berst við Tý ok hefir hvártveggi bana. Þórr drepr Miðgarðsorminn ok stígr framm níu fet um eitr ormsins. Úlfrinn gleypir Óðin ok er þat hans bani. | Þá snýr Viðarr framm ok stígr ǫðrum fǿti í neðra kept. Hann hefir þann skó er allan aldr hefir verit til samnat. Þat eru bjórar er menn taka ór skóm sínum fyrir tám ok hæli. Því skaltu þeim bjórum á brott kasta, sá maðr er at því vill hyggja at koma ásum at liði. Annarri hendi tekr hann enn efra kept hans ok rífr í sundr gin hans, ok verðr þat úlfsins bani. Loki berst við Heimdall ok verðr hvárr annars bani. Þá slǫngvir Surtr eldi yfir jǫrðina ok brennir heiminn allan. Sem hér segir:[4]

[1] GkS 2365 4to has *engi*, and the prose just before this stanza reads *engi þyrmir* 'no one will spare'. The last two lines are lacking in the Codex Regius version of *Snorra Edda*.

[2] The form without breaking appears three times in this story, but the more usual form *kjǫptr* is also found. See Noreen 1923, § 91.

[3] The Codex Regius version reads *Heljar sinnar* 'Hel's people'. The scribe of DG 11 4to seems to be still thinking of the *hellur* 'stone slabs' of the previous chapter.

[4] Cf. *Vǫluspá* 46/5–8, 47/1–3 and 48/4; 48/1–2, 5–6, 8; 57.

age of winds, age of wolves,
until the world falls in ruins.
Yet will a man
show mercy to another.

'The wolf will swallow the sun and injury is certain to men. Then the other wolf will swallow the moon. Stars will disappear. The earth will shake. Rocks and trees will become uprooted from the earth and will fall down. Fetters and bonds will break. Then the Fenriswolf will get free. Then the sea will surge onto the land because the Miðgarðr serpent will make its way into the dwelling places of giants. Then the ship Naglfari which is made of dead men's nails will be loosed from its moorings. It is for this reason that a man must not die with untrimmed nails, that this man will add much material to the ship Naglfari which the gods wished should not soon be finished, and the men too. But in this surge of the sea Naglfari will be launched. Hrymr will be its captain. Fenriswolf will go with mouth agape, and its lower jaw will be along the earth and its upper one along the sky. It would gape wider if more space were available.

'The Miðgarðr serpent will spit poison and on one side up above him the sky will then split open. And amid this turmoil Múspell's lads will ride. Surtr will ride in front. Before him and behind him will be fire burning. His sword will be as bright as the sun. But when they ride, Bifrǫst will break. Múspell's lads will ride onto the field Vígriðinn, Fenriswolf and the Miðgarðr serpent. Loki will also be there and Hrymir with him. The stone slabs will also accompany Loki. Múspell's lads have their own battle array and that will be bright. The field Vígriðinn is a hundred leagues each way.

'Heimdallr will blow on Gjallarhorn and wake up all the gods for their meeting. Óðinn will ride to Mímir's spring and receive from Mímir advice for himself. Then the ash Yggdrasill will shake and nothing will then be unafraid in heaven and on earth. The Æsir will put on their armour for the meeting and all the Einherjar will come onto the field. Óðinn will ride in front with his golden helmet and will have his spear Gungnir in his hand and will make for Fenriswolf. Þórr will fight with the Miðgarðr serpent, Freyr against Surtr and he will fall since he will not have his good sword.

'The dog Garmr will then have got free from Gnipalundr and will fight against Týr and both will be killed. Þorr will kill the Miðgarðr serpent and step forward nine paces through the serpent's poison. The wolf will swallow Óðinn and that will be the cause of his death. Then Viðarr will come forward and step with one foot on the lower jaw. He has a shoe for which the material has been being collected throughout all time. It is the waste pieces that people take from their shoes at the toes and heel. Therefore you must throw those pieces away, anyone that is concerned to give assistance to the Æsir. With one hand he will grasp its upper jaw and tear apart its mouth, and this will be the cause of the wolf's death. Loki will fight against Heimdallr and each will bring about the death of the other. Then Surtr will fling fire over the earth and burn the whole world. As it says here:

54 (52) Hátt blæss Heimdallr,
         horn er á lopti.
         Mælir Óðinn
         við Mímis hǫfuð.
         Skelfr Ygdrasils
         askr standandi,
         ymr it alna tré;
         æsir eru á þingi.

55 (53) Hvat er með ásum
         hvat með ásynjum?
         Stynja dvergar
         fyrir steins dyrum.
         Viti þér enn eða hvat?

56 (60) Sól mun sortna
         sigrfold⟨ar⟩innar,[1]
         hverfa af himni
         heiðar stjǫrnur.
         Geisar eimi
         ok aldrnari,
         leikr hár hiti
         viðr himin sjálfan.

Gangleri segir: Hvat verðr þá eptir er brendr er heimrinn ok dauð goðin ǫll ok menn?

Hár segir: Hverr skal þá búa í nokkurum heimi.

Þá segir Þriði: Margar eru vistir góðar ok margar illar. Bezt er at vera á Gimlé meðr Surti, ok gott er til drykkjar í Brimlé eða þar sem heitir Sindri. Þar byggja góðir menn.

Á Nástrǫndum er mikill salr ok illr. Dyrr horfa norðr. Hann er ofinn af orma hryggjum. En orma hǫfuð hanga inn um gluggana ok blása þeir eitri svá at ár falla af ok vaða þeir menn þær er eru eiðrofar ok morðvargar. Sem hér segir:[2]

57 (62) Sal veit ek standa
         sólu fjarri
         Nástrǫndum á,
         norðr horfa dyrr.
         Falla eitrdropar
         inn um ljóra.
         Sá er undinn salr
         orma hryggjum.

[1] *sigrfoldinnar* must be wrong, but is hardly a misreading or scribal error for *sígr fold í mar*, though maybe Snorri took it as that; cf. st. 13 of *Háttatal*.
[2] Cf. *Vǫluspá* 38 and 39/1–4.

54 Loud blows Heimdallr,
    his horn is aloft.
    Óðinn speaks
    with Mímir's head.
    There shakes Yggdrasill's
    ash as it stands,
    the ancient tree groans;
    Æsir are in council.

55 What is it with the Æsir,
    what is it with the Ásynjur?
    Dwarfs groan
    before the doorways in the rock.
    Know you yet, or what?

56 The sun will go dark
    of the victorious earth,
    vanish from the sky
    bright stars.
    Steam surges
    and life's nourisher (fire),
    high flame flickers
    against the very sky.'

Gangleri says: 'What will happen then after the world is burned and all the gods and men are dead?'

High says: 'Each one shall then dwell in some world.'

Then says Third: 'There will be many good mansions and many that are bad. The best place to be will be in Gimlé with Surtr, and there will be plenty to drink in Brimlé or in the place that is called Sindri. There good men will dwell.

'On Nástrandir is a large hall and a bad one. The doorways face north. It is woven of serpents' bodies. And serpents' heads hang in through the windows and they spit poison so that rivers flow from them and the people wade in them that are oathbreakers and murderers. As it says here:

57 I know a hall that stands
    far from the sun
    on Nástrands,
    north face the doors.
    Poison drops flow
    in through the smoke-hole.
    This hall is woven
    from snakes' backs.

58 (63)   Skulu þar vaða
          þunga strauma
          menn meinsvarar
          ok morðingjar.
Í Hvergelmi er verst:[1]
          Þar kvelr Níðhǫgr
          nái framgengna.
Þá segir Gangleri: Hvárt lifa þá nokkur guðin eða er þá nokkur jǫrðin eða himinninn?
Hár segir: Upp skýtr jǫrðunni ór sænum ok er hon grøn ok ósánir akrar. Viðarr ok Váli lifa ok svartalogi hefir eigi grandat þeim, ok byggva þeir á Eiðavelli, þar sem fyrrum var Ásgarðr, ok þar kómu synir Þórs Magni ok Móði ok hafa þar Mjǫlni. Þar kemr Baldr ok Hǫðr frá Heljar, talast við ok minnast á rúnar sínar, rǿða um tíðindi, Miðgarðsorm ok Fenrisúlf. Þá finna þeir í | grasinu gulltǫflur er æsir hafa átt.[2]
59 (64)   Viðarr ok Váli
          byggja vé guða
          þá er sloknar svartalogi.
          Móði ok Magni
          skulu Mjǫllni hafa
          Vignigs synir at vígroði.[3]
En í holdi Mímis leynast meyjar í svartaloga:[4]
60 (65)   Líf ok Lífþræsir
          er þar leynast meyjar
          í Mímis holdi,
          morgin dǫggva þær
          ok þar um aldr alast.
Sólin hefir dóttur getit eigi ófegri en sik, ok ferr hon leið hennar:[5]
61 (66)   Eina dóttur
          berr Álfrǫðull
          áðr henni Fenrir fari;
          sú mun renna
          eða ríða,[6]
          reginbrautir mær.

[1] Cf. Vǫluspá 39/7–8.
[2] Cf. Vafþrúðnismál 51.
[3] The other manuscripts and GkS 2365 4to have vígþroti.
[4] Cf. Vafþrúðnismál 45. GkS 2365 4to and the Codex Regius version include as line 5: þau sér at mat hafa 'they shall have as their food'.
[5] Cf. Vafþrúðnismál 47.
[6] GkS 2365 4to and the Codex Regius version have: (þá) er regin deyja 'when gods die'.

58   There shall wade
      heavy streams
      perjured people
      and murderers.

'It is worst in Hvergelmir:

      There Níðhǫggr torments
      the bodies of the dead.'

Then says Gangleri: 'Will there be any gods alive then, and will there be anything of the earth or the sky?'

High says: 'The earth will shoot up out of the sea and it will be green and crops unsown. Viðarr and Váli will be alive and the dark fire will not have harmed them, and they will dwell on Eiðavǫllr, where Ásgarðr had been previously, and Þórr's sons Magni and Móði will come there and bring Mjǫllnir there. Baldr and Hǫðr will come there from Hel's (abode), talk together and discuss their mysteries, speak of what has happened, the Miðgarðr serpent and Fenriswolf. Then they will find in the grass the golden playing pieces that had belonged to the Æsir.

59   Viðarr and Váli
      will dwell in the gods' holy places
      when the dark fire goes out.
      Móði and Magni
      shall have Mjǫllnir,
      Vignigr's sons in the battle-glow.

'But in Mímir's flesh maidens will lie hidden in the dark fire:

60   Life and Lífþræsir
      when maidens lie hidden there
      in Mímir's flesh,
      they bedew the morning
      and shall be nourished there for ever.

'The sun will have begotten a daughter no less fair than herself, and she will go her way:

61   One daughter
      shall Álfrǫðull bear
      before Fenrir catches her;
      she will run
      or ride,
      the maiden, the mighty ways.'

Nú er Gangleri heyrir þetta þá verðr gnýr mikill ok er hann á sléttum velli. Ok er æsirnir heyra þetta sagt, gáfu þeir sér þessi nǫfn ásanna, at þá er langar stundir liði efaðist menn ekki at allir væri einir, þeir æsir er nú er frá sagt ok þessir æsir er nú vóru, ok var Ǫku-Þórr kallaðr Ása-Þórr.[1]

32 Frá heimboði ása með Ægi

Þessir æsir þágu heimboð at Ægi í Hlésey. Áðr hafði Óðinn honum heim boðit. Um kveldit lét Óðinn bera sverð í hǫllina ok lýsti þar af sem logum bjǫrtum. Þórr var þar, Njǫrðr, Freyr, Týr, Heimdallr, Bragi, Viðarr, Váli, Ullr, Hǿnir, Forseti, Loki. Ásynjur: Slík, Frigg, Freyja, Gefjun, Iðunn, Gerðr, Sigun, Skolla,[2] Nanna. Bragi segir Ægi frá mǫrgum tíðindum:

Óðinn, Loki ok Hǿnir fóru um fjall, fundu øxnaflokk, taka eitt nautit ok snúa til seyðis, rjúfa tysvar seyðinn ok var eigi soðit. Þá sá þeir ǫrn yfir sér ok lézk hann valda at eigi var soðit. Gefit mér fylli ok mun soðit. Þeir játa því. Hann lætr sígast á seyðinn, tók annat uxalærit ok bóguna báða. Loki þreif upp stǫng ok laust á bak erninum. En hann brá sér upp við hǫggit ok flýgr. Stǫngin var fǫst við bak erninum, en hendr Loka vóru fastar við annan stangar enda.

Ǫrninn flýgr svá at fǿtr Loka námu niðri við jǫrðu ok grjóti. En hendr hugði hann slitna mundu ór axlarliðum ok biðr friðar. Ǫrninn lézt hann eigi mundu lausan láta nema Iðunn kǿmi þar með epli sín. Loki vill þetta ok ferr brott með eiði.

Hann teygir hana eptir eplunum ok biðr hana hafa sín epli, ok hon fór. Þar kom Þjazi jǫtunn í arnarham ok flaug með hana í Þrúðheim.

Æsir I gerðust ǿfrir mjǫk ok spurðu hvar Iðunn væri. En er þeir vissu, var Loka heitit bana nema hann fǿri eptir henni meðr valsham Freyju. Hann kom til Þjaza jǫtuns er hann var róinn á sæ. Loki brá henni í hnotar líki ok flaug með hana. Þjazi tók arnar ham ok flaug eptir þeim. En er æsir sá hvar valrinn fló þá tóku þeir byrði af lokar spánum ok slógu eldi í. Ǫrninn fekk eigi stǫðvat sik at fluginum ok laust eldi í fiðrit, ok drápu þeir jǫtunninn fyrir innan Ásgrindr.

En Skaði dóttir hans tók ǫll hervápn ok vill hefna hans. En þeir buðu henni at kjósa mann at fótum af liði þeira. Hon sá eins mans fǿtr fagra. Hon mælti þá: Þenna kýs ek. Fátt mun ljótt á Baldri. En þat var Njǫrðr.

En þat varð at sætt at æsir skyldu hlǿgja hana, en hon hugði at þat mætti engi gera. Loki batt sér geitar skegg undir hreðjarnar, ok létu þau ymsi eptir ok skrækti hvártveggja hátt. Þá lét hann fallast í kné Skaða, ok þá hló hon. Þá var sætt ger með þeim.

[1] On this chapter break see the Introduction, p. xcii above.
[2] Both *Slík* and *Skolla* are otherwise unknown. The Codex Regius version has *slíkt sama ásynjur* for *Ásynjur: Slík,* and *Fulla* for *Skolla*.

Now when Gangleri hears this, then there comes a great noise and he is on open ground. And when the Æsir hear tell of this, they gave themselves these names of the Æsir, so that when long periods of time had passed people should not doubt that they were all the same, those Æsir that stories have just been about and these Æsir that existed now, and Qku-Þórr was called Ása-Þórr.

32 Of the Æsir's invitation to a feast with Ægir

These Æsir accepted an invitation to a feast with Ægir on Hlésey. Previously Óðinn had invited him to a feast. In the evening Óðinn had swords brought into the hall and light shone from them like bright flames. Þórr was there, Njǫrðr, Freyr, Týr, Heimdallr, Bragi, Viðarr, Váli, Ullr, Hønir, Forseti, Loki. Ásynjur: Slík, Frigg, Freyja, Gefjun, Iðunn, Gerðr, Sigun, Skolla, Nanna. Bragi tells Ægir about many things that had happened:

'Óðinn, Loki and Hønir travelled over a mountain, came upon a herd of oxen, take the one ox and set it in an earth oven, open the earth oven twice and it was not cooked. Then they saw an eagle above them and it said it was responsible for it not cooking.

' "Give me my fill and it will be cooked."

'They agree to this. It let itself drop onto the earth oven, took one ox-ham and both shoulders. Loki snatched up a pole and struck the eagle on its back. But it leapt up at the blow and flies. The pole was stuck to the eagle's back, and Loki's hands were stuck to the other end of the pole.

'The eagle flies so that Loki's feet banged down against the earth and stones. But his arms he thought would be torn from his shoulder joints and he begs for mercy. The eagle said he would not let him go unless Iðunn came there with her apples. Loki agrees to this and gets away by means of his oath.

'He entices her after the apples and tells her to bring her own apples, and she went. The giant Þjazi came there in eagle shape and flew with her into Þrúðheimr.

'The Æsir got absolutely furious and asked where Iðunn was. And when they knew, Loki was threatened with death unless he went after her by means of Freyja's falcon shape. He came to the giant Þjazi's when he had gone to sea in a boat. Loki turned her into the form of a nut and flew with her. Þjazi took eagle's shape and flew after them. So when the Æsir saw where the falcon was flying, then they took loads of wood-shavings and set them on fire. The eagle could not stop in its flight and its feathers caught fire, and they killed the giant within the Áss-gates.

'So his daughter Skaði took all her weapons of war and wants to avenge him. But they offered her that she should choose herself a husband by his feet from their company. She saw one man's feet that were beautiful. Then she said:

' "I choose that one. There can be little that is ugly about Baldr."

'But it was Njǫrðr.

'But this was in the terms of settlement, that the Æsir were to make her laugh, but she thought that no one would be able to do this. Loki tied a nanny-goat's beard to himself under his testicles and they drew each other back and forth and both squealed loudly. Then he let himself drop into Skaði's lap, and then she laughed. Then the settlement between them was complete.

Óðinn gerði þat til fǫðurbóta við Skaða at hann tók augun Þjaza ok kastaði á himininn ok gerði af stjǫrnur. Auðvaldi hét faðir Þjaza. En er synir Auðvalda tóku arf, tók hverr munnfylli af gulli. Er nú gullit kallat munntal jǫtna, en í skáldskap mál þeira.

33 Hér segir frá því at æsir sátu at heimboði at Ægis ok hann spurði Braga hvaðan af kom skáldskaprinn. Frá því er Kvasir var skapaðr. Hér hefr mjǫk setning skáldskapar

Ægir spyrr: Hvaðan af kom skáldskaprinn?

Bragi svarar: Guðin hǫfðu ósætt við vani ok gerðu friðstefnu ok gengu til kers eins ok spýttu í hráka sínum ok skǫpuðu ór mann er heitir Kvasir.

Hann leysti ór ǫllum hlutum, ok er hann kom til dverganna Falas ok Galas, kǫlluðu þeir hann á einmæli ok drápu hann. Létu renna blóð hans í tvau ker ok einn ketil er Óðrǿrir heitir, en kerin heita Són ok Boðn. Þeir blǫnduðu við hunangi við blóðit ok heitir þat þá mjǫðr, ok sá er af drekkr verðr skáld ok frǿðamaðr. Dvergarnir sǫgðu at þeir hefði tapast í mannviti.

Dvergarnir buðu til sín jǫtni þeim er Gillingr hét ok buðu honum á sjó
f. 20r, p. 37 at róa ok hvelfðu skipi undir honum. Þat spurði Suttungr sun hans, ok flytr dvergana í flǿðisker. Þeir bjóða mjǫðinn í fǫðurbǿtr. Suttungr hirðir hann í Hnitbjǫrgum ok til gæzlu Gunnlǫðu dóttur sína.

Því heitir skállskaprinn Kvasis blóð eða Sónar eða farskostr dverganna, fyrir því at sá mjǫðr flutti þeim fjǫrlausn ór skerinu, eða Suttunga mjǫðr eða Hnitbjarga lǫgr.

Ægir spyrr: Hversu komst Óðinn at miðinum?

Bragi segir: Hann fór þar sem vóru níu þrælar ok slógu hey. Hann bauð at brýna ljá þeira. Hann tók hein ór pússi sínum ok gáfu þeir við hǫfuð sín. Síðan brá hverr ljánum á háls ǫðrum.

Þá kom Óðinn til Bauga ok nefndist Bǫlverkr. Baugi lézt eigi hafa vel haldit húskǫrlum sínum. Hann bauð at taka upp einn verk þeira níu ok hafa til einn drykk af Suttunga miði. Hann lézt ráð eiga á miðinum, en Suttungr vill einn hafa.

Bǫlverkr vann um sumarit níu manna verk, en at vetri vill hann kaupit. Fara þá til Suttungs ok beiða hann mjaðarins. Hann synjar. Þeir fóru ok tekr Bǫlverkr nafarinn Roða ok borar Hnitbjǫrg meðr, ok þá brást hann í orms líki ok skreið nafars raufina. ok hvíldi hjá Gunnlǫðu þrjár nætr ok drakk þrjá drykki af miðinum, ok var hann þá uppi allr, sitt . . . ór hverju kerinu. Hann brást þá í arnar ham ok flaug, en Suttungr í annan arnar ham ok flaug eptir honum.

Æsir settu út í garðinn ker sín. Óðinn spýtti miðinum í kerin. En sumum repti hann aptr, er honum varð nær farit ok hafa þat skáldfífl ok heitir arnarleir, en Suttunga mjǫðr þeir er yrkja kunna.

Því heitir skáldskaprinn fengr Óðins ok fundr ok drykkr ok gjǫf.

Óðinn did this for Skaði in compensation for her father that he took Þjazi's eyes and threw them into the sky and made stars of them. Þjazi's father was called Auðvaldi. And when Auðvaldi's sons took possession of their inheritance, each took a mouthful of gold. Now the gold is called mouth-tale of giants, and in poetry [it is called] their speech.

33. Here it tells about how the Æsir sat at a feast at Ægir's and he asked Bragi where the poetry came from. Of how Kvasir was created. Here more or less begins the rule for poetry.

Ægir asks: 'How did the poetry originate?'

Bragi replies: 'The gods had a dispute with Vanir and they arranged a peace-conference and went to a vat and spat their spittle into it and from it made a man that is called Kvasir.

'He found solutions to everything, and when he came to the dwarfs Falarr and Galarr, they called him to a private discussion and killed him. They poured his blood into two vats and a pot that is called Óðrørir, and the vats are called Són and Boðn. They mixed honey with the blood and then it is called mead, and he that drinks of it becomes a poet and a scholar. The dwarfs said they had perished in intelligence.

'The dwarfs invited the giant that was called Gillingr to stay with them and invited him to go to sea in a boat and they overturned the boat under him. His son Suttungr heard of this and carried the dwarfs onto a skerry. They offer the mead as compensation for his father. Suttungr put it for safe keeping in Hnitbjǫrg and his daughter to look after it.

'That is why the poetry is called blood of Kvasir or of Són or dwarfs' transportation, beause this mead brought them deliverance from the skerry, or Suttungi's mead or the liquid of Hnitbjǫrg.'

Ægir asks: 'How did Óðinn get hold of the mead?'

Bragi says: 'He went where there were nine slaves and they were mowing hay. He offered to hone their scythes. He took a whetstone out of his pouch and they gave their heads for it. After that they all cut each other's throats with their scythes.

'Then Óðinn came to Baugi's and gave his name as Bǫlverkr. Baugi said he had not kept his servants very well. He offered to take over the work of those nine on his own and get for it one drink of Suttungi's mead. He said he had control over the mead, but Suttungr wants to have it to himself.

'Bǫlverkr did the work of nine men during the summer, and when winter came he wants his payment. They go then to Suttungr and ask him for the mead. He refuses. They went and Bǫlverkr takes the auger Roði and bores a hole in Hnitbjǫrg with it, and then he turned himself into the form of a snake and crawled through the auger-hole, and slept with Gunnlǫð three nights and drank three draughts of the mead, and then it was all gone, one [draught] from each vat. He then turned himself into the shape of an eagle and flew, and Suttungr into another eagle shape and flew after him.

'The Æsir put their vats out in the courtyard. Óðinn spat the mead into the vats. But some he farted backwards, since it was such a close thing for him, and poetasters have that and it is called eagle's shit, but Suttungi's mead those who can compose

'Therefore the poetry is called Óðinn's booty and find and drink and gift.'

34 Hér segir hversu skilja skal skáldskap

Þá mælti Ægir: Hvé mǫrg eru kyn skállskaparins?
Bragi segir: Tvenn: mál ok háttr.
Ægir spyrr: Hvat heitir mál skáldskaparins?
Bragi segir: Tvent, kent ok ókent.
Ægir segir: Hvat er kent?
Bragi segir: At taka heiti af verkum manns eða annarra hluta eða af því er hann þolir ǫðrum eða af ætt nokkurri.
Ægir segir: Hver dǿmi eru til þess?
Bragi segir: At kalla Óðin fǫður Þórs, Baldrs eða Bezlu eða annarra barna sinna, eða ver Friggjar, Jarðar, Gunnlaðar, Rindar, eða eiganda | Valhallar eða stýranda guðanna, Ásgarðs eða Hliðskjálfar, Sleipnis eða geirsins, óskmeyja, einherja, sigrs, valfalls; gervandi himins ok jarðar, sólar. Kalla hann aldinn Gaut, hapta guð, hanga guð, farma guð, Sigtýr.

En þat er at segja ungum skáldum er girnast at nema skáldskapar mál ok heyja sér orðfjǫlða með fornum heitum eða skilja þat er hulit er ort, þá skili hann þessa bók til skemtanar. En ekki er at gleyma eða ósanna þessar frásagnir eða taka ór skáldskapnum fornar kenningar er hǫfuðskáldin hafa sér líka látit. En eigi skulu kristnir menn trúa né á sannast at svá hafi verit.

35 Saga Þórs ok Hrungnis

Nú skal segja af hverju þær kenningar eru er áðr eru dǿmi sǫgð.

Svá sagði Bragi, at Þórr var farinn í Austrveg at berja trǫll, en Óðinn reið Sleipni í Jǫtunheima ok kom til jǫtuns þess er Hrungnir hét.

Hrungnir spyrr hvat manna sá sé er ríðr lopt ok lǫg með gullhjálminn, sagði at hann átti furðu góðan hest. Óðinn segir at þar fyrir vill hann veðja hǫfði sína[1] at engi hestr skal jafngóðr með jǫtnum. Hrungnir segir at sá er góðr hestr. En hafa lézt hann mundu miklu sterkara hest. Sá heitir Gullfaxi.

Hrungnir varð reiðr Óðni. Hleypr nú upp á hest sinn ok hyggr at taka Óðin ok launa honum ofryrði sín. Óðinn hleypir svá mikinn fyrir at hann var á ǫðru leiti fyrir. En Hrungnir hafði svá mikinn móð at eigi fann hann hvar hann fór fyrri en hann kom inn um Ásgrindr. En er hann kom at hallardyrum buðu æsir honum til drykkju. Hann gekk í hǫllina, bað fá sér at drekka. Vóru teknar þær skálir er Þórr var vanr at drekka af ok svelgr Hrungnir af hverri. Ok nú gerist hann drukkinn. Skorti þar eigi stór orð. Hann lézt mundu taka upp Valhǫll ok fǿra í Jǫtunheima en søkkva Ásgarði ok drepa guðin ǫll nema Freyju ok Sif. Þær vill hann hafa með sér.

Freyja ein þorir at skenkja honum, ok drekka lézt hann mundu allt ǫl ása. En er ásum leiddust ofryrði hans, þá nefna þeir Þór. Ok því næst kemr Þórr í hǫllina ok hefir á lopti hamarinn ok var allreiðr ok spurði hverr því réði

[1] Sic, for *sínu*.

34 Here it tells how one shall understand poetry

Then spoke Ægir: 'How many categories are there in poetry?'
Bragi says 'Two: language and verse form.'
Ægir asks: 'What is language of the poetry called?'
Bragi says 'Two things, using a kenning and not using a kenning.'
Ægir says: 'What is using a kenning?'
Bragi says 'Taking a term from a person's deeds or other things or from what he suffers from another or from some relationship.'
Ægir says: 'What examples are there of this?'
Bragi says 'Calling Óðinn father of Þórr, Baldr or Bezla or of others of his children, or the husband of Frigg, Jǫrð, Gunnlǫð, Rindr, or possessor of Valhǫll or ruler of the gods, Ásgarðr or Hliðskjálf, Sleipnir or the spear, adoptive maids, Einherjar, victory, the fallen slain, maker of heaven and earth, the sun, calling him ancient Gautr, god of fetters, god of the hanged, god of cargoes, Sigtýr (Victory god).

But this must be said to young poets that desire to learn the language of poetry and furnish themelves with a wide vocabulary using traditional terms or understand what is composed obscurely, then let him take this book as entertainment. But these narratives are not to be consigned to oblivion or demonstrated to be false, nor are ancient kennings that major poets have been happy to use to be removed from the poetry. Yet Christian people are not to believe or be convinced that it has been thus.

35 The story of Þórr and Hrungnir

Now shall be told the origin of the kennings of which examples have earlier been given.

So said Bragi, that 'Þórr was gone to eastern parts to thrash trolls, but Óðinn rode Sleipnir into the world of giants and came to the giant's that was called Hrungnir.

'Hrungnir asks what sort of person this is that rides sky and sea with the golden helmet, saying that he had a marvellously good horse. Óðinn says he will wager his head that no horse as good would be found among the giants. Hrungnir says that it is a good horse. But he said he would have a much stronger horse. It is called Gullfaxi.

'Hrungnir was angry with Óðinn. He leapt up on his horse, intending to get Óðinn and pay him back for his boasting. Óðinn gallops so hard ahead that he kept ahead on the next rise in the ground. But Hrungnir was in such great fury that he did not notice where he was before he came in through the Ass-gates. But when he came to the hall entrance, the Æsir invited him in for a drink. He went into the hall, demanded to be given a drink. The goblets that Þórr normally drank from were brought out and Hrungnir took deep draughts from each one. And now he became drunk. There was no lack of big words. He said he was going to lift up Valhǫll and take it to the world of giants and bury Ásgarðr and kill all the gods except Freyja and Sif. Those he wants to keep with him.

'Only Freyja dares to bring him drink, and he said he was going to drink all the Æsir's ale.

'But when the Æsir got tired of his blustering, then they invoke the name of Þórr. And the next thing was that Þórr enters the hall with his hammer raised and in great anger and asked who was responsible for a cunning giant

er jǫtunn hundvíss skal þar drekka, eða hverr seldi Hrungni grið at vera í Valhǫllu, eða hví Freyja skal skenkja honum sem at gildi ása.

Þá svarar Hrungnir ok leit eigi vinar augum til Þórs, segir at Óðinn bauð honum ok lézt vera á hans griðum. Þá segir Þórr at þess boðs skal hann gjalda áðr hann komi út. Hrungnir segir at Ása-Þór er þat lítill frami at drepa hann vápnlausan. Hitt er meiri raun ef hann þorir at berjast við mik at landamæri á Grjótúnagerði, ok hefir þat verit mikil fólska er ek lét heima eptir skjǫld minn ok hein. En ef ek hefða hér vápn mín þá skyldi nú reyna hólmgǫngu. En at ǫðrum kosti legg ek þér við níðingskap ef þú vilt drepa mik vápnlausan.

Þórr vill fyrir engan mun bila at koma til einvígis er honum var hólmr skoraðr, því at engi hafði honum þat fyrri veitt. Fór þá Hrungnir brott leið sína ok hleypti ákafliga til þess er hann kom heim um nóttina ok varð hans ferð allfræg með jǫtnum.

Ok er at stefnudegi kom millum þeirra Þórs, þóttust jǫtnar hafa mikit í ábyrgð hvárr sigr fengi. Þeim var ills ván af Þór ef Hrungnir léti fyrir, því at hann var sterkastr. Þá gerðu jǫtnar mann á Grjótúnagarði af leiri, níu rasta hávan ok þriggja rasta breiðr undir hǫndina. En ekki fengu þeir hjarta svá mikit at honum dygði eða hǫfði fyrri en þeir tóku ór meri nokkurri, ok varð honum þat ekki stǫðugt þá er Þórr kom. Hrungnir átti hjarta þat er gert var af hǫrðum steini ok tindótt með þrimr hornum, sem síðan er gert ristubragð þat er Hrungnishjarta heitir. Af steini var ok hǫfuð Hrungnis. Skjǫldr hans var ok gjǫrr ór steinum ok viðum ok þykkr. Hann hafði skjǫldinn fyrir sér. Hann stóð á Grjótúnagǫrðum ok beið Þórs, en hein hafði hann fyrir vápn ok reiddi um ǫxl ok var ekki dælligr. Á aðra hlið honum stóð leirmaðrinn er nefndr er Mǫkkrkálfi ok var hann allhræddr. Svá er sagt at hann méi þá er hann sá Þór.

Þórr fór til hólmstefnunnar ok Þjálfi. Þá rann Þjálfi framm, þar sem Hrungnir stóð, ok mælti til hans: Þú stendr óvarliga, jǫtunn, hefir fyrir þér skjǫldinn, en Þórr hefir sét þik ok ferr hann et neðra í jǫrðu ok mun koma neðan at þér.

Þá skaut hann skildinum undir fǿtr sér ok stóð á, en tvíhendi heinina. Því næst sá hann eldingar ok heyrði þrumur stórar. Sá hann þá Þór í ásmóði. Fór hann ákafliga ok reiddi hamarinn ok kastaði um langa leið til Hrungnis. Hrungnir fǿrir upp heinina báðum hǫndum ok kastar í móti. Mǿtir hon hamrinum á flugi ok brotnar heinin í sundr. Fell annarr hlutr á jǫrð ok eru þar af heinbjǫrg ǫll, en annarr hlutr brast í hǫfði Þór svá at hann fell framm á jǫrð.

Hamarinn Mjǫllnir kom í mitt hǫfuðit Hrungni ok lamðist haussinn í smán mola, ok fell hann framm yfir Þór svá at fótr hans lá á hálsi Þór. En Þjálfi vó at Mǫkkrkálfa ok fell hann viðr lítinn orðstír.

Þá gekk Þjálfi at Þór ok skyldi taka fót Hrungnis af hálsi Þór ok fekk hvergi valdit. Þá gengu til allir æsir ok fengu eigi valdit. Þá kom til Magni, son Þórs ok Járnsǫxu. Hann var þá þrínættr. Hann kastaði fǿti Hrungnis af

drinking there, and who had guaranteed Hrungnir safety while he was in Valhǫll, and why Freyja should be serving him drink as if at the Æsir's banquet.

'Then Hrungnir replies, looking at Þórr with no friendly eyes, says that Óðinn had invited him and declared that he was under his protection. Then Þórr says that this invitation shall cost him something before he gets out. Hrungnir says that it is little honour to Þórr of the Æsir to kill him when he is unarmed.

' "It will be a greater test if he dares to fight with me on the frontier at Grjótúnagerði, and it has been a great folly to have left behind at home my shield and whetstone. But if I had my weapons here then we should hold a duel now. But the alternative is that I declare you guilty of baseness if you go and kill me when I am unarmed."

'Þórr was eager not to let anything stop him from going to single combat when he had been challenged to a duel, for no one had ever done him that honour before. Then Hrungnir went off on his way and galloped mightily until he got home at night, and his journey was very widely talked of among the giants.

'And when the day appointed for the meeting between him and Þórr came, the giants felt they had a great deal at stake as to which one won the victory. They would have little good to look forward to from Þórr if Hrungnir yielded, for he was strongest. Then the giants made a person at Grjótúnagarðr of clay, nine leagues high and three leagues broad under its arm. But they could not get a heart big enough to do for him or fit him until they took one out of a mare, and that turned out not to be steady in him when Þórr came. Hrungnir had a heart that was made of solid stone and sharply pointed with three points like the symbol for carving that is called Hrungnir's heart has since been made. Hrungnir's head was also of stone. His shield was also made of stones and wood and thick. He held the shield in front of him. He stood at Grjótúnagarðar and waited for Þórr, but he had a whetstone as weapon and carried it on his shoulder and was not pleasant to look at. On one side of him stood the clay man, who is named Mǫkkrkálfi, and he was quite terrified. It is said that he wet himself when he saw Þórr.

'Þórr went to keep his appointment for the duel, and Þjálfi. Then Þjálfi ran on ahead to where Hrungnir was standing, and spoke to him:

' "You are standing unguardedly, giant, you are holding your shield in front of you, but Þórr has seen you and he is travelling by the lower route underground and is going to come at you from below."

'Then he shoved his shield beneath his feet and stood on it, and held the whetstone in both hands.

'Next he saw lightnings and heard great thunders. Then he saw Þórr in an Áss-rage. He was travelling at an enormous rate and swung his hammer and threw it over a great distance towards Hrungnir, Hrungnir raised his whetstone with both hands and threw it in return. It met the hammer in flight and the whetstone broke in two. One piece fell to the ground and from it have come all whetstone rocks, but the other piece crashed into Þórr's head so that he fell forwards to the ground.

'The hammer Mjǫllnir hit the middle of Hrungnir's head and the skull was shattered in small fragments and he fell forwards over Þórr so that his leg lay on Þórr's neck. But Þjálfi attacked Mǫkkrkálfi and he fell with little glory.

'Then Þjálfi went up to Þórr and went to remove Hrungnir's leg from Þórr's neck and was unable to manage it. Then all the Æsir went up and were unable to manage it. Then Magni, son of Þórr and Járnsaxa, arrived. He was then three nights old. He threw Hrungnir's leg off Þórr's neck and spoke:

hálsi Þór ok mælti: Sé þar ljótan harm faðir at ek skylda svá at koma. Ek hugða at jǫtun þenna munda ek hafa lostit í Hel með hnefa mínum ef ek hefða fyrri funnit hann.

Þá stóð Þórr upp ok fagnaði vel syni sínum ok sagði at hann mundi verða mikill maðr fyrir sér. Ok vil ek gefa þér hestinn Gullfaxa, er Hrungnir hefir átt.

Þá mælti Óðinn, segir at Þórr gerir rangt er hann gaf þann enn góða hest gýgjar syni.

Þórr fór heim til Þrúðvanga ok stóð heinarbrotit í hǫfði honum. Þá kom til vǫlva sú er Gróa heitir, kona Aurvalda ens frøkna. Hon gól galdra sína yfir honum til þess er heinin losnaði. En er Þórr fann þat at honum þótti ván at á brott mundi nást heinin, þá vildi hann launa Gróu lækningina ok gera hana fegna. Hann segir henni þau tíðindi at hann hafði vaðit norðr yfir Élivága ok borit meis á baki sér norðan, ok í Aurvandil, norðan ór Jǫtunheimum, ok þat til jartegna at ein tá hans hafði staðit niðr ór meisinum, ok var sú frerin svá at hann braut af ok kastaði á himin ok gerði af stjǫrnu þá er nú heitir Aurvantá.[1] Þórr segir at eigi mundi langt til at Aurvandill | mundi norðan koma. Gróa varð svá fegin at hon munði enga galdra, ok varð heinin eigi laus, ok stendr hon enn þar í hǫfði Þór.

Eptir þessi sǫgu hefir ort Þjóðólfr enn hvinverski í Haustlǫng.

Þá mælti Ægir: Mikill þikki mér Hrungnir fyrir sér. Vann Þórr nokkut meira þrekvirki þá er hann átti viðr trǫll?

Þá segir Bragi:

36 Frá Geirrøð jǫtni ok Þór

Mikillar frásagnar er þat vert er Þórr fór til Geirraðargarða. Þá hafði hann ekki hamarinn Mjǫlni eða megingjarðar eða járngreiprnar ok olli því Loki.

Hann fór með Þór, því at Loka hafði þat hent, er hann flaug með valsham Friggjar at skemta sér, at hann[2] flaug í Geirraðargarða ok sá þar hǫll mikla, ok settist þar á ok sá inn í glugginn. Geirrøðr sá í móti honum ok mælti at taka skyldi fuglinn ok fǿra honum. En sendimaðr komst nauðiliga upp á hǫllina. Þat þótti Loka gott er hann komst nauðuliga til hans, ok ætlaði sér stund um, at fljúga eigi fyrri en hann hefði farit áðr allt torleiðit. Ok er maðrinn sótti at honum beindi hann fluginn ok spyrndi við fast, ok eru þá fǿtrnir fastir.

Var Loki tekinn ok fǿrðr Geirrøði, en er hann sá augu hans, þá grunaði hann at maðr mundi vera, ok bað hann svara. En Loki svaraði engu. Þá læsti hann Loka í kistu sinni ok svelti hann þrjá mánuðr. En þá er hann tók hann ór kistunni ok beiddi hann orða ok spurði hverr hann væri, hann sagði. Ok til fjǫrlausnar sér vann hann Geirrǿði þess eiða at hann kǿmi Þór í Geirraðargarða svá at hann hefði hvárki hamarinn né járngreiprnar né megingjarðar.

[1] In the Codex Regius version *Aurvandilstá* (Aurvandill in Codex Wormianus is written Ǫrvandill; many scribes sometimes used au as a spelling for ǫ and vice versa).

[2] *at hann* repeated in DG 11 4to.

' "Isn't it a terrible shame, father, that I should arrive so. I would have thought that I would have knocked this giant into Hel with my fist if I had met him first."

'Then Þórr got up and and welcomed his son warmly and said he would grow up to be a powerful person.

' "And I have decided to give you the horse Gullfaxi, which used to be Hrungnir's."

'Then Óðinn spoke, saying that it was wrong of Þórr to give that fine horse to a giantess's son.

'Þórr went home to Þrúðvangar and the fragment of whetstone remained in his head. Then there arrived the sorceress that is called Gróa, wife of Aurvaldi the Bold. She chanted her spells over him until the whetstone began to come loose. But when Þórr felt that it seemed likely to him that the whetstone was going to be got out, then he wanted to repay Gróa for her treatment and give her pleasure. He tells her these tidings, that he had waded north across Élivágar and on his way back from the north had carried a basket on his back with Aurvandill in it, from the north out of the world of giants, and there was this proof that one of his toes had stuck down out of the basket and this got frozen, so he broke it off and threw it into the sky and out of it made the star that is now called Aurvantá. Þórr says that it would not be long until Aurvandill would come from the north. Gróa was so pleased that she could remember none of her spells, and the whetstone did not get free and is still stuck in Þórr's head.

'Þjóðólfr of Hvinir has composed a passage based on this story in *Haustlǫng*.'

Then spoke Ægir: 'Hrungnir seems to me to be very mighty. Did Þórr achieve any greater exploit in his dealings with trolls?'

Then says Bragi:

36 Of the giant Geirrøðr and Þórr

'The story of how Þórr went to Geirrøðr's courts is worth detailed treatment. On that occasion he did not have the hammer Mjǫllnir or the girdle of might or the iron gauntlets, and that was Loki's doing.

'He went with Þórr, for it had befallen Loki, when he had gone flying with Frigg's falcon shape for fun, that he had flown into Geirrøðr's courts and seen there a great hall, and he alighted on it and looked in the window. Geirrøðr looked out at him and said that the bird was to be caught and brought to him. But the person sent got with difficulty up onto the hall. Loki was pleased that he got to him with difficulty, and planned to wait a while, not to fly until he had already performed the whole of the difficult climb. And when the man came at him he beat his wings and jumped hard upwards, and now his feet are stuck.

'Loki was captured and brought to Geirrøðr, and when he saw his eyes, then he suspected that it must be a man, and demanded that he answer. But Loki made no reply. Then he locked Loki in his chest and starved him for three months. But when he took him out of the chest and demanded that he speak and asked who he was, he told him. And to redeem his life he swore Geirrøðr oaths that he would make Þórr come to Geirrøðr's courts without him bringing either his hammer or his iron gauntlets or his girdle of might.

Þórr kom til gistingar til gýgjar er Gríðr heitir. Hon var móðir Viðars ens þǫgla. Hon segir Þór satt frá Geirrøði at hann er it mesta trǫll ok hundvíss jǫtunn ok illr viðreignar. Hon léði honum megingjarða ok járngreipa er hon átti ok staf sinn er Gríðarvǫlr heitir. Þá kom Þórr til ár þeirar er Vimur heitir, allra á mest. Þá spenti hann sik megingjǫrðum ok studdist forstreymis við Gríðarvǫl, en Loki helt undir megingjarðar. Ok þá er Þórr kom á miðja ána óx áin svá at braut um herðar Þór.

Þá kvað Þórr:

62 (72) Vaxat þú Vimur
         alls mik þik vaða tíðir
         jǫtlna garða í;
         veiztu enn ef þú vex
         at þá vex mér ásmegin
         jamhátt upp sem himinn.

Þá sér Þórr uppi í gjúfrunum at Gjálp, dóttir Geirraðar, stóð þar tveim megin árinnar ok gerði hon árvǫxtinn.

Þá tók Þórr upp ór áinni einn stein mikinn ok kastaði ok mælti svá at At ósi skal á stefna. Eigi misti hann. Ok í því bar hann at landi ok fekk tekit rísrunn einn ok steig svá ór áinni. Ok því er þat orðtak at reynir er bjǫrg Þórs.

En er Þórr kom til Geirraðar þá var þeim vísat fyrst í gestahús til herbyrgis, ok var einn stóll at sitja á, ok sat Þórr þar. Þá varð hann þess varr at stóllinn fór undir honum upp undir ráfit. Þórr stingr þá stafnum Gríðarveli upp undir ráfit ok lét sígast á stólinn fast. Þá varð skrækr mikill ok fylgði brestr. Þar hafði verit undir stólinum dǿtr Geirraðar, Gjálp ok Gneip ok hafði hann brotit hrygginn í þeim báðum.

Þá kvað Þórr:

63 Einu neytta ek
    alls megins
    jǫtna gǫrðum í,
    þá er Gjálp ok Gneip,
    dǿtr Geirraðar,
    vildu hefja mik til himins.

Þá lætr Geirrøðr kalla Þór inn í hǫllina til leika við sik. Þar vóru eldar stórir eptir endilangri hǫll. En er Þórr kom gagnvart Geirrøði þá tók Geirrøðr með tǫng járnsíu glóandi ok kastar at Þór, en Þórr í móti með járngreipunum ok fǿrði á lopt járnsíuna. En Geirrøðr hljóp undir súlu sína at forða sér. Þórr fǿrði á lopt síuna ok laust í gegnum járnsúluna ok í gegnum Geirrøð, gegnum vegginn ok svá í gegnum jǫrðina fyrir útan hǫllina.

Eptir þessi sǫgu hefir ort Eilífr Guðrúnarson í Þórsdrápu.

'Þórr lodged for a night with a giantess that is called Gríðr. She was Viðarr the silent's mother. She tells Þórr the truth about Geirrøðr, that he is a very great troll and a cunning giant and awkward to deal with. She lent him a girdle of might and some iron gauntlets that she had and her staff, which is called Gríðarvǫlr. Then Þórr came to the river that is called Vimur, greatest of all rivers. Then he buckled on the girdle of might and supported himself on the side away from the current with Gríðarvǫlr, but Loki held on beneath the girdle of might. And when Þórr got to the middle of the river the river rose so that it splashed over Þórr's shoulders.

'Then said Þórr:

62   Do not rise, Vimur,
        since I desire to wade you
        into giants' courts;
        be sure if you still rise
        that then will rise in me Áss-strength
        as high up as the sky.

'Then Þórr saw up in the ravines that Geirrøðr's daughter Gjálp was standing astride the river and it was she causing the rise in the river.

'Then Þórr picked up out of the river a great stone and threw it and spoke thus, that

'"At its outlet must a river be stemmed."

'He did not miss. And at that moment he reached the bank and managed to grasp a bush and thus climbed out of the river. And hence it is a saying that the rowan is Þórr's salvation.

'And when Þórr got to Geirrøðr's, then they were shown first into a guest apartment as lodging, and there was one seat to sit on, and Þórr sat there. Then he realised that the seat was moving under him up under the roof. Þórr then pushed the staff Gríðarvǫlr up under the roof and pressed himself down hard on the seat. Then there was a great scream accompanied by a great crack. There under the seat it had been Geirrøðr's daughters Gjálp and Gneip and he had broken both of their backs.

'Then said Þórr:

63   Once I used
        all my strength
        in giants' courts,
        when Gjálp and Gneip,
        daughters of Geirrøðr,
        tried to lift me to the sky.

'Then Geirrøðr had Þórr called into the hall for games with him. There were great fires there along the length of the hall. And when Þórr came opposite Geirrøðr, then Geirrøðr picked up with tongs a glowing lump of molten iron and threw it at Þórr, but Þórr in response with the iron gauntlets also raised the molten lump of iron into the air. So Geirrøðr ran under his pillar for protection. Þórr raised the molten lump into the air and struck it through the iron pillar and through Geirrøðr, through the wall and so through the ground outside the hall.

Eilífr Guðrúnarson has composed a passage based on this story in Þórsdrápa.'

Part II

Skáldatal
Genealogy of the Sturlungs
List of Lawspeakers

[Skáldatal]

Starkaðr inn gamli var skáld. Hans kvæði eru fornust þeira sem menn kunnu. Hann orti um Danakonunga. Ragnarr konungr loðbrók var skáld, Áslaug kona hans ok synir þeira.

Ragnarr konungr
    Bragi gamli Boddason

Eysteinn beli konungr
    Bragi gamli
    Erpr lútandi
    Grundi prúði
    Kálfr þrǿnski
    Refr rytski
    Ormr óframi
    Ǫvaldi, enn Ávalldi
    Fleini skáld
    Rǫgnvaldr skáld

Erpr lútandi vá víg í véum ok var ætlaðr til dráps. Hann orti um Sor (Sǫr? Saurr?) konung at Haugi ok þá hǫfuð sitt.

Bjǫrn at Haugi
    Bragi gamli

Eiríkr Refilsson
    Álfr hinn litli

Styrbjǫrn sterki
    Úlfr Súlujarl

Eríkr sigrsæli
    Þorvaldr Hjaltason

Óláfr sǿnski
    Gunnlaugr ormstunga
    Hrafn Ǫnundarson
    Óttarr svarti

Ǫnundr Óláfsson
    Sighvatr skáld Þórðarson
    Óttarr svarti
    Sighvatr skáld

Ingi Steinkelsson
    Markús Skeggjason

Sǿrkvir Karlsson
    Einarr Skúlason
    Halldórr skvaldri

[List of poets]

Starkaðr the Old was a poet. His poems are the most ancient of those that people know. He composed about the kings of the Danes. King Ragnarr loðbrók was a poet, his wife Áslaug and their sons.

King Ragnarr
    Bragi the Old Boddason

King Eysteinn beli (belly)
    Bragi the Old
    Erpr lútandi (the Bowing)
    Grundi prúði (the Courteous)
    Kálfr þrønski (of Þrándheimr)
    Refr rytski (the Russian)
    Ormr óframi (the Shy)
    Ǫvaldi, again Ávalldi
    Fleini the Poet
    Rǫgnvaldr the Poet

Erpr lútandi committed homicide in holy places and was going to be killed. He composed about King Sor (Saurr?) at Haugr and received his head.

Bjǫrn at Haugr
    Bragi the Old

Eiríkr Refilsson
    Álfr the Small

Styrbjǫrn sterki (the Strong)
    Úlfr jarl of Súla

Eríkr sigrsæli (the Victorious)
    Þorvaldr Hjaltason

Óláfr the Swede
    Gunnlaugr Serpent-Tongue
    Hrafn Ǫnundarson
    Óttarr the Black

Ǫnundr Óláfsson
    Sighvatr the Poet Þórðarson
    Óttarr the Black
    Sighvatr the Poet

Ingi Steinkelsson
    Markús Skeggjason

Sørkvir Karlsson
    Einarr Skúlason
    Halldórr skvaldri (the Clamorous)

Knútr Eiríksson
    Hallbjǫrn hali
    Þorsteinn Þorbjarnarson
Sørkvir Karlsson
    Sumarliði skáld
    Þorgeirr Danaskáld
Eiríkr Knútsson
    Grani Hallbjarnarson
Eiríkr Eiríksson
    Óláfr Þórðarson
Jón jarl Sørkvisson
    Einarr Skúlason
    Halldórr skvaldri
Sóni[1] jarl Ívarsson
    Halldórr skvaldri
Karl jarl Sónason
    Halldórr skvaldri
Birgir jarl Magnússon
    Sturla Þórðarson

Þjóðólfr hinn hvinverski orti um Rǫgnvald heiðumhæra Ynglingatal, brǿðrung Haralds ins hárfagra, ok talði þrjá tigu langfeðga hans ok sagði frá hvers þeira dauða ok legstað.

Haraldr inn hárfagri
    Auðunn illskælda
    Þorbjǫrn hornklofi
    Ǫlvir núfa
    Þjóðólfr ór Hvini
    Úlfr Sebbason
    Guttormr sindri
Eiríkr blóðøx
    Egill Skallagrímsson
    Glúmr Geirason
Hákon konungr góði A⟨ðalsteins⟩ f⟨óstri⟩
    Eyvindr skáldaspillir
    Guttormr sindri
Haraldr gráfeldr
    Glúmr Geirason
    Kormakr Ǫgmundarson

[1] Or *Soni*. Cf. Lind 1905–1931.

Knútr Eiríksson
	Hallbjǫrn hali (Tail)
	Þorsteinn Þorbjarnarson
Sørkvir Karlsson
	Sumarliði the Poet
	Þorgeirr Danaskáld (Poet of the Danes)
Eiríkr Knútsson
	Grani Hallbjarnarson
Eiríkr Eiríksson
	Óláfr Þórðarson
Jarl Jón Sørkvisson
	Einarr Skúlason
	Halldórr skvaldri
Jarl Sóni Ívarsson
	Halldórr skvaldri
Jarl Karl Sónason
	Halldórr skvaldri
Jarl Birgir Magnússon
	Sturla Þórðarson

Þjóðólfr of Hvinir composed *Ynglingatal* about Rǫgnvaldr heiðumhæri (Nobly Grey), cousin of Haraldr the Finehaired and enumerated thirty of his forebears and told about each of their deaths and burial places.

Haraldr the Finehaired
	Auðunn illskælda (Evil-Composing)
	Þorbjǫrn hornklofi (Raven)
	Ǫlvir núfa (Stub-Nose)
	Þjóðólfr from Hvinir
	Úlfr Sebbason
	Guttormr sindri (Spark)
Eiríkr Blood-Axe
	Egill Skallagrímsson
	Glúmr Geirason
King Hákon the Good Æþelstan's foster-son
	Eyvindr skáldaspillir (Despoiler of Poets)
	Guttormr sindri
Haraldr Greycloak
	Glúmr Geirason
	Kormakr Ǫgmundarson

Óláfr Tryggvason
    Hallfreðr vendræðaskáld
    Bjarni Gullbráskáld
    Gizurr Gullbráskáld
    Sighvatr skáld
Óláfr hinn helgi
    Sighvatr skáld
    Þorfinnr munnr
    Óttarr svarti
    Bersi Torfuson
    Þórðr Kolbeinsson
    Þormóðr Kolbrúnarskáld
    Hofgarða-Refr
Magnús góði Óláfsson
    Þórðr Kolbeinsson
    Skapti Þóroddsson
    Arnórr jarlaskáld
    Oddr Keikinaskáld
    Refr skáld
    Þjóðólfr skáld
Haraldr konungr Sigurðarson
    Sighvatr skáld
    Þjóðólfr Arnórsson skáld
    Bǫlverkr bróðir hans
    Valþjófr skáld
    Oddr Kikinaskáld
    Stúfr blindi
    Arnórr jarlaskáld
    Illugi Bryndǿlaskáld
    Grani skáld
    Sneglu-Halli
    Valgarðr á Velli
    Halli stirði
    Steinn Herdísarson
Óláfr kyrri
    Arnórr jarlaskáld
    Steinn Herdísarson
    Atli litli
    Vilborg skáld
    Þorkell Hamarskáld

Óláfr Tryggvason
    Hallfreðr Troublesome Poet
    Bjarni Gullbráskáld (Poet of Golden Eyelash)
    Gizurr Gullbráskáld (Poet of Golden Eyelash)
    Sighvatr the Poet
Óláfr the Saint
    Sighvatr the Poet
    Þorfinnr Mouth
    Óttarr the Black
    Bersi Torfuson
    Þórðr Kolbeinsson
    Þormóðr Poet of Kolbrún
    Hofgarða-Refr
Magnús the Good Óláfsson
    Þórðr Kolbeinsson
    Skapti Þóroddsson
    Arnórr Jarls' Poet
    Oddr Keikinaskáld (Poet from Kikin?)
    Refr the Poet
    Þjóðólfr the Poet
King Haraldr Sigurðarson
    Sighvatr the Poet
    Þjóðólfr Arnórsson the Poet
    Bǫlverkr his brother
    Valþjófr the Poet
    Oddr Kikinaskáld (Poet from Kikin?)
    Stúfr the Blind
    Arnórr Earls' Poet
    Illugi, poet of the people of Brynjudalr
    Grani the Poet
    Sneglu-Halli
    Valgarðr at Vǫllr
    Halli stirði (the Stiff)
    Steinn Herdísarson
Óláfr the Quiet
    Arnórr Earls' Poet
    Steinn Herdísarson
    Atli the Small
    Vilborg the Poet
    Þorkell Hamarskáld (Poet from Hamarr)

Magnús berfǿttr
- Þorkell hamarskáld
- Ívarr Ingimundarson
- Halldórr sk⟨v⟩aldri
- Bjǫrn krepphendi
- Bárðr svarti
- Gils Illugason,[1]
- Einarr Skúlason
- Ívarr Ingimundarson
- Halldórr skvaldri
- Þórarinn stuttfeldr[2]
- Þorvaldr Blǫnduskáld
- Árni fjǫruskeifr
- Ívarr Ingimundarson
- Einarr Skúlason
- Einarr Skúlason
- Halldórr skvaldri
- Hallr munkr
- Einarr skáld
- Ívarr Ingimundarson
- Einarr Skúlason
- Þorvarðr Þorgeirsson
- Kolli skáld
- Halldórr skvaldri

Sigurðr Haraldsson
- Einarr Skúlason
- Bǫðvarr balti

Óláfr Haraldsson
- Þorbjǫrn Gaurss⟨on⟩

Eysteinn Haraldsson
- Einarr Skúlason
- Sigurðr skrauti

Magnús Erlingsson
- Þorbjǫrn Skakkaskáld
- Súgandi skáld
- Hallr Snorrason

[1] The spaces in this part of the list are where other kings' names have been omitted, see *Edda Snorra Sturlusonar* 1848–87: III 263.
[2] The name written twice.

Magnús Bare-Legs
    Þorkell hamarskáld
    Ívarr Ingimundarson
    Halldórr skvaldri
    Bjǫrn krepphendi (Crippled Hand)
    Bárðr the Black
    Gils Illugason,
[Sigurðr Jórsalafari]
    Einarr Skúlason
    Ívarr Ingimundarson
    Halldórr skvaldri
    Þórarinn stuttfeldr (Short-Cloak)
    Þorvaldr Poet of Blanda (Mixture)[1]
    Árni fjǫruskeifr (Crooked Beach?)
[Eysteinn Magnússon]
    Ívarr Ingimundarson
    Einarr Skúlason
[Haraldr gilli]
    Einarr Skúlason
    Halldórr skvaldri
    Hallr Monk
[Magnús blindi]
    Einarr the Poet
[Sigurðr Slembir]
    Ívarr Ingimundarson
[Ingi Haraldsson]
    Einarr Skúlason
    Þorvarðr Þorgeirsson
    Kolli the Poet
    Halldórr skvaldri
Sigurðr Haraldsson
    Einarr Skúlason
    Bǫðvarr balti (Bear)
Óláfr Haraldsson
    Þorbjǫrn Gaursson
Eysteinn Haraldsson
    Einarr Skúlason
    Sigurðr skrauti (Ornamental)
Magnús Erlingsson
    Þorbjǫrn Skakkaskáld (Poet of [Erlingr] skakki (Crooked))
    Súgandi the Poet
    Hallr Snorrason

[1] Either a place or a river or a nickname.

Markús Stefánsson
Þórðr Hallsson
Skáld-Máni
Hákon herðibreiðr
Þorbjǫrn gauss
Argrímr[1] Bergþórsson

f. 24r, p. 45 Sverrir konungr
Þorsteinn Ketilsson
Sumarliði Þorbjarnarson
Arnórr Sǫrlason
Hallbjǫrn hali
Blakkr skáld Unásson Stefánssonar
Ljótr skáld
Bragi skáld
Sighvatr Egilsson
Snorri Bútsson[2]
Þorbjǫrn Skakka⟨skáld⟩
Hákon konungr Sverrisson
Ljótr skáld
Bragi Hallsson
Ingi
Ingi Bárðarson
Snorri Sturluson
Ljótr Sumarliðason
Játgeirr Torfason
Hǫskuldr liði
Runólfr skáld
Hákon konungr Hákonarson
Snorri Sturluson
Óláfr Þórðarson
Sturla Þórðarson
Játgeirr Torfason
Árni langi
Óláfr Leggsson
Gizurr jarl
Guttormr kǫrtr
Magnús Hákonarson
Sturla Þórðarson

[1] Probably a copying error for *Ásgrímr* or *Arngrímr*
[2] Written 'Búzson'.

Markús Stefánsson
Þórðr Hallsson
Skáld-Máni (Poet-)
Hákon Broad Shoulder
    Þorbjǫrn gauss (Gabbler)
    Argrímr Bergþórsson
King Sverrir
    Þorsteinn Ketilsson
    Sumarliði Þorbjarnarson
    Arnórr Sǫrlason
    Hallbjǫrn hali
    Blakkr the Poet son of Unás Stefánsson
    Ljótr the Poet
    Bragi the Poet
    Sighvatr Egilsson
    Snorri Bútsson
    Þorbjǫrn Skakkaskáld
King Hákon Sverrisson
    Ljótr the Poet
    Bragi Hallsson
    Ingi
Ingi Bárðarson
    Snorri Sturluson
    Ljótr Sumarliðason
    Játgeirr Torfason
    Hǫskuldr liði (Companion)
    Runólfr the Poet
King Hákon Hákonarson
    Snorri Sturluson
    Óláfr Þórðarson
    Sturla Þórðarson
    Játgeirr Torfason
    Árni langi (the Tall)
    Óláfr Leggson
    Jarl Gizurr
    Guttormr kǫrtr (Tiny?)
Magnús Hákonarson
    Sturla Þórðarson

Eiríkr Magnússon
 Þorsteinn Ǫrvendilsson
 Þorvaldr Helgason
 Jón murti Egilsson
 Þorsteinn Ingjaldsson
 Guðmundr skáld

Eyvindr skáldaspillir orti um Hákon jarl inn ríka kvæði þat sem heitir Ynglingatal ok talði þar langfeðga hans til Óðins ok sagði frá dauða hvers þeira ok legstað.[1]

Hákon jarl Grjótgarðsson
 Þjóðólfr ór Hvini

Sigurðr Hlaðajarl
 Kormakr Ǫgmundarson

Hákon jarl inn ríki
 Eyvindr Finsson
 Einarr skálaglamm
 Tindr Hallkelsson
 Skapti Þóroddsson
 Þorfinnr munnr
 Eilífr Guðrúnarson
 Vigfúss Víga-Glúmsson
 Þorleifr Hákonarskáld
 Hvannar-Kálfr

Eiríkr Hákonarson
 Hallfreðr vendræðaskáld
 Gunnlaugr ormstunga
 Hrafn Ǫnundarson
 Þórðr Kolbeinsson
 Halldórr úkristni

Sveinn jarl
 Eyjólfr dáðaskáld
 Skúli Þorsteinsson

Hákon jarl Eiríkssson
 Bersi Torfuson

Ormr jarl Eilífsson

Hákon jarl Ívarsson

Sigurðr jarl Hávarðsson

[1] Here is added at the side in a later hand (fifteenth century according to *Edda Snorra Sturlusonar* 1848–87: III 265) *Hákon konungr Magnússon, Magnús konungr Eiríksson*.

Eiríkr Magnússon
  Þorsteinn Ǫrvendilsson
  Þorvaldr Helgason
  Jón murti Egilsson
  Þorsteinn Ingjaldsson
  Guðmundr the Poet

Eyvindr skáldaspillir composed about Jarl Hákon the Great the poem that is called *Ynglingatal* and enumerated in it his ancestors to Óðinn and told about each of their deaths and burial places.

Jarl Hákon Grjótgarðsson
  Þjóðólfr from Hvinir
Sigurðr Jarl of Hlaðir
  Kormakr Ǫgmundarson
Jarl Hákon the Great
  Eyvindr Finsson
  Einarr skálaglamm (Scales-Tinkle)
  Tindr Hallkelsson
  Skapti Þóroddsson
  Þorfinnr Mouth
  Eilífr Guðrúnarson
  Vigfúss Víga-Glúmsson
  Þorleifr Poet of Hákon
  Hvannar-Kálfr (Angelica-)
Eiríkr Hákonarson
  Hallfreðr Troublesome Poet
  Gunnlaugr Serpent-Tongue
  Hrafn Ǫnundarson
  Þórðr Kolbeinsson
  Halldórr the Unchristian
Jarl Sveinn
  Eyjólfr dáðaskáld (Poet of (Great) Deeds)
  Skúli Þorsteinsson
Jarl Hákon Eiríksson
  Bersi Torfuson
Jarl Ormr Eiríksson
Jarl Hákon Ívarsson
Jarl Sigurðr Hávarðsson

f. 24v, p. 46 Erlingr skakki
   Þorbjǫrn Skakkaskáld
   Súgandi skáld
  Eiríkr jarl Sigurðarson
  Philippus jarl Birgisson[1]
  Skúli jarl
   Snorri Sturluson
   Óláfr Þórðarson
  Hákon jarl galinn
   Ívarr Kálfsson
   Steinn Kálfsson
   Steinn Ófeigsson
  Skúli hertogi
   Ljótr skáld
   Þorsteinn Ófeigsson
   Snorri Sturluson
   Óláfr Þórðarson
   Játgeirr Torfason
   Ljótr skáld
   Álfr Eyjólfsson
   Sturla Þórðarson
  Knútr jarl Hákonarson
   Guðmundr Oddsson
   Teitr skáld
   Roðgeirr Aflason
   Þórálfr prestr
   Óláfr Þórðarson
  Sveinn konungr tjúguskegg
   Óttarr svarti
  Knútr konungr inn ríki
   Sighvatr skáld
   Óttarr svarti
   Þórarinn loftunga
   Hallvarðr Háreksblesi
   Bersi Torfason
   Steinn Skaptason
   Arnórr jarlaskáld
   Óttarr keptr

[1] See Introduction p. lxxvii.

Erlingr skakki (Crooked)
    Þorbjǫrn Skakkaskáld
    Súgandi the Poet
Jarl Eiríkr Sigurðarson
Jarl Philippus Birgisson
Jarl Skúli
    Snorri Sturluson
    Óláfr Þórðarson
Jarl Hákon galinn (Mad)
    Ívarr Kálfsson
    Steinn Kálfsson
    Steinn Ófeigsson
Duke Skúli
    Ljótr the Poet
    Þorsteinn Ófeigsson
    Snorri Sturluson
    Óláfr Þórðarson
    Játgeirr Torfason
    Ljótr the Poet
    Álfr Eyjólfsson
    Sturla Þórðarson
Jarl Knútr Hákonarson
    Guðmundr Oddsson
    Teitr the Poet
    Roðgeirr Aflason
    Þórálfr Priest
    Óláfr Þórðarson
King Sveinn Fork-Beard
    Óttarr the Black
King Knútr the Great
    Sighvatr the Poet
    Óttarr the Black
    Þórarinn Praise-Tongue
    Hallvarðr Háreksblesi (Hárekr's Pony?)
    Bersi Torfason
    Steinn Skaptason
    Arnórr Earls' Poet
    Óttarr keptr (Jaw)

Sveinn konungr Álfífuson
    Þórarinn loftunga
Sveinn konungr Úlfsson
    Þorleikr fagri
Knútr inn helgi
    Kálfr Mánason
    Skúli Illugason
    Markúss Skeggjason
Eiríkr Sveinsson
    Markúss Skeggjason
Eiríkr eymuni
    Halldórr skvaldri
Sveinn svíðandi
    Einarr Skúlason
Valdimarr Knútsson
    Þorsteinn kroppr
    Arnaldr Þorvaldsson
Knútr Valdimarsson
    Þorgeirr Þorvaldsson
Valdimarr gamli
    Óláfr Þórðarson
    Játgeirr Torfason
    Þorgeirr Danaskáld
    Súgandi skáld
Sveinn jarl
    Þjóðólfr ór Hvini
Sigvaldi jarl
    Þórðr Sigvaldaskáld
Aðalsteinn Englakonungr
    Egill Skallagrímsson
Aðalráðr konungr
    Gunnlaugr ormstunga

Úlfr inn óargi var hessir ágætr í Noregi í Naumudali, faðir Hallbjarnar hálftrǫlls, faðir Ketils hǿings. Úlfr orti drápu á einni nótt ok sagði frá þreklvirkjum sínum. Hann var dauðr fyrir dag.

Þorleifr spaki
    Þjóðólfr ór Hvini

King Sveinn Álfífuson
    Þórarinn Praise-Tongue
King Sveinn Úlfsson
    Þorleikr the Fair
Knútr the Saint
    Kálfr Mánason
    Skúli Illugason
    Markús Skeggjason
Eiríkr Sveinsson
    Markús Skeggjason
Eiríkr eymuni (Ever-Remembered)
    Halldórr skvaldri
Sveinn svíðandi (Smarting)
    Einarr Skúlason
Valdimarr Knútsson
    Þorsteinn kroppr (Trunk)
    Arnaldr Þorvaldsson
Knútr Valdimarsson
    Þorgeirr Þorvaldsson
Valdimarr the Old
    Óláfr Þórðarson
    Játgeirr Torfason
    Þorgeirr Poet of the Danes
    Súgandi the Poet
Earl Sveinn
    Þjóðólfr from Hvinir
Earl Sigvaldi
    Þórðr Poet of Sigvaldi
King Æþelstan of the English
    Egill Skallagrímsson
King Æþelred
    Gunnlaugr Serpent-Tongue

Úlfr inn óargi (the Fearless) was an excellent lord in Norway in Naumudalr, father of Hallbjǫrn Half-Troll, father of Ketill Salmon. Úlfr composed a *drápa* in one night and told of his great deeds. He was dead before dawn.

Þorleifr spaki (the Wise)
    Þjóðólfr from Hvinir

Arinbjǫrn hersir
    Egill Skallagrímsson
Þorsteinn Þóruson
    Egill Skallagrímsson
Erlingr Skjálgsson
    Sighvatr skáld
Guðbrandr í Dǫlum
    Óttarr svarti
Ívarr hvíti
    Sighvatr skáld
Hárekr ór Þjóttu
    Refr Gestsson
Einarr fluga
    Refr skáld
Kálfr Árnason
    Bjarni Gullbráskáld
Úlfr stallari
    Steinn Herdísarson
Eysteinn orri
    Þorkell Hamarskáld
Víðkunnr Jónsson
    Ásu-Þórðr
Gregoríus Dagsson
    Einarr Skúlason
Nikulás Skjaldvararson
    Súgandi skáld
Eindriði ungi
    Einarr Skúlason
Ívarr selki
    Arnórr Kálfsson
Sigurðr munkr
    Arnórr Kálfsson
Arnbjǫrn Jónsson
    Óláfr Herdísarson
Gautr á Meli
    Steinvǫr Sighvatsdóttir
    Óláfr Herdísarson
    Dagfinnr Guðlaugsson

Lord Arinbjǫrn
    Egill Skallagrímsson
Þorsteinn Þóruson
    Egill Skallagrímsson
Erlingr Skjálgsson
    Sighvatr the Poet
Guðbrandr in the Dales
    Óttarr the Black
Ívarr the White
    Sighvatr the Poet
Hárekr from Þjótta
    Refr Gestsson
Einarr Fly
    Refr the Poet
Kálfr Árnason
    Bjarni Gullbráskáld
Úlfr the Marshal
    Steinn Herdísarson
Eysteinn Grouse
    Þorkell Hamarskáld
Víðkunnr Jónsson
    Ásu-Þórðr
Gregoríus Dagsson
    Einarr Skúlason
Nikulás Skjaldvararson
    Súgandi the Poet
Eindriði the Young
    Einarr Skúlason
Ívarr selki (Seal)
    Arnórr Kálfsson
Sigurðr Monk
    Arnórr Kálfsson
Arnbjǫrn Jónsson
    Óláfr Herdísarson
Gautr at Melr
    Steinvǫr Sighvatsdóttir
    Óláfr Herdísarson
    Dagfinnr Guðlaugsson

[Ættartala Sturlunga]

Adam faðir Sechz, faðir Enos, fǫður Canaans, fǫður Malalie, fǫður Jareth, fǫður Enon, fǫður Matusalam, fǫður Lameck, fǫður Nóa, fǫður Japeth, fǫður Japhans, fǫður Zechims, fǫður Ciprus, fǫður Cretus, fǫður Celius, fǫður Saturnus af Crít, fǫður Jupiter, fǫður Dardanus, fǫður Ericonii, fǫður Eroas, fǫður Ilus, fǫður Laomedon, fǫður Priami hǫfuðkonungs í Tróju, fǫður þeira Ectoris. Múnon eða Mennon hét konungr í Trója, hann átti Tróan, dóttur Príami konungs, ok var þeira son Trór, er vér kǫllum Þór. Hann var faðir Lorica, en son hans hét Hereðei, hans son Vengeþórr, hans son Vingener, hans son Meða, hans son Magni, hans son Sesef, hans son Beðvigg, hans son Atra, hans son Trinam, hans son Heremeth, hans son Skjaldun, en vér kǫllum Skjǫld, hans son Bíaf, þann kǫllum vér Bjár, hans son Guðólf⟨r⟩, hans son Finn, hans son Frialaf, er vér kǫllum Friðleif. Hann átti þann son er nefndr er Óðinn. Skjǫldr var son Óðins, faðir Friðleifs, fǫður Friðfróða, fǫður Herleifs, fǫður Hávars handramma, fǫður Fróða ins frøkna, fǫður Vémundar vitra, fǫður Ólǫfar, móður Fróða friðsama, fǫður Friðleifs, fǫður Fróða ins frøkna, fǫður Ingjalds Starkaðarfóstra, fǫður Hrøreks slǫngvanbauga, fǫður Haralds hilditannar, fǫður Hrøreks, fǫður Þórólfs váganefs, fǫður Vémundar orðlokars, fǫður Valgarðs, fǫður Hrafns heimska, fǫður Jǫrundar goða, fǫður Úlfs aurgoða, fǫður Svarts, fǫður Lǫðmundar, fǫður Gríms, fǫður Svertings, fǫður Vigdísar, móður Sturlu í Hvammi, fǫður Snorra ok Sighvats ok Þórðar ok Helgu móður þeira Egils ok Gyðu.

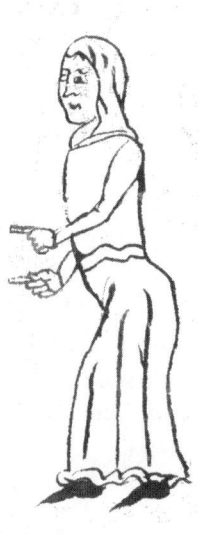

[Genealogy of the Sturlungs]

Adam father of Seth, father of Enos, father of Cainan, father of Mahaleel, father of Jared, father of Enoch, father of Methuselah, father of Lamech, father of Noah, father of Japheth, father of Javan, father of Kittim, father of Ciprus, father of Cretus, father of Celius, father of Saturnus of Crete, father of Jupiter, father of Dardanus, father of Ericthonius, father of Tros, father of Ilus, father of Laomedon, father of Priam high king in Troy, father of Hector and his brothers. Múnon or Mennon was the name of a king in Troy, he was married to Tróan, daughter of King Priam, and their son was Trór, whom we call Þórr. He was father of Lorica, and his son was called Hereðei, his son Vengeþórr, his son Vingener, his son Meða, his son Magni, his son Sesef, his son Beðvigg, his son Atra, his son Trinam, his son Heremeth, his son Skjalldun, but we call him Skjǫldr, his son Biaf, him we call Bjár, his son Guðólfr, his son Finn, his son Frialaf, whom we call Friðleifr. He had a son whose name is Óðinn. Skjǫldr was son of Óðinn, father of Friðleifr, father of Friðfróði, father of Herleifr, father of Hávarr the Strong-Handed, father of Fróði the Brave, father of Vémundr the Wise, father of Ólǫf, mother of Fróði the Peaceful, father of Friðleifr, father of Fróði the Brave, father of Ingjaldr foster-son of Starkaðr, father of Hrørekr Ring-Slinger, father of Haraldr War-Tooth, father of Hrørekr, father of Þórólfr váganef, father of Vémundr Word-Plane, father of Valgarðr, father of Hrafn the Foolish, father of Jǫrundr goði, father of Úlfr goði of Aurr (?), father of Svartr, father of Lǫðmundr, father of Grímr, father of Svertingr, father of Vigdís, mother of Sturla in Hvammr, father of Snorri and Sighvatr and Þórðr and Helga mother of Egill and Gyða.

DG 11 4to f. 25r

DG 11 4to f. 26r

[Lǫgsǫgumannatal][1]

Úlfljótr hét maðr er fyrst sagði lǫg upp á Íslandi. At hans ráði var alþingi sett. En hann hafði eigi lagauppsǫgu á Íslandi svá at þat sé vitat. En Hrafn Høingsson, hinn fyrsti lǫgsǫgumaðr á Íslandi, sagði lǫg upp tuttugu vetr, Þórarinn Ragabróðir, son Óleifs halta tuttugu sumur, Þorkell máni Þorsteinsson tólf sumur, Þorgeirr frá Ljósavatni Þorkelsson fjórtán sumur, á hans dǫgum kom Kristni til Íslands. Grímr frá Mosfelli Svertingsson tvau sumur, Skapti Þóroddsson goða fjǫgur sumur ok tuttugu. Hann andaðist á inu sama ári ok Óláfr konungr inn helgi fell. Steinn Þorgeirsson þrjú sumur, Þorkell I Tjǫrvason tuttugu sumur, Gellir Bǫlverksson níu sumur, Gunnarr inn spaki Þorgrímsson þrjú sumur, Kolbeinn Flosason þrjú sumur. Þat sumar sem hann tók lǫgsǫgu fell Haraldr konungr á Englandi. Gellir hafði lǫgsǫgu í annat sinni þrjú sumur Gunnarr í annat sinn eitt sumar, Sighvatr átta sumur. Markús Skeggjason tók lǫgsǫgn þat sumar er Gizurr biskup hafði verit einn vetr hér á landi ok hafði lǫgsǫgu tuttugu ok fjǫgur sumur. Gunnarr Úlfheðinsson níu sumur, Bergþórr Hrafnsson sex sumur, Gunnarr Þorgeirsson tólf sumur, Hrafn Úlfheðinsson fjǫgur sumur, Finnr Hallsson sjau sumur, Gunnarr Úlfheðinsson tíu sumur, Snorri Húnbogason fimmtán sumur, Styrkárr Oddason tíu sumur, Gizurr Hallsson tvau sumur ok tuttugu, Hallr Gizurarson fjǫgur sumur, Styrmir Kárason tvau sumur, Snorri Sturluson fjǫgur sumur, Teitr Þorvaldsson tvau sumur, Snorri Sturluson í annat sinn.

[1] On the Lawspeakers' lengths of office see Introduction p. lxxviii.

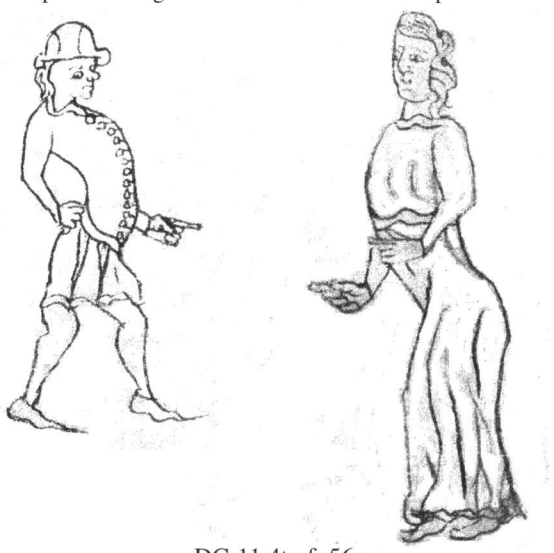

DG 11 4to f. 56r

[List of Lawspeakers]

It was a man called Úlfljótr who first proclaimed the law in Iceland. On his advice the General Assembly was instituted. But he did not hold the office of lawspeaker in Iceland as far as is known. But Hrafn Hǿingsson, the first lawspeaker in Iceland, proclaimed the law for twenty winters, Þórarinn brother of Ragi, son of Óleifr halti (the Lame) twenty summers, Þorkell Moon Þorsteinsson twelve summers, Þorgeirr from Ljósavatn Þorkelsson fourteen summers, in his days Christianity came to Iceland. Grímr from Mosfell Svertingsson two summers, Skapti son of Þóroddr goði four and twenty summers. He died in the same year as King Óláfr the Saint fell. Steinn Þorgeirsson three summers, Þorkell Tjǫrvason twenty summers, Gellir Bǫlverksson nine summers, Gunnarr the Wise Þorgrímsson three summers, Kolbeinn Flosason three summers. That summer when he took on the lawspeaking, King Haraldr fell in England. Gellir held the office of lawspeaker a second time for three summers, Gunnarr for a second time one summer, Sighvatr eight summers. Markús Skeggjason took on the office of lawspeaker the summer that Bishop Gizurr had been one winter here in this country, and held the office of lawspeaker for four and twenty summers. Gunnarr Úlfheðinsson nine summers, Bergþórr Hrafnsson six summers, Gunnarr Þorgeirsson twelve summers, Hrafn Úlfheðinsson four summers, Finnr Hallsson seven summers, Gunnarr Úlfheðinsson ten summers, Snorri Húnbogason fifteen summers, Styrkárr Oddason ten summers, Gizurr Hallsson two and twenty summers, Hallr Gizurarson four summers, Styrmir Kárason two summers, Snorri Sturluson four summers, Teitr Þorvaldsson two summers, Snorri Sturluson a second time.

DG 11 4to f. 37v

DG 11 4to f. 26v

Part III

Skáldskaparmál

37 Hér hefr skáldskapar mál ok heiti margra hluta

Hversu skal kenna skáldskapinn? Svá at kalla Kvasis blóð eða dverga drykkju eða fylli, eða margskonar lǫg Óðrøris eða Boðnar eða Sónar, eða farskostr dverga, Suttunga mjǫð eða lǫg Nitbjarga, fengr eða fundr Óðins, drykkr hans ok gjǫf ok drykkr ásanna.

38 Frá því eptir hverjum heitum skáldin hafa kveðit

Enn skal láta heyra dǿmin hvernig skáldin hafa sér látit líka at yrkja eptir þessum heitum ok kenningum.

Svá sem segir Arnórr jarlaskáld at Óðinn heiti Alfǫðr:

1 (1) Nú hykk, slíðrhugaðs, segja
– síð lætr mér stríðum –
þýtr Alfǫðrs, ýtum
jarls kosta, brim hrosta.

Hér kallaði hann skáldskapinn hrosta brim Alfǫðr.

Hávarðr halti kvað svá:

2 (2) Nú er jódraugum ægis
arnar flaug um hauga;
hyggeka heimboð þiggi
Hangaguðs af vangi.

Svá kvað Víga-Glúmr:

3 (3) Lattit[1] herr með hǫttu
Hangatýs at ganga;
þótti þeim at hætta
þekkiligt fyrir brekku.

Svá kvað Refr:

4 (4) Opt kemr, jarðar leiptra
er Baldr hniginn skaldi
hollr, at helgum fullum
hrafnásar, með stafni.

Svá kvað Eyvindr skáldaspillir:

5 (5) Ok Sigráð
hinn er svǫnum veitti
hróka bjór
Haddingja

---

[1] The manuscript has 'latið' which could be for *látit* (allow), *láti-t* (do not allow) or *latti-t* (did not hold back). *-ð* for *-t* in positions of low stress is frequent in DG 11 4to; *-tt-* is usually indicated by *t* with a dot above, which might here have been omitted. Since the infinitive with *at* follows, the last is likely to be what was intended. Cf. verse 133.

37 Here begins Skáldskaparmál and terms for many things

How shall the poetry be referred to?

Thus, by calling it Kvasir's blood or dwarfs' drink or fill, or many kinds of liquid of Óðrørir or Boðn or Són, or means of dwarfs' conveyance, Suttungi's mead or liquid of Nitbjǫrg, Óðinn's booty or find, his drink and gift and Æsir's drink.

38 Of using which terms poets have composed

We shall present further examples of how the poets have found it fitting to compose using these terms and kennings.

As Arnórr Earls' Poet says that Óðinn is called All-father:

1   Now I plan to tell men
          —long takes my torment to leave off—
          the virtues of the hostile earl;
          All-father's malt-surf pounds (resounds).

Here he has called the poetry All-father's malt-surf.

Havarðr the Lame said this:

2   Now for sea-steeds' (ships') trunks (warriors)
          there is eagles' flight over mounds in store;
          I do not expect they will receive the invitation to visit
          of the god of the hanged (Óðinn) from the field.

So said Víga-Glúmr:

3   The army did not hold back from advancing
          with Hangatýr's (Óðinn's) hoods (helmets);
          they thought it pleasant
          to venture down the slopes.

So said Refr:

4   Often one comes to the holy cups (of mead, i.e. poetry)
          of the raven-god (Óðinn) (i.e. I compose poetry);
          Baldr (god) of earth's brightness (gold) (i.e. the man),
          loyal to the poet, has fallen by the prow.

So said Eyvindr skáldaspillir:

5   And Sigráðr,
          him who raven beer (blood)
          of the Haddingjar
          gave to the swans

> Farmatýs
> fjǫrvi næmðu
> jarðráðendr
> á Áglói.[1]

Svá kvað Glúmr Geirason:

6 (6)   Þar vóru[2] þrafna hyrjar
        – þeim stýrðu guð beina –
        sjálfr í søkiálfi
        Sigtýr Atals dýra.

Svá kvað Eyvindr:

7 (7)   Gǫndul ok Skǫgul
        sendi Gautatýr
        at kjósa um konunga
        hvárr Yngva ættar
        skyldi með Óðni fara
        ok í Valhǫllu vera.

Svá kvað Úlfr Uggason:

8 (8)   Ríðum at vilgi víðu,
        víðfrægr, en menn líða,
        Hroptatýr, um hapta
        hróðrmál, sonar báli.

Svá kvað Þjóðólfr hvinverski:

[(9)   Valr lá þar á sandi
        vitinn inum eineygja
        Friggjar faðmbyggvi.
        Fǫgnuðum dáð slíkri.][3]

Svá kvað Hallfrøðr:

9 (10)   Sannyrðum spenr sverða
         snarr þiggjandi viggjan
         barhoddaða[4] byrjar
         biðkván und sik Þriðja.

Hér eru þau dømi at jǫrð er kǫlluð kona Óðins í skáldskap.

[1] This name is usually written Ǫgló. Cf. verse 176.

[2] The plural form is doubtless because the verb is followed by a plural noun, though it is not the subject.

[3] DG 11 4to f. 27r line 23 leaves a space for Þjóðólfr's verse. Its text is supplied from Faulkes 1998: 8. AM 157 8vo omits the reference to Þjóðólfr as well as the verse.

[4] Both *viggjan* and *barhoddaða* must be errors. Other manuscripts have *viggjar, barrhaddaða* ('biaʀ-' GkS 2367 4to). The translation incorporates these readings.

of Cargo-god (Óðinn, whose swans are ravens),
land-rulers
deprived of life
at Ágló.

So said Glúmr Geirason:

6   It was Victory-god (Óðinn) of the fiery staff (spear)
    —gods brought them help—
    himself in the attacking elf (viking)
    of Atall's (sea-king's) beasts (ships).

So said Eyvindr:

7   Gǫndul and Skǫgul
    Gautatýr (Óðinn) sent
    to choose among kings
    which of Yngvi's line
    should go with Óðinn
    and be in Valhǫll.

So said Úlfr Uggason:

8   Let us ride, but men suffer,
    widely famous Hroptatýr (Óðinn),
    to [your] son's very broad pyre
    at the glorious time of the gods.

So said Þjóðólfr of Hvinir:

    [The fallen lay there on the sand,
    destined for the one-eyed
    dweller in Frigg's embrace (Óðinn).
    We rejoiced in such achievement.]

So said Hallfreðr:

9   The bold wind-steed (ship) taker (seafarer, Earl Hákon)
    lures under himself (wins) with the true language of swords (battle)
    the pine-haired deserted wife of Third
    (Óðinn, whose wife is Jǫrð, the land of Norway).

Here there are examples of land being called Óðinn's wife in poetry.

Svá kvað Eyvindr:

10 (11) Hermóðr ok Bragi,
 kvað Hroptatýr,
 gangið í gegn grami.

Svá kvað Kormakr:[1]

11 (12) Eykr með ennidúki
 jarðllútr[2] día fjarðar
 breyti Húnn sá er beinan
 bindr. Seið Yggr[3] til Rindar.

Svá kvað Steinþórr:

12 (13) Forngervum á ek fyrðum
 farms Gunnlaðar arma,
 horna fors[4] at hrósa
 hlítstyggs ok þó litlum.

Svá kvað Egill Skúlason:[5]

13 (15) Blóta ek eigi af því
 bróður Vílis
 goð jarðar
 at ek gjarn sjá;
 þó hefir Mímis vinr
 mér um fengit
 bǫlva bǿtr
 er ek betra telk.

14 (16) Gáfumst íþrótt
 úlfs um baggi[6]
 vígi vanr
 vammi firrða.

Hér er hann kallaðr goð jarðar ok Mímis vinr ok úlfs baggi.

[1] This verse, like all those attributed here to Kormakr, is taken to be from his *Sigurðardrápa*. The form is *hjástælt* (the name is given in the list of stanzas, though not in the main text of DG 11 4to). The characteristic of this form is that there should be a 'forn minni' (traditional statement) at the end of each half-stanza. The one here perhaps relates to the story of Óðinn's lengthy wooing of Rinda in Saxo Grammaticus, *Historia Danorum* III.

[2] So all manuscripts. Usually taken to be an error for *jarðhljótr* 'land-getter'.

[3] Written 'ykr'.

[4] Masculine nouns are not infrequently endingless in the dative in Old Icelandic.

[5] From Egill Skallagrímsson's *Sonatorrek*. Only GkS 2367 4to has the poet's patronymic thus; AM 242 fol. and Codex Trajectinus omit it. Probably DG 11 4to was derived from a manuscript in which it was abbreviated 'Sk.', and a copyist confused the name with that of Einarr Skúlason.

[6] *Baggi* 'bundle' is obviously an error for *bági* 'enemy', which is what is found in other manuscripts and in *Egils saga*.

So said Eyvindr:

10 'Hermóðr ok Bragi,'
   said Hroptatýr,
   'go to meet the prince.'

So said Kormakr:

11 The one who worships the land (Earl Sigurðr), the Húnn (sea-king)
   that binds it on, honours with a head-band the productive provider
   of the deities' fiord (poetry, whose provider is the poet).
   Yggr (Óðinn) won Rindr by spells.

So said Steinþórr:

12 I must boast to men
   about [my] long ago brewed horn-cascade (mead, i.e. poetry)
   of the mediocrity-avoiding cargo of Gunnlǫð's arms (Óðinn)
   though it be meagre.

So said Egill Skúlason:

13 I do not worship
   Vílir's brother,
   god of earth,
   because I am eager;
   yet has Mímir's friend
   granted me
   a grief-comforter
   that I count better.

14 He gave me a skill,
   the wolf's enemy
   accustomed to battle,
   which is without blemish.

Here he is called god of earth and Mímir's friend and the wolf's enemy.

Svá kvað Refr:

15 (17) Þér eigu vér veigar,
 Valgautr, salar brautar
 fárs hrannmara fannar
 framr valdr, rammar gjalda.

Svá kvað Einarr skálaglamm:

16 (18) Hljóta mun ek, en heitir,
 Hertýs, um þat frýju,
 fyrir ǫrþeysi at ausa
 austr um gnoðar flausta.[1]

Svá kvað Úlfr Uggason:

17 (19) Kostigr ríðr at kesti
 kyngóðr, þeim er goð hlóðu,
 hrafnfreistaðar, hesti
 Heimdallr, at mǫg fallinn.

Svá segir í Eiríksmálum:[2]

18 (20) Hvat er þat drauma, Óðinn,[3]
 er ek hugðumst fyrir dag rísa,
 Valhǫll ryðja
 fyrir vegnu fólki;
 vektat ek einherja
 bæða ek upp rísa
 bekki at strá,
 borðker at leyðra,
 valkyrjur vín bera
 sem vísi kømi.

Svá kvað Kormakr:

19 (21) Allgildan bið ek aldar
 allvald um mér halda
 ýs bifvangi Yngva
 ungr. Fór hrókr með gunni.[4]

[1] Óðinn's ship's bilge-water is an unusual kenning for the mead of poetry, but clearly this is what it was meant to be. The ship may perhaps be taken to be a reference to Óðinn's stomach as he flew back to Ásgarðr in the form of an eagle with the mead in it.

[2] Eiríksmál is an anonymous poem composed for the fallen Eiríkr blóðøx. It is preserved apparently complete in Fagrskinna.

[3] Codex Wormianus and Fagrskinna have kvað before Óðinn.

[4] See note to verse 11 above. The proverbial statement in other manuscripts is Fór Hroptr með Gungni 'Óðinn went taking Gungnir (his spear)', which is undoubtedly more appropriate and provides a proper aðalhending. Hrókr, usually taken to be the shag (bird), which is not a bird of prey, might sometimes have meant raven (cf. English rook).

So said Refr:

15   To you, Slaughter-Gautr (Óðinn), bold ruler
          of the hall (sky) of the damager (sun)
          of the snowdrift (ice) of the road (sea) of wave-horses (ships),
          we owe the strong cups (of the mead of poetry).

So said Einarr skálaglamm:

16   I shall have to pour out Host-god's (Óðinn's)
          ship's bilge-water (the mead of poetry) (i.e. compose poetry)
          before the one who sails ships fast (Earl Hákon),
          but I am threatened with criticism for that.

So said Úlfr Uggason:

17   Splendid, well-born Heimdallr
          rides his horse to the pyre
          that gods raised for the fallen
          son (Baldr) of the raven-tester (Óðinn).

So it says in *Eiríksmál*:

18   What sort of dream is that, Óðinn,
          when I dreamed I rose up before dawn
          to clear up Valhǫll
          for slain people;
          I would not have aroused the Einherjar,
          bade them get up
          to strew the benches,
          clean the beer-cups,
          the valkyries to serve wine
          as if a ruler were coming?

So said Kormakr

19   I who am young bid the excellent great power-wielder (Earl Sigurðr)
          of Yngvi's people (Norwegians) hold over me
          his quivering bow-land (hand).
          The raven followed the battle.

Svá kvað Þorvaldr:

20 (22) Sagði hitt er hugði
 Hliðskjálfar gramr sjálfum,
 hlífarstyggs þar er hǫggnir
 Háreks liðar váru.

Svá kvað Bragi:

21 (24) Þat erum sýnt, er snimma
 sonr Alfǫðrs vildi
 afls við úri þaktan
 jarðar reist um freista.

Svá kvað Einarr skálaglamm:

22 (25) Því at fjǫlkostigr flestu
 feðr[1] ræðr við son Bestlu,
 tekit hefi ek, Mǫrðr,[2] til mærðar,
 mæringr, en þú færa.

Svá kvað Þorvaldr blǫnduskáld:

23 (26) Nú hefi ek margt
 í miði greipar[3]
 búkar Bors
 burar, arfa.

39 Hér segir hversu skáldin hafa kent skáldskapinn

Hér skal heyra hvernig skáldin hafa kent skáldskapinn eptir þeim heitum er áðr eru rituð.

Svá sem hér: at kalla Kvasis dreyra eða dverga skip, mjǫð jǫtna, mjǫð Suttunga, mjǫð Óðins ok ása, fǫðurgjǫld jǫtna; lǫgr Óðrøris ok Sónar ok Boðnar, ok lǫgr Hnitbjarga, fengr ok fundr ok farmr ok gjǫf | Óðins. Svá sem hér er kveðit, er orti Einarr:

24 (27) Hugstórar bið ek heyra,
 heyr jarl, Kvasis dreyra,
 foldar vǫrð ok fyrða
 fjarðleggjar brimdreggjar.

[1] Other manuscripts have *flestr* 'most', which provides a proper *aðalhending*; *feðr* is not a normal nominative form.

[2] All other manuscripts have *morðs,* which gives good sense and is translated here. But the reading is clear in DG 11 4to, and the scribe may have taken the word as the vocative of the name Mǫrðr.

[3] It is difficult to make sense of the readings of DG 11 4to here, but if *búkar* is taken as a genitive form, *greipar búks* may contain a reference to Óðinn in eagle shape. *Bors* is written 'Bærs'.

So said Þorvaldr:

20 Hliðskjálf's king (Óðinn)
 told the man himself what he thought
 where shy of (reluctant to use) shield Hárekr's
 troops were cut down.

So said Bragi:

21 It is obvious to me how
 All-father's son (Þórr) wanted
 soon to test his strength against
 the water covered earth-serpent.

So said Einarr skálaglamm:

22 For [your] very splendid father
 achieves less than you, prince,
 with Bestla's son (Óðinn) in most matters;
 I have attempted poetry in praise of battle.

So said Þorvaldr blǫnduskáld:

23 Now I have a great deal
 of the mead of the clutches
 of the body of Borr's heir,
 his son (Óðinn, whose mead is poetry; i.e. I have made poetry).

39 Here it tells how the poets have referred to the poetry

Here shall be made known how the poets have referred to the poetry using the terms that were noted above.

As here: to call it Kvasir's blood or dwarfs ship, giants' mead, Suttungi's mead, Óðinn's mead and the Æsir's, compensation for the death of giants' father; liquid of Óðrørir and Són and Boðn, and liquid of Hnitbjǫrg, Óðinn's booty and find and cargo and gift. As is said in this poem, which Einarr composed:

24 Hear, earl! I bid the defender of the land hear
 Kvasir's blood (poetry) and noble foaming
 yeast of fiord-bones men
 (men of the rocks, giants, whose foaming yeast is the mead of poetry).

Ok enn kvað Einarr:

25 (28) Ullar gengr um alla
    asksǫng[1] þess er hót magnar
    birkis bǫðvar serkjar
    bergs grymilá dverga.[2]

Svá kvað Ormr Steinþórsson:

26 (29) At væri burs bjórs
    bríkar ok mitt lík –
    rekkar nemi dauðs drykk –
    Dvalins í einn sal.[3]

Ok sem Refr kvað:

27 (30) Grjótaldar tel ek gildi
    geðreinar Þorsteini;
    berg-Møra glymr bára;
    bið ek lýða kyn hlýða.

Svá kvað Egill:

28 (31) Buðumst hilmir lǫð,
    nú á ek hróðrs um kvǫð;
    ber ek Óðins mjǫð
    á Engla bjǫð.

Svá kvað Glúmr Geirason:

29 (32) Hlýði! Hapta beiðis
    hefr mildinga gild⟨i⟩;
    því biðjum vér þǫgnar,
    þegna tjón at fregnum.

Svá kvað Eyvindr:

30 (33) Vilra[4] ek hljóð
    at Hárs líði
    meðan Gillingr
    gjǫldum yppir,

[1] Here there is no doubt about the reading, but the hending, the context and the other manuscripts all indicate that this is an error for -sǫgn. *Ullar askr* is a kenning for shield, see Faulkes1998: 194, note to 67/21.

[2] The context is clear, and *grymilá* must mean the mead of poetry, but the meaning of the first element and the function of *bergs* are obscure. Cf. Bergljót Kristjánsdóttir 1996: 203.

[3] This is clearly the second half of a stanza, thought to be part of Ormr's *Snjófríðar drápa*. See Ólafur Halldórsson 1990: 223. The dwarf-name Dáinn means 'dead', so that *dauðr* 'dead' can be used to mean 'dwarf' (*ofljóst*, wordplay).

[4] *vilra* is obviously an error for *vilja*; *Gillingr* ought to be genitive, to make the normal kenning *Gillings gjǫld* for poetry, and *yppir* should be *yppik*, as in other manuscripts.

And Einarr also said:

25 The . . . liquid of the dwarfs of the mountain
(giants, whose liquid is poetry) washes over (is heard by) all the crew
of Ullr's ash-ship (shield warriors) of the battle-shirt (coat of mail)
birch (warrior) who increases threats (encourages battle).

So said Ormr Steinþórsson:

26 . . . that the plank (tree) of beer's (woman's)
son's corpse and mine should be
in one Dvalinn's (dwarf's) hall (cave, sepulchre);
let men pay attention to [my] Dáinn's (dwarf's) drink (poem).

And as Refr said:

27 I utter for Þorsteinn a feast (the mead) of rock-men's (giants')
thought-land (breast); crag-Mørir's wave (sea of men of Mørr
of the crags, giants' sea) crashes (i.e. poetry resounds);
I bid mankind listen.

So said Egill:

28 The prince offered me hospitality;
now I have a duty of praise;
I bring Óðinn's mead (poetry)
to the land of the English.

So said Glúmr Geirason:

29 Listen! The feast (mead) of the gods' ruler
(Óðinn, whose mead is a poem) for princes begins;
we crave silence, for we
have heard of the loss of men.

So said Eyvindr:

30 I desire silence
for Hárr's (Óðinn's) ale (poetry)
while Gillingr/while I utter
utters payment/Gillingr's payment (a poem),

meðan hans ætt
í hverlegi
gálga grams
til goða teljum.

Svá kvað Einarr skálaglamm:

31 (34)　Eisar vargr[1] fyrir vísa,
　　　　　verk Rǫgnis mér hǫgna,[2]
　　　　　þýtr Óðrøris alda
　　　　　aldrhafs[3] við fles galdra.

32 (36)　Svá kvað Einarr Guðrúnarson:[4]
　　　　　Verði þér, en jarðar
　　　　　æs gert um kon mæran,
　　　　　á sæfreinju Sónar
　　　　　sáð, vingjǫfum báðir.

Svá kvað Vǫlu-Steinn:[5]

33 (37)　Heyr, Mímis vinr, mínar,[6]
　　　　　mér er fundr gefinn Þundar,
　　　　　við góma sker glymja
　　　　　Glaumber⟨g⟩s, Egill, strauma.

Svá kvað Ormr Steinþórsson:

34 (38)　Seggir þurfut ala ugg,
　　　　　engu sný ek í Viðurs feng
　　　　　háði, kunnum hróðursmíð
　　　　　haga, um minn brag.

Svá kvað Úlfr Uggason:

[1] DG 11 4to and the Codex Regius have *vargr* (wolf), which does not suit the context here; Codex Wormianus and Codex Trajectinus *vágr* (wave), which must be part of a kenning for poetry. There is no obvious determinant except *aldrhafs*, so it is perhaps a half-kenning.

[2] All manuscripts have a spelling of *hǫgna*, which has usually been emended to *hagna*, which at least makes sense.

[3] *Aldrhaf* is an unknown word. It may belong as part of one of the kennings for poetry ('of the ancient sea?). Cf. Faulkes 1998: 162, note to verse 34.

[4] In other MSS attributed to Eilífr Guðrúnarson. The text is obscure in both Codex Regius and Uppsala Edda versions; *sæfreinju* is probably intended as acc. of *sefrein* 'sedgeland', in other MSS part of a kenning for 'tongue'; but perhaps it means 'mind-land'.

[5] On Vǫlu-Steinn and his poetry see Finnur Jónsson 1920–1924, I: 510, Jón Helgason 1953: 138; *Íslendingabók. Landnámabók* 1968: 160, 184–86; *Skj* A I 98.

[6] Emending *mínar* to *mína* seems unavoidable.

> while his descent
> in pot-liquid (poetry)
> of the lord of gallows (Óðinn)
> we trace to gods.

So said Einarr skálaglamm:

31   The wave (of mead?) rushes (is poured) before the prince,
          Rǫgnir's (Óðinn's) works (poetry) benefit me,
          Óðrørir's swell (mead of poetry) pounds *aldrhafs*
          against songs' skerry (my teeth).[1]

So said Einarr Guðrúnarson:

32   You both must, but earth's *æs*
          made about High kin (Hákon),
          Són's seed (the mead of poetry) on the mind-land (breast)
          with friendly gifts.

So said Vǫlu-Steinn:

33   Hear, Egill, Mímir's friend—
          Þundr's (Óðinn's) find (poetry) is granted me—
          my streams (poetry) of Glaumr's (giant's) rock (Hnitbjǫrg)
          resounding against gum-skerries (my teeth; cf. verse 31).

So said Ormr Steinþórsson:

34   People do not need to nurse fear about my poetry;
          in Viðurr's (Óðinn's) booty (poetry)
          I weave no spite;
          we know how to order a work of praise.

So said Úlfr Uggason:

---

[1] See Faulkes 1998: 108/17–18.

35 (39)   Hjaldrgegnis tel ek Hildar
          herreifum Óleifi,
          hann vil ek at gjǫf Grímnis
          geðfjarðar lá, kveðja.

Skáldskapr er kallaðr sjár eða lǫgr Óðrøris áðr mjǫðrinn væri gjǫrr, ok þar gerðist hann í katlinum, ok er hann fyrir því kallaðr hverlǫgr Óðins. Svá kvað Eyvindr:

36 (40)   meðan hans ætt
          í hverlegi
          gálga grams
          til goða teljum.[1]

Enn er kallaðr skáldskaprinn far eða lið dverganna. Líð heitir ǫl, lið heitir skip. Svá er tekit til dømanna at skáldskaprinn er nú kallaðr fyrir því skip dverganna.[2] Svá sem hér segir:

37 (41)   Bæði er til bróður
          bergjarls ok skip dverga
          sólar vind at senda
          seinfyrnd gǫtu eina.

40 Frá kenningu Þórs

Hvernig skal kenna Þór?

Svá at kalla son Óðins ok Jarðar, fǫður Magna ok Móða ok Þrúðar, ver Sifjar, stjúpfǫður Ullar, stýranda ok eiganda Mjǫlnis ok megingjarða ok Bilskirnis, verjanda Ásgarðs ok Miðgarðs, dólg ok bana jǫtna ok trǫllkvenna, veganda Hrungnis ok Geirraðar ok Þrívalda, dróttinn Þjálfa ok Rǫsku, fóstra Vingnis ok Lóru.

Svá kvað Bragi skáld:

38 (42)   Vaðr lá Viðris arfa
          vilgi slakr, né raktist,
          á Eynæfis andri,
          Jǫrmungandr at sandi.

Svá kvað Ǫlvir:

39 (43)   Ǿstist allra landa
          umgerð ok sonr Jarðar.

Svá kvað Eilífr:

[1] See verse 30 above.
[2] On the word-play between *lið* and *líð* see Faulkes 1998: 109/11–22 and note on p. 226.

35	I utter for host-joyful Óleifr
	Hildr's (valkyrie's) noise-(battle-)meeter's (Óðinn's)
	mind-fiord's (breast's) liquid (a poem);
	I want to greet him with Grímnir's (Óðinn's) gift (poetry).

Poetry is called sea or liquid of Óðrørir before the mead was made, and it was made in that cauldron, and hence it is called Óðinn's pot-liquid.

So said Eyvindr:

36	... while his descent
	in pot-liquid (poetry)
	of the lord of gallows (Óðinn)
	we trace to gods.

The poetry is also called the dwarfs' vessel or lið. Ale is called líð, a ship is called lið. This is the origin of the expression whereby the poetry is now as a result called the dwarfs' ship. As it says here:

37	Both are to be sent to my brother,
	rock-earl's (giant's) sun's
	(giant-maiden's) wind (thoughts)[1]
	and unforgettable dwarfs' ships (poetry) the same way.

40 Of referring to Þórr

How shall Þórr be referred to?

By calling him son of Óðinn and Jǫrð, father of Magni and Móði and Þrúðr, husband of Sif, stepfather of Ullr, controller and owner of Mjǫllnir and the girdle of might and of Bilskirnir, defender of Ásgarðr and Miðgarðr, enemy and slayer of giants and trollwives, killer of Hrungnir and Geirrøðr and Þrívaldi, lord of Þjálfi and Rǫskva, foster-son of Vingnir and Lóra.

So said Bragi the Poet:

38	Viðrir's (Óðinn's) heir's (Þórr's) line lay
	by no means slack on Eynæfir's (sea-king's) ski (boat),
	nor did Jǫrmungandr (the Miðgarðr serpent)
	uncoil itself onto the sand.

So said Ǫlvir:

39	The encircler of all lands (the Miðgarðr serpent)
	and Jǫrð's son (Þórr) became violent.

So said Eilífr:

---

[1] Cf. Faulkes 1998: 108/28.

40 (44)　　Reiðr stóð Rǫsku bróðir;
　　　　　vá gagn faðir Magna.¹
　　　　　Skalf eigi Þórs né Þjálfa
　　　　　þróttarsteinn við ótta.

Svá kvað Eysteinn Valdason:
41 (45)　　Leit á brattar brautir
　　　　　baugs hvassligum augum,
　　　　　østist orð at flausti,
　　　　　yggs búð, faðir Þrúðar.

Svá kvað Eysteinn:
42 (46)　　Sinn bjó Sifjar rúni
　　　　　snarla fram meðr karli,
　　　　　hornstraum getum Hrímnis
　　　　　hræfa,² veiðarfǿri.

Svá kvað Bragi:
43 (48)　　Hamri fórk³ í hǿgri
　　　　　hǫnd þá er allra landa
　　　　　eigi ǫflug bára
　　　　　endiseiðs um kendi.

Svá kvað Gamli:
44 (49)　　Þá er gramr, hinn er svik samðit
　　　　　snart Bilskirni hjarta
　　　　　grundar fisk með grandi
　　　　　gljúfrskeljungs mun rjúfa.

Svá kvað Þorbjǫrn dísarskáld:
45 (50)　　Þórr hefir Yggs með árum
　　　　　Ásgarð af þrek varðan.

Svá kvað Bragi:
46 (51)　　Ok borðróins barða
　　　　　brautar þvengr inn ljóti
　　　　　á haussprengju⁴ Hrungnis
　　　　　harðgeðr neðan starði.

¹ The alliteration depends on the earlier forms *Vreiðr* and *Vrǫsku*. V before r continued to be pronounced into the tenth century in Iceland.

² *hræfa* 'suffer' is obviously an error for *hreyfa* 'move' or *hrǿra* 'stir', which is the reading of the other manuscripts and provides the required aðalhending.

³ Other manuscripts have 'forsc' or 'fort', which sound more convincing. The speaker is not Þórr, so the first person is inappropriate.

⁴ It is odd to have a feminine word in a kenning for Þórr. Other manuscripts have -*sprengi*.

| 40 | Rǫskva's brother (Þjálfi) stood enraged;
Magni's father (Þórr) struck a victorious blow.
Neither Þórr's nor Þjálfi's power-stone (heart)
shook with terror. |
|---|---|

So said Eysteinn Valdason:

| 41 | Þrúðr's father (Þórr) looked with piercing eyes
at the steep ways of the ring (the Miðgarðr serpent?),
words grew violent on the boat,
the terrifying one's (giant's) dwelling. |
|---|---|

So said Eysteinn:

| 42 | Once Sif's beloved (Þórr)
quickly brought out fishing gear
with the old fellow (the giant).
We can move Hrímnir's (giant's) horn-flow (mead, poetry). |
|---|---|

So said Bragi:

| 43 | I wielded the hammer in my right
hand when the not mighty
wave felt the coalfish
that surrounds all lands (the Miðgarðr serpent). |
|---|---|

So said Gamli:

| 44 | When the angry one (Þórr), he who did not in his heart
plan treachery quickly against Bilskírnir (Þórr's hall),
will destroy the seabed fish
with the gorge-whale's (giant's) destruction (Mjǫllnir). |
|---|---|

So said Þórbjǫrn dísarskáld:

| 45 | Þórr has with Yggr's (Óðinn's) angels (the Æsir)
defended Ásgarðr with might. |
|---|---|

So said Bragi:

| 46 | And the ugly thong (serpent)
of the side-oared beaked ship's road (sea)
stared up spitefully at
Hrungnir's skull-splitter (Þórr). |
|---|---|

Svá kvað Eilífr:

47 (53) Þreyngvir gein við þungum
þangs rauðbita tangar
kveldrunninna kvenna
kunnleggs alinmunni.

Svá kvað Úlfr Uggason:

48 (54) Þjokkvǫxnum kve⟨ð⟩st þikkja
þiklings fyrir miklum
hafra mæs[1] at hǫfgum
hætting[2] megindrætti.

Ok enn þetta:

49 (55) Fullǫflugr lét fellir
fjall-Gauts hnefa skjalla,
ramt mein var þat, reyni
reyrar leggs við eyra.

50 (56) Víðgenrir laust Vimrar
vaðs af frǫmum naðri
hlusta grunn við hrǫnnum.
Hlaut innan svá minnum.[3]

Hér er hann kallaðr jǫtunn Vimrar vaðs. Á heitir Vimur er Þórr óð yfir þar er hann sótti til Geirraðargarða.

Svá kvað Vetrliði skáld:[4]

51 (57) Leggi brauztu Leiknar,
lamðir | Þrívalda,
steyptir Starkaði,
stéttu um Gjálf dauða.

Svá kvað Þorbjǫrn dísarskáld:

52 (58) Ball í Keilu kolli,
Kallandi brauztu alla,
áðr draptu Lit ok Lóða,
léztu dreyra Búseyru,

---

[1] *mæs* may have been conceived as genitive of *mærr* 'famous' with assimilation of *-rs*.
[2] *hætting* is usually feminine.
[3] It is somewhat unusual for a complete eight-line stanza to be quoted in *Skáldskaparmál*. GkS 2367 4to and Codex Trajectinus have 'Enn kvað Úlfr' after line 4, Codex Wormianus has *ok*, DG 11 4to has the capital V in *Víðgenrir* out in the margin. The stanza as it is in DG 11 4to has been divided in two here. The stanza as a whole is arranged as st. 6 of *Húsdrápa* in *Skj* and the last line is a *stef* 'refrain' (or perhaps part of a *klofastef* 'split refrain') and recurs in st. 9. It refers to the images on the walls of Óláfr pái's hall.
[4] The events referred to in this and the following verse are not known from elsewhere.

So said Eilífr:

47 The oppressor (Þórr) of the kinfolk (trolls)
    of evening-faring women (trollwives)
    yawned with his arm's mouth (fist)
    over the heavy red lump of tongs-weed (iron).

So said Úlfr Uggason:

48 The stockily built one (the giant) is said to have thought
    there was great danger from the enormous
    heavy haul of the goats'
    famous stumpy one.

And also this:

49 The most mighty fell-Gautr's (giant's) feller (Þórr)
    made his fist crash—
    a mighty hurt was that—
    on the reed-bed bone (rock) frequenter's (giant's) ear.

50 Víðgenrir (a giant, i.e. the enemy) of Vimur's ford (Þórr)
    struck the ear-bed (head)
    from the bold serpent by the waves.
    Within [the hall] have appeared these motifs (pictures).

Here he is called giant of Vimur's ford. Vimur is the name of a river that Þórr waded when he was on his way to Geirrøðr's courts.

So said Vetrliði the Poet:

51 You broke Leikn's bones,
    you pounded Þrívaldi,
    you cast down Starkaðr,
    you trod over the dead Gjálf.

So said Þorbjǫrn dísarskáld:

52 There was a clang on Keila's crown,
    you broke Kallandi completely,
    before that you slew Litr and Lóði,
    you made Búseyra bleed,

> heptuð Hangankjǫptu,
> Hyrrærin dó fyrri,
> þó var meirr en mæra[1]
> Svívǫr numin lífi.

41 Frá kenningu Baldrs

Hverneg skal kenna Baldr? Svá at kalla hann son Óðins ok Friggjar, ver Nǫnnu, fǫður Forseta, eiganda Hringhorna ok Draupnis, dólg Haðar ok Heljar sinna, grátagoð. Úlfr Uggason hefir kveðit eptir sǫgu Baldrs langa hríð í Húsdrápu.

42 Frá kenningu Njarðar

Hversu skal kenna Njǫrð? Svá at kalla hann vanagoð eða vananið eða van, fǫður Freys ok Freyju, fégjafa d.[2]

43 Frá kenningu Freys

Hvernig skal kenna Frey? Svá at kalla hann son Njarðar, bróður Freyju ok vanaguð ok vananið ok van, ok árgoð ok fég⟨j⟩afaguð. Freyr er kallaðr Belja dólgr.

Svá kvað Eyvindr skáldaspillir:

53 (61) Þá er ofræstr[3]
         jarla bági
         Belja dólgr
         byggja vildi.

Hann er eigandi Skíðblaðnis ok galtar þess er Gullinbusti heitir.

Svá sem hér er sagt:[4]

54 (62) Ívalda synir
         gengu í árdaga
         Skíðblaðni at skapa,
         skipa bezt
         skírum Frey,
         nýtum Njarðar bur.

---

[1] The other manuscripts have *þó var snemr en sama* 'yet was the dusky'. This makes the alliteration regular.

[2] *d.* is possibly an abbreviation for *dróttinn* or else an error for *g.* = *goð*. Cf. Grape et al. 1977: 137. Note the kenning *fégjafaguð* for Freyr in the next chapter.

[3] This appears to be an adjective or past participle with *bági*. GkS 2367 and Codex Trajectinus have *útrǫst* 'outlying land', object of *byggja*; Codex Wormianus has *útræstr* (cleared out?), participle with *bági*. The DG 11 4to reading may be for *ófrestr* (undelayed, unhesitant?). The context of this subordinate clause is unknown.

[4] Cf. *Grímnismál* 43.

you halted Hangankjapta,
Hyrrærin died previously,
yet after that the famous
Svívǫr was deprived of life.

41 Of referring to Baldr

How shall Baldr be referred to?

By calling him son of Óðinn and Frigg, husband of Nanna, father of Forseti, owner of Hringhorni and Draupnir, enemy of Hǫðr and of the companions of Hel, god of lamentations.

Úlfr Uggason composed a long passage on the story of Baldr in *Húsdrápa*.

42 Of referring to Njǫrðr

How shall Njǫrðr be referred to?

By calling him god of the Vanir or descendant of Vanir or a Vanr, father of Freyr and Freyja, god of wealth-giving.

43 Of referring to Freyr

How shall Freyr be referred to?

By calling him son of Njǫrðr, brother of Freyja and god of the Vanir and descendant of Vanir and a Vanr, and harvest god, and god of wealth-giving. Freyr is called Beli's enemy.

So said Eyvindr skáldaspillir:

53   . . . when the unhesitant
         opponent of earls,
         Beli's enemy,
         wished to settle.

He is possessor of Skíðblaðnir and of the boar that is called Gullinbursti.

As it is said here:

54   Ívaldi's sons set to work
         in days of yore
         to build Skíðblaðnir,
         best of ships,
         for bright Freyr,
         bountiful son of Njǫrðr.

Svá sem segir Úlfr Uggason:[1]

55 (63) Ríðr á borg til borgar
         boðfróðr sonr Óðins,
         Freyr, ok fólkum stýrir,
         fyrstr enum gulli bysta.

Hann heitir ok Sligrugtanni.

44 Frá kenningu Heimdalls

Hvernveg skal kenna Heimdall? Svá at kalla hann son níu mœðra eða vǫrð goða, sem fyrr er sagt, eða hvíta ás; mensøki Freyju; um þat er kveðit í Heimdallargaldri, ok er síðan kallat hǫfuð m⟨j⟩ǫtuðr Heimdallar.[2] Sverðit heitir manns mǫtuðr. Heimdallr er eigandi Gulltopps, hann er tilsøkir Vágaskers ok Singasteins, þá er hann deildi til Brísingamens við Loka. Hann heitir ok Vindgler. Úlfr Uggason kvað í Húsdrápu langa stund eptir þessi frásǫgn ok er þess þar getit at þeir vóru í sela líki. Hann er ok son Óðins.

45 Frá kenningu Týs ok Braga

Hverninn skal kenna Tý? Svá at kalla hann hinn einhenda ás ok úlfs fóstra, vígagoð, son Óðins.

Hvernig skal kenna Braga? Svá at kalla hann ver Iðunnar, frumsmið bragar ok enn síðskeggja ás, ok af hans nafni er sá kallaðr skeggbragi er mikit skegg hefir. Son Óðins.

46 Frá kenningu Viðars ok Vála

Hversu skal kenna Viðar? Svá at kalla hann inn þǫgla ás, eiganda járnskós, dólg ok bana Fenrisúlfs, hefniás guðanna, byggiás fǫðurtoppa[3] ok son Óðins, bróður ásanna.

Hvernig skal kenna Vála? Svá at kalla hann son Óðins ok Rindar, stjúpson Friggjar, bróður ásanna, hefniás . . .[4] ok Baldrs ok dólg Haðar ok bana hans, byggjanda fǫðurtúna.

47 Kendr Hǫðr ok Ullr

Hvernveg skal kenna Hǫð?

[1] On this verse see Introduction p. lii.

[2] On this curious kenning, the origin of which is unknown, see Faulkes 1998: 225, note to 108/8–9.

[3] *Toppr* means 'lock of hair', 'mast top'. Other manuscripts have *fǫðurtopta* (*topt* = homestead). Cf. *fǫðurtúna* under Váli.

[4] The word *Óðins* (which is incorrect) seems to have been written here and then erased, but the scribe forgot to erase the following *ok*; see Grape et al. (1977: 138).

So says Úlfr Uggason:

55   Freyr, battle-skilled son of Óðinn,
          rides first to the pyre
          on the golden-bristled boar,
          and governs hosts.

It is also called Sligrugtanni.

44 Of referring to Heimdallr

How shall Heimdallr be referred to?

By calling him son of nine mothers or guardian of the gods, as was said above, or the white Áss; recoverer of Freyja's necklace; a passage in *Heimdallargaldr* is devoted to this story, and since then the head has been called Heimdallr's doom. The sword is called man's doom. Heimdallr is owner of Gulltoppr, he is the visitor to Vágasker and Singasteinn, when he contended with Loki for the Brísingamen. He is also called Vindgler. Úlfr Uggason composed a long passage in *Húsdrápa* based on this story, and it is mentioned there that they were in the form of seals. He is also son of Óðinn.

45 On referring to Týr and Bragi

How shall Týr be referred to?

By calling him the one-handed god and feeder of the wolf, battle-god, son of Óðinn.

How shall Bragi be referred to?

By calling him Iðunn's husband, inventor of poetry and the long-bearded Áss, and from his name a man is called 'beard-*bragi*' who has a big beard. Son of Óðinn.

46 On referring to Viðarr and Váli

How shall Viðarr be referred to?

By calling him the silent Áss, possessor of the iron shoe, enemy and slayer of Fenriswolf, the god's avenging Áss, the dweller in his father's homestead and son of Óðinn, brother of the Æsir.

How shall Váli be referred to?

By calling him son of Óðinn and Rindr, Frigg's stepson, brother of the Æsir, Baldr's avenging Áss and Hǫðr's enemy and his slayer, dweller in his father's courts.

47 Hǫðr and Ullr referred to

In what way shall Hǫðr be referred to?

Svá at kalla hann blinda ás, Baldrs bana, skjótanda mistilteins, son Óðins, Heljar sinna, vana[1] dólg.
Hvernig skal kenna Ull?
Svá at kalla son Sifjar, stjúpson Þórs, ǫndurás, bogaás, veiðiás, skjaldarás.

48 Frá kenningu Hǿnis ok Loka

Hverninn skal kenna Hǿni?
Svá at kalla hann sessa eða sinna eða mála Óðins ok enn skjóta ás ok enn langa for[2] ok aurkonung.[3]
Hversu skal kenna Loka?
Kalla hann son Fárbauta ok Heljar[4] Laufeyjar ok Nálar, bróður Býleifts ok Helblinda; faðir Vánargands, þat er Fenrisúlfr, ok Jǫrmungands, þat er Miðgarðsormr, ok Heljar ok Nara ok Ála; ok frænda ok fǫðurbróður, vársinna[5] ok sessa Óðins ok ása ok kistuskrúð Geirraðar; þjófr jǫtna, haf⟨r⟩s ok Brísingamens ok Iðunnar epla; Sleipnis frænda, ver Sigunar, goða[6] dólg, hárskaða Sifjar, bǫlva smið; hinn slǿgi áss, rǿgjandi ok vélandi guðanna, ráðbani Baldrs, hinn búni[7] áss, þrætudólgr Heimdallar ok Skaða.

49 Kend Frigg ok Freyja

Hverneg skal kenna Frigg?
Svá at kalla hana dóttur Fjǫrguns, ǫmmu Óðins, móður Baldrs, elju Jarðar ok Rindar ok Gunnlaðar ok Geiðar.[8]
Hvernig skal kenna Freyju?
Kalla hana dóttur Njarðar, systur Freys, kona Óðins, móðir Hnossar, eigandi valfalls ok Sess⟨r⟩úmnis ok fressa ok Brísingamens, vana goð, vana dís, hit grátfagra goð.
Svá skal kenna aðrar ásynjur ok nefna annarrar nafni ok kenna við | eign eða verk sín eða ættir.

50 Frá kenningu Iðunnar

Hversu skal kenna Iðunni?
Svá at kalla hana konu Braga ok gætandi eplanna ok eplin ellilyf ásanna. Hon er ok ránfengr Þjaza.
Ása er rétt at kalla einn hvern annars nafni ok kenna við verk sín eða ætt.

[1] Other manuscripts have *Vála*.
[2] Perhaps to be read *fǫr* 'journey', though this is feminine (*for* means 'mud', but is feminine too). Other manuscripts have *fót* 'foot' or 'leg'. AM 157 8vo has *aur* 'mud'.
[3] Written 'avr konvng', perhaps for *ǫrkonung* 'arrow-king'.
[4] See Grape et al. 1977: 138.
[5] See Introduction pp. lxiii–lxiv.
[6] Written 'gaða' in DG 11 4to.
[7] Other manuscripts have *bundni* 'bound'.
[8] Corrected in the margin to Gerðar (see Grape et al. 1977: 138).

By calling him the blind Áss, slayer of Baldr, shooter of mistletoe, son of Óðinn, companion of Hel, enemy of Vanir.

How shall Ullr be referred to?

By calling him son of Sif, stepson of Þórr, ski-Áss, bow-Áss, hunting Áss, shield-Áss.

48 Of referring to Hœnir and Loki

How shall Hœnir be referred to?

By calling him Óðinn's table-companion or comrade or confidant and the swift Áss and the long foot and mud-king.

How shall Loki be referred to?

By calling him son of Fárbauti and Laufey and Nál, brother of Býleifstr and Helblindi, father of Vánargandr, that is Fenriswolf, and of Jǫrmungandr, that is the Miðgarðr serpent, and of Hel and Nari and Áli, and relative and uncle, foster-brother and table-companion of Óðinn and the Æsir and Geirrøðr's casket-ornament; thief from giants, of goat and Brísingamen and Iðunn's apples; relative of Sleipnir, husband of Sigun, enemy of gods, damager of Sif's hair, maker of mischief; the cunning Áss, calumniator and tricker of the gods, contriver of Baldr's death, the prepared Áss, wrangler with Heimdallr and Skaði.

49 Frigg and Freyja referred to

How shall Frigg be referred to?

By calling her daughter of Fjǫrgunn, grandmother of Óðinn, mother of Baldr, rival of Jǫrð and Rindr and Gunnlǫð and Gerðr.

How shall Freyja be referred to?

By calling her daughter of Njǫrðr, sister of Freyr, wife of Óðr, mother of Hnoss, possessor of the fallen slain and Sessrúmnir and tomcats and Brísingamen, deity of Vanir, lady of Vanir, the tear-fair deity.

Other Ásynjur shall be referred to thus and called by the name of another one and referred to by their possession or deeds or descent.

50 Of referring to Iðunn

How shall Iðunn be referred to?

By calling her Bragi's wife and keeper of the apples and the apples the Æsir's old-age cure. She is also the giant Þjazi's booty.

It is normal to call Æsir one by the name of another and refer to them by their deeds or descent.

51 Hversu kenna skal himininn

Hversu skal kenna himininn? Svá at kalla hann Ymis haus ok þar af jǫtuns haus ok erfiði eða byrði dverganna eða hjálm Vestra ok Austra, Suðra, Norðra; land sólar ok tungls ok himintungla, vápna[1] ok veðra; hjálmr eða hús lopts ok jarðar ok sólar. Svá kvað Arnórr jarlaskáld:

56 (105)   Engr Skjǫldungr sitr aldri
           jammildr á við skildan,
           þess varð grams und gǫmlum
           gnóg rausn Ymis hausi.

Ok enn kvað hann:

57 (106)   Bjǫrt verðr sól at svartri,
           søkkr fold í mar dǫkkvan,
           brestr erfiði Austra,
           allr glymr sjár und fjǫllum.

Svá kvað Bǫðvarr balti:

58 (106)   Alls engi varð Inga
           undir sólar grundu
           bǫðvar hvatr, né betri
           brǿðr, landreki ǿðri.

Svá kvað Þjóðólfr hvinverski:

59 (108)   Ók at ísarnleiki
           Jarðar sonr en dulði
           móður, svall Meila blóði
           mána vegr und honum.

Svá kvað Ormr Barreyja⟨r⟩skáld:

60 (109)   Hvégi er, Draupnis drógar
           dís, ramman spyr ek vísa,
           sá ræðr, valdr, fyrir veldi
           vagnbrautar, mér fagnar.

Svá kvað Bragi:

61 (110)   Hinn er varp á víða
           vinda ǫndurdísar
           yfir manna sút[2] margra
           munnlaug fǫður augum.

Svá kvað Steinn Herdísarson:

[1] See Introduction pp. lx–lxi.
[2] Other manuscripts have *sjǫt* (men's dwelling = earth) a more normal concept here.

51 How the sky shall be referred to

How shall the sky be referred to?

By calling it Ymir's skull and hence giant's skull and toil or burden of the dwarfs or helmet of Vestri and Austri, Suðri, Norðri; land of sun and moon and stars, weapons and winds, helmet or house of air and earth and sun.

So said Arnórr Earls' Poet:

56 No prince as generous
   will ever sit on shield-hung plank (ship with shields on the sides)
   —this ruler's magnificence was ample—
   under Ymir's old skull (the sky).

And he also said:

57 The bright sun will beome a black one,
   earth will sink into the dark sea,
   Austri's toil (the sky) will split,
   all the sea will crash under the mountains.

So said Bǫðvarr Bear:

58 Never any battle-keen land-ruler
   beneath the sun's ground (sky)
   became more excellent or better
   then Ingi's brother.

So said Þjóðólfr of Hvinir:

59 Jǫrð's son drove to iron-game.
   but kept his mother in the dark;
   the moon's way (sky) swelled
   with Meili's blood under him.

So said Ormr Barreyjaskáld:

60 However mighty, goddess (lady) of Draupnir's band (gold ring),
   I learn the lord is—he rules his realm—
   the ruler of the Wain's (constellation's) way
   (sky) will welcome me.

So said Bragi:

61 He who threw into the winds'
   wide basin the ski-goddess's (Skaði's)
   father's (Þjazi's) eyes
   above the sorrow of many men.

So said Steinn Herdísarson:

62 (112)   Hás kveð ek helgan ræsi
           heimtjalds at brag þeima,
           mærð telst fram, en fyrða
           fyrr, því at hann er dýrri.

Svá kvað Arnórr:
63 (113)   Hjalp, dýrr konungr, dýrum,
           dags grundar, Hermundi.

Ok enn kvað hann:
64 (114)   Sannr stillir hjálptu snjǫllum,
           sóltjalda, Rǫgnvaldi.

Svá kvað Hallvarðr:
65 (115)   Knútr verr jǫrð sem ítran
           alls dróttinn sal fjalla.

Sem Arnórr kvað:
66 (116)   Mikáll vegr þat er misgert þikkir
           manvits fróðr ok allt it góða;
           tiggi skiptir síðan seggjum
           sólar hjálms á dømistóli.

52 Kend jǫrðin

Hversu skal jǫrð kenna?

Svá at kalla hana Ymis hold ok móður Þórs, dóttur Ánas, brúði Óðins, elju Friggjar ok Gunnlaðar ok Rindar, sværu Sifjar, gólf ok bǫnd[1] veðrahallar, sjár dýranna, dóttur Náttar, systur Auðs ok Dags.

Svá kvað Eyvindr skáldaspillir:
67 (117)   Nú er álfrǫðull elfar
           jǫtna dólgs um fólginn,
           rof eru ramrar þjóðar
           rík, í móður líki.

Svá kvað Hallfrøðr:
68 (118)   Ráð lukust at sá síðan
           snjallráðr konungs spjalli
           átti eingadóttur
           Ánas[2] viðrgrǿna.

[1] Other manuscripts have *botn* 'base'.
[2] Jǫrð's father is Ónarr/Ánarr/Annarr, see indexes in Faulkes 2005 and 1998. *Ánas* is for *Ánars* with assimilated r. In other manuscripts Jǫrð is *viði gróin* 'tree-grown', more plausible than *viðrgrǿnn*, which anyway ought to be *viðrgrǿnn* if the first element is *viðr* 'tree'.

62 I address the holy ruler (God)
    of the world's high tent (sky)
    with this poem, rather than men,
    for he is more worthy; praise is uttered.

So said Arnórr:

63 Save, dear king of day's ground (the sky)
    the dear Hermundr.

And he also said:

64 True ruler of sun's tents (the sky),
    save brave Rǫgnvaldr.

So said Hallvarðr:

65 Knútr protects the land
    as the lord of all [defends] the splendid hall of the mountains (sky).

As Arnórr said:

66 Michael, full of wisdom, weighs
    what seems ill done and all the good;
    The ruler of sun's helmet (the sky) then
    divides men up on his judgment seat.

52 The earth referred to

How shall the earth be referred to?

By calling it Ymir's flesh and mother of Þórr, daughter of Ánarr, bride of Óðinn, rival of Frigg and Gunnlǫð and Rindr, mother-in-law of Sif, floor and bonds of winds' hall, sea of the animals, daughter of Night, sister of Auðr and Day.

So said Eyvindr skáldaspillir:

67 Now the river's elf-disk (sun of the river = gold)
    is hidden in the body of giants' enemy's (Þórr's)
    mother (Jǫrð, Earth, i.e. the ground);
    the fall of a powerful people is mighty.

So said Hallfrøðr.

68 The match was later consummated
    by which that wise-ruling king's crony (the earl)
    married (gained possession of) the tree-green only daughter
    of Ánarr (Jǫrð, Earth, the land of Norway).

Svá kvað Þjóðólfr:

69 (120) Útan bindr við enda
  elju gers glǫðuðr hersa.[1]

Svá kvað Hallvarðr:[2]

70 (121) Því hykk fleygjanda[3] frægjan,
  ferr jǫrð und menþverri
  ítran, eina at láta
  Auðs systur, mjǫk trauðan.

71 (122) Dólgs húss hefir dáðar
  siðar latr staðit fjarri
  endr, þá er elju Rindar,
  ómilda tók skyldir.[4]

53 Frá kenningu sjóvarins

Hvernig skal kenna sæ? Svá at kalla hann Ymis blóð, heimsøkir guðanna, ver Ránar, fǫður Ægis dóttir[5] þeirra er svá heita: Himinglæva, Dúfa, Blóðughaða,[6] Hefring, Uðr, Rán, Bylgja, Bára, Kólga; land Ránar ok Ægis dǿtra, skipa, kjalar ok stála, súða, sýgju,[7] fiska, ísa; sækonunga leið ok braut. Eigi síðr hring eyjanna, hús sanda ok skerja, dorgar land ok sæfugla, byrjar.

Svá kvað Ormr Barreyja⟨r⟩skáld:

72 (123) Útan gnýr á eyri
  Ymis blóð fara góðra.

Svá kvað Refr skáld:

73 (124) Vágþeysta bar vestan,
  vætti ek lands fyrir brandi,
  hvalmæris skefr hlýra
  hádýr um lǫg báru.

[1] In the Codex Regius version there are four lines in this verse, which is there not too difficult to interpret. See *Skj* B I 346. Obviously *elju gers* ought to be a kenning for *Jǫrð* (land); it is *elgvers* 'of the elk's sea' in GkS 2367 4to.

[2] Written 'Hallv'', which must be for Hallvarðr. Other manuscripts have 'Hallf.' = Hallfrøðr.

[3] This seems to be a half-kenning (one lacking a determinant) for 'generous king' (distributor of gold or weapons). Half-kennings are not too uncommon in skaldic verse, though there are no other certain ones in Snorri's *Edda* except in the *þulur* of names of swords (*eldr, logi, snyrtir, herðir, skerðir*; see Faulkes 1998: 118–20; Meissner 1921, 150–51).

[4] DG 11 4to has no attribution, but in other manuscripts and sources (e.g. Fagrskinna) it is attributed to Þjóðólfr (Arnórsson) and the text is markedly different (see Faulkes 1988: 182 and references there). Here the defective alliteration underlines the corruption of the text.

[5] Obviously an error for *dǿtra*.

[6] Obviously an error for *Blóðughadda*.

[7] I.e. *sýju*.

So said Þjóðólfr:

69 The gladdener of lords (king)
    binds [ships] around the edge of the rival of *gerr*.

So said Hallvarðr:

70 So I think the famed distributor (ruler)
    —land comes under the splendid
    neck-ring diminisher (generous ruler)—very reluctant to leave
    Auðr's sister (the land of Norway) alone (abandon it).

71 Once the one reluctant for the practice of valour (battle)
    held back when the one who lays duties upon (rules)
    the enemy's (giant's) house (rock, stony land)
    took the ungracious rival of Rindr (Jǫrð, the land of Norway).

53 Of referring to the sea

How shall the sea be referred to?

By calling it Ymir's blood, visitor to the gods, husband of Rán, father of Ægir's daughters, whose names are Himinglæva, Dúfa, Blóðughaða, Hefring, Uðr, Rán, Bylgja, Bára, Kólga; land of Rán and Ægir's daughters, of ships, of keel and stem, planks, strake, fish, ice; sea-kings' way and road. No less ring of the islands, house of sands and skerries, land of fishing-tackle and seabirds, of sailing wind.

So said Ormr Barreyjarskáld:

72 Out on the sandbank of good vessels
    Ymir's blood (sea) roars.

So said Refr the Poet:

73 Wave-impelled roller was carried from the west
    over the sea; it sprays the rowlock-animal (ship)
    of the whale-praiser (sea-king?) on its bows;
    I expect (to see) land over the prow.

Ok enn kvað hann.

74 (126) Fører bjǫrn þar er bára
brestr undinna¹ festa
opt í Ægis kjapta
úrsvǫl ⟨G⟩ymis² vǫlva.

Hér er sagt at allt er eitt Ægir ok Hlér ok Gymir.

Ok enn kvað hann:

75 (127) Enn snjágnípu Sleipnir
slítr í vindriðinn hvítum
Ránar rauðum steini
runnit brjótt ór munni.³

Svá kvað Einarr Skúlason:

76 (128) Harðr hefir ǫrt fyrir jǫrðu
élvindr, svana strindar
blakr⁴ lætr í sæ søkkva
snægrund,⁵ skipi hrundit.

Ok enn þetta:

77 (129) Margr ríss, en drífr dorgar
dynstrǫnd í sviklǫndum,
spend verða stǫg stundum,
stirðr k⟨e⟩ipr, fira greipum.

78 (130) Grams bera gyllta spánu,
gǫfug ferð er sú jǫfra,
skýtr hólmnfjǫturr⁶ heiða
hrafni, snekkju⟨r⟩, stafna.⁷

Ok enn kvað hann:

79 (132) Sundr springr svalra landa
sverði gjǫrð fyrir bǫndum.

¹ Written 'unðina'.

² Both the next line of prose and the alleration show that *Ymis* is an error for *Gymis*.

³ *briott* must be an error for 'brioft' (*brjóst*).

⁴ *blakr* is probably for *blakkr* 'horse' (so Codex Wormianus and AM 757 a 4to). GkS 2367 4to has 'blackleitr'.

⁵ *Snægrund* (DG11 4to, Codex Trajectinus and Codex Wormianus) could mean 'snow-covered land', but has also been interpreted as 'Iceland'. GkS 2367 4to has *sægrund* 'seabed'. See Faulkes 1998: 182.

⁶ *Hólmn-* is obviously an error for *hólm-*.

⁷ Verses 77 and 78 are written as one stanza in DG 11 4to, but the content shows that this is a mistake. *Snekkjur* for *snekkju* is necessary to provide a subject for *bera* in line 1, though no manuscript has the *-r*.

And he also said:

74 Gymir's spray-cold spae-wife (Rán, the raging sea)
    often brings the twisted-rope bear (ship)
    into Ægir's jaws (under the waves)
    where the wave breaks.

Here it is implied that they are all the same, Ægir and Hlér and Gymir. And he also said:

75 Again Sleipnir (horse, i.e. ship) of the snowy-crest (wave),
    wind-tossed, tears its breast,
    covered in red paint
    from Rán's white mouth (the sea's grasp).

So said Einarr Skúlason:

76 A hard storm-wind has driven the ship
    fast along the coast;
    the swans' bank (sea) steed (ship)
    makes Iceland sink into the sea (beneath the horizon).

And also this:

77 Many a firm rowlock lifts
    and the fishing-tackle's sounding strand (sea) drives into
    deceptive lands (dangerous coasts or land that appears to be sea?);
    stays are sometimes made tight by men's grasps.

78 The king's warships
    have gilded ornaments;
    this is a glorious expedition for the princes;
    the island-fetter (sea) pushes on the horse of bright stems (ship).

And he also said:

79 The belt of cool lands (sea) springs
    apart for the gods before the sword.

Sem Snæbjǫrn kvað:

80 (133) Hvat⟨t⟩ kváðum hrœra grjóta
  her grimmastan skerja
  út frá jarðar skauti
  eylúðrs níu brúðir,
  þær er, lunds, | fyrir lǫngu,
  liðmildr skipa Hildir
  baugskerðir rístr barði,
  ból Amlóða mólu.

Hér er kallat hafit Amlóða kvern.[1]

Enn kvað Einarr Skúlason:

81 (134) Viknar Rán í, raknar
  reksaumr, flugastraumi;
  dúks hrindr bǫl, þar er bleikir
  bifgrund, á stag rifjum.

54 Frá kenningu sólar

Hvernig skal kenna sól?

Svá at kalla hana dóttur Mundilfeta, systur mána, konu Glens; eldr himins ok jarðar ok lopts.

Svá kvað Skúli Þorsteinsson:

82 (135) Glens beðja veðr gyðju
  guðblíð vé; síðan
  ljós kemr gǫrt meðr geislum
  gránsetrs ofan Mána.

Svá kvað Einarr Skúlason:

83 (136) Hvargi er Beita borgar
  bar grimmustum skála
  hár, vin hollum árum,
  heims vafrlogi sveimar.[2]

55 Kendr vindrinn

Hvernig skal kenna vind?

Svá at kalla son Fornjóts, bróður elds ok Ægis; brjótr viðar, skaði eða bani eða hundr eða vargr viðar eða seglreiða.

Svá kvað Sveinn í Norðrsetudrápu:

84 (137) Tóku fyrst til fjúka
  Fornjóts synir ljótir.

---

[1] *Amlóða kvern* does not actually appear in the verse here, but is perhaps implied.
[2] Cf. Faulkes 1989: 140 and 183, where the text is that of GkS 2367 4to emended.

As Snæbjǫrn said:

80   We said the nine brides (waves) of the island-box (sea)
were turning the most grim
host of rocky skerries (mill) fast
out beyond the land's edge,
they who long ago ground a dwelling
for Amlóði; the help-generous Hildir (warrior)
of the tree (man) of ships,
the ring diminisher (generous ruler), cuts [the sea] with his prow.

Here the sea is called Amlóði's mill.

Einarr Skúlason also said:

81   Rán (the sea) gives way in the rushing current;
the hammered nails come undone;
the sail's harmer (wind) pushes the reefs against the stay
where the shaking ground (sea) becomes white.

54 Of referring to the sun

How shall the sun be referred to?

By calling it daughter of Mundilfeti, sister of the moon, wife of Glenr, fire of the sky and the air.

So said Skúli Þorsteinsson:

82   God-blithe bedfellow of Glenr (the sun)
steps across the goddess's sanctuary; afterwards
the light of Máni (the moon) comes readily down
with beams of the grey setting (of the sun?).

So said Einarr Skúlason:

83   Wherever the hall (ship) of Beiti's (sea-king's)
stronghold (sea) was carried,
the high wandering flame (sun) of the world hovers,
friend to the most fearsome gracious angels.

55 The wind referred to

How shall wind be referred to?

By calling it son of Fornjótr, brother of fire and Ægir; breaker of tree, damager or slayer or dog or wolf of tree or rigging.

So said Sveinn in *Norðrsetudrápa*:

84   Fornjótr's ugly sons
began first to send blizzards.

56 Kendr eldr

Hversu skal kenna eld?
Svá at kalla hann bróður vinds ok Ægis, bana ok grand viðar ok húsa, Hálfs bana, sól húsa.

57 Vetrinn

Hvernig skal kenna vetr?
Svá at kalla hann son Vindsvals ok bana orma, hríðmál.
Svá kvað Ormr Steinþórsson:

85 (138) Réð ek þenna mǫg manni
Vindsvals únáð blindum.

Svá kvað Ásgrímr:

86 (139) Sigbjóðr var síðan
seimǫrr í Þrándheimi,
þjóð veit þínar iðnir,
þann orms trega sannan.

58 Kent sumar

Hvernig skal kenna sumar?
At kalla son Svásaðar ok líkn. Mannlíkn má kalla.
Svá kvað Egill Skallagrímsson:

87 (140) Upp skulum órum sverðum
úlfs tannlituðr glitra,
eigum dáð at drýgja
í dalmiskunn fiska.

59 Kendr maðrinn

Hverneg skal kenna manninn?
Hann skal kenna við verk sín, þat er hann veitir eða gerir eða þiggr. Hann má ok kenna við eignir sínar, þat er hann gefr eða hann á, ok við ættir þær er hann er af kominn; svá þær er af honum kómu.
Hverneg skal hann kenna við þessa hluti?
Svá at kalla hann vinnanda eða fremjanda verka sinna eða fara sinna eða athafnar, víga eða sæfara, eða skipa eða vápna. Hann er ok reynir vápnanna ok viðr víganna, allt eitt ok vinnanda. Viðr heitir tré ok reynir I heitir tré. Af þessum heitum hafa skáldin kallat manninn ask eða hlyn, lund eða ǫðrum viða heitum. Karlmann skal kenna ok til víga eða skipa eða fjár.
Mann er ok rétt at kenna til allra ása heita. Kent er ok við jǫtna heiti ok er þat flest háð eða lastmæli. Vel þikkir kent við álfa.

56 Fire referred to

How shall fire be referred to?

By calling it brother of wind and Ægir, slayer and damager of tree and houses, Hálfr's killer, sun of houses.

57 The winter

How shall winter be referred to?

By calling it son of Vindvalr and death of snakes, storm-season.

So said Ormr Steinþórsson:

85   This Vindsvalr's son (winter) I devised
            trouble[1] for a blind man.

So said Ásgrímur:

86   Afterwards the gold-generous
            battle-challenger was in Þrándheimr—
            everyone knows your achievements—
            that true (hard?) serpent's sorrow (winter).

58 Summer referred to

How shall summer be referred to?

By calling it son of Svásuðr and comfort. It can be called man's comfort.

So said Egill Skallagrímsson:

87   Stainer of wolf's teeth (with blood, i.e. warrior),
            we shall wave our swords in the sun;
            we have deeds to perform
            in the valley-fish's (snakes') mercy (summer).[2]

59 The man referred to

How shall the man be referred to?

He shall be referred to by his actions, what he gives or does or receives. He can also be referred to by his property, what he gives or he owns, and by the family lines he is descended from; also those that descend from him.

How shall he be referred to by these things?

By calling him achiever or performer of his actions or his expeditions or activities, killings or sea-journeys, or by ships or weapons. He is also trier (*reynir*) of the weapons and doer (*viðr*) of the killings, which is the same thing as achiever. *Viðr* is a word for tree and there is a tree called *reynir* (rowan). On the basis of these terms, the poets have called the man ash or maple, *lundr* (grove, tree) or by other tree-names. A male person may also be referred to by killings or ships or wealth.

It is also normal to refer to a man using all the names of Æsir. Names of giants are also used, and that is mostly as satire or criticism. Using names of elves is thought complimentary.

[1] Or happiness, see Introduction p. cxxiv.
[2] For another interpretation of this kenning see Heimir Pálsson 2004.

Konu skal kenna til alls kvenbúnaðar, gulls ok gimsteina, ǫls ok víns eða annars drykkjar þess er hon gefr eða selr, svá ok til ǫlgagna ok allra þeira hluta er henni samir at veita eða gefa. Rétt er ok at kenna hana svá at kalla hana selju eða lág þess er hon miðlar. En selja ok lág, þat eru tré. Fyrir því er kona kend til kenningar ǫllum viðar heitum. En fyrir því er kona kend til gimsteina eða glersteina: þat var í forneskju kvenna búnaðr er kallat er steinasørvi er þær hǫfðu á hálsi sér. Nú er svá fǿrt til kenningar at konan er kend við stein ok við ǫll steins heiti. Kona er ok kend við ǫll ásynja heiti eða valkyrur, nornir eða dísir. Konu er rétt at kenna við alla athǫfn sína eða við eign eða við ætt.

60 Kent gullit

Hvernig skal kenna gull?

Svá at kalla þat eld Ægis ok barr Glasis; haddr Sifjar, hǫfuðbǫnd Fullu, grátr Freyju, skúr Draupnis ok dropa ok regn augna Freyju, Otrgjǫld, sáð Fýrisvallar, haugþak Hǫlga, eldr Ægis ok Ránar ok allra vatna ok handar ok grjót ok sær[1] handar, Fróða mjǫl.

Svá segir Eyvindr:[2]

88 (143)   Fullu skein á fjǫllum
              fal⟨l⟩sól brá vallar
              Ullar kjóls um allan
              aldr Hákonar skáldum.

Svá kvað Skúli Þorsteinsson:

89 (144)   Margr hlaut um morgin
              morðelds þar er hlyn felldum
              Freyju tár at fleiri,
              fárbjóðr; at því várum.

Ok enn hefir Einarr kveðit svá at Freyju kallar hann móður Hnossar eða konu Óðs. Svá sem hér segir:[3]

90 (146)   Eigi þverr fyrir augna
              Óðs beðvinu Róða
              ræfr, eignis⟨t⟩ sá, regni
              ramsvel⟨l⟩, konungr elli.

Hér getr þess at Freyju má kalla systur Freys.[4]

Ok enn segir hann:

---

[1] Other manuscripts have *sker* (reef). Misreading 'scer' as *sær* is an understandable error.
[2] Cf. verse 261.
[3] Cf. verse 139; *ræfr* needs to be emended to *ræfs*
[4] The verse illustrating the kenning 'Freyr's sister' in the Codex Regius version is here omitted (see Faulkes 1998: 44). There is a similar error at the end of f. 34v.

A woman shall be referred to by all female adornment, gold and jewels, ale or wine or other drink that she gives or serves, also by ale-vessels and all those things that it is proper for her to provide or give. It is also normal to refer to her by calling her server (*selja*) or *lág* (usually spelt *lóg*, dispenser) of what she hands out. But *selja* (willow) and *lág* (log), these are trees. Hence a woman is referred to for kennings by all tree-names. And the reason a woman is referred to by gemstones or beads is that there was in antiquity a female adornment that is called 'stone-chain' that they wore round their necks. It has now been made into a kenning, so that the woman is referred to in terms of stone and all words for stone. A woman is also referred to using all the names of Ásynjur or valkyries, norns or *dísir* (divine ladies). It is normal to refer to a woman by any of her activities or by her possession or descent.

60 The gold referred to

How shall gold be referred to?

By calling it Ægir's fire and Glasir's foliage, Sif's hair, Fulla's snoods, Freyja's weeping, Draupnir's shower and dripping and rain of Freyja's eyes, otter-payment, seed of Fyri plain, Hǫlgi's mound-roof, fire of Ægir and Rán and all kinds of waters and of the arm and stones and sea of the arm, Fróði's meal.

So says Eyvindr:

| 88 | The falling sun (gold) of the plain (forehead) of Fulla's eyelashes shone on poets' fells (arms) of Ullr's boat (shield) throughout the life of Hákon. |

So said Skúli Þorsteinsson:

| 89 | Many a danger-threatener (warrior) got the more Freyja's tears (gold) in the morning where we felled maple (warrior) of death-flame (sword); we were busy at it. |

And moreover Einarr has composed poetry calling Freyja mother of Hnoss or wife of Óðr. As it says here:

| 90 | Róði's (sea-king's) strong roof-ice (shield-wall ice, = axe) is not the worse for the eye-rain (tears, i.e. gold) of Óðr's bedfellow (Freyja); may this king reach old age. |

Here it is mentioned that Freyja can be called Freyr's sister.

And he says further:

91 (148)　　Nýtt buðumst Njarðar dóttur
　　　　　　nálægt var þat stála,
　　　　　　vel um hrósa ek því vísa,
　　　　　　varn[1] sævar, ǫl, barni.
Hér er hon kǫlluð dóttir Njarðar.
Ok enn segir hann:
92 (149)　　Gaf sá er eining ofrar
　　　　　　ógnprúðr vana brúlðar
　　　　　　þings vafrloga þrǫngvir
　　　　　　þróttǫflga mér dóttir.[2]
　　　　　　Ríkr leiði mey mækis
　　　　　　mótvaldr á beð skáldi
　　　　　　Gefnar glóðum drifna
　　　　　　Gautreiks svana brautar.
Hér er hon kǫlluð Gefn ok vanabrúðr, ok til allra heita Freyju er rétt at kenna grátinn ok kalla svá gullit. Marga lund er þeim kenningum breytt, kallat hagl ok regn eða él ok dropar eða skúrir ok forsar augna hennar eða knjá eða hlýra ok brá eða hvarma. Orð eða ráð jǫtna, sem fyrr var sagt.
Svá kvað Bragi:
93 (150)　　Þann átta ek vin verstan
　　　　　　vazt[3] rǫdd ok mér beztan
　　　　　　Ála undirkúlu
　　　　　　óniðjaðan þriðja.
Hann kallaði sæinn vazta undirkúlu[4] en jǫtun Ála steins, en gull ráð jǫtuns.
Gull er kallat otrgjǫld eða nauðgjǫld ásanna eða rógmálmr, ból eða byggð Fáfnis eða málmr Gnitaheiðar eða byrðr Grana ok arfr Fáfnis, Niflunga skattr eða arfr, Kraka sáð.[5]
Svá kvað Eyvindr skáldaspillir:
94 (185)　　Bárum Ullr á[6] alla
　　　　　　ímunlauks á hauka
　　　　　　fjǫllum Fýrisvalla
　　　　　　fræ Hákonar ævi.

[1] = vǫrn. Rhyming of *a* and *ǫ* is not uncommon in skaldic verse.
[2] Either an error for *dóttur* or an early example of the confusion of case-endings. According to Björn K. Þórólfsson 1925: 29–30, the earliest example of such confusion is nominative *bróður* in Flateyjarbók.
[3] Written '[v]atzt'.
[4] The writer of the prose has misunderstood this kenning, which is for rock, not the sea.
[5] The stories behind these kennings appear here in the Codex Regius version, but much later in the Uppsala version. Gold = *otrgjǫld* does, however, appear in the list at the beginning of ch. 60 above.
[6] Clearly an error for *of* (so other manuscripts) or *um* (cf. verse 262).

91 I was offered beneficial help (ǫl 'ale'= líð; lið = help);
    this was close to (a kind of) defence of the sea's
    stems (prows of a ship, i.e. a shield); I am very proud of this wise
    child (Hnoss, i.e. hnoss 'treasure') of Njǫrðr's daughter (Freyja).

Here she is called Njǫrðr's daughter.
 And he says further:

92 The battle-gallant urger (warrior) of the assembly (battle)
    of the moving flame (sword), who upholds unity (friendship),
    gave me a daughter (Hnoss, treasure) of Vanr-bride (Freyja)
    with lasting strength.
    May the mighty controller (leader) of the sword-meeting (battle)
    lead Gefn's (Freyja's) maiden (Hnoss, treasure)
    decked in embers (gold) of Gautreikr's (sea-king's)
    swans' path (sea) to the poet's bed.

Here she is called Gefn and Vanr-bride, and it is normal to qualify weeping by any of the names for Freyja and to call gold that. These kennings are varied in many ways, calling it hail or rain or storm or drops or showers and cascades of her eyes or knees or cheeks and eyelashes or eyelids. Words or counsel of giants, as was said above.
 So said Bragi:

93 I had this third friend, unrelated, who was harshest to the voice
    of Áli (a god) of the ball beneath fishing-grounds (rock; Áli
    of rock is a giant, his voice is gold, being harsh to it is
    to be generous) and kindest to me.

He called the sea the ball beneath fishing-grounds and the giant Áli of rock and gold the giant's voice.
 Gold is called otter-payment or Æsir's forced payment or strife-metal, lair or abode of Fáfnir or metal of Gnitaheiðr or burden of Grani and Fáfnir's inheritance, Niflungs' treasure or inheritance, Kraki's seed.
 So said Eyvindr skáldaspillir:

94 Battle-leek (sword) Ullr (warrior),
    we used to wear on hawk-fells (our arms)
    Fyri plains' seed (gold rings)
    throughout Hákon's life.

Svá kvað Þjóðólfr:

95 (186) Eyss landreki ljósu
 lastvarr Kraka barri
 á hlémildra holdi
 hoskir[1] kálfur mér sjálfum.

Svá kvað Skúli Þorsteinsson:

96 (187) Þá er ræfrvita Reifnis
 rauð ek fyrir Sǫl[2] til auðar
 herfylgnis[3] bar ek Hǫlga
 haugþak saman baugum.[4]

Í Bjarkamálum eru tǫlð mǫrg gulls heiti. Svá segir þar:

97 (188) Gramr hinn gǫfgasti
 gladdi hirð sína
 Fenju forverki,
 Fáfnis miðgarði,
 Glasis glóbarri,
 Grana fagrbyrði,
 Draupnis dýrsveita,
 dúni Grafvitnis.

98 (189) Ýtti ǫrr hilmir,
 aldir við tóku,
 Sifjar svarðfestum,
 svelli dalnauðar,
 tregum otrsgjǫldum,
 tárum Marþallar,
 eldi Órunar,
 Iðja glysmálum.

99 (190) Gladdi gunnveitir
 —gengum fagrbúnir—
 Þjaza þingskilum
 þjóðir hermargar,
 Rínar rauðmálmi,
 rógi Niflunga,

[1] An error for *hauk* (verse 264 below) or *hauks* (other manuscripts); *hlémildra* is similarly an error for *hlémildar* (verse 264 and other manuscripts).

[2] DG 11 4to is damaged here and the reading is unclear (see Grape et al. 1977: 142). AM 157 8vo reads 'fol' but omits the next two lines. Jón Sigurðsson and Jón Rúgmann read 'savl'. Other manuscripts have *Svǫlð*.

[3] Probably an error for *-fylgins* (so some other manuscripts).

[4] Grape et al. 1977: 61 (cf. 142) read *bauga*, but *baugum* (with nasal stroke above u), as in most other manuscripts, would also fit.

So said Þjóðólfr:

95   The fault-shunning land-director (ruler)
pours Kraki's bright barley (gold)
onto my own hawk-lands (arms)
that provide security for flesh.

So said Skúli Þorsteinsson:

96   When I reddened Reifnir's (sea-king's) roof-fire
(shield-fire, i.e. sword) off Sǫl to gain wealth,
I amassed warlike Hǫlgi's
mound-roof (gold) in rings.

In *Bjarkamál* many terms for gold are listed. So it says there:

97   The most glorious prince
gladdened his men
with Fenja's labour,
Fáfnir's Miðgarðr,
Glasir's glowing foliage,
Grani's fair burden,
Draupnir's precious sweat,
Grafvitnir's pillow.

98   The generous lord pushed,
men received,
Sif's scalp-strings,
ice of bow-forcer (arm),
reluctant otter's payment,
Marþǫll's tears,
fire of Órun (a river),
Iði's shining talk.

99   The battle-giver gladdened
—we advanced beautifully adorned—
with Þjazi's assembly-agenda (talk)
the multitudinous hosts,
with the Rhine's red metal,
Niflungs' strife,

vísi hinn vígdjarfi;
vakti hann Baldr þeygi.[1]

Gull er kallat eldr handar eða liðs eða leggjar, því at þat er rautt, en silfr snjór, svell ok héla, því at þat er hvítt. Með sama hætti skal kenna gull eða silfr til sjóðs eða diguls, en | hvártveggja gull ok silfr má vera grjót handa ok hálsgjǫrð nokkurs þess er títt var at hafa men. Hringar eru bæði gull ok silfr ef eigi er annan veg breytt.

Svá kvað Þorleifr fagri:

100 (191) Kastar gramr á glæstar
gegn valstǫðvar þegnum
ungr vísi gefr eisu
armleggs digulfarmi.

Svá kvað Einarr skálaglamm:

101 (192) Liðbrǫndum kná landa
landfrǿkn jǫfurr branda;[2]
hykka ek ræsis rekka
Rínar grjót um þrjóta.

Svá kvað Einarr Skúlason:

102 (193) Blóðeisu liggr bæði
bergs tveim megin, geima
sjóðs, á ek søkkva stríði,
snær ok eldr, at mæra.

Ok enn kvað hann:

103 (194) Dǿgr þrymr hvert, en hjarta
hlýrskildir ræðr mildum[3]
Heita blaks um hvíta
hafleygr digulskafli.
Aldri má fyrir eldi
áls hrynbrautar skála,
ǫll vinnr folka fellir
framræði, snæ bræða.

Hér er gull kallat snær skálanna.

[1] It is impossible to say who did not wake whom, but the line may relate to the episode in *Hrólfs saga* where Bǫðvarr bjarki fights in the form of a bear while his human body lies apparently asleep until awakened by Hjalti. GkS 2367 4to has *varði hann Baldr þǫgli* 'the silent Baldr defended him'.

[2] An infinitive is required after *kná* (a meaningless auxiliary, = does). The only possibility is to emend *branda* to *granda*, the reading of the other manuscripts.

[3] *mildum* must be emended to *mildu* to agree with *hjarta* and *blaks* must be read as *blakks*. Single consonants for double are common with this scribe. Cf. verse 76.

the battle-bold ruler;
Baldr did not wake him at all.

Gold is called fire of arm or joint or limb, since it is red, and silver snow, ice and frost, since it is white. In the same way gold or silver should be referred to in terms of purse or crucible, and either gold and silver may be meant by rocks of the arms and neck-ring of some person whose custom it was to wear a necklace. Rings mean both gold and silver if it is not varied in some other way.

So said Þorleifr fagri:

100   The reliable prince throws
         the crucible's load onto thanes'
         adorned falcon-perches (arms);
         the young ruler gives arm-cinders (gold).

So said Einarr skálaglamm:

101   The land-bold prince of lands
         does harm (gives away) joint-brands (gold rings);
         I do not think the ruler's men
         will run short of Rhine's rock (gold).

So said Einarr Skúlason:

102   Both purse's snow (silver) and ocean's fire (gold)
         lie on each side of the blood-ember's (axe's)
         head; I must praise
         the one that fights destroyers (vikings).

And he said further:

103   Sea-flame (gold) rests every day
         on the white crucible-snowdrift (silver),
         and he who adorns the sides of Heiti's (sea-king's) steed (ship)
         with shield rules with generous heart.
         Never can the scales-snow (silver) be melted
         before the fire (gold, fire that gives no heat)
         of the eel's surging path (sea); the feller of hosts
         achieves all glorious exploits.

Here gold is called snow of the scales.

Svá kvað Þórðr mauraskáld:

104 (195) Sér á seima rýri
sigðirs látrs at átti
hrauns glaðsendir handa
Hermóðr fǫður góðan.

61 Kendr maðrinn

Maðr er kallaðr brjótr gulls, sem kvað Óttarr:

105 (196) Góðmennis þarf ek gunnar
gullbrjótanda at njóta;
hér er almennis[1] inni
inndrótt með gram svinnum.

Svá kvað Einarr skálaglamm:

106 (197) Gullsendir lætr grundar,
glaðar þengill herdrengi,
hans mæti kná ek hljóta,
hljó⟨t⟩, Yggs mjaðar njóta.

En gullvǫrpuðr sem Þorleikr kvað:

107 (198) Hirð viðr grams með gerðum
gullvǫrpuðr sér holla.

Svá kvað Þorvaldr blǫnduskáld:

108 (199) Gullstríðir verpr glóðum,
gefr auð konungr rauðan,
óþjóðar bregðr eyðir,
armleggs, Grana farmi.

62 Kend konan til gulls

Kona er kend til gulls, kǫlluð selja gulls. Sem kvað Hallar-Steinn:

109 (201) Svalteigar mun selju
salts Viðblindi[2] galtar
rǫfkastandi rastar
reyrþvengs muna lengi.

Hér eru hvalir kallaðir Viðblindi galtar. Viðblindi var jǫtunn ok dró hvali upp í hafi sem fiska. Teigr hvala er sær, rǫf sævar er gull. Kona er selja gulls, þess er hon gefr. Selja heitir tré. | Kona er ok kend við allskyns tré kvenkend. Hon er lág kǫlluð þess er hon lógar. Lág heitir tré þat er fellt er í skógi.

[1] The other manuscripts have *alnennin*. The leaf is damaged in DG 11 4to. Grape et al. 1977 read *almennis*, which is confirmed by Jón Sigurðsson (see Grape et al. 1977: 143).

[2] Other manuscripts have *Viðblinda* (except AM 748 I b 4to: *Viðblinnis*), and the genitive is required by the context.

So said Þórðr mauraskáld:

104   Glad giver of arm-rock (gold ring),
it can be seen in the diminisher (generous giver) of gold wire
that sword-lair's (shield's) Hermóðr (the warrior)
had a good father.

61 The man referred to

Man is called breaker of gold, as Óttarr said:

105   I need the favour of the noble battle-band
which follows the gold-breaker (generous man);
in here is a domestic troop of many men
with a wise prince.

So said Einarr skálaglamm:

106   Gold-sender (an unusual kenning for the poet) lets
ground getter (king)—the prince gladdens
the men of his army; I can receive his treasure—
enjoy Yggr's (Óðinn's) mead (poetry).

And gold-thrower, as Þorleikr said:

107   With a prince's deeds the gold-thrower (generous man)
makes his court loyal to himself.

So said Þorvaldr blǫnduskáld:

108   Gold-harmer (generous man) throws arms'
embers (gold rings), the king gives red wealth (gold),
destroyer of evil people
shifts Grani's load (gives away gold).

62 Woman referred to in terms of gold

Woman is referred to in terms of gold, called dealer of gold. As Hallar-Steinn said:

109   The thrower of the amber (gold)
of Víðblindi's boar's (whale's) salty cool land (sea)
will long remember the giver
of reed-thong's (serpent's) league (land, i.e. gold).

Here whales are called Víðblindi's boars. Víðblindi was a giant and drew whales up from in the sea like fish. The land of whales is sea, amber of the sea is gold. Woman is dealer (*selja*) of the gold that she gives. *Selja* (willow) is the name of a tree. Woman is also referred to by all kinds of feminine trees. She is called log (*lág*) of what she gives away (*lógar*). Log is a word for a tree that is felled in a wood.

Svá kvað Gunnlaugr ormstunga:

110 (202) Alin var rýgr at rógi,
runnr olli því gunnarr,[1]
lág var ek auðs at eiga
óðgjarn, fira bǫrnum.

Kona er kend mǫrk. Svá kvað Hallar-Steinn:

111 (203) Ek hefi óðar lokri
ǫlstafna þér skafna
væn mǫrk skála verki
vandr stefknarrar branda.

Ok enn sem hann kvað:

112 (204) Þú munt fús sem fleiri,
fljóðs hirði-Bil, tróður
grǫn⟨n⟩ er[2] gæfu þinni
grjóts Hjaðninga brjótask.

Svá kvað Ormr Steinþórsson:

113 (205) Skorða var í fǫt førð
fjarðbeins afar hrein
nýrri, sǫng nadd-Freyr
nisting, um mjaðar Hrist.

Sem hann kvað enn:

114 (207) Því at hjóls hrynbáls
hramma þat ek ber fram
Billings á burar full
bjarkar hefi ek lagit mark.

115 (208) Aura stendr fyrir órum
eik fǫgrbúin leiki.[3]

Svá sem hér segir:

116 (209) Ǫng, rekkr, skala okkr
álmr dynskúrar málma,
svá bauð lind í landi
líns, hugrekki dvína.

Maðr er kendr til viða, sem fyrr er ritat, kallaðr reynir vápna eða víga, ferða ok athafnar, skipa ok alls þess er hann ræðr eða reynir.

[1] The final consonant is in a hole in the manuscript, but seems to be R. Other manuscripts have *gunnar* and AM 157 8vo appears to have 'gunn*ar*', which must be correct.

[2] The context requires *við*, as in other manuscripts.

[3] There is no indication in DG 11 4to that this is a separate item from the preceding other than a rather large initial A, but the verse form is quite different and the break is clearly marked in the Codex Regius version.

So said Gunnlaugr ormstunga:

110 The lady was born to bring strife
among the sons of men; the battle-bush (warrior, her father)
was the cause of this; I was frantically eager
to possess the wealth-log (lady).

Woman is called forest. So said Hallar-Steinn:

111 Fair forest of hall of ale-vessels,
I, careful in my craftsmanship, have
smoothed for you with poetry's plane
the prow (beginning) of a refrain-ship (poem).

And as he said further:[1]

112 You will, like other poles (women)
of Hjaðnings' rocks (gold ornaments) eagerly strive
against your good fortune, slender Bil (goddess,)
who looks after a woman (i.e. young girl, servant?).

So said Ormr Steinþórsson:

113 Fiord-bone's (rock's, precious stone's) prop (the woman)
was put into exceedingly pure clothes
with new sewing; spear-Freyr (the warrior, poet)
sang over the Hrist (valkyrie, i.e. woman) of mead.

As he said further:

114 For in the Billingr's (dwarf's or giant's) son's drink (poem)
that I am performing, I have fixed the likeness
of the birch (valkyrie, warlike woman) of the paws
(arms) of the wheel's (shield's) clanging fire (sword).

115 The fairly-adorned coin-oak (woman)
stands in the way of our pleasure.

As it says here:

116 So did linen-linden (woman) instruct:
warrior, no courage shall diminish
in us in the land, elm (warrior)
of clashing weapon-shower (battle).

Man is referred to in terms of trees, as was written above, called rowan (*reynir*) of weapons or battles, of expeditions and activity, of ships and of everything he has in his power or puts to the test (*reynir*).

[1] The Codex Regius version has a differing text which uses quite different kennings. See Faulkes 1998: 63.

Svá kvað Úlfr Uggason:

117 (210) En stirðmálugr starði
storðar leggs fyrir borði
fróns á fólka reyna
fránleitr ok blés eitri.

Viðr ok meiðr sem kvað Kormakr:

118 (211) Meiðr er mǫrgum øðri
morðreins í dyn fleina;
hjǫrr fær hildibǫrrum
hjarl Sigurði jarli.

Lundr, sem kvað Hallfreðr vendræðaskáld:

119 (212) Álþollum stendr Ullar
austr at miklu trausti
røkilundr hinn ríki
randfárs brynjaðr[1] harri.

Þollr ok búss, sem Arnórr kvað:

120 (213) Rekr ǫndurt vár randir
reggbúss saman leggja,
rógskýja hélt Rýgjar
regni haustnótt gegnum.

Askr, sem kvað Refr:

121 (214) Gakk í gulli stokkna
gjǫfrífr Hás drífu
askr við ørinn þroska
eggþeys sæing meyjar.

Hlynr, sem hér segir:

122 (215) "Heill[2] kom þú!" – handar svella
hlynr kvaddi svá brynju.

Bǫrr, sem Refr kvað:

123 (216) Alls bǫðgeði bjóða
bǫrr hygg til þess hjǫrva;
ǫngstǫðvar hefi ek eigi
ein ráðin Þorsteini.

[1] DG 11 4to is damaged. Grape et al. 1977: 23 followed Jón Sigurðsson, reading 'brymaþr' (i.e. *brumaðr* 'budded'), but AM 157 8vo and Jón Rúgmann make it clear that 'bryniaþr' is the original reading.
[2] If the warrior is greeting the coat of mail, it ought to be *heil* (feminine). The Codex Regius and Codex Wormianus have *brynja* as the subject.

So said Úlfr Uggason:

117   But the harsh-speaking one (the serpent) stared
with piercing look over the gunwale
at the testers (Þórr and Eymir) of the people (giants) of the region
of lands' bones (rocks) and blew poison.

Tree and pole, as Kormakr said:

118   Pole (warrior) of battle-reindeer (warship)
is superior to many in spear-din (battle);
the sword wins land
for the battle-keen Earl Sigurðr.

Grove, as Hallfreðr vendræðaskáld said:

119   The grove (warrior) that cultivates Ullr (a warrior god),
the powerful mail-coated lord (warrior)
of shield-danger (battle), provides channel-trees (seafarers)
with great support in the east.

Tree and box, as Arnórr said:

120   Early in the spring the ship-box (seafarer, warrior)
forces shields to be brought together (fights a battle);
through the autumn night continued
Rýgr's (giantess's) rain (battle) of strife-clouds (shields).

Ash, as Refr said:

121   Gift-ready (generous) Hár's (Óðinn's) storm (battle)
ash (warrior), go with plenty of
manly deeds of edge-wind (battle)
into the maiden's gold-adorned bed.[1]

Maple, as it says here:

122   'Hello!' — thus maple (warrior) of arm-ice (sword)
greeted the coat of mail.

Spruce, as Refr said:

123   Sword-table (shield) maple (warrior),
regard all this with warlike mind;
I have not any advice for Þorsteinn
for these straits.

---

[1] The context is unknown, but if the 'maiden' is symbolic: she may represent Hildr (the valkyrie) or Hel, and her bed battle or death.

Stafr, sem kvað Óttarr svarti:

124 (217) Helztu þar er hrafn ne svelta,[1]
 hvatráðr ertu, láði,
 ógnar stafr fyrir jǫfrum
 ýgr tveim við kyn beima.

Þorn, sem kvað Arnórr.

125 (218) Hlóð, en hála týðu
 hirðmenn ara grenni,[2]
 auðar þorn fyrir ǫrnu
 ungr valkǫstu þunga.

63 Kend orrostan

Hvernveg skal kenna orrostu?
 Svá at kalla veðr vápna eða hlífa eða Óðins eða vápna eða valkyrju eða herkonunga eða gný eða glym. Svá kvað Hornklofi:

126 (219) Háði gramr þar er gnúði[3]
 geira hregg við seggi,
 rauð fnýstu ben blóði,
 bengǫgl at dyn Skǫglar.

Svá kvað Eyvindr:

127 (220) Ok sá hallr
 at Hás veðri
 hǫsvan serk
 Hrungnis bar.

Svá kvað Bragi:

128 (221) Þótta ek þá er ótta[4]
 ár, sagt er þat, várum,
 hǿfr at Hlakkar drífu,
 hyrrunnar vel Gunnar.

Svá kvað Einarr:

129 (222) Glymvindi setr Gǫndlar,
 gnestr hjǫrtaka, mestum
 Hildar segl þar er hagli,
 hraustr þengill, drífr strengjar.

Svá kvað Einarr skálaglamm:

---

[1] The context requires *svalta* as in Codex Regius and Codex Trajectinus.
[2] *æ* is written here for *e*.
[3] The context requires *gnúðu* as in other manuscripts.
[4] This word makes no sense. Other manuscripts have various spellings of *ǿri* 'younger'

Stave, as Óttarr the Black said:

124   Where the raven was not short of food
      you held onto territory, fierce battle-stave
      in the face of two princes;
      you are quick to act against mankind.

Thorn, as Arnórr said:

125   Young wealth-thorn (man) piled up
      heavy heaps of slain men
      for the eagles, and his men supported
      the feeder of eagles greatly.

63 Battle referred to

How shall battle be referred to?

By calling it weather of weapons or shields or of Óðinn or weapons or valkyrie or war-kings or [their] clash or noise. So said Hornklofi:

126   The prince waged storm of spears (battle)
      against men where wound-goslings (arrows)
      thundered in Skǫgul's din;
      red wounds spewed blood.

So said Eyvindr:

127   And this man, partial to Hár's (Óðinn's) weather (battle)
      wore Hrungnir's grey shirt (mail-coat).

So said Bragi:

128   Once upon a time I seemed well suited to
      Hlǫkk's (valkyrie's) snowstorm (battle),
      so it is said, when we were younger
      bushes (warriors) of Gunnr's (valkyrie's) fire (sword).

So said Einarr:

129   The bold monarch sets up Hildr's (valkyrie's) sail (his shield)
      in the greatest Gǫndul's (valkyrie's) noisy wind (storm of battle)
      where hail from strings (arrows) drives;
      there is clashing from drawing of swords.

So said Einarr skálaglamm:

130 (223) Ne sigbjarka serkir
         sómniðjungum rómu
         Hás við Hǫgna skúrir
         hleiðut¹ fast um reiðir.²

Sem hér segir:

131 (224) Odda gnýs við éli
         oddnets þinul setja.

Ok enn þetta:

132 (225) Hnigu fjándr at glym Gǫndlar
         grams und arnar hramma.

64 Kend vápnin

Vápn ok herklæði skal kenna til orrostu ok til Óðins ok valmeyja ok herkonunga, kenna hjálm hǫtt þeira eða fald, en brynju serk eða skyrtu, en skjǫld tjald. En skjaldborg er kǫlluð hǫll eða ræfr, veg⟨g⟩r³ eða gólf. Skildir eru kallaðir, ok kendir við herskip, sól eða tungl eða lauf eða blik eða garðr skipsins. Skjǫldr er kallaðr skip Ullar eða fótr Hrungnis, er hann stóð á skildinum. Á fornum skjǫldum var títt at skrifa rǫnd þá er kǫlluð er baugr, ok við þann baug eru skildir kendir. Hǫggvápn, sverð eða exar, eru kǫlluð el⟨d⟩ar blóðs eða benja. Sverð heita Óðins eldar, en geir kalla menn trǫllkvenna heitum ok kenna við blóð eða benjar, skóg eða eik. En lagvápn eru vel kend til orma eða fiska. Skotvápn eru mjǫk kend til hagls eða drífu eða rotu. Ǫllum þessum heitum eða kenningum er marga vega breytt, því at þat er flest ort í lofkvæðum er þessar kenningar þarf við.

133 (226) Lattit herr með hǫttu
         Hangatýs at ganga;
         þóttit⁴ þeim at hætta
         þekkiligt | fyrir brekku.

Svá kvað Einarr skálaglamm:

134 (227) Hjálmfaldinn bauð hildi
         hjaldrǫrr ok Sigvaldi,
         hinn er fór í gný Gunnar
         gunndjarfr Búi sunnan.

Róða serkr sem Tindr kvað:

¹ I.e. *hléðut*.
² It is difficult to make sense of this verse without emendation. Cf. Faulkes 1998: 194; *sómmiðjungar* 'bow-giants' would make a comprehensible kenning for warriors.
³ AM 157 8vo has *veggur*.
⁴ Written 'þot*r*iþ'. Cf. verse 3, where it reads *þótti*.

130   Battle-birches' (warriors') shirts (coats of mail)
       did not firmly protect the honour-descendants
       (noble warriors?) in Hár's (Óðinn's) tumult (battle)
       from Họgni's showers (rain of weapons) over the ships.

As it says here:

131   Set edge-rope (rim) of point-net (net which catches sharp missiles,
       shield) against storm of clash of points (crashing of sharp missiles).

And also this:

132   The prince's enemies sank beneath eagle's claws
       in Gọndul's din (battle).

64 The weapons referred to

Weapons and armour shall be referred to in terms of battle and Óðinn and death-maidens (valkyries) and war-kings, helmet referred to as their hood or cap, and mail-coat as shirt or tunic, and shield as curtain. And shield-wall is called hall or roof, wall or floor. Shields are spoken of and referred to in terms of warships, as sun or moon or leaf or gleam or fence of the ship. A shield is called Ullr's ship or Hrungnir's foot, since he stood on his shield. On ancient shields it was customary to decorate the border that is called the circle, and shields are referred to in terms of this circle. Cutting weapons, swords or axes, are called fires of blood or wounds. Swords are called Óðinn's fires, and people call a spear by names of trollwives and refer to them in terms of blood or wounds or forest or oak. And thrusting weapons it is fine to refer to as snakes or fish. Missiles are frequently referred to as hail or snowfall or rainstorm. All these names or kennings are varied in many ways, for most compositions are in the form of praise poetry, where those kennings are particularly required.

133   The army did not hold back from advancing
       with Hangatýr's (Óðinn's) hoods (helmets);
       they thought it not pleasant
       to venture down the slopes.

So said Einarr skálaglamm:

134   Helm-capped battle-bold Búi,
       who went from the south
       to Gunnr's (valkyrie's) din (battle)
       and war-keen Sigvaldi offered battle.

Róði's shirt, as Tindr said:

135 (228) Þá er hring- fáinn Hanga
hrynserk við ǫrr -brynju
hruðumst hríðmara Róðar[1]
rastar varð at kasta.

Hamðis skyrta, sem Hallfreðr kvað:

136 (229) Ólítinn brestr úti
undfúrs sú ... juls runnum
hart á Hamðis skyrtur
hryn-Gjálp Egils vápna.

Sǫrla fǫt, sem hann kvað enn:

137 (230) Þaðan verða fǫt fyrða,
fregn ek gjǫrla þat, Sǫrla,
rjóðast bjǫrt í blóði
benfúr méils skúrum.

Sem Grettir kvað:

138 (231) Héldu Hlakkar tjalda
hefjendr saman nefjum,
Hildar veggs ok hjuggust
hregg-Nirðir til s⟨k⟩eggjum.[2]

Róða ræfr, sem Einarr kvað:[3]

139 (232) Eigi þverr fyrir augna
Óðs beðvinu Róða
ræfr⟨s⟩ eignist sá, regni
ramsvel⟨l⟩, konungr elli.

Hildar veggr, sem Grettir kvað ok áðr er ritat.

Skips sól, sem Einarr kvað:

140 (233) Leygr rýðr ætt á ægi
Óláfs skipa sólar,
ylgr brunar hvatt, ins helga,
hrægjǫrn í spor ǫrnum.

Hlýrtungl, sem hér segir:

141 (234) Dagr var fríðr sá er fǫgrum
fleygjendr alimleygjar

[1] Presumably an error for *Róða* (so other manuscripts), though the kenning *Róða serkr* does not appear in this or any other skaldic verse. See Faulkes 1998: 195. The alliteration in this line would be correct if we read *riðmara* 'tossing steeds' (so other manuscripts).
[2] DG 11 4to has *seggjum* 'men', but most manuscripts have *skeggjum*.
[3] The same verse is quoted as no 90.

135 When we cleared our storm-steeds (ships) of Róði's (sea-king's)
league (the sea), the liberal one,
shining in Hangi's (Óðinn's) ringing shirt (mail-coat),
had to throw off his ring-mail coat.

Hamðir's tunic, as Hallfreðr said:

136 No small clashing Gjálp (giantess, damaging storm)
of Egill's weapons (arrows) crashes hard
on the outside of Hamðir's tunics (mail-coats)
of *su* . . . *juls* wound-fire (sword) bushes (warriors).

Sǫrli's clothes, as he also said:

137 As a result, Sǫrli's bright clothes (mail-coats)
— I learn precisely of this — must be
reddened with men's blood
by wound-fire (swords) in weapon-showers (battle).

As Grettir said:

138 The raisers (warriors) of Hlǫkk's (valkyrie's) curtains (shields)
held their noses together,
and Hildr's (valkyrie's) wall's (shield's) storm- (battle-)
Njǫrðrs (warriors) jabbed beards together (held a conference).

Róði's roof, as Einarr said:

139 Róði's (sea-king's) strong roof-ice (shield-wall ice, = axe)
is not the worse for the eye-rain (tears, i.e. gold)
of Óðr's bedfellow (Freyja);
may this king reach old age.

Hildr's wall, as Grettir said and was quoted above.
  Ship's sun, as Einarr said:

140 St Óláfr's kin reddens flame (sword)
of ship's sun (shield) at sea;
corpse-greedy she-wolf rushes
forward fast on the tracks of eagles (to find carrion after a battle).

Bows-moon, as it says here:

141 That was a fine day when flingers away (generous givers)
of forearm-flame (gold rings) pressed

á hranferil hringa
hlýrtungli mér þrungðu.[1]

Garðr skips, sem hér segir:

142 (235) Svá fór gegn í gǫgnum
garð steinfarinn barða,
sá var, gunnstǿrir geira
gunnar hǿfr, sem næfrar.[2]

Askr Ullar,[3] sem Þjóðólfr kvað:

143 (236) Ganga él um yngva
Ullar skips með fullu,
þar er samnaglar siglur
slíðrdúkanðar[4] ríða.

Ilja blað Hrungnis, sem kvað Bragi:

144 (237) Vilið Hrafnketill heyra
hvé hreingróit steini
Þrúðar skal ek þengils
þjófs iljablað leyfa?

Bragi skáld kvað þetta um bauginn á skildinum:

145 (238) Nema svá at góð ens gegna
gjǫld baugnafrs[5] vildi
meyjar hjóls, en ek merkða
mǫg Sigrúnar, Hǫgna.

Hann kallaði skjǫldinn Hildar hjól en bauginn nǫf hjólsins.

Baugjǫrð, sem Hallfreðr[6] kvað:

146 (239) Rauðljósa sér ræsir
– rítr[7] brestr sundr in hvíta –

[1] In the Codex Regius version attributed to Refr. Line 2 *alim-* is *alm-* in GkS 2367 4to, but Codex Wormianus and Codex Trajectinus have *alin-* which is obviously correct. Damage to DG 11 4to, f. 34r, makes line 3 difficult to decipher. Grape et. al. 1977 read *hrannferil* but Lasse Mårtensson 2010 reads *hran-*. This probably needs to be read *hryn-*, and *fǫgrum* in line 1 *fǫgru*, in order to make sense.

[2] Damage to f. 34 makes the verse difficult to decipher and interpret. Here the gaps in the text are filled in accordance with Grape et al. 1977: 154, which is based largely on Jón Rugman and supported partly by AM 157 8vo, though there the kenning *garðr barða* is unaccountably replaced by *grand branda*.

[3] Gaps in the text are filled in accordance with Grape et al. 1977: 65 and are fully supported by AM 157 8vo.

[4] Obviously an error for *slíðrdúkaðar*; *samnaglar* must be emended to *samnagla*.

[5] Must be read *-nafaðs* to accord with the prose.

[6] *Hallvarðr* in other manuscripts. Cf. verse 70 above.

[7] *Rítr* is plural. It ought to be singular (*rít*).

a fair bows-moon (shield) on my
ringing ring-track (arm).

Skip's fence, as it says here:

142   The reliable increaser (warrior) of battle of spears
went through the paint-covered
vessel's fence (shield) as through bark;
this man was fit for battle.

Ullr's ash(-ship), as Þjóðólfr said:

143   Storms (fighting) of Ullr's ship (shield)
rage totally round the prince
where the rivet-masts (swords)
sheath-clothed (having sheaths for sails) wave.

Hrungnir's sole-blade, as Bragi said:

144   Will you hear, Hrafnketill, how I shall praise
the prince's sole-blade (shield)
of the thief of Þrúðr (Hrungnir)[1]
which has fine colour growing on it?

Bragi the Poet composed this about the circle on the shield:

145   Unless it be that one desired good recompense
for the reliable circle-hubbed (that has a circle for its hub) wheel
(shield) of Hǫgni's maid (Hildr, which is also the name
of a valkyrie and a word for battle), but I noted Sigrún's son.

He called the shield Hildr's wheel and the circle the hub of the wheel.
Land of the circle, as Hallfreðr said:

146   The impeller (warrior) of the movement (flight)
of points (arrows or spears) sees red-bright (golden)

---

[1] The story of Hrungnir's theft of Þrúðr has not been preserved.

baugjǫrð brodda ferðar
– bjúgleit – í tvau fljúga.

Sverð er Óðins eldr, sem Kormakr kvað:

147 (241) Svall, sá er gekk með gjallan
Gauts eld með styr | belldi
glaðbræðanda Gríðar,
gunnr. Komst Ruðr ór brunni.[1]

Hjálms eldr, sem kvað Úlfr Uggason:

148 (242) Fullǫflugr[2] lét falla
fram hafsleipni hramma
Hildr en H⟨r⟩opts um gildar
hjálms eld⟨s⟩ þá er mar felldu.

Brynju eldr, sem kvað Glúmr Geirason:

149 (243) Heimþyntan[3] let hvína
hryneldr at þeim brynju
foldar vǫrðr sá er fyrðum
fjǫrnharðan sik varði.

Randar íss[4] ok grand hlífa, sem Arnórr[5] kvað:

150 (244) Ráðvǫndum þá ek rauðar
randar ís at vísa—
grand berið hjálms í hendi—
hramþey[6] drifinn meyju.

Øx heitir ok trǫllkona hlíf⟨a⟩[7], sem kvað Einarr:

151 (245) Sjá megu rétt hvé Ræfils
ríðendr við brá Gríðar
fjǫrnis fagrt um skornir
foldviggs drekar liggia.

Spjót er kallaðr ormr, sem Refr kvað:

152 (246) Kná myrkdreki markaðr
minn þar er ýtar finna

[1] The verse form shows that this verse is from *Sigurðardrápa*. Ruðr (confirmed by AM 157 4to) is Urðr or Uðr in other manuscripts. Cf. p. 30 above.
[2] Must be emended to *Fullǫflug* (feminine with Hildr).
[3] Obviously an error for *Hein*-; hryneldr in line 2 is for hryneld.
[4] The manuscript has *ís*. Single consonant for double is common in DG 11 4to.
[5] In the other manuscripts attributed to Einarr (Skúlason).
[6] Other manuscripts have *hvarm*-, which must be correct.
[7] DG 11 4to is damaged, but may have had *trǫllkonu hlíf* 'protector of trollwife', though the kenning must be *trǫllkona hlífa* 'trollwife, i.e. damager of shields, as in other manuscripts.

circle-land (shield) fly in two;
the white curved-looking shield breaks apart.

A sword is Óðinn's fire, as Kormakr said:

147 Battle raged. He who advanced with ringing
Gautr's (Óðinn's) fire (sword) waged
war with the feeder (warrior) of Gríðr's (giantess's)
steed (wolf). Ruðr rose from the spring.

Helmet's fire, as Úlfr Uggason said:

148 The most powerful Hildr of bear's paws (giantess) made the
sea-Sleipnir (horse of the sea, ship) go down (to the sea),
but Hroptr's (Óðinn's) ones (warriors, berserks) who make
good use of helmet's fire (sword), when they felled the horse . . .[1]

Mail-coat's fire, as Glúmr Geirason said:

149 The land's defender (king), who defended
himself against men mighty strongly,
made the hone-scraped ringing fire
of the mail-coat swish at them.

Shield's ice and damager of protective armour, as Arnórr said:

150 I received red shield's ice, covered with
maiden's (Freyja's) eyelid-thaw (tears, i.e. gold)
from the ruler careful of his actions;
carry helmet's damager (sword) in your hands.

An axe is also called trollwife of protective armour, as Einarr said:

151 Riders (seafarers) of Ræfill's (sea-king's) land's (the sea's)
horses (ships) can see how beautifully engraved
dragons lie just by the brow (curved edge)
of the Gríðr (giantess, i.e. axe) of the life-protector (armour).

A spear is called snake, as Refr said:

152 My fierce engraved dark
dragon of the shield (spear)

---

[1] The sentence would presumably have been completed in the second half-verse.

øfr á aldar [lófum
eikinn b]orðs á leika.¹

Ǫrvar eru kallaðar hagl boga eða strengjar eða hlífa eða orrostu, sem Einarr kvað:

153 (247) Brak-Rǫgna skóg bogna,
barg óþyrmir varga,
hagl ór Hlakkar seglum
hjǫrs, rakliga fjǫrvi.²

Orrosta er kǫlluð Hjaðninga veðr eða él, en vápn Hjaðninga eldr eða vendir. Orrosta er veðr Óðins, sem fyrr er ritat. Svá kvað Víga-Glúmr:

154 (255) Rudda ek sem jarðar,
orð lék á því forðum,
með veðrstǫfum Viðris
vandar, mér til handa.³

Viðris veðr er orrosta en vǫndr vígs sverðit, en menn stafir sverðsins. Hér er bæði vápn ok orrosta kent ok haft til kenningar mannsins, ok er þat rekit kallat er svá er ort. Skjǫldr er land vápnanna en vápn eru hagl eða regn þess lands ef nýgervingar er ort.

65 Frá kenningu skips

Hvernig skal kenna skip?

Svá at kalla hest eða dýr sækonunga eða sævar eða skipreiða eða byrjar.

Báru fákr sem Hornklofi kvað:

155 (256) Hrjóðr lét hæstrar tíðar
harðr skipa bǫrðum
báru fáks ins bleika
barnungr á lǫg þrungit.

Geitis marr, sem kvað Erringar-Steinn:

156 (257) Enn þó at ófrið sunnan
ǫll þjóð segi skáldi,
hlǫðum Geitis mar grjóti,
glaðir nennum vér þenna.

---

¹ The leaf in DG 11 4to is damaged, and the letters in square brackets are supplied from other manuscripts. The last two lines in AM 157 8vo read 'øfur á alldar lofum eiki borðs á leiki.' The á in the last line must be an error for at (so in other manuscripts).

² Rakliga: single k for double; skóg (also in Codex Wormianus) is obviously an error for skók (thus AM 157 8vo, Codex Trajectinus and AM 748 I b 4to) and Rǫgna for Rǫgnir.

³ The manuscript is damaged, but readings can be corrected from the prose that follows. This shows that the first word in line 4 should be vandar 'of the rod', as in all other medieval manuscripts of Snorra Edda that include the verse, though DG 11 4to is illegible and AM 157 8vo has Vandils, like Egils saga. All medieval manuscripts have jarlar in line 1 except DG 11 4to ('-rþar'; AM 157 8vo has jarðar). Codex Wormianus and AM 748 I b 4to have landa in line 4. See Heimir Pálsson 2010d and Faulkes 1998: 198.

can play savagely in men's hands
where men meet (in battle).

Arrows are called hail of bow or string or defensive armour or battle, as Einarr said:

153 Sword-crash Rǫgnir (warrior) shook bows'
hail (arrows) from Hlǫkk's sails (shields);
the one who does not spare wolves (criminals)
saved his life bravely.

Battle is called the Hjaðnings' weather or storm, and weapons the Hjaðnings' fire or rods. Battle is Óðinn's weather, as was written above. So said Víga-Glúmr:

154 I cleared space for myself as for territory—
I had a reputation for that once—
with staves (warriors) of the rod
of Viðrir's (Óðinn's) weather (battle).

Viðrir's weather is battle and rod of battle is the sword, and men staves of the sword. Here both weapons and battle are referred to by kennings and used in a kenning for the man, and this is called *rekit* (extended) when one composes thus. A shield is land of the weapons and weapons are hail or rain of that land if one composes allegorically (using *nýgervingar*).

65 Of referring to a ship

How shall a ship be referred to?

By calling it horse or wild animal of sea-kings or of the sea or ship's tackle or of a fair wind. Wave's steed as Hornklofi said:

155 The harsh clearer (attacker) of wave's pale steed (ship),
a child in age, caused ships' bows
to be impelled on the sea
at the most auspicious time.

Geitir's horse, as Erringar-Steinn said:

156 Even though all people tell the poet
of this war in the south,—
let us load Geitir's (sea-king's) horse (ship) with stones—
gladly we undertake this.

Hér er kallaðr sunddýr.[1]

157 (259) Sveigja lét fyrir Sygju
  sólborðs goti norðan,
  gustr skaut Gylfa rastar
  Glaumi suðr, Raumi.
  En slóðgoti síðan
  sæðin⟨g⟩s fyrir skut bæði ...[2]

Hér er skip kallat sólborðs hestr en sær Gylfa land, sæðin⟨g⟩s slóð særinn ok hestr skipit ok enn lauks hestr. Laukr heitir siglutréit.

Svá kvað Markús:

158 (260) Bjǫrn gekk fram á fornar
  flóðs hafskipa slóðir,
  skrúðǫrðigr braut skorðu
  skers gunnfjǫturr bersi.[3]

Hér er skipit kallat rasta bjǫrn ok bersi ok bjǫrn skorðu. Skipit er kallat hreinn. Svá kvað Hallvarðr sem áðr er ritat,[4] ok hjǫrtr, sem kvað Haraldr konungr:

159 (261) Sneið fyrir Sikiley víða
  súð; várum þá prúðir,
  brýnt[5] skreið vel til vánar
  vengis hjǫrtr und drengjum.

Eldr,[6] sem Einarr kvað:

160 (262) Baugs getr með þér þeygi
  þýðr drengr vera lengi —
  elg búum flóðs — nema fylgi,
  friðstøkkvir, þér nokkut.

Sem Máni kvað:

---

[1] *Kallaðr* ought to be neuter. The verse illustrating this kenning is omitted, perhaps because this was the end of a gathering.

[2] Here two lines are omitted (*—hestr óð lauks fyrir Lista—* | *lagði Kǫrmt ok Agðir*) in which the kenning *lauks hestr* was illustrated. See Faulkes 1998: 75. *Siggju* for *Sygju* in line 1 and *fyrir Aumar* for *Raumi* in line 4 would make this verse correspond better to the geography of Norway. *Sveggja* for *Sveigja* 'bend' in line 1 gives a verb more applicable to a ship's movements. These readings are all in the Codex Regius version.

[3] The first half of this stanza, in which the kennings *veturliði rastar, rasta bjǫrn* are illustrated, are omitted (see Faulkes 1998: 75). *-fjǫturr*: double consonant for single.

[4] This is a reference to the verse of Hallvarðr that has been omitted (no 258 in the Codex Regius version; see note 1 above). But cf. *morðreinn* in verse 118.

[5] Written 'brvnt'; *v* for *y/ý* is quite common in manuscripts.

[6] Error for *elgr* 'elk'. An attempt to correct it has been made by a later hand (see Grape et al. 1977: 158). AM 157 8vo has *eldur* 'fire'.

Here it is called straits-animal.

157   The gunwale's horse (ship) went tossing
        from the north past Sigg;
        a gust shot the steed (ship) of
        Gylfi's (sea-king's) league (sea) south by Aumar.
        And afterwards the horse (ship) of the gull's
        track (sea) [put] both [Kǫrmt
        and Agðir] past the stern;
        [the leek-horse waded past Listi.]

Here a ship is called gunwale's horse and the sea Gylfi's land, the sea the gull's track and the ship its horse, and also leek-horse. Leek is a word for mast-tree.

So said Markús:

158   The flood's bear (ship) went forward
        on the old ocean-ships' tracks;
        the stocks-grizzly (ship) with its proudly raised ornaments
        broke the skerry's war-fetter (surrounding breakers).

Here the ship is called bear of currents and grizzly and stocks-bear. A ship is called reindeer. So said Hallvarðr as is written above, and hart, as King Haraldr said:

159   The hull cut past broad Sicily;
        we were splendid then;
        the poop-hart (ship) glided swiftly beneath men
        quite in accordance with expectations.

Elk, as Einarr said:

160   A man cannot stay long with you,
        kind driver away of the ring's peace (generous man),
        unless something goes with you.
        Let us get the flood-elk (ship) ready.

As Máni said:

161 (263) Hvat muntu hafs á akri¹
hengiligr meðr drengjum
karl, því at kraptr þinn fǫrlast,
kinngrár, mega vinna.

Vargr, sem Refr kvað:
162 (264) En hoddvargr hlýddi
hlunnvitnis skal ek runni
hollr til hermðarspialla,
heimvandil⟨s⟩² Þorsteini.

Ok oxa³ er skip kallat ok skíð eða vagn eða reið. Svá kvað Eyvindr:⁴
163 (265) Meita fór at móti
mjǫk síð um dag skíði
ungr með jǫfnu gengi
út ver formum hersis.

Svá kvað Styrkárr Oddason:
164 (266) Ok eptir ítrum støkkvi
ók Hǫgna lið vǫgnum
hlun⟨n⟩s á Heita fannir
hyrjar flóðs af móði.

Ok sem Þorbjǫrn kvað:
165 (267) Hafræðar⁵ var hlǿðir
hlun⟨n⟩s í skírnarbrunni
Hvíta-Kristr⁶ sá er hæsta
hoddsviptir fekk giptu.

66 Hversu kenna skal Krist

Hversu skal kenna Krist?

Svá at kalla hann skapara himins ok jarðar, engla ok sólar, stýranda himinríkis ok engla, konung himna, sólar ok Jórsala ok Jórdánar ok Grikklands, ráðanda postula ok heilagra manna. Forn skáld hafa kent hann við Urðarbrunn ok Róm. Svá kvað Eilífr Guðrúnarson:

[1] Most manuscripts of *Snorra Edda* and both of the third grammatical treatise have *otri* 'otter', which is obviously correct. *Hafs akr* 'sea's field' is not a possible kenning for 'ship' and o can easily be read as a, and t as c in early manuscripts.

[2] *Heimvandill* is not a possible kenning for sword, and the other manuscripts have *hein-*. This word is also unusual, but is parallelled by the name of the sword Dragvandill in *Egils saga*. The genitive ending -s is, however, still required.

[3] This ought to be nominative *oxi*. The sentence is perhaps altered from a source that read 'skip kǫllum vér ok oxa'. The word is not in the other manuscripts, nor is *oxi* found in skaldic verse in a kenning for ship.

[4] *Eyjólfr dáðaskáld* in the other manuscripts.

[5] Should be *-reiðar*, as in the other manuscripts

[6] Should be genitive *Krists*, as in AM 157 8vo.

161   What will you, slouching, grey-cheeked
         old man, be able to achieve with the fellows
         on the otter of the sea (ship)?
         For your strength is fading.

Wolf, as Refr said:

162   But the hoard-wolf (enemy, i.e. generous man) was obedient
         to Þorsteinn. I shall stand by
         the bush (seafarer) of the slipway-wolf (ship)
         in the hone-rod's (sword's) angry conference (battle).

And a ship is also called ox and ski or waggon or carriage. So said Eyvindr:

163   Young, he went out across the sea in the guise of a lord
         to a meeting (battle) very late in the day
         on a Meiti's (sea-king's) ski (ship)
         with a following of the same size.

So said Styrkárr Oddason:

164   And Hǫgni's troop drove slipway-waggons (ships)
         over Heiti's (sea-king's) snowdrifts (waves)
         in fury after the splendid
         flood-fire (gold) scatterer (generous man).

And as Þorbjǫrn said:

165   The loader of the slipway's sea-carriage
         was in the baptismal pool,
         the hoard-robber (generous man) who received
         White-Christ's highest grace.

66 How Christ shall be referred to

How shall Christ be referred to?

By calling him creator of heaven and earth, of angels and the sun, ruler of the kingdom of heaven and angels, king of the heavens, the sun and Jerusalem and Jordan and Greece, master of apostles and saints. Early poets have referred to him in terms of Urðarbrunnr and Rome. So said Eilífr Guðrúnarson:

166 (268) Setbergs, kveða sitja
suðr¹ at Urðarbrunni,
svá hefir rammr konungr remðan
Róms banda sik lǫndum.

Svá kvað Skapti Þóroddsson:

167 (269) Máttr er munka | dróttinns
mestr; aflar guð flestu.
Kristr skóp ríkr ok reisti
Róms hǫll, verǫld alla.

Himna konungr, sem Markús kvað:

168 (270) Gramr skóp grund ok himna
glyggran⟨n⟩s sem her dyggvan.
Einn stillir má ǫllu
aldar, Kristr, um valda.

Svá kvað Eilífr:

169 (271) Hrócs lýtr halgum cruce²
heims ferð ok lið beima.
Sǫnn er en ǫll dýrð ǫnnur
einn sólkonungr hreinni.

Maríuson, sem Eilífr kvað:

170 (272) Hirð lýtr himna dýrðar
hrein Maríu sveini;
mátt³ verr mildingr dróttar,
maðr er hann ok guð, sannan.

Engla konungr, sem Eilífr kvað:

171 (273) Minni er en menn um hyggi
mætr guð vinum betri;
þó er engla gramr ǫllu
ǫrr, helgari ok dýrri.

Jórdánar konungr, sem kvað Sighvatr:

172 (274) Endr réð engla senda
Jórdánar gramr fjóra,
fors þó hans um hersis
heilagt skop⟨t⟩, ór lopti.

---

[1] To provide *aðalhending* in this line, the form *sunnr* would need to be substituted.

[2] The *-c-* in *Hrócs* and *cruce* would presumably have been pronounced ts. GkS 2367 4to has *z* in both words. The scribe of DG 11 4to generally only uses c for k when it must have stood in his exemplar.

[3] *Verja* in this sense normally takes the dative. The Codex Regius version has *vinnr*.

166 They say he has his throne south at
 Urðr's spring; thus has the mighty king of
 Rome (Christ) extended his realm
 over lands of flat-rock divinities (giants).

So said Skapti Þóroddsson:

167 The might of the lord of monks
 is greatest; God is able to do most things.
 Great Christ created the whole world
 and built Rome's hall.

King of the heavens, as Markús said:

168 Wind-hall's (sky's) prince (Christ) created the earth
 and the heavens as well as the virtuous host (of angels).
 Alone the ruler of men, Christ,
 can control all things.

So said Eilífr:

169 The host (angels) of the world's roof (the heavens)
 and the troop of men bow to the Holy Cross.
 The sun's king alone is finer
 than all other true glory.

Mary's son, as Eilífr said:

170 The pure court (angels) of the splendour of the heavens
 bows to Mary's boy (Christ);
 the ruler of the host (of angels) wields true power,
 he is man and God.

King of angels, as Eilífr said:

171 Glorious God is kinder to his lesser
 friends than people imagine;
 yet the generous lord of angels
 is holier and more glorious than anything.

King of Jordan, as Sighvatr said:

172 Once Jordan's prince did send
 four angels from the sky;
 a cascade washed
 the holy locks of its lord.

Grikkja konungr, sem Arnórr kvað:

173 (275) Bǿnir hefi ek beini
bragna fjalls¹ um snjallan
Grikkja vǫrð ok Garða;
gjǫf launa ek svá jǫfri.

Svá kvað Eilífr kúlnasveinn:

174 (276) Himins dýrð lofar hǫlða,
hann er alls konungr, spjalli.

Hér er Kristr kallaðr konungr manna en síðan alls konungr. Enn kvað Einarr Skúlason:

175 (277) Lét sá er landfólks gætir
líknbjartr himinríki
umgeypnandi opna
alls heims fyrir gram snjǫllum.

67 Hér segir frá konungum

Þar koma saman kenningar ok verðr sá at skilja er rǽðr af stǫðu skáldskaparins um hvárn kveðit er konunginn, því at rétt er at kalla Miklagarðs keisera Grikkja konung, ok svá þann konung er rǽðr Jórsala landi, kenna þann Jórsala konung. Svá ok Rómaborgar konung, kenna hann Róms konung ok Engla konung þann er Englandi rǽðr. En sú kenning er áðr var rituð at kenna Krist konung manna, þá kenning má eiga hverr konungr. Konunga alla er rétt at kenna svá at kalla þá landráðendr eða landvǫrðu eða landsǿki eða vǫrð landfólks eða hirðstjóra.

Svá kvað Eyvindr skáldaspillir:

176 (278) Farmatýs
fjǫrvi næmði
jarðráðendr
á Ǫglói.²

Svá kvað Glúmr Geirason:

177 (279) Hilmir rauð und hjálmi
heina lautr³ á Gautum;
þar varð í gný geira
grundar vǫrðr um fundinn.

¹ Other manuscripts have *falls*. The scribe of DG 11 4to can hardly have thought *beinir bragna fjalls* 'benefitter of men's mountain' a satisfactory kenning for God and *Grikkja vǫrð* a human king, in view of the preceding prose, and the *j* must have been inadvertent.
² Cf. verse 5 above.
³ Other manuscripts, and DG 11 4to in verse 211, have *laut*, which must be correct.

King of Greeks, as Arnórr said:

173   I offer prayers about the brave
      causer (war-leader) of men's falling (in battle)
      to the defender of the Greeks and Russia;
      thus I repay the prince for his gift.

So said Eilífr kúlnasveinn:

174   The friend of men praises the splendour
      of heaven; he is king of everything.

Here Christ is called king of men and after that king of everything. Also Einarr Skúlason said:

175   Bright with mercy, the embracer
      of the whole world, who keeps watch
      over the people of earth, made the kingdom
      of heaven open for the brave lord.

67 Here it tells about kings

Here kennings become ambiguous, and the person interpreting has to distinguish from the context of the poetry which king is being referred to, for it is normal to call the emperor of Constantinople king of the Greeks, and similarly the king that rules Palestine, to refer to him as king of Jerusalem. So also the king of the city of Rome, to refer to him as king of Rome, and the king of the English (*Englar* = the English or angels) him who rules England. And the kenning that was quoted above, referring to Christ as king of men, this kenning can be applied to any king. It is normal to refer to all kings in such a way as to call them land-rulers or land-defenders or land-attackers or defence of the people or governors of the court.

So said Eyvindr skáldaspillir:

176   . . . of Cargo-god,
      land-rulers
      deprived of life
      at Ógló.

So said Glúmr Geirason:

177   The helmeted prince reddened
      whetstone's hollow (sword) on Gauts;
      there in the din of spears (battle) was
      the land's protector (king) to be found.

Sem Þjóðólfr kvað:

178 (280) Hár skyli hirlðar stjóri
hugreifr sonum leifa
arf ok óðaltorfu,
ósk mín er þat, sína.

Svá kvað Einarr:

179 (281) Snáks berr fold um frøknu
fólkvǫrðr—konungs orða
frama telr gipt með gumnum—
geðsnjallr skarar fjalli.

Rétt er ok þá konunga, er undir honum eru skattkonungar, at kalla hann konung konunga. Keiseri er øztr konunga ok þar næst sá konungr er þjóðlandi ræðr, jafn í kenningum ǫllum hverr við annan. Þar næst eru þeir menn er jarlar heita eða skattkonungar, ok eru þeir jafnir í kenningum við konunga, nema eigi má þá kalla þjóðkonunga er skattkonungar eru. Svá kvað Arnórr jarlaskáld um Þorfinn jarl:

180 (282) Nemi drótt vina[1] sótti
snarlyndr konungr jarla.

Þar næst eru í kenningum þeir menn er hersar heita. Kenna má þá sem konunga eða jarla svá at kalla þá gullbrjóta ok auðmildinga eða merkismenn eða fólkstjórar, eða kenna hann oddvita liðsins eða orrostu, fyrir því at þjóðkonungr hverr sá er ræðr fyrir mǫrgum lǫndum, þessa setr hann landsstjórnarmenn með sér, skattkonungar[2] ok jarla at dǿma landslǫg ok verja land fyrir ófriði, þau lǫnd er konungi eru fjarri. Skulu þeira dómar vera jafnréttir sem sjálfs konungs. En í einu landi eru mǫrg herǫð ok er þat háttr konunga at setja þar réttar⟨a⟩ yfir svá mǫrg herǫð sem hann gefr til valds, ok heita þeir hersar, en lendir menn í danskri tungu en greifar í Saxlandi, en barónar í Englandi. Þeir skulu ok vera réttir dómarar ok réttir landvarnarmenn fyrir því ríki er þeim er fengit til forráða. Þá skal bera merki fyrir þeim í orrostu, ok eru þeir jafnréttir herstjórnarmenn sem konungar eða jarlar.

68 Hér segir hverir fremstir eru

Þar næst eru þeir menn er hǫlðar heita, þeir menn er réttnefndir eru, þeir bǿndr er gildir eru at ættum ok réttum. Þá má svá kenna at kalla veitanda fjár ok gætanda ok sætti manna. Þessar kenningar megu ok eiga konungar eða jarlar ok hǫfðingjar. Þeir hafa þar með sér þá menn er heita hirðmenn eða húskarlar.

[1] The other manuscripts have *hvé sjá*, which must be correct. They also include a second couplet.
[2] Error for *skattkonunga*.

As Þjóðólfr said:

178   May the high, joyful governor (King Haraldr)
      of the court bequeath to his sons
      inheritance and his native land.
      That is my wish.

So said Einarr:

179   Brave in disposition, the people's defender
      wears snake's land (gold) over his bold hair-fell (head);
      the king's gift with words (eloquence)
      recounts his glory among men.

It is also normal with those kings, under whom there are tributary kings, to call him king of kings. An emperor is highest of kings, and after him any king that rules over a nation, each one indistinguishable in all kennings from any other. Next are the men that are called earls or tributary kings, and they are indistinguishable in kennings from kings, except that those that are tributary kings must not be called national kings. This is how Arnórr Earls' Poet spoke of Earl Þorfinn:

180   Let the court learn how the keen-spirited
      king of earls (Earl Þorfinnr) pursued the sea.

Next in kennings are those men called lords. They can be referred to like kings or earls by calling them gold-breakers and wealth-bountiful ones or standard-men (one that has a standard carried before him) or commanders of the host, or referred to as leaders of the army or of battle, for every national king that rules over many lands, he appoints these as governors of the land together with himself, tributary kings and earls to administer the laws of the land and defend the land from hostility, those lands that are far away from the king. Their judgments are to be considered as valid as those of the king himself. And in a single land there are many districts, and it is the custom of kings to appoint administrators of justice over as many of these districts as he delegates power over, and they are called lords, and landed men in Scandinavia and counts in Germany, but barons in England. They are also supposed to be proper judges and proper defenders of the land for the realm that is given to them to govern. Then a standard is to be carried before them in battle, and they are as legitimate army commanders as kings or earls.

68 Here it says who are foremost

Next to them are the men called *hǫlðar* (freeholders), the men properly so called, the yeomen that have full status as regards lineage and legal rights. They may be referred to by calling them payers and keepers of money and pledges of truce among men. These kennings can also be applied to kings or earls and chieftains. They have there with them the men that are called *hirðmenn*

En lendir menn hafa með sér handgengna menn þá er í Danmǫrk ok Svíþjóð eru kallaðir | hirðmenn, en í Noregi eru húskarlar kallaðir, ok sverja þeir þó eiða konungi. Hirðmenn konunga vóru mjǫk húskarlar kallaðir í fyrnd. Svá kvað Þorvaldr blǫnduskáld:

181 (283) Konungr heill, ok svá snjallir,
    sóknǫrr, við lof gervan
    óð hafa menn í munni
    minn, húskarlar þínir.

Þetta orti Haraldr konungr Sigurðarson:

182 (284) Fullǫflugr bíðr fylla,
    finn ek opt at drífr minna,
    hilmis stól, á hæla.
    húskarla lið jarli.

Hǫfðingja má svá kenna at kalla þá in⟨n⟩drótt eða heiðing[1] eða verðung. Svá kvað Sigvatr:

183 (285) Þar frá ek víg at vatni
    verðung jǫfurs gerðu,
    nadda él, it nýja,[2]
    næst tel ek øng in smæstu.

Ok enn þetta:

184 (286) Þeygi var sem þessum
    þengill, á jó sprengir
    mjǫk fyrir, mála kveðjur
    mær⟨r⟩ heiðingum bæri.[3]

Heiðfé heitir máli eða gjǫf er hǫfðingjar veita, jarlar eða hersar. Hirðmenn eru svá kendir at kalla hann runnar[4] eða sessar eða málar. Svá kvað Hallfreðr:

185 (288) Gramr rúni lætr glymja
    gunnlíkr[5] sá er hvǫt líkar
    hǫgnar[6] hamri slegnar,
    heiptbráðr und sik váðir.

Svá kvað Snæbjǫrn:

[1] See Grape et al. 1977: 218. Codex Wormianus and Codex Trajectinus have *heiðmenn*.

[2] In *Edda Snorra Sturlusonar* 1848–87 II *nýta*. See Grape et al. 1977: 160. Other manuscripts have *nýla* 'recently'.

[3] See Introduction, p. lxxx–lxxxi

[4] Obviously an error for *rúnar* 'confidants', cf. the following verse.

[5] Obviously an error (anticipation of following *líkar*) for *gunnríkr* (so the other manuscripts).

[6] Perhaps for *hǫggnar*, though it spoils the rhyme. Other manuscripts have the well-known kenning for mail-coat *Hǫgna váðir* 'Hǫgni's clothes'.

(retainers) or housecarles. But landed men have the men in their service that in Denmark and Sweden are called *hirðmenn*, but in Norway are called housecarles, and yet they swear oaths to the king. Retainers of kings were generally called housecarles in ancient times.

So said Þorvaldr blǫnduskáld:

181 Hail, battle-keen king and also
   your brave housecarles; people
   have my poetry, filled with
   praise, in their mouths.

King Haraldr Sigurðarson composed this:

182 The very powerful one is waiting
   to fill the prince's throne; I have often
   seen a smaller troop of housecarles
   surging at the heels of an earl.

Chieftains can be referred to by calling them a domestic troop or stipendiaries or mercenaries. So said Sigvatr:

183 I have heard that there at the lake
   the prince's mercenary troop
   fought the recent battle;
   I count none of the smallest point-storms (battles) second to it.

And also this:

184 It was not like a renowned prince
   bringing these paid troops
   (empty) promises of pay; the horse
   was on the point of collapsing.

Stipend-money is called wages and gift that chieftains give, earls or lords. Retainers are referred to by calling them bushes or bench-mates or gossips. So said Hallfreðr:

185 Battle-powerful prince, your confidant,
   he whom action pleases, hasty in fighting,
   makes the hewed hammer-forged clothes (mail-coat)
   jangle beneath him.

So said Snæbjǫrn:

186 (289) Stjórnviðrar¹ lætr styðja
stáls dǫglinga máli
hlemmisverð við harðri
húflangan skæ þúfu.

Svá kvað Arnórr:

187 (290) Bera sýn um mik mínir,
mærð kendr taka² enda
þessum þengils sessa,
þung mein synir ungir.

Konungs spjalli, sem Hallfreðr kvað:

188 (291) Ráð lukust at sá síðan
snjallráðr konungs spialli.³

Svá skal kenna mann við æt⟨t⟩ir sínar, sem Kormakr kvað:

189 (292) Heyri sonr á Sýrar
sannreynis fentanna—
ǫrgreipa⟨r⟩ læt ek uppi—
⟨j⟩ast-Rín Haraldr⁴ mína.

Hann kallaði jarlinn sannreyni konungsins en Hákon var son Sigurðar jarls.

En Þjóðólfr kvað svá:

190 (293) Eykr Óláfs feðr
Járnsǫxu veðr
harðræðit hvert
svá hróðrs er vert.

Ok enn:

191 (294) Svá Jarizleifr um sá
hvat jǫfurr brá;
hófs⟨t⟩ hlýri frams
ens helga grams.

Svá kvað Arnórr:

192 (296) Réð Heita konr hleyti
herþarfr við mik gerva;
stórr⁵ lét oss um orkat
jarls mæg⟨ð⟩ at því frægðar.

Ok enn kvað hann um Þorfinn jarl:

¹ For either *stjórnviðar* or *stjórnviðjar* 'steering-timber' (-oar) or 'steering-tie' (the band attaching the steering oar to the side of a ship).
² Error for *kend tekr*.
³ See verse 68, where the sentence is completed in lines 3–4, as it is here in other manuscripts.
⁴ In view of the following prose, this ought to be *Haralds* (as in other manuscripts).
⁵ Error for *stór*.

186 The gossip of rulers makes
the long-sided steering-oar horse (ship)
lean resounding prow-swords (brands, ornamental strips along
the sides of the prow) on hard mound (rock).

So said Arnórr:

187 My young sons suffer evident
heavy anxiety about me;
the praise-poem addressed to this prince's
bench-mate comes to an end.

King's crony, as Hallfreðr said:

188 The match was later consummated
by which that wise-ruling king's crony (the earl) . . .

So shall a man be referred to in terms of his descent, as Kormakr said:

189 Let Haraldr son of Sýr listen
to my yeast-Rhine (ale, i.e. mead of poetry) of the true
experiencer (giant) of fen-teeth (rocks);
I raise my eager hands.

He called the earl the true tester of the king, and Hákon was the son of Earl Sigurðr.

And Þjóðólfr said this:

190 Every difficult undertaking
increases Járnsaxa's (giantess's) wind (courage)
in Óláfr's father,
so that praise is due.

And again:

191 So Jarizleifr saw
how the prince reacted;
the brother of the bold saintly ruler (i.e. Haraldr harðráði)
became renowned.

So said Arnórr:

192 Beneficial to the people, the kinsman (brave sea-warrior) of Heiti
(sea-king) decided to bring about a family connexion with me;
in this great links with the earl by marriage
caused glory to be built up for us.

And in addition he said about Earl Þorfinnr:

193 (297) Bitu sverð, en þar þurði,
þungjǫrr¹ yfir Mǫn sunnan
Rǫgnvalds kind, en² randir
ramligt folk, ins gamla.

Ok enn kvað hann:

194 (298) Ættbøti firr ítran
allríks—en ek bið líknar
trúrar tiggja dýrum—
Torf-Einars, guð, meinum.

Ok enn kvað Einarr skálaglamm:

195 (299) Ne ættstuðill ættar
ógnherði⟨r⟩ mun verða—
skyldr em ek hróðri at halda—
Hilditanns inn mildri.

69 Hér segir hversu kend er setning skáldskapar

Hvernig er kend³ setning skáldskaparins? Svá at nefna hvern hlut sem heitir. Hver eru ókend nǫfn skáldskaparins? Hann heitir bragr ok hróðr, mærð ok lof ok leyfð. Svá kvað Bragi gamli þá er hann ók um skóg nokkurn síð um kveld. Þá stefjaði trǫll á hann ok spurði hverr þar føri. Hann svarar:

196 (300b) Skáld kalla mik
skapsmið Viðurs.
Gauks gjafrǫtuð
grepp óhneppan.
Yggs ǫlbera
óðs spár-Móða,
hagsmið bragar.
Hvat er skáld nema þat?

Svá kvað Kormakr:⁴

197 (301) Hróðr geri ek um mǫg mæran
meirr Sigurð⟨a⟩r fleira;
happsønis⁵ geld ek honum
heið. Sitr Þórr í reiðu.

Svá kvað Þórðr Kolbeinsson:

¹ Error for *-gjǫr*.
² Error for *und*.
³ It is clear from what follows that both here and in the heading *kend* is an error for *ókend*: 'What is the rule for poetry without using a kenning?'.
⁴ See note to verse 11 above.
⁵ *happsønis* must be an error for *haptsønis*. AM 157 8vo has *happsønum*.

| 193 | Thinly-made swords bit for Rǫgnvaldr
the Old's offspring (Earl Þorfinnr) in the south
across Man, and a powerful host
rushed forward beneath their shields there. |

And in addition he said:

| 194 | God, keep the splendid
glory of the family of all-powerful
Torf-Einarr from harm; and I pray
for true grace for the worthy prince. |

And in addition Einarr Skálaglamm said:

| 195 | There will not be a family pillar
of the line of Hilditǫnn
who is a more generous battle-promoter;
I am under an obligation to continue his praise. |

69 Here it says what the rule is for poetry in kennings

What is the rule for poetry in kennings? By naming each thing by its (normal) name. What terms are there for poetry without kennings? It is called rhyme and praise, encomium, eulogy and laud. So said Bragi the Old when he was driving through a certain forest late in the evening. Then a trollwife accosted him in verse and asked who was going there. He replies:

| 196 | Poets call me
Viðurr's (Óðinn's) thought-smith,
getter of Gaukr's (Óðinn's) gift,
lack-nought hero,
server of Yggr's (Óðinn's) ale
poetry's prophecy-Móði (a god),
skilled smith of rhyme.
What is a poet other than that? |

So said Kormakr:

| 197 | I shall continue to make more praise
about the renowned son of Sigurðr;
I shall pay him the stipend (mead) of the gods'
atoner (Óðinn). Þórr sits in his chariot. |

So said Þórðr Kolbeinsson:

198 (302) Mjǫk lét margar snekkjur,
 mærðar ǫrr, sem knǫrru,
 óðr vex skáldi, ok skeiðar
 sk⟨j⟩aldhlynr á brim dynja.

Mærð, sem kvað Úlfr:

199 (303) Þar kemr á, er æri
 endr bar ek mærð á hendi,
 ofra ek svá, til sævar,
 sverðregns, lofi þegna.

Hér ok lof kendr skáldskaprinn. Svá kvað Ormr Steinþórsson:

200 Ek hefi orðgnótt mikla,
 opt finnum þat; minni
 fram tel ek leyfð fyrir lofða
 ljós⟨s⟩ en ek munda kjósa.[1]

70 Um nǫfn guðanna

Hverneg eru nǫfn guðanna? Þau heita bǫnd, sem kvað Eyjólfr dáðaskáld:

201 (304) Dregr land at mun banda.[2]

Ok hǫpt, sem Þjóðólfr kvað:

202 (305) Tormiðlaðr var tívum
 tálhrein⟨n⟩ meðal beina.
 Hvat, kvað þú, hapta snytrir
 hjálmfaldinn, því valda.

Rǫgn sem Einarr kvað:

203 (306) Rammaukinn[3] kveð ek ríki
 rǫgn Hákonar magni.

Þolnar,[4] sem Eyvindr kvað

204 (307) Þolnar át
 en vér gátum
 stillis lof
 sem steina brú.

Díar, sem Kormakr kvað:

[1] This verse is only in DG 11 4to.
[2] The other manuscripts have three lines comprising part of a *klofastef* in *Bandadrápa*. Cf. *Skj* A I 300–302.
[3] Must be an error for *Rammaukin*.
[4] This is not a known word, and the other manuscripts have *Jólnar*, and in the first line of the quotation *Jólna sumbl*; a later hand in DG 11 4to has written *Jólnar* in the margin. The first line in DG 11 4to probably ought to be *Jólna át*.

| 198 | The shield-maple (warrior) frequently made many cruisers,
as well as freighters and cutters
thunder on the surf; the rhapsody,
liberal with encomium, develops in the poet.

Encomium, as Úlfr said:

| 199 | There the river reaches the sea (the poem ends)
in which I have again presented an encomium
for the sword-rain (battle) deliverer (warrior);
thus I raise the eulogy of thanes.

Here poetry [is] also referred to as eulogy. So said Ormr Steinþórsson:

| 200 | I have a great abundance of words,
we often realise that; I perform
less laud for the lord of light (God)
than I would choose.

70 Of names for the gods

What names are there for the gods? They are called bonds, as Eyjólfr dáðaskáld said:

| 201 | Draws land [under himself] to the pleasure of the bonds.

And fetters, as Þjóðólfr said:

| 202 | Middlingly free of deceit, he was a slow
provider of service to the gods.
Something, you said, helmet-capped
educator (Óðinn) of the gods, was behind it.

Powers, as Einarr said:

| 203 | I declare the most puissant powers
imbue with strength the rule of Hákon.

Yule-beings, as Eyvindr said:

| 204 | But yule-beings' (the gods') food (the mead of poetry),
our ruler's eulogy,
we have produced,
like a bridge of masonry.

Deities, as Kormakr said:

205 (308) Eykr með ennidúki
jarðr lútr día fjarðar
þar breyti Húnn sá er beinan
bindr. Seið Yggr til Rindar.[1]

71 Um nǫfn heimsins

f. 37v, p. 72 Þessi nǫfn heims[2] eru rituð en eigi hǫfum vér funnit | í kvæðum ǫll þessi. En þessi heiti þikki mér óskylt at hafa nema kveðit[3] sé til. Hann heitir himinn, hlýrnir, heiðþyrnir, leiptr, hrjóðr, víðbláinn.

Hverninn skal kenna himininn?[4] Kalla hann Ymis haus ok erfiði ok byrði dverga, hjálm Austra, Vestra, Norðra, Suðra; land sólar ok tungls ok himintungla, vápna[5] eða veðra, hjálm eða hús lopts ok jarðar.

72 Um nǫfn stundanna

Þessi eru nǫfn stundanna: ǫld, forðum, aldr, fyrir lǫngu, misseri, vetr, sumar, haust, vár, mánuðr, vika, dagr, nótt, morginn, aptann, kveld, árla, snemma, síðla, í sinn, fyrra dag, í næst,[6] í gær, stund, mél. Þessi eru heiti nætrinnar í Ǫlvismálum:

206 (380) Nótt heitir með mǫnnum,
njóla Helju,
kǫlluð er gríma með guðum;
ǫldurg[7] kalla jǫtnar,
álfar svefngaman,
dvergar draum.

73 Hér segir um nǫfn sólar ok tungls

Tungl:[8] narinn, múlinn, mýlinn, ný, hríð, ártali, fengari, klárr, skyndir, skjálgr, skrámr.

Sól: sunna, rǫðull, eyglóa, anskip,[9] sýin, fagrahvel, línuskin, Dvalins leika, álfrǫðull.

Hvernig skal kenna sól?[10] Kalla hana dóttur Mundilfeta, systur mána, konu Gle⟨n⟩s, eldr himins ok lopts.

---

[1] See verse 11; *jarðr lútr* here must be an error for *jarðlútr* there. *Yggr* written *ykr*.
[2] What follows shows that here and in the heading above *heims* ought to be *himins*.
[3] Or *kvæðit*?
[4] Cf. ch. 51.
[5] See Introduction pp. lx–lxi.
[6] Written *nets* (apparently).
[7] Other manuscripts have *ósorg* 'sorrow-free', GkS 2365 4to has *óljós* 'unlight'.
[8] The beginning of this list seems somewhat confused. Other manuscripts have *máni* 'moon' for *narinn*, *nið* 'waning moon' for *hríð*; *múlinn* and *mýlinn* seem to be spellings of the same word, the meaning of which is uncertain.
[9] Other manuscripts have *alskír* 'all-bright'; *sýin* is for *sýni*.
[10] Cf. ch. 54.

205 The one who worships the land (Earl Sigurðr), the Húnn (sea-king)
that binds it on there, honours with a head-band
the productive provider of the deities' fiord (poetry,
whose provider is the poet). Yggr (Óðinn) won Rindr by spells.

71 Of names for the world

These names for world are written down, but we have not found all these in poems. So it seems to me unnecessary to use these terms unless the poem is extant. It is called heaven, twin-lit, bright-drier, lightning, coverer, wide-blue.

How shall the sky be referred to? By calling it Ymir's skull and toil and burden of dwarfs, helmet of Austri, Vestri, Norðri, Suðri; land of sun and moon and stars, of weapons or winds, helmet or house of air and earth.

72 Of names for times

These are the names for times: age, formerly, period, long ago, season, winter, summer, autumn, spring, month, week, day, night, morning, evening, nightfall, early, betimes, late, at once, day before yesterday, next, yesterday, hour, while. These are names of the night in *Alvíssmál* (verse 30):

206 Its name is night among men,
obscurity for Hel,
it is known as mask among gods,
giants call it the old one (?),
elves sleep-joy,
dwarfs dream.

73 Here it tells of names for sun and moon

Moon: *narinn*, horned, pointed, waxing moon, *hríð*, year-counter, shiner, clear, hastener, squinter, pale one.

Sun: daystar, disc, ever-glow, *anskip*, sight, fair wheel, line-shine, Dvalinn's toy, elf-disc.

How shall the sun be referred to? By calling it daughter of Mundilfeti, sister of the moon, wife of Glenr, fire of heaven and sky.

74¹

Konungr er nefndr Hálfdan, er inn gamli var kallaðr, er allra konunga var ágætastr. Hann gerði blót mikit at miðjum vetri ok blótaði til þess at hann lifði í konungdǿmi sínu þrjú hundruð vetra. En hann fekk þau andsvǫr at hann mundi eigi lifa meirr en einn mikinn aldr eins manns, en engi mundi kona í ætt hans né ótiginn maðr. Hann var hermaðr mikill ok fór víða um Austrvegu. Þar drap hann í einvígi þann konung er Sigtryggr hét. Hann fekk Alurg dóttur Emundar konungs ór Hólmgarði. Þau áttu átján sonu ok vóru níu senn bornir. Þeir hétu svá: Þengill, Ræsir, Gramr, Gylfi, Hilmir, Jǫfurr, Tiggi, Skúli, Skylli,² Harri. Þeir eru svá ágætir at í ǫllum frǿðum eru nǫfn þeira hǫfð fyrir tignarnǫfn sem konunga nǫfn eða jarla. Þeir áttu engi bǫrn ok fellu allir í bardaga.

Svá kvað Arnórr:

207 (390) Þengill var þegar ungr
þess³ gerr ǫrr vígǫrr;
haldast bið ek hans aldr;
hann tel ek yfirmann.

Svá kvað Markús:

208 (391) Ræsir lét af roðnum hausi
Rínar sól á marfjǫll skína.

Svá kvað Egill:

209 (392) Gramr hefir gerðihǫmrum
grundar upp um hrundit.⁴

Svá kvað Eyvindr:

210 (393) Lék við ljóðmǫgu,
skyldi land verja,
Gramr⁵ enn glaðværi
stóð und gullhjálmi.

Svá kvað Glúmr Geirason:

211 (394) Hilmir rauð und hjálmi
heina laut á Gautum.⁶

---

¹ Half of f. 37v was left blank and f. 38r begins with a large initial. This indicates that a new independent section of *Skáldskaparmál* is beginning, but there is no heading.

² Other manuscripts have *Skyli eða Skúli*. By omitting *eða*, DG 11 4to gets a list of 10 sons.

³ Other manuscripts have *þreks*, but it does not seem possible to read the damaged abbreviation in DG 11 4to as that word.

⁴ The next two lines of Egill's verse include the remainder of the sentence. See *Egils saga* 145.

⁵ The other manuscripts have *Gylfi* here, in accordance with the list of kings above.

⁶ See verse 177 above.

74

There is a king named Hálfdan, who was called the Old, who was the most renowned of all kings. He held a great sacrifice at midwinter and offered a sacrifice in order to be granted that he should live in his kingdom for three hundred winters. But the reply he got was that he might live no longer than one long life of one man, but there would be neither woman in his line nor non-noble male. He was a great warrior and travelled widely over eastern parts. There he killed in single combat a king that was called Sigtryggr. He married Alurg, daughter of King Emundr of Hólmgarðr. They had eighteen sons and nine were born at a time. Their names were as follows: Þengill, Ræsir, Gramr, Gylfi, Hilmir, Jǫfurr, Tiggi, Skúli, Skylli, Harri. They are so renowned that in all records their names are used as honorific titles equivalent to the titles of of kings or earls. They had no children and all fell in battle.

So said Arnórr:

207   The prince was already at an early age
      full of this: liberal, vigorous in battle;
      I pray his life may last;
      I consider him a superman.

So said Markús:

208   The ruler made the Rhine's sun (gold) shine from the
      red-coloured skull (figurehead) on the mere's mountains (waves).

So said Egill:

209   The ruler has raised up the fence-cliffs (brows)
      of my [mask's] ground (face) [from my eyes].

So said Eyvindr:

210   He was merry with the sons of the people,
      he had to defend the land,
      the cheerful ruler,
      he stood beneath his golden helmet.

So said Glúmr Geirason:

211   The helmeted prince reddened
      whetstone's hollow (sword) on Gauts.

Svá kvað Óttarr:

212 (395) Jǫfurr gefi[1] upphaf,
ofrast mun konungs lof,
háttu nemi hann rét⟨t⟩
hróðrs míns, bragar síns.

Tiggi, sem Stúfr kvað:

213 (396) Tíreggjaðr hjó Tiggi
tveim hǫndum lið beima,
reifr gekk herr und hlífar,
hizi suðr fyrir Nizi.

Svá kvað Hallfreðr:

214 (397) Skiliðr em ek við Sky⟨l⟩ja;
ská⟨l⟩mǫld hefir því valdit;
vætti ek virða dróttinns;
villa er mest ok dul flestum.

Svá kvað Markús:

215 (398) Harra kveð ek at hróðrgerð dýrri
hauklundaðan Dana grundar.

75 Capitulum

Enn áttu þau Hálfdan aðra níu sonu, er svá hétu: Hildir, er Hildingar eru frá komnir, Nemir er Niflungar eru frá komnir, Qði er Qðlingar eru frá komnir,[2] Dagr er Dǫglingar eru frá komnir—þat er ætt Hálfdanar milda. Buðli er af Buðla ætt, þat eru Buðlungar. Lofði var herkonungr. Honum fylgði þat lið er Lofðungar hétu. Hans | ættmenn eru kallaðir Lofðungar. Þaðan kom Eylimi, móðurfaðir Sigurðar Fáfnisbana. Sigarr, þaðan kómu Siklingar. Þat er Siggeirs ætt, mágs Vǫlsungs, ok Sigars er hefndi Hagbarðs.

Af Hildinga ætt var kominn Haraldr inn granrauði, móðurfaðir Hálfdan⟨a⟩r svarta. Af Niflunga ætt var Gunnarr konungr. Af Ynglinga ætt var Eiríkr inn málspaki.

Þessar eru konunga ættir ágætar: frá Yngvar eru Ynglingar, frá Skildi í Danmǫrku eru Skjǫldingar, frá Vǫlsungi í Frakklandi eru Vǫlsungar. Skelfir hét einn ágætr konungr. Hans ættmenn hétu Skilfingar. Sú kynslóð eru í Austrvegum.

Þessar ættir er nú eru nefndar hafa menn sett svá í skáldskapinn at halda ǫll nǫfn þessi fyrir tignarnǫfn.

[1] The other manuscripts have *heyri* 'hear'.
[2] Yngvi is missing here, and Bragi after Dagr. Sigarr is therefore the ninth son in this list, and the rest of the kings listed here were not sons of Hálfdan the Old.

So said Óttarr:

212   Let the prince grant the beginning
of his rhyme; the king's eulogy shall be raised;
may he note properly
the forms of my praise.

Tiggi, as Stúfr said:

213   Glory-spurred ruler hewed
with both hands the troop of warriors
there south of the Nissan; the host
went cheerful beneath their shields.

So said Hallfreðr:

214   I am parted from the ruler;
the time of swords has caused this;
I look for the lord of men's return;
for most this is regarded as the greatest error and delusion.

So said Markús:

215   I salute in a highly-wrought work of praise
the hawk-spirited lord of Danish ground.

75 Chapter

Hálfdan and his wife had a further nine sons, whose names were: Hildir, whom the Hildingar are descended from, Nemir whom the Niflungs are descended from, Qði whom the Qðlings are descended from, Dagr whom the Dǫglings are descended from—this is the line of Hálfdan the Generous. Buðli is from the line of the Buðlar, these are Buðlungs. Lofði was a war-king. His following was a troop known as Lofðungs. His descendants were known as Lofðungs. From them is descended Eylimi, Sigurðr Fáfnisbani's grandfather. Sigarr, from him are descended the Siklings. This is the line of Siggeirr, who was related by marriage to Vǫlsungr, and of Sigarr who avenged Hagbarðr.

From the Hilding line was descended Haraldr the Red-Whiskered, grandfather of Hálfdan the Black. From the Niflung line came King Gunnarr. From the Yngling line came Eiríkr the Eloquent.

The following are great kings' lines: from Yngvarr come Ynglings, from Skjǫldr in Denmark come Skjǫldings, from Vǫlsungr in Francia come Vǫlsungs. Skelfir was the name of a great king. His descendants were called Skilfings. That family is in eastern parts.

These family lines that have just been named have been used in the poetry in such a way as to treat all these names as honorific titles.

Sem Einarr kvað:

216 (399) Frá ek við hólm at heyja
Hildingar fram gengu,
lind varð grǿn, en⟨n⟩ gróna
geirþing, vam[1] springa.

Sem Grani kvað:

217 (400) Dǫglingr fekk at drekka
danskt blóð ara jóði.

Svá kvað Gamli Gnævaðarskáld:

218 (401) Ǫðlingr drap sér ungum
ungr naglfara á tungu
innan borðs ok orða
aflgerð meðalkafla.

Bragningr. Svá kvað Jórunn:

219 (402) Bragningr rauð í blóði,
beið herr konungs reiði,
hús hlutu opt fyrir eisum,
óþjóðar slǫg, rjóða.

Svá kvað Einarr:

220 (403) Beit Buðlungs hjǫrr,
blóð fell á dǫrr.

Svá kvað Arnórr:

221 (404) Siglinga[2] venr snekkju⟨r⟩
stýrir lútar[3] gramr konr úti.
Hann litar herskip innan,
hrafns góð er þat, blóði.

Svá kvað Þjóðólfr:

222 (405) Svá lauk Siklings ævi
snjalls at vér erum allir.[4]

223 (406) Skjǫldungr, mun þér annarr aldri
ǿðri gramr und sólu fǿðast.

Vǫlsungr. Svá kvað Arnórr:[5]

[1] The other medieval manuscripts have *í tvau* 'in two'. AM 157 8vo has 'van*ar*' 'hope's'.

[2] Obviously an error for *Siklinga*, which is the reading of AM 157 8vo.

[3] Line 2 has two syllables too many, but if *snekkju* is made plural (as in the other manuscripts) some sense can be made of this otherwise incomprehensible line.

[4] The complement of *erum* is in the couplet that is omitted after this one. DG 11 4to runs the remaining couplet together with the next one, which is by Arnórr.

[5] This attribution belongs with the preceding couplet. The next verse is by Þorkell.

As Einarr said:

216　　I have heard that the kings went forward
　　　 to hold a spear-parliament (battle)
　　　 by the island covered with vegetation;
　　　 the green shield was made to split *vam* . . .

As Grani said:

217　　The king gave eagle's bairn
　　　 Danish blood to drink.

So said Gamli Gnævaðarskáld:

218　　The young king launched himself as a young
　　　 man abroad into the mighty word-activity
　　　 (argument, i.e. battle) between haft's tongue
　　　 (sword) and sword's board (shield).

Bragningr. So said Jórunn:

219　　The king reddened weapons
　　　 in wicked people's blood; the host suffered
　　　 the king's wrath; because of embers (fire),
　　　 they often got to redden houses.

So said Einarr:

220　　The king's blade bit,
　　　 blood fell on darts.

So said Arnórr:

221　　The descendant of kings accustoms the dipping
　　　 warships to be out (at sea), the ruler steers.
　　　 He colours warships on the insides
　　　 with blood; this is a benefit to the raven.

So said Þjóðólfr:

222　　The brave king's life ended in such a way
　　　 that we are all [in a difficult situation].

223　　Another king more excellent than you, ruler,
　　　 will never be born beneath the sun.

Vǫlsungr. So said Arnórr:

224 (407) Mér réð at senda
um svalan ægi
Vǫlsunga niðr
vápn gullbúit.

Ynglingr, sem Arnórr[1] kvað:

225 (408) Engi varð á jǫrðu
ógnbráðr áðr þér náði
austr sá er eyjum vestan
Ynglingr und sik þryngvi.

Yngvi. Svá kvað Markús:

226 (409) Eiríks lof verðr ǫld at heyra,
engi maðr veit fremra þengil,
Yngvi helt við orðstír langan
jǫfra sessi, í verǫld þessi.

Skilfingr, sem Valgarðr kvað:

227 (410) Skilfingr heltstu þar er skulfu
skeiðr fyrir land it breiða—
auðit var þar suðr um síðir—
Sikiley liði miklu.

76

Skáld heita greppar ok er rétt í skáldskap at kenna svá hvern mann er vill. Rekkar vóru kallaðir þeir menn er fylgðu Hálfi konungi. Af þeirra nafni eru rekkar kallaðir hermenn, ok er rétt at kenna svá alla menn. Lofðar heita þeir menn í skáldskap. Skatnar heita þeir menn er fylgðu Skata konungi ok af hans nafni er hverr skati kallaðr er mildr er. Bragnar hétu þeir menn er fylgðu Braga konungi inum gamla. Virðar heita þeir menn er meta mál manna, fyrðar ok firar. Verar heita landvarnarmenn. Víkingar ok flotnar, þat eru skipaherr. Beimar hétu þeir menn er fylgðu Beima konungi. Gumnar ok gumar heita fólkstjórar, sem gumi heitir í brúðfǫr. Gotnar hétu þeir menn er fylgðu Gota konungi, er Gotland er við kent. Hann heitir af nafni Óðins ok dregit af Gauts nafni. Þeir heita drengir er millum landa fara, þeir konungs drengir er þeim þjóna eða ríkum mǫnnum. Þeir heita vaskir menn er batnandi eru. Seggir heita ok kníar, liðar, þat eru fylgðarmenn, þegnar, hǫlða, svá heita bóndr. Ljónar heita þeir er um sættir ganga.

77 Hér segir fornǫfn

Kappar heita ok kempur, garpar, snillingar, hreystimenn, afarmenn, harðmenni, hetjur. Þessi standa þar í móti, at kalla mann blauðan, þirfing, blótamann, skauð eða skræfu, vák, vámenn,[2] ljóska, sleyma, dási, drokr, dusilmenni.

[1] This verse is by Óttarr svarti, see *Hkr* II 172–3.
[2] *vák, vámenn* written as *vakvamenn*.

224   The descendant of kings
        decided to send me
        a gold-adorned weapon
        across the cool ocean.
Yngling, as Arnórr said:
225   No battle ardent ruler who subjected
        islands in the west under himself
        appeared on the landscape
        in the east (Norway) until they got you (St Óláfr).
Yngvi. So said Markús:
226   This generation must hear Eiríkr's praise,
        no one knows of a more outstanding ruler
        in this world; the king held the throne
        of princes with long-lasting renown.
Skilfingr, as Valgarðr said:
227   King, you took a great force
        past the broad land of Sicily
        where warships quivered; there
        in the south it was granted in the end.

76

Poets are called *greppar*, and it is normal in poetry to refer thus to any man one desires. The men in King Hálfr's following were known as *rekkar* (heroes). From their name warriors are known as *rekkar*, and it is normal to refer to all men thus. Those men are called *lofðar* in poetry. The men that were in the following of King Skati are called *skatnar*, and from his name everyone that is generous is known as *skati*. The men that were in the following of King Bragi the Old were called *bragnar*. Men who assess people's cases are called *virðar*, *fyrðar* and *firar*. Defenders of the land are called *verar*. Vikings and sailors, these are a naval host. The men that were in the following of King Beimi are called *beimar*. Leaders of a host are called *gumnar* and *gumar*, just as there is a *gumi* (groom) in a bridal party. The men that were in the following of King Goti, whom Gotland is named after, are called *gotnar*. He is called after one of Óðinn's names, and it was derived from the name Gautr. They are called *drengir* that travel from land to land, king's *drengir* those that serve them or powerful men. They are called valiant men that are ambitious. Warriors are also called *kníar*, *liðar*, these are followers, *þegnar*, *hǫlða* this is what landowners are called. Those that negotiate settlement of disputes are called *ljónar*.

77 Here substitutions are listed

Heroes are also called champions, fighting cocks, valiant ones, bravoes, tough ones, braves. These are contrary to them in meaning, calling a man effeminate, milksop, weakling, coward or craven, wretch, men of woe, cunt, dastard, useless one, sluggard, good-for-nothing.

78 Høverskra manna nǫfn

Ǫrr maðr heitir mildingr, mæringr, skati, þjóðskati, gullskiptir, mannbaldr, auðkýfingr, sælkeri. ~~kendr~~ Sinkr heitir maðr ok er svá kallat: hnøggr, gløggr, mælingr, vesalingr, gjǫflati. Spekingr, ráðvaldr, snyrtimaðr, ofláti, glæsimaðr. Raumi, skrapr, skrokkr, skeiðklofi, flangi, slinni, fjósni, ljóðir. Heitir þræll kefsir, þræll, þjónn, ǫnnungr, þírr. Lýðr heitir landsfólk.

Maðr heitir einn hverr,
ái ef tveir eru,
þorp ef þrír eru,
fjórir eru fǫruneyti,
flokkr fimm menn,
sveit ef sex eru,
sjau fylla sǫgn,
átta fylla ámælisskor,
nautar eru níu,
tugr eru tíu,
ærir eru ellefu,
toglǫð tólf,
þyss er þrettán,
ferð er fjórtán,
fundr er þar er fimmtán finnast,
seta eru sextán,
sók⟨n⟩ eru sautján,
ørnir þikkja óvinir þeim er átján møta,
neyti eru nítján,
drótt er tuttugu,
þjóð eru þrír tigir,
fólk er fjórir tigir,
fylki eru fimm tigir,
samnaðr sex tigir,
svarfaðr sjau tigir,
aldir átta tigir,
herr er hundrað.[1]

79 Hér segir frá viðrkenningum

Enn eru þær kenningar er menn láta ganga fyrir nǫfn manna. Þat kǫllum vér fornǫfn manna. Þat eru viðkenningar at nefna annan hlut réttu nafni ok kalla þann er hann nefnir til þess er hann er eigandi, eða svá at kalla hann

---

[1] In most cases Roman numerals are used. 90 is lacking in all manuscripts.

78 Names for courteous men

A generous man is called munificent one, illustrious one, *skati*, splendid-*skati*, gold distributor, prince of men, money-bags, affluent one. A man is called avaricious and is said to be stingy, close, tight-fisted, churl, gift-grudger.

Sage, decision-maker, elegant man, show-off, dandy.

Rough, blatherer, scrag, hewer of wood, clown, good-for-nothing, yokel, common person. A slave is called captive, slave, servant, labourer, serf. The folk of a country are called the people.

> An individual is called a man,
> forefather if there are two,
> a bunch if there are three,
> four are a company,
> a flock is five men,
> it is a troop if there are six,
> seven complete a crew,
> eight complete an accusation-tally,
> nine are mates,
> ten are a decade,
> eleven make up an embassy,
> twelve are a train,
> thirteen is a crowd,
> fourteen is an expedition,
> it is an assembly when fifteen meet,
> sixteen are an occupation,
> seventeen are a congregation,
> his enemies seem plenty to one whom eighteen meet,
> nineteen are companionship,
> twenty is a household,
> thirty are a people,
> forty is a folk,
> fifty are a county,
> sixty a muster,
> seventy a tumult,
> eighty a population,
> a hundred is a host.

79 Here it tells about circumlocutions

There are also the terms that are put in place of men's names. We call these substitutions for persons. They are circumlocutions to name something else by its normal name and call the one that he is referring to in terms of

réttu nafni þess er hann nefndi, fǫður hans eða afa. Ái heitir, sonr, arfuni, arfi; bróðir heitir blóði, lifri, niðr, nefi, komr,[1] kundr, kynstafr, niðjungr, ættstuðill, æt⟨t⟩bornir, afspringr.

Heita ok mágar sifjungar, ⟨h⟩leytamenn, spjalli, aldarþópti, halfrýmisfélagi. Heitir dólgr ok andskoti, søkkvi, skaðamaðr, þrǫngvir, ósvip⟨r⟩uðr.[2] Þessi kǫllum vér viðrkenningar, ok þó at maðr sé kendr við bǿi sína eða skip, eða þat er nafn á, eða eign sína, þá er eignarnafn á.

80 Frá sannkenningu

Þetta kǫllum vér sannkenningar at kalla mann spekimann, ætlanarmann, orðspakan, ráðsnjallan, auðmildingr, úsløkinn, gæimann, glæsimann. Þetta eru forn nǫfn.[3]

81 Frá kvenna nǫfnum úkendum

Þessi eru kvenna nǫfn úkend: víf, brúðr. Fljóð heita þær konur er mjǫk fara með dramb eða skart. Snótir heita þær er orðnǿfrar eru. Drósir heita þær konur er kyrrlátar eru. Svarri ok svarkr þær er mikillátar eru. Ristill heitir sú kona er skǫruglynd er. Rýgr heitir sú er ríkust er. Feima heitir sú er ófrǫm er sem ungar meyjar ok þær konur er úðjarfar eru. Sæta heitir sú kona er bóndi hennar er af landi farinn. Hæll heitir sú kona er bóndi hennar er veginn útanlands. Ekkja heitir sú kona er bóndi hennar er andaðr, þær konur eljur er einn mann eigu. Kona er kǫlluð beðja eða mála ok rúna bónda síns, ok er þat viðkenning.

82 Hversu kenna skal hǫfuðit

Hǫfuð skal kalla svá at kalla erfiði háls eða manns byrðr, land hjálms ok hattar ok heila ok l hárs ok brúna, svarðar, eyrna, augna, munns, Heimdallar sverð, ok er rétt at kenna sverðs heiti ok nefna hvert er vill ok kenna við eitthvert nafn Heimdallar. Hǫfuð heitir úkent hauss, hjarnskjal⟨l⟩,[4] kollr. Augu heita sjón eða lit eða viðrlit. Þau má svá kenna at kalla sól, tungl, skjǫldu eða gler eða gimsteina eða stein eða[5] brá eða brúna, hvarma eða ennis. Eyru heita hlustir. Þau má svá kenna at kalla land eða jarðar heitum nokkurum eða munn eða sjón, augu heyrnarinnar ef nýgervingar eru.

83 Kendr muðr

Munn skal svá kenna at kalla land eða hús tungu eða tanna eða góma, varra, ok ef nýgervingar eru, þá kalla menn munn skip, en varrar borð eða tungu

---

[1] Obviously an error for *konr*.
[2] The Codex Regius version seems to have had *ósvifruðr* (written 'osvifr rvðr' in GkS 2367 4to). The scribe of DG 11 4to has occasionally interpreted insular f (ꝼ) as p.
[3] Obviously an error for *fornǫfn* 'substitutions'.
[4] Possibly for *hjarnskál* 'brain pan'.
[5] This word is redundant.

what he is possessor of, or thus, to call him the father or grandfather of the one that he named by his normal name. He is called great-grandfather, son, inheritor, heir; a brother is called consanguinean, cognate, relative, kinsman, kin, relation, scion, descendant, pillar of a family, legitimate ones, offspring.

Relations by marriage are also called affinitives, connections, gossip, rowing-bench mate of men, rowing-bench partner.

An opponent is also called enemy, destroyer, injurer, oppressor, unyielding one. These we call circumlocutions, also if a man is referred to by his dwellings or ships, or whatever has a name, or one of his possessions that has a proper name.

80 Of true description
We call them true descriptions, calling a person sage, thinker, eloquent, wise in counsel, liberal with wealth, unsluggish, heedful person, dandy. These are ancient names.

81 Of non-periphrastic terms for women
The following are non-periphrastic terms for women: wife, bride. The women that always go around with pomp and finery are called *fljóð*. Those that are clever in speech are called *snótir*. Those that are gentle in behaviour are called *drósir*. Those that are arrogant ar called *svarri* and *svarkr*. A woman that is of independent character is called *ristill*. One that is very rich is called *rýgr*. One that is retiring like young girls and those women that are timid is called *feima*. The woman whose husband has left the country is called *sæta*. The woman whose husband has been slain abroad is called *hæll*. The woman whose husband is dead is called a widow, those women that are married to the same man *eljur*. A woman is known as the bedfellow or gossip and confidante of her husband, and that is circumlocution.

82 How the head shall be referred to
The head shall be called by calling it toil of the neck or a man's burden, land of helmet and hat and brains and hair and eyebrows, scalp, ears, mouth, Heimdallr's sword, and it is normal to refer to sword-names and to name whichever one wishes and refer to it in terms of some name for Heimdallr. Without periphrasis the head is called skull, brain-skin, crown. Eyes are called sight and glance or look. They may be referred to by calling them sun, moon, shields or glass or jewels or stone of eyelashes or eyebrows, eyelids or forehead. Ears are called auricles. They may be referred to by calling them land or by any terms for earth or mouth or sight, eyes of the hearing if allegory is being used.

83 Mouth referred to
The mouth shall be referred to by calling it land or house of tongue or teeth or gums, lips, and if allegory is being used, then people call the mouth a

rǿðit eða stýrit. Tennrnar eru stundum kallaðar grjót munnsins eða góma, tungu eða ~~varra~~ orða.
Tunga er réttkent sverðsheiti ok kend til máls eða munns.
Skegg heitir barð eða kanpr, þat er stendr úr vǫrrum.
Hár heitir lauf, haddr þat er konur hafa. Hár er svá kent at kallat skógr eða viðarheiti nokkuru ok kent til hauss eða hǫfuðs, en skegg kenna menn við hǫku ok kinnr eða kverkr.
Hjarta heitir negg. Þat skal svá kenna at kalla korn eða stein eða epli eða hnot eða mýl ok kenna við brjóst eða hug. Kalla má ok hús eða berg eða jǫrð hugarins.
Brjóst má svá kenna at kalla hús eða garð eða[1] hjarta, skip anda eða lifrar, hemmar[2] land hugar ok munns.

84 Hér segir enn frá nýgervingum
Hugr heiti sefi, ást, elskugi, vili,[3] munr. Huginn má svá kenna at kalla vind trollkvenna ok rétt at nefna hverja er vill, ok svá at nefna jǫtna eða kenna þá til konu hans eða móður hans eða dóttur. Hugr heitir ok geð, þekkinn,[4] eljun, nenning, vit, skaplyndi, trygð, hugr.
Hugr heitir ok geð, þokki, reiði, fjandskapr, ráð, fár, girnd, bǫl, harmtregi, úskap, grellskapr,[5] lausung, geðleysi, þunngeði, gessinn,[6] harðgeði, óþverri.

85 Hér segir hversu heitir hǫndin
Hǫnd heitir mund, armr, hrammr. Á hendi heitir ǫlbogi, armleggr, úlfliðr, fingr, greip, hreifi, nagl, gómr, jaðarr, kvikva, | vǫðvi, aflvǫðvi, æðar, sinar, kǫgglar, knúi. Hǫnd má kalla jǫrð vápna eða hlífa, við axla ok erma, lófa, hreifa, jǫrð gullhringa ok vals ok hauks ok allra heita hans, ok í nýgervingum fót axla ok bognauð.[7]

86 Hversu kendir eru føtrnir
Fót má kenna tré ilja, rista, leista. Má kalla fótinn tré eða stoð þessa. Við skíð, skúa ok brǿkr eru føtr kendir. Á føti heitir lær, kné, kálfi, bein, leggr, rist, jarki, il, tá. Við allt þetta má svá kenna fótinn, kalla hann tré ok kenna við þessa hluti.

87 Kent málit
Mál heitir orð, orðtak, snilli, tala, saga, senna, þræta, þjarka, sǫngr, galdr, kveðandi, skjal, skval, glaumr, þys⟨s⟩, þrapt, skálp, dólska, ljóðæska. Heitir ok rǫdd ok[1] hljómr, ómun, þytr, gnjǫll,[8] gnýr, glymr, þrymr, rymr, brak, svipr, svipan, gangr.

[1] This word is redundant.
[2] Obviously an error; *heimar* does not fit the context. The other manuscripts have *eljunar* 'energy'.
[3] Written 'villi'.
[4] This must be an error for *þokkinn*, although *þokki* comes again in the next sentence.
[5] Written 'grezlſkapr'.
[6] Perhaps for *gessni* 'greed'.   [7] Written *baugnauð*.
[8] Probably an error for *gjǫll*.

ship, and the lips gunwale or the tongue the oar or the rudder. The teeth are sometimes called rocks of the mouth or gums, of the tongue or words.

The tongue is correctly referred to by a term for sword and referred to in terms of speech or mouth.

Facial hair is called beard or moustache, that which grows from the lips.

Hair is called foliage; head of hair in the case of women. Hair is referred to by calling it forest or by some term for tree and referring to it in terms of skull or head, but the beard people refer to in terms of chin and cheeks or throat.

The heart is called bosom. It shall be referred to by calling it corn or stone or apple or nut or ball and referring to it in terms of breast or thought. It can also be called house or crag or ground of the thought.

Breast can be referred to by calling it house or enclosure of the heart, ship of spirit or liver, land of energy, thought and mouth.

84 Here it tells again of allegory

Thought is called mind, love, affection, desire, pleasure. The thought shall be referred to by calling it wind of trollwives and it is normal to use the name of any one of them you wish, and also to use names of giants or refer to them in terms of his wife or his mother or daughter. Thought is also called disposition, the attitude, energy, liking, wit, temperament, troth, thought.

Thought is also called disposition, attitude, anger, enmity, intention, hostility, lust, evil, grief-sorrow, bad temper, wrath, duplicity, inconstancy, frivolity, greedy, defiance, restlessness.

85 Here it tells how the upper limb is called

The upper limb is called hand, arm, paw. On the upper limb is what is called elbow, upper arm, wrist, finger, grasp, palm, nail, fingertip, side of the hand, quick, muscle, biceps, veins, sinews, joints, knuckles. The upper limb can be called ground of weapons or shields, tree of shoulders and sleeves, palms, wrists, ground of gold rings and of falcon and hawk and all terms for it, and in allegory leg of shoulders and bow-forcer.

86 How the legs are referred to

The leg can be called tree of the soles, insteps, stocking-feet. The leg can be called tree or pillar of these. Legs are referred to in terms of skis, shoes and breeches. On the leg is what is called thigh, knee, calf, shank, shin, instep, side of the foot, sole, toe. In terms of all these the leg can be referred to, calling it tree and referring to it in terms of these things.

87 The speech referred to

Speech is called words, vocabulary, eloquence, tale, story, wrangle, dispute, quarrelling, song, incantation, recitation, chat, babble, noisy merriment, clamour, squabbling, chatter, impertinence, childishness. Voice is also called sound, resonance, whistling, din, clash, boom, clamour, roaring, crash, thud, crack, clatter.

Vit heitir speki, ráð, skilning, skǫrungskapr. Heitir undirhyggja vélræði, brigðræði. Heitir ok øði ólund. Tvíkend er reiði, ef maðr er í illum hug, reiði heitir ok fargervi skips eða hross. Far er ok tvíkent, fár er reiði, far er skip. Þvílík orðtǫk hafa menn mjǫk til at yrkja fólgit.

88 Kendr vargrinn

Vargr heitir dýr ok er rétt at kenna við blóð eða hræ, svá at kenna lund hans. Eigi er rétt at kenna við fleiri dýr. Vargr heitir ok úlfr, sem Þjóðólfr kvað:

228 (318) Gera var gisting byrjuð
gnógr en úlfr úr skógi,
sannr Freki skal vekja
Sigurðr, kom norðan.[1]

Hér er Geri kallaðr. Freki, sem Egill kvað:

229 (319) Þá er und Freki
en[2] odd⟨b⟩reki
gnúði hrafni
á hǫfuðstafni.

Vitnir:

230 (320) Elfr var unda gjálfri
eitrkǫld roðin heitu;
vitnis fell með vatni
varmt eldr[3] í munn Karmtar.

Ylgr, sem Arnórr kvað:

231 (321) Svalg áttbogi ylgjar
ógóðr, en var blóði
grøðir grǿnn at rauðum,
brandvǫxnum[4] ná, blandinn.

Vargr sem Illugi kvað:

232 (322) Vargs var muðr[5] þar er margan —
menskerðir stakk sverði
myrkaurriða markar —
minn dróttinn rak flótta.

[1] Some sense can be made of this garbled verse by changing *gnógr* to *gnóg* (so the other manuscripts) and *Sigurðr* to *Sigurð* (other manuscripts *Sigurðar*).

[2] Other manuscripts have *sleit* 'tore'. The verse is from Egill's *Hǫfuðlausn*.

[3] The verse is from Einarr Skúlason's *Elfarvísur* and is also in many manuscipts of *Heimskringla*. Most manuscripts have *ǫlðr* 'ale', and *eldr* 'fire' is likely to be a misreading of that word. Kǫrmt is an island, and most other manuscripts have *men* 'necklace', which provides a more normal kenning for the sea.

[4] Obviously an error for *grand-* (so other manuscripts).

[5] Obviously an error for *munr*. Three other quatrains from this poem about Haraldr harðráði are extant; lines 2–3 in all four are 'ancient motifs' referring to the Vǫlsung story.

Wisdom is called sagacity, counsel, understanding, genius. Dissembling is called deception, shiftiness. Fury is also called bad temper. *Reiði* can refer to two things, if a man is in a bad mood, *reiði* is also the term for the tackle of a ship or a horse. *Fár* can also refer to two things, fury is *fár*, a ship is *far*. People frequently use such vocabulary so as to compose with concealed meaning.

88 The wolf referred to

There is an animal called a warg, and it is normal to refer to it in terms of blood or corpse so as to indicate its nature. It is not normal to use such kennings for other animals. A warg is also called wolf, as Þjóðólfr said:

228   Sufficient fare was brought
to Geri (a wolf, i.e. men were killed in battle), and the wolf came
from the north out of the forest;
a true Freki (wolf) shall waken Sigurðr.

Here it is called Geri. Freki, as Egill said:

229   When Freki [tore] wound (i.e. in battle),
and point-breaker (wave of pointed weapons, i.e. blood)
washed over the prow (beak)
of the raven's head.

Watcher:

230   Deadly cold Elfr was reddened
with hot wound-surge (blood);
the watcher's (wolf's) warm ale (blood, drink for the wolf)
flowed with water into the mouth of Kǫrmt (sea).

She-wolf, as Arnórr said:

231   Evil relatives of she-wolf (wolves)
swallowed much harmed corpse,
and green swell turned to red,
mixed with blood.

Warg, as Illugi said:

232   It was pleasure for the warg
where my lord drove many a rout.
The neck-ring diminisher (generous man, Sigurðr) stabbed
with his sword the dark forest-trout (dragon, Fáfnir).

Heiðingi, sem hér segir:

233 (323) Heiðingja sleit hungri,
hár⟨r⟩ gylðir naut sára,
granar rauð gramr af eiri,[1]
gekk úlfr í ben rekka.

Sem Þjóðólfr kvað:

234 (324) Óð, en, ørnu, náði
missveit[2] Freka beitu,
Geira ylðir[3] naut gylðir,
Gjálfar[4] stóð í blóði.

89 Kendr bjǫrn

Bjǫrn: fetvíðr, húnn, vetrliði, bersi, fress, íugtanni, ifjungr, glúmr, vilskarfr,[5] bera, Jóreykr, frekr, blóm⟨r⟩, ysonigr.[6]

90 Frá hirti ok hesta nǫfnum ágætum

Hjǫrtr: mótrauðnir,[7] dalarr, dallr, Daninn, Dvalinn, Dyraþórr, Dyneyrr, Eikþyrnir.[8]

235 (325) Hrafn ok Sléttfeti,
hestar ágætir,
Valr ok Léttfeti,
var þar Tjaldari,
Gulltoppr ok Goti,
getit heyrða ek Sóta,
Mór ok Lungr
með Mari.

236 (326) Vingr ok Stúfr
með Skæfaxa;
Óðin knátti á baki bera;
Sil⟨f⟩rintoppr ok Simr;
svá heyrða ek Fáks getit;
Gullfaxi ok Jór með guðum.

[1] *af eiri* is clearly an error for *á Fenri* (so the other manuscripts).
[2] Written 'missveita' with the *a* cancelled; clearly an error for *íms sveit*.
[3] I.e. *Gera ǫlðra* as in some other manuscripts.
[4] Written 'giolfar'. Obviously to be read *Gjálpar*.
[5] For *-skarpr*.
[6] Error for *ysjungr* (so other manuscripts).
[7] For *-troðnir*. Other manuscripts have *dalr* for *dallr*.
[8] This word written by a later hand. See Grape et al. 1977: 165. It is found in *Gylfaginning* (p. 58 above, written Tak-), like the four preceding hart names (p. 30).

Heath-dweller, as it says here:

233 The heath-dweller's (wolf's) hunger was sated (corpses were provided, battle was fought), the grey howler (wolf) fed on wounds, the prince reddened Fenrir's chops, the wolf went to drink from wounds.

As Þjóðólfr said:

234 Gjálp's stud (giantess's horses, wolves) waded in plenty of blood, and the dusky one's (wolf's) troop (pack) got Freki's food (carrion); the howler (wolf) enjoyed Geri's ales (blood).

89 Bear referred to

Bear: wide-stepper, cub, winter-survivor, grizzly, snarler, greedy-tooth, hooded one, dark one, shrivelled-gut, she-bear, Jórekr, greedy one, snorer, bustler.

90 Of the hart and famous names of horses

Hart: heath-treader, antlered one, curved horned one, Daninn, Dvalinn, Dyraþórr, Dyneyrr, Eikþyrnir.

235 Hrafn and Sléttfeti,
famous horses,
Valr and Léttfeti,
Tjaldari was there,
Gulltoppr and Goti,
I have heard Sóti mentioned,
Mór and Lungr
with Marr.

236 Vingr and Stúfr
with Skæfaxi;
it could carry Óðinn on its back;
Silfrintoppr and Simr;
also I heard Fákr mentioned;
Gullfaxi and Jór among the gods.

237 (327) Blótughóf⟨i⟩[1] hét hestr
er bera kváðu
ungan at ríða.
Gils ok Falófnir,
Glæx[2] ok Skeiðbrimir;
þar var ok Gyllis um getit.

91 Frá hestum[3]

238 (328) Dagr reið Hrafni
en Dvalinn Móðni,
Họð Hjálmþír
en Haki Faxa,
reið bani Belja
Blóðughófa,
en Skæfaði
skati Haddingja.

239 (329) Vésteinn Vali
en Vífill Stúfa,
Meinþjófr Mói,
en Muninn Vakri,
Áli Hrafni
en til ís⟨s⟩ riðu,
en annarr austr
undir Aðilsi,
grár hvarfaði
geiri undaðr.

240 (330) Bjọrn reið Blakki,
en Bjár⟨r⟩ Kerti,
Atli Glaumi,
en Aðils Slungni,
Họgni Họlkni,
en Haraldr Fọlkni.
Gunnarr Gota,
Grana ríðr Sigurðr.

241 (331) Gamalla øxna heiti
hefi ek gjọrla fregit,

[1] Error for *Blóðughófi*.
[2] Error for *Glær*.
[3] Called *Alsvinnsmál* in the Codex Regius version. The preceding *þula* is called *Þorgrímsþula*, and verse 241 is also said to be from *Þorgrímsþula*.

237   There was a horse called Blóðughófi
       which they said carried
       the young one riding;
       Gils and Falófnir.
       Glær and Skeiðbrimir;
       Gyllir was also mentioned there.

91 Of horses

238   Dagr rode Hrafn
       and Dvalinn Móðnir,
       Hjálmþír Hǫðr
       and Haki Faxi,
       the slayer of Beli
       rode Blóðughófi,
       and Skæfaðr
       the prince of the Haddings.

239   Vésteinn Valr
       and Vífill Stúfi,
       Meinþjófr Mór
       and Muninn Vakr,
       Áli Hrafn,
       when they rode to the ice,
       and another one east
       under Aðils,
       grey, it wandered
       wounded with a spear.

240   Bjǫrn rode Blakkr
       and Bjárr Kǫrtr,
       Atli Glaumr
       and Aðils Slungnir,
       Hǫgni Hǫlknir
       and Haraldr Fǫlknir.
       Gunnarr Goti,
       Sigurðr rides Grani.

241   Names of ancient oxen
       I have precisely heard,

þeirra Rauðs ok Høfis;[1]
Reginn ok Hlýrr,
Himinrjóðr ok Arfli,
Arfr ok Arfuni.

92 Frá orma heitum

Þessi eru orma heiti: ormr, dreki, Fáfnir, Jǫrmungandr, naðr, Níðhǫgr, naðra, lin⟨n⟩r, Góinn, Móinn, Grafvitnir, Grábakr, Ófnir, Súgrínir.

93

Tveir eru fuglar þeir er eigi þarf annan veg at kenna en kalla blóð eða hræ ⟨drykk⟩ þeirra. Þat er hrafn eða ǫrn. Alla aðra fugla karlkenda má kenna við blóð. Sem Þjóðólfr kvað:

242 (333) Blóðorra lætr barri
bragningr ara fagna;
Gauts berr sík[2] á sveita
svans verð konungr Hǫrða;
Geirsoddum lætr grøðir
g(runn) h(vert) st(ika) ⟨sunnar⟩
h(irð) þ(at) ⟨er⟩ h(ann) s(kal) v(arða)
hrægamms ara s(ævar).[3]

f. 41v, p. 80 Krákr, Huginn, Muninn, borginmóði, árflognir, ártali, holdboði. Svá kvað Einarr skálaglamm:

243 (334) Fjallvǫndum gaf fylli,
fullr varð, en spjǫr gullu,
herstefnandi hrǫfnum,
hrafn á ylgjar tafni.

Svá kvað Einarr Skúlason:

244 (335) Dólgstála[4] kná ek dýrum
dýr⟨r⟩ magnandi at stýra—
Hugins fermu bregðr harmi
harnar[5]—bliksólar garmi.

Ok enn kvað hann:

[1] Written with double *s*.
[2] Other manuscript have *sigð* 'sickle', i.e. sword: the king kills men.
[3] The abbreviations have been expanded with the help of the Codex Regius version. See Lasse Mårtensson and Heimir Pálsson 2008.
[4] Possibly an error for *-stara*, which provides a sort of *skothending*. Other manuscripts have *-skára* 'gulls'.
[5] The verse form shows that this word must be *harmr*. On this verse see Grape et al. 1977: 166 and Faulkes 1998: 212.

of Rauðr and Hǫfir;
Reginn and Hlýrr,
Himinrjóðr and Arfli,
Arfr and Arfuni.

92 Of names for serpents

These are names for serpents: worm, dragon, Fáfnir, Jǫrmungandr, adder, Níðhǫggr, viper, snake, Góinn, Móinn, Grafvitnir, Grábakr, Ófnir, Súgrínir

93

There are two birds that there is no need to refer to in any other way than by calling blood or corpses their drink. These are the raven or eagle. All other masculine birds can be referred to in terms of blood. As Þjóðólfr said:

242   The ruler lets blood-grouse (ravens) delight in eagle's barley;
       the king of people of Hǫrðaland (Haraldr harðráði) brings
       Gautr's ditch (mead of poetry) to the blood-swan's (raven's)
       food (the fallen slain, i.e. he composes about them);
       the one (king) who benefits (feeds) the corpse-vulture (raven)
       of the eagle's sea (blood) lets
       his followers fence every shallow
       that he has to defend with spear-points.

Crow, Huginn, Muninn, secure-mood, early flier, year-counter, flesh-marker. So said Einarr skálaglamm:

243   The army musterer gave
       mountain haunting ravens their fill,
       and spears rang; the raven
       got full on she-wolf's food.

So said Einarr Skúlason:

244   Splendid strengthener of warfare-starlings, I can
       wield the splendid dog (enemy, i.e. sword) of the gleaming
       sun (shield); the troubler (eater, i.e. eagle) of Huginn's (raven's)
       food (carrion) puts an end to his trouble (gets fed).

And again he said:

245 (336) En við hjaldr þar er hǫlðar,
haugþrútinn,[1] svelgr lúta,
Muninn drekkr blóð ór benjum
blásvartr, Munins[2] hjarta.

Svá kvað Víga-Glúmr:[3]

246 (337) Þá er dynfúsar dísir,
dreyra más, á eyri,
bráð fekk borginmóði,
blóðskjaldaðir stóðum.

Svá kvað Skúli Þorsteinsson:

247 (338) Mundi opt þar er undir
árflogin[4] gaf ek sára
Hlǫkk í hundraðs[5] flokki
hvítinga mik líta.

94 Frá kenningu arnarins

Ǫrn: ari, gemlir, hreggskornir, geirlǫðnir, hrímnir, ym⟨i⟩r, andhrímner, egþirr,[6] gin⟨n⟩arr, undskorinnnir, gallófnir. Svá kvað Einarr:

248 (339) Sámleitum rauð sveita—
sleit ǫrn Gera beitu,
fekst arnar matr járnum—
Járnsǫxu grǫn faxa.

Svá kvað Þjóðólfr:

249 (341) Segjǫndum fló sagna
snótar úlfr at móti
í gemlis ham gǫmlum
glamma á[7] fyrir skǫmmu.

Ok sem hér segir:

250 (342) Hreggskornis vil ek handa
háleitan mjǫk[8] vanda.

[1] Error for *hug-*. Emending *-þrútinn* to *þrútit* (so the Codex Regius version) would make this refer to the king's heart.
[2] Obviously dittography from the previous line. Other manuscripts have *konungs*.
[3] See Heimir Pálsson 2010d.
[4] Must be an error for *árflogni* (dat.) (so the other manuscripts).
[5] Written 'hvndraz'.
[6] Double r for single. The four preceding names are not in the Codex Regius version, but appear in other manuscripts in *þulur* for eagle and hawk (*Skj* A 1 686–7).
[7] Error for *ó*, the detached negative prefix to *skǫmmu* (tmesis).
[8] Error for *mjǫð* (so other manuscripts).

245	But the king's heart swells at the battle, where heroes sink down; blue-black Muninn (raven), swollen with determination, drinks blood from wounds.

So said Víga-Glúmr:

246	When we with bloody shields withstood the ladies (valkyries) eager for noise (battle) on the sandbank, secure-mood (the raven) got food (carrion) of the gore-gull (eagle).

So said Skúli Þorsteinsson:

247	The Hlǫkk (lady) of (who serves) drinking horns would often see me where I gave wounds to the early-flier of wounds (raven) in a company of a hundred.

94 Of referring to the eagle

Eagle: erne, old one, storm-cleaver, spear-offerer, screamer, croaker, the one that is dark in front, sharp-claw, deceiver, wound-cleaver, shrill crier. So said Einarr:

248	He reddened with blood the chops of the dark-looking steed (wolf) of Járnsaxa (giantess); eagle tore Geri's (wolf's) food (carrion); erne's meat was provided by irons (weapons).

So said Þjóðólfr:

249	The lady wolf (snatcher of Iðunn, Þjazi) flew noisily to meet the commanders (leaders) of the crew (the Æsir) no short time ago in an old old-one's (eagle's) form.

And as it says here:

250	I will work carefully the noble mead (poetry) (that is) in storm-cleaver's (Óðinn's in eagle shape) hands.

Svá kvað Skúli:

251 (343) Vakist[1] þar er vellis[2] ekla
víðis áðr ok síðan
grepp⟨r⟩ heyrir þá góðum[3]
gallófnis vel spjalli.

95 Kendr eldr

Eldr, sem hér segir:

252 (370) Eldr brennat svá sjaldan,
svíðr dyggr jǫfurr bygðir,
blása rǫnn fyrir ræsi
reyk, er Magnúss[4] kveikir.

Logi, sem Valgarðr kvað:

253 (371) Reykr stóð en steyptist
steinóðr logi innan.

Eisa, sem Atli kvað:

254 (374) Óxu ok eisur vaxa
allmǫrg[5] loga hallar.

Eimr sem hér segir:

255 (375) Brunnu allvalds inn⟨i⟩,
eldr hykk at sal felldi
eimr skaut á her hrími,
hjálmgerr[6] við Nið sjálfa.

Hyrr, sem Arnórr kvað:

256 (376) Eymðit ráð við Rauma
reiðir[7] Eydana meiðir.
Heit dvínuðu Heina,
herr[8] gerði þá kyrra.

Funi, sem Einarr kvað:

257 (377) Funi kyndist fljótt.

Bruni,[9] sem Valgarðr kvað:

[1] *Vaki ek* in other manuscripts.
[2] Perhaps an error for *vells*. The line is a syllable too long.
[3] Perhaps an error for *góðu* (so other manuscripts).
[4] Double s for single.
[5] The other manuscripts have two more lines in which the word *hús* appears.
[6] Double r for single. This verse is attributed to Þórðr Sjáreksson in *Fagrskinna*.
[7] Obviously an error for *reiðr* (so other manuscripts).
[8] Clearly this ought to be *hyrr* 'burning', as is shown by the prose.
[9] Here and in the following verse, other manuscripts have *brími* 'fire'.

So said Skúli:

251   I stay awake early and late
where [there is] dearth of wealth;
shrill-crier's (eagle's) ocean's (blood's) fellow (warrior)
then listens well to the good news.

95 Fire referred to

Fire, as it says here:

252   Fire does not burn so seldom
that Magnús kindles; the worthy
prince singes dwellings; buildings
belch smoke because of the ruler.

Flame, as Valgarðr said:

253   Smoke rose up, and
furious flame poured out.

Ember, as Atli said:

254   Embers of the hall grew and grow,
very many [houses] are on fire.

Smoke, as it says here:

255   The all-powerful one's (king's) vaulted lodgings
burned by the Nið itself;
I think it was fire that brought down the hall,
smoke shot soot on the host.

Burning, as Arnórr said:

256   The angry Island-Danes' injurer
did not soften his treatment of the Raumar (people of Raumaríki).
The defiance of the Heinir (people of Heiðmǫrk) dwindled;
the army made them submissive.

Blaze, as Arnórr said:

257   The blaze was kindled quickly.

Heat, as Valgarðr said:

258 (378) Bjartr sveimaði bruni.

Leygr, sem Halldórr kvað:

259 (379) En knáttust þar þeira,
þú vart aldrigin, skjaldar
leygr þaut um sjǫ⟨t⟩, sigri,
sviptr, gersimum skipta.

96 Hér segir frá bardaga Heðins ok Hǫgna

Orrosta er kǫlluð Hjatningja veðr eða él, ok vápn Hjaðninga eldar eða vendir. En sú saga er til þess, at konungr hét Hǫgni. Hann átti þá dóttur er Hildr hét. Hana tók at herfangi Heðinn Hjarrandason. Þá var Hǫgni farinn í konungastefnu, ok er hann spurði at herjat ⟨var⟩ ríki hans ok brott tekin dóttir hans Hildr, þá fór hann með liði sínu at leita Heðins ok spurði til hans at hann fór norðr undan. Ok er hann kom í Noreg spurði hann at honum hafði komit lið ór Orkneyjum, ok er hann kom þar sem heitir Háey, þar var fyrir Heðinn með sitt lið. Þá kom Hildr á fund fǫður síns ok bauð honum sætt af hendi Heðins, en í ǫðru lagi segir hon at hann sé búinn at berjast ok kveðr hann engrar vægðar eiga ván af honum. Hǫgni svaraði stutt dóttur sinni ok er hon hitti Heðin sagði hon honum at faðir hennar vill enga sætt, ok bað hann búast til bardaga. Ok svá gera þeir, ganga upp á land ok fylkja liðinu. Kallar Heðinn á Hǫgna mág sinn ok bauð honum sætt ok mikit gull at bótum. Þá svarar Hǫgni: Of síð bauðtu þetta, því at nú hefi ek sverðit Dánuleif ór slíðrum dregit, er dvergar hafa gert ok manns bani verðr hvert sinn er brugðit er ok aldri bilar í hǫggi ok ekki sár grǿr þat er þar skeinist af. Þá svarar Heðinn: Sverði hǿlir þú þar en eigi sigri. Þat kalla ek hvert hollt er dróttinnhollt er.

Þá hófu þeir þá orrostu er Hjaðningaveðr er kallat ok bǫrðust þann dag allan. At kveldi fóru þeir til skipa. En Hildr gekk um nóttina ok vakti upp með fjǫlkyngi alla þá menn er um daginn hǫfðu fallit.

Annan dag gengu konungar á land ok bǫrðust, ok svá allir þeir er fellu enn fyrra dag. Fór svá orrostan hvern dag eptir annan at allir menn ⟨er⟩ fellu ok ǫll vápn er þar lágu á vígvelli þá urðu at grjóti ok svá hlífar. Ok er dagaði stóðu allir upp inir dauðu menn ok bǫrðust, ok ferr svá allt til Ragnarǫkkrs.

97 Hér segir um kenning gulls

Hví er gull kallat barr Glasis eða lauf hans? Í Ásgarði er hann, sem hér segir at

260 (142) Glasir stendr
með gulligu laufi
fyrir Sigtýrs sǫlum.

Sá er viðr frægr með guðum ok mǫnnum.

258   The bright heat surged.
Lowe, as Halldórr said:
259:    But they were able to divide their
       treasures for themselves there;
       you were never bereft of victory;
       shield's lowe (the sword) thundered through dwellings.

96 Here it tells of the battle of Heðinn and Hǫgni

Battle is called the Hjaðnings' weather or storm, and weapons Hjaðnings' fires or rods. And there is this story that tells the origin of it, that there was a king called Hǫgni. He had a daughter that was called Hildr. She was abducted in a raid by Heðinn Hjarrandason. At the time Hǫgni was away at a conference of kings, and when he learnt that his kingdom had been raided and his daughter Hildr carried off, then he set out with his army to find Heðinn and got wind of him that he was travelling away north. And when he got to Norway he learnt that troops had joined him from Orkney, and when he got to the place called Hoy, he found Heðinn there with his force. Then Hildr came to see her father and offered him atonement on Heðinn's behalf, but alternatively she says that he is ready to fight and declares he has no hope of his giving way at all. Hǫgni's reply to his daughter was curt, and when she got back to Heðinn, she told him that her father was not interested in atonement, and told him to prepare for battle. And this is what they do, go ashore and marshall their troops. Heðinn calls out to his father-in-law Hǫgni and offered him atonement and a great deal of gold to make amends. Then Hǫgni replies:

'Too late have you offered this, for I have now drawn the sword Dánuleif from its sheath, which dwarfs have made and becomes the death of someone every time it is drawn, and a stroke from it never fails and no wound heals that that is inflicted by it.'

Then Heðinn replies: 'You can boast like this of your sword, but not of victory. In my opinion whatever serves its master is serviceable.'

Then they began the battle that is known as the Hjaðnings' weather, and they fought all that day. In the evening they went to their ships. But Hildr went during the night and woke up by magic all the men that had fallen during the day.

The next day the kings went ashore and fought, and so did all those that had fallen the previous day. The battle went on one day after another so that all the men that fell and all the weapons that lay there on the battlefield then turned to stone, and shields too. And when day came all the dead men got up and fought, and so it all goes on until the twilight of the gods.

97 Here it tells about referring to gold

Why is gold called Glasir's foliage or its leaves? It is in Ásgarðr, as it says here that
260   Glasir stands
       with golden foliage
       before Sigtýr's (Óðinn's) halls.
This tree is famous among gods and men.

98 Frá vélum dvergsins við Loka

Hví er gull kallat haddr Sifjar?
En þat bar til þess at Loki Laufeyjarson hafði þat gert til lævísi at klippa hár allt af Sif. En er Þórr varð varr tók hann Loka hǫndum ok mundi lemja hvert bein í honum áðr hann sverði þess eið at ⟨hann⟩ skal[1] fá af svarta álfum at þeir gera hadd af gulli til handa Sifju þann er svá skal vaxa sem annat hár. Eptir þat fór Loki til dverga þeira er hétu Ívalda synir, ok gerðu þeir haddinn ok skipit Skíðblaðni ok geirinn Gungni, er Óðinn á. Þá veðjaði Loki hǫfði sínu við dverginn, hvárt bróðir dvergsins mundi gert geta jamgóða gripi sem þessir vóru aðra þrjá, ok er þeir kómu til smiðju lagði dvergrinn í aflinn svínskinn ok bað blása at ok létta eigi blástrinum fyrr en hann tøki ór þat er hann hafði í látit aflinn. Ok þegar hann var út genginn ok hinn blés, þá settist á hann fluga ein ok krop⟨p⟩aði hann. En hann blés sem áðr, þar til er smiðrinn kom til ok tók ór aflinum, ok var þat gǫltr ok bustin ór gulli á. Því næst lagði hann í aflinn gullit ok bað hann blása þar til er hann kømi til. Þá kom flugan ok settist á háls honum ok krop⟨p⟩aði hálfu fastara en it fyrra sinn. En hann blés þar til er smiðrinn kom ok tók ór aflinum gullhring er Draupnir heitir. Þá lagði hann járn í afl ok bað hann blása, segir at ónýtt mun ef hann lætr falla blástrinn. Þá settist flugan á millum augna honum ok kroppaði svá at hann sá ekki. Þá greip hann til hendi sinni sem skjótast ok sveipti af sér fluguna meðan belgrinn lagðist niðr. Þá kom smiðrinn ok sagði nær hafa at ónýtast mundi ǫll smíðin í aflinum. Þá tók hann ór aflinum hamar ok fekk alla gripina honum í hendr brǿðr sínum ok bað hann fara til Ásgarðs með gripina at leysa veðjan sína.

En er þeir Loki báru saman gripina, þá settust æsir á dómstóla sína, ok skyldi þat atkvæði standast er Óðinn lagði á ok Þórr ok Freyr. Þá gaf Loki Óðni geirinn Gungni, en Þór haddinn er Sif skyldi hafa, en Frey Skíðblaðni ok sagði skyn á ǫllum gripunum, at geirrinn man eigi í hǫggvi stað nema, en haddrinn var þegar holdfastr er hann kom á hǫfuð Sif, en Skíðblaðnir hafði byr hvert er fara skyldi ok segl kom upp, en mátti vefja | saman ok hafa í pungi sér, ef þat vildi.

Þá bar dvergrinn saman sína gripi. Hann gaf Óðni hringinn ~~Gungn~~ Draupni ok sagði at ina níundu hverja nótt mundu drjúpa af honum átta hringar jafnhǫfgir sem hann. En Frey gaf hann gǫltinn ok sagði at hann mundi renna nótt ok dag meira en einn hestr lopt ok lǫg, ok aldri verðr svá myrkt af nótt at eigi sé ørit ljóst þar sem hann er, svá lýsti af bustinni. Þór gaf hann hamarinn Mjǫlni ok sagði hann ljósta mega svá stórt sem hann vildi hvat sem fyrir yrði, at eigi mundi hann bila, ok ef hann yrpi honum, mundi hann eigi

---

[1] *Skal* is written twice. In *Edda Snorra Sturlusonar* 1848–87: II the first is replaced by *hann*.

98 Of the dwarf's tricks against Loki

Why is gold called Sif's head of hair?

Now it is the origin of this that Loki Laufeyjarson had done this for love of mischief, cut off all Sif's hair. And when Þórr found out, he caught Loki and was going to break every one of his bones until he swore an oath that he would get black elves to make a head of hair for Sif of gold that would grow like any other hair. After this Loki went to some dwarfs that were called Ívaldi's sons, and they made the head of hair and the ship Skíðblaðnir and the spear Gungnir which belongs to Óðinn. Then Loki wagered his head with the dwarf on whether the dwarf's brother would succeed in making precious things as good as these were, another three, and when they got to the workshop, the dwarf put a pig's hide into the forge and gave instructions to blow and not to stop the blowing before he took out what he had put into the forge. And when he was gone out and the other was blowing, then a fly settled on him and nibbled him. But he went on blowing as before until the smith came up and took [his work] out of the forge, and it was a boar with bristles of gold on it. Next he put the gold into the forge and told him to blow until he returned to it. Then the fly came came and settled on his neck and nibbled twice as hard as the previous time. But he went on blowing until the smith came and took from the forge a gold ring that is called Draupnir. Then he put iron in the forge and told him to blow, saying it will be no good if he let there be any pause in the blowing. Then the fly settled between his eyes and nibbled so that he could not see. Then he snatched at it with his hand as quick as he could and swept the fly off him while the bellows was on its way down. Then the smith came and said it had come close to all the work in the forge being ruined. Then he took from the forge a hammer and handed over all the precious things to him, his brother, and told him to go to Ásgarðr taking the precious things to redeem his stake.

And when he and Loki brought the precious things together, then the Æsir took their places on their judgment seats and the decision that Óðinn imposed, together with Þórr and Freyr, was to be final. Then Loki gave Óðinn the spear Gungnir, and Þórr the head of hair that Sif was to have, and Freyr Skíðblaðnir, announcing the features of all the precious things, that the spear will never not stop in its thrust, and the head of hair was immediately attached to the skin when it came onto Sif's head, and Skíðblaðnir had a fair wind wherever it was intended to go and the sail was hoisted, while it could be folded up and kept in one's pocket if desired.

Then the dwarf put together his precious things. He gave Óðinn the ring Draupnir, saying that every ninth night there would drip from it eight rings equal to it in weight. And he gave Freyr the boar, saying that it would run night and day faster than any single horse across sky and sea, and it never gets so dark due to the night that it is not bright enough wherever it is, there was so much light shed from its bristles. To Þórr he gave the hammer Mjǫllnir saying he could strike as heavily as he liked, whatever the target, so that it would would not fail, and if he threw it, he would not miss, nor would it fly

missa ok eigi fljúga svá langt at eigi mundi hann søkja heim hǫnd, ok ef hann vildi mundi hann vera svá lítill at hafa mátti í serk sér. En lítit var forskeptit. Ok var þat dómr þeira at hamarrinn var beztr gripanna ok mest vǫrn fyrir hrímþussum, ok dømðu þeir at dvergrinn ætti veðféit. Þá bauð Loki at leysa hǫfuð sitt, en dvergrinn sagði at þess var engi ván. Tak þú mik þá, kvað Loki. Ok hann vildi taka hann. Þá var hann víðs fjarri. Loki átti skúa þá er hann báru lopt ok lǫg. Þá bað hann, dvergrinn, Þór at hann skyldi taka hann, ok hann gerði svá. Þá vildi dvergrinn hǫggva af hǫfuð hans, en Loki sagði at hann á hǫfuðit en eigi hálsinn. Þá tók dvergrinn kníf ok þveng ok vill rifa saman varrar Loka ok vill stinga raufar á vǫrrunum, en knífrinn beit eigi á. Þá mælti dvergrinn at betri væri alr bróður hans. Ok svá skjótt sem hann nefndi, þá kom hann ok hann beit varrarnar. Hann rifaði saman varrar Loka, en Loki reif ór æsunum. Sá þvengr er munnr Loka er saman saumaðr með heitir Vartari.

99 Frá kenningu gulls

Hér heyrir at gull er kent til hǫfuðbanda Fullu, er Eyvindr kvað:[1]

261 (143) Fullu skein á fjǫllum
fjallsól brá vallar
Ullar kjóls um allan
aldr Hákonar skáldum.

100 Loki drap Otr son Hreiðmars

Þat er sagt at æsir fóru at kanna heim, Loki, Óðinn, Hønir. Þeir gengu at á nokkurri ok gengu í fors nokkurn, ok þar var otr einn ok hafði tekit lax einn ór forsinum. Þá tók Loki upp stein einn ok kastar at | otrinum. Kom í hǫfuðit ok hafði hann þegar bana. Loki hrósar veiði sinni, at hann hafði veitt í einu hǫggi otr ok lax. Tóku þeir otrinn ok laxinn, báru eptir sér. Kómu at bø nokkurum. Gengu inn. Þar bjó Hreiðmarr[2] bóndi, mikill ok fjǫlkunnigr. Beiddust æsir at hafa þar nátturðar dvǫl eða náttstað ok kóðust hafa vistina með sér ok sýndu bónda veiði sína. Ok er Hreiðmarr sá veiðina kallar hann á sonu sína, Regin ok Fáfni, segir at Otr bróðir þeirra var veginn. ok svá hverr þat hefir gert.

Nú ganga þeir feðgar at ásum, taka þá hǫndum ok binda þá, segja at otrinn var son Reiðmars. Æsir bjóða fjǫrlausn svá mikla sem Reiðmarr vill. Varð þat at sætt með þeim ok binda svardǫgum. Þá var otrinn fleginn. Tók Hreiþmarr otrbelginn ok mællti við þá at þeir skyldi fylla belginn af gulli rauðu ok hylja hann[3] allan ok skal þat vera at sætt með þeim.

Þá mælti Óðinn at Loki skyldi fara í Svartálfaheim. Hann kom til dvergs þess er Andvari heitir. Hann var svá margkunnigr at hann var stundum fiskr í

---

[1] See verse 88; *fjall-* in line 2 here is an error for *fall-*.
[2] Written sometimes *Hreiðmarr*, sometimes *Reiðmarr* in the manuscript.
[3] Written *hans*.

so far that it would not find its way back to his hand, and if he wanted, it would be so small that it could be kept inside his shirt. But the handle where it came out through the head was small.

And this was their decision, that the hammer was the best of the precious things, and the greatest defence against frost giants, and they decreed that the dwarf had won the stake.

Then Loki offered to redeem his head, but the dwarf said there was no chance of that.

'Catch me then,' said Loki.

And he tried to catch him. Then he was far away. Loki had some shoes that bore him across sky and sea. Then he, the dwarf, bade Þórr that he should catch him, and he did so. Then the dwarf was going to cut off his head, but Loki said that the head is his but not the neck. Then the dwarf got a knife and a thong and is going to stitch up Loki's lips and was going to pierce holes in his lips, but the knife would not pierce them. Then said the dwarf that his brother's awl would be better. And as soon as he spoke his name, then he came and he pierced his lips. He stitched Loki's lips together, but Loki tore tore out the holes. The thong that Loki's mouth is sewn together with is called Vartari.

99 Of referring to gold

In this verse, which Eyvindr composed, you can hear how gold is referred to in terms of Fulla's snoods:

261   The falling sun (gold) of the plain (forehead)
of Fulla's eyelashes shone
on poets' fells (arms) of Ullr's boat (shield)
throughout the life of Hákon.

100 Loki killed Otter son of Hreiðmarr

It is said that Æsir went to explore the world, Loki, Óðinn, Hønir. They came to a certain river and went into a certain waterfall, and there was an otter there and it had caught a salmon from in the waterfall. Then Loki picked up a stone and threw it at the otter. It hit its head and it was killed immediately. Loki was triumphant at his catch, that he had got in one blow otter and salmon. They picked up the otter and the salmon, taking them along with them. They came to a certain dwelling. They went in. In it lived Master Hreiðmarr, big and skilled in magic. The Æsir asked if they could stay there for supper or a night's lodging, saying that they had their provisions with them and showed the farmer their catch. And when Hreiðmarr saw their catch, he called to his sons Reginn and Fáfnír, saying that their brother Otter was slain, and also who had done it.

Now the father and his sons went up to the Æsir, took them prisoner and tied them up, saying that the otter was Hreiðmarr's son. The Æsir offer ransom for their lives, as much as Hreiðmarr wants. These terms were agreed between them and they confirm it with oaths. Then the otter was skinned. Hreiðmarr took the otter-skin and announced to them that they were to fill the skin with red gold and cover it entirely, and these were to be the terms of their settlement.

Then Óðinn said that Loki was to go into the world of black elves. He came across the dwarf that is called Andvari. He was so skilled in magic that

vatni. Loki tók hann hǫndum ok lagði á hann fjǫrlausn at hann skyldi greiða allt þat gull er hann átti í steini sínum.

Þá svipti dvergrinn undir hǫnd sér einum litlum gullbaug. Þat sá Loki ok bað hann fram láta bauginn. Dvergrinn bað hann eigi taka af sér bauginn ok lézt mega ǫxla sér fé af bauginum. Loki kvað hann eigi skyldu hafa einn pe⟨n⟩ing ok tók af honum bauginn ok gekk út.

Dvergrinn mælti at sá baugr skyldi verða at bana hverjum er ætti. Loki sagði at honum þótti þat vel ok sagði því haldast mega þann formála at hann mundi flytja þeim til handa er hafa skyldi ok þá tøki við.

Hann fór í brott ok kom til Hreiðmars ok sýndi Óðni gullit, en er hann sá bauginn, sýndist honum afar fagr ok tók af fénu. Hreiðmarr fylldi nú otrbelginn sem mest má hann ok setti upp síðan er fullr var. Þá gekk Óðinn til ok skyldi hylja belginn með gullinu, ok þá mælir hann við Reiðmar at hann skal til ganga ok sjá hvárt eigi er hulðr. Leit á vandliga ok sá eitt granahár ok bað þat hylja, en at ǫðrum kosti væri lokit sætt.

Dregr Óðinn nú fram | hringinn ok hulði granahárit ok sagði at þá var hann lauss frá gjaldinu.

Ok er Óðinn hafði tekit geirinn en Loki skúa sína ok þurftu þá ekki at óttast, þá mælir Óðinn at þat skyli haldast er Andvari hafði mælt um at sá baugr skyldi verða þess bani er ætti, ok þat helz⟨t⟩ síðan.

Nú er sagt hví gullit heitir otrgjǫld eða nauðgjǫld ásanna eða rógmálmr.

Nú tók Hreiðmarr gullit at sonargjǫldum, en Fáfnir ok Reginn[1] beiddust af nokkurs í bróðurgjǫld. Þeir drápu fǫður sinn. Fáfnir lagðist á féit ok varð at ormi, en Reginn fór á brott.

101 Frá því er Hrólfr seri gullinu

Hrólfr konungr var ágætr konungr af mildi ok frøknleik. En þat er eitt mark um mildi hans at bóndason einn, sá er Vǫggr hét, hann kom í hǫll Hrólfs konungs. Konungr var ungr, grannleitr á vǫxt. Þá gekk Vǫggr at hásætinu ok sá á hann. Þá mælti konungr: Hvat viltu mér, sveinn, er þú sér á mik? Vǫggr svarar: Þá er ek var heima var mér sagt at Hrólfr konungr væri mestr maðr á norðrlǫndum. En nú sitr hér í hásætinu kraki einn lítill, ok er sá konungr kallaðr. Þá svarar konungr: Þú hefir, sveinn, gefit mér nafn, at ek skal heita Hrólfr kraki. En þat er títt at gjǫf skal fylgja hverri gjǫf nafnfesti. Ne sé ek þik enga gjǫf hafa mér at gefa þá er sømiliga sé. Nú skal sá ǫðrum gefa er heldr hefir til, ok tók gullhring af hendi sér ok gaf honum.

Þá mælti Vǫggr: Gefðu allra konunga heilastr. Þess strengi ek heit at verða þess manns bani er þinn verðr.

Þá mælti Hrólfr konungr: Litlu verðr Vǫggr feginn.

[1] Written *Regins*.

he was sometimes a fish in water. Loki captured him and imposed on him as a ransom that he was to pay all the gold that he had in his cave.

Then the dwarf slipped under his arm one small gold ring. Loki saw this and told him to hand over the ring. The dwarf begged him not to take the ring off him, and said he could multiply wealth for himself from the ring. Loki said he was not going to have one penny, and took the ring off him and went out.

The dwarf pronounced that this ring should turn out to be the death of whoever possessed it. Loki said he was happy for that to be so, and said this pronouncement should have the power to remain valid inasmuch as he would convey it into the hands of those that were to have it and would then possess it.

He went off and came to Hreiðmarr's place and showed Óðinn the gold, and when he saw the ring, it seemed to him extremely beautiful and he removed it from the treasure. Hreiðmarr now filled the otter-skin as tightly as he could and after that stood it up when it was full. Then Óðinn went up and had to cover the skin with the gold, and then he said to Hreiðmarr that he should go up and see whether it is not covered. He looked at it closely and saw a single whisker and ordered it to be covered, but otherwise that would be the end of any agreement.

Now Óðinn takes out the ring and hid the whisker and said that now he was quit of the payment.

And when Óðinn had taken his spear and Loki his shoes and they had now had no need to fear, then Óðinn declared that it should remain valid, what Andvari had pronounced, that this ring should turn out to be the death of whoever possessed it, and this was subsequently fulfilled.

Now it has been told why the gold is called otter-payment or the Æsir's forced payment or strife-metal.

Now Hreiðmarr took the gold as atonement for his son, but Fáfnir and Reginn demanded some of it in atonenent for their brother. They slew their father. Fáfnir lay down on the treasure and turned into a serpent, but Reginn went away.

101 Of how Hrólfr sowed the gold

King Hrólfr was a notable king for generosity and valour. And this is one illustration of his humility, that a peasant's son that was called Vǫggr, he entered King Hrólfr's hall. The king was young, thin-looking in build. Then Vǫggr approached the throne and looked at him. Then said the king:

'What do you want with me, boy, that you look at me?'

Vǫggr replies: 'When I was at home I was told that King Hrólfr was the greatest man in the northern lands. But now there sits here on the throne a little pole (*kraki*), and it is called king.'

Then replies the king: 'You, boy, have given me a name, that I shall be called Hrólfr kraki. Now it is customary for a gift to accompany any name-giving. I do not see that you have any gift to give me that would be suitable. Now instead, he shall he give to the other that has something to give.'

And he took a gold ring from his arm and gave it him. Then said Vǫggr:

'May you be blessed above all kings in your giving. I solemnly vow to be the slayer of the man that becomes your [slayer].'

Then said King Hrólfr: 'It does not take much to please Vǫggr.'

102 Capitulum

Annat mark var þat um frøknleik hans at konungr réð fyrir Uppsǫlum er Aðils hét. Hann átti Yrsu, móður Hrólfs konungs kraka. Hann hafði ófrið við þann konung er Áli hét inn upplenski. Þeir bǫrðust á vatnsísi þeim er Vænir heitir. Aðils sendi orð Hrólfi at hann kømi til liðs við hann, ok hét mála ǫllu liði hans, því er føri með honum. En konungr skyldi sjálfr eignast þrjá kostgripi, þá er hann kyri af Svíþjóð. Hrólfr konungr mátti eigi fara fyrir ófriði þeim er hann átti við Saxa, en þó sendi hann Aðilsi kappa sína tólf. Í þeirri orrostu fell Áli konungr. Þá tók Aðils af honum dauðum hjálminn Hildisvín | ok hestinn Hrafn. Þá beiddust þeir berserkirnir Hrólfs at taka mála sinn, þrjú pund gulls hverr þeirra, ok flytja Hrólfi kostgripi þá, er þeir keri honum. Þat var hjálmrinn Hildigautr ok brynjan Finnsleif, er á hvárigu festi járn, ok gullhringinn Svíagrís⟨s⟩, er átt hǫfðu langfeðgar Aðils. En konungr varnaði allra gripa, ok eigi galt hann málann. Fóru berserkir brot⟨t⟩ ok unðu illa sínum hlut, sǫgðu Hrólfi konungi.

Hrólfr býr ferð sína til Uppsala ok kom skipum sínum í ána Fýri ok reið til Uppsala ok tólf berserkir hans griðalausir. Yrsa móðir hans fagnaði honum vel ok fylgði honum til herbyrgis ok eigi til konungs hallar. Vóru þá gervir eldar fyrir þeim ok gefit ǫl at drekka. Þá kómu menn Aðils inn ok báru skíð á eldinn ok gerðu svá mikinn at klæði manna Hrólfs konungs brunnu af þeim, ok mæltu: Er þat satt at Hrólfr ok kappar hans hafa svá mælt at þeir mundi hvárki flýja eld né járn?

Þá stóð Hrólfr upp ok mælti: Aukum vér nú eldana at Aðils húsum! Tók skjǫld sinn, kastar á eldinn ok hljóp yfir eldinn meðan skjǫldrinn brann. Konungr mælti: Flýrat sá eld, er yfir hleypr. Svá fór þá hverr at ǫðrum hans manna. Tóku þá er eldana hǫfðu keykt ok kǫstuðu á eldinn. Þá kom Yrsa drottning, móðir hans, ok fekk Hrólfi dýrshorn fullt af gulli ok með Svíagrís, ok bað þá fara til liðs síns.

Þeir riðu ofan á Fýrisvǫll. Þá sá þeir at Aðils konungr reið eptir þeim með her sínum alvápnaðum ok vill drepa þá. Þá tók Hrólfr hendi sinni í hornit ok seri gullinu um gǫtuna. En er Svíar sá þat, hljópu ⟨þeir⟩ ór sǫðlunum ok lesa upp gullit. En Aðils bað þá ríða ok reið ok sjálfr fremstr. Þá er Hrólfr konungr sá at Aðils reið nær honum, tók hann hringinn Svíagrís ok kastaði til Aðils ok bað hann þiggja at gjǫf. Aðils tók með spjótsoddinum ok laut eptir. Þá leit Hrólfr konungr aptr ok sá at Aðils laut niðr, ok mælti: Svínbeygða ek nú þann er øztr er með Svíum. Skilja at þessu.

Þvi er gullit kallat Kraka sáð eða Fýrisvallar. Svá kvað Eyvindr skáldaspillir:

262 (185)   Bárum Ullr um alla
        ímunlauks á hauka
        fjǫllum Fýrisvallar
        fræ, | Hákonar ævi.[1]

---

[1] Cf. verse 94.

102 Chapter

There is another illustration of his valour, that a king was ruling over Uppsala that was called Aðils. He was married to Hrólf kraki's mother Yrsa. He was at war with the king that was called Áli the Upplander. They fought on the ice of the lake that is called Vænir. Aðils sent word to Hrólfr that he should come to his aid, and promised a salary to all his followers that went with him. And the king himself was to get three treasures of his choice from Sweden. King Hrólfr could not go because of the hostilities in which he was engaged with Saxons, but still he sent Aðils his twelve champions. In this battle King Áli fell. Then Aðils took from him as he lay dead the helmet Hildisvín and his horse Hrafn. Then Hrólfr's berserks asked to be given their salary, three pounds of gold for each of them, and to take for Hrólfr the treasures that they chose for him. These were the helmet Hildigautr and the mail-coat Finnsleif, neither of which iron could penetrate, and the gold ring Svíagríss that had belonged to Aðils's ancestors. But the king refused all the treasures, and he did not pay the salary either. The berserks left and were greatly displeased with their treatment, telling King Hrólfr.

Hrólfr set off for Uppsala and brought his ships into the river Fýri and rode to Uppsala, and his twelve berserks, without waiting to negotiate terms of entry. His mother Yrsa welcomed him warmly and took him to a private room and not to the king's hall. Then fires were made for them and they were given ale to drink. Then Aðils's men came in and heaped wood on the fire and made it so huge that King Hrólfr's men's clothes were burning off them, and said:

'Is it true that Hrólfr and his champions have said this, that they would flee neither fire nor iron?'

Then Hrólfr stood up and said: 'Let us now add to the fires in Aðils's buildings.'

He took his shield, threw it on the fire and leapt over the fire while the shield was burning. The king said:

'He flees not fire that leaps over it.'

Then one after another of his men did the same. They took those that had lit the fires and threw them on the fire. Then his mother, Queen Yrsa, came and gave Hrólfr an animal's horn full of gold and the ring Svíagríss as well, and bade them go to their troops.

They rode down onto Fýri plain. Then they saw that King Aðils was riding after them with his army fully armed and is intending to kill them. Then Hrólfr took in his hand from in the horn and sowed the gold over the road. And when the Swedes saw this, they leapt from their saddles and gather up the gold. But Aðils told them to ride and also rode in front himself. When King Hrólfr saw that Aðils was riding close to him, he took the ring Svíagríss and threw it to Aðils and told him to accept it as a gift. Aðils picked it up with the point of his spear, and stooped down for it. Then King Hrólfr looked back and saw that Aðils was stooping down and said:

'I have made him that is highest among the Swedes grovel like a pig.'

They part with this.

This is why the gold is called Kraki's or Fýri plain's seed. So said Eyvindr skáldaspillir:

262 Battle-leek (sword) Ullr (warrior),
    we used to wear on hawk-fells (our arms)
    Fýri plain's seed (gold rings)
    throughout Hákon's life.

Svá kvað Þjóðólfr:[1]

263 (186) Auð sær Y⟨r⟩su byrðar
indrótt jǫfurr sinni
bjartplógaðar² bauga
brattakr valaspak⟨r⟩a.

Ok enn:

264 (186) Eyss landreki ljósu
látr³ varr Kraka barri
á hlémyldar⁴ holdi
haukkálfar⁵ mér sjálfum.

103 Hér segir hví gull er kallat Fróða mjǫl

Gull er kallat mjǫl Fróða því at Fróði konungr keypti ambáttirnar Fenju ok Menju, ok þá fannst kvernsteinn einn svá mikill í Danmǫrku at engi fekk dregit, en sú náttúra fylgði at allt mjǫl, þat er undir var malit, varð at gulli.⁶ Ambáttirnar fengu dregit steininn. Konungr lét þær mala gull um hríð. Þá gaf hann þeim eigi meira svefn en kveða mátti ljóð eitt. Síðan mólu þær her á hendr honum. Sá var hǫfðingi fyrir er Mýsingi hét, spekingr mikill.

104 Hér segir hví gull er kallat haugþak Hǫlga

Konungr hét Hǫlgi, faðir Þorgerðar Hǫlgabrúðar. Þau vóru blótuð ok var haugr gerr at þeim, ǫnnur fló af gulli en ǫnnur af silfri, þriðja af moldu. Hafa hér eptir skáldin kveðit, sem fyrr er ritat.

---

[1] Verses 263 and 264 comprise one complete stanza in the Codex Regius version; cf. verse 95.
[2] *-plógaðan* would enable this adjective (participle) to go with *-akr*.
[3] *last-* verse 95 and other manuscripts, which is obviously correct.
[4] For *-mild-*, as verse 95 and other manuscripts.
[5] For *-kálfur*, as verse 95 and other manuscripts.
[6] The manuscript has *gullit*.

So said Þjóðólfr:

263   The prince sows the brightly-ploughed
steep field of limb-peaceful (resting quietly on the arms)
rings (arms) with wealth of Yrsa's
load to his domestic troop

And again:

264   The fault-shunning land-director (ruler)
pours Kraki's bright barley (gold)
onto my own hawk-lands (arms)
that provide security for flesh.

103 Here it says why gold is called Fróði's meal

Gold is called Fróði's meal because King Fróði bought the slave-girls Fenja and Menja, and then there was found a millstone in Denmark so huge that no one was able to move it, but it had this property, that all the meal that was ground under it turned to gold. The slave-girls were able to move the stone. The king made them grind gold for a while. Then he allowed them no more sleep than for the time it takes to sing one song. After that they ground out an army against him. He was the leader of it that was called Mýsingr, a great sage.

104 Here it says why gold is called Hǫlgi's mound-roof

There was a king called Hǫlgi, father of Þorgerðr Hǫlgabrúðr. They were both worshipped and a mound was made for them, one layer of gold and the second of silver, the third of earth. The poets have used this in poems, as is written above.

265 Blíð er mær við móður,
 mála drekkr á ekkju,
 kvíðir kerling eiðu,
 kveðr dóttir vel beðju,
 opt finnr ambátt hǫptu,
 æ er frilla grǫm sværu,
 kiljar kvæn við elju,
 kann nipt við snǫr skipta.

266 Brottu er svarri ok sværa,
 sveimar rýgr ok feima,
 brúðr er í fǫr með fljóði,
 fat ek drós ok man kjósa,
 þekki ek sprund ok sprakka,
 spari ek við hæl at mæla,
 firrumst ek snót ok svarra,
 svífr mér lang⟨t⟩ frá vífi.[1]

267 Stendr þat er stórum grandar
 sterkviðri mér Herkju,
 í hneggverǫld hyggju;
 hefi ek stríð borit víða.
 Þar kemr enn ef un⟨n⟩a
 ítr vildi Bil skáldi
 at blíðr grør Gríðar
 glaumvindr í sal þindar.[2]

---

[1] See Introduction p. lxv.
[2] See Introduction p. xcvi.

265 A maiden is agreeable to her mother,
her female friend drinks to the widow,
an old lady is apprehensive about her ma,
her daughter welcomes her (female) bedfellow,
a slave-girl often finds a female captive,
a concubine is always hostile to her mother-in-law,
a wife always quarrels with her rival,
a sister knows how to share with a daughter-in-law.

266 The arrogant woman and the mother-in-law are away,
the powerful woman and bashful woman wander about,
the bride is in company with the woman,
I managed to choose girl and maid,
I know lady and splendid woman,
I hold back from speaking with a widow,
I avoid the lady and the arrogant woman,
I drift far from my wife.

267 This trollwife's storm (passionate emotion)
that greatly disturbs thought resides in my
heart-world (breast);
I have borne strife (anxiety) far and wide.
It may reach the point yet if
the beautiful goddess (lady) would love the poet
that the giantess's merry wind (joyful thoughts)
will grow happily in my diaphragm's hall (breast).

Part IV

Second Grammatical Treatise

105 Hér segir af setningu háttalykilsins

Hvat er hljóðs grein?

Þrenn.

Hver?

Þat er ein grein hljóðs er þýtr veðr eða vatn eða sær eða bjǫrg eða jǫrð eða grjót hrynr. Þetta hljóð heitir gnýr ok þrymr ok dunur ok dynr. Svá þat hljóð er málmarnir gera eða manna þyssinn. Þat heitir ok gnýr ok glymr ok hljómr. Svá þat ok er viðir brotna eða vápnin mǿtast. Þetta heita brak eða brestir eða enn sem áðr er ritat.

Allt eru þetta vitlaus hljóð, en hér um fram er þat hljóð er stafina eina skortir til málsins. Þat gera hǫrpurnar ok enn heldr hin meiri sǫngfǿrin, en þat heitir sǫngr.

Ǫnnur hljóðs grein er sú sem fuglarnir gera eða dýrin ok sækykvindin. Þat heitir rǫdd, en þær raddir heita á marga lund. Fuglarnir syngja ok gjalla ok klaka. Ok enn með ymsum háttum ok nǫfnum ok kunnǫstum eru greind ymsa vega dýra nǫfnin ok kunnu menn skyn hvat kykvendin þikkjast benda með mǫrgum sínum látum. Sækykvendin blása eða gella. Allar þessar raddir eru mjǫk skynlausar at viti flestra manna.

En þriðja hljóðs grein er sú sem menninir hafa. Þat heitir hljóð ok rǫdd ok mál. Málit gerist af blæstrinum ok tungubragðinu við tenn ok góma ok skipan varranna. En hverju orðinu fylgir minnit ok vitit. Minnit þarf til þess at muna atkvæði orðanna, en vitit ok skilningina til þess at hann muni at mæla þau orðin er hann vill.

Ef maðr fær snilld málsins þá þarf þar til vitit ok orðfrǿði ok fyriræltan ok þat mjǫk at hǿgt sé tungubragðit. Ef tennrnar eru skǫrðóttar ok missir tungan þar, þat lýtir málit. Svá ok ef tungan er of mikil, þá er málit blest. Nú er hon of lítil, þá er sá holgómr. Þat kann ok spilla málinu ef varrarnar eru eigi heilar.

Muðrinn ok tungan er leikvǫllr orðanna. Á þeim velli eru reistir stafir þeir er mál allt gera ok hendir málit ymsa, svá til at jafna sem hǫrpustrengir eða eru læstir[1] lyklar í simphóníe.

---

[1] 'locked'. Probably for *leystir* 'released'.

105 Here it tells of the arrangement of the key to forms

What are the classes of sounds?

Threefold.

Which?

It is one class of sounds when wind whistles or water or sea or rocks or earth or stones crash down. This sound is called clash and din and noise and clatter. Also the sound that weapons make or a crowd of people. This is also called clash and ringing and roar. Also when timbers break or weapons meet each other. This is called crash or crack and so on as was written above.

All these are meaningless sounds, but besides these there is the sound that only lacks letters to be speech. This is made by the harps and even more so the larger musical instruments, and this is called music.

The second class of sounds is that which birds make or the animals and the sea-creatures. This is called voice, but these voices have names of various kinds. The birds sing and scream and twitter. And moreover by means of various methods and names and techniques, the names of animals[' voices] are distinguished, and people understand the sense of what the animals seem to be indicating by many of their sounds. Sea-creatures blow or scream. All these voices are pretty well irrational according to most people's understanding.

But the third class of sounds are those that people use. These are called utterance and voice and speech. The speech is made by the breath and the movement of the tongue against teeth and gums and the arrangement of the lips. And every word is accompanied by the memory and the intelligence. The memory in necessary in order to remember the pronunciation of the words, and the intelligence and the understanding in order that one may remember to speak the words that one wishes.

If a person gets skill in speech, then it is necessary to have for it the intelligence and knowledge of words, and forethought, and especially for the movement of the tongue to be supple. If the teeth have gaps between them and the tongue does not cover there, this spoils the speech. Also if the tongue is too large, then the speech is defective. Then if it is too small, then the person has a hollow palate. It can also spoil the speech if the lips are not sound.

The mouth and the tongue are the playing field of the words. On this field the letters are erected which form all speech and the speech reaches many, as for example the strings of a harp or when the keys of a symphonia (a kind of hurdy-gurdy) are released.

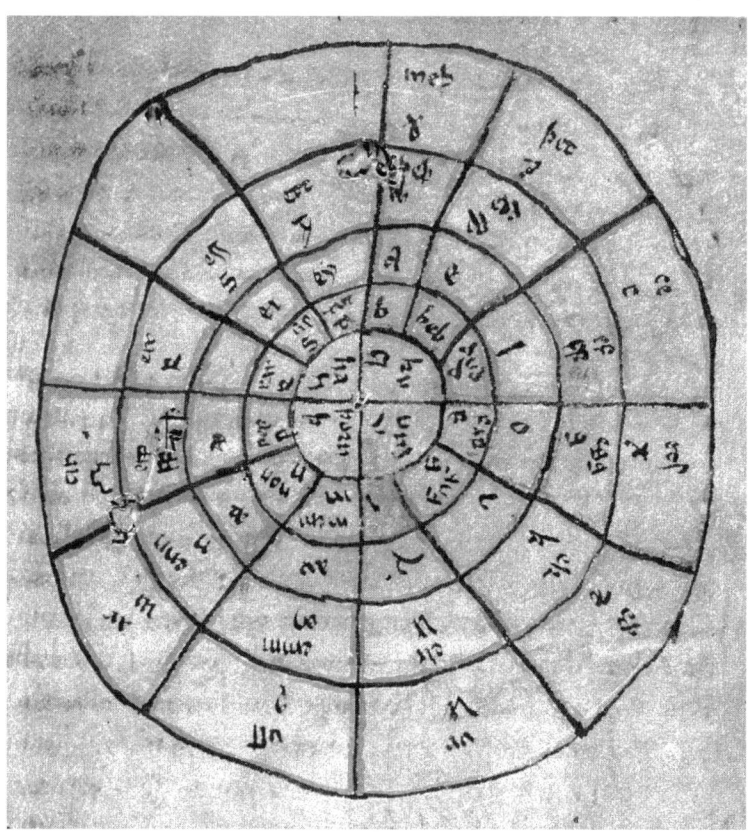

DG 11 4to f. 46r

DG 11 4to f. 47r

106

Í fyrsta hring eru fjórir stafir. Þá má til enskis annars nýta en vera fyrir ǫðrum stǫfum: q, v, þ, h.[1]

Í ǫðrum hring eru stafir ellefu[2] þeir sem heita málstafir. Hverr þeirra má vera bæði fyrir ok eptir í málinu, en engi þeira gerir mál af sjálfum sér: b, d, f, g, k, l, m, n, p, r, ſ, s, t, en nǫfn þeira eru hér sett eptir hljóði þeira.

Í þriðja hring eru tólf stafir er hljóðstafir heita. Þessi grein er þeira stafa: Fyrst heita ⟨hljóð⟩stafir ok skal svá rita: a, e, j, o, v, y. Ǫnnur grein er sú er heita límingar ok skal svá rita: æ, a/ ỿ. Þessir eru tveir.[3] Hér eru tveir hljóðstafir | saman límðir því at þessi stafinn hefir hvern hlut af hljóði hinna, er hann er af gerr. En þriðja grein er þat er heita lausaklofar ok skal svá rita: ey, ei. Þessir eru tveir ok skal svá rita at rita tvá stafi óbreytta ok gerr einn af því at hann tekr hljóð hinna beggja, en fyrir ritsháttar sakir er þessa stafi óhǫgt saman at binda. Nú er enn tólfti stafr er skiptingr heitir, þat er i.[4] Þat er réttr hljóðstafr ef málstafr er fyrir honum ok eptir honum í samstǫfunni, en ef hljóðstafr er næst eptir honum, þá skiptist hann í málstaf ok gerast þá af honum mǫrg full orð, svá sem er *já*, eða *jǫrð* eða *jór*. Ǫnnur skipting hans er þat at hann sé lausaklofi svá sem þeir er áðr eru ritaðir, ok enn svá ef málstafr stendr fyrir honum, en hljóðstafr næst eptir, svá sem er *bjǫrn* eða *bjór*⟨*r*⟩ eða *bjǫrg*. Þessir[5] stafir einir saman gera mǫrg full orð, en skamt mál gera þeir. En ef *á* gerir heilt orð þá mets⟨t⟩ svá sem þú nefnir *yfir*, en *í* þau sem *fyrir innan*. En *ó* eða *ú*, þau skipta um orðunum, svá sem er *satt* eða *úsatt*. Menn kalla einn við *ý*, en *æ*, þat er veinun, en *ey* heitir þat land sem sjór eða vatn fellr umhverfis. Þat er kallat *ey* eða *æ* er aldri þrýtr. Hljóðstafir hafa ok tvenna grein, at þeir sé styttir eða dregnir. En ef skýrt skal rita þá skal draga yfir þann stafinn er seint skal leiða, sem hér: Á því ári sem Ari var fǫddr, þat er í mínu minni. Optliga skipta orða leiðingar ǫllu máli hvárt inn sami hljóðstafr er leiddr seint eða skjótt. Lofat er þat í ritshætti, at rita af límingum heldr en af lykkju en fullt a, ok er þat svá: ę, ǫ.

[1] There is a close reconstruction of the diagram in Grape et al. 1977: 169. Anne Holtsmark (1960: 417) calls these four letters *hǫfuðstafir* 'chief letters', the word used in Codex Wormianus. The scribe here has made various mistakes in the text. For instance, he places the *hǫfuðstafir* not here in the first circle, but in the second, after the words *þeir sem heita*. He adds f (written ꝼ), which belongs to the second circle, and y, which belongs in the third, and lists the others as þ, h, h, q.

[2] Codex Wormianus has 'xii' here, which is doubtless correct. The thirteen letters in DG 11 4to are really only twelve, because the scribe includes both s and ſ, which are only graphic variants representing the same sound.

[3] In fact there are three, as it says in Codex Wormianus.

[4] This is what is known as the semi-vowel j, which can be used as a consonant or a vowel.

[5] Before this word Codex Wormianus has 'á, í, ó, ý:'.

106 [The circular diagram]

In the first circle there are four letters. They can be used for nothing else than to be in front of other letters: q, v, þ, h.

In the second circle there are twelve letters, which are called consonants. Each of them can be both before and after [others] in speech, but none of them can make speech on their own: b, d, f, g, k, l, m, n, p, r, ſ, s, t, and their names are put here after each of their sounds.

In the third circle there are twelve letters that are called vowels. This group comprises these letters: first there are those called vowels and are to be written thus: a, e, j, o, v, y. The second group is that which is termed ligatures, and are to be written thus: æ, a/ ay. There are three of these. In these there are two vowels that are joined together because here the letter includes each part of the sound of the other two it is constructed from. And the third group is that which is called diphthongs, and are to be written thus: ey, ei. There are two of these and they are to be written by writing two letters without alteration, making one, because it takes on the sounds of the other two, but because of the way they are written it is not possible to join these letters together. Now comes the twelfth letter that is called the changeable, this is j. This is a true vowel if a consonant is in front of it and after it in the syllable, but if a vowel is next after it, then it changes into a consonant, and then many complete words can be made with it, such as *já* 'yes', or *jǫrð* 'earth' or *jór* 'stallion'. Another of its changes is when it is [part of] a diphthong like those that are written above, and likewise if a consonant stands in front of it and a vowel next after, such as *bjǫrn* 'bear' or *bjórr* 'beer' or *bjǫrg* 'help'. [á, í, ó, ý:] These letters on their own form many complete words, but they form short utterances. But if *á* 'on' forms a complete word, then it is regarded as the same as if you say *yfir* 'over', and *í* the [same] as these, *fyrir innan* 'inside'. But *ó* or *ú*, these transform words, as in *satt* 'truth' versus *úsatt* 'untruth'. People call a certain tree *ý* (accusative of *ýr* 'yew'), and *æ*, this is a wail 'oh', while *ey* 'island' is the word for the land that sea or a lake flows round. That is said to be *ey* or *æ* 'always' that never stops. Vowels also have two types, that they can be shortened or lengthened. And if the writing is to be clear, then there should be a stroke above the letter that is to be pronounced long, as here: *Á því ári sem Ari var fǫddr, þat er í mínu minni* 'In the year that Ari was born, this is in my memory'. Frequently the pronunciation of words changes the whole meaning, depending on whether the same vowel is pronounced long or short. It is permitted in spelling with ligatures to write it rather with a hook than with a complete a, and that is like this: ę, ǫ.

Í fjórða hring eru tólf stafir svá ritaðir: B, D, F, G, K, L, M, N, P, R, S, T.[1] Þessir stafir gera ekki annat, en menn vilja hafa þá fyrir ritsháttar sakir ok er settr hverr þeirra einn fyrir tvá málstafi, því at sum orð eða nǫfn endast ⟨í⟩ svá fast atkvæði at engi málstafr fær einn borit, svá sem er hóll eða fjall eða kross eða hross, framm, hramm. Nú þarf annat hvárt at rita tysvar einn I málstaf eða láta sér líka þanneg at rita.

Í fimta hring eru ritaðir þeir þrír stafir er kallaðir eru undirstafir: ð, z, x. Þessum staf má við engan staf koma nema þat sé eptir hljóðstaf í hverri samstǫfu, en fjórði stafr er c, ok hafa sumir menn þann ritshátt at hafa hann fyrir konung,[2] en hitt eina er rétt hans hljóð at vera sem aðrir undirstafir í enda samstǫfu.

Titlar eru svá ritaðir hér sem í ǫðrum ritshætti.

107

Stafa setning sjá sem hér er rituð er svá sett til máls sem lyklar til hljóðs ⟨í⟩ músika ok regur[3] fylgja hljóðstǫfum svá sem þeir lyklum. Málstafir eru ritaðir með hverri regu bæði fyrir ok eptir, ok gera þeir mál af hendingum þeim[4] sem þeir gera við hljóðstafina fyrir eða eptir. Kǫllum vér þat lykla sem þeir eru í fastir, ok eru þeir hér svá settir hér sem í spacione[5] sem lyklar í simphoníe ok skal þeim kippa eða hrinda ok drepa svá regustrengina ok tekr þá þat hljóð sem þú vilt haft hafa. Þessar hendingar eru meiri en þær sem fyrr eru ritaðar ok hinar minstu þeira sem stafat[6] sé til, því at hér er í hending einn hljóðstafr ok einn málstafr, ok gerir svá margar hendingar sem nú er ritat áðr í stafasetninginni. Hér standa um þvert blað ellifu hljóðstafir, en um endilangt blað tuttugu málstafir. Eru þeir svá settir sem lyklar í simphoníe, en hljóðstafir sem strengir. Málstafir eru tólf þeir sem bæði hafa hljóð hvárt sem kipt er eða hrundit lyklinum. En átta þeir er síðarr eru ritaðir hafa hálft hljóð við hina. Sumir taka hljóð er þú kippir at þér, sumir er þú hrindir frá þér. Þessir hljóðstafir standa um þvert: a, e, i, o, y, v, ę, ǫ, ǽ, ei, ey. Þessir eru tólf málstafir: b, d, f, g, k, l, m, n, p, r, ſ, t. Þessir eru málstafir ok hafa hálft hljóð við hina: ð, þ, z, y, c, h, x, q.

[1] DG 11 4to uses double consonants rather than small capitals, but it is clear from what follows that here it is saying that it is possible to use capitals instead of double consonants to indicate length. This is the same practice as is recommended in the first grammatical treatise, and capitals are used in the corresponding place in Codex Wormianus.
[2] Doubtless a misunderstanding of '*k.*', which is often used as an abbreviation for *konung(r)* 'king' in manuscripts.
[3] This is a hapax legomenon. Raschellà (1982: 72–73) adduces evidence that it means 'line'.
[4] Written *þeiri* in DG 11 4to.
[5] Raschellà reckons that this is the same word as *spázía* 'margin' ('spacione' = *spázíunni*), but here refers to the columns in the diagram. The preceding *sem* seems to be redundant.
[6] For *stafar*?

In the fourth circle there are twelve letters written thus: B, D, F, G, K, L, M, N, P, R, S, T. These letters indicate nothing else but that people like to use them for the sake of spelling and each one of them is put for two consonants, since some words or names end with such hard pronunciation that no single consonant can sustain it, like *hóll* 'hillock' or *fjall* 'mountain' or *kross* 'cross' or *hross* 'horse', *framm* 'forward', *hramm* 'paw' (accusative case). So it is necessary either to write one consonant twice or to be pleased to write it thus.

In the fifth circle are written the three letters that are known as subsidiary letters: ð, z, x. Such a letter can go with no letter unless it comes after a vowel in every syllable, but the fourth letter is c, and some people use this spelling, putting it for k, but the only correct sound for it to be is at the end of a syllable like other subsidiary letters.

Tittles are written here just as in other spelling systems.

107 [The rectangular diagram]

The arrangement of letters that is written here is applied to speech like the keys to sound in music, and lines correspond to vowels as they do to keys. Consonants are written along each line both before and after, and they form speech from the rhymes that they make with the vowels before or after them. We call them keys that they are attached to, and they are put here in the columns like keys in a symphonia, and they have to be pulled or pushed and thus strike the line-strings, and then this takes on the sound that you want to have used. These rhymes are longer than those that are written above, and the shortest of those that there are letters for, because here there is in a rhyme one vowel and one consonant, and it makes as many rhymes as now has just been written in the arrangement of letters. Here there stand across the page eleven vowels, and from top to bottom of the page twenty consonants. They are arranged like the keys in a symphonia, and the vowels like strings. There are twelve consonants that have sounds whether the keys are pushed or pulled. But the eight that are written afterwards form half the number of sounds that the others have. Some get sound if you pull them towards youself, some when you push them away from you. These vowels stand across [the page]: a, e, i, o, y, v, ę, ǫ, a⁄, ei, ey. These are the twelve consonanats: b, d, f, g, k, l, m, n, p, r, s, t. These are the consonants that have half the number of sounds that the others have: ð, þ, z, y, c, h, x, q.

Part V

Háttatal

f. 48r p. 93 Fyrst er dróttkvæðr háttr: Lætr sá er Hákon heitir.
Kendr háttr: Fellr um fúra stilli.
Rekit: Úlfs bága verr ægis.
Sannkent: Stinn sár þróast stórum.
Tvíriðit: Óðharða spyr ek eyða.
Nýgervingar: Sviðr lætr sóknar naðra.
Oddhent: Hjálms fylli spekr hilmir.
Klofinn spyr ek hjálm.
Sextánmælt: Vóx iðn. Vellir roðnan.[1]
Áttmælt: Jǫrð verr siklingr sverðum.
Fjórðungalok: Ýskelfir kann úlfum auðmildr.
Stælt: Hákon veldr ok hǫlðum.
Hjástælt: Manndýrðir fá mæ⟨r⟩ðar.
Langlokum: Hákon ræðr með heiðan.
Afleiðingum: Þeim er grundar grimmu.[2]
Drǫgur: Setr um vísi vitran.
Refhvǫrf: Síks glóðar verr søkir.
Ǫnnur refhvǫrf: Blóð fremr h(lǫkk)[3] en.
Þriðju refhvǫrf: Segl skekr um hlyn Huglar.
Hélir hlýr fyrir stáli hafit.
Ǫnnur en minni: Lung frá ek lýða þengils.
En þriðja: Himinglæva strýkr h(ávar)[3].
Refhvarfabróðir: Firrit hǫnd með harra.
Dunhent: Hreintjǫrnum gleðr horna.
Tilsagt: Rǫst gefr ǫðlingr ástar.
Orðr kviðu[4] háttr: Fúss brýtr fylkir eisu.
Álagsháttr: Ískalda braut eisu eik varð súð en bleika.
Tvískelft: Vanbaugs veiti sendir.
Detthent. Tvær mun ek hilmi hýrum heims vistir ótvistar.
Draugsháttr: Þoll bið ek hilmis hylli halda grøn⟨n⟩a skjalda.
Bragarháttr: Stáls dynblakka støkkvi stinngeðs samir minnast.
Liðhendum: Él þreifst skarpt um Skúla skýs snarvinda lindar.
Veggjat: Lífs var rán at raunum reidd sverð skapat mjǫk ferðum.
Flagðalag: Flaust bjó fólka treystir fagrskjǫlduðustum[5] eldum.
Príhent: Hristist hvatt þá er reistist.[6]

[1] Error for *roðna*.
[2] Presumably an error for *grímu* (two consonants written for one).
[3] Both *hlǫkk* and *hávar* are abbreviated '.h.'
[4] Certainly for *orðskviðuháttr*.
[5] Written 'fagr fkiolldvzvztvm'. See Introduction, p. cxxiv.
[6] On this list of verses see Lasse Mårtensson 2010.

[List of verses]

First is the form for court poetry: *Lætr sá er Hákon heitir.*
Form using kennings: *Fellr um fúra stilli.*
Extended [kennings]: *Úlfs bága verr ægis.*
Truly described: *Stinn sár þróast stórum.*
Doubly strengthened: *Óðharða spyr ek eyða.*
Allegory: *Sviðr lætr sóknar naðra.*
Front-rhymed: *Hjálms fylli spekr hilmir.*
Klofinn spyr ek hjálm.
Sixteen-sentenced: *Vóx iðn. Vellir roðna.*
Eight-sentenced: *Jǫrð verr siklingr sverðum.*
Quarter-ends: *Ýskelfir kann úlfum auðmildr.*
Inlaid: *Hákon veldr ok hǫlðum.*
Abutted: *Manndýrðir fá mærðar.*
Late conclusions: *Hákon ræðr með heiðan.*
Deducings: *Þeim er grundar grímu.*
Drawings: *Setr um vísi vitran.*
Fox-turns: *Síks glóðar verr søkir.*
Second fox-turns: *Blóð fremr hlǫkk en.*
Third fox-turns: *Segl skekr um hlyn Huglar.*
Hélir hlýr fyrir stáli hafit.
The second lesser: *Lung frá ek lýða þengils.*
The third: *Himinglæva strýkr hávar.*
Fox-turns' brother: *Firrit hǫnd með harra.*
Echoing rhyme: *Hreintjǫrnum gleðr horna.*
Annotated: *Rǫst gefr ǫðlingr ástar.*
Proverb form: *Fúss brýtr fylkir eisu.*
Extension form: *Ískalda braut eisu eik varð súð en bleika.*
Double-shaken: *Vanbaugs veiti sendir.*
Falling-rhyme: *Tvær mun ek hilmi hýrum heims vistir ótvistar.*
Ghost's form: *Þoll bið ek hilmis hylli halda grǫnna skjalda.*
Poetic form: *Stáls dynblakka støkkvi stinngeðs samir minnast.*
Help-rhymes: *Él þreifst skarpt um Skúla skýs snarvinda lindar.*
Wedged: *Lífs var rán at raunum reidd sverð skapat mjǫk ferðum.*
Ogre-form: *Flaust bjó fólka treystir fagrskjǫlduðustum eldum.*
Triple-rhymed: *Hristist hvatt þá er reistist.*

Háttatal, er Snorri Sturluson orti um Hákon konung ok Skúla hertuga

Hvat eru hættir skáldskaparins?
Þrennir.
Hverir?
Setning, leyfi, fyrirboðning.
Hvat er setning hátta?
Tvenn.
Hver?
Tala ok grein.
Hvat kallast ⟨tala⟩setning háttanna?
Þrenn.
Hver?
Sú er ein tala hvé margir hættir hafa funnist í kvæðum hǫfuðskáldanna. Ǫnnur er sú hvé mǫrg vísuorð standa í einu eyrindi ok[1] hverjum hætti. En þriðja er sú hvé margar samstǫfur eru settar í hvert vísuorð í hverjum hætti.
Hvat er grein setningar háttanna?
Tvenn.
Hver?
Málsgrein ok hljóðsgrein.
Stafasetning gerir mál allt. En hljóð greinir þat at hafa samstǫfur langar eða skammar, harðar eða linar, ok þat er setning hljóðsgreina er vér kǫllum hendingar. Sem hér er kveðit:

Dróttkvæðr háttr i[2]

1   Lætr sá er Hákon heitir,
    hann rǿkir lið, bannat
    jǫrð kann frelsa, fyrðum,
    friðrofs, konungr, ofsa.
    Sjálfr ræðr allt ok Elfar
    einn stillir sá milli
    gramr of gipt at fremri
    Gandvíkr jǫfurr landi.

Hér er stafasetning sú er hætti ræðr ok kveðandi gerir, þat eru tolf stafir í erindi ok eru þrír settir í hvern fjórðung. Í hverjum fjórðungi eru tvau vísuorð. Hverju vísuorði fylgja sex samstǫfur. Í ǫðru vísuorði er settr sá stafr fyrir í vísuorðinu er vér kǫllum hǫfuðstaf. Sá stafr ræðr kveðandi. En í fyrsta vísuorði mun sá stafr finnast tysvar standa fyrir samstǫfur. Þá stafi kǫllum vér stuðla. Ef hǫfuðstafr er samhljóðandi þá skulu stuðlar vera inn sami stafr, sem hér er:

[1] Obviously an error for *í*.
[2] The Roman numerals after the heading of each of the first seven stanzas mark the numbers of the verses in ordinary *dróttkvætt*. Cf. Faulkes 2007: st. 6/17–21.

Háttatal, which Snorri Sturluson composed about King Hákon and Duke Skúli

What kinds of verse form are there in the poetry?
 They are of three kinds.
 What are they?
 [Those that are in accordance with] rule, licence, prohibition.
 What kinds of rule for verse forms are there?
 Two.
 What are they?
 Number and distinction.
 What is it that is called number rule for verse forms?
 It is threefold.
 What are they?
 One kind of number is how many verse forms have been found in poems of the major poets. The second is this, how many lines there are in one stanza in each verse form. The third is this, how many syllables are put in each line in each verse form.
 What kinds of distinction are there in the rule for verse forms?
 Two.
 What are they?
 Distinction of meaning and distinction of sound.
 Spelling forms all speech. But sound is distinguished by having syllables long or short, hard or soft, and there is a rule of distinctions of sound that we call rhymes. As in this verse:

Court poetry form i

1   He that is called Hákon
     causes peace-breaking arrogance
     to be banned to men; he takes care of troops;
     the king knows how to free the land.
     Himself, this ruler alone controls
     the land all the way between Gandvík
     and the Elfr, the sovereign, the prince so much
     the greater in good fortune.

Here there is one aspect of spelling that determines the verse form and creates the poetical effect, that there are twelve staves (alliterating sounds) in the stanza, and three are put in each quarter-stanza. In each quarter-stanza there are two lines. Each line comprizes six syllables. In the second line there is put at the head in the line the stave that we call the chief stave. This stave determines the alliteration. But in the first line this stave will be found twice at the beginning of syllables. These staves we call props. If the chief stave is a consonant, then the props must be the same letter, as here:

Lætr sá er H(ákon) h(eitir),
h(ann) r(ǿkir) l(ið), b(annat).[1]

En rangt er ef þessir stafir standa fyrir samstǫfur optar eða sjaldnar en svá í fjórðungi. En ef hljóðstafr er hǫfuðstafrinn, þá skulu stuðlar ok vera hljóðstafir, ok er þá fegra at sinn hljóðstafr sé hverar þeira. Þá má ok hlýða at hljóðstafr standi fyrir optar í fornǫfnum eða málfyllingum þeim er svá kveðr at: at ek[2] eða ek, eða svá: en, er, at, ok, io[3], af, of, um; ok er þat leyfi, en eigi setning rétt.

Ǫnnur stafasetning er sú er fylgir setning hljóðs þess er hátt gerir ok kveðandi. Skal sú grein í dróttkvæðum | hætti svá vera at fjórðungr vísu skal þar saman fara at allri stafasetning ok hljóða. Skal í fyrra vísuorði svá greina þá setning:

Jǫrð kann frelsa fyrðum

Hér er svá: jǫrð, fyrð. Þá er ein samstafa í hvárri ok fylgir sinn hljóðstafr hvárri ok svá hǫfuðstafr, en einn stafr hljóðs er í hváru orðinu ok inn sami málstafr eptir hljóðstaf. Þessa setning hljóðfalls kǫllum vér skothending. En í ǫðru vísuorði er svá:

Friðrofs konungr ofsa

Svá er hér rofs ok ofs. Þat er einn hljóðstafr ok svá þeir er eptir fara í báðum orðunum. En upphafsstafrinn greinir orðin. Þetta heita aðalhendingar. Svá skal hendingar setja í dróttkvæðum hætti at in síðari hending í hverri vísu⟨orði⟩, sú er heitir viðrhending, hon skal standa í þeiri samstǫfu er ein er síðarr. En sú er frumhending heitir stendr stundum í upphafi orðs ok kǫllum vér þá oddhending, en stundum í miðju orði ok kǫllum vér þá hluthending. Þessi er dróttkvæðr háttr. Með þessum hætti er flest ort þat er vandat er. Þessi er upphaf allra hátta svá sem málrúnar eru fyrir ǫðrum rúnum.

Kendr háttr ij

Hvat er breytt setning háttanna?
 Tvá vega.
 Hverneg er?
 Með máli ok hljóðum.
 Hversu skal með máli skipta?
 Tvá vega.
 Hvernen?
 Halda eða skip⟨t⟩a háttunum.

[1] Abbreviated 'h. h. h. r. l. b.'.
[2] Should probably be omitted.
[3] The Codex Regius version has 'i, o,', the latter usually emended to *á*, and DG 11 4to perhaps should be read *í, á*.

> Lætr sá er <u>H</u>ákon <u>h</u>eitir,
> <u>h</u>ann rǿkir lið, bannat.

But it is wrong if these staves stand at the beginning of syllables more often or less often than this in a quarter-stanza. And if the chief stave is a vowel, then the props must also be vowels, and it is then more elegant for each of them to be a different vowel. It is then also acceptable for initial vowels to come more frequently in pronouns or particles of the following kinds: *at* 'that' or *ek* 'I', or these: *en* 'but', *er* 'when', *at* 'to', *ok* 'and', *í* 'in', *á* 'on', *af* 'from', *of* 'about', *um* 'around'; and this is licence, and not the proper rule.

There is a second aspect of spelling that is involved in the rule for the sound that constitutes the verse form and poetical effect. This distinction in court poetry form requires this, that the quarter-stanza in it should agree in all the arrangement of letters and sounds. In the odd lines this rule is analysed thus:

> J<u>ǫrð</u> kann frelsa f<u>yrð</u>um.

Here there is *jǫrð*, *fyrð*. Now there is one syllable in each and each contains a different vowel and also initial letter, but the same letter of sound is in each word and the same consonant after the vowel. This rule of assonance we call *skothending* 'half-rhyme'. But in the even lines it is thus:

> Frið<u>rofs</u> konungr <u>ofs</u>a

Here there is *rofs* and *ofs*. There is the same vowel and also the [same sounds] that follow in both the words. But the words are distinguished by their initial letters. This is called *aðalhendingar* 'full rhymes'. The rhymes in court poetry form must be so arranged that the second rhyme in each line, which is called *viðrhending* 'accessory rhyme', it must be in the last syllable but one. But the one that is called *frumhending* 'anterior rhyme', sometimes comes at the beginning of the line, and then we call it *oddhending* 'front-rhyme', and sometimes in the middle of the line, and then we call it *hluthending* 'mid-rhyme'. This is court poetry form. This is the form most often used for elaborate poetry. This is the foundation of all verse forms, just as speech-runes are the principal kind of runes.

The form using kennings ii

How is the rule for the verse forms varied?
    In two ways.
    What are they?
    In meaning and in sounds.
    How may it be changed in meaning?
    In two ways.
    How?
    By keeping or changing the verse forms.

Hvé skal breyta háttunum ok halda sama hætti?
Svá at kenna eða styðja eða reka eða sannkenna, eða yrkja at nýgervingum.
Hvat eru kendir hættir?
Svá sem þetta:

2   Fellr um fúra stilli
         fleinbraks limvaka[1]
         Hamðis fǫng þar er hringum
         hylr ættstuðill skylja;
         hollt felr Hildigelti
         heila ljós, en deilir
         gulls í gelmis stalli
         gunnseið skǫrungr reiðir.

Hér eru ǫll heiti kend í þessi vísu, en hendingar ok orðalengð ok stafaskipti skulu fara sem fyrr var ritat.

Kenningar eru með þrennu móti greindar. Fyrst heita kenningar, annat tvíkent, þriðja rekit. Þat er kenning at kalla fleinbrak orrostuna. Þat er tvíkent at kalla fleinbraks fúr sverðit, en þá er rekit, ef lengra er.

Rekit[2] iij

3   Úlfs bága verr ægis
         ítr báls hatti mála;
         sett eru bǫrð yfir bratta
         brúns Míms vinar rúnu.
         Orms váða kann eiðu
         allvaldr | gǫfugr; halda
         menstilli máttu móður
         mellu dólgs til elli.[3]

Sannkent iiij

Hvat eru sannkenningar?
    Svá sem þetta:

[1] The Codex Regius version has *limu axla*, which fits the metre and internal rhyme-scheme properly, and *bǿs* in line 6 instead of *ljós*, and these differences lead to a rather different meaning. Note that Hermann Pálsson (1954) interprets the verse in a quite similar way to the one given here.

[2] This stanza actually illustrates *tvíkent*, and there is no stanza that systematically illustrates *rekit*, though there is one example in line 4.

[3] In order to make the text grammatical and comprehensible, the following emendations based on the Codex Regius version need to be made: *hati* for *hatti*, *málu* for *mála*, *fyrir* for *yfir*, *brún* for *brúns*, *menstillir* for *menstilli*.

How may the verse forms be varied and the same form be kept?

By using kennings or *styðja* 'supporting' or extending [kennings] or using true descriptions, or by composing with allegory.

What are forms using kennings?

As follows:

2 Watcher (protector) of limbs (i.e. mailcoat) falls around
the controller (warrior) of the fire (sword) of the spear-clash (battle)
where the upholder of the ruler's dynasty covers
Hamðir's (hawk's) grasps (his arms) with rings (ring-mail);
the outstanding one (King Hákon) conceals
his gracious brains' light (eye) with a battle-boar (helmet),
and the distributor of gold wields
his battle-fish (sword) in hawk's perch (hand).

Here in this stanza all the concepts are expressed by kennings, but the rhymes and length of lines and distribution of staves (alliteration) have to go as was prescribed above.

Kennings are categorised in three classes. First there are kennings, second doubly modified, third extended. It is a kenning to call the battle 'spear-clash', it is doubly modified to call a sword 'spear-clash's fire', and then it is extended if there are more elements.

Extended iii

3 The splendid hater (distributor) of the fire of the sea (gold) defends
the beloved (wife, Jǫrð, i.e. land) of the wolf's enemy (Óðinn);
ships are placed over the steep brow (shore) of Mímr's
friend's (Óðinn's) wife (Jǫrð, i.e. the land);
the noble mighty ruler knows the serpent's
harmer's (Þórr's) mother (Jǫrð, i.e. land);
may you, controller of necklaces (generous ruler) keep trollwife's
enemy's (Þórr's) mother (Jǫrð, i.e. your realm) until old age.

Truly described iiii

What are true descriptions?

As follows:

4   Stinn sár þróast stórum,
       sterk egg frǫmum seggjum
       hvasst skerr hlífar traustar;
       Óðs drengr gǫfugr þengill;[1]
       hrein sverð litar harða
       hverr drengr; gǫfugr þengill—
       ítr mun[2] furast undrum—
       unir bjartr snǫru hjarta.

Þat er sannkenning at styðja svá orðit meðr réttu efni at kalla stinn sár, því at hǫfug eru stór sár, en rétt er mælt at þróist. Ǫnnur sannkenning er sú at sárin þróast stórum. Nú er eitt vísuorð ok tvær sannkenningar.

Nú ferr svá með sama hætti unz ǫll er uppi vísan, ok eru hér sextán sannkenningar sýndar í átta vísuorðum. En þó fegra⟨r⟩ þat mjǫk í kveðandi at eigi sé jammjǫk eptir þeim farit.

Sannkenningar hafa þrenna grein, heitir ein stuðning, ǫnnur sannkennng, þriðja tvíriðit.

Tvíriðit[3] **v**

5   Óðharða spyr ek eyða
       egg fullhvǫtum seggjum;
       dáðrǫkkum veldr dauða
       drengr[4] ofrhugaðr þengill;
       hamdøkkum fær Hlakkar
       hauk mundriða[5] aukin⟨n⟩—
       veghrossin[6] spyr ek vísa—
       vald⟨r⟩ ógnþorinn skjaldar.

Hér fylgir stuðning hverri sannkenning, sem eggin er kǫlluð óðhǫrð en fullhvatir menn. Þat er sannkenning: hǫrð egg en hvatir menn. Þat er stuðning er annat sannanarorð fylgir sannkenningu.

Nýgjǫrvingar vj

6   Sviðr lætr sóknar naðra
       slíðrbraut jǫfurr skríða;

---

[1] This line is obviously an erroneous anticipation of line 6. The Codex Regius version has *hár gramr lifir framla*.

[2] Perhaps for *mund* 'hand', but the Codex Regius has *rǫnd* 'shield', which makes better sense and has *skothending*.

[3] This stanza illustrates *stuðning* (in lines 1–4). No stanza illustrates *tvíriðit*.

[4] The Codex Regius version has *dreng*, which provides a dative noun for *dáðrǫkkum*.

[5] The Codex Regius version has *munnroða*, which gives better sense than *mundriða* 'sword'.

[6] I.e. *veghrǫsinn*, as in the Codex Regius version, and this gives acceptable sense.

4   Severe wounds increase greatly,
       strong edge cuts sharply
       trusty shields for bold men;
       the high prince lives honourably;
       each warrior colours mightily
       clean swords (with blood); the noble prince,
       radiant, rejoices in a bold heart;
       the fine shield is furrowed (damaged) amazingly.

It is a true description to support the word with correct material so as to call wounds severe, for great wounds are heavy, and it is normal to say that it increases. Another true description is this, [to say] that severe wounds increase greatly. So there is one line and two true descriptions.

Now it goes on thus in the same manner until the whole verse is finished, and there are here sixteen true descriptions to be found in eight lines. And yet it adds great beauty to the poetical effect even if they are not imitated so precisely.

True descriptions are of three kinds, one is called support, the second true description, the third doubly strengthened.

Doubly strengthened v

5   I hear that mighty hard edge
       destroys very brave men;
       the most valiant prince causes the death
       of deed-bold warrior;
       the battle-daring wielder of the shield (warrior)
       causes the mouth-reddening (with blood)
       of Hlǫkk's dark-coated hawk to be increased;
       I hear the ruler is proud of his glory.

Here support accompanies each true description, as when the edge is called mighty hard and men very brave. This is true description: hard edge and brave men. It is support when another confirmatory word accompanies the true description.

Allegory vi

6   The wise prince makes the adders of battle (swords)
       creep the scabbard-path (be drawn);

opt ferr rógs ór réttum
ramsnákr fetilhamsi;
spennir[1] sverða sennu
sveita bekks at leita;
orm⟨r⟩ þyrr vals at varmri
víggjǫll sefa stígu.

Þat eru nýgervingar at kalla sverðit ⟨orm⟩ ok kenna rétt, en kalla slíðrar gǫtur hans, en fetlana ok umgerð hams hans. Þat heldr til náttúra hans ormsins, at hann skríðr ór hamsi ok til vats. Því er svá at hann ferr at leita blóðs bekkjar ok skríðr hugar stígu, þat eru brjóst manna. Þá eru nýgervingar vel kveðnar at þat | mál er upp er tekit haldist um alla vísuna. En ef sverðit er ormr kallat, en síðan fiskr eðr vǫndr eðr annan veg breytt, þat kalla menn nykrat[2] ok þikkir þat spilla.

Nú er dróttkvæðr háttr með fimm greinum ok er þó enn sami háttr réttr ok óbrugðinn ok er optliga þessar greinir samar eða allar í einni vísu ok er þat réttr. Kenningar auka orðafjǫlða. Sannkenningar fylla og fegra mál. Nýgervingar sýna kunnǫstu ok orðfimi.

Þat er leyfi háttanna at hafa samstǫfur seinar eða skjótar, svá at dragist fram eða aptr ór réttri tǫlu setningar, ok mega finnast svá seinar at fimm samstǫfur sé í einu orði, ǫðru ok enu fjórða, sem hér er:[3]

Oddhent vij

7 Hjálms fylli spekr hilmir
hvatr Vinlés skatna;
hann kann hjǫrvi þunnum
hræs þjóðár vel ræsa.
Ýgr hilmir lætr eiga
ǫld dreyrfá skjǫldu;
styrks[4] rýðr stillir hersum
sterkr járngrá serki.

Hér eru allar oddhendingar inar fyrri hendingar, ok er þó dróttkvæðr háttr at heiti.

Nú skal sýna svá skjótar samstǫfur ok svá settar hverja nær annarri, at af því eykr lengð orðsins:

---

[1] *spennir* 'clasps', written in a later hand apparently as a correction (see Grape et al. 1977: 173), conflicts with the rules of the verse form. The Codex Regius version has *linnr kná*. *Kná* is occasionally found with *at*, e.g. Faulkes 1998: stt. 145/1, 246/1.

[2] Cf. *finngálknat* in the third and fourth grammatical treatises (Ólsen 1884: 80, 131); *nykr* and *finngálkn* are both fabulous monsters.

[3] On the metre of this stanza see Faulkes 2007: 50.

[4] The Codex Regius version has *styrs*, which improves the rhyme and the kenning.

the mighty war-snake (sword) often
goes from the straight baldric-slough;
the sword-quarrel serpent (sword)
does seek the stream of blood;
the worm of the slain (sword) rushes along the mind's path
(through a man's breast) to the warm war-river (stream of blood).

It is allegory to call the sword a snake and use an appropriate determinant, and to call the scabbard its paths and the straps and fittings its slough. It is in accordance with a snake's nature that it creeps from its slough and to water. Therefore it is so that it goes to seek the stream of blood and creeps the paths of thought, that is men's breast. Allegory is then well composed when the idea that is taken up is maintained throughout the whole stanza. But if the sword is called a snake, and then a fish or a wand or varied in some other way, this is said to be made monstrous and it is considered to spoil it.

Now the court poetry form has been presented with five distinct variants, and yet it has been the same verse form, normal and without departure from it, and frequently the same or all of these variant features are found in a single stanza, and that is normal. Kennings enlarge the vocabulary resources. True descriptions expand and enhance the sense. Allegory displays art and verbal skill.

It is a licence in the verse forms to have slow or quick syllables so that there is a drawing on or back from the normal number of the rule, and they can be found so slow that there are five syllables in a line, the second and the fourth, as there is here:

Front-rhymed vii

7   The bold king quietens men
    with Vinlér's helmet-filler (Heimdallr's head[1]);
    he knows how to make mighty corpse-rivers
    (rivers of blood) flow fast with slender sword.
    The terrible prince makes men
    have gore-stained shields;
    the strong ruler reddens (with blood)
    lords' iron-grey battle-shirts (mail-coats).

Here all the first rhymes [in each line] are front-rhymes, and yet [it is] court poetry form by name.

Now shall be demonstrated such quick syllables and ones placed so close to each other that as a result the length of the line is increased:

[1] I.e. a sword; see p. 146 above.

Ǫnnur oddhending
8   Klofinn spyr ek hjálm fyrir hilmis
hjarar egg; duga seggir;
því eru heldr, þar er skekr skjǫldu
skafin sverð lituð ferðar.
Bila munat gramr þar er gumnar
gullar[1] rítr nái líta;
draga þorir hann fyrir hreinan
hvatan brand, þrimu randa.[2]

Hér er í fyrsta ok þriðja vísuorði níu samstǫfur, en í ǫðru ok inu fjórða sjau. Hér er þat sýnt hversu flestar samstǫfur mega vera í vísuorði með dróttkvæðum hætti, ok af þessu má þat vita at átta ok sjau megu vel hlýða í fyrsta ⟨ok⟩ í þriðja vísuorði. Í þessi vísu eru allar frumhendingar hlut⟨h⟩endum ok dregr þat til at hengja[3] má orðit at sem flestar samstǫfur standi fyrir hendingar.

Þat er annat leyfi háttanna at hafa í dróttkvæðum hætti eitt orð eða tvau í vísu með álǫgum eða detthent eða dunhent eða skjálfhent eða með nokkurum þeim hætti | er eigi[4] spilli kveðandi.

Þriðja leyfi er þat at hafa aðalhendingar í fyrsta ok þriðja vísuorði.

Fjórða leyfi er þat at skemma svá samstǫfur at gera eina ór tveimur ok taka ór annarri hljóðstaf.

Þat er it fimmta leyfi at skipta tíðum í vísuhelmingi.

Sétta at hafa í dróttkvæðum hætti samhendingar eða hluthendingar.

Sjaunda at hafa eitt málsorð í báðum vísuhelmingum ok þikkir þat spilla í einstaka vísum.

Átta at nýta, þótt samkvætt verði við þat er áðr er ort, vísuorð eða skemmra.

Níunda at reka til ennar fimmtu kenningar, en ór ættum ef lengra er rekit, en þó at þat finnist í fornskálda verkum, þá látum vér nú þat ónýtt.

Tíunda ef vísu fylgir drag eða stuðill. Ok þó at þat sé í síðara helmingi, ef maðr er nefndr eða kendr í fyrra helmingi, þótt þá sé eigi nafn annan veg en hér[5] eða hinn eða sá eða sjá.

Ellipta er þat at er eða en eða at má hafa optar í vísuhelmingi, sem Refr kvað:

Sæll er heinn[6] er hranna
hádýra vel stýrir—
tíðir[7] erumk vitnis váða
víngerð—unir sínu.

---

[1] I.e. *gular* (double consonant for single).
[2] On the features of this stanza, the use of resolution and the possibility of reducing the number of syllables by adopting contracted forms, see Faulkes 2007: 50. In spite of the heading, this stanza has no *oddhendingar*.
[3] Obviously an error for *lengja*.
[4] *er eigi* are the final words on f. 50r and they are repeated at the top of 50v.
[5] Error for *hann*. This whole sentence probably belongs with the seventh *leyfi* above.
[6] Obviously an error for *hinn* (so the Codex Regius version and AM 157 8vo).
[7] Error for *tíð*.

Second front-rhyme

8   I hear that helmet is cloven before the prince's
    sword-edge; men act well;
    so where shields are shaken, troops'
    burnished swords are quite coloured (with blood).
    The king will not give way where men
    get to see yellow shields;
    he dares to draw polished, keen
    sword in the face of the noise of shields (battle).

Here there are nine syllables in the first and third lines and seven in the second and fourth. This is an example of the maximum number of syllables that can be in a line in the court poetry form, and from this it can be seen that it is easily acceptable to have eight and seven in the first and in the third lines. In this stanza the first rhymes in each line are with mid-rhyme, and it makes it possible to lengthen the line, that as many syllables as possible come before the rhymes.

It is a second licence of the verse-forms to have in court poetry form one or two lines in a stanza with extensions or falling-rhymed or echoing-rhymed or shivering or with some variation that does not spoil the poetic form.

It is a third licence to have full rhymes in the first and third lines.

It is a fourth licence to shorten syllables so as to make one out of two and take away the vowel from one of them.

It is the fifth licence to vary tenses in the half-stanza.

The sixth, to have coincident rhymes or mid-rhymes in court poetry form.

The seventh, to have the same word in both half-stanzas, and this is considered a defect in single-stanza poems.

The eighth, to make effective use of repetition of what has been uttered earlier, a line or less.

The ninth, to extend [a kenning] to a fifth determinant, but it is out of proportion if it is extended further, and even if it is found in the works of ancient poets, we consider it now unacceptable.

The tenth, if a stanza has an appendage or a buttress (an additional line at the end?). And [this applies] even if it is in the second half-stanza, if a man is named or referred to in the first half-stanza, even though it is then not a name in any other form than *hann* 'he' or *hinn* 'the other' or *sá* 'this person' or *sjá* 'that person'.

The eleventh is that *er* 'is, who' or *en* 'but' or *at* 'that' may be put more often in a half-stanza, as Refr said:

> Happy is that steerer of the tall animals
> of the waves (ship) who is well content
> with his lot. I am practised
> in the wolf's danger's (Óðinn's) wine-making (composing poetry).

Tólfta er atriðsklauf.

Hér segir af sextán málum

Hvat er tíðaskipti?
Þrennt.
Hvernig?
Þat er var, þat er er, þat er verðr.

Hver setning fær nǫfn háttum ok greina svá tǫlu háttanna ena fyrstu, en halda annarri ok enni þriðju tǫlu setningar. Þat er sem fyrr var ritat,[1] at hafa átta vísuorð í eyrindi ok in þriðja tala at hafa sex samstǫfur í vísuorði ok sǫmu setning hendinganna.

Háttum er skipt með ymsum orðtǫkum ok er þessi einn háttr er kallaðr er sextánmælt.

9   Vex iðn. Vellir roðna.
      Verpr lind. Þrimu snerpir.
      Felsk gagn. Fylkir eignast.
      Falr hitnar. Setst[2] vitni⟨r⟩.
      Skekr rǫnd. Skildir bendast.
      Skelfr askr. Griðum raskar.
      Brandr gellr. Brynjur sundrast.
      Braka spjót. Litast ǫrvar

Hér eru tvau mál fullkomin í hverju vísuorði, en orðalengð ok samstǫfur ok hendingar ok stafaskipti sem í dróttkvæðum hætti.

Nú er breytt dróttkvæðum hætti ok enn með máli einu saman:

Áttmæltr háttr

10   Jǫrð verr siklingr sverðum.
      Sundr rjúfa spjǫr undir.
      Blind[3] skerr[4] í styr steinda.
      Støkkr hauss af bol lausum.
      Falla fólk á velli.
      Fremr mildr jǫfurr hildi.
      Egg bítr á lim lýti.
      Liggr skǫr sniðin hjǫrvi.

Hér er mál fyllt í hverju vísuorði.

---

[1] See p. 262 above.
[2] I.e. *seðst*.
[3] The Codex Regius version has *Lind*. It is difficult to see any sense in *Blind* ('blind', feminine adjective).
[4] Codex Wormianus also has *skerr*, GkS 2367 4to *sekr*, Codex Trajectinus *skekr*.

The twelfth is tmesis.

Here it tells of sixteen sentences

What is variation of tenses?
 Of three kinds.
 How?
 That which was, that which is, that which shall be.

Each rule gives its name to the verse forms, and thus they make a distinction in the the first kind of number that relates to the verse forms, but they keep the second and the third kinds of number in the rule. This means, in accordance with what was written before, having eight lines in the stanza, and the third kind of number, having six syllables in the line, and the same rule for the rhymes.

The verse forms are altered by various turns of phrase, and this is one verse form that is called sixteen-sentenced:

9   Labour grows. Fields go red (with blood).
           Lime-spear is thrown. Battle grows harsh.
           Victory is concealed (uncertain). The ruler gains possessions.
           Dart grows hot. Wolf is sated.
           Targe is shaken. Bucklers are bent.
           Ash(-spear) quivers. Peace is disturbed.
           Brand resounds. Mail-coats are split apart.
           Spears crack. Arrows are dyed (red with blood).

Here there are two complete sentences in each line, but the length of lines and the syllables and the rhymes and alliteration as in court poetry form.

Now the court poetry form is varied and again in meaning only:

Eight-sentenced form

10   The king defends his land with swords.
           Spears tear wounds open.
           The coloured shield is cut in battle.
           The head flies from the unattached body.
           Hosts fall on the field.
           The generous prince wages war.
           The edge bites blemishes on limbs.
           The scalp lies cut by sword.

Here a sentence is completed in every line.

Þessi er inn þriði

11 Ýskelfir kann úlfum
    allmildr búa hildi;
    lætr gylðis kyn gáti
    gunnsnarr und sik harri;
    fær gotna vinr vitni
    valbjór afar stóran;
    vargr tér ór ben bergja
    blótdrykk ok grǫn rjóða.

Hér lýkr máli í tveim vísuorðum.

Sá er nú skal rita er enn fjórði þeira er breyt⟨t⟩ir eru, en inn fimmti at háttum:[1]

12 Hákon veldr ok hǫlðum—
    harðráðum guð jarðar
    tiggja lér með tíri—
    teitr þjóðkonungr[2] heiti.
    Vald á víðrar foldar—
    vindræfurs jǫfurr gæfu
    ǫðlingi skóp ungum—
    ǫrlyndr skati gjǫrla.

Þetta er it fyrsta:

    Hákon veldr ok hǫlðum
    teitr þjóðkonungs heiti.

En annat ok it þriðja vísuorð er sér um mál kallat.

13 Manndýrðir fær mærðar
    mæt ǫld fira gætir
    lætr auðgjafa ítrum
    ǫll. Stóð sær á fjǫllum.
    Rjóðr vendils gátst[3] randa
    røki-Njǫrð at søkja,
    høf ferð var sú handa,[4]
    heim. Skaut jǫrð ór geima.

---

[1] Stt. 2–8 were not considered to be fully varied from *dróttkvætt*. Taking st. 1 as being the basic form, st. 12 is the fifth type. Stt. 12 and 14 are quoted and discussed in the third grammatical treatise (Ólsen 1884: 136).

[2] Obviously an error for *þjóðkonungs*, cf. the two lines quoted again below.

[3] Error for *gat*.

[4] Error for *harða*.

This is the third

11   The very generous bow-shaker (warrior)
       knows how to prepare battle for wolves;
       the battle-keen lord makes warg's kin
       subject to himself with food;
       the friend of men gives the watcher (wolf)
       a very great deal of corpse-beer (blood);
       warg does taste sacrifice-drink
       from wound and redden its lips.

Here the sentence ends in two lines.

The one that shall be written now is the fourth of those that have variation, but the fifth in the [number of] verse-forms:

12   Hákon possesses as well as subjects—
       God grants the firm-ruling
       prince land with glory—
       happy, the name of great king.
       Power over a wide realm—
       the lord (God) of the winds' roof (heaven) has bestowed
       grace on the young nobleman—
       the generous prince has completely.

This is the first [inlaid]:

       Hákon possesses as well as subjects
       happy, the name of great king.

But the second and the third lines are said to be separate in sense.

13   The protector of men gains
       glorious achievements; all noble mankind
       allows the splendid wealth-giver
       glories. The sea lay over the mountains.
       The reddener (warrior) of the wand (sword) was able
       to visit the Njǫrðr (king) who cultivates shields (fights battles)
       at home; that journey was very
       proper. The earth sprang out of the sea.

Hér er it fyrsta vísuorð ok annat ok it þriðja sér um mál, ok hefir þó þat mál eina samstǫfu með fullu orðinu af enu ⟨fjórða⟩, en þær fimm samstǫfur er eptir fara lúka heilu máli, ok skal orðtak við forn minni.[1]

Þessi er inn sjaundi:

14   Hákon ræðr með heiðan—
        hefir drengja vinr fengit,
        land[2] verr buðlungr brandi
        breiðfelld, mikit veldi.
        Rógleiks sjáir[3] ríki
        remmi-Týr at stýra,
        ǫld fagnar því, eignu—
        orðróm konungdómi

Hér hefr upp mál í inu fyrsta vísuorði, en lýkr í inu síðarsta, ok eru þau sér um mál.

15   þeim er, grundar grímu
        gjaldseiðs ok var faldinn,
        drátt mun[4] enn þess, átti
        áðr hans faðir ráða.
        Gunnhættir kná grýtu,[5]
        gramr býr við þrek, stýra,
        stórt ræðr hann, en hjarta
        hvetr, buðlunga setri.

Hér er enn fyrri vísuhelmingr leiddr af inni fyrri vísu ok fylgir þat vísuorð er afleiðingum er kallat, er síðast var í enni fyrri vísu. Þessum vísuhelmingi er svá breytt ok er sá vísuhelmingr eigi ella réttr at máli.

16   Setr um vísa vitran
        vígdrótt, en þar hníga,
        ýr[6] dregst, við skotskúrum
        skjaldborg, í gras aldir.
        Vápnrjóðr stikar víða,
        vellbrjótr á lǫg, spjótum,
        þrøngr at sverða sǫngvi,
        sóknharðr þrimu jarðar.

Þat málsorð er fyrst í þessi, er síðarst var í hinni fyrri, ok er hin síðari svá dregin af inni fyrri. Þat heita drǫgur.

---

[1] The two traditional statements here are reminiscent of *Vǫluspá* 4 and 59. This form is called *hjástælt* in the Codex Regius version and the list of verses on p. 260 above.

[2] Error for *lǫnd* (thus the Codex Regius version).

[3] Error for *náir* (thus the Codex Regius version).

[4] *drátt mun* is clearly an error for *drótt man* though *muna* does not normally have a genitive object (genitive would have been correct after *muna til* or *minnast*).

[5] For *grýttu* (single consonant for double).   [6] Written 'vr'; *v* for *y* occurs elsewhere.

Here the first line and the second and the third belong together in sense, and yet this sentence includes one syllable comprising a complete word from the fourth, and the five syllables that follow complete a full sentence, and the expression has (to be) with traditional statements.

This is the seventh:

14   Hákon rules with bright—
The friend of warriors has gained
great power; the prince defends
his extensive lands with the brand.
The Týr (god) that encourages the play
of hostility (war, i.e. the king) is able to rule
his own kingdom; men welcome this.
—glory the kingdom

Here a sentence begins in the first line and is completed in the last, and they make up a separate statement.

15   which his father had to rule previously,
being crowned with the fish of the
ground-money's (serpent's) helmet (helmet of terror);[1]
the court still remembers this.
He who risks battle is able
to rule the princes' bouldered seat (Norway);
the king is endowed with great fortitude;
he rules forcefully, and his valour spurs him on.

Here the first half-stanza follows on from the preceding stanza, and the line that is called deducings (antecedent), which was last in the preceding stanza, is linked to it. This half-stanza is thus a variation, and the half-stanza would not otherwise be correctly expressed.

16   The war-band sets a shield-wall
around the wise ruler
against missile-showers, and men
sink there into the grass; bow is drawn.
The battle-hard weapon-reddener (warrior)
thrusts far and wide with spears
at the uproar of the land (battle); the gold-breaker (generous king)
presses onward onto the sea to the song of swords (battle).

The word is first in this [stanza] that was last in the preceding one, and the second is thus drawn from the first. This is called drawings.

[1] Cf. the *ǿgishjálmr* of *Fáfnismál* 16. The expression means that the king held men in awe.

Hér segir um refhvǫrf

Þessi háttr er inn tíundi, er vér kǫllum refhvǫrf. Í þeim hætti skal velja saman þau orðtǫk er ólíkust eru at greina ok hafa þó einnar tíðar fall bæði orð, ef vel skal vera. Nú er til þessa háttar vant at finna ǫll orð gagnstaðlig, ok eru hér því sum orð dregin til hǿginda. En sýnt er þat í þessi vísu at orðin munu finnast, ef vandlega er at leitat, ok mun þat sýnast at flest frumsmíð stendr til bóta. Sem hér er kveðit:

17   Síks glóðar verr sǿkir
        slétt skarð hafi jarðar.
        Hlífgranda rekr hendir
        heit kǫld loga ǫldu.
        Fljót⟨t⟩ válkat skilr fylkir
        friðlæ, rǫðuls sævar,
        ránsið ræsir stǫðvar
        reiðr, glaðr, frǫmum meiðum.

Hér er í fyrsta vísuorði svá kveðit: Síks glóðar. Sík er vatn, glóð er eldr, en eldr ok vatn hatar hvárt annat. Verr ok sǿkir: þat er ólíkt at verja eða sǿkja. Annat vísuorð er svá: Slétt skarð hafi jarðar. Sær er haf. Land er jǫrð. En þat er ⟨í⟩ eitt fall mælt at sá ferr af hafi til jarðar. Þriðja vísuorð er svá: Hlífgranda rekr hendir. Þat er ljóst refhvǫrf ok svá rekr hendir. Sá flytr brott er rekr, en sá stǫðvar er hendir. Svá er it fjórða: Heit kǫld, þat eru ljós orð ok svá loga ǫldu. Logi er eldr, alda er sær. Fimmta er svá: Fljótt válkat. Fljótt er þat er skjótt er, en válkat þat er seint er. Ok svá: skilr fylkir. Sá skilr er dreifir, en sá er fylkir er[1] samnar. Sétta orð er svá: Frið læ. Friðr er sætt, læ þat er vél. Rǫðull sævar. Rǫðull er sól ok gengr hon fyrir eld í ǫllum kenningum ok ⟨sær⟩ er enn sem fyrri móti eldi. Sjaunda er svá: rán er þat er ósiðr er, ok svá ræsir stǫðvar. Svá[2] flytr er ræsir, en sá heldr aptr er stǫðvar. | Átta vísuorð er svá: Reiðr glaðr frǫmum meiðum. Reiðr ok glaðr, þat er ljóst mælt ok svá frǫmum meiðum. Þat er újafnt at un⟨n⟩a mǫnnum frama eða meizla. Hér eru sýnd í þessi vísu sextán orðtǫk sundrgreinilig, ok eru flest ofljóst til rétts máls at fǿra, ok skal svá þá upp taka: Síks glóð, þat er gull; sǿkir gulls er maðr; hann verr skarð jarðar hafi slétt, þat eru Firðir. Svá heitir fylkir[3] í Noregi. Hlífgrandi eru vápn kend. ⟨Hendir⟩ loga ǫldu, þat er maðr. Hann rekr kǫld heit með sverðinu, þat er at hegna ósiðu. Fljótt válkat má þat kalla er skjótt ráðit er; þat skilr hann af ófriðinum at[4] konungr heitir fylkir. Ránsið ræsir stǫðvar sævar rǫðuls frǫmum meiðum.

[1] Redundant.
[2] Error for *Sá*.
[3] Obviously an error for *fylki*.
[4] Redundant; *þat* refers to the previous sentence, *konungr heitir fylkir* is an independent statement.

Here it tells about fox-turns
This verse form is the tenth, which we call fox-turns (antithesis). In this verse form the expressions are to be chosen to be together that are most unlike in signification, and yet both words are to have the same cadence if it is to be effective. Now it is for this verse form difficult to find all the words of opposite meanings, and so some words are stretched [in meaning] for convenience. But it is demonstrated in this stanza that the words will be found if they are sought for carefully, and it will be apparent that most first attempts can bear improvement. As it says here:

17   The ditch-glede's (gold's) attacker (generous king)
defends the sea-smoothed land-cleft (fjords, Firðir in Norway).
The wave-flame (gold) thrower (generous king) drives away
cold threats with shield-damager (sword).
The happy war-leader perceives hastily-weighed
peace-destruction (warfare); the angry ruler
puts a stop to the plundering habit
of bold sea-sun (gold) trees (warriors).

Here in the first line it is expressed thus: *Síks glóðar*. *Sík* 'ditch' is water, *glóð* 'glede' is fire, and fire and water are each opposed to the other. *Verr* 'defends' and *søkir* 'attacker/attacks': it is different to defend and attack. The second line is thus: *Slétt skarð hafi jarðar*. *Sær* is sea, *jǫrð* is land. And so it is said in one phrase that one goes from sea to land. The third line is thus: *Hlífgranda* 'shield harm' *rekr hendir*. This is an obvious case of fox-turns, and similarly *rekr* 'drives' *hendir* 'thrower/throws catches'. He that drives moves something away, but he that catches stops something. Similar is the fourth: *Heit* 'hot' *kǫld* 'cold', these words are obvious, and similarly *loga ǫldu*. *Logi* 'flame' is fire, *alda* 'wave' is sea. The fifth is thus: *Fljótt válkat*. *Fljótt* 'hast(il)y' is what is quick, *válkat* 'weighed/hovered' what is slow. And similarly: *skilr* 'perceives/divides' *fylkir* 'leader/musters'. He that scatters divides, but he that musters gathers. The sixth line is thus: *Frið læ*. *Friðr* 'peace' is reconciliation, *læ* 'destruction/fraud', that is machination. *Rǫðull sævar*. *Rǫðull* is the sun, and it is used for fire in all kennings, and *sær* 'sea' is again as before contrary to fire. The seventh is thus: *rán* 'plundering' is what is not *siðr* 'habit/morality', and similarly *ræsir* 'ruler/impels' *stǫðvar* 'puts a stop to'. He that impels moves something, but he that puts a stop to holds something back. The eighth line is thus: *Reiðr glaðr frǫmum meiðum*. *Reiðr* 'angry' and *glaðr* 'happy', the meaning is obvious, and also *frǫmum* 'bold/advance' *meiðum* 'trees/injure'. It is quite different to grant people advancement or injuries. Here are demonstrated in this stanza sixteen phrases of contrary meanings and most of them have to be turned to their proper meaning by means of word-play, and this is how it is to be understood: ditch-glede, i.e. gold; gold's attacker is a man; he defends clefts of land smoothed by the sea, i.e. Firðir. This is the name of a district in Norway. Weapons are referred to as shield-damager. Thrower of wave's flame, i.e. man. He drives away cold threats with his sword, this is to punish bad habits. Hastily-weighed may be said of what is quickly decided; he perceives this from the warfare. A king is called war-leader. The ruler puts a stop to the plundering habit of bold sea's sun's trees.

Annat refhvarf

Þessi eru ǫnnur vísuorð,[1] ok eru hér hálfu færi vísuorð þau er refhvǫrfum eru sett, ok eru þau tvenn í ǫðru vísuorði ok eru þau kǫlluð en mestu:

18   Blóð fremr, hlǫkk at háðist
heldr slitnar dul, vitni;
skjǫldr, en skatnar fellir,[2]
skelf⟨r⟩ harðr, taka varða.
Fal[3] látið[4] her hvítan
hollr gramr rekinn framðan;
en tiggja sonr seggjum
svalr brandr dugir grandar.

Hér eru þau refhvǫrf í ǫðru vísuorði: heldr ok slitnar, dul vitni. Dul er laun, en vitni sǫnnun. En í fjórða orði er svá: skelf⟨r⟩ harðr, taka varða. Í sétta vísuorði er svá: hollr gramr, rekinn framðan. Átta vísuorð[5] er svá: Svalr brandr. Brandr er elds heiti. Dugir grandar. Þetta er ofljóst. Hér eru ok ǫnnur máltǫk þau er til máls skulu taka, svá at kalla blóð frumvitni,[6] þat er vargr. En í[7] dul eða kaun[8] slitnar eða rofnar en hlǫkk háðist, þat er orrosta. Ok í ǫðrum fjórðungi er svá ⌜at harðr skjǫldr ⟨skelfr⟩, en skatnar taka at varða ríki. Ok[9] í þriðja fjórðungi er svá: hollr gramr lætr her framðan, fal hvítan rekinn. Sá er framiðr er framarr er settr. Í fjórða fjórðungi er svá at svalr brandr grandar seggjum en tiggja sun dugir.

19   Segl skekr ok hlyn, Huglar—
hvast drífa skip—rastar,
en fell um gram, Gylli
grun⟨n⟩ djúp harra[10] unna.
Ne Rán við⟨r⟩ hal hánum,
hafraust stafar flaustum,
hrǫnn fyrir hafi[11] þunnum
heil klofnar, frið, deilu.

Hér er eitt orð í hvárum | vísuhelmingi þat er refhvǫrfum er ort ok tvenn í hvárum, sem hér er: grun⟨n⟩ djúp, hata unna. En í efra helmingi er svá: heil klofnar, frið deilu. Þetta eru kǫlluð mestu[12] refhvǫrf ok þó minnst af þessum.

---

[1] Error for *refhvǫrf*.
[2] The Codex Regius version has *foldir* (AM 242 4to 'fellder'); *foldir* is the only reading that fits.
[3] Written *Fall* in DG 11 4to.
[4] All manuscripts have *látið/látit* here, but the following prose has *lætr*, which is clearly correct. The line then lacks a syllable, and the Codex Regius version reads *of her* 'over the army' in the prose.
[5] Written *-orði*.
[6] The other manuscripts have *fremr vitni*, in keeping with the verse text above.
[7] Redundant.   [8] The other manuscripts have *laun*, which is obviously correct.
[9] From ⌜ is repeated after the next *svá*, and then crossed out.
[10] Error for *hata* (thus the Codex Regius version).
[11] Probably for *húfi* (thus the other manuscripts).   [12] Written 'messo'.

Second fox-turns

This is another fox-turns, and here there are only half as many lines that have fox-turns put in them, and there are two of them in alternate lines, and this is said to be the greatest:

18 Blood benefits wolf, it rather breaks concealment
(there are clear reports) that battle is waged;
hard shield shakes
and men begin to defend lands.
The gracious prince causes the white spear
to be thrust, the host to be advanced;
cool sword harms,
but the king's son helps, men.

Here there are these fox-turns in the second line: *heldr* 'rather/holds' and *slitnar* 'breaks', *dul* 'concealment' *vitni* 'wolf/witness'. Concealment is hiding, but witness demonstration. And in the fourth line it is thus: *skelfr* 'shakes/trembling' *harðr* 'hard/firm', *taka* 'begin/seize' *varða* 'defend'. In the sixth line it is thus: *hollr* 'true/gracious' *gramr* 'prince/angry', *rekinn* 'thrust/driven off' *framðan* 'advanced'. The eighth line is thus: *svalr* 'cool' *brandr* 'sword/brand'. Brand is a word for fire. *Dugir* 'helps' *grandar* 'harms'. This is word-play. Here too it is another signification of the words that must be taken for the sense as follows, saying that blood benefits *vitni(r)*, i.e. the wolf. And concealment or secrecy is broken or breached and *hlǫkk*, i.e. battle, is waged. And in the second quarter-stanza it is thus, that hard shield shakes, and men begin to defend lands. And in the third quarter-stanza it is thus: gracious prince causes the host to be advanced, the white spear to be thrust. He is advanced that is moved forward. In the fourth quarter-stanza it is thus, that cool sword harms men, but the king's son helps them.

19 Sail shakes and the deep crashes down
above the king and the current-maple (ship);
ships drive fast; and the shallows near Hugl hate (are dangerous to)
the Gyllir (horse) of the waves (ship).
Rán (the rough sea) does not grant to him, the man,
peace; the voice of the sea allots
cruisers strife; the entire wave
breaks before the thin planks.

Here there is one line in each half-stanza that is composed with fox-turns, and there are two in each, as follows: *grunn* 'shallow' *djúp* 'deep', *hata* 'hate' *unna* 'waves/love'. And in the latter half-stanza it is thus: *heil* 'entire' *klofnar* 'breaks', *frið* 'peace' *deilu* 'strife'. This is called the greatest fox-turns and yet [is]the least of those.

20 Hélir hlýr fyrir stáli,
    hafit fellr en svífr þelli,
    ferr, dvǫl firrist harða,
    framm mót lagar glammi.
    Vindr rekr, váðir bendir,
    vefr rekkr[1] á haf snekkjur;
    veðr þyrr; vísa iðnir
    varar fýsir skip lýða.

Hér er eitt refhvǫrf[2] í hverju vísuorði, ok flest ofljóst.

21 Lung frá ek lýða þengils—
    lá reis of skut—geisa,
    en sverð of her herða;
    hljóp stóð um gram bjóða.
    Þik[3] fær þungra skeiða
    þrǫngt rúm skipat lǫngum;
    stál lætr styrjar deilir
    stinn kløkk í mar søkkva.

Hér eru refhvǫrf í ǫðru hverju vísuorði.

22 Himinglæva strýkr hávar—
    hren[4] skilja søg—þiljur;
    lǫgstígu bil lǫgis[5]
    ljótr fagrdrasill[6] brjóta.
    Lýskeims[7] náir ljóma—
    líðr ár—of gram blíðum,
    unnr rekkir kjǫl kløkkvan
    kǫld, eisa; far geisar.

Hér eru ein refhvǫrf í hverjum helmingi.

23 Firrist hǫnd með harra
    hlumr; líðr vetr at[8] sumri;
    en flaust við lǫg Lista
    lǫng taka hvíld at gǫngu.

[1] *rekkr* is for *rekr*, *þyrr* is written 'þvʀ'. Lines 3 and 8 lack rhyme. Lines 3 and 5 lack antithesis. The Codex Regius version has *ferð* 'crew/movement' for *ferr*, *réttr* 'straight' for *rekkr* and *lýsa* 'illumine, shed glory on' for *lýða*.

[2] Error for *refhvarf*.

[3] The Codex Regius version has *Þjóð*, which gives both rhyme and sense.

[4] Error for *hrǫnn*. The Codex Regius version has *sog* (pl.) 'keel' for *søg* 'stormy sea'.

[5] Line 3 reads *lǫgstíga vill lǫgir* in the Codex Regius version.

[6] I.e. *-drasil* (double consonant for single.

[7] Error for *Lýsheims*.

[8] The Codex Regius version has *af* 'from', which makes the ending of voyages more natural.

20 The bow (/warms) freezes before the stem,
    the sea (/lifted) falls and the timber glides,—
    stopping is avoided with difficulty—
    travels forwards against (/back) the water's uproar.
    Wind drives, it bends the sails,
    the cloth (/folds) drives (/unfolds) warships on the sea;
    wind (/paces) whistles (/rushes) past; the business of the king
    makes the men's ship eager (/urges) for the harbour (/warns).

Here there is one fox-turn in every line, and most involve word-play.

21 I have heard that the troop's king's longship—
    the water (/lay down) rose up above the stern—rushed,
    and that swords were tempered throughout the host; the stud
    of horses (/stood still) of boards (ships) galloped round the king.
    People are able for a long time to man
    the narrow bench (/spacious) of the heavy warships;
    the battle-dealer (warrior) makes the stiff stem
    sink softly(/flexible) into the sea.

Here there are fox-turns in every other line.

22 Himinglæva (a wave) strokes the high
    planks; the keel parts the wave;
    the ugly ocean tries to break
    the fair horse of the sea-paths.
    There manages to shine around the happy
    king the fish-home's (sea's) fire (gold),
    cold wave encourages pliant keel;
    oar moves; vessel speeds.

Here there are single fox-turns in each half-stanza.

23 The oar-handle is separated from the hand
    among the lord's men; winter passes to summer;
    and the long vessels take a rest
    from travelling across the sea near Listi.

él[1] móðir lið lýða—
létt skipast hǫll—it rétta,
en skál of gjǫf gela[2]
gulls, svífr, tóm, en fulla

Hér er í ǫðru vísuorði ok inu fjórða þau er gagnstaðlig orð eru hvárt ǫðru sem refhvǫrf, en standa eigi saman, ok er ein samstafa milli þeira, ok lúkast eigi bæði ⟨í⟩ eina tíð. Þessir hættir er nú eru ritnir eru dróttkvæðir at hætti, hendingum ok orðalengð, svá sem hér er. Hér eru sex samstǫfur í hverju vísuorði ok aðalhendingar í ǫðru ok enu fjórða en skothent í fyrsta ok þriðja.

Hér segir hversu skipta skal hættinum

Hvernig skal skipta dróttkvæðum hætti með hendingum eða orðalengð? Sem hér er:

24   Hreintjǫrnum gleðr horna—
horn náir lítt at þorna—
mjǫðr hegnir bǫð bragna—
bragningr skipa sagnir;
folkhǫmlu gefur framla
framlyndr viðum gamlar,[3]
hinn er heldr fyrir skot skjǫldu,
Skjǫldungr hunangs ǫldur.[4]

Hér er það málsorð fyrst í ǫðru ok inu fjórða vísuorði er | síðast er í fyrsta ok þriðja.

25   Ræst[5] gaf ǫðlingr ⟨j⟩astar—
ǫl[6] virði ek svá—firðum;
þegn[7] fellir brim bragna—
bjór⟨r⟩ forn er þat—horna;
máls kann mildingr heilsu—
mjǫðr heitir svá·—veita;
stryks[8] kemr í val veiga—
vín kalla ek þat—galda.[9]

[1] The Codex Regius version has 'avl' = ǫl 'ale' for él 'storm'.
[2] The Codex Regius version has góla = góliga.
[3] Written 'gamlair', but Grape et al. 1977: 175 point out that signs of an attempt at correction are visible.
[4] Written 'olldr'.
[5] Obviously an error for rǫst.
[6] Written 'oll'.
[7] Error for þǫgn.
[8] Error for strúgs.
[9] Error for galli.

> The good (/straight) ale wearies the company of men,
> the hall (/aslant) is easily filled when empty,
> but the full golden bowl passes
> over the gifts splendidly.

Here in the second line and the fourth are those which are words of contrary meaning to each other like fox-turns, but they do not stand together, and there is one syllable between them, and they do not have the same cadence. These verse forms that have now been written are court poetry in form, rhymes and length of lines just as they are here. Here there are six syllables in every line and full rhymes in the second and the fourth but half-rhymes in the first and third.

Here it says how the verse form may be varied

How may court poetry form be varied in rhymes or line length?
   As it is here:

24   The prince gladdens the ships' crews
           with pure lakes of horns (ale)
           The horn does not get to dry out too much.
           Mead keeps back men's [desire for] battle.
           The bold-hearted king, he who
           holds shields in front of missiles,
           gives generously old honey-waves (mead)
           to army-rod (sword) trees (warriors).

Here the word is first in the second and fourth line that is last in the first and third.

25   The king gave currents of yeast—
           that is what I adjudge ale to be—to men;
           Men's silence is dispelled by surf—
           that is old beer—of horns;
           the prince knows how speech's salvation—
           that is what mead is called—is to be given;
           in the choicest of cups comes—
           this is what I call wine—dignity's destruction.

26 Fúss brýtr fylkir eisu
 fens—bregðr hǫnd á venju.
 Ránhegnir gefr Rínar
 rǫf—spyrr ætt at jǫfrum.
 Mjǫk trúir ræsir rekka
 raun—sér gjǫf til launa.
 Ráð á lofðungr lýða
 lengr—vex hverr af gengi.
27 Ískalda skar ek ǫldu
 eik—var súð in bleika
 reynd—til ræsis fundar
 ríks. Em ek kunnr at slíku.
 Brjótr þá hersis heiti
 hátt—dugir sømð at vátta—
 auðs af jarla prýði
 ítrs. Vara slíkt til lítils.

Hér hefr upp annat ok it fjórða vísuorð með fullu orði ok einni samstǫfu, ok leiðir orð af inum fyrra vísuhelmingi[1] ok orðinu. En þær fimm samstǫfur er þá eru um mál er eptir eru.

Þessi er enn fyrsti háttr ritaðr þeira er breyttir sé af dróttkvæðum hætti með fullu háttaskipti, ok héðan í frá skal nú rita þær greinir er skipt er dróttkvæðum hætti ok breytt með hljóðum ok hendingaskipti eða orðalengð, stundum við lagt, stundum af tekit.

28 Van⟨d⟩baugs veit⟨t⟩i sendir
 vígrak⟨k⟩r, en gjǫf þakkak
 skjaldbrags[2] skylja mildum
 skipre⟨i⟩ði menn,[3] heiða.
 Fann næst fylkir unna
 fall[4] dýr at gjǫf stýra[5]
 stálhreins; styrjar deili⟨s⟩
 stórlæti fáir møta.

Hér er í fysta ok þriðja vísuorði þat er háttum skiptir. Hér standa stuðlar, hljóðfyllendr svá nær at ein samstafa er í milli þeira. Þe⟨i⟩r gera skjálfhendar,[6] ok eru hin fyrri upphǫf vísuorðs. En hendingar standast sem fyrst. En ⟨ef⟩ frumhending er í þeiri samstǫfu er næst er enni fyrstu, þá bregst eigi skjálfhenda.

[1] *-helmingi* is a mistake, and is corrected with the next two words; *inum* must be changed to *inu*.
[2] I.e. *skjaldbraks*.
[3] Error for *mér*.
[4] Error for *fǫl* (thus the Codex Regius version).
[5] Error for *stýri*.
[6] Error for *-hendur*.

26 The leader is eager to distribute fen's
fire (gold)—the hand tends to act in accordance with custom.
The punisher of plundering gives Rhine's
amber (gold)—princes become famous among men.
The ruler greatly trusts his men's
experience—a gift looks to its recompense.
The king has power over his men for the
future—each man gains from companionship.

27 I cut the ice-cold wave with
oak—the pale planking was put to the
test—to meet the powerful
ruler. I am renowned for such.
The breaker of splendid wealth (generous man, the poet)
received—it is worth reporting the honour—
the noble name of lord from the honourer of
earls (King Hákon). Such a thing was not a small benefit.

Here the second and fourth line begins with a complete word consisting of a single syllable, and [this] word belongs in sense to the previous line. But the five syllables that follow [are] about the statement that comes next.

This is the first verse form [that is] written of those that are varied from court poetry form with a complete change of form, and from now on we shall exemplify the distinctions by which court poetry form is varied and changed in alliteration and arrangement of rhymes or length of lines, [which is] sometimet increased and sometimes reduced.

28 The war-bold shield-wand (sword) provider
gave me a skip's rigging,
and I thank the prince unsparing
of shield-crash (battle) for the splendid gift.
The ruler next found available as a gift
waves-animals (ships) for the stem-deer (ship)
steersman (the poet); few men experience
the munificence of the hostility-dealer.

Here the variation in the form is in the first and third lines. There the props (alliterating staves), the alliterating syllables, stand so close [to each other] that there is one syllable between them. They constitute shiverings, and the first ones [of each pair] form the beginnings of the lines. But the rhyming syllables come as early as possible. But if the first rhyme is in the syllable that is next to the first, this does not affect the shiverings.

29   Tvær man ek hilmi hýrum
     heimsvistir ótvistar,
     hlaut ek ásamt at sitja
     seimgildi fémildum;
     fúss gaf fylkir hnossir,
     fleinstýrir[1] margdýrar;
     hollr var hersa stilli
     hátt spenn fjǫlni ennum.[2]
Hér skiptast hættir í ǫðru ok fjórða, og ræðr en fjórða samstafa háttum.

30   Þoll bið ek hilmis hylli
     halda | grǫnna skjalda;
     askr beið af því þroska
     þilju Hrungnis ilja;
     vígfoldar mót valdi
     vandar margra landa
     nýtr váttu oss til ítra⟨r⟩
     elli dólga fellir.[3]
Hér er í ǫðru ok þriðja[4] vísuorði þat er háttum skiptir ok ræðr hér en þriðja samstafa.[5]

31   Stáls dynblakka støkkvi
     stinngeðs samir minnast—
     álms bifsøki aukum
     Yggs[6] feng—á lof þengils;
     odds bláferla jarli
     ǫrbrjót ne skal þrjóta—
     Hárs saltunnum hrannir
     hrørum—odd at skera.[7]
Hér skiptir háttum í ǫðru[8] ok þriðja vísuorði. Hér standa stuðlar sem first má, en hendingar svá at ein samstafa er í milli. Þat greinir háttuna.

[1] Error for *fleinstýri*.
[2] This line in the Codex Regius version reads *hoddspennir fjǫlmennum*. The text in DG 11 4to is incomprehensible.
[3] This interpretation of the second half of the stanza conflicts with the youthful age of the king. The Codex Regius version, having *njót* for *mót* and *vartu* for *váttu* gives the more appropriate (and straightforward) meaning 'Battle-land wand-wielder, enjoy many lands until splendid old age; you have been beneficial to us, feller of enemies.'
[4] Error for *fjórða* (thus the Codex Regius version). See Faulkes 2007: 57.
[5] The Codex Regius version adds: *Nú hefur upp annat kvæði* 'Here begins the second poem'. This will be about Jarl Skúli.
[6] Written 'ygſ'.
[7] *odd at skera* is meaningless. The Codex Regius version reads *óð at stǿra*.
[8] Error for *fyrsta*.

29 I remember two not unenjoyable
    visits to the friendly prince,
    I got to sit in company with
    the generous gold-payer;
    the ruler eagerly gave most
    valuable treasures to the spear-guider (the poet),
    the hoard-spender (or -grasper; the poet) was loyal
    to the controller of lords with his great company.

Here the forms are varied in the second and fourth [lines], and it is the fourth syllable [which is long and stressed] that is significant for the form.

30 I pray that the green shields' tree (the poet)
    may keep the prince's favour;
    Hrungnir's sole-plank (shield) ash (the poet)
    has gained advancement from this;
    you fought, feller of enemies of many lands,
    beneficial to us, until splendid old age
    against the wielder (warrior) of the
    wand (sword) of battle-land (shield).

Here what varies the forms is in the second and fourth line, and here it is the third syllable [which is long and stressed] that is significant.

31 It befits the impeller (sailor, the poet) of the noisy stem-horses
    (ships) to recall the glory of the firm-minded prince (Skúli);
    we activate Yggr's (Óðinn's) gain (poetry)
    for him who seeks to make the bow quiver (the warrior).
    The eager breaker (warrior, the poet) of the point's (arrow's)
    dark paths (shields) shall not cease
    to extend eulogy for the earl; we stir
    the waves (the mead of poetry) of Hárr's hall-vats.

Here the verse forms are varied in the first and third line. Here the props (alliterating staves) stand as far apart as possible, and the rhyme syllables so that there is one syllable between them. This distinguishes the verse forms.

292 Uppsala Edda

32   Él þreifst skarpt um Skúla
    skýs snarvinda lindar,
    egg varð hvǫss í hǫggum
    hræs dynbrunnum runnin;
    seimþreytir bjó sveita
    snjallr ilstafna hrafni;
    valr[1] varð und fót falla
    framm þrábarni arnar.

Hér skiptir háttum í ǫðru ok fjórða vísuorði. Standa hendingar ⟨báðir samt⟩ nær enda ok lúkast báðar í einn hljóðstaf ok er betr at samhljóðandi sé eptir aðra.[2]

33   Lífs var rán at raunum
    – reidd sverð – skapat mjǫk ferðum;
    stǫng óð þrátt at þingi
    þjóðsterk; liðu framm merki;
    hrauð um hilmis bróður
    hvǫss egg friðar ván seggjum;
    spjót náðu blá bíta;
    bóndmenn hlutu þar renna.

Hér er háttaskipti í ǫðru ok fjórða vísuorði ok er þar ein samstafa í sett svá at tvær eru síðarr ok aukit því lengð orðsins.[3]

34   Flaust bjó fólka treystir
    fagrskjǫlduðustum[4] eldum;[5]
    leið skar bragnings bróðir
    bjartveggjuðustu hreggi;[6]
    hest rak hilmir rasta
    harðsveipaðastan reipum;
    sjár hlaut við þrǫm þrjóta
    þunghúfu⟨ðu⟩stu⟨m⟩ lungi.

Hér skiptir háttum í ǫðru ok fjórða vísuorði. Er hér aukit samstǫfu ok fullnat orðtak sem framast má, ok eptir þá samstǫfu eru þrjár samstǫfur ok er rétt dróttkvætt ef hon er ór tekin.[7]

[1] The Codex Regius version has *Páll*, taken to be Páll dróttseti 'king's steward', killed probably in 1213, though not in battle; he was executed by Skúli for treachery. Maybe the wording of lines 7–8 does not necessarily mean he fell in battle.
[2] See Introduction pp. xc–xci.
[3] See Faulkes 2007: 58.
[4] See Introduction p. cxxiv.
[5] Error for *ǫldum*.
[6] GkS 2367 4to and Codex Trajectinus have *reggi*, 'ship', but DG 11 4to and AM 242 fol. have *hreggi* 'storm', which hardly makes sense.
[7] See Faulkes 2007: 58.

32 The sharp storm (battle) of the keen
spear-wind cloud (shield) raged around Skúli,
the sharp edge was flooded with rushing
corpse-streams (blood) amid the blows;
the brave gold exhauster (generous man) covered
the raven's sole-stems (claws) with blood;
the slain had to fall down beneath
the foot of the eagle's beloved offspring.

Here the verse forms are varied in the second and fourth line. The rhyme syllables stand both together near the end and they both have the same sound in the ending and it is better that one of them is followed by a consonant.

33 Robbing of life was made very much
a reality for soldiers; swords [were] brandished;
mighty strong standard advanced irresistibly
to the assembly (battle); banners went forward;
Sharp edge deprived men of hope
of peace around the king's (Ingi's) brother (Skúli);
dark spears got to bite;
peasants there had to flee.

Here there is variation of verse forms in the second and fourth line, and there one syllable is inserted before the last two and thus the length of the line is increased.

34 The tester of armies (Skúli) provided a craft
with the most beautifully shielded men;
the king's brother cut the sea
with the most brightly sailed cruiser;
the prince drove the current-horse (ship)
with most tightly twisted ropes;
the sea had to resound against the side
of the most heavily planked longship.

Here the verse-forms are varied in the second and fourth line. A syllable is added here and the expression amplified as far as it can be, and after that syllable there are three syllables and it is normal court poetry form if it is taken out.

35   Reist at Vágsbrú vestan,
       var⟨r⟩síma bar fjarri,
       heitfastr hávar rastir
       hjálm-Týr svǫlu stýri;
       støkkr vóx er bar b⟨l⟩akka
       brims | fyrir jǫrð it grimma
       herfjǫlð, húfar svǫlðu,
       hrannláð bóndmanna.¹

Hér er skjálfhent eða² aðalhending í þriðja vísuorði í hvárum helmingi, en at ǫðru sem dróttkvætt. Þenna hátt fann fyrst Þorvaldr veili. Þá lá hann í útskeri nokkuru, kominn af skipsbroti ok hafði fátt klæða, en veðr kalt. Þá orti hann kvæði er kǫlluð er Kviðan skjálfhenda eða Drápan steflausa.

36   Hristist³ hvatt þá er reistist
       herfǫng mjǫk lǫng véstǫng;
       samði fólk en⁴ framði
       fullsterk hringserk grams verk;
       hǫnd lék, herjum reyndist
       hjǫrr kaldr, allvaldr mannbaldr;
       egg-, frá ek breiða bjuggu
       bragning fylking, stóð -þing.

Hér eru þrennar aðalhendingar samt í ǫðru ok hinu fjórða vísuorði ok fylgir samstafa fyrir hverja.

37   Vann, kann virðum banna
       vald, gjald, hǫfundr aldar,
       ferð verð fólka herði
       fest mest, sú er bil lestir;
       hátt þrátt hǫlða áttar,
       hrauð auð jǫfurr rauðum,
       þat, gat þengill skatna
       þjóð, stóð um gram, bjóða.

Hér er í fyrsta ok þriðja vísuorði tvær aðalhendingar sem⁵ í upphafi, en hin þriðja at hætti við enda.

38   Farar snarar fylkir byrjar,
       freka breka lemr á snekkjum,
       vaka taka vísa rekkar,
       viðar skriðar at þat biðja;

¹ Written 'bondm*ann*a' but needs to be read *búandmanna* to provide the correct number of syllables.
² Error for *með*.
³ Error for *hristust* (the subject is *herfǫng*).
⁴ Written as *enn*.   ⁵ Error for *samt*.

35 The helmet-Týr (warrior), true to his word,
    cut deep currents with cold steering-oar
    from the west to Vágsbrú;
    the line of the wake stretched far;
    the peasants' flight increased when
    the grim wave-land (sea) bore a great multitude
    of horses of the surf (ships) past the coast.
    The planks were made cold.

Here there is shivering with full rhyme in the third line in each half-stanza, but otherwise [it is] like court poetry form. This verse-form was invented by Þorvaldr veili. He was at the time lying on a certain outlying skerry, having escaped from a shipwreck, and he had little clothing, and the weather was cold. Then he composed a poem that is called the Shivering Poem or the Refrainless Drápa.

36 Armour was shaken violently when
    the very long standard was raised;
    the army donned the mail-shirt
    and carried out the prince's most mighty deeds;
    cold sword waved in the hand,
    the great ruler proved an outstanding one to the hosts;
    I heard that the leader drew up the broad battle-line,
    the parliament of edges (battle) took place.

Here there are three full rhymes together in the second and fourth line and there is a syllable in front of each one.

37 Deserving men who put an end
    to hesitation caused very great payment
    to be made to the promoter of battles (war-leader); the judge of men
    knows how to stop men's arrogance;
    the prince of men was able forcefully to teach
    the company of the clan of landowners
    [good] behaviour; the prince gets rid of (gives away)
    red wealth (gold); this continued around the king.

Here there are in the first and third line two full rhymes together at the beginning, and the third as usual at the end.

38 The war-leader undertakes swift journeys,
    strong waves lash the warships,
    the ruler's men begin to stay awake,
    after that they urge on the timber's (ship's) movement;

svipa skipa sýjur heppnar
sǫmum frǫmum[1] í byr rǫmmum;
Haka skaka hrannir blǫkkum
hliðar; miðar und kjǫl niðri.

39   Ok hjaldrreifan hófu
hoddstiklanda miklir,
morðflýtir kná mǿta
málmskúrar dyn, h⟨j⟩álmar
hjaldrs þá er hilmir[2] foldar
hugfǿrum gaf stǿri,
ógnsvellir fær allan,
jarldóm, gǫfugr sóma.

Hér skiptir háttum í fjórða[3] vísuorði ok leiðir í því orði máltak af fyrra vísuhelmingi, ok dregst þat vísuorð með hljóðfyllingum mjǫk eptir skjálfhendu enni nýju.

40   Hverr fremr hildi barra?
Hverr er mælingum fyrri?[4]
Hverr gerir hǫpp at stǿrri?
Hverr kom auð at þverra?
Veldr hertugi hjaldri,
hann er first blikurmanni,
hann á happ[5] at sýnni,
hann vélir blik spannar.

Þessum hætti er breytt til dróttkvæðs ⟨með orðum⟩.

41   Velr ítrhugaðr ýtum
otrgjǫld jǫfurr snotrum;
opt hefir þings fyrir þrøngvi
þungfarmr Grana sprungit;
hjǫrs vill rjóðr at ríði
reiðmálmr Gnitaheiðar;
vígs er hreytt at hættis
hvatt Niflunga skatti.

Þat eru liðhendur er inn sami stafr stendr fyrir hendingar, ok er réttr ortr liðhendr háttr at í ǫðru ok fjórða vísuorði sé oddhending ok skothending við þær hendingar er í fyrra orði eru ok verðr þá einn upphafsstafr allra þeira þriggja hendinga.

[1] Error for þrǫmum.
[2] First written 'hilldinir', then the *d* erased. See Grape et al. 1977: 176.
[3] Error for *fimta*.
[4] I.e. *firri*.
[5] Error for *hǫpp* (*sýnni* requires it to be plural).

Uppsala Edda

the fortunate planks flex the fine
ships' gunwales in the powerful wind;
the waves shake the sides of Haki's (sea-king's) horses (ships);
there is movement down under the keel.

39 And great helmets enhanced the glory of
the battle-happy treasure-thrower (generous lord);
the urger of killing (war-leader) does
meet the metal-storm clash (battle)
when the king of the land gave
the courageous battle-increaser
an earldom; the honourable
war-sweller receives all glory.

Here the verse forms are varied in the fourth line and in this line the sense continues from the previous half-stanza, and in the alliteration this line is very similar to the new shivering.

40 Who wages harsh war?
Who is further from being a niggard?
Who achieves the greater success?
Who caused wealth to diminish (by his generosity)?
The duke brings about war,
he is furthest from being a miser,
he has the clearer success,
he cheats (gives away) the gleam of the palm (gold).

This verse form is a verbal variation of court poetry form.

41 The splendid-minded prince selects
otter's payment (gold) for wise men;
often has the heavy burden of Grani (gold) broken
(been distributed) because of the assembly-compeller (war-leader);
the sword-reddener desires the metal-load (gold)
of Gnitaheiðr to be scattered;
the treasure of the Niflungs (gold) is flung
energetically in the presence of the battle-darer.

Those are help-rhymes when the same letter stands in front of the rhymes, and it is correctly composed help-rhyme form when in the second and fourth line there is front-rhyme and half-rhyme with the rhymes that are in the previous line, and then there is the same initial letter for all these three rhyming syllables.

42 Alrauðum drífr auði
 ógnrakkar¹ firum hlakkar,
 veit ek, hvar vals á reitu
 verpr hringdropa snerpir;
 snjallr lætr á fit falla
 fagrregn jǫfurr þegnum,
 ógnflýtir verr ýtum
 arm, Marþallar hvarma.

Hér eru aðalhendingar í fyrsta ok þriðja vísuorði, en gætt at taka ór skothendum.²
Enn er sá háttr er vér kǫllum hina minni alhendu. Þar eru skothendur í hinu fyrsta vísuorði í báðum helmingum, svá sem hér segir:

43 Samþykkjar fremr søkkum
 snar⟨r⟩ Baldr hjarar aldir;
 gunnhættir kann Grotta
 glaðdript hraða skipta;
 féstríðir kná Fróða
 friðbygg liði tryggva;
 fjǫlvinjat hylr Fenju
 falr meldr alinveldi.

Þá er rétt ort in minni alhenda at haldit sé vísulengð saman. En ef ein er skothenda í fulla alhendu, svá at skothendur sé þar sumar eða allar í vísuorði, þá er þat eigi rétt.

44 Frama skotnar gramr;³ gotnum
 gjǫf sannas⟨t⟩ ref⁴ spannar;
 menstiklir venr miklar
 manndýrðir innan skýrðar;
 herfjǫlð—bera hǫlðar—
 hagbáls lagar stála
 friðast sjaldan við valdi—
 va⟨lla⟩nds⁵ svala branda.

Hér eru tvennar aðalhendingar í hverju vísuorði. Þessi þikkir vera vandastr ok fegrstr, ef vel er kveðit, þeira hátta er kvæði sé af ort, ok er þá full alhending ef eigi finnsk í at, ek, en, eða þau smáorð er þeim fylgja, nema þau standi í hendingum. En eigi hafa allir menn þat varast ok er þat því eigi rangt, sem kvað Klǿingr biskup:

¹ Error for *ógnrakkr.*
² Error for *skothendur.*
³ Error for *gram.*
⁴ Error for *rǫf.*
⁵ Haplography (*a* to *a*) causing the loss of a syllable and spoiling the rhyme.

42 There is scattering of the all-red wealth (gold),
I know, where the attack-bold
battle-sharpener (warrior) throws ring-droplets
(gold, cf. Draupnir) on men's hawk-lands (arms);
the bold prince makes the fair
rain of Mardǫll's eyelids (gold)
fall on subject's limbs,
the attack-hastener (war-leader) covers men's arms.

Here there are full rhymes in the first and third lines, but care has been taken to leave out half-rhymes.

Next is the verse form that we call the lesser fully-rhymed. In it there are half-rhymes in the first line in both half-stanzas, as it says here:

43 The swift sword-Baldr (warrior) benefits
men with the destroyers of unity (gold ornaments);
the battle-darer knows how to quickly
share out Grotti's joy-bringing snow (silver);
money's enemy (generous man) does entrust
men with Fróði's peace-barley (gold);
Fenja's meal (gold), freely available, covers
the realm of the forearm, which has many resting-places.

The lesser fully-rhymed is correctly composed if the pattern is maintained throughout the stanza. But if there is one half-rhyme in complete fully-rhymed, so that some or all [of the rhymes] in a line there are half-rhymes, then it is not correct.

44 Glory befalls the prince; the gift to men
turns out to be palm's amber (gold);
the necklace-thrower (generous man) makes customary
his great virtues made evident from within;
the multitude of finely-made sea-pyres (gold ornaments)
is seldom left in peace (it is given away)
with the steel-wielder (warrior); yeomen
wear cool hawk-land's (arms') brands.

Here there are two pairs of full rhyme in each line. This is considered to be the most demanding and most beautiful, if it is composed well, of the verse forms that poems are made from, and it is then full complete rhyme if there is not found in it *at* 'that', *ek* 'I', *en* 'but', or those particles of that kind, unless they form part of the rhyme-scheme. But not everyone has avoided this, and so it is not wrong, as in Bishop Kløingr's verse:

Bað ek sveit á glað Geitis;
ger¹ er hríð at fǫr tíðum;
drǫgum hest | á lǫg lesti;²
lið flýtr, en skip³ nýtum.

45 Lætr undin brot brotna
bragningr fyrir sér hringa;
sá tekr fyrir men meina⁴
mæt⟨t⟩ orð of sik fæt⟨t⟩ir;
armr kná við blik blikna
brimlands viðum randa
þar er hǫnd at lið liðnar
lýslóðar berr glóðir.

Hér er í fysta vísuorði og þriðja tvíkveðit at einni samstǫfu ok haft þat til hendinga, ok kǫllum vér því þetta stamhent at tvíkylpt er til hendingar.

46 Virðandi gefr virðum
verbál liðar skerja;
gleðr vellbroti vellum
verðung afar þungum;
ýtandi fremr ýta
auðs sæfuna rauðum,
þar er mætum gram mæti
marblakks skipendr þakka.

Hér eru þær hendingar er⁵ í ǫðru ok fjórða vísuorði svá settur⁶ sem skothendur í dróttkvæðum hætti.

47 Seimþverrir gefr seima
seimerr⁷ liði beima,
hringmildan spyr ek hringum
hringkenning⁸ brott þinga;
baugstøkkvir fremr baugum
bauggrimmr hjarar drauga;
vinnr gullbroti gulli
gullheitr skaða fullan.

Hér er þrim sinnum haft samhending, tysvar í fyrsta ok þriðja vísuorði, en í ǫðru ok enu fjórða er haldit afhending sem í dunhendum hætti.

¹ Error for *gǫr*.
² Error for *lesta*.
³ Error for *skrið* (to provide the rhyme).
⁴ The Codex Regius version has *menja*, which provides the correct rhyme and meaning (misreading of *ni* as *in*).
⁵ Redundant.   ⁶ Error for *settar*.   ⁷ Obviously an error for *seimǫrr*.
⁸ The Codex Regius version has *hringskemmi*, which is clearly correct. Line 3 is written twice, the second time crossed out.

I ordered the troop onto Geitir's steed (ship);
attack is carried out repeatedly on the journey;
we drag the cargo-horse onto the sea;
the vessel floats, and we enjoy motion.

45   The prince makes twisted ring-fragments
fragment before him (distributes gold);
because of the necklaces this necklace-diminisher (generous man)
receives fitting renown about himself;
the shield-trees' (warriors') limb does gleam with the gleam
of the surf-land (gold) where the hand wears
fish-path (sea) embers (gold rings)
with which the arm is armed.

Here in the first line and the third, one syllable is repeated, and this forms the rhymes, and we call this stammering-rhymed because the rhyme is produced by double hammering.

46   The valuer of limb-skerries (gold jewellery)
gives men depth-pyres (gold);
the gold-breaker (generous man) gladdens his following
with extremely heavy gold ornaments;
the wealth-pusher honours men
with red sea-blaze (gold)
where the sea-steed's (ship's) crew thank
the splendid prince for splendid objects.

Here the rhyme-syllables in the second and fourth line are in the positions of the half-rhymes in court poetry form.

47   The gold-generous gold-diminisher
gives the troop of men gold;
I hear the ring-liberal ring-spoiler
disposes of rings;
the bracelet-hating bracelet-flinger honours
sword-trunks (warriors) with bracelets;
the gold-breaker, threatener of gold,
causes complete destruction to gold.

Here coincident rhyme (one falling on the same syllables as the alliteration) is used three times, twice in the first and third line, but in the second and fourth, off-rhyme (the same rhyme in the even lines as at the end of the preceding odd lines) is kept as in echoing-rhymed form.

48 Auðkendar verr auði
   auð-Týr boga nauðir;
   þar er auðviðum auðit
   auðs í gulli rauðu;
   heiðmǫnnum býr heiðis
   heiðfrøkn jǫfurr reiðir;
   venr heiðfrǫmuðr heiðar
   heiðgjǫf vala leiðar.

Hér halda samhendingar um alla vísulengð[1] ok taka með aðalhending ina síðarri í ǫðru ok fjórða vísuorði.

49 Hjaldrremmir tekr Hildi,
   hringr brestr at gjǫf, flesta;[2]
   hnígr und Hǫgna meyjar
   hers valdandi tjald;
   Heðins málu[3] býr hvílu
   hjálmlestandi flestum;
   morðaukinn þiggr mæki
   mund Hjaðninga sprund.

Hér er í fyrsta[4] orði stýft ok tekin af sú samstafa er dróttkvæðum hætti skal leggja með hending.

50 Yggs drósar rýfr eisa
   ell[5] móðsefa tjǫld;
   glóð støkkr í haf[6] Hlakkar
   hugtúns firum brún;
   geðveggr | sýnir[7] glugga
   glæs dynbrími hræs;
   hvattr er hyrr at slétta
   hjaldrs gnapturna aldrs.

Hér er stýft annat ok it fjórða vísuorði.

51 Herstefnir lætr hrafn
   hungr⟨s⟩ fullseðjast ungr;
   ilspornar[8] getr ǫrn
   aldrlausastan haus;

---

[1] It should be *vísuhelming* ('half-stanza') as in the Codex Regius version.
[2] Error for *festa*.
[3] Error for *mála*.
[4] Error for *fjórða*.
[5] Error for *ǫld* (thus the Codex Regius version).
[6] So AM 242; GkS 2367 4to and Codex Trajectinus have *hof*, which must be correct.
[7] The Codex Regius version has *geðveggjar svífr*, which must be correct.
[8] Error for *ilspornat*.

48 The wealth-Týr (prince) covers the easily-picked out
(because of the rings on them) bow-forcers (men's arms)
with wealth; there wealth is granted
to wealth-trees (men) in red gold;
the payment-bold prince adorns
the soldiers' hawk-carts (arms on which hawks are carried);
the payment performer accustoms the bright
falcon-paths (arms) to payment gift.

Here the coincident rhymes continue throughout the whole length of the stanza and are consonant with the second full rhyme in the second and fourth line.

49 The battle-strengthener (ruler) engages himself to Hildr (a valkyrie,
personification of battle); the ring is broken as a gift;
the ruler of the host moves under
Hǫgni's daughter's (Hildr's) tent (his shield);
Heðinn's beloved (Hildr) prepares a bed (selects for death)
for most helmet-damagers (warriors);
the lady of the Hjaðnings (Hildr) receives a wedding gift,
a sword famous for slaying.

Here the fourth line is docked (catalectic) and the syllable that in court poetry form has to be placed next to the rhyme-syllable is omitted.

50 The fire (sword) of Yggr's (Óðinn's) maid (valkyrie) tears
the tents of men's mood-thought (breast);
Hlǫkk's burnished ember (sword) flies
into the temple of men's thought-enclosure (breast);
the clashing corpse-flame (sword) glides through
the window of the transparent wall of thought (breast-wound);
the battle-fire (sword) is sharpened to slice off
the jutting towers of life (heads).

Here the second and fourth line is docked.

51 The young battle-leader lets the raven
fully sate its hunger;
the eagle is able to tread underfoot
the completely lifeless skull;

vilja borg en vargr
vígsára klífr grár;
opt sólgit fær ylgr—
jǫfurr góðr vill svá—blóð.

Hér eru ǫll vísuorð stýfð. Þessir hættir er nú eru ritnir eru greindir í þrjá staði, því at menn hafa ort svá at í einni vísu var annarr helmingr stýfðr, en annarr tilstýfðr[1] ok eru þat háttafǫll. Sá er enn þriði er alstýfðr er, því at þar eru ǫll vísuorð stýfð.

52 Sær skjǫldungs[2] niðr skúrum
    skǫpt darraðar lyptast;
    hrindr gunnfara[3] grundar
    glygg um frǿknum tiggja;
    geisa vé fyrir vísa;
    veðr stǫng at hlyn[4] Gungnis;
    styrk eru mót und merkjum
    hjálms[5] vin[6] ítrum hilmi.

Hér eru skothendur í ǫllum vísuorðum en at ǫðru sem dróttkvæðr háttr.

53 Stjóri venst at stǿra
    stór verk dunu geira;
    halda kann með hildi
    hjaldr-Týr und sik foldu;
    harri skilr und[7] hverri
    Hjarranda fǫt snerru;
    falla þá til fyllar
    f⟨j⟩allvargs jǫru þollar.

Í þessum hætti eru liðhendur með tvennum hætti, en aðrar á þá lund at ina fyrri hending í fyrsta ok þriðja vísuorði . . .[8]

Hættir fornskálda

Nú skal rita þá háttu er fornskáldin hafa kveðit, ok eru nú settir saman þótt þeir hafi ort sumt með háttafǫllum, ok eru þessir hættir dróttkvæðir kallaðir í fornkvæðum, en sumir finnast í lausavísum, svá sem orti Ragnarr konungr loðbrók með þessum hætti:

[1] Error for tví- (thus AM 242 4to and Codex Trajectinus).
[2] Written as skjǫldungrs, but the r is cancelled (see Grape et al. 1977: 108).
[3] Error for gunnfana; glygg is written 'glvgg'.
[4] The Codex Regius version has hlym 'din', giving a kenning for battle.
[5] hjálms for málms 'metal's' (thus the Codex Regius version) destroys the alliteration.
[6] Error for um (misreading of 'vm' as vin).
[7] The Codex Regius version has slítr í; the DG 11 4to reading makes no sense.
[8] Sentence incomplete in all manuscripts.

but the grey wolf climbs upon the battle-wounded
stronghold of the will (breast);
the she-wolf is often able to drink
blood, the good prince wishes it so.

Here all lines are docked. These verse forms that have just been written are divided into three types, because people have composed so that in a single stanza one half-stanza was docked, and the other docked in two lines [only], and this is a metrical inconsistency. The third type is all-docked, for there all lines are docked.

52 The prince's spear-showers
    are strewn down, shafts are lifted;
    storm pushes the battle-flags
    around the valiant lord of the land;
    the banners rush before the prince;
    the pole [of the banner] advances against maple of
    Gungnir (warrior); the powerful helmet-meetings (battles) take place
    under the standards around the splendid prince.

Here there are half-rhymes in all lines but otherwise [it is] like court poetry form.

53 The spear-din controller (battle-leader) becomes accustomed
    to carry out great deeds;
    the battle-Týr (warrior) knows how to hold land
    under himself with warfare;
    the lord cuts Hjarrandi's (Óðinn's)
    clothing (mail-coats) in every fray;
    then there fall combat-trees (warriors)
    as food for the mountain-wolf.

In this verse form there are help-rhymes in two ways, and in the first case such that the earlier rhyme in the first and third line . . .

Verse forms of ancient poets

Now shall be written the verse forms used by ancient poets, and they have now been made consistent, though they have in some cases composed with metrical inconsistencies, and these verse forms in ancient poems are said to be in court poetry form, and some of them are found in single-stanza poems, as King Ragnarr loðbrók composed using this form:

54 Skýtr at Skǫglar veðri—
en skjǫldungi[1] haldist—
Hildar hleimidrífu[2]
of hvítum þrǫm rítar,
en í søfis sveita
at sverðtogi ferðar
rýðr aldar vinr odda—
þat er jarls megin—snarla.

Hér er í fyrsta ok þriðja vísuorði háttleysa, en í ǫðru ok enu fjórða aðalhendingar. En hǫfuðstafrinn stendr svá, er kveðandi ræðr, í ǫðru ok enu fjórða vísuorði, ⟨at⟩ þar er fyrir sett samstafa ein eða tvær, en at I ǫðru sem dróttkvætt.

55 Hverr sæi jǫfri øgri[3]
jarl forvitrum betra[4]
eða gjarnara at grøða
glym harðsvelldan skjalda?
Stendr af stála skúrar
styrr ólítill Gauti
þá er fólks jaðarr foldir
ferr sigmǫrkum varða.

Hér er í fyrsta ok þriðja vísuorði háttleysa, en í ǫðru ok enu fjórða skothent ok riðhent.

56 Hverr ali blóði bysta
ben⟨s⟩ rauðsylgjum ylgjar,[5]
nema svá at gramr of gildi
gráð dog[6] margan vargi?
Gefr oddviti undir
egg nýbitnum[7] vitni;
hann ⟨s⟩ér Fenris fitjar
fram klóboðnar[8] roðna.

Hér er í fyrsta vísuorði ok þriðja háttleysa, en í ǫðru ok enu fjórða alhendingar ok riðhent.

[1] I.e. skjǫldum eigi. Rhymes in ǫ and a can form full rhymes in early poetry.
[2] Error for hlemmidrífu.
[3] Error for øgi.
[4] Here the scribe first wrote snarla 'swiftly' (influenced by the preceding verse?), but corrected it himself above the line, though without deleting snarla.
[5] Error for ylgi.
[6] Error for dag.
[7] Error for nýbitnar.
[8] Error for -loðnar (thus the Codex Regius version).

54 Hildr's resounding snowstorm (rain of weapons)
    is shot in Skǫgul's wind (battle) —
    but they cannot defend themselves with shields —
    around the white rim of the targe,
    but in the sweat (blood) of the queller (sword)
    at the troop's sword-drawing (battle)
    the friend of men (Skúli) reddens points (of weapons)
    energetically. Such is the earl's power.

Here there is lack of form (there are no rhymes) in the first and third line, but in the second and fourth [there are] full rhymes. But the chief stave, that determines the alliteration, is positioned in the second and the fourth line in such a way that there it is preceded by one or two syllables, but in other respects [it is] as court poetry.

55 Who can have seen an earl better
    than the most wise prince, the terrifying one,
    or more eager to increase
    the mightily swollen clash of shields (battle)?
    No small tumult arises
    from the steel-shower Gautr (warrior)
    when the people's protection goes
    to defend lands with battle-standards.

Here there is lack of form in the first and third line, but in the second and fourth it is half-rhymed and rocking-rhymed (with rhymes close together at the end).

56 Who would nourish the bloody-bristled
    she-wolf with the wound's red drinks
    unless it were that the prince satisfies
    the wolf's greed many a day?
    The leader provides the watcher (wolf)
    with wounds newly pierced by edge;
    he sees Fenrir's (wolf's) shaggy-(prickly-)clawed
    limbs in front redden (with blood).

Here there is lack of form in the first line and the third, but in the second and the fourth full rhymes and rocking-rhymed.

Index of Names

d. = died
Ls = Lǫgsǫgumannatal, the list of lawspeakers
R indicates that the name is differently written in GkS 2367 4to
Skt = Skáldatal, K = Skáldatal in the Kringla manuscript
ÆS = Ættartala Sturlunga, the genealogy of the Sturlungs

Aðalráðr konungr m. (Skt, 10th–11th century) King Eþelred II of England 114
Aðalsteinn Englakonungr m. (Skt, 10th century) King Æþelstan of England) 114
Adam m. (ÆS) 6, 118
Aðils m., a king in Uppsala 226, 242
Affríka f., Africa 8
Ágló/Ǫgló n., an area in Trøndelag 126, 194
Ái m., a dwarf 26
Alfaðir/Alfǫðr m., a name of Óðinn 10, 12, 20, 24, 28, 34, 36, 48, 52, 58, 124, 132
Álfheimar m. pl., the world of elves 32
Álfr m., a dwarf 26
Álfr hinn litli m. (Skt, a poet of King Eiríkr Refilsson) 100
Álfr Eyjólfsson m. (Skt, 13th century, a poet of Duke Skúli Bárðarson) 112
Álfrǫðull m., a name for the sun 84
Áli m., son of Loki (cf. Faulkes 1998: 168, note to 20/2) 148
Áli inn upplenski m., enemy of King Aðils 242
Áli/Váli m., a god (son of Óðinn and Rindr) 46, 164, 226
Alurg Emundardóttir f., wife of Hálfdan gamli 208
Alþjófr m., a dwarf 26
Amlóði m., a legendary person, possibly the one named by Saxo Grammaticus Amleth, i.e. Hamlet 158
Ámsvartnir m., a lake 48
Ánarr m., the father of Jǫrð 152
Andrímnir m., a cook 56
Andvari m., a dwarf 26, 238, 240
Angrboða f., a giantess, mother to Fenrisúlfr, Miðgarðsormr and Hel 46
Annarr m., a dwarf 26
Annarr m. (cf. Atra) son of Sefsmeg 8
Arfli m., an ox 228
Arfr m., an ox 228
Arfuni m., an ox 228
Argrímr/Arngrímr/Ásgrímr Bergþórsson m. (Skt, 13th century, a poet of Hákon herðibreiðr) 108
Arinbjǫrn hersir m. (Skt, 10th century, a Norwegian) 116
Arnaldr Þorvaldsson m. (Skt, 12th century, a poet of the Danish king Valdimarr Knútsson) 114
Arnbjǫrn Jónsson m. (Skt, 13th century, a Norwegian chieftain) 116
Árni fjǫruskeifr m. (Skt, a poet of Sigurðr Jórsalafari (K)) 106
Árni langi m. (Skt, 13th century, a poet of King Hákon Hákonarson) 108
Arnórr Kálfsson m. (Skt, 12th century, a poet of the Norwegian chieftain Ívarr selki and of Sigurðr munkr) 116
Arnórr Sǫrlason m. (Skt, 12th century, a poet of Sverrir Sigurðarson) 108
Arnórr Þórðarson m. jarlaskáld (Skt, 11th century, a poet of Magnús góði, Haraldr harðráði, Óláfr kyrri and Knútr ríki) 104, 112, 124, 150, 152, 174, 176, 184, 194 (other MSS Einarr Skúlason), 196, 200, 208, 212, 214, 222, 232
Ás(a)brú f., a name of Bifrǫst 28
Ása-Þórr = the god Þórr m. 38, 66, 70, 86, 92
Ásgarðr m., the home of the 'historical' Æsir 10, 12, 20, 24, 76, 84, 90, 138, 140, 234, 236
Ásgarðr inn forni m. 20
Ásgrímr m., a poet 160
Ásgrindr f. pl., the gates of Ásgarðr 86, 90

Index of names

Asía f. 8
Askr m., the first man 20
Áslaug f., a poetess (Skt), daughter of Sigurðr Fáfnisbani 100
Ásu-Þórðr m. (Skt, 12th century, a poet of the Norwegian chieftain Víðkunnr Jónsson) 116
Atall m., a sea-king 126
Atli m., a legendary person 226
Atli litli m. (Skt, 11th century, a poet of Óláfr kyrri) 104, 232
Atra m., son of Beðvigg (ÆS) 118
Atra m. (cf. Annarr), son of Sefsmeg 8
Atríðr m., a name of Óðinn 36
Auðr m., brother (more correctly son) of Nátt 152, 154
Auðumla (Auðhumla) f., a cow 16
Auðunn illskælda m. (Skt, a Norwegian poet of Haraldr hárfagri) 102
Auðvaldi m., father of Þjazi 88
Aurgelmir m. (= Ymir), a giant 16
Aurvaldi/Aurvandill m., a giant 94
Aurvangar m. pl. 26
Aurvantá f., R Aurvadilstá, a star 94
Austri m., a dwarf 18, 26, 150, 206
Austr-Saxland n., East Saxony 8
Austrvegir m. pl., the eastern Baltic lands 208, 210
Austrvegr m., the world of giants (Scythia) 60, 90
Ávalldi/Ǫvaldi m. (Skt, poet(s) of King Eysteinn Beli) 100
Baldr inn góði/hvíti m., a god 28, 38, 40, 46, 74, 76, 84, 86, 90, 124, 144, 146, 148, 168, 298
Baldr m. = Beldeg, son of King Óðinn 8
Bambǫrr m., a dwarf 26
Báleygr m., a name of Óðinn 36
Bára f., a wave, daughter of Ægir 154
Bárðr svarti m. (Skt, a poet of Magnús berfǿttr) 106
Baugi m., a giant, brother of Suttungr 88
Beðvigg m., son of Sefsmeg/Sesef (ÆS) 118
Beimar m., followers of King Beimi 214
Beimi m., a legendary king 214
Beiti m., a sea-king 158
Beldeg m. = Baldr, son of King Óðinn 8
Beli m., a giant 54, 144, 226
Bergelmir m., a giant 18
Bergþórr Hrafnsson m. (Ls) 120
Bersi Torfuson/Torfason m. (Skt, d. 1030, a poet of Óláfr helgi, Jarl Hákon Eiríksson and Knútr inn ríki) 104, 110, 112
Beyzla/Bestla f., mother of the god Óðinn 18, 132
Bezla f., daughter of the god Óðinn 90
Bíaf see Bjárr
Biblindi m., a name of Óðinn 36
Bifrǫst f., a bridge 22, 24, 28, 34, 44, 60, 80
Bil f., daughter of Viðfiðr 22, 54, 172, 246
Bileygr m., a name of Óðinn 36
Billingr m., a dwarf or giant 172
Bilskirnir m., Þórr's hall 38, 138, 140
Birgir Magnússon m. (Skt, a Swedish jarl 1248–1266) 102
Bivur (Bívurr?) m., a dwarf 26
Bjarkamál n. pl., a poem 166
Bjarni m. Gullbráskáld m. (Skt, 10th and 11th century, a poet of Óláfr Tryggvason and Kálfr Árnason) 104, 116
Bjárr/Bíaf m. = Bǫrr, son of Skjaldun/Skjǫldr (ÆS) 8, 118, 226
Bjǫrn m., a legendary person 226
Bjǫrn m. at Haugi (Skt, 9th century, king in Uppland, Sweden) 100
Bjǫrn krepphendi m. (Skt, around 1100, a poet of Magnús berfǿttr) 106
Bláinn m., a dwarf (?) 24
Blakkr m., a horse 226
Blakkr m. skáld Unásson Stefánssonar (12th century, a poet of King Sverrir Sigurðarson) 108
Blíkjand(a)bǫl n., Hel's bed-hangings 48
Blóðughaða/Blóðughadda f., a wave, daughter of Ægir 154
Blótughófi/Blóðughófi m., a horse 226
Boðn f., a vat containing the mead of poetry 88, 124, 132

Borr/Burr m., father of the god Óðinn 16, 18, 20, 132
Bragi gamli m., a legendary king 214
Bragi gamli Boddason m. (Skt, a poet of the kings Ragnarr loðbrók, Eysteinn beli and Bjǫrn at Haugi) 60, 100, 138, 140, 150, 164, 176 (verse 128 is probably by Hólmgǫngu-Bersi), 182, 202
Bragi m., a god of poetry 42, 44, 86, 88, 90, 94, 128 (this may be Bragi Boddason), 146, 148
Bragi m. skáld Hallsson (Skt, 12th century, a poet of Sverrir Sigurðarson and his son Hákon Sverrisson) 108
Bragningr m., a descendant of Bragi Hálfdanarson (who is not mentioned in DG 11 4to) 212
Breiðablik n. pl., Baldr's dwelling 32, 40
Brimlé n., a hall 82
Brísingamen n., a necklace of Freyja 52, 146, 148
Buðlar m. pl., descendants of Buðli 210
Buðli m., one of King Hálfdan's 18 sons 210
Buðlungr m., a member of the family of Buðli Hálfdanarson 210, 212
Búi m., a warrior 178
Buri m., grandfather of the god Óðinn 16
Búseyra f., a giantess (?); a possible reading would be *Bús eyru*, and then Búr m. would be a giant 142
Byggvir m., a well 22
Býleiftr/Býleiptr m., brother of Loki 46, 148
Bylgja f., a wave, daughter of Ægir 154
Bǫðvarr balti m. (Skt, 12th century, a poet of Sigurðr Haraldsson) 106, 150
Bǫlverkr m., a name of Óðinn 36, 88
Bǫlverkr Arnórsson m. (Skt, 11th century, brother of Þjóðólfr Arnórsson, a poet of Haraldr harðráði) 104
Bǫlþorn m., a giant, grandfather of the god Óðinn 18
Bǫrr m., a dwarf 26
Bǫrr m. = Bíaf, son of Skjaldun 8
Canaan (Cainan) m. (ÆS) 118

Celius m. (ÆS) 118
Ciprus m. (ÆS) 118
Cretus m. (ÆS) 118
Crít (Crete) f. (ÆS) 118
Dagfinnr Guðlaugsson (Skt, 13th century, a poet of the Norwegian chieftain Gautr á Meli) 116
Dagr m., brother (more correctly son) of Nátt 152
Dagr m., one of King Hálfdan's 18 sons 210, 226
Dani (Dáni?) m., a dwarf 26
Daninn (R Dáinn) m., a stag 30, 224
Danir m. pl., Danes 100, 102, 114, 210
Danmǫrk f., Denmark 10, 198, 210, 244
Dánuleif (in other sources Dáinsleif) f., a sword 234
Dardanus m. (ÆS) 118
Dolgþvari m., a dwarf 26
Dori (Dóri?) m., a dwarf 26
Dramir m., a dwarf 26
Draupnir m., a ring 76, 144, 150, 162, 166, 236
Drómi m., a fetter 48
Dúfa f., a wave, daughter of Ægir 154
Dúfr m., a dwarf 26
Durinn m., a dwarf 24
Dvalinn m., a dwarf 26, 30, 134
Dvalinn m., a legendary person 226
Dvalinn m., a stag 30, 224
Dyneyrr m., a stag 30, 224
Dyraþrór/Dyraþórr m., a stag 30, 224
Dyrinn (= Durinn?) m., a dwarf 24
Dǫglingr m., father of Dagr 20
Dǫglingr m., descendant of Dagr Hálfdanarson 210, 212
Ector m. (ÆS) Hector 118
Edda f., book title 6
Egill m., an unknown man 136
Egill m., an archer, brother of Vǫlundr 180
Egill Skallagrímsson m. (Skt, 10th century, a poet of Eiríkr blóðøx, Aðalsteinn Englakonungr, Arinbjǫrn hersir and Þorsteinn Þóruson) 102, 114, 116, 128, 134, 160, 208, 222

Index of names

Egill Skúlason m. = Egill Skallagrímsson 128
Egill Sǫlmundarson m. (ÆS) 118
Eiðavǫllr (R Iðavǫllr) m., an open place in Ásgarðr 84
Eikinskjalli m., a dwarf 26
Eikþyrnir m., a stag, maybe the same as Takþyrnir 224
Eilífr m., a poet 192 (R adds the nickname kúlnasveinn), 194
Eilífr Guðrúnarson m. (Skt, 10th century, a poet of Hákon inn ríki) 96, 110, 136 (written Einarr), 138, 142, 190
Einarr m. fluga (Skt, 12th century, a Norwegian chieftain) 116
Einarr Guðrúnarson m. = Eilífr Guðrúnarson 136
Einarr skálaglamm m. (Skt, 10th century, a poet of Hákon inn ríki) 110, 130, 132, 134, 136, 168, 170, 176, 178, 186, 202, 204, 228
Einarr Skúlason m. (11th and 12th century, a poet of the Swedish king Sørkvir Karlsson, his son the jarl Jón Sørkvisson, the Danish king Sveinn svíðandi and the Norwegian kings Sigurðr Jórsalafari (K), Eysteinn Magnússon, Haraldr gilli, Magnús blindi, Ingi Haraldsson (K), Sigurðr Haraldsson, Eysteinn Haraldsson and the chieftains Gregoríus Dagsson and Eindriði ungi) 100, 106, 114, 116, 156, 158, 162, 168, 180, 184, 188, 194, 196, 212, 228, 230, 232
Eindriði ungi m. (Skt, 12th century, a Norwegian chieftain) 116
Eir f., a goddess 52
Eiríkr blóðøx m. (Skt, a Norwegian king, 10th century) 102
Eiríkr Eiríksson m. (Skt, king of Sweden 1222–1250) 102
Eiríkr eymuni m. (Skt, 12th century, a Danish king) 114
Eiríkr Hákonarson m. (Skt, 10th century, a Norwegian jarl) 110
Eiríkr inn málspaki m., a legendary king 210

Eiríkr Knútsson m. (Skt, a Swedish king, d. 1216) 102
Eiríkr Magnússon m. (Skt, king of Norway 1280–99) 110
Eiríkr Refilsson m. (Skt, 9th century king) 100
Eiríkr sigrsæli m. (Skt, 10th century, king in Uppland, Sweden) 100
Eiríkr jarl Sigurðarson m. (Skt, a Norwegian jarl? 11th century? No poets) 112
Eiríkr Sveinsson m. (Skt, 11th century, a Danish king) 114, 214
Eldrímnir m., a pot 56
Elfr f. (Göta älv, river in Sweden)) 262
Élivágar f. pl., rivers 14, 16, 94
Eljúðnir m., Hel's hall 48
Elli f., the personification of old age 72
Em(b)la f., the first woman 20
Emundr m., king in Hólmgarðr 208
Enea f. = Evrópa (Europe) 8
England n., England 194, 196
Englar m. pl., the English 134, 194
Enon (Enoch) m. (ÆS) 118
Enos m. (ÆS) 118
Eremóð m., son of Ítrman 8
Ericonius (Ericthonius) m. (ÆS) 118
Eríksmál n. pl., a poem 130
Erlingr skakki m. (Skt, a Norwegian jarl, 11th century) 112
Erlingr Skjálgsson m. (Skt, 11th century, a Norwegian) 116
Eroas (Tros) m. (ÆS) 118
Erpr lútandi m. (Skt, a poet of King Eysteinn Beli) 100
Erringar-Steinn m., a poet 186
Eva f. Eve 6
Evrópa f. (Europe) = Enea 8
Eydanir m. pl., the Danes living on the islands 232
Eyjólfr dáðaskáld m. (Skt, 11th century, a poet of Jarl Sveinn) 110, 204
Eylimi m., legendary king, the grandfather of Sigurðr Fáfnisbani 210
Eymir m. (other MSS Hymir), a giant 72, 74
Eynæfir m., a sea-king 138

Eysteinn beli konungr m. (Skt, a Danish king, 9th century) 100
Eysteinn Haraldsson m. (Skt, 12th century, king of Norway) 106
Eysteinn orri m. (Skt, 11th century, a Norwegian chieftain) 116
Eysteinn Valdason m., a poet 140
Eyvindr Finnsson skáldaspillir m. (Skt, 10th century, a Norwegian poet of Hákon Aðalsteinsfóstri, Hákon jarl inn ríki) 102, 110, 124, 126, 128, 134, 138, 144, 152, 162, 164, 176, 190 (other MSS Eyjólfr dáðaskáld), 194, 204, 208, 238
Fáfnir m., son of Hreiðmarr, a serpent 164, 166, 228, 238, 240
Fáfnismál n. pl., a poem 30 note
Fákr m., a horse 224
Falarr m., a dwarf 88
Fallanda forað n., Hel's gate 48
Falófnir m., a horse 28, 226
Falr m., a dwarf 26
Fárbauti m., a giant, father of Loki 46, 148
Farmaguð m., a name of Óðinn 36
Farmatýr m., a name of Óðinn 36, 126, 194
Faxi m., a horse 226
Fenja f., a giantess 166, 244, 298
Fenrir m. (= Fenrisúlfr, Loki's son), a wolf 22, 84, 224 (MS af eiri)
Fenrisúlfr m. (Loki's son), a wolf 44, 46, 48, 80, 84, 146, 148
Fensalir m.pl., the hall of Frigg 50, 74
Fiðr m., a dwarf 26
Fili m., a dwarf 26
Fimbulþul f., a river 14, 58
Finn m. (ÆS) 118
Finnr m., son of Guðólfr 8
Finnr Hallsson (Ls) 120
Finnsleif f., a mail-coat 242
Firðir m. pl. a district in western Norway 280
Fjǫlnir m., name of Óðinn 12, 36
Fjǫlsviðr m., a name of Óðinn, 36
Fjǫrgyn/Fjǫrgun m., father of Frigg 20, 148

Fjǫrni f., a river (R and *Grímnismál* Fjǫrm) 14, 58
Fleini skáld (Skt, a poet of King Eysteinn Beli) 100
Fólkvangr m., the dwelling of Freyja 42
Fornjótr m., father of the wind 158 (Cf. *Orkneyinga saga* chs 1–3)
Forseti m., a god (son of Baldr and Nanna) 46, 86, 144
Frakkland n., land of the Franks 8, 210
Fránang(r)sfors m., a waterfall 78
Freki m., a wolf 56, 222, 224
Freyja f., a goddess 42, 52, 60, 62, 76, 86, 90, 92, 144, 146, 148, 162, 164
Freyr m., a god 42, 52, 54, 62 note, 76, 80, 86, 144, 146, 148, 162, 172, 236
Frialaf see Frjálafr
Friðfróði (= Fróði Friðleifsson) m. (ÆS) 118
Friðleifr/Frialaf/Frjálafr m. (ÆS) son of Finn(r) 8, 118
Friðleifr Fróðason m. (ÆS) 118
Friðleifr Skjaldarson m. (ÆS) 8, 118
Frigg/Frigida f., wife of the god Óðinn 8, 34, 36, 50, 52, 74, 76, 86, 90, 94, 126, 144, 146, 148, 152
Frigida/Frigg f., wife of King Óðinn 8
Frjálafr/Frialaf/Friðleifr m. (ÆS) son of Finn(r) 8, 118
Fróði friðsami m. (ÆS) 118
Fróði inn frøkni m. (ÆS) 118
Fróði Friðleifsson/Frið-Fróði m., a legendary king 162, 244, 298
Frosti m., a dwarf 26
Fundinn m., a dwarf 26
Fylla/Fulla f., a goddess, serving-maid of Frigg 52, 76, 162, 238
Fýri n. or f., a river 58, 242
Fýrisvǫllr/Fýrisvellir m. 162, 164, 242
Folknir m., a horse 226
Galarr m., a dwarf 88
Gamli gnævaðarskáld m., a poet 140, 212
Gandálfr m., a dwarf 26
Gandvík f., the White Sea 262
Ganglati m. (the slow to go), Hel's slave 48

Index of names

Gangleri m., assumed name of Gylfir 10, 12, 14, 18, 22, 24, 28, 30, 34, 38, 42, 44, 48, 50, 56, 58, 60, 64, 74, 82, 84, 86
Gangleri m., a name of Óðinn 36
Ganglǫt f. of Ganglati, Hel's serving-maid 48
Garðar m. pl., Russia 194
Garðrofa f., a mare 54 note
Garmr m., a dog (wolf?) 60, 80
Gaukr m. a name of Óðinn 202
Gautar m. pl., the inhabitants of Gautland 194, 208
Gautatýr m., a name of Óðinn 126
Gautr á Meli (Skt, 13th century, a Norwegian chieftain) 116
Gautr m., a name of Óðinn, also in a kenning for a giant (fjall-Gautr) 36, 90, 142, 184, 214, 228, 306
Gautreikr m., a sea-king 164
Gefjun f., a goddess 52, 86
Gefn f., a name of Freyja 52, 164
Geiðr = Gerðr 148
Geirahǫð f., a valkyrie 54
Geiri m., a wolf, see Geri
Geirraðargarðar m. pl., a dwelling of the giant Geirrøðr 94, 142
Geirrøðr m., a giant-king 36, 94, 96, 138, 148
Geirumul f., a river 58
Geitir m., a sea-king 186, 300
Geldnir m., a name of Óðinn 36
Gelgja f., a rope 50
Gellir Bǫlverksson (Ls) 120
Gerðr f., daughter of the mountain giant Gymir, beloved of the god Freyr 54, 86, 148
Geri m, a wolf 56, 222, 224 (MS Geiri) 230
Gillingr m., a giant 88, 134
Gils m., a horse 28, 226
Gils (Gísl) Illugason (Skt, 12th century, poet of Magnús berfǿttr) 106
Gimlé n., also Vingólf 12, 34, 82
Ginarr m., a dwarf 26
Ginnungagap n., the great abyss 16, 18, 28
Gipul f., a river 58
Gizurr m. Gullbráskáld (Skt, a poet of Óláfr Tryggvason) 104
Gizurr Hallsson (Ls) 120
Gizurr [Ísleifsson] m. (Ls) 120
Gizurr jarl Þorvaldsson (Skt, 1208–68, a poet of King Hákon Hákonarson) 108
Gjallarhorn n. 28, 44, 80
Gjálp/Gjálf f., a giantess, daughter of Geirrøðr 96, 142, 180
Gjǫful f., a river 58
Gjǫll/Gjallará f., a river 14, 76
Gjǫll f., a stone slab 50
Gjǫll f., a valkyrie 54
Glaðheimr m., a temple 24
Glaðr m., a horse 28
Glapsviðr m., a name of Óðinn 36
Glasir m., a tree 162, 166, 234
Glaumr m., a horse 188, 226; a giant 136
Gleifnir/Gleipnir m., a fetter 44, 48
Glenr m., the husband of Sól 158, 206
Glitnir m., Forseti's hall in heaven 32
Glóni m., a dwarf 26
Glúmr Geirason (Skt, a poet of Haraldr gráfeldr) 102, 126, 134, 184, 194, 208
Glæx/Glær m., a horse 226
Gná f., a goddess 52, 54
Gneip f., a giantess, daughter of Geirrøðr 96
Gnipalundr m. (R Gnipahellir) 80
Gnitaheiðr f. 164, 296
Góni/Góinn m., a serpent 32, 228
Goti m., a horse 224, 226
Goti m., a legendary king 214
Gotland n. 214
Grábakr m., a serpent 32, 228
Gráð f. a river 58
Grafvitnir m., a serpent 32, 166, 228
Grafvǫlduðr m., a serpent 32
Gramr m., one of King Hálfdan's 18 sons 208
Grán f., a river 58
Grani Hallbjarnarson m. (Skt, a poet of the Swedish king Eiríkr Knútsson) 102
Grani m., Sigurðr Fáfnisbani's horse 164, 166, 170, 226, 296

Grani skáld (Skt, 11th century, a poet of Haraldr harðráði) 104, 212
Gregoríus Dagsson (Skt, 12th century, a Norwegian chieftain) 116
Grettir Ásmundarson m., a poet 180
Gríðarvǫlr m., a pole 96
Gríðr f., a giantess, mother of Viðarr 184, 246
Grikkir m. pl., Greeks 194
Grikkland n., Greece 190
Grímnir m., a name of Óðinn 36, 138
Grímnismál n. pl. 20 note, 28 note, 30 note, 36 note, 38, 40 note, 44 note, 46 note, 54, 56 note, 58 note, 60 note, 62 note
Grímr Lǫðmundarson m. (ÆS) 118
Grímr m., a name of Óðinn 36
Grímr Svertingsson m. (Ls) 120
Grjótúnagarðr m., -garðar m. pl., -gerði n. 92
Grotti m., a mill 298
Gróa f., giantess, wife of Aurvaldi 94
Grundi prúði m. (Skt, a poet of King Eysteinn Beli) 100
Guðbrandr m. í Dǫlum (Skt, 11th century, a Norwegian chieftain) 116
Guðmundr Oddsson m. (Skt, 13th century, a poet of Jarl Knútr Hákonarson) 112
Guðmundr m. skáld (Skt, 13th century, a poet of Eiríkr Magnússon) 110
Guðólfr m. (ÆS) 118
Guðólfr m., son of Jat 8
Guðr/Gunnr f., a valkyrie; also a common noun for battle 54, 176, 178
Gullfaxi m., a horse 90, 94, 224
Gullinbu(r)sti m., Freyr's boar 76, 144
Gullintanni m. (the god Heimdallr) 44
Gulltoppr m., a horse 28, 44, 76, 146, 224
Gundró f., a river (R Gunnþrá, Gunnþró or Gunnþróin) 14, 58
Gungnir m., Óðinn's spear 80, 236, 304
Gunnarr Gjúkason m., a legendary king 210, 226
Gunnarr Úlfheðinsson m. (Ls) 120
Gunnarr Þorgeirsson m. (Ls) 120
Gunnarr inn spaki Þorgrímsson m. (Ls) 120
Gunnlaugr Illugason m. ormstunga (Skt, a poet of King Óláfr sǫnski, Jarl Eiríkr Hákonarson and Aðalráðr king in England) 100, 110, 114, 172
Gunnlǫð f., daughter of Suttungr 88, 90, 128, 148, 152
Guttormr kǫrtr m. (Skt, 13th century, a poet of King Hákon Hákonarson) 108
Guttormr sindri m. (Skt, a Norwegian poet of Haraldr hárfagri and Hákon Aðalsteinsfóstri) 102
Gyða Sǫlmundardóttir f. (ÆS) 118
Gylfi m., a legendary king in Sweden 10
Gylfi m., a sea-king 188
Gylfi m., one of King Hálfdan's 18 sons 208
Gylfir m., calling himself Gangleri 10
Gyllir m., a horse 28, 226, 282
Gymir m., a mountain giant, father of Gerðr 54, 156
Gǫmul f., a river 58
Gǫndul f., a valkyrie 126, 176, 178
Hábrók f., a hawk 60
Haddingjar m. pl., warriors 124, 226
Hagbarðr m., a legendary hero 210
Haki m., a legendary person 226
Hákon Aðalsteinsfóstri m. (Skt, king of Norway, 10th century) 102, 114, 162, 164, 238, 242
Hákon jarl Eiríksson m. (Skt, 11th century, a Norwegian jarl) 110
Hákon jarl galinn m. (Skt, 12th and 13th century, a Norwegian jarl) 112
Hákon jarl Grjótgarðsson m. (Skt, 10th century) 110
Hákon Hákonarson m. (Skt, king of Norway 1217–1263) 6, 108, 260, 262, 264, 276, 278
Hákon herðibreiðr m. (Skt, 13th century, king of Norway) 108
Hákon jarl Ívarsson m. (Skt, a Norwegian jarl, 11th century. No poets) 110
Hákon jarl Sigurðarson m. inn ríki/the Great (Skt, 10th century) 110, 200, 204
Hákon Sverrisson Sigurðarsonar m. (Skt, 13th century, a Norwegian king) 108

Index of names

Háleygjatal n., wrongly referred to as Ynglingatal, a poem 110
Hálfdan inn gamli m., a king 208, 210
Hálfdan inn mildi m., a king 210
Hálfdan inn svarti m., a king 210
Hálfr m., a legendary king 160, 214
Hallar-Steinn m., a poet 170, 172
Hallbjǫrn m. hálftrǫll 114
Hallbjǫrn hali m. (Skt, 12th century, a poet of the Swedish king Knútr Eiríksson and the Norwegian king Sverrir Sigurðarson) 102, 108
Halldórr skvaldri m. (Skt, 11th and 12th century, a poet of the Swedish king Sørk-vir Karlsson, Jarl Jón Sørkvisson, Jarl Sóni Ívarsson and Jarl Karl Sónason, the Norwegian kings Magnús berføttr, Sigurðr Jórsalafari (K), Haraldr gilli (K), Ingi Haraldsson (K) and the Danish king Eiríkr eymuni) 100, 102, 106, 114, 234
Halldórr úkristni m. (Skt, 10th century, a poet of Eiríkr Hákonarson) 110
Hallfreðr/Hallfrøðr Óttarsson m. vendræðaskáld (the nickname always spelt thus in DG 11 4to) (Skt, d. c. 1007, a poet of King Óláfr Tryggvason and Jarl Eiríkr Hákonarson) 104, 110, 126, 152, 174, 180, 182, 198, 200, 210
Halli stirði m. (Skt, 11th century, a poet of Haraldr harðráði) 104
Hallr Gizurarson m. (Ls) 120
Hallr munkr m. (Skt, 12th century, a poet of Haraldr gilli (K) 106
Hallr Snorrason m. (Skt, 12th century, a poet of Magnús Erlingsson) 106
Hallvarðr Háreksblesi m. (Skt, 11th century, a poet of Knútr ríki) 112, 152, 154, 188
Hamðir m., see the eddic poem *Hamðismál* 180; a hawk 266
Hamskerpir m., a horse 54 note
Hangaguð m., a name of Óðinn 36, 124
Hangankjapta f., a giantess 144
Hangatýr m., a name of Óðinn 124, 178
Hangi m., a name of Óðinn 180
Happaguð m., a name of Óðinn 36
Hár m., a dwarf 26
Hár m., name of Óðinn 12, 14, 18, 22, 24, 26, 28, 34, 36, 38, 42, 44, 50, 56, 58, 60, 64, 74, 82, 174, 176, 178; Hárr 134, 290
Haraldr m., a legendary person (perhaps Haraldr Hilditǫnn) 226
Haraldr gráfeldr m. (Skt, a Norwegian king, 10th century) 102
Haraldr hilditǫnn m. (ÆS) 118, 202
Haraldr inn granrauði m., a king 210
Haraldr inn hárfagri m. 102
Haraldr Sigurðarson harðráði m., (Skt, Ls, king of Norway 1046–66) 10 note, 104, 120, 188, 198, 200
Hárbarðr m., a name of Óðinn 36
Hárekr m., a warrior (?) 132
Hárekr m. ór Þjóttu (Skt, 12th century, a Norwegian chieftain) 116
Harri m., one of King Hálfdan's 18 sons 208, 210
Háttatal n., a poem by Snorri Sturluson 6, 262
Hatti Hróðrvitnisson m., a wolf (R Hati) 22
Haustlǫng f., a poem 94
Hávarðr halti m., a poet 124
Hávarr handrammi m. (ÆS) 118
Heðinn Hjarrandason m., a legendary warrior 234, 302
Hefring f., a wave, daughter of Ægir 154
Heiðrún f., a goat 58
Heimdallargaldr m., a poem 44, 146
Heimdallr m., a god 42, 44, 76, 80, 82, 86, 130, 146, 148, 218
Heinir m.pl., the inhabitants of Heiðmǫrk 232
Heiti m., a sea-king 168, 190, 200
Hel f., daughter of Loki; also the name of her abode 12, 46, 62, 74, 76, 80 (cf. note 3), 84, 94, 144, 148, 206
Helblindi m., brother of Loki 46, 148
Helblindi m., a name of Óðinn 36
Helga Sturludóttir f. (ÆS) 118
Helgrindr f. pl., Hel-gates 14, 76
Heptifili m., a dwarf 26
Hereðei m. (ÆS) 118

Heremeth m. (ÆS) 118
Herfjǫtra f., a valkyrie 54
Hergelmir m. (most often Hvergelmir),
  a well 14
Herjann m., a name of Óðinn 12, 36
Herkja f., a giantess 246
Herleifr m. (ÆS) 118
Hermóðr m., Óðinn's son 74, 76, 128, 170
Hermundr m., brother of Gunnlaugr ormstunga 152
Herteitr m., a name of Óðinn 36
Hertýr m., a name of Óðinn 130
Hildigautr m., a helmet 242
Hildigǫltr m., a helmet 266
Hildingar m.pl., descendants of Hildir Hálfdanarson 210, 212
Hildir m., one of King Hálfdan's 18 sons 210
Hildir m., a warrior 154
Hildisvín n., a helmet 242
Hilditannr m. = Haraldr hilditǫnn 202
Hildr f., a valkyrie; also a common noun for battle 54, 138, 176, 180, 182, 184, 302, 306
Hildr Hǫgnadóttir 234
Hilmir m., one of King Hálfdan's 18 sons 208
Himinbjǫrg n. pl., a place in heaven 34, 44
Himinglæva f., a wave, daughter of Ægir 154, 260
Himin(h)rjóðr m., an ox 74, 228
Hjaðningar/Hjatningar m. pl., followers of Heðinn 172, 186, 234, 302
Hjaðningaveðr n. pl., a battle 234
Hjarrandi m., a name of Óðinn 304
Hjálmberi m., a name of Óðinn 36
Hjálmskíði m. the god Heimdallr 44
Hjálmþír m., a legendary person 226
Hjúki m., son of Viðfiðr 22
Hleiðólfr m., a dwarf 26
Hlésey f, Læsø, island off Denmark (?) 86
Hliðskjálf f., a watchtower 20, 54, 78, 90, 132
Hlín f., a goddess 52
Hlýrr m., an ox 228

Hlǫkk f., a valkyrie 54, 176, 180, 186, 230, 268, 302
Hnikarr m., a name of Óðinn 36
Hnikuðr m., a name of Óðinn 36
Hnitbjǫrg/Nitbjǫrg n. pl., home of the giant Suttungr 88, 124, 132
Hnoss f., daughter of Freyja 52, 148, 162
Hofgarða-Refr m. see Refr Gestsson
Hófvarpnir m., a horse 52, 54
Holl f. (or Hǫll), a river 58
Hólmgarðr m., Novgorod 208
Hornklofi m. = Þorbjǫrn hornklofi
Hrafn m., a horse 224, 226, 242
Hrafn heimski m. (ÆS) 118
Hrafn Høingsson m. (Ls) 120
Hrafn Úlfheðinsson m. (Ls) 120
Hrafn Ǫnundarson m. (Skt, a poet of King Óláfr sønski and Jarl Eiríkr Hákonarson) 100, 110
Hrafnketill m., an unknown person 182
Hreiðmarr/Reiðmarr m., the father of Fáfnir, Otr and Reginn 238, 240
Hríðr f., a river (Grímnismál 28) 14
Hrímfaxi m., Nótt's horse 20
Hrímnir m., a giant 140
Hringhorni m., Baldr's boat 76, 144
Hrist f., a valkyrie 54, 172
Hrólfr kraki (Kraki) m., king in Denmark 164, 166, 240, 242, 244
Hroptatýr m., a name of Óðinn 126, 128
Hroptr m., a name of Óðinn 184
Hrungnir m., a giant 90, 92, 94, 138, 140, 176 (in a kenning that really requires a name of a warrior or valkyrie), 178, 182, 290
Hrungnishjarta n., a figure 92
Hrymr m., a giant 80
Hræsvelgr m., a giant 60
Hrørekr Haraldsson m. (ÆS) 118
Hrørekr slǫngvanbaugi m. (ÆS) 118
Hrǫnn f., a river 58
Hugi m., personification of thought 68, 70
Huginn m., a raven 56, 228
Hugl f., Huglo, island off Norway 282
Hugstari m., a dwarf 26

Index of names

Hungr n., Hel's plate 48
Húnn m., a sea-king 128
Húsdrápa f., a poem 144, 146
Hvammr m. (ÆS) a farm in Iceland 118
Hvannar-Kálfr (Skt, 10th century, a poet of Jarl Hákon inn ríki) 110
Hvergelmir m., see Hergelmir, a well 28, 30, 58, 84
Hvíta-Kristr m., Christ 190
Hyndluljóð (Vǫluspá in skamma), a poem 16 note
Hyrrokin f., a giantess 76
Hyrrærin (= Hyrrokin?) f., a giantess 144
Hæn f., name of Freyja 52
Hǿfir m., an ox 228
Hǿnir m., a god 40, 86, 148, 238
Hǫðr m., a god 44, 74, 76, 84, 144, 146
Hǫðr m., a horse 226
Hǫgni m., a legendary warrior or king 178, 182, 190, 226, 234, 302
Hǫlgi m., a legendary king 162, 166, 244
Hǫlknir m., a horse 226
Hǫrðar m. pl., the inhabitants of Hǫrðaland 228
Hǫskuldr liði m. (Skt, 13th century, a poet of King Ingi Bárðarson) 108
Iðavǫllr m. 24
Iði m., a giant 166
Iðunn f. (Bragi's wife), a goddess 44, 86, 146, 148
Illugi Bryndǿlaskáld m. (Skt, 11th century, a poet of Haraldr harðráði) 104, 222
Ilus m. (ÆS) 118
Ingi m. (Skt, a 13th century poet, not mentioned in K, and presumably an erroneous anticipation of the next king's name, Ingi Bárðarson. Cf. *Edda Snorra Sturlusonar* 1848–87: 278) 108
Ingi Bárðarson m. (Skt, king of Norway 1204–17) 108
Ingi Steinkelsson m. (Skt, king in Sweden, d. c. 1111) 100
Ingjaldr Starkaðarfóstri m. (ÆS) 118
Ísland (Ls) n. Iceland 120
Ítrman m., son of Atra 8

Ívaldi m., a dwarf 144, 236
Ívarr hvíti m. (Skt, 11th century, a Norwegian chieftain) 116
Ívarr Ingimundarson m. (Skt, 12th century, a poet of Magnús berfǿttr, Sigurðr Jórsalafari (K) and Sigurðr slembir (K)) 106
Ívarr Kálfsson m. (Skt, 12th century, a poet of Jarl Hákon galinn) 112
Ívarr selki m. (Skt, 12th century, a Norwegian chieftain) 116
Jafnhár m., name of Óðinn 12, 14, 16, 28, 34, 36, 64
Jálkr m., a name of Óðinn 36
Jap(h)eth m. (ÆS) 118
Japhan (Javan) m. (ÆS) 118
Jareth (Jared) m. (ÆS) 118
Jarizleifr m., Yaroslav 200
Járnsaxa f., a giantess, mother of Magni 92, 200, 230
[Járnviðjur f. pl., those who dwell in Járnviðr] 22
Járnviðr m., 'Ironwood', a mythical forest 22
Jat m., son of Bjáf 8
Játgeirr Torfason (Skt, 13th century, a poet of the Norwegian kings Ingi Bárðarson and Hákon Hákonarson, of Duke Skúli Bárðarson and of the Danish king Valdimarr gamli) 108, 112, 114
Jón Murti Egilsson m. (Skt, 13th century, a poet of Eiríkr Magnússon) 110
Jón jarl Sǫrkvisson m. (Skt, 12th century) 102
Jór m., a horse 224
Jórdán f., the river Jordan 190, 192
Jóreykr m., the name of a bear 224
Jórsalir m. pl., Jerusalem 190, 194
Jórunn [skáldmær] f., a poetess 212
Jótland n., Jutland 8
Jupiter m. (ÆS) 118
Jǫfurr m., one of King Hálfdan's 18 sons 208, 210
Jǫrð f. (Earth), giantess/goddess, Þórr's mother 20, 54, 90, 138, 148, 150, 152

Jǫrmungandr m., a name of Miðgarðsormr 46, 148, 228
Jǫrundr goði Hrafnsson m. (ÆS) 118
Jǫruvellir m. pl. 26
Jǫtunheimar m. pl. 20, 24, 38, 46, 60, 64, 80, 90
Kálfr Árnason m. (Skt, 11th century, a Norwegian chieftain) 116
Kálfr Mánason m. (Skt, 11th century, a poet of the Danish king Knútr inn helgi) 114
Kálfr þrǫ́n(d)ski m. (Skt, a poet of King Eysteinn Beli) 100
Kallandi (other MSS Kjallandi) f., a giantess 142
Karl jarl Sónason m. (Skt, a Danish king, 9th century) 102
Keila f., a giantess (?) 142
Kerlaugar f. pl., two rivers 28
Ketill høingr m., an ancestor of many important Icelanders 114
Kili m., a dwarf 26
Kjalarr m., a name of Óðinn 36
Klǿingr m., an Icelandic bishop 298
Knútr inn ríki m. (Skt, 11th century, a Danish king) 112
Knútr Eiríksson m. (Skt, king of Sweden, d. 1195) 102
Knútr Hákonarson m. jarl (Skt, 13th century, a Norwegian jarl) 112
Knútr inn helgi Sveinsson m. (Skt, 11th century, a Danish king) 114
Knútr m., son of Sveinn tjúguskegg 152
Knútr Valdimarsson m. (Skt, 12th century, a Danish king) 114
Kolbeinn Flosason m. (Ls) 120
Kólga f., a wave, daughter of Ægir 154
Kolli skáld m. (Skt, 12th century, a poet of Ingi Haraldsson (K)) 106
Kormakr Ǫgmundarson m. (Skt, a poet of King Haraldr gráfeldr and Sigurðr Hlaðajarl) 102, 110, 128, 130, 174, 184, 200, 202, 204
Kraki m. = Hrólfr kraki 164, 166, 244
Kristr m., Christ 192, 194
Kvasir m., the wisest god 78, 88, 124, 132
Kǫr f., Hel's bed 48
Kǫrmt f., a river 28, 222
Kǫrtr m., a horse 226
Lameck (Lamech) m. (ÆS) 118
Laomedon m. (ÆS) 118
Laufey or Nál f., mother of Loki 46, 148
Leikn f., a giantess (?) 142
Léraðr m., a tree 58
Léttfeti m., a horse 28, 224
Líf n./f., a human survivor 84
Lífþræsir m., a human survivor 84
Listi m., Lister in southern Norway 284
Litr m., a dwarf or a giant 26, 76, 142
Ljótr m. skáld Sumarliðason (?) (Skt, 12th century, a poet of Sverrir Sigurðarson, Ingi Bárðarson and Duke Skúli Bárðarson) 108, 112
Lóði m., a giant 142
Lofarr m., a dwarf 26
Lofði m., one of King Hálfdan's 18 sons 210
Lofðungar m., followers or descendants of Lofði Hálfdanarson 210
Lofn f., a goddess 52
Logi m., personification of fire 68
Lokasenna f. 34 note
Loki Laufeyjarson m., the trickster, one of the Æsir, but half-giant 34, 46, 50, 60, 62, 64, 68, 72, 74, 78, 80, 86, 94, 96, 146, 148, 236, 238
Loptr m., a name of Loki 34, 46
Lóra (Hlóra) f., foster-mother of Þórr 138
Lorica/Lórriði m. (ÆS) 118
Lórriði m., son of Tror/Þórr 8
Lungr m., a horse 224
Lyngvi m., an island 48
Lǿðingr m., a fetter 48
Lǫðmundr Svartsson m. (ÆS) 118
Magi/Magni m., son of Móða/Meða (ÆS) 8, 118
Magni m., son of Þórr 84, 92, 138, 140
Magnús Erlingsson m. (Skt, 12th century, king of Norway) 106
Magnús Hákonarson m. (Skt, king of Norway 1263–1280) 108

Index of names

Magnús berfǿttr Óláfsson m. (Skt, king of Norway 1093–1103) 106
Magnús góði Ólafsson m. (Skt, king of Norway 1035–47) 104, 232
Malalie (Mahaleel) m. (ÆS) 118
Mánagarmr m., a wolf 22
Máni skáld/Skáld-Máni (Skt, 12th century, a poet of Magnús Erlingsson) 108, 188
Máni m., son of Mundilferi 20, 22, 60, 158, 206
Maríuson m., Mary's son, Christ 192
Markús Skeggjason m. (Skt, Ls, lawspeaker 1084–1107, a poet of Ingi Steinkelsson and the Danish kings Knútr inn helgi and Eiríkr Sveinsson) 100, 114, 120, 188, 192, 208, 210, 214
Markús Stefánsson m. (Skt, 12th century, a poet of Magnús Erlingsson) 108
Marr m., a horse 224
Marþǫll (Mardǫll) f., name of Freyja 52, 166, 298
Matusalam (Methuselah) m. (ÆS) 118
Meða (cf. Móða) m. (ÆS) 118
Meili m., a rather obscure person, usually taken to be Þórr's brother and Óðinn's son, but in DG 11 the scribe seems to see him as a giant 150
Meinþjófr m., a legendary person 226
Meiti m., a sea-king 190
Menja f., a giantess 244
Menon/Mennon/Múnon m. (ÆS) king in Troy 8, 118
Miðgarðr m., error for Útgarðr 68 note
Miðgarðr m. 18, 20, 138
Miðgarðsormr m., Miðgarð serpent, son of Loki 46, 72, 74, 80, 84, 148
Miðjarðarsjár m. Mediterranean Sea 8
Mikáll m., archangel 152
Mikligarðr m., Constantinople 194
Mímir m., a giant 28, 80, 82, 84, 128, 136
Mímisbrunnr m., a well 28, 80
Mímr m. = Mímir (?) 266
Mist f., a valkyrie 54
Mjǫðvitnir m., a dwarf 26
Mjǫl(l)nir m., Þórr's hammer (as a rule written with a single l in DG 11, only twice with ll) 38, 64, 76, 84, 92, 94, 138, 236
Móða (cf. Meða) f., son of Vingenir 8
Móðguðr f., guardian of Gjallar brú 76
Móði m., son of Þórr 84, 138, 202
Móðnir m., a horse 226
Móðsognir m., a dwarf 24
Móni/Móinn m., a serpent 32, 228
Mór m., a horse 224, 226
Mosfell n., a farm in Iceland 120
Mundilferi m., father of Máni and Sól (the third vowel in other MSS o, ǫ, a and ǿ [œ]), in Skáldskaparmál twice Mundilfeti 20, 158, 206
Muninn m., a legendary person 226
Muninn m., a raven 56, 228, 230
Múnon/Men(n)on m. (ÆS) 118
Múspells megir m. pl., Múspell's sons or men of Múspell, the world of fire; Múspell was perhaps sometimes taken to be the name of a person (a giant) 22, 24, 54, 62, 80
Múspellsheimr m. the world of fire = Múspell 16, 18, 22
Mýsingi m., a legendary hero 244
Mǿrir m. pl., the people of Møre in Norway 134
Mǫkkrkálfi m., a giant 92
Mǫn f., (Isle of) Man 202
Naglfari m., a ship 62, 80
Nál (Laufey) f., mother of Loki 46, 148
Nani (Náni?) m., a dwarf 26
Nanna Nefsdóttir f. (other MSS Nepsdóttir), a goddess 46, 76, 86, 144
Nari/Narfi m., son of Loki 46, 78, 148
Nástrandir f. pl. 'the shores of the dead' 82
Naumudalr m., a valley in Norway 114
Nemir m., one of King Hálfdan's 18 sons 210
Nið f., a river in Norway 232
Níðhǫg(g)r m. (always written with a single g in U) a serpent 28, 30, 84, 228
Niði m., a dwarf 26

Nif(l)heimr m., the world of mists 12, 14, 16, 28, 46, 62
Niflungar m.pl., descendants of Nemir Hálfdanarson 164, 166, 210, 296
Nikaðr, Nikuðr m., names of Óðinn 12
Nikulás Skjaldvararson (Skt, 12th century, a Norwegian chieftain) 116
Niningr (Níningr?) m., a dwarf 26
Nitbjǫrg = Hnitbjǫrg 124
Niz f., a river in Sweden 210
Njǫrðr m., a god 40, 42, 86, 144, 148, 164, 180, 276
Nóatún n. pl., dwelling of Njǫrðr 40, 42
Nói (Noah) m. (ÆS) 118
Norðri m., a dwarf 18, 26, 150, 206
Norðrsetudrápa f., a poem 158
Noregr, m., Norway 10, 114, 198, 234
Nori (Nóri?) m., a dwarf 26
Nótt f., daughter of Nóri 20, 152
Nýi m., a dwarf 26
Nýráðr m., a dwarf 26
Nǫtt f., a river 58
Oddr keikinaskáld m. (Skt, 11th century, a poet of Magnús góði and Haraldr harðráði) 104
Óðinn m., a god, son of Borr 18, 28, 34, 36, 50, 56, 60, 62 note, 66 (in error), 76, 78, 80, 82, 86, 88, 90, 92, 94, 110, 124, 126, 130, 132, 138, 144, 146, 148, 152, 176, 178, 184, 186, 214, 224, 236, 238, 240
Óðinn m., a king = Vodden, son of Frjálafr/ Friðleifr (ÆS) 8, 10, 118
Óðr m., husband of Freyja 52, 148, 162, 180
Óðrǫrir m., a pot, containing the mead of poetry 88, 124, 132, 136, 138
Ófnir m., a serpent 32, 228
Óir m., husband of Hnoss 52
Óláfr sǿnski m. (Skt, 11th century, king in Uppland, Sweden) 100
Óláfr Haraldsson hinn helgi m. (Skt, Ls, Norwegian king 1015–1030) 104, 120, 180, 200
Óláfr kyrri Haraldsson m. (Skt, 12th century, a Norwegian king, d. 1093) 104
Óláfr Haraldsson = Óláfr kyrri? 106
Óláfr Herdísarson m. (Skt, 13th century, a poet of the Norwegian chieftains Arnbjǫrn Jónsson and Gautr á Meli) 116
Óláfr Leggsson m. (Skt, 13th century, a poet of King Hákon Hákonarson) 108
Óláfr Tryggvason m. (Skt, king of Norway 995–1000) 104
Óláfr Þórðarson hvítaskáld m. (Skt, 13th century, a poet of the Norwegian king Hákon Hákonarson, Skúli Bárðarson jarl, later hertogi (jarl, duke), Jarl Knútr Hákonarson, the Danish king Valdimarr gamli and the Swedish king Eiríkr Eiríksson) 102, 108, 112, 114
Óleifr halti m. (Ls) 120
Óleifr m. = Óláfr Hǫskuldsson pái 138
Ólǫf Vémundardóttir f. (ÆS) 118
Ómi m., a name of Óðinn 12, 36
Onni (Ǫnni?) m., a dwarf 26
Ori m., a dwarf 26
Ormr m. Barreyja(r)skáld (poet of Barra in the Hebrides) 150, 154
Ormr óframi m. (Skt, a poet of King Eysteinn Beli) 100
Ormr jarl Eilífsson m. (Skt, a Norwegian jarl? 11th century? No poets) 110
Ormr Steinþórsson m., a poet 134, 136, 160, 172, 204
Orr (Ǫrr?) m., a dwarf 26
Órun f., a river 166
Óski m., a name of Óðinn 12, 36
Otr m., son of Hreiðmarr 238
Otrgjǫld n. pl., the compensation paid for Otr 162
Óttarr keptr m. (Skt, 11th century, a poet of Knútr ríki) 112
Óttarr svarti m. (Skt, a poet of King Óláfr sǿnski, Ǫnundr Ólafsson, Óláfr hinn helgi, Sveinn tjúguskegg, Knútr ríki and Guðbrandr í Dǫlum) 100, 104, 112, 116, 170, 176, 210
Philippus jarl Birgisson m. (Skt, 11th century? A Norwegian jarl? No poets) 112
Príamus m. king in Troy (ÆS) 8, 118

Index of names

Ráðgríðr f., a valkyrie 54
Ráðsviðr m., a dwarf 26
Ragnarr konungr loðbrók (Skt, a poet) 100, 304
Ragnarøkkr n., the twilight of the gods 50, 78, 234
Rán f., a goddess, wife of Ægir 154, 156, 158, 162, 282
Rán f., a wave, daughter of Ægir 154
Randgríðr f., a valkyrie 54
Ratakostr (R Ratatoskr) m., a squirrel 30
Rauðr m., an ox 228
Raum (= Aumar?) f., islands in Norway 188
Raumar m., inhabitants of Raumaríki 232
Refr rytski m. (Skt, a poet of King Eysteinn Beli) 100
Refr Gestsson (Hofgarða-Refr) m. (Skt, 11th century, a poet of Óláfr helgi, Magnús góði and chieftains Hárekr ór Þjóttu and Einarr fluga) 104, 116, 124, 130, 134, 154, 174, 184, 190
Reginleif f., a valkyrie 54
Reginn m., an ox 228
Reginn m., one of Hreiðmarr's sons 238, 240
Reiðgotaland n., a name for Jutland 8
Reiðmarr, see Hreiðmarr
Reifnir m., a sea-king 166
Rekkr m., a dwarf 26
Rerir m., son of Sigi 8
Riflindi m., a name of Óðinn 12
Rín f., a river (the Rhine) 166, 168, 200, 208, 288
Rindr f., Óðinn's mistress, mother of Váli, counted among the goddesses 46, 54, 90, 128, 146, 148, 152, 154, 206
Roðgeirr Aflason m. (Skt, 13th century, a poet of Jarl Knútr Hákonarson) 112
Roði m., an auger, in other MSS Rati 88
Róði m., a sea-king 162, 178, 180,
Róm n., Rómaborg f., Rome 8, 190, 192, 194
Rósta f., a valkyrie 54

Ruðr (Urðr?) f. 184
Runólfr skáld m. (Skt, 13th century, a poet of the king Ingi Bárðarson) 108
Rýgr f., a giantess 174
Ræfill m., a sea-king 184
Ræsir m., one of King Hálfdan's 18 sons 208
Rǫgnir m., a name of Óðinn 136, in a kenning for a warrior 186
Rǫgnvaldr heiðumhæri m. (Skt, a Norwegian king c. 900) 102
Rǫgnvaldr m. the Old, Mǿrajarl 202
Rǫgnvaldr m. skáld (Skt, a poet of King Eysteinn Beli) 100
Rǫgnvaldr Brúsason m., jarl of Orkney (d. 1046) 152
Rǫsk(v)a f., Þórr's serving maid, sister of Þjálfi 64, 138, 140
Saðr m., a name of Óðinn 36
Saga/Sága f., a goddess 52
Sálkr m., a name of Óðinn 12
Sanngetall m., a name of Óðinn 36
Saturnus af Krít m. (ÆS) 118
Saxland n., Saxony 8, 10, 196
Sefsmeg/Sesef m., son of Magi/Magni 8, 118
Semingr m., son of King Óðinn, ancestor of the kings of Norway 10
Sesef/Sefsmeg m. (ÆS) 8, 118
Sessrúmnir/Sessvarnir m., Freyja's hall 42, 148
Sibil f. = Sif, wife of Tror/Þórr 8
Síð f., a river 58
Síðhǫttr m., a name of Óðinn 36
Síðskeggr m., a name of Óðinn 36
Sif f., Sibil, wife of Tror/Þórr 8, 46, 90, 138, 140, 148, 152, 162, 166, 236
Sigarr m., a descendant of Sigarr Hálfdanarson 210
Sigarr m., one of King Hálfdan's 18 sons 210
Sigfǫðr m., a name of Óðinn 36
Siggeirr m., a legendary king 210
Sighvatr Egilsson m. (Skt, 12th century, a poet of Sverrir Sigurðarson) 108
Sighvatr Sturluson m. (ÆS) 118

Sighvatr [Surtsson] m. (Ls) 120
Sighvatr/Sigvatr skáld Þórðarson m. (Skt, a poet of the kings Ǫnundr Ólafsson, Óláfr Tryggvason, Óláfr helgi Haraldsson, Haraldr harðráði Sigurðarson and Knútr ríki and the chieftains Erlingr Skjálgsson and Ívarr hvíti) 100, 104, 112, 116, 192, 198
Sigi m., son of King Óðinn 8
Sigráðr m., most likely a misreading for Sigurðr (jarl Hákonarson) 124
Sigrún f., a valkyrie 182 (see *Helgakviða Hundingsbani* I and II)
Sigtryggr m., king in Austrvegir 208
Sigtún n. pl., Sigtuna in Sweden 10
Sigtýr m., a name of Óðinn 90, 234
Sigun see Sigyn
Sigurðr Fáfnisbani m. 210, 226
Sigurðr Hlaðajarl m. (Skt, 10th century, son of Jarl Hákon) 110, 174, 200 (?)
Sigurðr munkr m. (Skt, 12th century, Norwegian) 116
Sigurðr skrauti m. (Skt, 12th century, a poet of Eysteinn Haraldsson) 106
Sigurðr Hákonarson m., a Norwegian jarl (d. 962) 202
Sigurðr Haraldsson m. (Skt, a Norwegian king, 12th century) 106
Sigurðr Hálfdanarson m. sýr, father of Haraldr Sigurðarson 222
Sigurðr jarl Hávarðsson m. (Skt, a Norwegian jarl? 11th century? No poets) 110
Sigvaldi jarl (Skt, 10th century, a Danish jarl) 114, 178
Sigvatr see Sighvatr
Sigyn/Sigun f., wife of Loki 46, 78, 86, 148
Sikiley f., Sicily 188
Siklingr m., a descendant of Sigarr Hálfdanarson 210, 212
Silfrintoppr m., a horse 224
Simr m. (in a *þula* Simir), a horse 224
Simul f., a pole 22
Sindri m., a hall 82
Singasteinn m. 146
Sinir m., a horse 28

Sjǫfn f., a goddess 52
Skaði f., daughter of Þjazi, wife of Njǫrðr 40, 42, 78, 86, 88, 148
Skafiðr m., a dwarf 26
Skáld-Máni see Máni skáld
Skapti Þóroddsson m. (Skt, d. 1030, a poet of Magnús góði and Jarl Hákon inn ríki; Ls) 104, 110, 120, 192
Skati m., a legendary king 214
Skegǫld f., a valkyrie 54
Skeiðbrimir m., a horse 28, 226
Skelfir m., a legendary king 210
Skíðblaðnir m., a ship 60, 62, 64, 144, 236
Skilfingr m., a descendant of King Skelfir 210, 214
Skinfaxi m., Dagr's horse 20
Skirfir m., a dwarf 26
Skírnir m., messenger of the gods 48, 54
Skjal(l)dun/Skjǫldr, son of Heremeth/ Eremóð (ÆS) 8, 118
Skjǫldr/Skjal(l)dun, son of Heremeth/ Eremóð (ÆS) 8, 118
Skjǫldr m., son of King Óðinn (ÆS) 8, 118, 210
Skjǫldungr m., descendant of Skjǫld; ruler 8, 150, 210, 212, 286
Skoll m., a wolf (R Skǫll) 22
Skolla f., a goddess (a mistake for Fulla?) 86
Skrýmir m., a giant 66
Skuld f., a norn 30, 54
Skúli m., one of King Hálfdan's 18 sons 208
Skúli Bárðarson m. jarl, later hertogi (Skt, 13th century, a Norwegian jarl, later duke) 6, 112, 260, 262, 292
Skúli Illugason m. (Skt, 11th century, a poet of the Danish king Knútr inn helgi) 114
Skúli Þorsteinsson m. (Skt, 11th century, a poet of Jarl Sveinn) 110, 158, 162, 166, 230, 232
Skyl(l)i m., one of King Hálfdan's 18 sons 208, 210
Skæfaðr m., a horse 226
Skæfaxi m., a horse 224
Skǫgul f., a valkyrie 54, 126, 306

Index of names

Sleipnir m., a horse 28, 60, 76, 90, 148, 156
Sléttfeti m., a horse 224
Slíðr f., a river (Vǫluspá, Grímnismál (Slíð)) 14
Sligru(g)tanni m. (in GkS 2367 4to the name is Slíðrugtanni, which is easier to inter-pret, cf. Ásgeir Bl. Magnússon 1989), Freyr's boar 76, 146
Slík f., a goddess? 86
Slintoppr m. (WT Silfrintoppr), a horse 28
Slungnir m., a horse 226
Sneglu-Halli m.(Skt, 11th century, a poet of Haraldr harðráði) 104
Snorri Bútsson m. (Skt, 12th century, a poet of Sverrir Sigurðarson) 108
Snorri Húnbogason m. (Ls) 120
Snorri Sturluson m. (Skt, ÆS, Ls, 13th century, a poet of the Norwegian kings Ingi Bárðarson and Hákon Hákonarson, Skúli Bárðarson jarl, later hertogi (jarl, duke)) 6, 108, 112, 118, 120, 262
Snotra f., a goddess 52
Snæbjǫrn m., a poet 158
Sor m. konungr at Haugi (Skt, a king at Uppsala) 100
Sól f., daughter of Mundilferi, wife of Glórnir/Glenr 20, 54, 60, 158, 206
Són f., a vat containing the mead of poetry 88, 124, 132, 136
Sóni (or Soni) Ívarsson m. (Skt, around 1100) 102
Sóti m., a horse 224
Starkaðr inn gamli m. (Skt, a poet) 100
Starkaðr m., a giant 142
Steinn Herdísarson m. (Skt, 11th century, a poet of Haraldr harðráði, Óláfr kyrri and Úlfr stallari) 104, 116, 150
Steinn Kálfsson m. (Skt, 12th century, a poet of Jarl Hákon galinn) 112
Steinn Ófeigsson m. (Skt, 12th century, a poet of Jarl Hákon galinn) 112
Steinn Skaptason m. (Skt, 11th century, a poet of King Knútr ríki) 112
Steinn Þorgeirsson m. (Ls) 120
Steinvǫr Sighvatsdóttir f. (Skt, 13th century, a poet of the Norwegian chieftain Gautr á Meli) 116
Steinþórr m., a poet 128
Stúfr/Stúfi m., a horse 224, 226
Stúfr Þórðarson blindi m. (Skt, 11th century, a poet of Haraldr harðráði) 104, 210
Sturla Þórðarson m. (1214–84) (Skt, a poet of Jarl Birgir Magnússon, King Hákon Hákonarson, duke Skúli Bárðarson and King Magnús Hákonarson) 102, 108, 112
Sturla Þórðarson í Hvammi m. (ÆS) 118
Styrbjǫrn sterki m. (d. c. 985) son of Óláfr II of Sweden, nephew of Eríkr sigrsæli 100
Styrkárr Oddason m., a poet (Ls) 120, 190
Styrmir Kárason m. (Ls) 120
Suðri m., a dwarf 18, 26, 150, 206
Súgandi skáld (Skt, 12th and 13th century, a poet of the Danish king Valdimarr gamli and the Norwegian chieftain Nikulás Skjaldvararson, King Magnús Erlingsson and Jarl Erlingr skakki) 106, 112, 114, 116
Súgrínir m., a serpent 228
Sultr m., Hel's knife 48
Sumarliði m. skáld (Skt, a poet of the Swedish king Sørkvir Karlsson and the Norwegian king Sverrir Sigurðarson) 102, 108
Surtr/Svartr m., a giant 14, 80, 82
Suttungr/Suttungi m., a giant, son of Gillingr 88, 124, 132 (the form in *Suttunga mjǫð* could be pl., 'the mead of the Suttungar')
Svaðilferi m. (other MSS Svaðilfæri (Svaðilfǫri), Svaðilfari), a horse 60, 62
Svarnishaugr m. (other MSS Svarinshaugr) 26
Svartálfaheimr m. world of black elves 48, 238
Svartr/Surtr m. (ÆS) a giant 14
Sváfnir m., a serpent 32
Svartr Úlfsson m. 118

Svásaðr m., father of summer 160
Sveinn jarl m. (Skt, 11th century, a Danish jarl) 110, 114
Sveinn m., a poet 158
Sveinn svíðandi m. (Skt, 12th century, a Danish king) 114
Sveinn tjúguskegg m. (Skt, a Danish king 992–1014) 112
Sveinn Álfífuson m. (Skt, 11th century, king of Norway) 114
Sveinn Úlfsson m. (Skt, 11th century, a Danish king) 114
Sverrir Sigurðarson m. (Skt, 12th century, king of Norway) 108
Svertingr Grímsson m. (ÆS) 118
Svíagríss m., a ring 242
Svíar m. pl., Swedes 242
Sviðrir/Sviðurr m., names of Óðinn, 12, 36
Svipall m., a name of Óðinn 36
Svívǫr f., a giantess 144
Svíþjóð f., Sweden 10, 198
Svoll (Svǫl?) f., a river 58
Svǫlnir m., a name of Óðinn 10
Sygja (= Sigg?) f., a mountain in Norway 188
Sylgr f., a river (*Grímnismál* 28) 14
Syn f., a goddess 52
Sýr f., a name of Freyja 52
Sýr m. (Sow), the nickname of Sigurðr Hálfdanarson 200
Særímnir m., a boar 56
Søgr m., a tub 22
Søkin f. a river 58
Søkkvabekkr m., Saga/Sága's dwelling 52
Sørkvir Karlsson m. (Skt, a Swedish king, R Kolsson, evidently taken to be different from the next, as they have different poets) 100
Sørkvir Karlsson m. (Skt, a Swedish king, d. 1210), 102
Sǫl f., an island (?) 166
Sǫrli m., Hamðir's brother 180
Takþyrnir m. (R Eirþyrnir, Codex Wormianus Eikþyrnir) a stag 58; cf. Eikþyrnir
Tangnjóstr m., one of Þórr's goats 38

Tangrisnir m., one of Þórr's goats 38
Teitr m. skáld (Skt, 13th century, a poet of Jarl Knútr Hákonarson) 112
Teitr Þorvaldsson m. (Ls) 120
Tiggi m., one of King Hálfdan's 18 sons 208, 210
Tindr Hallkelsson m. (Skt, 10th century, a poet of Jarl Hákon inn ríki) 110, 178
Tjaldari m., a horse 224
Torf-Einarr m., jarl in Orkney 202
Trinam m. (ÆS) 118. Cf. Ítrmann
Tróan/Trója(m) f. (ÆS), daughter of King Príamus 8, 118
Trója f. (ÆS) Troy 8, 10, 118
Trór/Þórr m. (ÆS) son of King Men(n)on/ Múnon 8, 118
Týr m., a god 42, 44, 48, 50, 80, 86, 146, 278, 294, 302, 304
Uðr/Urðr f., a norn 30. Cf. Ruðr
Uðr f., a wave, daughter of Ægir 154
Úlfljótr m. (Ls) 120
Úlfr aurgoði m. (ÆS) 118
Úlfr inn óargi m. 114
Úlfr stallari (Skt, a Norwegian chieftain) 116
Úlfr Súlujarl (Skt, 10th century poet of Styrbjǫrn sterki) 100
Úlfr Sebbason m. (Skt, a Norwegian poet of Haraldr hárfagri) 102
Úlfr Uggason m., a poet 126, 130, 136, 142, 144, 146, 174, 184, 204
Ullr m., a god, (son of Sif) 46, 86, 134, 138, 148, 162, 164, 174, 178, 182, 238, 242
Uppsalir m. pl., Uppsala 242
Urðarbrunnr m., Urðr's spring 28, 32, 190, 192
Urðr/Uðr f., a norn 30
Útgarða-Loki m., a giant 64, 68, 70, 72
Útgarðr m., dwelling of giants 68
Vafþrúðnismál n. pl., a poem 16 note, 18 note, 58 note, 84 note
Vágasker n. 146
Vágsbrú f., a place in Þrándheimr 294
Vakr m., a horse 226

Index of names

Valaskjálf f., a building in heaven 34
Valdimarr gamli m. (Skt, 13th century, a Danish king) 114
Valdimarr Knútsson m. (Skt, 12th century, a Danish king) 114
Valfǫðr see Val(s)fǫðr
Valgarðr m. á Velli (Skt, 11th century, a poet of Haraldr harðráði) 104, 214, 232
Valgarðr Vémundarson m. (ÆS) 118
Valgautr m., a name of Óðinn 130
Valhǫll f., the hall of the gods 36, 54, 58, 74, 90, 92, 126, 130
Váli m., a dwarf (Váli Þjórr written Valiþior) 26
Váli m., son of Loki 78
Váli/Áli m., a god (son of Óðinn and Rindr) 46, 54, 84, 86, 146
Valr m., a horse 224, 226
Val(s)fǫðr m., a name of Óðinn 28, 36
Valþjófr m. skáld (Skt, 11th century, a poet of Haraldr harðráði) 104
Vam f., a river 50
Vanadís f., a name of Freyja 52
Vanaheimr m., the world of Vanir 40
Vánargandr m., a name of Fenrisúlfr 148
Vandill m., a sea-king 186 note 3
Vár f., a goddess 52
Vartari m., a thong 238
Vé m., son of Borr 18
Veðrlaufnir m., a hawk 30
Vegdreg m. (R Veggdegg), son of King Óðinn 8
Veglun f., a river 58
Vémundr orðlokarr m. (ÆS) 118
Vémundr vitri m. (ÆS) 118
Vengeþór/Vingiþór m., son of Lórriði or Heredei 8, 118
Veratýr m., a name of Óðinn 36
Verðandi f., a norn 30
Vésteinn m., a legendary person 226
Vestrfál n., Westphalia 8
Vestri m., a dwarf 18, 26, 150, 206
Víð f., a river 58
Viðarr þǫgli m., son of Þórr 46, 80, 84, 86, 96, 146

Víðbláinn m., a heaven 34
Viðblindi m., a giant 170
Viðfiðr m., father of Bil and Hjúki 22
Víðgenrir m., a giant 142 (R Víðgymnir)
Víðkunnr Jónsson m. (Skt, 12th century, a Norwegian chieftain) 116
Víðleiptr f., a river 14
Viðrir m., a name of Óðinn 12, 138, 186
Viðurr m., a name of Óðinn 36, 202
Vífill m., a legendary person 226
Víga-Glúmr m., a poet 124, 186, 230
Vigdís Svertingsdóttir f. (ÆS) 118
Vigfúss Víga-Glúmsson (Skt, 10th century, a poet of Jarl Hákon inn ríki) 110
Viggr m., a dwarf 26
Vignig m., (other MSS Vignir) Þórr 84
Vígriðinn m., a battlefield 80
Viktólfr m., ancestor of prophetesses 16
Vilborg f. skáld (Skt, 11th century, a poet of Óláfr kyrri) 104
Vili/Vílir m., son of Borr 18, 128
Vilmeiðr m., ancestor of supernatural beings 16
Vimur f., a river 96, 142
Vina (Vína?) f., a river 58
Vindálfr m., a dwarf 26
Vindgler/Vinlér (R Vindlér) m., a name of Heimdallr 146, 270
Vindglóð f., a sanctuary (R Vingólf n.) 24
Vindsvalr m., the father of winter 160
Vingener/Vingenir m. (ÆS) son of Vingiþórr 8, 118
Vingiþórr/Vengeþórr m. (ÆS) son of Lórriði or Heredei 8, 118
Vingnir m., foster-father of Þórr 138
Vingólf n., a house in heaven 36
Vingr m., a horse 224
Vinlér see Vindgler
Vinþǫll f. a river 59 (Vin, Þǫll in the Codex Regius version)
Virfir m., a dwarf 26
Vitr m., a dwarf 26
Vodden m. = King Óðinn, son of Frjálafr 8
Vænir m., a lake in Sweden 242

Vǫggr m. 240
Vǫlsungr m., son of Rerir 8, 210
Vǫlsungar m. pl., descendants of Vǫlsungr, 8, 210, 212, 214
Vǫluspá f., a poem 14, 18 note, 22 note, 24, 28, 32 note, 34, 62, 78 note, 80 note, 82 note, 84 note
Vǫluspá in skamma (part of *Hyndluljóð*), a poem 16 note
Vǫlu-Steinn m., a poet 136
Vǫr f., a goddess 52
Ygdrasill m., an ash tree (always with single g in DG 11) 26, 28, 30, 32, 60, 80, 82
Yggr m., a name of Óðinn 128, 140, 170, 202, 206, 290
Ylgr f., a river (*Grímnismál* 28) 14
Ymir m. (= Aurgelmir), a giant 6, 14, 16, 18, 20, 24, 150, 152, 154, 206
Ynglingatal n. (a poem) error for Háleygjatal 110
Ynglingatal n. (Skt) a poem 102
Ynglingr m., a descendant of Yngvarr Hálfdanarson 10, 210, 214
Yngvarr m., ancestor of the Ynglings 210
Yngvi m., a dwarf 26
Yngvi m., son of King Óðinn, ancestor of the Ynglings, rulers of Norway 10, 126; Yngvi's people = Norwegians 130; a ruler in general 214
Yrsa f., mother and sister of Hrólfr kraki 242, 244
Zechim (= Kittim) m. (ÆS) 118
Þekkr m., a name of Óðinn 36
Þengill m., one of King Hálfdan's 18 sons 208
Þjálfi m., Þórr's servant 64, 66, 68, 70, 72, 92, 138, 140
Þjazi m., a giant 40, 42, 86, 88, 148, 166
Þjóðnunja (Þjóðnuma) f., a river 58
Þjóðólfr hvinverski m. (Skt, 10th century, a Norwegian poet of Haraldr hárfagri, Jarl Hákon Grjótgarðsson, Þorleifr spaki and the Danish jarl Sveinn) 10, 94, 102, 110, 114, 126, 150, 204, 230

Þjóðólfr Arnórsson m. (Skt, d. 1086, a poet of Magnús góði and Haraldr harðráði) 104, 154, 166, 182, 196, 200, 212, 222, 224, 228, 244
Þjór m., a dwarf 26
Þolmóðnir m., Hel's threshold 48
Þórálfr prestr m. (Skt, 13th century, a poet of Jarl Knútr Hákonarson) 112
Þórarinn loftunga (Skt, 11th century, a poet of Knútr ríki and Sveinn Álfífuson) 112, 114
Þórarinn stuttfeldr m. (Skt, a poet of Sigurðr Jórsalafari (K)) 106
Þórarinn Ragabróðir Óleifsson m. (Ls) 120
Þorbjǫrn m. dísarskáld, a poet 140, 190 (?)
Þorbjǫrn gauss m. (Skt, 13th century, a poet of Hákon herðibreiðr) 108
Þorbjǫrn hornklofi m. (Skt, a Norwegian poet of Haraldr hárfagri) 10 note, 102, 176, 186
Þorbjǫrn m. Skakkaskáld (Skt, 12th century, a poet of Magnús Erlingsson, Sverrir Sigurðarson, Jarl Erlingr skakki) 106, 108, 112
Þorbjǫrn Gaursson m. (Skt, 12th century, a poet of Óláfr Haraldsson) 106
Þórðr Hallsson m. (Skt, 12th century, a poet of Magnús Erlingsson) 108
Þórðr m. mauraskáld, a poet 170
Þórðr Kolbeinsson m. (Skt, c. 1000, a poet of Óláfr helgi, Magnús góði and Jarl Eiríkr Hákonarson) 104, 110, 202
Þórðr m. Sigvaldaskáld (Skt, 10th century, a poet of the Danish jarl Sigvaldi) 114
Þórðr Sturluson m. (ÆS) 118
Þorfinnr munnr m. (Skt, d. 1030, a poet of Óláfr helgi and Jarl Hákon inn ríki) 104, 110
Þorfinnr jarl Sigurðarson m., jarl in Orkney 196, 200
Þorgeirr m. Danaskáld (Skt, 13th century, a poet of the Swedish king Sørkvir Karlsson and the Danish king Valdimarr gamli) 102, 114
Þorgeirr Þorkelsson m. (Ls) 120

Index of names

Þorgeirr Þorvaldsson m. (Skt, 12th century, a poet of the Danish king Knútr Valdimarsson) 114

Þorgerðr Hǫlgabrúðr f., a legendary woman 244

Þorinn m., a dwarf 26

Þorkell m. hamarskáld (Skt, c. 1100, a poet of Óláfr kyrri, Magnús berfǿttr and chieftain Eysteinn orri) 104, 106, 116

Þorkell Tjǫrvason m. (Ls) 120

Þorkell máni Þorsteinsson m. (Ls) 120

Þorleifr spaki m. (Skt, 10th century) 114

Þorleifr m. Hákonarskáld (Skt, 10th century, a poet of Jarl Hákon inn ríki) 110

Þorleikr/Þorleifr fagri m. (cf. Faulkes 1998: 189; Skt, 11th century, a poet of the Danish king Sveinn Úlfsson) 114, 168, 170

Þormóðr m. Kolbrúnarskáld (Skt, d. 1030, a poet of Óláfr helgi) 104

Þórólfr váganef m. (ǼS) 118

Þórr/Ása-Þórr/Ǫku-Þórr m., a god 28, 38, 46, 54, 60, 62, 64, 66, 68, 70, 72, 74, 76, 78, 80, 84, 86, 90, 92, 94, 96, 138, 140, 142, 148, 152, 202, 236, 238

Þórr/Trór m., son of King Men(n)on/Múnon 8, 118

Þórsdrápa f., a poem 96

Þorsteinn m., an unknown person 134, 174

Þorsteinn kroppr m. (Skt, 12th century, a poet of the Danish king Valdimarr Knútsson) 114

Þorsteinn Ingjaldsson m. (Skt, 13th century, a poet of Eiríkr Magnússon) 110

Þorsteinn Ketilsson m. (Skt, 12th century, a poet of Sverrir Sigurðarson) 108

Þorsteinn Ófeigsson m. (Skt, 13th century, poet of Skúli hertogi) 112

Þorsteinn Þorbjarnarson m. (Skt, a poet of the Swedish king Knútr Eiríksson) 102

Þorsteinn Þóruson m. (Skt, 10th century, a Norwegian) 116

Þorsteinn Ǫrvendilsson m. (Skt, 13th century, a poet of Eiríkr Magnússon) 110

Þorvaldr m., a poet 132

Þorvaldr m. blǫnduskáld (Skt, a poet of Sigurðr Jórsalafari (K)) 106, 132, 170, 198

Þorvaldr Helgason m. (Skt, 13th century, a poet of Eiríkr Magnússon) 110

Þorvaldr Hjaltason m. (Skt, a poet of Eiríkr sigrsæli) 100

Þorvarðr Þorgeirsson m. (Skt, 12th century, a poet of Ingi Haraldsson (K)) 106

Þrándheimr m., Trøndelag in Norway 160

Þriði m., a name of Óðinn 12, 14, 16, 34, 36, 64, 82, 126

Þrívaldi m., a giant 138, 142

Þrór m., a name of Óðinn 36

Þrúðheimr m., dwelling of Þjazi and Skaði 40, 42, 86 (here probably an error for Þrymheimr)

Þrúðr f., a valkyrie 54

Þrúðr f., daughter of Þórr 138, 140, 182

Þrúðvangr m., dwelling of Þórr 38, 94

Þuðruðr m., a name of Óðinn 36

Þundr m., a name of Óðinn 136

Þviti m., a stone 50

Þǫkt (other MSS Þǫkk) f., a giantess 76

Ægir m., a giant (personification of the ocean) 86, 88, 90, 154, 156, 158, 160, 162

Ægis døtr f. pl. waves, daughters of Ægir 154

Ækin f., a river 58

Ǫði m., one of King Hálfdan's 18 sons 210

Ǫðlingr, descendant of Ǫði Hálfdanarson 210, 212

Ǫgló = Ágló

Ǫku-Þórr m. = Þórr 38, 64, 68, 86

Ǫlvir m. (h)núfa (Skt, a Norwegian poet of Haraldr hárfagri) 102, 138

Ǫlvismál (Alvíssmál) n. pl. a poem 206

Ǫndlangr m., a heaven 34

Ǫnundr Ólafsson m. (Skt, king, son of Óláfr sǿnski, 11th century) 100

Ǫrboða f., mother of Gerðr 54

Ǫrmt f., a river 28

Ǫvaldi/Ávalldi m. (Skt, poet(s) of King Eysteinn Beli) 100